THE ROUTLEDGE INTERNATIONAL HANDBOOK OF YOUNG CHILDREN'S RIGHTS

Written to commemorate 30 years since the United Nations Convention on the Rights of the Child (UNCRC), *The Routledge International Handbook of Young Children's Rights* reflects upon the status of the rights of children aged 0–8 years around the world, whether they are respected or neglected, and how we may move forward. With contributions from international experts and emerging authorities on children's rights, Murray, Blue Swadener and Smith have produced this highly significant textbook on young children's rights globally.

Containing sections on policy, along with rights to protection, provision and participation for young children, this book combines discussions of children's rights and early childhood development, and investigates the crucial yet frequently overlooked link between the two. The authors examine how policy, practice and research could be utilised to address the barriers to universal respect for children, to create a safer and more enriching world for them to live and flourish in.

The Routledge International Handbook of Young Children's Rights is an essential resource for students and academics in early childhood education, social work and paediatrics, as well as for researchers, policymakers, leaders and practitioners involved in the provision of children's services and paediatric healthcare, and international organisations with an interest in or ability to influence national or global policies on children's rights.

Jane Murray is Associate Professor and Co-Director at the Centre for Education and Research, University of Northampton, UK. She has published extensively on early childhood education and social inclusion, and is Editor of the *International Journal of Early Years Education*.

Beth Blue Swadener is Professor of Justice and Social Inquiry and Social and Cultural Pedagogy in the School of Social Transformation at Arizona State University, USA.

Kylie Smith is Associate Professor in the Melbourne Graduate School of Education's Social Transformation and Education Hub at the University of Melbourne, Australia.

THE ROUTLEDGE INTERNATIONAL HANDBOOK SERIES

For more information about this series, please visit: www.routledge.com/Routledge-International-Handbooks-of-Education/book-series/HBKSOFED

THE ROUTLEDGE INTERNATIONAL HANDBOOK OF YOUNG CHILDREN'S RIGHTS

Edited by Jane Murray, Beth Blue Swadener and Kylie Smith

Routledge
Taylor & Francis Group

LONDON AND NEW YORK

First edition published 2020
by Routledge
2 Park Square, Milton Park, Abingdon, Oxon, OX14 4RN

and by Routledge
52 Vanderbilt Avenue, New York, NY 10017

Routledge is an imprint of the Taylor & Francis Group, an informa business

British Library Cataloguing-in-Publication Data
A catalogue record for this book is available from the British Library

Library of Congress Cataloging-in-Publication Data
Names: Murray, Jane, 1962- editor. | Blue Swadener, Beth, editor. | Smith, Kylie, 1968- editor.
Title: The Routledge international handbook of young children's rights / [edited by] Jane Murray,
Beth Blue Swadener, Kylie Smith.
Description: New York : Routledge, 2019. |
Series: Routledge international handbooks | Includes bibliographical references and index. |
Identifiers: LCCN 2019035253 (print) | LCCN 2019035254 (ebook) | ISBN 9780367142018 (hardback) |
ISBN 9780367142025 (ebook)
Subjects: LCSH: Children (International law) | Children–Legal status, laws, etc. | Children's rights. |
Convention on the Rights of the Child (1989 November 20)
Classification: LCC K639 .R67 2019 (print) | LCC K639 (ebook) | DDC 341.4/8572–dc23
LC record available at https://lccn.loc.gov/2019035253
LC ebook record available at https://lccn.loc.gov/2019035254

ISBN: 978-0-367-14201-8 (hbk)
ISBN: 978-0-367-14202-5 (ebk)

Typeset in Bembo
by Swales & Willis, Exeter, Devon, UK

We dedicate this book to the young children to whom the rights belong,
and to those who champion those rights

CONTENTS

ACKNOWLEDGEMENTS

Thank you from Jane, Beth and Kylie:

To the team at Routledge – always wonderful colleagues.

To the authors, researchers and research participants whose footprints are in this book forever.

To our excellent editorial assistants, Jemima Murray, Grethel Ochoa Bobadilla and Bruce Hurst: you have been an outstanding team and we have been so grateful for your consistent, thoughtful and thorough work.

To Professor Laura Lundy for her advice, support and expertise.

Thank you from Jane:

To Beth and Kylie for being exceptional colleagues. It has been such a privilege and pleasure to work with you both on this project.

To Professors Chris Pascal and Tony Bertram for your tireless work in co-constructing the early childhood field in Europe and beyond.

To Stephen Murray for all your encouragement and support.

To Jemima, Richard, Will, Rosie, Fergus and Chrissie for love and laughter.

Thank you from Beth:

I would like to thank and acknowledge Daniel Swadener for his support and understanding as I've worked on the handbook, as well as his sense of when I needed a break (for a Harley ride or cultural event).

I would like to acknowledge the great teamwork and consistently open and timely communication and collaboration: thank you to my fellow editorial team, Kylie and Jane.

Thank you from Kylie:

I would like to thank Bruce Hurst who has supported the development and completion of the handbook. His willingness to step in and out of tasks is always done with consideration and support.

I would also like to acknowledge the ongoing inspiration of rights-based work by Laura Lundy, Sheralyn Champbell and Glenda MacNaughton. Their critical gaze continues to help me consider the possibilities, tensions, gaps and inequities of children's rights.

Finally, I would like to thank Jane and Beth for first inviting me to be a co-editor and second for their guidance and enthusiasum throughout the process.

AUTHOR BIOGRAPHIES

Vina Adriany is associated with the Department of Early Childhood Education, Universitas Pendidikan Indonesia. Her research focuses on the issues of gender and social justice in early childhood education (ECE) as well as the impact of neoliberalism in ECE. She has published a number of peer-reviewed articles and book chapters on the topic. She has also been invited as a Visiting Lecturer to Sutan Qaboos University, Oman, and Gothenburg University and University West, Sweden. She was a Guest Editor for the *Policy Futures in Education* (PFIE) Special Edition on Neoliberalism and Practices of ECE in Asia.

Priscilla Alderson is Professor Emerita of Childhood Studies, University College London, UK. Recent books include *The Politics of Childhoods Real and Imagined* (2016, Routledge), *Childhoods Real and Imagined: An Introduction to Childhood Studies and Critical Realism* (2013, Routledge), *The Ethics of Research with Children and Young People* (2011/2020, Sage, with Virginia Morrow) and *Young Children's Rights* (2000/2008, Jessica Kingsley/Save the Children).

Vinnarasan Aruldoss is an assistant professor at BITS-Pilani, Dubai Campus. Previously, he held Research Fellowships at University of Sussex and Goldsmiths, University of London on the ERC-funded Connectors Study. His doctoral research at the University of Edinburgh explored children's lived experiences in the early years institutions, and his postdoctoral research investigated the relationship between childhood, politics and public life. His research interests include childhood, sociology of education, social policy, early years intervention, and social theories of power, inequality and injustice.

Caralyn Blaisdell is a lecturer in Early Years Education at the University of Strathclyde. She is an experienced Early Years Practitioner whose work focuses on children's rights and early learning and childcare. She is particularly interested in exploring how young children's voice, agency and contributions to social life are recognised, and how recognition occurs within interdependent social relationships.

Petra Büker is Professor at the Institute of Education at University of Paderborn, Germany. She is working in the field of early childhood education and primary school pedagogy. The main focus of Petra's research work is on child-centred pedagogy, rights-based participation of children, transition processes, documentation of children's learning processes, heterogeneity, intersectionality, interculturality, and inclusion in kindergarten and primary school.

Margaret Coady is an honorary research fellow at the Youth Research Centre, University of Melbourne and a founding researcher at the Centre for Applied Philosophy and Public Ethics. She has lectured on children's rights at universities in many countries, including China, England, Singapore and South Africa. Her main research interests are children's rights, professional ethics and the history of ideas in the education of young children.

Aline Cole-Albäck is an associate lecturer in Early Childhood Studies at Oxford Brookes University, and PhD candidate on the combined programme at the Centre for Research in Early Childhood (CREC) and Birmingham City University in England. It was while working as an early years teacher in England, and prior to that as a parent volunteer in schools in Germany and the USA, three very different education systems, that Aline's interest in and research on children's rights in early childhood education and care developed, the focus of her doctoral thesis.

John M. Davis is a professor of education at the University of Strathclyde. His research focuses on childhood, disability, inclusion and social justice, and seeks to support children, young people, parents and professionals to develop creative and innovative solutions to their life issues. His work has also examined international approaches to multi-professional working and increased our understanding of the factors that foster creative and innovative learning

Ludovica De Panfilis is Head of the Unit of Bioethics at the Azienda USL – IRCCS in Reggio Emilia, Italy. She is a Researcher, Bioethicist and Trainer in Bioethics and Medical Ethics.

Cristina Devecchi is a co-director of the Centre for Education and Research at the University of Northampton. She is responsible for PhD students' admission and progression at the Faculty of Education and Humanities, and has carried out a number of national and international projects on inclusion, leadership and professional identity in all phases of education.

Sue Dockett is an emeritus professor at Charles Sturt University Australia. While she has recently retired from the university sector, she remains an active researcher and writer, exploring issues related to the transition to school, young children's participation and play.

Johanna Einarsdottir is a professor of education at the School of Education, University of Iceland. She holds an honorary doctorate from the University of Oulu in Finland and was awarded the Distinguished Alumni Achievement Award from the University of Illinois in 2018.

Sonya Gaches is a lecturer at the University of Otago College of Education in Dunedin, New Zealand. Prior to this, she was an Assistant Professor of Practice in Early Childhood Education at the College of Education at the University of Arizona and an Early Childhood Classroom Teacher of toddlers and early primary grades for over 20 years. Sonya's teaching and research interests include teachers' and children's classroom experiences and children's rights, and how these interact with policies and practices.

Megan Gallagher has worked in various roles within education for 25 years and is currently a Primary Teacher working in Otago, New Zealand. She was awarded Master of Education (with Distinction) from Otago University in 2017.

Philip Garner has been professionally engaged in education for almost 50 years. He has worked in both mainstream and specialist settings and in universities. His principal involvement has been in special education and the initial preparation and professional development of teachers, both in the UK and internationally.

Luca Ghirotto is Head of the Qualitative Research Unit at the Azienda USL – IRCCS in Reggio Emilia, Italy, and Researcher in Special and Inclusive Education at the Department of Human Sciences, University of Verona.

Rebekah Grace is a senior research fellow and the Deputy Director of the Centre for Translational Research and Social Innovation in the School of Nursing and Midwifery at Western Sydney University. Her research focuses on the service and support needs of children and families who experience adversity.

Margo Greenwood, Academic Leader of the National Collaborating Centre for Aboriginal Health, is an Indigenous scholar of Cree ancestry. She is also Vice President of Aboriginal Health for the Northern Health Authority in British Columbia and Professor in both the First Nations Studies and Education programmes at the University of Northern British Columbia. Her academic work crosses disciplines and sectors, and focuses on the health and well-being of indigenous children and families and public health.

Amita Gupta is a professor of early childhood education and former department chair in the School of Education at the City College of New York, CUNY. Her research interests in comparative and international education utilise postcolonial theoretical frameworks to examine cross-cultural issues in young children's development and education, and the impact of globalisation on early childhood teacher preparation and practice.

Shelly-Ann Harper is currently the early childhood development specialist in the UNICEF Eastern Caribbean Area Office. In this capacity, she oversees UNICEF's early childhood development programme in collaboration with governments in 12 island states. She is a certified teacher with more than 25 years of experience.

Rochelle L. Hostler is the International Baccalaureate Primary Years Programme Coordinator at the Kent State University Child Development Center and a Lecturer for the School of Teaching, Learning and Curriculum Studies at Kent State University.

Daniela S. Jadue-Roa is in the Faculty of the University of Chile and conducts research on ethical issues and child participation in research, children's transition from kindergarten to first grade, and learning agency development.

Casey Khaleesi has been an educator in Arizona for 30 years and an advocate for listening to and learning from children and youth. She currently teaches special education and has worked with all levels of education. She recently completed her MA in Social and Cultural Pedagogy at Arizona State University. Her thesis examined middle school children's embodied experiences of high-stakes testing.

Laura Lundy is Co-Director of the Centre for Children's Rights and a Professor in the School of Social Sciences, Education and Social Work at Queen's University Belfast. She is Co-Editor-in-Chief of the *International Journal of Children's Rights*. The 'Lundy model' of child participation has been adopted by international organisations including the European Commission and World Vision.

George Kent is Professor Emeritus with the University of Hawaii and Adjunct Professor with the University of Sydney in Australia and also with Saybrook University in California. He is Deputy Editor of *World Nutrition* and Associate Editor of *Public Health Nutrition*.

Matías Knust lives in Santiago de Chile. He co-founded the Children's International Foundation for Research, Education and Peace (CIFREP) in 2018 to develop further the field of education in Chile. Matias teaches bachelor's students at universities and translates educational textbooks into Spanish in order to make the teaching and methods of forest, nature and wilderness education in Chile better known.

Kristina Konstantoni is a lecturer in childhood studies and co-director of the Centre for Education for Racial Equality in Scotland. Kristina was the programme director of the BA Childhood Practice at the University of Edinburgh. Kristina's research focuses on children's experiences of intersecting inequalities, children's rights in humanitarian crises (austerity and refugee crises), children's peer relationships and educators' social justice pedagogies. Kristina has been involved in research and knowledge exchange projects linked to children and young people's intersecting identities, inequalities, participation and rights. She has published widely in the fields of childhood studies and children's rights.

Sheila Long is a lecturer in the Department of Humanities at the Institute of Technology Carlow, Ireland. Her teaching and research interests centre on interdisciplinary children's rights education for professionals who work with children and young people, particularly ECEC students. She holds a doctorate in childhood studies from Queen's University Belfast.

Vera Lopez is a professor in the School of Social Transformation at Arizona State University. Lopez's research areas include delinquency, substance use and prevention research, with a major focus on system-involved Latina girls. She is the author of *Complicated Lives: Girls, Parents, Drugs, and Juvenile Justice* (2017, Rutgers University Press).

Eunice Lumsden is head of early years at the University of Northampton and a fellow of the Royal Society of Arts. Before entering higher education, she spent 20 years as a social worker. She has been a government adviser in England and internationally on the professionalisation of early years.

Angeles Maldonado is a mother and human rights scholar activist studying race, migration, discourse and social movements in Arizona. She is the CEO for Ybarra Maldonado Law Group and the Founder and Executive Director of the Institute for Border Crit Theory, whose mission is to foreground the voices and experiences of people of color living in the borderlands (through social justice education and pedagogy, borderland research and the publication of counter-narratives of resistance). Dr Maldonado believes strongly that migration is a fundamental human right and all borders must be resisted.

Lisa McClean-Trotman is a communication for development specialist for UNICEF. She is based at the UNICEF Eastern Caribbean Area Office.

Lynn McNair is Head of Cowgate Under 5's Centre in Edinburgh, Scotland, and is a Senior Teaching Fellow at the University of Edinburgh. Lynn has more than 30 years' experience working in early years education and was awarded an OBE for Services to Early Years Education in 2009. Lynn is a Trained Froebelian, attaining her certificate at the Froebel Institute, Roehampton University, London, UK. She is an award-winning author. Finally, Lynn would say her passion for egalitarianism, emancipation, democracy and a belief that children are rich, active, resourceful beings came from being a mother to Kurt and

Mischa, and what she learned as she observed them playing freely as children. This way of being with children, trusting in them in their abilities and capabilities, is where she puts her energy into her work with children today.

Alison Moore is Placement Manager at University College Cork in Ireland. Until recently, she led a group of children's centres in Birmingham, England, managing multidisciplinary teams and delivering support to children under 5 and their families, including early years care, education, family support and mental health. She is a PhD Candidate on the Combined Programme at the Centre for Research in Early Childhood (CREC) and Birmingham City University. Alison's roots lie within early years, with 40 years' experience, and her research reflects her belief in Article 12 of the UNCRC.

Luigina Mortari is Full Professor of Qualitative Research Epistemology and Philosophy of Care at the University of Verona, Italy, where she founded and currently leads the Caring Education Research Center (CERC).

Peter Moss is an emeritus professor at the UCL Institute of Education, University College London. Recent publications include *Loris Malaguzzi and the Schools of Reggio Emilia: A Selection of His Writings and Speeches* (edited with colleagues from Reggio Emilia), *Alternative Narratives in Early Childhood Education* and *Parental Leave and Beyond: Recent International Developments, Current Issues and Future Directions* (edited with Ann-Zofie Duvander and Alison Koslowski).

Diana Paola Gómez Muñoz is a PhD researcher at the Early Childhood Research Centre at Dublin City University. She was awarded the title of Magister in Education by Universidad Nacional de Colombia, where she has been a member of the interdisciplinary research group Language and Cognition in Childhood since 2007. Diana is currently working towards her PhD on Early Childhood Development, Education and Care with and for Rural Populations and Contexts in Colombia.

Colette Murray is a lecturer in Early Childhood Care in Education at the Technological University Dublin. Her research interests centre on diversity and equality issues, and she has several publications on diversity and equality in early childhood care and education. She coordinates the Equality and Diversity Early Childhood National Network (EDENN) and was a founding member of the Diversity in Early Childhood Care, Education and Training (DECET) European Network.

Jane Murray is associate professor and co-director at the Centre for Education and Research, University of Northampton, UK. She has published extensively on early childhood education and social inclusion, and is editor of the *International Journal of Early Years Education*.

Mercy Musomi is the CEO of Girl Child Network and a Human Rights Crusader. She lives in Kenya and has travelled extensively to champion for the rights of children. She is passionate about gender equality and inclusion. She is a mother of four sons but has also defended the rights of thousands of girls.

Casey Y. Myers is an assistant professor in early childhood education at Kent State University. Her research interests include participatory research methodologies with young children and Anthropocene childhoods. Casey is the Coordinator of Studio and Research Arts at the Kent State University Child Development Center.

Anikó Varga Nagy is a senior lecturer in the Department of Child Education at the Faculty of Child and Adult Education, University of Debrecen, Hungary, where she teaches basic principles of pedagogy, family pedagogy, active exploration of the outside environment and associated methods. She is a Mentor Pedagogue of students' practical training in kindergartens. Her research interests are in the history of pedagogy, education for early childhood and kindergarten pedagogues' professionalism.

Zoi Nikiforidou is a senior lecturer in early childhood at Liverpool Hope University. Her research interests relate to aspects of cognition, pedagogy and risk. Zoi is a member of the OMEP UK executive committee and a co-convenor of the holistic well-being EECERA SIG.

Emma Nottingham is a senior lecturer in law at the University of Winchester. Her research specialises in children's rights in a range of contexts, including digital and social media and healthcare law.

Cathy Nutbrown is Professor of Education at the University of Sheffield. She researches in the field of early childhood education and is committed to finding ways of working 'with respect' with young children. Cathy is Editor-in-Chief of the Sage *Journal of Early Childhood Research*.

Sara M. Ólafsdóttir is a research assistant and assistant teacher at the School of Education, University of Iceland. Her research focus has been on children's perspectives on play, transition and belonging in early childhood education.

Ioanna Palaiologou has worked as a university academic in the UK for the last 20 years and is now returning to her career as a Child Psychologist. She is a Chartered Psychologist of the British Psychological Society, with specialisation in child development and learning theories, and was appointed as Associate Fellow of the BPS in 2015.

Sándor Pálfi is Vice Dean and Head of the Department of Child Education, and holds a Chair in Early Childhood Education within Early Childhood Teacher Education at the Faculty of Child and Adult Education, University of Debrecen, Hungary. He has a background as a Kindergarten Pedagogue. His research focus is on early childhood education, principles of project pedagogy in Hungary, and the interpretation of the child-based education approach in kindergarten and children's free play.

Kyriaki Patsianta is a lawyer specialising in European and international human rights law, and more specifically in children's rights. She has worked as a consultant for the Council of Europe (France) and the NGO Network for Children's Rights (Greece) while she has participated in research projects coordinated by the University of Exeter (UK).

Bob Perry is an emeritus professor at Charles Sturt University, Australia. He remains actively involved in research and publications focusing on transition to school, children's participation, working with families and young children's mathematics.

Erzsébet Rákó is an associate professor, Deputy Dean and Head of the Department of Child Education at the Faculty of Child and Adult Education, University of Debrecen, Hungary. Her research interests include the living conditions of children in child protection institutions.

Jenny Ritchie is an associate professor in Te Puna Akopai, the School of Education, at Te Herenga Waka, Victoria University of Wellington, Aotearoa New Zealand. Her research and teaching focus on social, cultural and ecological justice in early childhood care and education.

Sioned Saer is an early years lecturer at the University of Wales Trinity Saint David, and her interests focus on all aspects of safeguarding, child protection and citizenship, supporting the view that children have a voice and have a right to express their views under Article 12 of the UNCRC, as well as the principles of the Rights of Children and Young Persons (Wales) Measure 2011.

Cat Sewell works as an artist, facilitator, educator and play specialist with a range of early childhood settings. She has a Bachelor of Creative Arts from the Victorian College of the Arts, Melbourne University, and a Master of Creative Arts Therapy from the Royal Melbourne Institute of Technology.

Mere Skerrett, Māori indigenous researcher, teacher, mother, grandmother and tribal member. A foundation adherent of *Kōhanga Reo* (Māori language nests) and its schooling equivalent, Mere is a veteran Māori language activist, working in the area of indigenous children's rights and social justice. Tihei mauri ora.

Jo Smale is Manager for Families, Youth and Children at Darebin City Council, Melbourne, Australia.

Kylie Smith is Associate Professor in the Melbourne Graduate School of Education's Social Transformation and Education Hub at the University of Melbourne, Australia.

Heather Stewart is a child protection officer for UNICEF. She is based at the UNICEF Eastern Caribbean Area Office.

Jodi Streelasky is an assistant professor in the Department of Curriculum and Instruction at the University of Victoria, Canada. Her research examines children's use of multimodal forms of communication, outdoor education and young learners, and the inclusion of indigenous ways of knowing in early childhood classrooms.

Beth Blue Swadener is Professor of Justice and Social Inquiry and Social and Cultural Pedagogy at Arizona State University, USA. Her research focuses on childhood studies, internationally comparative social policy, with a focus on sub-Saharan Africa and children's rights and voices. She has published over 80 articles and book chapters and co-edited and authored 14 books, including *Children and Families 'At Promise', Power and Voice in Research with Children, Does the Village Still Raise the Child?, Decolonizing Research in Cross-Cultural Context, Children's Rights and Education* and *Reconceptualizing Early Childhood Care and Education: A Reader.*

Prospera Tedam joined the United Arab Emirates University in 2018 and has taught at the Open University, University of Northampton and Anglia Ruskin University. She is a UK-qualified social worker with practice experience in child protection, fostering and adoption, and she previously advised the UK Home Office on safeguarding involving children at risk of being returned to their countries of origin. Prospera has research interests concerning the rights of children in education settings in Ghana, harmful traditional and cultural practices, and social justice. She is a senior fellow of the Higher Education Academy.

Marek Tesar is an associate professor in childhood studies and early childhood education, and associate dean international, at the University of Auckland, New Zealand. He is the editor-in-chief of *Policy Futures in Education*, published by SAGE, and a book series editor for *Children: Global Posthumanist Perspectives and Materialist Theories*, published by Springer.

Eleonóra Teszenyi is a senior lecturer in Education and Specialist in Early Years Education at the University of Northampton, where she teaches on postgraduate and undergraduate programmes in early years. Before entering higher education in 2010, she worked in the early years sector in England for 19 years as an Early Years Teacher and Local Authority Advisory Teacher and she led practice in a children's centre. Eleonora's research interests focus on parental choice of childcare provision and mixed-age kindergartens in Hungary. She has several publications in the field of early childhood.

Glenda Tinney is an early years lecturer at the University of Wales Trinity Saint David. In recent years, she has been exploring the links between learning in nature, citizenship, sustainability and children's rights, with a specific focus on Article 29 of the UNCRC, the UN Sustainable Development Goals and the Well-Being of Future Generations (Wales) Act.

John Tobin holds the Francine V. McNiff Chair in International Human Rights Law in the Law School at the University of Melbourne, where he is also the co-director of the human rights programme. He has published widely on matters relating to children's rights and is editor of *The UN Convention on the Rights of the Child: A Commentary* (2019, Oxford University Press).

Michelle Trudgett is a proud Wiradjuri woman. She is the inaugural Director of the Centre for the Advancement of Indigenous Knowledges at the University of Technology Sydney. Her work has been recognised at the highest levels, including the 2018 National NAIDOC Scholar of the Year Award and the 2018 Neville Bonner National Teaching Excellence Award.

Mathias Urban is Desmond Chair of Early Childhood Education and Director of the Early Childhood Research Centre (ECRC) at Dublin City University (DCU), Ireland. He works on questions of diversity and equality, social justice, evaluation and professionalism in working with young children, families and communities in diverse sociocultural contexts. Before joining DCU, Mathias held the position of Froebel Professor of Early Childhood Studies at the University of Roehampton, London, UK. In 2018, Mathias was awarded the Marianne Bloch Distinguished Career Award by the international Reconceptualising Early Childhood Education network.

Nichola Welton is a senior lecturer in the discipline of Social Justice and Inclusion at the University of Wales Trinity Saint David. Her main areas of teaching and research focus on social justice and well-being with young people and communities. She is project-managing a four-year UNCRC training programme for key children and young people workforce sectors on behalf of the Welsh Government.

Tamaki Yoshida researched physical punishment in two primary schools in Tanzania for her PhD at the UCL Institute of Education. She has worked at the Japanese embassy in Dar es Salaam. Her areas of interest are children's agency, international development and critical realism.

Hani Yulindrasari is a senior lecturer and early career researcher at the Faculty of Education, Universitas Pendidikan Indonesia. She received her bachelor's degree in psychology (2002) from Gadjah Mada University, Indonesia, a master's degree in gender and development (2006) and a PhD in gender studies (2017) from the University of Melbourne, Australia. Her research interest is gender research in education and family settings.

Germán Camilo Zárate Pinto is a PhD researcher at the Early Childhood Research Centre at Dublin City University. He was awarded the title of Magister in Education by

Universidad Nacional de Colombia, where he is a member of the interdisciplinary research group Language and Cognition in Childhood. His current research work focuses on early childhood education, development, and care with post-war communities in Colombia.

FOREWORD

The UN Convention on the Rights of the Child, drafted over ten years, and adopted by the UN General Assembly in 1989, provides a radical and transformative lens through which to view childhood. It acknowledges the universality of children's needs and insists that they are entitled to have those needs met. It thereby establishes children as rights holders, moving beyond the traditional perspective of children merely as passive recipients of adult guidance and protection. It recognises them as social agents capable of and entitled to influence matters affecting their lives. And, perhaps most radical of all, every one of the rights embodied in the Convention, including civil and political, economic, social, cultural and protection rights, are acknowledged as applying to all children from birth (or conception, depending on the jurisdiction) up to the age of 18 years.

The potential impact of the Convention was strengthened by the evolution of the concept of a rights-based approach in which it is recognised that individual rights alone are insufficient to the attainment of real change. Also needed is an understanding of the core principles of human rights to inform the way in which those rights are implemented. Human rights are universal, inalienable, indivisible and accountable. In other words, they apply equally to everyone, including babies and very young children. They are 'portable' and therefore must be respected wherever the child is. Thus, for example, the right to protection from all forms of violence, including corporal punishment, must extend to the family and schools, as well as wider institutional settings. Their indivisibility means they cannot be implemented in isolation. The right of young children to health, for example, can only be realised if other rights, including family life, play and rest, an adequate standard of living, and protection from violence and exploitation, are also addressed. And there must be mechanisms in place to hold governments to account if they fail to meet their obligations to children.

The Committee on the Rights of the Child, the international body charged with monitoring states' implementation of the Convention, has further identified four rights that must also be understood as core principles: non-discrimination, the best interests of the child, optimum development and the right of children to be heard. Together, these principles provide a rigorous approach to guiding the actions of duty bearers – in other words, those with obligations for implementing the Convention.

The Convention applied through the perspective of a rights-based approach has real significance for the realisation of rights for young children. While all rights apply to all children, the way in which they are implemented must necessarily be informed by the age and evolving capacities of the child. A commitment to non-discrimination means that it is never acceptable to deny their rights. Rather, it demands that consideration is given to how to ensure their realisation in ways that are appropriate. For example, the right to protection from violence applies to every child, but the forms and locus of violence to which children are exposed, the potential perpetrators and the nature of protection will be influenced by the age of the child. Similarly, listening to the views of young children and taking them seriously is every bit as important as hearing the views of older children, but the tools needed, the type of space created and the support provided must be sensitive and appropriate to the developmental needs of young children if it is to be meaningful and effective. The Committee on the Rights of the Child has emphasised that the views and feelings of very young children, including babies, must be taken seriously, as expressed through, for example, body language, facial expression, attention, crying and laughing. The onus is on responsible adults to explore ways of listening to and hearing their forms of communication.

And so, 30 years on, it is timely to reflect on what these profound developments have actually achieved for young children. There is no doubt that the Convention has been a driving force for change. It has necessitated a fundamental review of laws, policies, service design and scope, budgetary allocations, professional training, government priorities and coordination, and mechanisms for monitoring and accountability. And in all regions, and in diverse economic, cultural, religious and political environments, governments have introduced child-focused legislation where none previously existed – in respect of child protection, access to justice, family law, school leaving age, child labour, sexual exploitation and age of marriage. Prior to 1989, the issue of violence against children barely registered on the international agenda, but now, although the problem remains extensive, it is widely understood to be a pervasive and damaging reality in the lives of millions of children, with devastating consequences for their immediate and long-term physical and emotional safety and health. And nearly half the world's countries have either already legislated its prohibition in all settings or are committed to so doing. Significant progress has been made in improving access to healthcare and education, poverty reduction, and hunger and malnutrition. The interpretation of the right to education as extending to early years has been a critical development, especially when supported by the growing evidence from neuroscience of the importance of the first 1,000 days of life. And the rights-based approach has been adopted to establish new methods of working – baby-friendly hospitals, child-friendly cities and communities, children's rights commissioners, rights-respecting schools and early years settings, and the application of children's rights impact assessments when developing legislation or policy.

However, huge challenges remain. As documented in this handbook, far too little attention has been afforded to the rights of young children. Although considerable efforts have been made to create opportunities for children to express their views and be taken seriously both as individuals and collectively, this commitment rarely extends to children under 8 years. Far too many young children are still denied early years care and education, go to bed hungry, face insecurity and violence, live in institutions, are discriminated against and excluded, and face a future with limited life chances and hope. Issues of privacy, freedom of expression and respect for dignity are rarely, if ever, discussed in relation to young children. A growing number of authoritarian and populist governments are seeking to put the clock back and once again render children invisible within the auspices of the family, giving back total authority to parents and removing any role for the state in providing protection. Indeed, governments generally have shown insufficient commitment to translating their commitments on paper into realities on the ground.

Furthermore, the world we now inhabit looks very different from the one in which the Convention was adopted. What progress has been made is under increasing threat as we confront the emerging crises of authoritarianism, climate change, huge and growing inequalities, conflict and war, migration, and the rapid digitalisation of our environments. Any one of these challenges could represent a potential barrier to progress, but collectively they constitute an existential threat to the lives of us all. Unfortunately, young children, who are the most vulnerable when their rights are violated, and the least able to act to protect themselves, are likely to suffer the most serious consequences. They therefore need powerful advocates. They need to be rendered visible. They need to be forcefully defended as subjects of rights.

This handbook provides a vital antidote to the many inadequacies in addressing the rights of young children. Drawing on the most recent research data, and highlighting both progress and failures, it provides a comprehensive depiction of the most critical issues affecting them and points to the way forward if we are to make more progress in the second 30-year lifespan of the remarkable treaty that is the UN Convention on the Rights of the Child. The rights, principles, standards and tools exist. It is up to everyone who cares about young children to make sure that they are applied rigorously and that governments, who invariably claim children to be their most precious resource, are not allowed to fail in ensuring that their rights are pushed up the political agenda and actually given the primary consideration to which they are entitled.

PART 1

Policy affecting young children's rights

1

INTRODUCTION

The state of young children's rights

Jane Murray, Beth Blue Swadener and Kylie Smith

The Routledge International Handbook of Young Children's Rights marks the 30th anniversary of the adoption of the United Nations Convention on the Rights of the Child (UNCRC) (Office for the High Commissioner for Human Rights (OHCHR), 1989). The UNCRC frames the human rights specifically for children, defining a child in its first article as 'a person below the age of 18, unless the laws of a particular country set the legal age for adulthood younger' (OHCHR, 1989). The Convention is a legacy of Eglantyne Jebb's work to secure the Geneva Declaration on the Rights of the Child (League of Nations, 1924), the first recognition by international governments of children's rights. However, nearly a century later, 'much remains to be done' (UNICEF, 2014a): many children are still at profound risk and in great need (UNICEF, 2018a).

Over the three decades since the UNCRC was adopted, powerful research evidence has built to reveal the importance for lifetime outcomes of the early childhood phase, from conception to 8 years (Heckman and Masterov, 2007; The Lancet, 2016; UNICEF, 2014b). Longitudinal studies have emerged showing the benefits of nurturing and stimulating early childhood experiences (e.g. Bakken, Brown and Downing, 2017; Schweinhart et al., 2005) alongside exponential developments in the field of neuroscience that reveal infants' significant capabilities, where previously these were hidden from view (Centre on the Developing Child, 2007; Goswami and Bryant, 2007; McCain and Mustard, 1999; Shonkoff and Phillips, 2000; Shore, 1997). This evidence has persuaded governments internationally of the benefits of investment in young children's early experiences, exemplified by the first global target for early childhood development: 'By 2030, ensure that all girls and boys have access to quality early childhood development, care and pre-primary education so that they are ready for primary education' (United Nations, 2015). Yet it may be argued that the attention given to school readiness in this international target aligns with an agenda more attuned to an adult concern – economics – than young children's needs and rights (Brooks and Murray, 2018; Moss and Urban, 2018; Murray, 2017a). Dominant views about children are primarily centred on the notion that they are 'pre-adult becomings' (Holloway and Valentine, 2000, p. 5) or 'deferred' citizens (Cheney, 2004, p. 13), meaning they have little agency to influence change until they are older or reach an age of majority. Valerie Polakow (1993) and others have long argued that existential framings of childhood are as critical as instrumental ones that emphasise cost–benefit analysis or later pay-offs of investments in early childhood.

The growing awareness across the world of the importance of early childhood has high-lighted the need to look afresh at UNCRC (OHCHR, 1989) and to examine its fitness for purpose in respect of the rights of infants and children up to 8 years in an array of sociocul-tural contexts, including the Global South. This need was recognised in the UNCRC Gen-eral Comment 7 (GC7) (OHCHR, 2006) and has also been addressed in a few sources in the literature (Alderson, Hawthorne and Killen, 2008; Kanyal, 2014). However, given the intensity of global policy, research and practice focusing on the early childhood years in recent decades, relatively little discourse has attended to rights as they are afforded specific-ally to infants and young children. Consultation with young children about matters affecting them is increasingly advocated and included in child rights-based research and programme planning designs (e.g., Lundy and Swadener, 2015; Murray, 2017b; Smith, 2013).

The UNCRC (OHCHR, 1989) itself marginalises younger children by predicating chil-dren's access to their rights on the notion of 'evolving capacities' (Lansdown, 2005; Van Beers, Invernizzi and Milne, 2008, p. 54), rather than seeing children from birth as compe-tent social actors (Dahlberg and Lenz Taguchi, 1994, p. 2; Prout and James, 1997) and infants and children up to 8 years as 'important people who have rights and are important human beings capable of understanding, communicating and influencing (their) own lives and those around (them)' (Harcourt, Perry and Waller, 2011: 7). Indeed, GC7 acknow-ledges 'young children as social actors from the beginning of life' (OHCHR, 2006, p. 2). Yet over a decade after its publication, GC7 (OHCHR, 2006) remains an addendum to UNCRC (OHCHR, 1989); the original convention has not yet been reframed to acknow-ledge fully the capacities of the youngest children, the world citizens who are experiencing the most critical period of their lives.

As a result of obscurity in policy and practice across the world, the rights of many infants and young children are not respected, so that they are denied play opportunities, a standard of living that meets their physical and social needs, or protection from sexual abuse and vio-lence. This international handbook is concerned with the ways rights of infants and young children up to 8 years translate from policy into practice. The book captures and critiques much of what has been achieved to date in realising the rights of infants and children up to 8 years, critically reviews the current state of rights for those children, and considers what remains to be done to secure and respect the rights of infants and young children younger than 8 years in particular. To achieve these aims, the handbook draws on international per-spectives characterised by empirical research evidence, praxis and expertise across multiple disciplines. This chapter begins that journey by setting in context the rights of infants and children younger than 8 years. We consider children's rights generally, reflecting on their history and definition and considering some of the problems concerning them, before out-lining the handbook's organisation and content.

A short history of children's rights

Following World War I, Eglantyne Jebb co-founded the Save the Children Fund (SCF) in 1919 and subsequently co-wrote the Declaration of the Rights of the Child, endorsed by the League of Nations in 1924 (Mahood, 2008; Milne, 2008). The 1924 Declaration 'recog-nised and affirmed for the first time the existence of rights specific to children' (Humanium, 2011), with a primary focus on protection and provision, and small consideration of partici-pation as 'rights-in-trust' (Archard, 2011).

International focus on human rights intensified after World War II, signalled in 1945 by the transformation of the League of Nations into the United Nations (United Nations, 2000).

Between 1945 and 1949, Nazi collaborators were tried at the Nuremberg Trials, resulting in the Nuremberg Code (United States Government, 1949). While the Nuremberg Trials were in session, the Universal Declaration of Human Rights emerged, framing 'childhood' as a phase when children are 'entitled to special care and assistance' (United Nations, 1948). The second Declaration of the Rights of the Child emerged from the United Nations General Assembly in 1959: this focused predominantly on protection, 'with little emphasis on empowering (children) as well' (Humanium, 2011; UNICEF, 2009). This was not a legally binding document, but three decades later, on 20 November 1989, the UNCRC was adopted by the United Nations General Assembly as a legal agreement (OHCHR, 1989). However, few of its authors were practising lawyers and few 'knew much about the real situation of children in any country including their own' (Milne, 2008, p. 51): they were an eclectic and elite group of UN diplomats, most of whom were based in Geneva or New York. Shortly after the UNCRC was adopted, it was ratified by all but two United Nations member states, the United States of America and Somalia (Gordon, Irving, Nandy and Townsend, 2007); Somalia ratified the UNCRC in 2015.

Like the UNCRC, the African Charter on the Rights and Welfare of the Child (ACRWC) is a comprehensive instrument that sets out rights and defines universal principles and norms for the status of children. The ACRWC was adopted by the Organisation of African Unity (OAU) in 1990 and was entered into force in 1999. The ACRWC calls for the creation of an African Committee of Experts on the Rights and Welfare of the Child (Committee of Experts), and its mission is to interpret, promote, protect and practise applying the rights established by the ACRWC. This allows for important cultural distinctions (e.g. a more communitarian approach for the African continent). The ACRWC and the UNCRC are the only international and regional human rights treaties that cover the whole spectrum of civil, political, economic, social and cultural rights.

Many consider the UNCRC (OHCHR, 1989) to have made a strong and positive contribution to children's rights internationally (Franklin, 1995; Milne, 2008; Reid, 1994). However, this is by no means a universal view (Byrne and Lundy, 2015), and in regard to younger children there seem to be particular challenges in translating policy into practice (McGrath et al., 2008; Te One, 2010).

The nature of rights

Feinberg (1970) proposes that 'a claim against someone whose recognition as valid is called for by some set of governing rules or moral principles' (p. 257); rights may be those rules or principles. Human rights are defined as 'basic rights and freedoms that all people are entitled to regardless of nationality, sex, national or ethnic origin, race, religion, language, or other status' (Amnesty International, 2011). A right affords 'power, prerogative and privilege' (Hohfeld, 1920, pp. 36–37). Rights may be framed as sets of 'jural opposites', for which they are juxtaposed with no rights – privilege/duty, power/disability, immunity/liability – or sets of 'jural correlates', for which they are associated with duties – privilege/no rights, power/liability, immunity/disability (Hohfeld, 1920, pp. 36–37). This construct creates tensions (e.g. between 'rights and duties' for which *claim rights* and *liberty rights* are given primacy over *power rights* and *immunity rights*) (Wilson, 2007). Any suggestion that *claim rights* should balance rights with responsibilities 'should be uncontroversial' (Ife and Fiske, 2006, p. 297), but *claim rights* may have a more pragmatic quality than *liberty rights* – 'rights of individuals to pursue their own lives without interference' (Jones and Welch, 2010, pp. 30–31) – because they acknowledge limitations that social contexts may impose.

Moral rights are so important that it would be 'wrong to deny it or to withhold' them (MacCormick, 1982, p. 160); Archard (2004) distinguishes between moral rights and legal rights, but suggests that a single right might be both. Equally, different types of rights tend to assume negative or positive connotations. Rights requiring protection may be regarded as 'negative rights', whereas positive rights are considered 'legal, institutional, customary' rights and fundamental rights, including liberty, self-determination, and freedom of thought, expression, religion or movement, and as such are viewed as 'moral, natural, human' rights (Archard, 2004; O'Neill, 1988, p. 445; Symonides, 2000). Welfare or provision rights are also regarded as positive rights, and may include rights to shelter, health, medicine, food and personal autonomy (Archard, 2011; Eddy, 2006; Griffin, 2000). However, there may be a finite supply of *welfare rights* so that they cannot be guaranteed for everyone, so it may be argued that a more apposite term for these is 'ethical rights' (Eddy, 2006; Griffin, 2000, p. 30).

While 'all people are entitled to ... basic rights' (Amnesty International, 2011), another way of categorising rights is predicated on age: adults' rights ('A Rights'), children's rights ('C Rights') and rights that both groups share ('A-C Rights') (Feinberg, 1980). Two types of 'C Rights' focus on 'being' and 'becoming' (Qvortrup, 1994): rights to goods such as food, shelter, love and freedom from harm and 'rights to an open future' (e.g. education) (Archard, 2011; Feinberg, 1980). However, 'C Rights' carry tensions: for example, when a child is positioned as a passive recipient of protection rights, other rights may be compromised (e.g. rights to liberty or freedom of expression and movement).

The nature of children's rights

The UNCRC (OHCHR, 1989) asserts that 'childhood is entitled to special care and assistance', and to that end the Convention incorporates social, cultural, political, civil and economic rights in its 54 articles, to which every child has an entitlement. While all 54 articles are considered equally important and interwoven, four rights are articulated in the Convention's General Principles: these are children's rights that also facilitate the other UNCRC rights (UNICEF, 2018b). The four General Principles are concerned with a child's rights to non-discrimination (Article 2), primacy afforded to his or her best interests (Article 3), life, survival and optimal development (Article 6) and being heard (Article 12) (OHCHR, 1989). Alongside the General Principles, other rights are divided into three groups: survival and development rights, sometimes termed protection rights, provision rights, and participation rights; these three groups of children's rights are widely referred to as the 'three Ps' (Bardy, 2000). There is some overlap across these groups; for example, Article 4, which is concerned with protection of children's rights, is included in all three Ps (UNICEF, 2014c).

Children's protection rights

UNCRC protection rights are concerned with keeping children safe (UNICEF, 2014c). They focus on protecting children from cruelty, exploitation, neglect and all types of abuse, including any they may encounter if they enter the criminal justice system. With these rights, children are also afforded 'special protection' during wartime. Specifically, child protection rights are captured in the following 16 articles (Table 1.1).

Table 1.1 Articles for children's protection rights

Article	Child protection rights focus
4	Protection of rights
11	Kidnapping
19	Protection from all violence
20	Children deprived of family environment
21	Adoption
22	Refugee children
32	Child labour
33	Drug abuse
34	Sexual exploitation
35	Abduction, sale and trafficking
36	Other forms of exploitation
37	Detention and punishment
38	War and armed conflicts
39	Rehabilitation of child victims
40	Juvenile justice
41	Respect for superior national standards: *national legislation that protects children's rights better than the CRC articles has primacy over CRC in that country*

Children's provision rights

Children's provision rights – or survival and development rights – are children's fundamental basic rights to life, survival and development, and include Article 6, which is the General Principle concerned with life, survival and optimal development (UNICEF, 2014c). Twenty-one articles feature children's provision rights (Table 1.2).

Children's participation rights

Children's participation rights are the smallest group of the three Ps and were a later addition to the Convention (Skelton, 2007). Indeed, children were not even consulted when the UNCRC was developed. These seven articles are concerned with children's rights to an active voice and incorporate Article 12, which is the General Principle concerned with the child's right to be heard (UNICEF, 2014c) (Table 1.3).

Some problems with children's rights

Policy is irrelevant if it does not translate into practice. Thus, the UNCRC (OHCHR, 1989) attempts to reify the Convention by stipulating how governments and adults should collaborate to ensure rights are respected and enacted for every child. Article 1 defines 'child', and Articles 42–54 are concerned with the United Nations' and States Parties' obligations concerning the UNCRC (OHCHR, 1989). However, while 195 States Parties ratified the UNCRC, few national governments have managed to implement the Convention fully (Lundy, Kilkelly, Byrne and Kang, 2012; UNICEF, 2016).

Table 1.2 Articles for children's provision rights

Article	Child provision rights focus
4	Protection of rights
5	Parental guidance
6	Survival and development
7	Registration, name, nationality, care
8	Preservation of identity
9	Provision for children separated from parents
10	Family reunification
14	Freedom of thought, conscience and religion
18	Parental responsibilities; state assistance
20	Provision for children deprived of family environment
22	Provision for refugee children
23	Provision for children with disabilities
24	Health and health services for children
25	Review of treatment in care to ensure it is in the best interests of the child
26	Provision of social security for children who are poor or in need
27	Provision of an adequate standard of living
28	Right to free primary education
29	Goals of education enable every child to develop fully, respect others and live peacefully
30	Children of minorities and indigenous groups learn about and practise their own culture, language and religion
31	Children have rights to leisure, play and culture
42	Provision for children to know about their rights

Table 1.3 Articles for children's participation rights

Article	Child participation rights focus
4	Protection of rights
12	Respect for the views of the child 'given due weight in accordance with the age and maturity of the child' (OHCHR, 1989)
13	Freedom of expression as long as it is not 'damaging to themselves or others'
14	Freedom of thought, conscience and religion
15	Freedom of association with others
16	Children's right to privacy
17	Children have a right to access children's books, mass media and information that promotes their health and well-being

Individual States Parties tend to prioritise UNCRC protection rights but focus less on children's provision and participation rights (Mayall, 2006; Parton, 2005). As indicated earlier in this chapter, tensions between children's protection and participation rights can arise, yet for children's rights to be respected and implemented, both are needed, as well as provision rights. Indeed, children are in a better position to reify their own rights if their participation rights are respected (Ruiz-Casares, Collins, Tisdall and Grover, 2017). Given opportunities to exercise their rights to participation, children have the capacity to demonstrate rational decision-making leading to competent actions (Kelly and Smith, 2017; Murray, 2016). Nevertheless, there is some divergence of opinion concerning how UNCRC participation rights have been taken up: while Skelton (2007) claims they have led to a 'paradigmatic shift in thinking about children' (p. 167), elsewhere it is argued that value attributed to them tends to be 'tokenistic' and that they lack clarity so are difficult to translate from policy to practice (Byrne and Lundy, 2015; Lansdown, 2010; Mayall, 2006: 11). Other concerns relate to tensions in cultures, including some indigenous cultures, in which children learn through observation and listening and less through exercising their voice. Child participation rights may also be read as oppositional to respect of elders or the larger community, though that view may be considered a misinterpretation of the intent of the UNCRC articles pertaining to children's participation rights (Ndimande and Swadener, 2013; Una, 2011). In other words, they are not intended to be in opposition to parental or community rights. Equally, it must be noted that the UNCRC itself is a document that is laden with Western cultural norms.

Evolving capacities

The notion of 'evolving capacities' is embedded in Article 12 and is a feature of the Convention that may exclude infants and the youngest children from accessing their rights. Article 12 is the participation right which states that children may express their views freely in matters affecting them only if the child is deemed 'capable of forming his or her own views', to which others then accord 'due weight in accordance with the age and maturity of the child'. Article 12 assumes that age may equate with capacity, but this claim is contestable. Lansdown (2005) queries the meaning of 'due weight', to what extent and at which ages it should be accorded and what account adults may take of the varied maturity of individual children. Whereas the World Bank (2010) defines 'capacity' as 'fully operational', Lansdown (2005) argues that children's 'acquisition of competencies will vary according to circumstances' and that their 'capacities can differ according to the nature of the rights to be exercised' (p. ix). In this way, argues Lansdown (2005), the idea of 'evolving capacities' balances recognition of children as rights-bearing active social agents with entitlement to protection, according to their 'relative immaturity and youth' (p. ix). However, it may be argued that the proposition that children's capacities evolve detracts from any possibility that they may be regarded as competent, capable, 'rich' social actors from birth (Dahlberg and Lenz Taguchi, 1994, p. 2; Prout and James, 1997).

Indeed, there is good evidence to suggest that humans can express their views regarding matters affecting them from birth. From birth, infants assert their identities, personhood, self-expression and intersubjectivity (Alderson et al., 2008; Meltzoff and Moore, 1977; Trevarthen, 2004). Equally, young children express their views through multiple modalities, including 'bodily cues and forms of non-verbal communication' (Bae, 2010, p. 208), and can plan and co-construct their own learning with adults (Garrick et al., 2010), a process for which they express their views regarding matters affecting them. However, adults may find it difficult to comprehend children's thoughts and actions because they 'try to interpret them in adult terms' (Hardman, 1973, p. 95), so the nature and extent of 'due weight' given to the 'views of the child' depends on the capacity of those people who accord the 'due weight' to identify and recognise children's capacities to form and express their own views in matters affecting them. As Van Beers et al. (2008) posit, 'reference to "evolving capacities" is often made when adults decide to include or exclude children from various aspects of social life' (p. 54). The alternative is for adults to provide stimulating, safe environments where all children are acknowledged to have capacity from birth to form and express their views and where adults ensure that respectful account is taken of children's views concerning matters that affect them (Bardy, 2000; Human Early Learning Partnership, 2012; Swadener and Polakow, 2011).

General Comment 7

As long ago as 2004, the UNCRC noted that infants and young children 'can only benefit from the protection rights recognised in the Convention', yet that 'the rights of babies and young children are too often overlooked', although 'early childhood is a crucial period for the sound development of young children' (Liwski, 2006, p. 8). This was the UNCRC rationale for developing GC7 (OHCHR, 2006). Equally, GC7 explicitly recognises, in an addendum to the original UNCRC, 'young children as social actors from the beginning of life, with particular interests, capacities and vulnerabilities, and of requirements for protection, guidance and support in the exercise of their rights' (OHCHR, 2006, p. 2).

The rights of many young children continue to be disregarded 14 years on from GC7 and 30 years on from the original Convention. For example, young children's rights to a standard of living that meets their physical and social needs, play opportunities, appropriate early education and protection from sexual abuse are not guaranteed. Indeed, the very chapters that make up this handbook do not cover all the UNCRC rights evenly or even comprehensively. Instead, they reflect the messy, complex reality that is the young children's rights zeitgeist, with all its flaws, disparities, strengths and weaknesses, 30 years after the Convention was adopted.

Conclusion

In the publication year of this handbook – 2019 – children are among large numbers of refugees and asylum seekers separated from their parents at the US border, held in detention off the coast of Australia, and detained in refugee camps throughout the world. Thirty years after the launch of the UNCRC, children across the world continue to experience poverty, being spoken for, marginalisation, and lack of rights to protection, provision and participation.

At the same time, young children are involved increasingly in matters that affect them, for example in climate protests, and in the research process of scholars in childhood studies, sociology of childhood, early childhood education and other fields. Examples are interwoven throughout the handbook's chapters.

Although the editors of this handbook are from three geographically widespread continents, they live in Majority World cultures. Nevertheless, the book's authors are from many nations across the globe, and they draw on extensive experience across multiple disciplines and vastly different cultural contexts to contribute research and critiques concerning young children's rights.

Our handbook is structured quite simply, belying the many complex nuances, levels and intersections that shape young children's rights. We have chosen to open with a section on policy that is relevant to young children's rights, illustrating how global policy concerning young children's rights is operating in some specific circumstances. This section opens with 'an assessment of the impact of General Comment No. 7 on law and policy on a global scale' from Laura Lundy. Next, Priscilla Alderson and Tamaki Yoshida critique babies' rights, then Margaret Coady and John Tobin draw attention to young children's rights policy and practice in Australia. Sheila Long critiques experiences from Ireland, then Vina Aldriny, Hani Yulindrasari and Marek Tesar share experiences from Indonesia.

The sections that follow are structured according to the 'three Ps' of the UNCRC (OHCHR, 1989): protection rights, provision rights and participation rights, each with its own introductory chapter. We have framed the handbook in the same way that the United Nations chose to frame rights 30 years ago, but we emphasise strongly that all the rights are inextricably interwoven.

It has been a tremendous privilege to work with the many contributors to this volume; we are in awe of the wonderful work they and their collaborators have done to shine a light on young children's rights, despite many challenges. Our handbook celebrates the many advances in young children's rights over the past 30 years, but it also highlights the significant work still to do. We commend it to you and urge you to engage actively with its content to advance further the field of young children's rights at every level in ways that position young children powerfully.

References

Alderson, Priscilla, Joanna Hawthorne, and Margaret Killen. 2008. "The Participation Rights of Premature Babies." In *Beyond Article 12: Essential Readings on Children's Participation*, edited by Henk Van Beers, Antonella Invernizzi, and Brian Milne, 57–65. Bangkok: Black and White Publications.

Amnesty International. 2011. "Human Rights Basics." www.amnestyusa.org/research/human-rights-basics

Archard, David. 2004. *Children, Rights and Childhood* (2e). London: Routledge.

Archard, David. 2011. "Children's Rights." In *The Stanford Encyclopedia of Philosophy (Summer 2011 Edition)*, edited by Edward N. Zalta. Stanford CA: Stanford University. http://plato.stanford.edu/entries/rights-children/.

Bae, Berit. 2010. "Realising Children's Right to Participation in Early Childhood Settings: Some Critical Issues in a Norwegian Context." *Early Years*, 30(3): 205–221.

Bakken, Linda, Nola Brown, and Barry Downing. 2017. "Early Childhood Education: The Long-Term Benefits." *Journal of Research in Childhood Education*, 31(2): 255–269.

Bardy, Marjatta. 2000. "The Three Ps of Children's Rights: Provision, Protection and Participation." *CYC-Online*, 16. www.cyc-net.org/cyc-online/cycol-0500-threepees.html.

Brooks, Elspeth, and Jane Murray. 2018. "Ready, Steady, Learn: School Readiness and Children's Voices in English Early Childhood Settings." *Education 3–13*, 46(2): 143–156.

Byrne, Bronagh, and Laura Lundy. 2015. "Reconciling Children's Policy and Children's Rights: Barriers to Effective Government Delivery." *Children and Society*, 29(4): 266–276.

Centre on the Developing Child. 2007. "The Science of Early Childhood Development." https://46y5eh11fhgw3ve3ytpwxt9r-wpengine.netdna-ssl.com/wp-content/uploads/2007/03/InBrief-The-Science-of-Early-Childhood-Development2.pdf

Cheney, Kristen E. 2004. *Pillars of the Nation: Child Citizens and Ugandan National Development*. Chicago, IL: University of Chicago Press.

Dahlberg, Gunilla, and Hillevi Lenz Taguchi. 1994. *Förskola och skola och om visionen om en mötesplats, [Preschool and school and the vision of a meeting-place]*. Stockholm: HLS Förlag.

Eddy, Katherine. 2006. "Welfare Rights and Conflicts of Rights." *Res Publica*, 12(4): 337–356.

Feinberg, Joel. 1970. "The Nature and Value of Rights." *Journal of Value Inquiry*, 4: 243–257.

Feinberg, Joel. 1980. "A Child's Right to an Open Future." In *Whose Child? Parental Rights, Parental Authority and State Power*, edited by William Aiken and Hugh LaFollette, 124–153. Totowa, NJ: Littlefield, Adams, and Co.

Franklin, Bob. 1995. "Children's Rights: An Overview." In *The Handbook of Children's Rights*, edited by Bob Franklin, 13–42. London: Routledge.

Garrick, Ros, Caroline Bath, Karen Dunn, Heloise Maconochie, Ben Willis, and Claire Wolstenholme. 2010. *Children's Experiences of the Early Years Foundation Stage*. London: Department for Education.

Gordon, David, Michelle K. Irving, Shaileen Nandy, and Peter Townsend. 2007. "The Extent and Nature of Absolute Poverty. Final Report to DFID: R8382." https://assets.publishing.service.gov.uk/media/57a08c37ed915d622c0011d7/R8382FR.pdf

Goswami, Usha, and Peter Bryant. 2007. *Children's Cognitive Development and Learning (Primary Review Research Survey 2/1a)*. Cambridge: University of Cambridge Faculty of Education.

Griffin, James. 2000. "Welfare Rights." *The Journal of Ethic*, 4(1/2): 27–43.

Harcourt, Deborah, Bob Perry, and Tim Waller. Eds. 2011. *Researching Young Children's Perspectives: Debating the Ethics and Dilemmas of Educational Research with Children*. London: Routledge.

Hardman, Charotte. 1973. "Can There Be An Anthropology of Children?" *Journal of the Anthropology Society of Oxford*, 4(1): 85–99.

Heckman, James, and Dimitriy Masterov. 2007. "The Productivity Argument for Investing in Young Children." *Review of Agricultural Economics*, 29(3): 446–493.

Hohfeld, Wesley N. 1920. *Fundamental Legal Conceptions, As Applied in Judicial Reasoning and Other Legal Essays*. New Haven, CT: Yale University Press.

Holloway, Sara L., and Gill Valentine. 2000. "Children's Geographies and the New Social Studies of Childhood." In *Children's Geographies: Playing, Living, Learning*, edited by Sara L. Holloway and Gill Valentine, 1–26. London: Routledge.

Human Early Learning Partnership. 2012. *Early Childhood Rights Indicators*. http://earlylearning.ubc.ca/documents/152/

Humanium. 2011. *Children's Rights Portal*. http://childrensrightsportal.org/references-on-child-rights/declaration-rights-child/

Ife, Jim, and Lucy Fiske. 2006. "Human Rights and Community Work." *International Social Work*, 49(3): 297–308.

Jones, Phil, and Sue Welch. 2010. *Rethinking Children's Rights*. London: Continuum.

Kanyal, Mallika. 2014. *Children's Rights 0-8: Promoting Participation in Education and Care*. London: David Fulton.

Kelly, Leanne M., and Kylie A. Smith. 2017. "Children as Capable Evaluators: Evolving Conceptualizations of Childhood in NGO Practice Settings." *Child and Family Social Work*, 22(2): 853–861.

Lansdown, Gerison. 2005. *The Evolving Capacities of Children: Implications for the Exercise of Rights*. Florence: UNICEF Innocenti Research Centre.

Lansdown, Gerison. 2010. "The Realisation of Children's Participation Rights." In *A Handbook of Children and Young People's Participation*, edited by Barry Percy-Smith and Nigel Thomas, 11–23. London: Routledge.

League of Nations. 1924. *Declaration on the Rights of the Child*. www.unicef.org/vietnam/01_-_Declaration_of_Geneva_1924.PDF

Liwski, Norberto. 2006. "Implementing Child Rights in Early Childhood." In *Guide to General Comment 7: Implementing Child Rights in Early Childhood*, edited by UNICEF and Bernard van Leer Foundation, 8–10. The Hague: Bernard van Leer Foundation.

Lundy, Laura, Ursula Kilkelly, Bronagh Byrne, and Jason Kang. 2012. *The UN Convention on the Rights of the Child: A Study of Legal Implementation in 12 Countries*. Belfast: Centre for Children's Rights.

Lundy, Laura, and Beth Blue Swadener. 2015. "Engaging with Young Children as Co-Researchers: A Child Rights-Based Approach." In *Handbook of Research Methods in Early Childhood Education, Volume II*, edited by Olivia Saracho, 657–676. Charlotte, NC: Information Age Publishing.

MacCormick, Neil. 1982. *Legal Rights and Social Democracy: Essays in Legal and Political Philosophy*. Oxford: Clarendon Press.

Mahood, Linda. 2008. "Eglantyne Jebb: Remembering, Representing and Writing a Rebel Daughter." *Women's History Review*, 17(1): 1–20.

Mayall, Berry. 2006. "Values and Assumptions Underpinning Policy for Children and Young People in England." *Children's Geographies*, 4(1): 9–17.

McCain, Margaret, and Fraser Mustard. 1999. *Reversing the Brain Drain: Early Years Study*. Toronto: Ontario Children's Secretariat.

McGrath, Gulliver, Zen McGrath, Sam Parsons, Kylie Smith, Greta Swan, and Sharon Saitta. 2008. "'You're Not Going to Like This But … ' Learning to Hear Children as Experts in Early Childhood Classrooms." In *Young Children as Active Citizens*, edited by Glenda MacNaughton, Patrick Hughes, and Kylie Smith, 148–159. Newcastle, UK: Cambridge Scholars Publishing.

Meltzoff, Andrew N., and M. Keith Moore. 1977. "Imitation of Facial and Manual Gestures by Human Neonates." *Science*, 198: 75–78.

Milne, Brian. 2008. "From Chattels to Citizens?" In *Children and Citizenship*, edited by Antonella Invernizzi and Jane Williams, 44–54. London: Sage.

Moss, Peter, and Mathias Urban. 2018. "The Organisation for Economic Co-operation and Development's International Early Learning Study: What's Going On?" *Contemporary Issues in Early Childhood*, 1–6. doi:10.1177/1463949118803269.

Murray, Jane. 2016. "Young Children are Researchers: Children Aged Four to Eight Years Engage in Important Research Behaviour When They Base Decisions On Evidence." *European Early Childhood Education Research Journal*, 24(5): 705–720.

Murray, Jane. 2017a. "Young Children are Human Beings." *International Journal of Early Years Education*, 25(4): 339–342.

Murray, Jane. 2017b. "Welcome in! How the Academy Can Warrant Recognition of Young Children as Researchers." *European Early Childhood Education Research Journal*, 25(2): 224–242.

Ndimande, Bekisizwe S., and Beth Blue Swadener. 2013. "Children's Rights and Cultural Tensions in South Africa." *International Journal of Equity and Innovation in Early Childhood*, 10(1): 79–92.

O'Neill, Onora. 1988. "Children's Rights and Children's Lives." *Ethics*, 98(3): 445–463.

Office of the High Commissioner for Human Rights (OHCHR). 1989. "Convention on the Rights of the Child." www.ohchr.org/EN/ProfessionalInterest/Pages/CRC.aspx

Office of the High Commissioner for Human Rights (OHCHR). 2006. "General Comment No.7. 2005. Implementing Child Rights in Early Childhood." www2.ohchr.org/english/bodies/crc/docs/AdvanceVersions/GeneralComment7Rev1.pdf

Parton, Nigel. 2005. *Safeguarding Childhood. Early Intervention and Surveillance in Late Modern Society*. Basingstoke: Palgrave MacMillan.

Polakow, Valerie. 1993. *Lives on the Edge: Single Mothers and Their Children in the "Other" America*. Chicago, IL: University of Chicago Press.

Prout, Alan, and Allison James. 1997. "A New Paradigm for the Sociology of Childhood." In *Constructing and Reconstructing Childhood* (2e), edited by Allison James and Alan Prout, 7–33. London: Falmer Books.

Qvortrup, Jens. 1994. "Introduction." In *Childhood Matters: Social Theory, Practice and Politics*, edited by Jens Qvortrup, Marjatta Bardy, Giovanni Sgritta, and Helmut Wintersberger, 1-26. Wien: Avebury.

Reid, Richard. 1994. "Children's Rights: Radical Remedies for Critical Needs." In *Justice for Children*, edited by Stewart Asquith and Malcolm Hill, 19–25. London: Martinus Nijhoff Publishers.

Ruiz-Casares, Monica, Tara M. Collins, E. Kay M. Tisdall, and Sonja Grover. 2017. "Children's Rights to Participation and Protection in International Development and Humanitarian Interventions: Nurturing a Dialogue." *The International Journal of Human Rights*, 21(1): 1–13.

Schweinhart, Lawrence J., Jean Montie, Zongping Xiang, W. Steven Barnett, Clive R. Belfield, and Miligros Nores. 2005. *Lifetime Effects: The High/Scope Perry Preschool Study through Age 40*. Ypsilanti, MI: High/Scope Press.

Shonkoff, Jack P., and Deborah A. Phillips. 2000. *From Neurons to Neighbourhoods*. Washington, DC: National Academy Press.

Shore, Rima. 1997. *Rethinking the Brain*. New York: Families and Work Institute.

Skelton, Tracey. 2007. "Children, Young People, UNICEF and Participation." *Children's Geographies*, 5(1): 165–181.

Smith, Kylie. 2013. "A Rights-Based Approach to Observing and Assessing Children in Early Childhood Classrooms." In *Children's Lives and Education in Cross-national Contexts: What Difference Could Rights Make?* edited by Beth Blue Swadener, Laura Lundy, Janette Habashi, and Natasha Blanchet-Cohen, 99–114. New York: Sage.

Swadener, Beth Blue, and Valerie Polakow. 2011. "Introduction to the Special Issue on Children's Rights and Voices in Research: Cross-National Perspectives." *Early Education and Development*, 22(5): 707–713.

Symonides, Janusz. 2000. *Human Rights: Concept and Standards*. Burlington, VT: UNESCO Publishing and Ashgate.

Te One, Sarah. 2010. "Advocating for Infants' Rights in Early Childhood Education." *Early Childhood Folio*, 14(1): 13–17.

The Lancet. 2016. "Advancing Early Childhood Development: From Science to Scale: An Executive Summary for the Lancet's Series." www.thelancet.com/pb-assets/Lancet/stories/series/ecd/Lancet_ECD_Executive_Summary.pdf

Trevarthen, Colwyn. 2004. *Learning about Ourselves from Children: Why a Growing Human Brain Needs Interesting Companions*. Edinburgh: University of Edinburgh Perception–in-Action Laboratories.

Una Children's Rights Learning Group. 2011. *Children's Rights in Cultural Contexts. Working Paper 8*. Belfast, Northern Ireland: Una (Queens College).

UNICEF. 2009. *The State of the World's Children 2009*. New York: United Nations Children's Fund.

UNICEF. 2014a. "Convention on the Rights of the Child." www.unicef.org/crc/

UNICEF. 2014b. "Early Childhood Development: The Key to a Full and Productive Life." www.unicef.org/dprk/ecd.pdf

UNICEF. 2014c. "Convention on the Rights of the Child: Rights under the Convention on the Rights of the Child." www.unicef.org/crc/index_30177.html

UNICEF. 2016. "The State of the World's Children 2016." www.unicef.org/sowc2016/

UNICEF. 2018a. "UNICEF Strategic Plan 2018–2021." www.unicef.org/publications/files/UNICEF_Strategic_Plan_2018-2021.pdf

UNICEF. 2018b. "How We Protect Children's Rights." www.unicef.org.uk/what-we-do/un-convention-child-rights/

United Nations. 1948. "The Universal Declaration of Human Rights." www.un.org/en/documents/udhr/index.shtml

United Nations. 2000. "About the United Nations: History." www.un.org/aboutun/history.htm

United Nations. 2015. "Sustainable Development Goals." www.un.org/sustainabledevelopment/sustainable-development-goals/

United States Government. 1949. *Nuremberg Code. Trials of War Criminals before the Nuremberg Military Tribunals under Control Council Law*. 10 (2): 181–182. Washington, DC: US Government Printing Office.

Van Beers, Henk, Antonella Invernizzi, and Brian Milne. 2008. *Beyond Article 12: Essential Readings on Children's Participation*. Bangkok: Black and White Publications.

Wilson, James G. S. 2007. "Rights." In *Principles of Health Care Ethics* (2e), edited by Richard E. Ashcroft, Angus Dawson, Heather Draper, and John R. McMillan, 239–246. Chichester: John Wiley.

World Bank. 2010. "Private Participation in Infrastructure Projects Database." https://ppi.worldbank.org/data

2

IMPLEMENTING THE RIGHTS OF YOUNG CHILDREN

An assessment of the impact of General Comment No. 7 on law and policy on a global scale

Laura Lundy

Introduction

The UN Committee on the Rights of the Child ('the Committee') published General Comment No. 7 ('GC7') (UN, 2005), its official guidance to governments on the implementation of children's rights in the early years, in 2005. The advice is far-reaching; it covers all aspects of young children's lives, not just early education and care, but also health, social security, family life, and play and leisure. Moreover, there is an explicit focus on recognising younger children's capacity for participation and agency as well as the particular situation of those who are more vulnerable to breaches of their rights, including children who are disabled, in poverty and living through conflict and displacement. One of the objectives of GC7 was to 'contribute to the realization of rights for all young children through formulation and promotion of comprehensive policies, laws, programmes, practices, professional training and research specifically focused on rights in early childhood' (UN, 2005, para. x).

Since then, scores of United Nations ('UN') member states have filed assessments of their progress in meeting the requirements of the United Nations Convention on the Rights of the Child (UN, 1989) ('the CRC' or 'the Convention') (in States Parties reports) and the Committee has published reports commenting on their progress and identifying areas of concern (in 'concluding observations'). The aim of this chapter is to assess the extent to and ways in which children's rights in the early years are addressed both by governments and the Committee on the Rights of the Child in the periodic monitoring process on the Convention. It does this through a documentary analysis of States Parties reports and concluding observations of countries submitted in the wake of GC7 in one specific year – 2017 (the most recent complete set). This includes 22 countries with very diverse social and economic profiles from each of the UN's five regions. The reports have been analysed to assess: the extent and ways in which governments prioritise children's rights in law and policy in the early years in its reporting to the Committee; the profile given to this group of children by the Committee and the issues that it addresses; what is regarded by the Committee as good practice in terms of law and policy; and the extent to which GC7 is influencing government and indeed the Committee on the Rights of the Child itself.

The method

Periodic reporting by the Committee is the primary enforcement mechanism of the CRC, as it is for most other UN human rights treaties. Every five years (although it often takes much longer in practice), states are required to reflect on their progress in implementing the CRC according to reporting guidelines which specify the information that the state is required to submit (Article 44 of the CRC; UN, 2015a). The concluding observations provide an easily accessible and reliable focus for documentary analysis: they are official documents, written by a single body of experts and publicly available online in English. For the purposes of this chapter, a documentary analysis was conducted of all 22 member states that were examined across the Committee's three sessions in one year – 2017. The countries cover a spectrum of UN member states across all five UN regions, including Bhutan, North Korea, Denmark, Moldova, Malawi, Lebanon, Tajikistan, Serbia and Vanuatu. The only region not well represented in this particular group is the Western European and Others region: Denmark is the only country from this group that reported in 2017 apart from the United States (which reported on two of the Optional Protocols but not the Convention itself, which it has not ratified). To supplement this, Ireland has been included as it appeared before the Committee in 2016.

While the Committee's reports present an independent evaluation of policy and practice against an agreed framework of international standards, their evidential basis, their purpose and their audience must be borne in mind (Prior, 2008). Not only do they need to be concise and accessible to fulfil their role in publicising breaches among rights-holders, but they are to a large extent dependent on the information presented to them by States Parties and others, which can be both ad hoc and lacking in independence and criticality. They cannot therefore be regarded as a complete factual account of the state of children's rights in signatory states, but a reliable evidence base of independent expert opinion on the issue (Lundy, 2012). The States Parties self-reports are similarly, if not more, limited. States will wish to present themselves as making meaningful progress in the implementation of the CRC. For the Committee, the aim is to hold the state to account while encouraging realistic progress and conveying consistent messages about the requirements of the CRC (Lundy, 2012). Nonetheless, while bearing these limitations in mind, the analysis of the published UN reports still yields valuable insights into the way in which young children's rights are being addressed in diverse global contexts.

The reports to the Committee and the Committee's concluding observations are all publicly available on the website of the Office of the High Commission on Human Rights (www.ohchr.org). They do not reference any individual person by name. Given that the analysis was based on a documentary analysis of these publicly available sources, no ethical issues were considered to arise.

The analysis is structured according to the widely used categorisation of children's rights known as the 'three Ps' – provision, participation and protection (Hammarberg, 1990) –

since these have been chosen to structure this collection. Quennerstedt (2010) provides a robust criticism of this framework, arguing that it can hamper research and result in key rights being omitted from consideration. She queries why children need a special categorisation for their rights and suggests a return to the traditional categories of social, economic, and civil and political rights. However, the latter have also been the subject of significant critique since; like the three Ps, there are many rights (education is a key example) that simply defy categorisation. Thus, bearing these limitations in mind and recognising that all rights are interrelated and interdependent, and no rights should be neglected because the subjects are young, the three Ps were employed here as a convenient structure to discuss the diverse range of rights that the Convention provides to young children.

The analytical strategy involved reading every concluding observation (and preceding States Parties report) that was published in 2017 in full. Every statement in the reports that referenced young children (defined as under 8 by the Committee) and the substantive issues addressed in General Comment No. 7 were copied into a separate file for coding and categorisation (using the three Ps as the overarching themes): children in the early years; maternal health, pregnancy or breastfeeding; early/preschool education; play; all references to children aged under 8 and/or babies (and related terms such as 'infants'); and General Comment No. 7 itself. These extracts formed the core data, which was then coded and themed within each of the core rights that fall within the three Ps. (e.g. nutrition, breastfeeding and the environment were the key themes that emerged under the right to health, which is one aspect of 'provision'). The discussion that follows presents the findings of the documentary analysis using examples from the reports to illustrate common or interesting examples that arose in the analysis, drawing on reports from across the 22 countries.

Provision

The first 'P' – 'provision' – is by far the most extensive, covering an array of the rights normally classified as social and economic: health, education, and play and leisure. These are considered individually below as they all appear in some form or other in relation to young children. The other key right in this category – the right to an adequate standard of living – is addressed only once in a way that is specific to young children: in Ecuador, the government was urged to ensure resources for 'the eradication of multidimensional poverty in early childhood' (UN, 2017a, para.10b). That said, the impact of poverty is undoubtedly a crosscutting theme across the reports, and rightly so since poverty and structural inequality are widely recognised as the biggest challenge to the enjoyment of children's human rights (Pemberton et al., 2012). A further area that has been included here is the right to family life and alternative care. This encompasses a package of rights that are particular to children and do not fit neatly into traditional categorisations.

Health and well-being

Health is generally where young children appear most frequently in the concluding observations. Of particular concern, yet neglected in children's rights research, is Article 6, which addresses the child's right to life, survival and development (Peleg, 2017). Mortality rates for under-fives are of regular concern to the Committee, often in developing countries (e.g. in Mongolia, where the Committee 'remains seriously concerned about risks to the life, survival and development of children caused by injuries and accidents, in particular burns among children below 5 years of age') (UN, 2017b, para. 19). The Committee also points out where mortality is disproportionate for the context. For example, in Serbia, it noted serious concern that 'the State party's infant mortality rate remains above the European Union average', an outcome that was linked to poor access to neonatal care for Roma children (UN, 2017g, para. 26).

Article 24 places states under an obligation to:

> ensure that all segments of society, in particular parents and children, are informed, have access to education and are supported in the use of basic knowledge of child health and nutrition, the advantages of breast-feeding, hygiene and environmental sanitation and the prevention of accidents.

Early childhood nutrition is a pervading concern. For example, while the Democratic Republic of Korea presented details of a National Strategy and Plan to Control Child and Maternal Malnutrition (2014–2018), the Committee expressed serious concern about the very high prevalence of undernourishment in the state, referencing a 2012 nutrition survey which suggested that 28 per cent of children under 5 years of age were suffering from stunting and 4 per cent were suffering from wasting, 'which could be conservative estimates' (UN, 2017c, para. 41). Similarly, in relation to Antigua and Barbuda, the Committee encouraged the state to undertake research into nutrition, especially among newborns, and to ensure 'the availability of essential micronutrients, including vitamins A and D, to children under 5 years of age, paying particular attention to children in rural areas and from low-income families' (UN, 2017e, para. 41)

Breastfeeding is one issue that is concretely connected to younger children and their rights. Given its recognised advantages for children's health and development, it is striking that GC7 simply repeats the wording of Article 24 and provides no further comment on the significance of breastfeeding and what states can do to support it. Inexplicably, the States Parties reporting guidelines, revised in 2015, do not ask states to report on the rates of children who are breastfed as this appears to be lumped in with 'nutrition'. However, the Committee will nonetheless often highlight states that are falling short in this regard. A typical recommendation is the following for Saint Vincent and the Grenadines:

> Collect information on breastfeeding; develop a national programme for the protection, promotion and support of the decision to breastfeed exclusively for a minimum of six months; fully implement the International Code of Marketing of Breast-milk Substitutes; provide appropriate support to mothers and babies through counselling in hospitals, clinics and the community at large; implement the baby-friendly hospital initiative throughout the country; and raise awareness of the importance of breastfeeding among families and the general public and on the role they can play in supporting breastfeeding through comprehensive campaigns.
>
> *(UN, 2017f, para. 50b)*

While children do not have a right to be breastfed (and nor can there be given that: (a) this is not always possible; and (b) it may not be the mother's choice), there is an argument that breastfed babies should have a right to be breastfed (see Kent, 2006). There are lots of barriers, cultural and otherwise, that impinge adversely on that. Key issues not explored in the comments or states' reports are, for example, whether the children of mothers in prison should be supported to breastfeed their children (Van den Bergh et al., 2011) or whether laws should require those who harass breastfeeding mothers to participate in compulsory educational and awareness programs (Kent, 2006).

Breastfeeding is one of the ways in which HIV can be transmitted to infants, and mother-to-child transmission of HIV is the most common way in which children become HIV-positive (UN, 2003b, para. 25). Many women do not take advantage of antiretroviral therapy and prophylaxis treatment, even though this can significantly reduce the child's chance of becoming HIV-positive, due to lack of awareness or stigma (Ferguson et al., 2012). The Committee encouraged Cameroon, for example, to intensify the accessibility and availability of free testing for HIV and accelerate the task-shifting of initiating treatment to nurses and midwives (UN, 2017l, para. 36). Likewise, in Tajikistan, it expressed concerned about the significant increase in HIV infection among children below the age of 10 years and delays in antiretroviral therapy initiation among pregnant women living with HIV (UN, 2017m, para. 6).

The impact of the environment on young children's health and development is receiving increasing attention, yet GC7 mentions it only in passing in relation to Article 6 (UN, 2005, para. 10). A recent report by the UN Special Rapporteur on the environment and human rights, John Knox, on the issue of children's rights and the environment has emphasised the potential adverse impact of environmental harms such as pollution and climate change on young children's development and survival (UN, 2018). For instance, concern is expressed about the fact that one-quarter of the total disease burden in children under the age of 5 is attributed to environmental exposures (UN, 2018, para. 15). In spite of the growing and overwhelming evidence of the disproportionate adverse impact of the environment on younger children, their specific needs and rights are rarely addressed specifically in law and policy. Moreover, the only mention in the 22 concluding observations was in relation to Mongolia, where it noted the efforts the government was making to assess severe air pollution, but expressed concern about the impact of increasing levels of air pollution on children, 'including reduced fetal growth, pre-term birth, reduced lung function leading to acute respiratory disease' (UN, 2017b, para. 6).

Education

Early childhood education provision is not specifically mentioned in Article 28 of the CRC and is quite low-key in GC7. However, the Committee has defined education in its widest sense and noted 'with appreciation that some States parties are planning to make one year of preschool education available and free of cost for all children' (UN 2005, para. 28). It also features in most (albeit not all) concluding observations. Many of the countries reported on specific early years strategies, and in some instances progress, in terms of increasing the numbers of children with access to early childhood education, was acknowledged by the Committee. There was no consistency in the overall comments, but more often than not the Committee encouraged states to extend their efforts in this regard, often linking this to Goal 4.2 of the UN Sustainable Development Goals. A typical recommendation from the Committee in relation to Barbados is as follows:

> Taking note of target 4.2 of the Sustainable Development Goals on ensuring that all girls and boys have access to quality early childhood development, care and pre-primary education, the Committee recommends that the State party further strengthen its efforts to improve access to quality early childhood care and education and collect disaggregated data on early childhood care.
>
> *(UN, 2017o, para. 52)*

Recommendations exactly like this appear throughout the reports. While it is somewhat formulaic, it also appears to be one area where GC7 may have had some impact. Most states report something on education in the early years. Vanuatu, for example, specifically linked its recent action plan to its human rights obligations: it said that its early childhood care and education policy was 'developed to promote and ensure equitable access to quality preschool centres in Vanuatu' and that the government had 'considered its international commitment to international human rights declaration and the articles of the Convention in its policy' (UN, 2017p, para. 41).

Play

A surprising finding from the documentary analysis was the lack of reference to the right to play for very young children. Play has long been established as crucial to development in the early years (Lester and Russell, 2010) and was strongly emphasised in GC7: 'Play is one of the most distinctive features of early childhood. Through play, children both enjoy and challenge their current capacities, whether they are playing alone or with others' (UN, 2005, para. 34). While governments may be taking increasing steps to include play in policy, that is not apparent from their reports to the Committee. Nor is the Committee actively monitoring or reporting on it.

Although the right to play is not exclusive to young children, it is recognised as especially important for them, so it is disappointing that it is referred to only twice in the concluding observations, and that when it does appear there is nothing specific for children under the age of 8. It has been argued that the right to play suffers from the fact that it has been clustered under education in the States Parties reporting guidelines (Davey and Lundy, 2011). However, it might have been expected to gain prominence after the publication of General Comment No. 17 on the right to play, rest and leisure (UN, 2013b). There are also a growing number of examples of children's right to play being addressed in law and policy: Ireland reported extensively on its national play and recreation strategies when it reported in 2013, pointing out that extra funding had led to the number of playgrounds in the country more than doubling – from fewer than 200 to over 561 – with more than 100 further playgrounds planned (UN, 2015b, section E). It is disappointing that play remains largely 'invisible' in other national policy frameworks in the early years (in relation to New Zealand, see Alcock, 2013) and is an area that would still benefit from more robust monitoring from the Committee.

Family life and alternative care

The CRC contains a package of rights that relate to the child's right to family life and care. For example, Article 7 gives children the right to know and be cared for by their parents and Article 9 requires states to ensure the right of the child who is separated from one or both parents to maintain personal relations and direct contact with both parents on a regular basis, except if it is contrary to the child's best interests. GC7 also acknowledges the particular need for young children to have stable care. It states that:

> Under normal circumstances, young children form strong mutual attachments with their parents or primary caregivers. These relationships offer children physical and emotional security, as well as consistent care and attention. Through these relationships children construct a personal identity and acquire culturally valued skills, knowledge and behaviours. In these ways, parents (and other caregivers) are normally the major conduit through which young children are able to realize their rights.
>
> *(UN, 2005, para. 16)*

One practical challenge to this right is for the children of prisoners. Some countries will make arrangements for young children to stay with parents, a response which in itself poses additional children's rights challenges (Alejos et al., 2005). This arose only once in the 2017 concluding observation when the Committee urged Moldova to:

> Take urgent measures to ensure that living conditions for children in prison with their mothers are adequate for the child's physical, mental, moral and social development, and seek alternative measures to institutional confinement for pregnant women and mothers with small children, wherever possible.
>
> *(UN, 2017q, para. 27)*

Where children are not staying with their imprisoned parents, there is also an obligation to secure ongoing contact, the absence of which can have significant adverse consequences for children and their rights (Minson, 2018).

A related issue is how and where young children receive care when they cannot live with parents since there are compelling reasons to ensure that they are not placed in institutions, not least the impact on their physical and cognitive development (van IJzendoorn et al., 2011). GC7 encourages governments to invest in and support forms of alternative care that 'can ensure security, continuity of care and affection, and the opportunity for young children to form long-term attachments based on mutual trust and respect, for example through fostering, adoption and support for members of extended families' (UN, 2005, para. 36(b)). Yet this continues to be a consistent cause of concern across the country reports. For example, Ecuador was criticised for describing children over the age of 4 as 'difficult to adopt' (UN, 2017a, para. 31). More often, the concern was about the placement of young children in institutional care (e.g. see the reports on Serbia, the Democratic People's Republic of Korea and Estonia). In relation to the latter, the Committee observed: 'At least one fifth of the children placed in shelters owing to separation from their families are reportedly under 3 years of age, shelters are insufficiently regulated, with the ratio of children to employees being too high' (UN, 2017h, para. 36). However, it is not only an issue for children who have been removed from their parents. For example, the Committee raised issues about the construction of regional boarding schools in Bhutan replacing schools in rural areas, which provide for children as young as 6 years, given the impact that may have on the child's development and right to family life (UN, 2017k).

Protection

Children, particularly young children, are more vulnerable to abuse and neglect. GC7 acknowledges this, observing that:

> Young children are especially vulnerable to the harm caused by unreliable, inconsistent relationships with parents and caregivers, or growing up in extreme poverty and deprivation, or being surrounded by conflict and violence or displaced from their homes as refugees, or any number of other adversities prejudicial to their well-being.
>
> *(UN, 2005, para. 36)*

In spite of this, in only one of the 22 concluding observations does the Committee highlight a specific child protection issue for children in the early years. It observes that 'sexual violence in Cameroon is prevalent, including against very young children' (UN 2017l, para. 18).

It is also notable that the recommendations for addressing child protection issues are directed largely towards older children, although there is regular reference to the need for 'three digits' helplines, which would be one way of making these helplines accessible to some younger children. For the very young, who cannot self-report violence and abuse, multisectoral systems of review and treatment are crucial and should be embedded into law and policy in ways that reflect the principles of the CRC (Reading et al., 2009). In GC7, the Committee urges States Parties to incorporate the particular situation of young children into all legislation, policies and interventions to promote physical and psychological recovery and social reintegration within an environment that promotes dignity and self-respect. However, there is limited evidence of particular laws and policies for younger children and, if anything, notable gaps in provision. For example, the Committee recommended that the *mandaturi* (school resource officers) in Georgia 'extend their mandate to kindergartens and childcare facilities and reinforce their capacity for the identification, reporting and management of cases of violence and abuse' (UN, 2017n, para. 21)

States Parties have particular responsibilities in relation to protect children from economic exploitation, including by setting minimum wages for child labour (Article 31 of the CRC). However, the Committee has acknowledged that:

> In some countries and regions, children are socialized to work from an early age, including in activities that are potentially hazardous, exploitative and damaging to their health, education and long-term prospects. For example, young children may be initiated into domestic work or agricultural labour, or assist parents or siblings engaged in hazardous activities. Even very young babies may be vulnerable to economic exploitation, as when they are used or hired out for begging.
>
> *(UN, 2005, para. 36(e))*

The legal response to this is often to prohibit children from working, and even those who argue that child labour should be regulated rather than banned accept that it should be prohibited completely for the very young (e.g. see Liebel, 2015). However, even when minimum age laws exist, there can be a problem with compliance. For example, the Committee welcomed Tajikistan's adoption of a new labour code in 2016 that defines the minimum age for employment as 15 years, but expressed concern that 'reportedly approximately a quarter of all children aged between 5 and 17 from families facing social and economic hardships are engaged in economic activity' (UN, 2017m, para. 4).

Participation

The UNCRC is one of the most comprehensive human rights treaties in the UN, giving children access not only to social and economic rights, but the full package of civil and political rights – the so-called participatory rights (Kilkelly and Lundy, 2006). Foremost among these is Article 12 of the CRC, which gives children a right to their views and to have their views given due weight. The right to express a view is afforded to all children who are capable of forming a view (mature or not) (Lundy, 2007). The right to have views given due weight – the second part of Article 12(1) – is subject to 'age and maturity', a qualification that is of particular relevance to younger children. That said, children's entitlement to be heard should not be shut down on the basis that they are not considered competent enough to express a mature view (UN, 2009). Nor should less weight be attached to their views just because they are young – the weight to be given to the child's views depends on the child, the issue under consideration and the context.

GC7 places huge emphasis on young children's entitlement to be heard, stressing that Article 12 of the CRC 'reinforces the status of the young child as an active participant in the promotion, protection and monitoring of their rights'. (UN, 2005, para. 7). While there is a growing body of literature on children's participation in the early years (often referencing the CRC), very little of it is explicitly children's rights-based (cf. Bae, 2010; Dunphy, 2012; MacNaughton et al., 2007). While there is a growing body of evidence that children can contribute to the development of early years policy and services using a rights-based approach (e.g. Lundy et al., 2011; Smith, 2014), this stands in stark contrast to the focus of States Parties reports and the Committee's concluding observations where specific references to young children's right to be heard are conspicuously absent. While the Committee's recommendations in relation to Article 12 of the UNCRC often refer to 'all children', and that of course includes young children, the specific examples it tends to give, such as youth parliaments, are very rarely spaces that are open to children under the age of 8.

There were only two areas where younger children's right to be heard was addressed specifically in the monitoring process and both were in relation to court proceedings. The Committee's report on Estonia notes that the national legislation states that a child who is 10 years or older shall be heard in decisions which concern him or her and that the court may also hear younger children. The Committee expressed its concern that in practice, there is often a tendency by judges to hear only children who are older than 10 years (UN, 2017h). That was a solid rights-based critique that reinforces younger children's right to be heard in court proceedings. Likewise, in relation to Tajikistan, the Committee expressed concern about a law restricting the right of the child to be heard only in family and adoption cases and only to children above 10 years of age (UN, 2017m, para. 16). There is a compelling case for children being heard in judicial proceedings – not least to counteract the perverse incentive to abuse younger children so that they cannot act as witnesses in criminal proceedings. While there is also a growing trend of younger children's views being heard in the courts, there is much more to be done before younger children's testimony is both sought and regarded as credible (Cashmore and Parkinson, 2008).

References to young children's other civil and political rights are even more rare. The one exception to this is in relation to the right to identity and birth registration under Article 8 of the CRC. This is crucial for all children, but the timing of registration connects it to the very young in particular. A typical set of concerns, on this occasion for the Central African Republic, is as follows:

> The enduring low rate of registered children and the major disparities between urban and rural areas; Birth registration not being freely provided to all children; The limited period for birth registration, as provided by article 134 of the Family Code; and limited awareness of the population of the importance of birth registration.
>
> *(UN, 2017i, para. 32)*

The child's right to freedom of conscience and religion, Article 14 in the CRC, has an additional clause that acknowledges parents' right to provide direction and guidance on this (Langlaude, 2008). However, the solitary mention of it in the 2017 reports provides an interesting assertion of the right to freedom of conscience for younger children. In relation to Tajikistan, the Committee commented on the fact that religious education could only be delivered from state-licensed institutions and only to children over 7 years of age, and that children were prohibited from entering mosques (UN, 2017m, para. 19).

Freedom of assembly and association is never mentioned specifically in relation to younger children in spite of current attention given to the work of children as human rights defenders. In fact, the Committee's recommendations could be interpreted to endorse the restriction of this right to older children. For example, in its comments on Romania, it suggests that legislation should support adolescents in organizing themselves in associations and formal groups, including outside (UN, 2017d, para. 20), thus indirectly endorsing a lack of regulation for children under the age of adolescence. This is at odds with the Committee's position in GC7 that: 'Respect for the young child's agency – as a participant in family, community and society is frequently overlooked, or rejected as inappropriate on the grounds of age and immaturity' (UN, 2005, para. 7).

Discussion

GC7 marked a watershed for understanding the rights of children in the early years, a landmark document in so many respects. It provides a rich foundation on which to build a world fit for young children, one that understands that they do not only require and are entitled to care and protection, but have a right to be heard and treated with respect. A core aim of the General Comment was to address the prevailing conception of young children and the neglect of their rights:

> The Committee is concerned that in implementing their obligations under the Convention, States parties have not given sufficient attention to young children as rights holders and to the laws, policies and programmes required to realize their rights during this distinct phase of their childhood.
>
> *(UN, 2005, para. 3)*

Given that this was a key driver, one would expect that States Parties would, in the wake of it, pay more attention to the specific experiences of laws and policies related to young children. One would also expect the Committee on the Rights of the Child would continue to monitor and highlight issues identified in GC7 as they arose in the reporting process. In the analysis above, I assessed the extent to which this is happening across a sample of States Parties. It is striking that in this analysis of the concluding observations of the Committee in 2017, GC7 itself is not mentioned once specifically and many of its core recommendations are neglected when the Committee reviews the performance of States Parties.

The fact that it has not been referred to specifically by the Committee does not mean that it has not had any effect or that countries are not paying any attention to the rights of younger children. States report on their progress in the early years following the reporting guidelines (UN, 2015a); this means that they are asked to address issues such as infant mortality and early years education. For example, Moldova's States Party report, just one example, devotes several paragraphs documenting a range of early years educational initiatives:

> Through a pilot mentoring program for early education system implemented by MoEd in 2013–2014, the following were achieved: (i) 30 national mentors who provide continuous training services trained, (ii) 3 training modules and 27 guidelines of education practices for teachers developed; (iii) 260 local mentors, 40 inspectors in mentoring and 7000 educators in implementing positive practices of early education trained; (iv) mentoring programs (individual and group) for 4000 teachers provided; (v) 130 mentoring centers in each administrative-territorial unit created in order to ensure the sustainability of mentoring programs.
>
> *(UN, 2016c, para. 221)*

Nonetheless, what the analysis also suggests is that attention to children's rights in the early years is essentially partial. Apart from the two exceptions noted earlier, their experiences and rights tend to get folded in to the general mix of childhood, a fact that undermines the claims in GC7 about the particularities of their experiences. One example of this is in relation to the United States (who also reported in 2017, but only in relation to the two Optional Protocols, which it has ratified). When commenting on its progress in relation to the Optional Protocol on the Sale of Children, the Committee said:

> Preventive efforts targeting children who are particularly at risk of becoming victims of the offences under the Optional Protocol remain insufficient. Those children include children living in poverty; migrant children; children living in difficult family situations; including runaway and homeless children; Native SC 19 American children, especially girls; boys who tend to be runaways or abandoned; lesbian, gay, bisexual and transgender children; adolescent girls; and 'in-system' children.
>
> *(UN, 2017j, para. 19)*

It is widely recognised that young children are more vulnerable to exploitation and abuse, and yet there is not one specific mention of them in this otherwise extensive list of children who are particularly at risk of becoming victims.

Going forward, it is recommended that the Committee on the Rights of the Child should take active steps to ensure that children in the early years are not neglected in the periodic monitoring processes. The review of States Parties' progress provides an unparalleled opportunity for it to direct the gaze of the world's governments to their implementation of the CRC for children aged under 8. It could amend its reporting guidelines to ask for more specific information on this age group across all rights when data are being disaggregated; it could ask governments who fail to mention young children in their States Parties reports to provide more detail under the formal 'list of issues'; and it could increase and strengthen its specific recommendations for the early years in its concluding observations. General Comment No. 7 provides a template for all this; it is time to put it to work.

Conclusion

Despite the rhetoric of GC7, there is still a lack of recognition of the particular experiences of young children in relation to the enjoyment of their rights in governments' reports to the Committee on the Rights of the Child, and indeed in the priorities of the Committee when it is monitoring progress on implementation. Even though under-eights are almost half of the childhood population, they are relatively invisible in law and public policy, and indeed in the published reports of the Committee on the Rights of the Child. Reading the 2017 reports, it is striking that the focus of the Committee tends to be on adolescents whose rights are the subject of two General Comments, including a recent one specifically for them (UN, 2016b). My intention is not to pit one group of children against another, but to argue that there is a need for governments and the Committee on the Rights of the Child to give younger children's rights the dedicated attention for which GC7 makes such a robust case. The chapters that follow highlight many instances where young children have been deprived of their rights, but they also provide a compelling case for increasing the attention given to them as rights-holders. They provide a multitude of interesting insights into the areas of children's rights that tend to receive priority in law and policy in the early years, and those that are neglected. In particular, they demonstrate ways in which young children can be engaged in making meaning in their own lives, and thus provide a rich platform to advocate for greater and more targeted engagement with a children's rights approach to law and policy for young children on a global scale.

References

Alcock, S., 2013. Searching for play in early childhood care and education policy. *New Zealand Journal of Educational Studies, 48*(1), pp. 19–33.

Alejos, M., Brett, R. and Zermatten, J., 2005. *Babies and small children residing in prisons*. Geneva: Quaker United Nations Office. p. 22.

Bae, B., 2010. 'Realizing children's right to participation in early childhood settings: some critical issues in a Norwegian context. *Early Years, 30*(3), pp.205–218.

Cashmore, J. and Parkinson, P., 2008. Children's and parents 'perceptions on children's participation in decision making after parental separation and divorce. *Family Court Review, 46*(1), pp.91–104.

Davey, C. and Lundy, L., 2011. Towards greater recognition of the right to play: an analysis of Article 31 of the UNCRC. *Children & Society, 25*(1), pp.3–14.

Dunphy, E., 2012. Children's participation rights in early childhood education and care: the case of early literacy learning and pedagogy. *International Journal of Early Years Education, 20*(3), pp.290–299.

Ferguson, L., Grant, A. D., Watson-Jones, D., Kahawita, T., Ong'ech, J. O. and Ross, D. A., 2012. Linking women who test HIV-positive in pregnancy-related services to long-term HIV care and treatment services: a systematic review. *Tropical Medicine & International Health, 17*(5), pp.564–580.

Hammarberg, T., 1990. The UN convention on the rights of the child–and how to make it work. *Human Rights Quarterly, 12*(1), pp.97–105.

Kent, G., 2006. Child feeding and human rights. *International Breastfeeding Journal, 1*(1), p.27.

Kilkelly, U. and Lundy, L., 2006. Children's rights in action: using the UN Convention on the Rights of the Child as an auditing tool. *Child & Family Law and Quarterly, 18*, p.331.

Langlaude, S., 2008. Children and religion under Article 14 UNCRC: a critical analysis. *The International Journal of Children's Rights, 16*(4), pp.475–504.

Lester, S. and Russell, W., 2010. *Children's right to play: an examination of the importance of play in the lives of children worldwide. Working Papers in Early Childhood Development, No. 57*. The Hague, The Netherlands: Bernard van Leer Foundation.

Liebel, M., 2015. Protecting the rights of working children instead of banning child labour. *The International Journal of Children's Rights, 23*(3), pp.529–547.

Lundy, L., 2007. Voice is not enough: conceptualising Article 12 of the United Nations Convention on the Rights of the Child. *British Educational Research Journal, 33*(6), pp.927–942.

Lundy, L., 2012. Children's rights and educational policy in Europe: the implementation of the United Nations Convention on the Rights of the Child. *Oxford Review of Education, 38*(4), pp.393–411.

Lundy, L., McEvoy, L. and Byrne, B., 2011. working with young children as co-researchers: an approach informed by the United Nations Convention on the Rights of the Child. *Early Education & Development, 22*(5), pp. 714–736.

MacNaughton, G., Hughes, P. and Smith, K., 2007. Young children's rights and public policy: practices and possibilities for citizenship in the early years. *Children & Society, 21*(6), pp.458–469.

Minson, S., 2018. Direct harms and social consequences: an analysis of the impact of maternal imprisonment on dependent children in England and Wales. *Criminology & Criminal Justice*, p.1748895818794790.

Peleg, N., 2017. Developing the right to development. *The International Journal of Children's Rights, 25*(2), pp.380–395.

Pemberton, S., Gordon, D. and Nandy, S., 2012. Child rights, child survival and child poverty: the debate. In *Global Child Poverty and Well-Being: Measurement, Concepts, Policy and Action*. Policy Press. pp.19–37.

Prior, L., 2008. Repositioning documents in social research. *Sociology, 42*(5), pp.821–836.

Quennerstedt, A., 2010. Children, but not really humans? critical reflections on the hampering effect of the "3 p's". *The International Journal of Children's Rights, 18*(4), pp.619–635.

Reading, R., Bissell, S., Goldhagen, J., Harwin, J., Masson, J., Moynihan, S., Parton, N., Pais, M. S., Thoburn, J. and Webb, E., 2009. Promotion of children's rights and prevention of child maltreatment. *The Lancet, 373*(9660), pp.332–343.

Smith, K., 2014. Discourses of childhood safety: what do children say? *European Early Childhood Education Research Journal, 22*(4), pp. 525–537.

United Nations. 1989. *UN Convention on the Rights of the Child.* Geneva: United Nations.

United Nations. 2018. *Report of the Special Rapporteur on the issue of human rights obligations relating to the enjoyment of a safe, clean, healthy and sustainable environment. A/HRC/37/58.* Geneva: United Nations.

United Nations, UN Committee on the Rights of the Child. 2003a. *General comment no.5 general measures of implementation UN/CRC/GC/2003/.* Geneva: United Nations.

United Nations, UN Committee on the Rights of the Child. 2003b. *HIV/AIDS and the rights of children UN/CRC/GC/2003/3.* Geneva: United Nations.

United Nations, UN Committee on the Rights of the Child. 2005. *Implementing child rights in early childhood general comment no. 7 (2005) UN/CRC/GC/2005/1.* Geneva: United Nations.

United Nations, UN Committee on the Rights of the Child. 2009. *General comment no.12 on the right of the child to be heard. CRC/C/GC/12.* Geneva: United Nations.

United Nations, UN Committee on the Rights of the Child. 2013b. *General comment no.17 on the right of the child to rest, leisure, play, recreational activities, cultural life and the arts (art. 31) to have his or her best interests taken as a primary consideration. CRC/C/GC/17.* Geneva: United Nations.

United Nations, UN Committee on the Rights of the Child. 2015a. *Treaty-specific guidelines regarding the form and content of periodic reports to be submitted by States parties under article 44, paragraph 1 (b), of the Convention on the Rights of the Child. CRC/C/58/Rev.3.* Geneva: United Nations.

United Nations, UN Committee on the Rights of the Child. 2015b. *Committee on the Rights of the Child consideration of reports submitted by States parties under article 44 of the Convention. Combined third and fourth periodic reports of Ireland due in 2009.* Geneva: United Nations.

United Nations, UN Committee on the Rights of the Child. 2016a. *General comment no.19 on public budgeting for the realization of children's rights (art.4). CRC/C/GC/19.* Geneva: United Nations.

United Nations, UN Committee on the Rights of the Child. 2016b. *General comment no. 20 (2016) on the implementation of the rights of the child during adolescence. CRC/C/GC/19.* Geneva: United Nations.

United Nations, UN Committee on the Rights of the Child. 2016c. *Consideration of reports submitted by States parties under article 44 of the Convention. Fourth and fifth periodic reports of States parties due in 2015. Republic of Moldova CRC/C/MDA(4-4).* Geneva: United Nations.

United Nations, UN Committee on the Rights of the Child. 2017a. *Concluding observations on the combined fifth and sixth periodic reports of Ecuador.* Geneva: United Nations.

United Nations, UN Committee on the Rights of the Child. 2017b. *Concluding observations on the fifth periodic report of Mongolia.* Geneva: United Nations.

United Nations, UN Committee on the Rights of the Child. 2017c. *Concluding observations on the fifth periodic report of the Democratic People's Republic of Korea.* Geneva: United Nations.

United Nations, UN Committee on the Rights of the Child. 2017d. *Concluding observations on the fifth periodic report of Romania.* Geneva: United Nations.

United Nations, UN Committee on the Rights of the Child. 2017e. *Concluding observations on concluding observations on the combined second and third periodic reports of Antigua and Barbuda.* Geneva: United Nations.

United Nations, UN Committee on the Rights of the Child. 2017f. *Concluding observations on concluding observations on the combined second and third periodic reports of St Vincent and the Grenadines.* Geneva: United Nations.

United Nations, UN Committee on the Rights of the Child. 2017g. *Concluding observations on concluding observations on the combined second and third periodic reports of Serbia.* Geneva: United Nations.

United Nations, UN Committee on the Rights of the Child. 2017h. *Concluding observations on concluding observations on the combined second to fourth periodic reports of Estonia.* Geneva: United Nations.

United Nations, UN Committee on the Rights of the Child. 2017i. *Concluding observations on the combined second to fourth periodic reports of the Central African Republic.* Geneva: United Nations.

United Nations, UN Committee on the Rights of the Child. 2017j. *Concluding observations on the combined third and fourth reports submitted by the United States of America under article 12 (1) of the Optional Protocol to the Convention on the Rights of the Child on the sale of children, child prostitution and child pornography.* Geneva: United Nations.

United Nations, UN Committee on the Rights of the Child. 2017k. *Concluding observations on the combined third to fifth periodic reports of Bhutan.* Geneva: United Nations.

United Nations, UN Committee on the Rights of the Child. 2017l. *Concluding observations on the combined third to fifth periodic reports of Cameroon.* Geneva: United Nations.

United Nations, UN Committee on the Rights of the Child. 2017m. *Concluding observations on the combined third to fifth periodic reports of Tajikstan.* Geneva: United Nations.

United Nations, UN Committee on the Rights of the Child. 2017n. *Concluding observations on the fourth periodic report of Georgia.* Geneva: United Nations.

United Nations, UN Committee on the Rights of the Child. 2017o. *Concluding observations on the second periodic report of Barbados.* Geneva: United Nations.

United Nations, UN Committee on the Rights of the Child. 2017p. *Concluding observations on the second periodic report of Vanuatu.* Geneva: United Nations.

United Nations, UN Committee on the Rights of the Child. 2017q. *Concluding observations on the combined fourth and fifth periodic report of the Republic of Moldova.* Geneva: United Nations.

Van den Bergh, B. J., Gatherer, A., Fraser, A. and Moller, L., 2011. Imprisonment and women's health: concerns about gender sensitivity, human rights and public health. *Bulletin of the World Health Organization, 89,* pp.689–694.

van IJzendoorn, M. H., Palacios, J., Sonuga-Barke, E. J., Gunnar, M. R., Vorria, P., McCall, R. B., Le Mare, L., Bakermans-Kranenburg, M. J., Dobrova-Krol, N. A. and Juffer, F., 2011. I. Children in institutional care: delayed development and resilience. *Monographs of the Society for Research in Child Development, 76*(4), pp.8–30.

3

BABIES' RIGHTS, WHEN HUMAN RIGHTS BEGIN

Priscilla Alderson and Tamaki Yoshida

Introduction

This chapter regards babies as real human beings. Every child is a different individual. Their thoughts and feelings and developing capacities form part of their humanity and 'inherent dignity'. These entitle each baby to 'the equal and inalienable rights of all members of the human family' (United Nations (UN), 1948, 1989). Academic analysis of babies can increase our understanding of humanity, of human rights at any age, and the human agency of rights-bearers. We take babies to be people aged up to about 12 to 15 months. As we discuss later, defining children in terms of age is not helpful from natural rights perspectives, although from legal rights perspectives it is sometimes necessary.

Rights are broadly justified on either legal or natural grounds. This chapter will review differences between the two approaches, and their relations to children's and babies' rights. We consider how human rights protect vulnerable human beings, how they provide for human flourishing, and how participation rights promote social inclusion for all age groups.[1] This chapter is informed by the United Nations (UN) international standard, and illustrated cross-nationally by our experiences of living with Ren (born in 2016) in Tokyo, Japan, and Kolbe (born in 2017) in Dorset, England. They reminded us each day of how, from birth and when they are awake, babies constantly and intensively think, explore, communicate, relate to other people, and enjoy and wonder at the world.

Two ways of justifying rights: legal and natural

Legal rights

Rights are legal concepts. To be more than empty claims, rights have to be carefully worded in terms that could be tested in law courts. For example, children do not have a right to love or to health because neither of these can be willed or enforced. The courts cannot order parents to love their child, or assure health to a child dying of cancer. Instead, the courts can enforce behaviours to protect children's rights not to be neglected or abused. The courts can only support children's rights to 'the highest attainable health and healthcare' (UN, 1989, Article 24) by working to prevent low standards and obvious abuses. However, in response to child abuse in the home, the revised Japanese Child Welfare Act (2016), in the spirit of the United Nations Convention on the Rights of the Child (UNCRC) Preamble, refers to the child as the subject rather than the object. It mentions the child's need for family-type care, and the 'child's rights to appropriate/adequate rearing, to be loved and to be protected' (UN, 1989).[2]

The advantage of national law is that it provides the strongest practical support for citizens' legally recognised rights, enforced by the courts (Freeman, 2011). The UNCRC (UN, 1989) is the most detailed statement of children's rights, ratified by every state except the USA. Yet, as international law, the UNCRC has the disadvantage of being less enforceable. However, governments that have ratified the UNCRC undertake to implement it in law and administration, and to respect children's 'economic, social and cultural rights … to the maximum extent of their available resources … [and] with international co-operation' (Article 4).

National legal rights are limited in that they reflect local cultures. For example, English and Japanese law still allow parents to hit their children, although by 2018 53 countries had banned all physical punishment. Hitting most commonly and seriously affects the youngest children (Children's Rights Alliance for England, 2018; Save the Children, 2018). For millennia, national laws have favoured property-owning men as rational rights-holders (Freeman, 2011). Only slowly over the past century have the rights of women, then young people, children and other disadvantaged groups been recognised. Babies seem to be the last group to become widely respected as entitled to human rights.

Legal rights are defined and enshrined by governments. Further limitations of national rights are shown: first, when government refuse to recognise and respect the rights of certain groups; second, greater dangers occur when governments actively violate certain of their citizens' rights; and third, other countries may refuse to help refugees and asylum seekers who try to escape from regimes that refuse to protect and provide for them (Freeman, 2011). These problems challenged the UN after World War II during the Nuremberg Trials of Nazi state-organised genocide (Sands, 2016). The agreed way forward was to promote older ideas of every human being's natural rights.

Natural rights

In contrast to rights recognised in law, the idea of natural rights assumes that everyone has human rights by virtue of being human. These rights are seen as universal and inalienable (Freeman, 2011). Human nature, in its innate human quest for equality and freedom, is central to natural rights. Over 2,000 years ago, Cicero (1943) claimed, 'we are born for Justice, and that right is based, not upon opinions, but upon Nature'. Some authorities justified rights through divine authority. For example, the US Declaration of Independence (1776) asserted, 'We hold these Truths to be self-evident, that all Men are created equal, that they are endowed by their Creator with certain unalienable Rights, that among these are Life, Liberty, and the Pursuit of Happiness'. The Declaration's main author, Thomas Jefferson, later added, 'Man [is] a rational animal, endowed by nature with rights and with an innate sense of justice' (Jefferson, 1903–1904, p. 441). The idea of 'innate' (inborn) relates to babies and will be discussed later.

Following the Nuremberg Trials, the UN justified natural rights in secular terms of promoting peace. The UN Charter (UN, 1945) and Declaration (UN, 1948), on which the Convention of the Rights of the Child is based (UN, 1989), and the European Convention (EC) (European Court of Human Rights (ECHR), 1950) were all agreed as major tools to protect all human beings and their rights. The Charter aimed 'to reaffirm faith in fundamental human rights, in the dignity and worth of the human person, in the equal rights *of men and women*' (UN, 1945, emphasis added). This changed into the more all-age-inclusive:

> recognition of the inherent dignity and of the equal and inalienable rights of *all members of the human family* is the foundation of freedom, justice and peace in the world [and prevents] the disregard and contempt for human rights [that] have resulted in barbarous acts which have outraged the conscience of mankind.
>
> *(UN, 1948, emphasis added)*

Whatever the local laws, the UN agreed that all governments should respect human rights.

Natural rights promote respect, justice and equality for all. This can involve extra support for the weak and vulnerable. Natural rights have emerged throughout history from mass social movements and protests against oppression and injustice (Freeman, 2011). Children's rights are sometimes discussed as if they began with the UNCRC (UN, 1989), such as in Article 31, the right to play. However, many UNCRC Articles originated in all-age human rights, enshrined in the Charter (UN, 1945) and the Declaration (UN, 1948). Article 31 stems from 'Everyone has the right to rest and leisure' (UN, 1948, Article 24) as an inalienable natural right.

One limitation of natural rights debates is that, despite the claims that they are equal, universal, inalienable and innate to all human beings, there has been little recognition of how they actually apply to babies, the main topic of this chapter. Another limitation is that some authors confine natural rights to negative rights, to freedoms *from* harm and injustice. Yet freedoms *to* goods and services, more fully recognised in legal rights, are also vital for everyone, especially the most dependent groups such as babies. The UN (1945, 1948, 1989) combined legal and natural rights in human rights. The next sections examine how human rights protect babies, provide for their human flourishing, and promote their social inclusion or participation.

Protection rights

Children's rights are criticised for being too different from adults' rights. It is as if children 'have to be protected and kept apart from the adult world for their own safety' (Gadda, 2008, p. 6) and as if adults do not also need similar protections. Yet protection is central to all-age international human rights (UN, 1945, 1948). Even freedom rights involve protection from the constraints and harms that interfere with freedom. For six decades, sociologists virtually ignored human rights and also the Holocaust (Alderson, 2012; Hynes et al., 2011). Then Zygmunt Bauman (2005) and Bryan Turner (2008) considered a new understanding of rights. Instead of emphasising the historical basis of rights in respect for rational men (Freeman, 2011), they also stressed how rights are essential to protect vulnerable human beings from suffering. Turner (2008) also cited children's need for protection and provision rights during their long, dependent childhood.

The Nuremberg Trials drew the world's attention to the need for strong, enforceable protection rights. During the trials, lawyers debated whether the Holocaust should be termed 'genocide', an attempt to destroy a whole ethnic group, the Jews (Sands, 2016). Genocide is one of many examples in which babies play a central though often hidden part, when one main genocidal method is to prevent all births in that ethnic group. Another method is to ensure that any babies who are born are of mixed, not pure, ethnicity, so rape is a routine part of warfare, to produce children who are fathered by the victors, in another form of genocide.

The most basic human right protects the right to life (Article 6), in terms of both survival and an adequate standard of living (Article 27). Babies, with their small, frail bodies, are at the highest risk of being killed or permanently disabled by disease, malnutrition and injury. For example, every year, an estimated 250,000 to 500,000 young children become blind for lack of vitamin A. Half of them die within a year (Empson, 2014, pp. 184–185). Many of those babies who survive face a lifetime of social exclusion, whereas working-age adults who become blind may be better able to continue with the partners, friendships and work they already enjoy.

Babies are also in greatest need of protection during natural disasters, floods or famine, earthquake or fires. However, as Aramaki (2013) criticises, adults are often prioritised during and after natural disasters. It is as if 'restoration of children's lives could be achieved if adults' everyday lives are restored' (p. 9, authors' translation). With climate change, disasters are increasing. Babies and children will live longest into the future when the effects of climate change will be much more severe (Intergovernmental Panel for Climate Change, 2018). Real concern to protect young children would respect their present and future rights, and present policies towards reducing greenhouse gas emissions would greatly change.

Natural disasters can increase violent social conflict, forced migration and separation of families, where, of all age groups, babies are least able to trace their family and reunite with them. UNCRC Article 22 concerns extra protection for refugee children and asylum seekers. Article 35 is about preventing babies from being stolen by criminals and trafficked for the international adoption market or the trade in human organs (Bagheri, 2016). Yet States too separate children from their families, legally when children need to be protected from their parents (Article 9). This sometimes occurs illegally. In 2018, US officials took babies and children from their immigrant parents at the Mexican border, leaving many parents unable to find their children (BBC, 2018).

All the UNCRC Articles, even seemingly adult-centred ones, apply to babies. Babies need rights to protect them from narcotics (Article 33). Thousands of babies each year are born addicted to the narcotics their mothers take, and they need intensive nursing care (Smith, 2017). Many also need protection from 'sexual exploitation and sexual abuse' (Article 34). Online pornography involves babies (Internet Watch Foundation, 2018). Protection from economic exploitation, hazardous work and long working hours (Article 32) affects babies. For example, pregnant women's stress and exhaustion can induce premature birth, when their newborn babies may need intensive hospital care and have many associated problems (Li et al., 2012).

The law is meant to protect the innocent and ensure that they are not wrongly imprisoned: 'No child shall be deprived of his or her liberty unlawfully or arbitrarily' (Article 37b). Nevertheless, many babies live in prisons when they stay with their mothers. In many countries, they have to leave their mothers behind in prison when they are a few months old. They then may have to be fostered and can lose contact with their family (Gordon, 2018). Women are usually imprisoned for petty theft and other crimes linked to poverty (Ministry of Justice, 2016). States that support young families with adequate income and housing (Article 27) can prevent much imprisonment of young parents. The states then save on the high costs of imprisonment, often followed by unemployment, homelessness and family breakdown, as well as the costs of the likely lifelong harmful effects on the young children. Numerous reports from around the world attest to the need of young children for protection and rescue, both by individual adults but also through laws as well as political and economic structures (Rutter, 2002).

Providers of services, such as healthcare, social care and criminal justice, learn many details about babies and their families. To prevent 'unlawful attacks on his or her honour and reputation', all States Parties (including all agencies of state services) must respect each baby's right to privacy (Articles 16.1 and 40.2.vii). This includes protecting babies' personal records as confidential.

Increasingly, wars are fought in civilian areas where homes, water systems and even hospitals are bombed (Bourke, 2014; Feinstein, 2012). This can deny healthcare to all ages, and babies are the group that most urgently needs expert emergency care in cases of infection or injury. Article 37 protects against 'torture or other cruel, inhuman or degrading treatment'. Article 38 protects children against physical, mental and sexual abuse during armed conflict. There is great concern about child soldiers, but little is said about the babies the young girl soldiers have. It is hard for former child soldiers to reunite with their families and communities, with respect for their right to promotion of their 'physical and psychological recovery and social reintegration' (Article 39) (Anderson, 2016). This can be still harder for girls who have illegitimate babies (Deno and Buccitelli, 2017). Wars and disasters leave many children deeply traumatised, haunted by memories of the suffering they have experienced and witnessed. Psychoanalysis reveals how trauma and subconscious fantasies remembered from the earliest months, even of seemingly 'minor' neglect or abuse, can affect children and adults most seriously and be the hardest to heal (Chertoff, 2009).

All UNCRC Articles apply 'without discrimination of any kind' (Article 2), and babies should be protected against discriminations of racism, sexism, and religious, class and other prejudices (Article 1). However, babies tend to suffer from discriminations and oppressions against their parents, to the extent of inheriting their family's debts and being born into low caste or lifelong indebted labour. Babies born outside wedlock and their mothers may endure severe discrimination (Hertzog, 2009), though far less so today in many societies.

The law is concerned with recognised legal persons and with property. Children used to be treated as their father's legal property, whereas today most children are respected as legal persons with rights and interests (Freeman, 2011; UN, 1989), although this varies (Twum-Danso, 2010), and babies are still at risk of being treated as property, to be disposed of as others decide. In the growing international surrogacy services, for example, women in India give birth to children who have developed from the egg and/or the sperm of individuals or couples in certain Australian states. Many of these babies are cherished by their intended parents, but some are treated as mere objects and may be rejected by all the adults concerned, and be left stateless, defenceless and bereft (McGuirk, 2016).

This links to perhaps the greatest discrimination against babies: doubt that they are fully human when differences between the fetus and the newborn baby may be blurred. A few leading bioethicists deny any difference between feticide and infanticide, arguing the newborn babies are 'pre-persons' without justified rights, though many bioethicists disagree (Rodger et al., 2018). Abortion of hundreds of thousands of unwanted female fetuses can merge into infanticide when girl babies are killed, starved or abandoned (Ahmad, 2010). Japanese law allows abortion up to 21 weeks gestation under specific conditions (Okamoto, 2014); English law allows the abortion of abnormal fetuses up to 24 weeks gestation, and also the quite frequent medically assisted ending of the life of severely impaired babies after birth (Larcher et al., 2014).

The UNCRC does not define when childhood begins (Article 1), but leaves that to each state, and most choose the moment of birth (UN, 2005). There are crucial differences between the fetus before birth and the infant after birth. The fetus has neither an independent existence nor, therefore, legal rights. In European law, women have autonomy rights to control their own body, and can refuse interventions during labour even if this could end the life of the fetus (*Konovalova v Russia* [2015], the European Court of Human Rights; *St George's Healthcare NHS Trust v S*, [1997]). However, from birth onwards, the baby has an independent existence and legal rights. Modern medicine can keep alive many babies who are barely conscious but endure severe discomfort, with limited hope of developing or enjoying a minimally reasonable quality of life. In the past, they would have died. This raises hard questions for parents and doctors about how the baby's right to life (Article 6) may conflict with the right to an adequate standard of living (Article 27) and the child's best interests (Article 3). Far from treating babies as disposable property or pre-persons, the adults try to make decisions in which 'the best interests of the child shall be a primary consideration' (Article 3) (Larcher et al., 2014). Real protection from poverty, neglect and abuse, and illness and injury is based on respect for every child and baby as a valued person and a world citizen, principles at the heart of UNCRC.

Provision rights

Provision rights ensure children are provided with all that they need to enjoy an adequate standard of living. Like protection rights, provision rights can be especially vital to support each baby's life, present well-being and future development. With education, for instance (Articles 28 and 29), babies are more likely to survive and thrive when their mothers are better educated (Boyden and Bourdillon, 2012), and they need care from well-educated health and welfare professionals.

People need to be aware of their rights in order that they may claim them for themselves and for others. When States Parties make the UNCRC 'widely known, by appropriate and active means, to adults and children alike' (Article 42), they strengthen practical respect for everyone's rights. They also do so when they show how human rights apply to babies and so actually are inalienable through life.

Babies benefit from public amenities and services: healthcare, public transport, nurseries, libraries, informal baby groups, parks, swimming pools, social services and legal services: 'States Parties shall take all appropriate measures to ensure that children of working parents have the right to benefit from child-care services and facilities for which they are eligible' (Article 18.3). All these need to be well-resourced, and young children are greatly affected by austerity cuts (Wickham et al., 2018). Around the world, many babies live in slums, not served by electricity or water services or rubbish collection. They are at the highest risk of illness and of dying from infections or heat or cold (World Health Organization (WHO), 2018). Babies are the least able to make formal complaints, and so they most depend on states ensuring routine review:

> that the institutions, services and facilities responsible for the care or protection of children shall conform with the standards established by competent authorities, particularly in the areas of safety, health, in the number and suitability of their staff, as well as competent supervision.
>
> *(Article 3.3)*

There should be 'periodic review of the treatment' of children in residential care (Article 25).

States should avoid separating families and should support the 'positive, humane and expeditious' reunion of children with parents if they are separated (Articles 9 and 10). Health visitors and social workers aim to support parents, but lack of time and resources increasingly lead them (in the UK and Japan) into separating families, by 'rescuing babies from failing families' (National Audit Office, 2018). Current care policies are influenced by theories from brain science. These are cited to suggest that babies must be highly stimulated during the first 1,000 days after birth, or else their lifelong development will be 'stunted' (Cusick and Georgieff, 2018). Gillies et al. (2017) show how, although the first years are very important for learning, they can be overemphasised. Undue stress on learning in the first months can result in unrealistic pressure on disadvantaged families. When brain theories suggest that these babies fail to learn later on through childhood, this can work to excuse poor services and schools. It can mistakenly shift blame away from inefficient schools and on to children's families (Gillies et al., 2017). The theories can also undermine the respect professionals should show to 'continuity in a child's upbringing and to the child's ethnic, religious, cultural and linguistic background' (Articles 20.3 and 21).

Good healthcare supports babies' present and lifelong health. States Parties should 'recognize the right of every child to the enjoyment of the highest attainable standard of health and to facilities for the treatment of illness and rehabilitation of health' (Article 24). This includes 'nutritious foods and clean drinking-water, taking into consideration the dangers and risks of environmental pollution'. Clean drinking water is crucial when babies have formula milk. Bottle-feeding rates are rising, despite the higher costs and higher infection and mortality rates (WHO, 2017). Formula milk is usually sweetened, which encourages young children to want the sweet foods avidly marketed by baby milk and food and drinks companies such as Nestlé (Changing Markets Foundation, 2017; WHO, 2017). This highlights how international trade policies can affect baby's rights from birth when they increase the risks of later obesity and diabetes. Seemingly small rights, such as to clean air and water, can expand into large concerns: ways in which whole cities are planned can either reduce or increase water and air pollution and traffic accidents (Kent and Thompson, 2014).

If babies had a right to be breastfed, that could override the rights and privacy of mothers who do not want to breastfeed; therefore, breastfeeding is treated as the mother's informed choice. Article 24.2e on healthcare rights requires that 'parents and children, are informed, have access to education and are supported in the use of basic knowledge of child health and nutrition, the advantages of breastfeeding, hygiene and environmental sanitation and the prevention of accidents'. Japanese women are allowed extra breaks if they 'request time to care for the infant of at least 30 minutes twice a day'.[3] Another healthcare right, 'abolishing traditional practices prejudicial to the health of children' (Article 24.3), relates to neonatal rituals.

The above health and welfare rights are greatly affected by each family's prosperity or poverty, and every child has 'the right to benefit from social security' (Article 26). 'With regard to economic, social and cultural rights, States Parties shall undertake such measures to the maximum extent of their available resources and, where needed, within the framework of international co-operation' (Article 4). Many parents of the youngest children especially need financial support, whether they stay at home with their children or pay others to care for them while they work. Yet child benefit and other supports are being reduced by global austerity policies in many countries, and have never been granted in others. Millions of refugee and asylum-seeking families are in great need. When basic rights, such as to an adequate standard of living, are ignored or violated by States, all of whom have ratified the UNCRC (except the USA), then rights become even more important. They are remedies for wrongs and rightful claims to campaign for.

Participation rights

Reviews of children's rights can make children seem like passive consumers of services. Instead, they are contributors who take an active part in their families and communities. As has been known for decades, in seemingly innate, universal capacities, newborn babies engage in the micro-dance and turn-taking of communicating with another person (Dunn, 1977; Murray and Andrews, 2005; Stern, 1977). They immediately engage in education, avidly learning about time and space, cause and effect, self and others. By 3 months, they show their early understanding of justice and kindness, long before these concepts can be explained to them in words (Bloom, 2014; Gopnik, 2010; Gopnik et al., 2001). Charles Darwin (1877, p. 289) noted his 6-month-old son's moral sympathy in his anxious concern when his nurse pretended to cry. Babies share in their own healthcare; even premature babies can soothe and calm themselves (Als, 1999). Babies 'organise' breastfeeding by creating the 'demand' that builds up the 'supply'. As Ren and Kolbe kept showing us, babies inform their carers when they feel tired, hungry, too hot or too cold. They soon start helping to dress, feed and wash themselves, all activities necessary to maintain health and prevent illness. They 'reward' their caregivers with smiles, happily share toys and food with others from around 6 months, and by 1 year they are keen to help with housework.

Babies actively make very determined choices. They can get very anxious or angry if their 'plans' are thwarted or delayed. They concentrate intensely on repeatedly trying to solve problems, such as to reach a toy or fit it together. They are pleased and excited when they can carry out their plans and solve problems. Researchers find that babies think like scientists and philosophers (Bloom, 2014; Gopnik, 2010). Babies show how rights are not abstract ideas, but respectful, living, interacting relationships through which both partners can benefit. This is endorsed in the Declaration: 'Everyone has duties to the community in which alone the free and full development of his [sic] personality is possible' (UN, 1948, Article 29.1). The African Charter on the Rights and Welfare of the Child (1990) states, 'Every child shall have responsibilities towards his family and society ... 1. to work for the cohesion of the family' (Article 31). Very young children start to fulfil these responsibilities, and, although they do not consciously do so, babies are the agents who create families through their arrival. They connect separate families together into new genetic alliances, and they regenerate societies.

New parents are often in closer contact with their own parents after their first baby is born than they may have been in preceding years, frequently visiting, or phoning with news about the baby, or relying on grandparents as carers. Ren's mother started to feel more included in the neighbourhood, talking to strangers after Ren had waved at them. Ren and Kolbe talk to dogs, and try to play with people sitting next to them on a train. Babies seem instinctively to be social and actively make contact with other people and animals. The UNCRC Preamble summarises vitally important matters that cannot be willed or enforced rights, but which rights are intended to promote. One clause recognises 'that the child, for the full and harmonious development of his or her personality, should grow up in a family environment, in an atmosphere of happiness, love and understanding' (UN, 1989). Babies greatly contribute to this atmosphere.

Participation rights involve agents as the rights-holders who actively participate. In our chapter on older children, we suggested six elements of human agency (Alderson and Yoshida, 2016), which can also apply to babies as agents: (1) Physical/verbal (or preverbal) activity by the unique embodied agent with (2) thought and conscious decision-making, purpose and motive. Early on, babies make and persistently carry out 'plans' such as reaching for a toy then playing with it, or waiting eagerly to be fed. (3) At all ages, agency occurs within powerful and enabling or constraining social relationships and structures. These evoke varying reactions in the agent, from voluntary/willing cooperation to active resistance, such as when babies happily accept or else protest when they are put into a cot or a pushchair. There is (4) some moral awareness about need and desire, harm and benefit to self and others (as Darwin noted above), and (5) time, space, resources and opportunity enhance and restrict limited human agency. Finally, (6) (babies') agency tends to affect others and cause change – as new parents very quickly realise.

Premature babies can clearly 'form and express views' (Article 12), of fear, pain, need, anxiety, trust and contentment (Alderson et al., 2005; Als, 1999). Carers have to give 'due weight' to babies' expressed views on when they need to feed, rest, be warmer or cooler, play, laugh or be comforted in order to be able to care for them adequately. Babies intensely take in, sort through and make sense of information (Article 17) (Gopnik et al., 2001). When around 6 months old, instead of lying still while his nappy was changed, Ren started wriggling and reaching for toys around him. No longer absorbed with looking at people's faces, he wanted to play with his favourite toys, find out more, and scream. A few months later, he would dance, run, talk and reach for more. He smiles and taps in time with songs that he likes, dances to them, and chooses songs to play by pressing buttons in his electronic songbook. Then, unexpectedly, he stops, and plays with another toy, eloquently expressing himself through many media (Articles 12 and 13).

Many faiths have ceremonies to welcome new babies into their faith group. To attend these, families depend on their 'freedom to manifest one's religion or beliefs' (Article 14) without fear of discrimination or persecution. 'Freedom of association and of peaceful assembly' (Article 15) is also vital for the safety and well-being of babies and their families, to enhance their health, and to avoid parents suffering from social exclusion and anxious isolation.

Babies have crucial civil rights, and States Parties should 'respect the right of the child to preserve his or her identity, including nationality, name and family relations as recognized by law without unlawful interference' (Article 8). Yet an estimated one-third of births still go unregistered, leaving babies technically stateless and unable to claim the rights owed to them by the State (for discussions of babies' 'identity', see Alderson, 2008, pp. 78–86, 2013, Chapter 6).

States should 'encourage the mass media to disseminate information and material of social and cultural [and educational] benefit to the child' (Article 17a) that are useful and respectful towards all ages of childhood.

Conclusion

The cited research on babies' thinking and our experiences on opposite sides of the world show how babies are far more like all other human beings than used to be believed, and that all UNCRC Articles apply to them to respect their inalienable human rights. Babies have different needs and vulnerabilities and levels of social advantage and disadvantage, yet they are highly aware and responsive in uniquely human ways. They expand earlier notions of humanity, beyond the rational adult versus the developing child. They show how preverbal babies too can reason and feel, fear and hope, have views and aims and moral relationships. Recent sociological interest in protection rights for all vulnerable human beings (Bauman, 2005; Turner, 2008) also opens the way for babies' rights to be more fully respected. Bauman (2005) and Alderson (2013) regard morality as partly innate and deeply integral to human nature. Morality is not merely a cultural veneer that has to be wholly taught to children. The research with babies we have cited, which confirms this view, can increase our understanding of humanity, human agency and human rights shared by all members of the human family.

Policies are needed that prevent violent conflict and cherish babies and children for themselves, as well as for being the future workers and citizens who will maintain peace and prosperity. Legacies of conflict and divided societies tend to generate further conflict (Bourke, 2014). In contrast, policies that centre on protecting and promoting babies' rights as all-age human rights can benefit the babies and also whole present and future societies. They recognise that 'the inherent dignity and … the equal and inalienable rights of all members of the human family is the foundation of freedom, justice and peace in the world' (UN, 1948, 1989).

Notes

1   All Articles in protection, provision and participation rights sections refer to the UNCRC.
2   Japanese Child Welfare Act (2016), www.japaneselawtranslation.go.jp/law/detail_main?id=11&vm=2
3   Japanese Labour Standards Act (Act No. 49 of 1947) – *Art. 67 Time for Child Care* (authors' translation).

References

African Commission on Human and People's Rights. 1990. "African Charter on the Rights and Welfare of the Child. OAU Doc. CAB/LEG/24.9/49." www.achpr.org/instruments/child/#a31

Ahmad, N. 2010. "Female Feticide in India." *Issues in Law & Medicine*, 26 (1): 13–29.

Alderson, P. 2008. *Young Children's Rights*. London: Jessica Kingsley/Save the Children.

Alderson, P. 2012. "Young Children's Human Rights: A Sociological Analysis." *International Journal of Children's Rights*, 20: 177–198.

Alderson, P. 2013. *Childhoods Real and Imagined: An Introduction to Dialectical Critical Realism and Childhood Studies*. London: Routledge.

Alderson, P., J. Hawthorne and M. Killen. 2005. "The Participation Rights of Premature Babies." *International Journal of Children's Rights*, 13: 31–50.

Alderson, P. and T. Yoshida. 2016. "Meanings of Children's Agency: When and Where Does Agency Begin and End?" In *Reconceptualising Agency and Childhood. New Perspectives in Childhood Studies*, edited by F. Esser, M. Baader, T. Betz and B. Hungerland, 75–88. London: Routledge.

Als, H. 1999. "Reading the Premature Infant." In *Developmental Interventions in the Neonatal Intensive Care Nursery*, edited by E. Goldson, 18–85. New York: Oxford University Press.

Anderson, R. 2016. "Family Involvement in the Reintegration of Former Child Soldiers in Sierra Leone: A Critical Examination." In *Children and War: Past and Present Volume II*, edited by G. Prontera, W. Aschauer, J. Buckley, H. Embachler, A. Lichtblau and J.-D. Steinert, 103–117. Warwick: Helion and Company Ltd.

Aramaki, S. 2013. "Kodomo ni Fusawashii Sekai no Souzou [Creating a World Fit for Children]." In *Kodomo no Kenri Ajia to Nihon [Children's Rights Asia and Japan]*, edited by S. Aramaki, A. Kita and A. Morita, 8–15. Tokyo: Sanseido.

Bagheri, A. 2016. "Child Organ Trafficking: Global Reality and Inadequate International Response." *Medicine, Health Care and Philosophy*, 19: 239–246.

Bauman, Z. 2005. *Modernity and the Holocaust*. Cambridge: Polity.

BBC News. 2018. "Trump Migrant Separation Policy: Children 'in Cages' in Texas." *BBC News*, 18th June 2018. www.bbc.co.uk/news/world-us-canada-44518942

Bloom, P. 2014. *Just Babies: The Origins of Good and Evil*. New York: Broadway Books.

Bourke, J. 2014. *Wounding the World: How Military Violence and War-Play Invade Our Lives*. London: Virago.

Boyden, J. and M. Bourdillon (Eds). 2012. *Childhood Poverty: Multidisciplinary Approaches*. Basingstoke: Palgrave Macmillan.

Changing Markets Foundation. 2017. *Milking It: How Milk Formula Companies are Putting Profits before Science*. Utrecht: Changing Markets Foundation.

Chertoff, J. 2009. "The Complex Nature of Exposure to Early Childhood Trauma in the Psychoanalysis of a Child." *Journal of American Psychoanalytical Association*, 57: 1425–1457.

Children's Rights Alliance for England. 2018. *State of Children's Rights in England*. London: CRAE.

Cicero. 1943. *De Legibus*. C. Keyes (trans) Book 1, section 28. London: Heinemann.

Cusick, S. and M. Georgieff. 2018. "The First 1,000 Days of Life: The Brain's Window of Opportunity." www.unicef-irc.org/article/958-the-first-1000-days-of-life-the-brains-window-of-opportunity.html

Darwin, C. 1877. "A Biographical Sketch of an Infant." *MIND*, 2: 285–294.

Deno, M. and A. Buccitelli. 2017. "Child Soldiers." In *Handbook of Children's Rights: Global and Multidisciplinary Perspectives*, edited by M. Ruck, M. Peterson-Badali and M. Freeman, 465–478. New York: Routledge.

Dunn, J. 1977. *Distress and Comfort*. Glasgow: Fontana.

Empson, M. 2014. *Land and Labour*. London: Bookmarks.

European Court of Human Rights. 1950. "European Convention on Human Rights." www.echr.coe.int/Documents/Convention_ENG.pdf

Feinstein, A. 2012. *The Shadow World: Inside the Global Arms Trade*. London: Penguin.

Freeman, M. 2011. *Human Rights*. Cambridge: Polity.

Gadda, A. 2008. "Rights, Foucault and Power: A Critical Analysis of the United Nation Convention on the Rights of the Child." *Edinburgh Working Papers in Sociology*, 31. University of Edinburgh. www.sociology.ed.ac.uk/__data/assets/pdf_file/0010/13015/WP31_Gadda.pdf

Gillies, V., R. Edwards and N. Horsley. 2017. *Challenging the Politics of Early Intervention*. Bristol: Policy.

Gopnik, A. 2010. *The Philosophical Baby: What Children's Minds Tell Us about Truth, Love, and the Meaning of Life*. London: Picador.

Gopnik, A., A. Meltzoff and P. Kuhl. 2001. *How Babies Think: The Science of Childhood*. London: Phoenix.

Gordon, L. 2018. *Contemporary Research and Analysis of the Children of Prisoners: Invisible Children*. Newcastle upon Tyne: Cambridge Scholars Publishing.

Hertzog, E. 2009. *Tough Choices: Bearing an Illegitimate Child in Japan*. Stanford, CA: Stanford University Press.

Hynes, P., M. Lamb, D. Short and M. Waites. 2011. "Sociology and Human Rights: Confrontations, Evasions and New Engagements." *International Journal of Human Rights*, 14 (6): 811–832.

Intergovernmental Panel on Climate Change. 2018. "Global Warming of 1.5^{0}." https://report.ipcc.ch/sr15/pdf/sr15_spm_final.pdf

Internet Watch Foundation. 2018. *Annual Report 2017*. Cambridge: Internet Watch Foundation.

Jefferson, T. 1903–1904. *The Writings of Thomas Jefferson*, Memorial Edition, edited by A. Lipscomb and A. Bergh. Washington, DC: Thomas Jefferson Memorial Association.

Kent, J. and S. Thompson. 2014. "The Three Domains of Urban Planning for Health and Well-being." *Journal of Planning Literature*, 29 (3): 239–256.

Larcher, V., F. Craig, K. Bhogal, D. Wilkinson and J. Brierley. 2014. *Making Decisions to Limit Treatment in Life-limiting and Life-threatening Conditions in Children: A Framework for Practice*. London: Royal College of Paediatrics and Child Health.

Li, H., N. Jia, Q. Su, Z. Zhu, X. Liu, M. Sungkur and S. Padari … 2012. "Effects of Prenatal Psychosocial Stress on Pregnancy Outcomes and Physical and Neurobehavioural Development in Infancy with Gender Difference." *European Journal of Psychotraumatology*, 3: 1.

McGuirk, R. 2016. "Parents Often Reject Surrogate Babies with Defects, Australian Review Says." *The Star*, Canberra, 4 February 2016. www.thestar.com/news/world/2016/02/04/parents-often-reject-surrogate-babies-with-defects-australian-review-says.html

Ministry of Justice. 2016. "Women and the Criminal Justice System Statistics 2015." www.gov.uk/government/statistics/women-and-the-criminal-justice-system-statistics-2015

Murray, L. and L. Andrews. 2005. *The Social Baby: Understanding Babies' Communication from Birth*. Richmond, UK: CP Publishing.

National Audit Office. 2018. "Financial Sustainability of Local Authorities 2018." www.nao.org.uk/wp-content/uploads/2018/03/Financial-sustainabilty-of-local-authorites-2018-Summary.pdf

Okamoto, E. 2014. "Japan Turns Pro-Life: Recent Change in Reproductive Health Policy and Challenges by New Technologies." *International Journal of Health Policy Management*, 2 (2): 61–63.

Rodger, D., B. Blackshaw and C. Miller. 2018. "Beyond Infanticide: How Psychological Accounts of Persons Can Justify Harming Infants." *The New Bioethics*, 24: 106–121.

Rutter, M. 2002. "Nature, Nurture, and Development: From Evangelism through Science toward Policy and Practice." *Child Development*, 73: 1–21.

Sands, P. 2016. *East West Street: The Origins of Genocide and Crimes Against Humanity*. London: Weidenfeld & Nicholson.

Save the Children, Sweden. 2018. "Map of the 53 Countries That Ban the Corporal Punishment of Children." https://brilliantmaps.com/corporal-punishment/

Smith, F. 2017. "Babies Fall Victim to the Opioid Crisis." *National Geographic*, September 2017. www.nationalgeographic.com/magazine/2017/09/science-of-addiction-babies-opioids/

Stern, D. 1977. *The First Relationship: Infant and Mother*. Glasgow: Fontana.

Turner, B. 2008. *The Body and Society*. London: Sage.

Twum-Danso, A. 2010. "The Construction of Childhood and the Socialisation of Children in Ghana." In *A Handbook of Children and Young People's Participation*, edited by B. Percy-Smith and N. Thomas, 133–140. London: Routledge.

United Nations (UN). 1945. "Charter of the United Nations Chapter XIV: The International Court of Justice." www.un.org/en/sections/un-charter/chapter-xiv/index.html

United Nations (UN). 1948. "Universal Declaration of Human Rights." www.un.org/en/universal-declaration-human-rights/

United Nations (UN). 1989. "Convention on the Rights of the Child." www.unicef.org.uk/Documents/Publication-pdfs/UNCRC_PRESS200910web.pdf

United Nations (UN), Committee on the Rights of the Child. 2005. *Implementing Child Rights in Early Childhood General Comment No. 7 (2005) UN/CRC/GC/2005/1*. Geneva: United Nations.

Wickham, S., B. Barr, D. Taylor-Robinson and M. Whitehead. 2018. "Assessing the Health Impact of Austerity and Rising Poverty in the UK." www.ohchr.org/Documents/Issues/EPoverty/UnitedKingdom/2018/Academics/University_of_Liverpool_Department_of_Public_Helath_and_Policy.pdf

World Health Organisation (WHO). 2017. "10 Facts on Breastfeeding." www.who.int/features/factfiles/breastfeeding/en/

World Health Organisation (WHO). 2018. "Children: Reducing Mortality." www.who.int/news-room/fact-sheets/detail/children-reducing-mortality

4

UNDERSTANDING CHILDREN'S RIGHTS IN EARLY CHILDHOOD

Policy and practice in Australia

Margaret Coady and John Tobin

Introduction

When the United Nations (UN) Committee on the Rights of the Child ('Committee') adopted the revised version of its General Comment No. 7 on Implementing Child Rights in Early Childhood in 2006 (United Nations Committee on the Rights of the Child (UNCRC), 2006a), its objectives were ambitious. Among them was a desire to 'contribute to the realisation of rights for all young children through formulation and promotion of comprehensive policies, laws, programmes, practices, professional training and research specifically focused on rights in early childhood' (UNCRC, 2006a, para. 2(g)). The aim of this chapter is to build on this objective by examining the implications for policy and practice in two areas related to early childhood: first, the provision of ECE; and, second, the home, and more specifically the relationship that is envisioned under the Convention on the Rights of the Child ('Convention', 20 November 1989, 1577 U.N.T.S. 3) (United Nations (UN), 1989) between young children, their parents and the state.

The account offered in relation to each of these domains is not comprehensive. The aim of this chapter is more modest and offers insights that will encourage an ongoing debate. The first section examines the idea and consequences of what is referred to as a rights-based approach to ECE. The central argument is that this approach emphasises the capacities rather than deficits of children, and has a role to play in advocacy, policy design, service provision and research within the ECE sector. The second section sets out on a more controversial path as it seeks to explore the demands of the Convention on both parents and the state when it comes to the period from 0–8 years known as early childhood (UNCRC, 2006a, para. 4). It sets the Convention in the political and philosophical context in which it was drafted and adopted.

ECE: what is the rights-based approach?

An implied right as a normative end

There is no *explicit* right to ECE under the Convention, and proposals made during drafting to include an explicit reference to care before preschool age were not adopted. Instead, Article 28 recognises a broad *right of the child to education*, which includes a requirement that *primary education* should be made compulsory and available free to all. The Committee has interpreted 'the right to education during early childhood as beginning at birth and closely linked to young children's right to ... development' under Article 6(2) (UNCRC, 2006a, para. 28). It has also called:

> on States parties to ensure that all young children receive education in the broadest sense ..., which acknowledges a key role for parents, wider family and community, as well as the contribution of organized programmes of ECE provided by the State, the community or civil society institutions.
>
> *(UNCRC, 2006a, para. 30)*

It has been further noted that:

> early childhood education has also been the subject of repeated concern in the Committee's concluding observations where it has variously recommended that states adopt a national policy for ECE and development, ensure that all children have access to early childhood care and education opportunities and allocate sufficient resources to ECE.
>
> *(Courtis and Tobin, 2019, p. 1064)*

Thus, the Committee has effectively taken the view that there is an 'implied right' to early childhood education (ECE) under the Convention which must be facilitated and enabled by the state progressively and in light of available resources (UNCRC 2006a, paras 30, 38), which is consistent with the ambitions of the Sustainable Development Goals to ensure that 'by 2030, ... all girls and boys have access to quality early childhood development, care and pre-primary education' (United Nations General Assembly (UNGA), 2015, Goal 4.2).

However, the recognition of an implied right to ECE under the Convention is only one side of the rights-based coin. It recognises the normative standard that all states are required to aspire and take appropriate measures to achieve. In this sense, it is a worthy end in itself, given research that confirms the value of ECE to the development of an individual child and the multiplier effects that flow to families and society. However, a rights-based approach is also concerned with the instrumental impact of human rights and how they can inform the development, provision and monitoring of the provision of ECE. The consequences of this side of the rights-based coin are now explored.

Understanding rights as a means to an end

A growing body of scholarship has been exploring the meaning of a rights-based approach in matters affecting children in a range of areas including ECE (MacNaughton, Hughes and Smith, 2007; Mentha, Church and Page, 2015; Quennerstedt, 2016). The focus here is on two key features of this approach: first, the implications of a rights-based approach on the conception of a child; and, second, the key principles that inform the implementation of this approach in the area of ECE.

Conceptions of childhood

The conception of children held by an educator or policymaker will impact on the design and provision of services to those children. Although there are multiple conceptions of childhood, we contrast three – a proprietary conception, a welfare-based conception and the rights-based conception. The proprietary approach reflects the historical position that children were literally conceived of as the property of their parents. There are remnants of this proprietary conception of children within most societies – the defence of reasonable chastisement that permits the use of violence and force by parents to discipline their child being one example. Traces of this model might be seen in the resistance experienced by an early ECE educator from a parent who seeks to assert exclusive parental control and authority over a child in circumstances where this authority does not align with a child's best interests. For the most part, however, societies have now moved beyond an *explicit* conception of a child as merely a chattel.

This transition has involved a shift to the welfare-based approach to children that emerged in the early twentieth century and has dominated the policy framework concerning children ever since. Under this model, children are primarily conceived of as being vulnerable and in need of protection. The core principle animating this model is that the best interests of children shall be the paramount consideration in all matters affecting them. It offers a counterpoint to the historical marginalisation of children's interests relative to those of adults. Under the welfare model, a more active role is anticipated for the state in providing protection, education and assistance to a child. However, the focus remains on the vulnerabilities of a child. It represents a deficit model of childhood whereby children are to be seen but not heard because it is assumed that they lack the necessary expertise and understanding on issues relevant to them.

In contrast, the UNCRC (2006a) has explained that a rights-based approach demands 'a shift away from traditional beliefs that regard early childhood mainly as a period for the socialization of the immature human being towards mature adult' (para. 5). It requires 'that children, including the very youngest children, be respected as persons in their own right' and that 'young children should be recognized as active members of families, communities and societies, with their own concerns, interests and points of view' (para. 5). In summary, it recognises the vulnerabilities of children, but it does not define them by reference to these vulnerabilities (Tobin, 2015). Instead, it offers a conception of children that recognises their evolving capacities, their expertise, their agency and their insight into matters which concern them. It demands that children are not only seen, but also heard, listened to and taken seriously.

The consequences of the three conceptions of childhood for the state are summarised in Table 4.1.

Table 4.1 Consequences of three conceptions of childhood

Conception	Consequences
Property	No need for state intervention or assistance; child invisible; subject to exclusive parental control
Welfare	Active role for state to protect and assist realisation of a child's best interests; child is seen but not heard
Rights	Active role for state to protect and assist child in realisation of rights; child must be seen, heard, listened to and taken seriously

Within the ECE context, there is a question as to the dominant conception of childhood. The answer can be differentiated at the *regulatory level*, where policy regarding the operation of this sector is determined; the *managerial level*, which concerns the values of those who are responsible for the management and operation of an ECE facility; and the *personal level*, which concerns the conception of a child held by the face-to-face provider of ECE services. A separate study would be required to answer these questions. Here, two key points are emphasised: first, the answer will have implications for the design and provision of ECE services; and, second, a rights-based approach anticipates a more active role for children than alternative models. This chapter examines the extent to which some core policy documents that regulate the early childhood sector in Australia advance a conception of children that is consistent with a rights-based approach. Of principal relevance are:

- The Education and Care Services National Law 2010 ('National Law') (Victoria State Government (VSG), 2010), which is the foundation for the regulation of ECE in Australia.
- The National Quality Framework ('NQF'), which was established by the Australian Children's Education and Care Quality Authority (ACECQA) in 2012 to outline the standards for service providers.
- *Belonging, Being & Becoming: The Early Years Learning Framework for Australia* ('*Belonging, Being & Becoming*') (Council of Australian Governments (CAG), 2009), which was adopted by the Australian Government Department of Education and Training (AGDET) to guide the provision of ECE in Australia.
- *Victorian Early Years Learning and Development Framework: For All Children from Birth to Eight Years* ('Victorian Early Years Framework'), which was adopted by the Victorian Curriculum and Assessment Authority (VCAA) (2016) to guide the provision of ECE in Victoria.

Importantly, the National Law lists in its objectives that 'the guiding principles of the national education and care services quality framework ... [include] ... (a) that the rights and best interests of the child are paramount' (VSG, 2010, s.3(3)). The NQF also provides that 'the dignity and rights of every child are maintained' (ACECQA, 2012, Element 5.1). Although there is no explicit reference to the idea of a rights-based approach in *Belonging, Being & Becoming*, it states that 'early childhood educators guided by the Framework will reinforce in their daily practice the principles laid out in the United Nations Convention on the Rights of the Child' (CAG, 2009, p. 5). Moreover, the ideas that underlie a rights-based approach are embraced in this policy document. Consider the following examples:

> Children actively construct their own understandings and contribute to others' learning. They recognise their agency, capacity to initiate and lead learning, and their rights to participate in decisions that affect them including their learning.
>
> Viewing children as active participants and decision-makers opens up possibilities for educators to move pre-conceived expectations about what children can do and learn. This requires educators to respect and work with each child's unique qualities and abilities.
>
> *(CAG, 2009, p. 10)*

The emphasis here is not on a deficit model of childhood, but on the capacities and agency of children. The Victorian Early Years Framework also makes it clear in its 'vision and purpose' that it 'upholds the image of the child as a rights holder and competent learner with capacities to learn from birth' (VCAA, 2016, p. 2). It further recognises all children as 'full members of society, capable of participating in their social worlds through their relationship with others' (VCAA 2016, p. 4).

It is clear that at the *regulatory level*, there is a strong commitment to the idea that children are rights-bearers with evolving capacities who enjoy a right to participate in all matters that affect them. Where the gap emerges, however, is in the detail of how to operationalise this approach. Thus, for example, *Belonging, Being & Becoming* demands that early years educators will 'reinforce in their daily practice the principles laid out in the Convention' (CAG, 2009, p. 5), but it does not actually identify with any precision what those principles are or how they are to be implemented. It is to these principles that we now turn.

Key principles of a rights-based approach

The orthodox view is that the key principles under the Convention (UN, 1989) are:

- The right to non-discrimination (Article 2).
- The right for the best interests of the child to be upheld (Article 6).
- The right to life and development (Article 6).
- The right to be heard (Article 12).

The Victorian Early Years Framework specifically lists these principles (VCAA, 2016, pp. 4, 37). It does not, however, explain how they are to be translated into practice within the context of ECE. Instead, it states simply that 'these principles are consistent with contemporary early childhood research and are embedded within the practices espoused in this Framework' (VCAA, 2016, p. 4). This chapter is not the place to undertake a detailed assessment of whether this claim is justified; it is sufficient to offer the following observations.

First, broadly speaking, there is often a strong alignment between the core principles under the Convention *and* best practice in early childhood. Take, for example, the key practice principles under the Victorian Early Years Framework (VCAA, 2016, p. 7), which include promotion of a child's identity, *also a specific right under Article* 7 of the Convention, a child's culture, *also a right under Article 30*, support for professionals to act in a child's best interests, which is *consistent with Article 3*, and measures to ensure early childhood professionals respond sensitively and positively to each child, an approach that is required to fulfil a child's *right to development under Article 6.*

It would be wrong to assume, however, that given the alignment between the Articles under the Convention and the practice principles under the Victorian Early Years Framework, there is no need to inquire further into what the Convention and a rights-based approach might add to the early childhood sector in Australia. As such, there remains a need to inquire further whether or not a rights-based approach demands more of ECE and can add value to the way in which such services are designed, provided and monitored.

The added value of a rights-based approach

We propose four possible areas where a rights-based approach can add value to the ECE sector: advocacy, policy design, service provision and research. First, in the context of *advocacy*, a rights-based approach can be used to support demands that a state has an obligation under international law to take all appropriate measures to secure a child's implied right to ECE under Article 28 of the Convention (UN, 1989). ECE is not merely a desirable experience for children or a sound economic investment; it is an entitlement that states are bound to secure for the benefit of children. Second, in the context of *policy design*, the so-called '4A model' developed by the UN Special Rapporteur on the Right to Education (United Nations Economic and Social Council, 1999) offers guidance about the qualities required for an effective ECE sector:

- *Availability* demands the provision of ECE services.
- *Accessibility* demands that services must be financially accessible to all children without discrimination, geographically accessible for children in remote and/regional communities, and physically accessible for children with a disability.
- *Acceptability* demands that services must be of appropriate quality and accommodate religious, cultural, gender and other sensibilities.
- *Adaptability* demands that service must be responsive to the specific needs of children within their local context.

The third area in which a rights-based approach provides guidance for the early childhood sector concerns the actual *provision* of ECE services. Table 4.2 provides a summary of the differences between historical models of service provision for children and a rights-based approach.

Table 4.2 reveals that under a rights-based approach, children are not merely vulnerable and dependent on adult assistance, but that their capacity, agency and expertise must be recognised and integrated into ECE services. The linchpin of this model is Article 12 of the Convention (UN, 1989), which demands that:

> State parties must assure to the child who is capable of forming his or her own views the right to express those views freely on matters affecting the child, the views of the child being given due weight in accordance with the age and maturity of the child.

The provision gives rise to a number of questions: When is a child capable of forming views? What matters affect children? How do children express their views? How much weight does 'due weight' demand? What is required of states to 'assure' children express their views? For present purposes, the critical issue is that answers to these questions must presume competence and capacity rather than incompetence. Significantly, all the documents that regulate the ECE sector in Australia adopt this position. The greater challenge, however, relates to the question of how best to develop appropriate systems that enable children to express their views meaningfully.

Table 4.2 Historical models and a rights-based approach

Historical conception of children	*Rights-based conception of children*
Victims	Agents
Vulnerable and in need of protection	Vulnerable and in need of protection
Incompetent	Evolving capacity with need for supported decision-making
Weak	Resilient
Passive recipients of welfare	Active agents and collaborators
Lacking in expertise	Possessing expertise

There is an increasing body of literature that seeks to address this issue (Hart, 1992; Lundy, 2007; Shier, 2001). Moving forward, the challenge for the sector in Australia, and other jurisdictions, is how to translate children's right to participate in all matters affecting them into practice. It will require not only a commitment to a rights-based approach at the regulatory level, but also a commitment and understanding of the consequences of this model at managerial and personal levels where understandings of children's agency and right to participate will vary (MacNaughton et al., 2007; Mentha et al., 2015). This will require not only education and training, but also research to assess what measures are effective in translating the principles under the Convention into practice (Quennerstedt, 2016). It is this area of research where a rights-based approach can also add value to the early childhood sector.

Table 4.3 outlines the features of a traditional research model on matters concerning children. In this model, children risk being reduced to an object of inquiry for researchers and have no role in the development of the research question, or the collection, evaluation and dissemination of data. In contrast, under a rights-based approach, children are conceptualised as subjects with whom researchers can potentially collaborate (Lundy, McEvoy and Byrne, 2011), and indeed as independent researchers themselves (Kellett, 2011, 2012). This opens up the possibility for children to have an active role in the development of research questions, and the collection, evaluation and dissemination of data. This is not to suggest that such a model is easy to implement, but rather that a rights-based approach is constantly seeking to recognise the evolving capacities and expertise of children and, where appropriate, forge collaborations with children.

Early childhood and the family: rights, regulation and the state

This section considers a more controversial aspect of the Convention (UN, 1989): its implications for relations between the state, family and child. We start this discussion by examining the philosophical and political context in which the Convention was drafted, providing an insight into the reasons for the Convention's controversial status.

Contrasting philosophical views of the family and of rights

The years before, during and after the drawing up and ratifying of the Convention (UN, 1989) saw divergent and often emotionally expressed views on the family and on children's rights. For example, Lasch (1977) analyses how the family came to be seen as a 'haven in a heartless world', while Zaretsky (2007) goes further in showing how the family became a political issue in the United States of America (USA) and was used as

Table 4.3 Research on, with, by and for children

Research on children *under a welfare model*	*Research* with, by and for children *under a rights-based approach*
Object of inquiry	Subject
Research on child	Research with and by children
No role in research question, methodology, evaluation or dissemination	Potential role in designing research question, research methodology, evaluation and dissemination
Seen but not heard	Seen, heard and actively involved

a rallying symbol by both left-wing and right-wing groups. Lasch (1977) argued that 'parental functions once confined to the private sphere had been appropriated by agents of a burgeoning welfare state, including doctors, psychiatrists, social workers, teachers, and child guidance experts' (p. 17).

At the same time, Holt (1975) was proclaiming rights for children that were in fact the same rights as adults had. With regard to family, Holt held children should be able to choose their own family. While extreme and unrealistic for general acceptance, Holt's rights were useful in pointing out just how many freedoms children were denied. Another philosophical group described as communitarians defended the traditional family. Communitarians tended to be critical of rights, which they saw as divisive, individualistic and destructive of the kind of community that children needed in order to develop.

In response to claims that the state was intervening too much into family life, Olsen (1985) wrote, 'because the state is deeply implicated in the formation and functioning of families, it is nonsense to talk about whether the state does or does not intervene in the family' (p. 837). Okin (1989), another US feminist philosopher, pointed out many ways the state intervened through taxation laws, marriage laws and divorce laws, labour laws, and so on to support the traditional family. She suggested that the gendered nature of the traditional family led to injustices between members of the family, that the private family could also be a site of violence between its members because of inequalities of power, and that talk of privacy and intimacy can hide violence against less powerful family members.

These tensions concerning different views of the family continued after the ratification of the Convention (UN, 1989). In 1996, Hafen and Hafen published *Abandoning Children to Their Autonomy: The United Nations Convention on the Rights of the Child*. Similar concerns about the view of the family embodied in the CRC led to a Senate Committee of the Parliament of the Commonwealth of Australia re-examining Australia's commitment to the Convention. Bruce Hafen from the USA put in a submission, and was invited to give evidence to the Senate committee. Hafen's conservative views were already well known in Australia. Hafen and Hafen (1996) claimed that 'avant-garde thinkers about liberation ideology' in the USA had failed in the courts in that country, so had gone to the international human rights forum where those rights had been accepted by countries which did not realise the Convention contained 'autonomy rights'. A majority (51 per cent) of the submissions to this committee opposed the Convention, many of them on the grounds of 'government interference in family life' (Joint Standing Committee on Treaties, Parliament of the Commonwealth of Australia 1998, p. ix). The way most submissions were produced may be criticised, but they indicated some powerful opposition to the Convention in Australia, and, given the evidence about the drafting of the Convention, in other states also. Kamchedzera (2012) and Quennerstedt, Robinson and l'Anson (2018) analyse the changes, rethinkings and rewordings of the draft CRC, and these indicate that the role of the parent was one of the most challenging for states to agree.

The family and the Convention

Article 5 in the Convention defines 'parent' broadly, referring to 'rights and duties of parents or, where applicable, the members of the extended family or community as provided for by local custom, legal guardians or other persons legally responsible for the child' (UN, 1989). While Article 5 establishes parents' duties and rights to guide and direct their children, it qualifies these in two ways: parents should guide the 'exercise by the child of the rights recognized in the present Convention', and should do so 'in a manner consistent with the evolving capacities of the child'.

These qualifications make an apparently traditional, even banal, statement of parents' rights innovative, even revolutionary. As Kamchedzera (2012) points out, Article 5 is 'a break from the largely welfarist approaches expressed in regional general human rights instruments' (p. 7), highlighting that previous global human rights statements only hinted at any view that was not welfarist. CRC advocates may welcome this qualification of parents' 'direction' but only see its relevance for older children, since the term 'capacity' has been seen to limit very young children's rights in the past. However, the Committee's General Comment No. 7 is clear that very young children also have 'concerns, interests and points of view' that should be noted and taken into account in all matters concerning their futures (UNCRC, 2006a, para. 5).

Equally important is the reference in Article 5 to 'the rights recognized in this Convention'. This commits parents to all the rights in the Convention, including the more contentious Articles. The 'right to be heard' guaranteed in Article 12 has been seen by some as the most significant Article in the Convention (Van Bueren, 1995). Article 12 does not mention the word 'family', but has important implications for the family. It 'disaggregates' the child's interests from those of the family as a whole, so is revolutionary in international law. The use of the word 'disaggregate' does not mean the child's rights are entirely separate from the family: the many references to parents' guidance and direction in the CRC would not allow for that interpretation. Van Bueren (1995) herself recognises that while children must be consulted in all decisions that affect them, their views are not necessarily determinative. Article 12 only demands that they be given 'due weight'.

To return to the detail of Article 5, Kamchedzera (2012) argues that because the state is 'a principal duty bearer', the word 'respect' in the first phrase of Article 5 entails that states 'should not interfere with the exercise of such rights and the discharge of the duties except to ensure the best interests of the child and compliance with other child rights principles' (pp. 26–27). However, the interference could be quite extreme, as Article 19 indicates by recognising that violence, neglect and sexual abuse occur in the home, and urging that states take 'all legislative, administrative, social and educational measures' in such cases to prevent detriment to the child. Together with General Comment 8 (United Nations Committee on the Rights of the Child (UNCRC), 2006b), Article 19 is aimed at protecting a child from all violence and neglect, effectively banning corporal punishment within and outside the family.

The CRC (UN, 1989) acknowledges that families have a crucial role in the education and care of children. However, unlike previous statements of children's rights, the CRC recognises that children from the earliest age have an essential role in claiming these rights by making known their concerns and points of view. Very young children may express claims to their rights in different forms, which parents are usually in the best position to interpret. Article 5 is directive that parents have a duty to ensure the child can exercise and enjoy CRC rights.

Moral rights and enforcement

Families are generally the best place for the child to experience one right that has had much attention in recent years: the right to receive love. While the word 'love' does not appear in the CRC (UN, 1989), it can be read into the several mentions of the word 'care' in the

CRC and in General Comment No. 7 (UNCRC, 2006a). Liao (2015, pp. 1–3) observes that the right to be loved appears in some national declarations of children's rights, and Principle 6 in the UN Declaration of the Rights of the Child (UNGA, 1959, p. 19) states that the child, 'for the full and harmonious development of his personality, needs love and understanding. He shall, wherever possible, grow up in the care and under the responsibility of his parents, and in any case in an atmosphere of affection'. This 1959 Declaration is acknowledged in the CRC Preamble (UN, 1989).

The idea of the child's right to be loved is interesting from an enforcement perspective. Empirical evidence (Liao, 2015) shows the need for the child to experience unconditional love from parents or substitutes, for full psychological and even physical development. Given the fundamental importance of love in a child's life, it is plausible to argue for it to be a right. Many parents would not find such love difficult, but some parents do find it hard to bond with their child. States have a range of interventions – legislative, administrative, social, and educational measures – at their disposal, but few would want legislative measures to be used punitively in the case of parents who found it difficult to love their child. Of course, if failure to feel love led to abuse or neglect, more drastic state action would be necessary, as envisaged in the CRC, but that would be covered by other laws. Despite the importance that a child experiences love and attachment, it may be difficult to claim that a child has a direct *legal* right to receive love. Nevertheless, it could be said that the child has an important *moral* right to be loved. In the case of some moral rights, such as those concerning justice within a family (Okin, 1989), it may be undesirable for the law to prescribe precise ways to attain such justice. Of course, the state can intervene in other ways, by using social and educational measures to encourage and enable parents to love their child and by using legislation such as labour laws to give parents more time to form attachments, to love their children, and to perform a fair share of family work.

There are many important moral norms that are ill-suited to legal coercion, including decisions within the family (Etinson, 2018, p. 17). Etinson cites Tasioulas (2012, p. 2) example of the division of labour within a household, which is an issue that affects very young children since the home is a place for them to learn about gender roles. Although rights to love and to gender justice in the family are important, the reasons they are not suited to legal enforcement are varied. Such rights may be difficult to regulate. The idea of policing parents' expressions of love for their children or of enforcing the amount of housework undertaken by each parent would be repugnant to most. Moreover, state intervention may inhibit parents' expressions of love and the sensitive discussion and moral choices required for justice and love to exist within the family. While the CRC (UN, 1989) encompasses state intervention to enforce some laws within the family, in particular to prevent abuse, it assumes a degree of privacy for the family, partly as a way of assuring children's rights.

On the difficult question of state intervention in the family, the CRC (UN, 1989) recognises, as do the feminist philosophers discussed earlier, the variety of ways in which a state ruled by laws already intervenes, and intervenes in ways other than by law. Appropriately for a convention on children's rights, the CRC (UN, 1989) concentrates on interventions to promote the rights of the child in the family. It recognises the child's right to privacy, restricting state intrusion into the family, while allowing for interventions that defend the rights of the child.

Conclusion

In this chapter, we have analysed the significance of the United Nations CRC (UN, 1989) in two different but related domains in the context of early childhood: ECE and the family. We have noted that the values within the Convention (UN, 1989) challenge traditional values in these domains.

In respect of ECE, the Convention offers a conception that children are not merely vulnerable and dependent on adult assistance. Instead, their evolving capacities, expertise and agency are not only recognised, but also celebrated in demands that active measures are taken to enable children's views to be expressed and taken into account in all matters that affect them. In Australia, the policy and regulatory frameworks strongly align with this rights-based conception of childhood, but the challenge is in securing effective implementation.

In regard to the family, policymaking is complex in Australia's pluralist and multicultural society. The Convention (UN, 1989) regards the family as the fundamental unit in society; it affirms parents' primacy in their children's upbringing, while recognising the potential for children – including young children – to enjoy interests that may be disaggregated from those of their parents. It also states that direction and guidance offered by parents to their children must gradually adjust in response to their evolving capacities and be consistent with their enjoyment of rights.

To this point, policy implications for families are consonant with those for early childhood educators. However, when it comes to enforcement, the situation is very different. On the basis of the policies enunciated in the first part of this chapter, early childhood educators are likely to be sanctioned for failure to follow CRC-inspired policies. However, family policy is more diffuse, covering criminal law, family law, health legislation, taxation legislation, and policies concerning provision of benefits and childcare. We have argued that sanctions are appropriate in some of these areas, such as family child abuse, but that there are other areas of family activity where state sanctions are not practicable or, even if practicable, undesirable.

References

Australian Children's Education and Care Quality Authority (ACECQA). 2012. "National Quality Framework." www.acecqa.gov.au/

Council of Australian Governments (CAG). 2009. *Belonging, Being & Becoming: The Early Years Learning Framework for Australia*. Canberra: Commonwealth of Australia.

Courtis, Christian and John Tobin. 2019. "Article 28: The Right to Education." In *The UN Convention on the Rights of the Child: A Commentary*, edited by John Tobin, 1056–115. Oxford: Oxford University Press.

Etinson, Adam, ed. 2018. *Human Rights: Moral or Political?* Oxford: Oxford University Press.

Hafen, Bruce C., and Jonathan O. Hafen 1996. "Abandoning Children to Their Autonomy: The United Nations Convention on the Rights of the Child." *Harvard International Law Journal* 37 (2, Spring): 449–92.

Hart, Roger A. 1992. *Children's Participation: From Tokenism to Citizenship. No. 4 of Innocenti Essays*. Florence: UNICEF International Child Development Centre, 1990–99.

Holt, John. 1975. *Escape from Childhood: The Needs and Rights of Children*. Harmondsworth: Penguin.

Joint Standing Committee on Treaties, Parliament of the Commonwealth of Australia. 1998. *United Nations Convention on the Rights of the Child: 17th Report, SCOT 17 Chapter 4*. Canberra: Commonwealth of Australia.

Kamchedzera, Garton. 2012. "Article 5: The Child's Right to Appropriate Direction and Guidance." In *A Commentary on the United Nations Convention on the Rights of the Child*, edited by André Alen, Johan Vande Lanotte, Eugeen Verhellen, Fiona Ang, Eva Berghmans, Mieke Verheyde, and Bruce Abramson, Leiden: Martinus Nijhoff.

Kellett, Mary. 2011. "Empowering Children and Young People as Researchers: Overcoming Barriers and Building Capacity." *Child Indicators Research* 4 (2): 205–219.

Kellett, Mary. 2012. "Child-Led Research from Inception to Reception: Methodological Innovation and Evolution Issues." *CM: Časopis Za Upravljanje Komuniciranjem* 7 (24): 5–25.

Lasch, Christopher. 1977. *Haven in a Heartless World: The Family Besieged*. New York: Basic Books.

Liao, Matthew S. 2015. *The Right to be Loved*. Oxford: Oxford University Press.

Lundy, Laura. 2007. "'Voice' Is Not Enough: Conceptualising Article 12 of the United Nations Convention on the Rights of the Child." *British Educational Research Journal* 33 (6): 927–942.

Lundy, Laura, Lesley McEvoy, and Bronagh Byrne. 2011. "Working with Young Children as Co-Researchers: An Approach Informed by the United Nations Convention on the Rights of the Child." *Early Education and Development* 22 (5): 714–736.

MacNaughton, Glenda, Patrick Hughes, and Kylie Smith. 2007. "Early Childhood Professionals and Children's Rights: Tensions and Possibilities around the United Nations *General Comment No. 7* on Children's Rights." *International Journal of Early Years Education* 15 (2): 161–170.

Mentha, Sue, Amelia Church, and Jane Page. 2015. "Teachers as Brokers: Perceptions of 'Participation' and Agency in ECE and Care." *International Journal of Children's Rights* 23 (3): 622–637.

Okin, Susan Moller. 1989. *Justice, Gender, and the Family*. New York: Basic Books.

Olsen, Frances E. 1985. "The Myth of State Intervention in the Family." *University of Michigan Journal of Law Reform* 18 (4): 835–864.

Quennerstedt, Ann. 2016. "Young Children's Enactments of Human Rights in ECE." *International Journal of Early Years Education* 24 (1): 5–18.

Quennerstedt, Ann, Carol Robinson, and John l'Anson. 2018. "The UNCRC: The Voice of Global Consensus on Children's Rights?" *Nordic Journal of Human Rights* 36 (1): 38–54.

Shier, Harry. 2001. "Pathways to Participation: Openings, Opportunities and Obligations." *Children & Society* 15 (2): 107–117.

Tasioulas, John. 2012. "Towards a Philosophy of Human Rights." *Current Legal Problems* 65 (1): 1–30.

Tobin, John. 2015. "Understanding Children's Rights: A Vision beyond Vulnerability." *Nordic Journal of Human Rights* 84 (2): 155–182.

United Nations. 1989. *UN Convention on the Rights of the Child*. Geneva: United Nations.

United Nations Committee on the Rights of the Child (UNCRC). 2006a. *Revised General Comment No. 7: Implementing Child Rights in Early Childhood, CRC/C/GC/7/Rev.1 (Sep. 20, 2006)*. www.refworld.org/docid/460bc5a62.html

United Nations Committee on the Rights of the Child (UNCRC). 2006b. "General Comment No. 8 (2006): The Right of the Child to Protection from Corporal Punishment and Other Cruel or Degrading Forms of Punishment (Arts. 19; 28, Para. 2; and 37, inter alia), 2 March 2007, CRC/C/GC/8." www.refworld.org/docid/460bc7772.html

United Nations Economic and Social Council. 1999. "Preliminary Report of the Special Rapporteur on the Right to Education, Ms. Katarina Tomasevski, Submitted in Accordance with Commission on Human Rights Resolution 1998/33, E/CN.4/1999/49 (Jan. 13, 1999)." https://undocs.org/E/CN.4/1999/49

United Nations General Assembly (UNGA). 1959. "Declaration of the Rights of the Child." www.ohchr.org/EN/Issues/Education/Training/Compilation/Pages/1DeclarationoftheRightsoftheChild(1959).aspx

United Nations General Assembly (UNGA). 2015. "Resolution 70/1, Transforming Our World: The 2030 Agenda for Sustainable Development, A/RES/70/1 (Oct. 21, 2015)." https://undocs.org/A/RES/70/1

Van Bueren, Geraldine. 1995. *The International Law on the Rights of the Child*. Dordrecht: Martinus Nijhoff.

Victoria State Government (VSG). 2010. "Education and Care Services National Law Act 2010. 69/2010." www.legislation.vic.gov.au/Domino/Web_Notes/LDMS/PubStatbook.nsf/f932b66241ecf1b7ca256e92000e23be/B73164FE5DA2112DCA2577BA0014D9ED/$FILE/10-069a.pdf

Victorian Curriculum and Assessment Authority (VCAA). 2016. *Victorian Early Years Learning and Development Framework: For All Children from Birth to Eight Years*. Melbourne: Department of Education and Training.

Zaretsky, Natasha. 2007. *No Direction Home: The American Family and the Fear of National Decline 1968–1980*. Chapel Hill: The University of North Carolina Press.

5

TOWARDS COMPREHENSIVE AND SYSTEMATIC CHILDREN'S RIGHTS EDUCATION FOR EARLY CHILDHOOD EDUCATION AND CARE STUDENTS

Experiences from Ireland

Sheila Long

Introduction

This chapter presents the argument that comprehensive, state-initiated and systematic children's rights education (CRE) for early childhood education and care (ECEC) educators is required to realise young children's rights. The United Nations Convention on the Rights of the Child (UNCRC) (United Nations (UN), 1989) is a comprehensive statement of 54 articles upholding children's human rights and the general rights and freedoms applicable to all humans under the earlier Universal Declaration of Human Rights (Alston and Tobin, 2005; United Nations General Assembly (UNGA), 1948). Lauded as the most widely ratified human rights treaty worldwide, the principles and provisions of the UNCRC are increasingly incorporated into national constitutions and considered by judicial bodies in international, regional and domestic law (Tobin, 2013). Young children have tended to be among the least enfranchised, powerful, visible and audible of rights-holders in political structures and decision-making processes internationally, regionally, nationally and locally. Therefore, they are particularly dependent on the development of a comprehensive and supportive legislative, policy and institutional environment for the realisation of their rights. Fundamental changes are also necessary in educational cultures, relations and experiences along with policies, pedagogies and practices in spaces that educate and care for young children (Quennerstedt, 2013). However, without state action on children's rights education, there is no reason to assume that these changes will be enacted (Jerome, Emerson, Lundy and Orr, 2015). This chapter examines this claim by drawing on the Republic of Ireland as a case study to analyse legislative, policy and institutional changes that followed the Republic of Ireland's ratification of the UNCRC in 1992. Highlighting lessons learned, the chapter discusses barriers, tensions and gaps that remain in ECEC educators' access to CRE and presents recommendations for future action.

The children's rights framework

The UNCRC is not a flawless instrument (Freeman, 2000), nor is it a 'perfect vehicle' for the realisation of children's rights in education (Lundy, 2012, p. 394). It was not created to be the final victory for children or to establish an ideal global childhood (Prout, 2005). Children's rights is not the only possible analytical framework for the field, as Nolan (2019) argues. Indeed, insights of the capabilities, well-being and human capital approaches are frequently used by ECEC policymakers. However, ambiguous policy landscapes can blur the meaning of the critical concepts that can enable us to understand and apply a rights-based approach in practice. While the children's rights discourse does not seek to stifle alternatives, it makes explicit the connection between the child as the rights-holder and the state as the duty-bearer, with each guaranteed entitlement the UNCRC provides valued as an end in itself, and not just the means to achieve some distant goal (Woodhead, 2006). The most enduring value of a children's rights perspective therefore, and the starting point for this chapter, is that it provides educationalists, both academic and in practice, with a compelling framework for holding governments to account. For those who seek change and share a common passion for social justice as it applies to young children, the possibilities for transformation that the UNCRC may provide in the public policy sphere are immeasurable (Lundy, 2012).

To prepare for their role as future duty-bearers under the UNCRC, ECEC students should acquire legal literacy in both domestic law and international human rights law as part of their education (Lundy and Sainz Martínez, 2018). Lack of systematic and comprehensive education on the UNCRC for professionals is commonplace among States Parties, an unsatisfactory situation that has been emphasised by the UNCRC monitoring body, the United Nations Committee on the Rights of the Child ('the Committee'):

> If the adults around children, their parents and other family members, teachers and carers do not understand the implications of the Convention and above all its confirmation of the equal status of children as subjects of rights, it is most unlikely that the rights set out in the Convention will be realised for many children.
>
> *(UN, 2003, para. 66)*

CRE is a field derived from the more established field of human rights education (HRE), but they are not entirely synonymous. Although its shape and focus changes depending on the educator, context and audience, CRE is anchored firmly in the international children's rights framework. It addresses knowledge and understanding of the UNCRC, adopts processes and pedagogies that respect children's rights, and prepares children and their educators to become active agents in promoting children's rights and holding duty-bearers to account (Jerome, 2016). Progress has been slow, however, in mainstreaming comprehensive and systematic CRE for ECEC educators (Jerome et al., 2015; Lundy, 2012; Nutbrown, 2018; Pardo and Jadue Roa, 2018). Those who have not received CRE as part of their initial education may fail to make explicit connections with the children's rights dimensions of their practice, particularly the role of the adult in propagating or addressing children's rights violations (Brian Howe and Covell, 2005). There have been calls in the ECEC literature for more research on CRE (Nutbrown, 2018; Robson, 2016; Zanatta, 2018), building on earlier research that sought to explore the potential of current and future ECEC educators to identify and position themselves as committed children's rights professionals (MacNaughton, Hughes and Smith, 2007). A recent study commissioned by UNICEF (Pardo and Jadue Roa, 2018) examined 26 different ECEC programmes across Chile and found that while it was claimed that programmes had embedded children's rights, there was scant evidence to support this assertion. Instead, they found uncertain formative models for professional practice which meant that ECEC educators were inadequately prepared as duty-bearers. These findings raise important questions about whether, to what extent and in what ways ECEC professionals acquire knowledge of the UNCRC (UN, 1989) to inform their practice with young children.

The young child's rights under Articles 28, 29 and 42 of the UNCRC

If the philosophy, culture and values that inform the education and practices of those who work with and for children are to be underpinned by the principles and standards of the UNCRC (UN, 1989), educators of young children need to know and understand their obligations and those of the state. As all rights are interrelated, the UNCRC provisions must be applied in a teleological manner, with reference to the overall spirit of the Convention and its drafters (Lundy, 2007). The young child's rights under Articles 28, 29 and 42 underpin CRE for young children and those who care for and educate them. Similar to other forms of education, ECEC has far-reaching importance, because the child's right to access education, under Article 28 of the UNCRC, acts as an enabler or multiplier which, when guaranteed, supports their holistic development and enhances all other rights and freedoms (Lundy and Tobin, 2018; Tomasevski, 2001). This point is clarified by the Committee in General Comment No. 7 (GC7), which highlights the link between education in its broadest sense, care and development, clarifies that a child's education begins at birth, and asserts that all children have the right to be educated in an environment of peace, understanding and tolerance (UN, 2005).

Given that the right to an education throughout all stages of childhood and beyond is affirmed by GC7 (UN, 2005), it can be argued that young children as the first rights-holders should also be the first learners of rights (Fritzche, 2007). This raises questions about the form of this learning. Critical to understanding the ECEC educator's role in this respect is the principle of evolving capacities, derived from Articles 5 and 14 of the UNCRC and emphasised in GC7 as the process whereby children progressively acquire understanding about their rights and about how they can best be realised (UN, 1989, 2005). A core concept, with strong links to child development and growing maturity, the concept of evolving capacities plays a balancing role between autonomy and protection and relates directly to all other rights (Hanson and Lundy, 2017). CRE for ECEC educators is therefore necessary to build the capacity of duty-bearers, so that they can build the capacity of babies and young children to engage progressively with their own rights and the rights of others (Jerome et al., 2015).

Articles 29 and 42 of the UNCRC illustrate states' obligation to ensure that educators of young children receive CRE. Often overlooked and underestimated (Lundy and Tobin, 2018), Article 29 highlights some of the knowledge, practices and values an ECEC educator would require to fully realise this right for all young children in ECEC contexts. If educators of young children receive up-to-date and accurate CRE as part of their professional formation, they can act as autonomous professionals, basing their interpretations and pedagogical decisions on their knowledge. Article 29, Section (b) requires that 'the education of the child shall be directed to … the development of respect for human rights and fundamental freedoms, and for the principles enshrined in the Charter of the United Nations' (UN, 1989). As it is an entitlement for all children, this requirement demonstrates the need for ECEC educators to access the complex body of knowledge about international human rights relating to children. CRE should not replace or usurp other important knowledge or philosophies central to ECEC theory and practice, but the foundational frames of reference in early childhood, with roots in theories and research spanning the biological and social sciences, cannot provide sufficient grounding in children's rights. Human rights draw on quite different ethical and legal principles (Woodhead, 2006).

As a general measure of implementation, Article 42 of the UNCRC serves a 'pan-Convention' function and is considered a cornerstone of CRE (Hanson and Lundy, 2017, p. 299): 'States Parties undertake to make the principles and provisions of the Convention widely known, by appropriate and active means, to adults and children alike' (UN, 1989). What might be considered 'appropriate and active means' for educators and the children they work with should be defined from within the ECEC profession itself, and contextualised to local conditions, cultures, traditions and resources (Jerome, 2016). It should, at minimum, emphasise the communicative, relational, participatory and playful dimensions of young children's learning and development within their sociocultural context (Woodhead, 2006).

For aspiring and established children's rights educators, and for others who seek out synergies between the UNCRC (UN, 1989) and ECEC, there can be no 'best practice' or 'one-size-fits-all' CRE model, only locally negotiated solutions (Jerome, 2016). The fine detail of what a CRE curriculum should look like and how children's rights-oriented ECEC educators must practice should be decided within the context where the educators and children are (Nutbrown, 2018). However, three practical points are important: (i) what is to be taught to ECEC students (curriculum); (ii) how it should be taught (pedagogy); and (iii) why it should be taught (purpose) (Jerome, 2018). Eight distinguishing features of CRE for ECEC can be distilled from three United Nations sources (UN, 1989, 2003; United Nations Children's Fund (UNICEF), 2014); these provide some clarity, structure and guidance to help ECEC educators understand CRE (Long, forthcoming), and are discussed critically here.

1. *An explicit education about the international children's rights framework*

A thorough grounding in children's rights should start with knowledge about all UNCRC provisions and principles and commentary of the Committee relevant to ECEC, and how these interact with law, policy and practice at national and regional levels. This is particularly important given competing discourses, vague and diluted language, and incomplete emphasis on particular principles to the exclusion of others in the policy landscape. Fuller interpretations from international children's rights law, moral philosophy and political science could be included, along with ECEC literature from some of its foundational frames, including psychology, sociology and education (Quennerstedt, 2013).

2. *A tailored approach for ECEC students*

CRE for ECEC students, as future duty-bearers under the UNCRC, needs to be appropriate and relevant for them, reflecting their own needs and local conditions, and specific to the contexts and knowledge interests of ECEC professionals (Quennerstedt, 2013). While generic CRE models and curricula are available online (e.g. UNICEF, 2014), contextualised local models or frameworks enable educators to be more responsive, since specific barriers, tensions and debates related to children's rights exist for different professional groups who work in practice with young children and their families. These need to be identified and engaged with by educators and students, with particular emphasis on the principle of evolving capacities and playful, nurturing and participatory pedagogies.

3. *A focus on resourcing relational processes and practice-based learning sites*

In general, the initial education of ECEC students depends on elements of practice-based learning. ECEC settings, the children in them and the wider systems that support them need to be secured and respected as a valuable resource for facilitating student learning about children's rights in practice.

4. *An established curricular entitlement for CRE*

CRE should be visible and given expression on programmes that educate future duty-bearers under the UNCRC (UN, 1989), with the young child positioned explicitly as a rights-holder. Whether embedded across an entire programme or developed as a stand-alone feature within a programme, this entitlement must be explicit in learning outcomes and recognisable as CRE for ECEC students, administrators and governments. CRE should receive comparable treatment to other modules or knowledge domains. Without this emphasis in initial ECEC educator programmes, single workshops, short courses and awareness-raising campaigns provide insufficient opportunities to nurture critically reflective ECEC educators.

5. *Participatory, experiential, democratic and critically reflective pedagogies and practices*

An intentional approach to teaching and learning about rights, rooted in human interactions and relationships, using participatory pedagogies, can enable students to learn to protect, promote and take action for children's rights. By provoking critical thinking and nurturing practices and confidence to cope with dilemmas, complexity and ambiguity, students can develop confidence to work with uncertainty in practice (Quennerstedt, 2013). Dialogue, group work, problem-based learning, reflective journaling and other experiential learning opportunities can open up spaces to question assumptions, provoke different ways of thinking and enable changes to occur initially at the individual and interpersonal level. CRE pedagogies and processes using critical and transformative pedagogies, alongside rights-based pedagogical principles (Osler and Sharkey, 2010), not only contain some of this dissonance safely and respectfully, but also ensure students receive education in, through and for rights.

6. *A critical orientation*

A critical orientation to the UNCRC (UN, 1989) and to related theory and practice can enable students to identify gaps between the ideal and realities and become thoughtful, critically reflective, respectful ECEC educators (Martinez Sainz, 2018). Time and space are required for ECEC students to reflect critically on the multiple theoretical lenses and policy agendas that inform their profession, which may have shaped (and blurred) understandings of CR. Such opportunities will enable ECEC students to develop the knowledge and confidence to adopt an informed and critical stance to policy and government actions (Nutbrown, 2018).

7. *Positioning ECEC students as future duty-bearers and stakeholders in their own education*

The purpose of CRE is to ensure that ECEC students are framed as future duty-bearers under the UNCRC (UN, 1989) and understand their obligations in helping to realise the rights of all young children they educate and care for. To do this, ECEC students must know what children's rights are, and how they can ensure that these rights are respected. Additionally, CRE can build students' skills to enable them to advocate and take action for children's rights in ECEC more broadly and as stakeholders in their own education, empowering them to question and make demands on decision-makers for the resources and learning spaces they will need as future educators and duty-bearers under the UNCRC (UN, 1989).

8. *Consultation and capacity-building of decision-makers*

A high level of support, leadership and knowledge of children's rights is required to main-stream CRE effectively in the initial education of ECEC students. To learn about CRE, students need quality learning experiences in a rights-compliant environment. In turn, this approach enables education providers to improve accountability, and may assist their governments in respect of data requirements they may have under Articles 28, 29 and 42 of the UNCRC (UN, 1989).

A comprehensive, systematic and interdisciplinary approach to CRE for ECEC, adapting or expanding on any of the features above, has the potential to empower ECEC students to become confident and knowledgeable about children's rights issues, while simultaneously experiencing CRE methodologies as an empowering learning process. The processes of their education could mirror much of the substance of a rights-based approach to ECEC (Smith, 2013), while also reinforcing and strengthening wider, interconnected and interdependent systems. Although there can be no one best way to proceed for any country in implementing CRE for ECEC, the next section adopts a case study approach to reflect on some of Ireland's efforts in implementing the UNCRC (UN, 1989) in the years 1992–2019. Four enabling factors have laid the groundwork for a systematic and comprehensive approach to CRE for ECEC students in the Republic of Ireland. These include the framing of ECEC as a children's rights issue, a constitutional change, participation at the core of policy and CRE as a curricular entitlement for young children. Some challenges remain, however, similar to findings from other countries (Jerome et al., 2015) in getting policy alignment to support CRE and training to translate from government to the level of the child.

The case study of Ireland

Singular in its historical, social and economic past, Ireland has become, like other countries, strongly influenced by regional and global education agendas set by the European Union, the OECD, the World Bank and UNICEF, among others. Notwithstanding these influences, it may be regarded as useful to reflect on and validate systems and processes where a child rights-based approach has been successfully embedded. This section does not provide an in-depth review of all of Ireland's obligations under the UNCRC (UN, 1989), nor is it an exhaustive analysis of all relevant legislation, policy, institutional and other changes and challenges pertaining to ECEC since engagement with the UNCRC reporting cycle. Though there has been much reform of law and policy, as well as improvements in practice, in Ireland, it is nonetheless important not to overstate achievements, nor to become complacent or reductionist, considering the low starting point and the ongoing challenges that remain for the ECEC profession there.

The framing of ECEC as a children's rights issue

The sustained and effective advocacy efforts of alliances and coalitions composed of non-governmental organisations (NGOs) and ECEC profession in Ireland successfully used the UNCRC as a 'blueprint' at policy level to create a vision and advance a positive agenda for young children (Hayes, 2013, p. 2). Decision-makers tend to pay attention to alliances; however, 30 years ago, relationships were weak between the government and the NGO sector. There were a few formal structures in place, but much fragmentation, particularly in areas such as family support, preschool care and community development, which made meaningful consultation difficult (Children's Rights Alliance (CRA), 1997). The sustained focus and analytical research and advocacy of influential ECEC scholars, such as Hayes and colleagues at the then Dublin Institute of Technology, and others since the 1990s, alongside the inception of the Irish Children's Rights Alliance in 1995, meant that the interests and rights of young children in ECEC contexts were foregrounded on decision-makers' agenda. Sustained energy and philanthropic funding helped to engage vital players to generate debate and advance collaborations among academics, educators, researchers and representative organisations in ECEC. More recently, campaigning on policy development has translated to action to increase funding, child and family support, and paid parental leave, and to extend and enhance quality ECEC services, while simultaneously addressing governance and accountability issues (Startstrong, 2016). Leading on the development of evidence-based policy and driving an ambitious agenda, civil society in Ireland has been pivotal in advancing children's rights in ECEC in Ireland and connecting and engaging with government structures and processes to do so.

A constitutional change

A second powerful catalyst for advancing children's rights in Ireland was a constitutional amendment. The Irish legal system consists of constitutional, statute and common law, while at the international level it operates a dualist system. This means that international treaties do not become part of Irish law unless a specific Act of the *Oireachtas* (parliament) is passed. Although the Irish Constitution recognised a small number of rights for children, historically the strong constitutional position of the family downplayed children's rights, particularly the best interests of the child, while favouring the integrity of the family (defined by the courts based on marriage) (Kilkelly, 2012). The subsequent 31st Amendment of the Constitution (Children) Act 2012, signed into law in April 2015, has brought greater recognition of children's individual rights. Through the limited adoption in its wording of two UNCRC principles – Article 3 (best interests) and Article 12 (respect for the views of the child) – the Irish Constitution now recognises that all children are individual rights-holders, although only those provisions that are expressly incorporated into national law can give rise to enforceable rights and duties (Lundy, Kilkelly, Byrne and Kang, 2012). That said, this altered landscape has led to much continued legal reform to ensure that domestic law is moving towards greater respect for children's rights and progress has been made in relation to structures, monitoring, and children's rights training of legal professions and participatory practices among child protection and welfare professionals (TUSLA Child and Family Agency, 2016). Following the constitutional changes, training has been provided to the children's workforce in the statutory sector, and a commitment has been made to provide training and a manual on participation for ECEC educators (Department of Children and Youth Affairs (DCYA), 2018). This would enable ECEC educators to consider what these two principles might mean for their profession, given that they too are tasked with making these rights real for the young children with whom they work.

Participation at the core of public policy

Internationally, lack of political leadership has been identified as a barrier to the implementation of the UNCRC (Jerome et al., 2015); however, since its inception in 2011, the DCYA in Ireland, with a full cabinet minister, has been instrumental in the mobilisation of political will and coordination of resources. Driving a children's rights agenda across government, policy decisions can be supported by evidence-based recommendations from expert advisory groups and comprehensive, disaggregated data on children's well-being and development from a longitudinal study (*Growing Up in Ireland*). This coherent approach to mainstreaming children's rights in policy and legislative processes is supported by a participation support team and hub that supports government departments, state agencies and NGOs in ensuring that children's views on all issues that affect their lives are heard in decision-making processes (DCYA, 2018). Thus, direct relationships with children and a coherent children's rights knowledge base has the potential to underpin government decision-making (Lundy et al., 2012), although until now representation and formal communication structures for children aged 0–6 years, in line with their evolving capacities, remain underdeveloped.

Following effective lobbying from the NGO sector, and criticism of the Committee in its first report, an ombudsperson's office was established in 2004 under the Ombudsman for Children Act 2002 (as amended). While promoting and raising awareness of the UNCRC (UN, 1989) is different from implementing CRE, this office takes participation and the Committee's ongoing recommendations on CRE of professionals seriously. As an independent body, it has a strong record of holding the government to account on children's rights issues and awareness-raising about the UNCRC (Lundy et al., 2012). A range of high-quality resources are available for primary and secondary school teachers to support them in their role (Ombudsman for Children's Office (OCO), 2018), although there are, as yet, no online resources for ECEC educators.

The principle of participation first appeared in Irish policy with the first Children's Strategy – *Our Children, Their Lives* (Department of Health and Children, 2000). The second and current children's strategy, published in 2014 – *Better Outcomes, Brighter Futures* – is far more ambitious in its remit (DCYA, 2014). It tracks government commitment to the child in a holistic way, from birth through to early adulthood. An interdisciplinary and cohesive overarching policy framework, it consists of aligned, constituent strategies that have established strong systems, structures and collaborative arrangements. In doing so, it brings together statutory, voluntary and community bodies, with a strong emphasis on local and national interagency activity to facilitate implementation (DCYA, 2014). Ireland was one of the first countries to publish a national strategy on children and young people's participation in decision-making, which was guided and strongly influenced by the UNCRC (UN, 1989) and the European Charter of Fundamental Rights (European Union, 2000). It provides a robust definition of the principle of participation as 'the process by which children and young people have active involvement and real influence in decision-making on matters affecting their lives, both directly and indirectly' (DCYA, 2015, p. 20). This ensured that the new constitutional principle would have impact beyond the courts.

A specific priority in this strategy was early education, which meant that young children's views are now seen as vital for all aspects of ECEC, from the mundane, everyday routines to the 'development of policy, legislation, research and services' (DCYA, 2015, p. 17). It also incorporated Lundy's model of participation, a legally sound, user-friendly conceptualisation of Article 12 that focuses attention for ECEC educators on participation as a process of four chronological aspects of participation: space, voice, audience and influence (Lundy, 2007).

When GC7 was published, governments were urged to develop:

> Rights-based, coordinated, multisectoral strategies in order to ensure that children's best interests are always the starting point for service planning and provision. These should be based around a systematic and integrated approach to law and policy development in relation to all children up to 8 years old.
>
> *(UN, 2002, para. 22)*

More than a decade later and following a large consultation process with the ECEC sector, expert advisory groups, young children, parents and the public, an early years strategy was published in Ireland, broadly fulfilling these recommendations. Promising commitments have been made to the development and use of appropriate methodologies and mechanisms for consulting and engaging with young children, publication of guidance on participation, and the development of child participation training programmes (DCYA, 2018). However, addressing only one principle in training would not be as effective for ECEC educators as comprehensive, systematic children's rights education that takes as its starting point the interconnections with all the rights of the child.

A curricular entitlement for children's rights education

In 1998, the United Nations Committee on the Rights of the Child emphasised to the Irish state that 'Children's rights should be incorporated in the curricula of all educational and pedagogical institutions and comprehensive training programmes on the Convention should be conducted for professional groups working with and for children' (UN, 1998, para. 33). The national quality and curricular frameworks in Ireland were subsequently embedded and demonstrably rooted in the UNCRC (Hayes, 2013). The purpose, content and quality of education articulated by Article 29 of the UNCRC is reflected in ECEC pedagogy in Ireland, influenced by the holistic definition of ECEC provided by *Aistear*, the national curricular framework (National Council for Curriculum and Assessment (NCCA), 2009), and *Siolta*, the national quality framework (Centre for Early Childhood Development and Education (CECDE), 2006). A curricular entitlement to CRE for young children under Articles 29 1 (b) and 42 is clearly articulated in *Aistear* (NCCA, 2009, p. 8). Simultaneously, *Aistear* as an overarching framework ensures cohesion of curricula, which is also important for strengthening links between initial practitioner education and transmission among colleagues in the workplace (Urban, Lazzari, Vandenbroek, Peeters and van Laere, 2011). There is clear potential for a cohesive approach to education and training about children's rights in Ireland due to a centralised department of education and a centralised curriculum authority (Lundy, 2012). With these frameworks and associated guidance, ECEC settings in Ireland, whether voluntary, community or private, have the potential to develop their own unique innovative and rights-based practices, deeply meaningful to their own children, where play and respectful, reciprocal relationships are central to the realisation of children's rights.

Barriers, tensions and gaps

To date, a possible side effect of the limited incorporation of the UNCRC into the Constitution is the elevation of the two incorporated guiding principles (best interests and participation) in policy and practice guidance. Reliance on a 'trickle-down' approach to learning about children's rights, based on policy and practice guidance that considers only some aspects of the UNCRC (UN, 1989), is insufficient preparation for UNCRC duty-bearers. Hanson and Lundy (2017) have argued that the four guiding principles of the UNCRC, of which the best interests and participation are the most visible in the Irish legal and policy landscape, can distort implementation of the UNCRC.

It can be difficult to establish whether, in what ways and to what extent ECEC students and educators receive CRE as part of their professional formation. The picture is complicated in Ireland by disparities in qualifications (500 qualifications of varying levels, from a vast range of jurisdictions, are recognised currently) and the absence of either a professional regulation body or a professional competency framework. The status and conditions of the profession, including low pay and high staff turnover, continue to generate vigorous debate. These interconnected problems and priorities impact on the quality and consistency of relationships young children require for the realisation of their rights in ECEC. However, CRE is not a panacea for the poor conditions of the ECEC educator, or chronic underfunding of the sector, nor should autonomous and professional ECEC educators, through CRE, be reduced to mere instruments for implementing the UNCRC (Quennerstedt, 2013). As indicated earlier in this chapter, CRE has transformative potential to empower not only children, but also ECEC educators.

Conclusion

This chapter has presented the argument that comprehensive, systematic CRE for ECEC educators, initiated and enacted by states, is required to realise young children's rights. To do so, it has drawn on the case of the Republic of Ireland, and has analysed legislative, policy and institutional changes since the Republic of Ireland's ratification of the UNCRC in 1992 until 2019. The progress, achievements, barriers, tensions and gaps influencing ECEC educators' CRE in Ireland have been discussed critically. Taking into account these points, the following recommendations are now proposed to the wider international audience as potential ways to secure more systematic and comprehensive CRE for ECEC students.

Comprehensive, coordinated analysis

Individual states should conduct comprehensive, coordinated national situation analyses with respect to CRE of ECEC students. Institutions that educate ECEC students should gather evidence to examine if and how knowledge of the UNCRC is explicitly embedded in their programmes.

Adopting eight features of CRE

While the understanding of key stakeholders, including students, educators, administrators and young children, is a vital element of CRE, it may also be useful to examine overall structures, relational processes, pedagogies, resource decisions and curricula on ECEC programmes against the eight features of CRE outlined above.

Monitoring and evaluation of CRE

Governments should monitor and evaluate CRE in ECEC as a general measure of implementation of the UNCRC and report on it to the Committee. This would enable governments to track public funding of ECEC educators as part of their ECEC professionalisation processes and hold institutions accountable for resourcing relevant programmes to ensure they meet required competences, in line with the UNCRC.

Building the capacity of decision-makers

There should be mobilisation and capacity-building of key decision-makers to ensure that ECEC programme providers understand their role in CRE, take it seriously, and resource it appropriately. This recommendation is particularly important for states where there are no national professional regulation requirements.

References

Alston, Philip and John Tobin. 2005. *Laying the Foundations for Children's Rights*. Florence: Innocenti Research Centre.

Centre for Early Childhood Development and Education (CECDE). 2006. *Síolta*. Dublin: CECDE.

Children's Rights Alliance (CRA). 1997. *Small Voices: Vital Rights. Submission to the United Nations Committee on the Rights of the Child*. Dublin: Children's Rights Alliance. www.childrensrights.ie/sites/default/files/submissions_reports/files/ShadowReportSmallVoices97_0.pdf.

Department of Children and Youth Affairs. 2014. *Better Outcomes, Brighter Futures: The National Policy Framework for Children and Young People*. Dublin: The Stationary Office.

Department of Children and Youth Affairs. 2015. *National Strategy on Children and Young People's Participation in Decision Making Processes 2015–2020*. Dublin: The Stationary Office.

Department of Children and Youth Affairs. 2018. *First Five: A Whole-of-Government Strategy for Babies, Young Children and Their Families*. Dublin: Government Publications.

Department of Health and Children. 2000. "National Children's Strategy: Our Children: Their Lives." www.dcya.gov.ie/documents/Aboutus/stratfullenglishversion.pdf.

European Union. 2000. "Charter of Fundamental Rights of the European Union." https://eur-lex.europa.eu/legal-content/EN/ALL/?uri=CELEX:32000X1218(01).

Freeman, Michael D.A. 2000. "The Future of Children's Rights." *Children and Society* 14 (4): 277–293, doi:10.1111/j.1099-0860.2000.tb00183.x.

Fritzche, K. Peter 2007. "Children's Rights Education as a Key to Human Rights Education." *Peace Matters*. 29. Utrecht: SIM. www.human-rights-education.org/images/HREUtrechtlast.pdf.

Hanson, Karl and Laura Lundy. 2017. "Does Exactly What It Says on the Tin? A Critical Analysis and Alternative Conceptualisation of the So-Called 'General Principles' of the Convention on the Rights of the Child." *International Journal of Children's Rights* 25: 285–306, doi:10.1163/15718182-02502011.

Hayes, Noirin. 2013. *Early Years Practice: Getting It Right from the Start*. Dublin: Gill & McMillan.

Brian Howe, R., and Katherine Covell. 2005. *Empowering Children: Children's Rights Education as a Pathway to Citizenship*. Toronto: University of Toronto Press.

Jerome, Lee. 2016. "Interpreting Children's Rights Education: Three Perspectives and Three Roles for Children." *Citizenship, Social and Economic Education* 15 (2): 143–156, doi:10.1177/2047173416683425.

Jerome, Lee. 2018. "Heros or Hypocrites? Thinking About the Role of the Teacher in Human Rights Education." *Human Rights Education Review* 1 (2): 58-75.

Jerome, Lee, Lesley Emerson, Laura Lundy, and Karen Orr. 2015. *Child Rights Education: A Study of Implementation in Countries with A UNICEF National Committee Presence*. Geneva: UNICEF.

Kilkelly, Ursula. 2012. "Children's Rights in Child Protection: Identifying the Bottom Line in Critical Times." In *Children's Rights and Child Protection: Critical Times, Critical Issues in Ireland*, edited by Deborah Lynch and Kenneth Burns, 29–44. Manchester: Manchester University Press.

Long, Sheila. forthcoming. "Children's Rights Education for Early Years." In *Conceptualising and Reconceptualising Children's Rights in Infant Toddler Early Childhood Education and Care: Transnational Conversations*, edited by Frances Press and Sandra Cheeseman, Berlin: Springer.

Lundy, Laura. 2007. "Voice Is Not Enough: Conceptualisng Article 12 of the United Nations Convention on the Rights of the Child." *British Education Research Journal* 33 (6): 927–942, doi:10.1080/01411920701657033

Lundy, Laura. 2012. "Children's Rights and Educational Policy in Europe: The Implementation of the United Nations Convention on the Rights of the Child." *Oxford Review of Education* 38 (4): 393–441, doi:10.1080/03054985.2012.704874.

Lundy, Laura, Ursula Kilkelly, Bronagh Byrne, and Jason Kang. 2012. *The UN Convention on the Rights of the Child: A Study of Legal Implementation in 12 Countries*. United Kingdom: UNICEF. www.qub.ac.uk/researchcentres/CentreforChildrensRights/filestore/Filetoupload,485596,en.pdf.

Lundy, Laura and Gabriela Sainz Martínez. 2018. "The Role of Law and Legal Knowledge for a Transformative Human Rights Education: Addressing Violations of Children's Rights in Formal Education." *Human Rights Education Review* 1 (2): 4–24, doi:10.7577/hrer.2560

Lundy, Laura and John Tobin. 2018. "The Aims of Education." In *The United Nations Convention on the Rights of the Child: A Commentary*, edited by John Tobin, 1116–1152. Oxford: Oxford University Press.

MacNaughton, Glenda, Patrick Hughes, and Kylie Smith. 2007. "Young Children's Rights and Public Policy: Practices and Possibilities for Citizenship in Early Years." *Children and Society* 21: 458–469, doi:10.1111/j.1099-0860.2007.00096.x.

Martinez Sainz, Gabriela. 2018. "Building Professional Agency in Human Rights Education: Translating Policy to Practice." *International Journal of Human Rights Education* 2 (1): 1–30. https://repository.usfca.edu/ijhre/vol2/iss1/

National Council for Curriculum and Assessment (NCCA). 2009. "Aistear." www.ncca.ie/en/early-childhood/aistear.

Nolan, Aoife. 2019. "Poverty and Child Rights." In *Oxford Handbook of Children's Rights*, edited by Jonathan Todres and Shani King, New York: Oxford University Press.

Nutbrown, Cathy. 2018. *Early Childhood Educational Research: International Perspectives*. London: Sage.

Ombudsman for Children's Office (OCO). 2018. "Children's Rights Education Materials." www.oco.ie/childrens-rights/education-materials/.

Osler, Audrey and Hugh Sharkey. 2010. *Teachers and Human Rights Education*. London: Trentham.

Pardo, Marcela and Daniela Jadue Roa. 2018. "Fledgling Embeddedness of the Child Rights Approach in ECEC Undergraduate Programmes in Chile: Any Possibilities for the Enactment of Children's Rights for Infants and Toddlers in ECEC Programs." 28th European Early Childhood Education Research Association Conference. Budapest: EECERA.

Prout, Alan. 2005. *The Future of Childhood: Towards the Interdisciplinary Study of Children*. London: Falmer Press.

Quennerstedt, Anne. 2013. "Children's Rights Research Moving into the Future – Challenges on the Way Forward." *International Journal of Children's Rights* 21: 233–247, doi:10.1163/15718182-02102006.

Robson, Jenny. 2016. "Early Years Teachers and Young Children's Rights." *Research in Teacher Education* 6 (1): 6–12.

Smith, Kylie. 2013. "A Rights-based Approach to Observing and Assessing Children in the Early Years Classroom." In *Children's Rights and Education*, edited by Beth Blue Swandener, Laura Lundy, Natasha Blanchet-Cohen and Janette Habashi, 99–115. New York: Peter Lang.

Startstrong. 2016. *Startstrong: The Impact of a Small Children's Rights Advocacy Organisation on Early Years Policy in Ireland*. Dublin: Startstrong. www.startstrong.ie/files/13297_start_strong_report16.pdf.

Tobin, John. 2013. "Justifying Children's Rights." *International Journal of Children's Rights* 21: 1–47, doi:10.1163/15718182-02103004.

Tomasevski, Katarina. 2001. *Human Rights in Education as a Prerequisite for Human Rights Education*. Stockholm: Swedish International Development Agency.

TUSLA Child and Family Agency. 2016. *Child and Youth Participation Toolkit*. www.tusla.ie/uploads/content/Tusla_-_Toolkit_(web_version).pdf.

United Nations (UN). 1989. *Convention on the Rights of the Child*. Geneva: United Nations.

United Nations Children's Fund (UNICEF). 2014. *Child Rights Education Toolkit: Rooting Child Rights in Early Childhood Education, Primary and Secondary School*. Geneva: UNICEF. www.unicef.org/crc/files/UNICEF_CRE_Toolkit_FINAL_web_version170414.pdf.

United Nations, United Nations Committee on the Rights of the Child. 1998. "Concluding Observations on the Second Periodic Report of Ireland." www.childrensrights.ie/sites/default/files/submissions_reports/files/UNCRC-ConclObs1998.pdf.

United Nations, United Nations Committee on the Rights of the Child. 2003. *General Comment No. 5 Implementation. UN/CRC/GC/2003/1.* Geneva: United Nations.

United Nations, United Nations Committee on the Rights of the Child (UNCRC). 2005. *Implementing Child Rights in Early Childhood General Comment No.7 (2005) UN/CRC/GC/2005/1.* Geneva: United Nations.

United Nations General Assembly (UNGA). 1948. "Universal Declaration of Human Rights, General Assembly Resolution 217 A." www.ohchr.org/EN/UDHR/Documents/UDHR_Translations/eng.pdf.

Urban, Mathias, Ariana Lazzari, Michel Vandenbroek, Jan Peeters, and van Laere Katrien. 2011. *Core Competence Requirements in Early Childhood Education and Care.* Brussels: European Commission/Directorate General in Education. https://download.ei-ie.org/Docs/WebDepot/CoReResearchDocuments2011.pdf.

Woodhead, Martin. 2006. "Changing Perspectives on Early Childhood: Theory, Research and Policy." *International Journal of Equity and Innovation in Early Childhood* 4 (2): 1–43. http://oro.open.ac.uk/id/eprint/6778.

Zanatta, Francesca. 2018. "Are We Really Doomed? Critical Pathways for Advancing Children's Rights through Theory and Practice." In *International Perspectives on Practice and Research into Children's Rights*, edited by Gabriela Martinez Sainz and Sonia Ilie, 35–56. Mexico: Centre for Human Rights Studies. https://cedhmx.org/index.php/publicaciones/.

6

SATU DESA, SATU PAUD – ONE VILLAGE, ONE CENTRE

Unpacking the meaning of children's participation within ECE policy and provision in Indonesia

Vina Adriany, Hani Yulindrasari and Marek Tesar

Introduction

This chapter examines the complex relations between early childhood education (ECE) provision in Indonesia and the notion of children's participation in this sector. Children's participation is part of the Indonesian government agenda, and we will demonstrate, utilising critical policy analysis, how this policy of 'participation' is positioned in contemporary Indonesia as a contested term. Furthermore, this analysis will yield how future directions of children's participation in the ECE context could be shaped.

Indonesia is one of the countries that ratified the United Nations Convention on the Rights of the Child (UNCRC) back in 1990 (United Nations (UN), 1989; United Nations Children's Fund (UNICEF), 2014). One of the central concepts in the UNCRC is Article 12, which states that children have the right to participate in decision-making processes that impact on their lives. This principle recognises children as individuals who have agency and the capacity to make informed decisions about their lives (Te One and Dalli, 2010). However, despite the Indonesian government's increasing attention to ECE, discussion of children's rights in Indonesia does not seem to take into account children in ECE settings. In the UNCRC review prepared by Save the Children (2010), for instance, the focus is on generic issues such as preventing child marriages and children living under specific detrimental circumstances, such as street children. While these issues are important, the absence of children's rights in the ECE context in this discussion represents a significant gap.

A brief overview of Indonesia

Indonesia is situated in South East Asia and is the world's largest archipelago, consisting of more than 17,000 islands. It is also one of the most ethnically diverse countries, with more than 300 indigenous ethnicities residing within it, each having their own language (World

Population Review, 2018). The Javanese form the largest ethnic group and Javanese is also the dominant culture in Indonesia, influencing many social, cultural and political practices (Geertz, 1976). Indonesia is the fourth most populous country in the world, with more than 260 million people, as well as being the world's most populous Muslim country. There are huge socio-economic disparities between the islands, communities and ethnicities, and between urban and rural areas. Even though it is not an Islamic state, Islam is increasingly influencing hegemonic values in Indonesia (Van Bruinessen, 2011). As such, Javanese and Islamic values are prevalent in both child-rearing and teacher education.

The Asian Development Bank (2016) notes that Indonesia is one of the countries that has experienced rapid economic growth and progress. However, this growth is not distributed evenly and is marked by rising inequality between different socio-economic groups within society (Yusuf, Sumner and Rum, 2014). Within this complex context, contemporary Indonesia is characterised by complexities, messiness and contradictions, and the case of ECE in Indonesia is an embodiment of these positions, on the one hand, and of dreams and ideas, on the other.

The notion of children's participation in the Indonesian context

The term *participation* is contested. From a historical perspective, children's participation was initially understood as child protection (Lansdown, 1994). However, latterly, the meaning of the term has expanded to include more of children's ability to make choices and decisions (Smith, 2007). This marks a paradigm shift from a traditional belief that positions children as irrational individuals, unable to be involved in any decision-making process, to the more progressive humanistic approaches that see children as people with voices and agency (Bae, 2010). However, despite the emphasis on children's capacity, the meaning of children's participation is always defined and understood from adults' perspectives (Mannion, 2007).

The adoption of the UNCRC in Indonesia commenced in 1990 through Presidential Decree No. 36 on Children's Rights. The introduction of this decree illuminates the extent to which the Indonesian government has exercised its power on a governmental and a civic level to account for the notion of children's rights in its activities. This decree was then followed by the passing of Law No. 23 Year 2002 on Child Protection. This law was modified again in 2014 when the government developed and passed Law No. 35 Year 2014 on Child Protection (Octarra, 2014).

One of the rights mentioned in the latest legislation is the right of children's participation. The word *participation* appears in at least three contexts. First, the term is stated in relation to the notion of children's protection. Second, the word is used when explaining the rights of children with disabilities. Third, it is used to indicate the responsibility of the government to provide children with opportunities that allow them to participate in the nation's development. Fourth, the word is specified again to illuminate the government's role in providing space that would permit children to participate, and finally the term is used when the law provides a working definition of the term *rights*. All legal instances of the term remain ambiguous, and the extent to which this law is translated into practice remains a problematic issue. It appears that the focus of child protection law in Indonesia is still on the issue of *protection*. This suggests the way children are constructed in Indonesia: that they are often conceived of as fragile, passive and in need of constant protection (Adriany, 2013). Nevertheless, the government has attempted to include the notion of children's participation in Ministry Regulation No. 3 Year 2011 on the Policy of Children's Participation in the Nation's Development. This regulation provided a more obvious definition of children's participation. Chapter 1, Article 1, Verse 2 of the law defines children's participation as 'children's involvement in the decision making process in everything that would affect them. This [participation] has to be done with consciousness, understanding, and personal will so that children can enjoy the benefit from the decision making process' (Ministry of Women's Empowerment and Child Protection of the Republic of Indonesia, 2011, para. 4).

Although there have been efforts to include the notion of children's participation more, the concept is only implemented in an orchestrated way, such as the establishment of the Children's Forum from village to state levels. Which children are selected to be representatives on the Children's Forum is unclear. At the same time, the use of the term 'participation' in the educational setting remains problematic. The term appears to only be understood in relation to children's enrolment rate. The fact that the regulation pertaining to children participation was developed by the Ministry of Women's Empowerment and Child Protection, and not by the Ministry of Education, suggests that the issue of children's rights is still seen as detached from educational issues.

Early childhood education in Indonesia

The practice of ECE in Indonesia can be traced back to precolonial and colonial times (Thomas, 1992). However, it is not the purpose of this chapter to provide an exhaustive historical review of ECE in Indonesia. Briefly, Indonesia gained its independence in 1945, and in 1950 the Indonesian government included ECE in the national education system through the Law of the Foundation of Education and Teaching in Schools (Thomas, 1988). There were two settings for young children as part of ECE: (a) kindergarten (*Taman Kanak-kanak/TK*); and (b) preschool (*prasekolah*), with both serving as pre-primary education for children aged 3 to 6 years old. Despite there being some attention from the Indonesian government towards institutionalised education and care of young children, the main focus of the government's policy and spending in the years from 1950 to 2001 was on primary education (Thomas, 1992).

Push for participation

In this section, we will demonstrate how the government's push for children's participation is limited to the notion of children's protection and children's access to ECE centres. To unpack this, we will start by discussing how ECE in Indonesia has become one of the government's foci.

Greater attention to ECE was forced by the global development agenda marked by the Dakar Framework Declaration in 2000, which included access to ECE as one of the goals of Education for All (Hasan, Hyson and Chang, 2013). This was followed by the Millennium Development Goals (MDGs), which clearly state ECE as one means to eradicate poverty (Adriany and Saefullah, 2015). Since then, ECE has become a national agenda item in Indonesia. As the Sustainable Development Goals (SDGs) replaced the MDGs in 2015, this focus continued, with the SDG framework explicitly positioning ECE as one of the global development goals. In addition to the SDGs, the new Global Strategy for Women's, Children's and Adolescents' Health has also identified ECE as a global priority (Dua et al., 2016). On a regional level, attention on ECE was encouraged by the Putrajaya Declaration in 2016 (UNESCO Bangkok, 2016). The global push also marks a neoliberal element of ECE in Indonesia in which ECE is positioned as a site that would improve a country's economic development in the future. Among the current rhetoric is ECE as human capital investment (Formen, 2017).

Until 2001, ECE was the responsibility of the Directorate of Kindergarten and Primary Education, which included both kindergarten and preschool. A new development started when the government established a directorate within the Indonesian Ministry of National Education (now the Ministry of Education and Culture) that is specifically responsible for ECE. The term ECE, literally translated as *Pendidikan Anak Usia Dini* (PAUD), is now commonly used to define *non-formal* kindergarten and preschool. Preschool is now responsible only for children aged 2 to 4 years old, while children aged 4 to 6 years old attend kindergarten (TK) (Hasan et al., 2013). The term *formal* kindergarten only applies to kindergarten (TK) and *Raudhatul Athfal* (RA), the Islamic kindergarten.

The terms *formal* and *non-formal* ECE form one of the complexities of ECE in Indonesia. In addition to the children's ages they are serving, formal and non-formal ECE are characterised by differences in the teachers' qualifications. Formal ECE teachers are required to have at least a bachelor's degree in ECE or psychology, while non-formal ECE teachers must have only some post-secondary training in ECE. This can be either a two-year diploma programme or ECE training from an accredited institution (Denboba, Hasan and Wodon, 2015). However, in reality, many non-formal ECE teachers have not even graduated from secondary education (World Bank, 2012a). Another difference is the number of hours children are enrolled in a centre. Children enrolled in formal ECE must have between 150 and 180 minutes of school per day for five or six days a week, while children in non-formal ECE are required to have at least 180 minutes per day, three days a week (Denboba et al., 2015). The regulatory differences between formal and non-formal ECE have contributed to the creation of a dualism between them (Adriany and Saefullah, 2015).

The new development was conceptualised as a result of the Education for All (EFA) initiative of the World Bank, with a loan of US$21.5 billion to reform ECE (World Bank, 2007). The main agenda was to increase children's access to (participation in) ECE services, and their focus was on non-formal ECE. The World Bank developed a pilot project in 11 districts in Indonesia focused on developing non-formal ECE (Hasan et al., 2013). The reason was that the children who could access ECE services were mostly middle- and upper-class children from predominantly urban areas. Hence, establishing non-formal ECE in rural areas was seen as a strategy to include more children and increase children's participation in ECE (Hasan et al., 2013; World Bank, n.d.). While it is not completely identical, an idea to push for more participation to ECE among children in the rural areas is similar to approaches taken by the UK government with 'Sure Start' and the US government with 'Head Start'. Behind the programme lies an idea that children in the rural areas and those from underprivileged backgrounds need to be *saved* so that they can develop fully. The idea of children's participation here seems to be rooted with the protectionist principle, as we mentioned earlier in the chapter.

In addition to protecting the children in rural areas, the idea of participation is also linked with children's gross ECE enrolment rate. The government, for instance, aims to reach 100 per cent child participation in ECE in 2030. The strategies adopted by the government are mostly focused on establishing and expanding non-formal ECE (Denboba et al., 2015). The influence of neoliberalism is evident here since children are reduced to numbers to justify the progress government makes in ECE, as we will demonstrate throughout the remainder of this chapter.

Increasing access to ECE through non-formal ECE, however, has failed to create equal quality within ECE services. As Adriany and Saefullah (2015) argue, the division between non-formal and formal kindergarten has often perpetuated the inequality. As we have indicated, the Teachers' and Lecturers' Law (2005) explicitly regulates that teachers in kindergarten should be university graduates, while non-formal ECE is operated by women volunteers (Yulindrasari, 2014) – and many of these women volunteers have not completed secondary school (World Bank, 2012b).

There is an additional complexity in this system. A strong proliferation of neoliberal forces in ECE in Indonesia has enabled and facilitated internationally franchised early childhood settings (both formal and non-formal) to be established in more prosperous urban areas (Thomas, 1992). These new forms of kindergarten often possess strong financial capital, especially compared with the non-formal ECE centres in rural areas that frequently struggle financially. Hence, the division between formal and non-formal kindergarten perpetuates the inequality between kindergartens in the rural and urban areas. Although the government attempted to resolve these tensions by establishing the Directorate of ECE and Community Education in 2010, tensions between formal and non-formal ECE persist (Adriany and Saefullah, 2015).

To increase participation of children in ECE, in 2013 the government allocated a budget of US$40 per child per annum to cover the operational costs of a child in ECE organisations (*Bantuan Operasional Penyelenggaraan*, BOP PAUD). As we have mentioned, ECE centres must run their services for three to six days per week and between 150 and 180 minutes per day. This initiative has been a pivotal milestone in ECE provision. In this period, children with special needs, children from low socio-economic backgrounds, and other marginalised children were prioritised to receive the operational allowance. In 2016, the new regulation of operational costs for ECE was introduced; however, it lacked an agenda focused on priority children. The cost is now distributed equally to all the children enrolled in ECE centres, provided they are registered on the online national database. To be eligible to receive this funding, each centre must have at least 12 pupils. Again, children are relegated into being mere numbers. In addition, the setting must also meet other prerequisites, such as making sure that the setting has an operating licence and meets the terms of all other relevant policies (Ministry of Education and Culture Republic of Indonesia, 2018). Teachers have complained that these changes have become an additional bureaucratic burden for them (Solehuddin and Adriany, 2017) and, as most of the ECE centres do not have administrative staff, the burden falls on teachers. The teachers' workload has sometimes doubled, which often means a reduction in contact time with children, for preparing resources and planning for classes, and for having pedagogical conversations. It is important to note that operational budgets cannot be used directly to benefit children despite being distributed to a centre on the basis of the number of children it has enrolled. Operational funding, for instance, cannot be used to pay for children's tuition (Ministry of Education and Culture Republic of Indonesia, 2018). Therefore, the operational budget allowance does not make ECE free for children.

In addition, the regulation states that the money cannot be used for procuring students' uniforms and shoes. Even though the policy also elaborates that an exception might be made for children from low socio-economic backgrounds, it emphasises that the funding cannot be used directly for children. Adriany's (2013) work demonstrates the extent to which items such as clothes, shoes and uniforms have become a signifier for peer inclusion or exclusion in kindergartens. The fact that the settings cannot use the funding for that purpose might illuminate the government's lack of understanding of the micropolitics and power relations that take place in a kindergarten (Alloway, 1997; MacNaughton, 2005; Tesar, 2014). Again, this raises questions about what the Indonesian government intends by promoting children's participation if children do not become the primary beneficiaries of the policy or have their voices heard.

Satu Desa, Satu Paud (one village, one centre)

The Indonesian government also provides a *Dana Desa* (village fund) for each village in rural areas. The fund is used for developing infrastructure; however, it can be allocated to establishing and administering early childhood centres. The catchphrase *Satu Desa, Satu Paud* (one village, one centre), which has been used since 2012 (Directorate of Early Childhood and Community Education, 2012), is now a policy set by the Directorate of Early Childhood and Community Education. However, the policy guidance to the village fund does not make it mandatory for a village to establish an ECE centre; instead, the leader of each village, in whom political power is vested, makes the decision. In many cases, therefore, ECE centres in villages are still operating on the basis of women's voluntary time (Newberry and Marpinjun, 2018).

In 2013, in addition to the operational allowance, the government launched another critical milestone in ECE development. It introduced the concept of Holistic and Integrative/HI Early Childhood Education (PAUD Holistic Integrative/PAUD HI).[1] This initiative provides a legal framework for HI ECE and for coordinating various agencies and ministries that are responsible for ECE (Ministry of National Development Planning/National Development Planning Agencies (BAPPENAS), 2013). Not only does this policy regulate, but it also recognises that ECE is a multisectoral unit. While recognition of ECE as a multisectoral unit is not a new concept, and various ministries have already organised various kinds of ECE providing specific services for young children, this change means there is now a coordinated strategy between agencies and ministries.

The Indonesian government is thus taking the initiative to encourage more children's participation in ECE; however, again, the promotion of participation is perpetuated by the language of neoliberalism with its emphasis on the human capital discourse (Adriany and Saefullah, 2015; Peach and Lightfoot, 2015; Penn, 2002). As we have mentioned, ECE is considered to be a good investment in Indonesia, and it attracts local and global players not traditionally associated with education. Hackman's (2005) claim that every cent spent in ECE will bring a higher return in the future is taken seriously in Indonesia. ECE is thus seen as a vehicle to achieve the country's future economic development with children as the objects of intercession. For example, in the Indonesian national curriculum, a child is constructed as a 'little scientist' (Ministry of Education and Culture Republic of Indonesia, 2014). The scientist discourse is preferred because science and STEM are a direct policy link to a country's economic progress (Adriany and Saefullah, 2015). The push for participation thus links to neoliberalism, where children are the inevitable key component of the successful economic model of the nation state (Peters and Tesar, 2017).

Saving the children, blaming the parents

The promotion of children's participation in ECE in Indonesia illustrates the prevalent force of neoliberal ideology. As Penn (2002, 2008, 2011) argues, the World Bank positions children in Global South countries such as Indonesia in a very particular way. There is an image, promoted through numerous discourses and agencies, that children in the Global South are somehow savage and in need of both protection and saving (Tesar, 2015a, 2016). Institutionalised ECE provision therefore shapes and saves the children from potential damage, as perceived by adults and the organisations funded through global and multinational players in economic growth. Various agendas have been pursued and subsequent programmes have been developed to stimulate children's development and their readiness to enter primary education (Hasan et al., 2013). Children and childhood continue to be proxies for national and international development goals, rather than these serving the children, so children remain the *objects* of these policies and investments, rather than their *subject*.

Children are not the only object of the World Bank's intervention. Parents are also included in their agenda, with emphasis on the 'correction' of certain behaviours and ideas. We mentioned earlier in the chapter that the Indonesian government's promotion of children's participation in ECE is connected with the notion of protecting children; the concept of *saving the children* is closely related with *blaming the parents* (Schaefer, 2010). The World Bank associates parents' behaviour in the village with inadequate and incorrect parenting practices, such as parents never reading books to their children and parents not teaching their children how to draw (Hasan, cited in Adriany and Saefullah, 2015). Many parenting programmes in Indonesia have been developed to correct certain – mostly precolonial – parenting styles and have resulted in the establishment of a specific department, the Directorate of Parenting, within the Ministry of Education and Culture of Indonesia. Institutions, including the World Bank, are investing in shaping both children and parenting in ways that mirror the Western middle class. The institutions – large global players that channel funding to Indonesia – ignore wider sociological factors that influence children's development, such as poverty levels and global inequality (Penn, 2017).

Retraining the teachers

In line with the idea of saving the children lies the concept of re-educating the teachers. Western aid – for example, from the World Bank – is not only used to establish non-formal ECE in the rural areas of Indonesia, but also to assist teachers' professional development in Indonesia (Chang et al., 2014). One of the most radical changes that the Indonesian government's introduction of the Teacher and Lecturer Law (2005) brought to the teaching workforce was that in-service teachers had to undergo training to be considered as professional teachers. Only once they are certified and become professional teachers will they be entitled to receive professional allowance money from the government. However, this policy regulates only those teachers who teach in formal kindergartens. Under this policy, non-formal teachers are not considered teachers. As such, the policy perpetuates the inequality between formal and non-formal ECE.

The teachers' reform programme focuses on the notion of child-centredness. This term comes from developmental psychology, in particular Piaget's theory of child development, with its strong emphasis on children's activities being developmentally appropriate (Adriany and Warin, 2014). In this conception, a child's individuality is strongly promoted (Marsh, 2003). Although a certain version of child-centredness has existed in Indonesian ECE since the Dutch colonial presence and the establishment of Froebelian kindergartens, within the neoliberal discourse this has become state-sponsored practice in ECE (Adriany, 2013; Newberry, 2012). Hence, child-centredness has become the dominant discourse in Indonesian ECE, not necessarily because it carries more *truth*, but because it contains more *power*.

One may also assume that the adoption of child-centredness in ECE in Indonesia is the government's attempt to take into account children's voice in the education process. Within child-centredness lies an idea to place children as the focus. However, Bae's research (2010) has revealed that the concept of child-centredness is often reduced to children's freedom and individualisation rather than children's participation. As Tzuo (2007) points out:

A child-centered curriculum focuses more on the importance of children's individual interests and their freedom to create their own learning through choosing from various classroom activities. In contrast, teacher-directed curriculum places more stress on the teachers' control over children's exploration of learning.

(p. 33)

Hence, the adoption of child-centredness in Indonesian ECE practice appears to be more influenced by neoliberalism principles than incorporating children's voice in the education process.

One of the implications of the construction of child-centredness as the new *regime of truth* is that it becomes the only way for formal teachers to understand reality. Formal teachers often perceive non-formal teachers as less competent because they do not incorporate child-centredness into their teaching (Adriany and Saefullah, 2015). Practices in non-formal ECE are seen as not developmentally appropriate, and are believed to be detrimental for the children. Saving the children is at the centre of the interest of adults in order to justify how the teachers' practices in non-formal ECE need to be changed, if not corrected.[2]

Indonesian ECE is further complicated as the World Bank, on the one hand, supports the establishment of non-formal ECE in villages but, on the other, collaborates in the teacher reform programme for formal and non-formal teachers that, in turn, situate non-formal teachers as 'the other' (Arndt, 2015). This demonstrates the complexity of power relations and how they operate within a discourse. Power is not necessarily only oppressive; it may simultaneously be a productive force, and all adults and children participate, shape and form this discourse (Tesar, 2015b). As such, the discourse of child-centredness is celebrated by both formal and non-formal teachers. Hence, the World Bank's view of children and childhood continues to be promoted, prevalent and dominant in Indonesia (Hackman, 2005).

Conclusion

This chapter argues that the notion of participation in ECE in Indonesia has been shaped and formed by many forces over the years, and most recently by the neoliberal practices and major global players who push particular agendas by channelling funding and influencing how children should learn, play and develop in Indonesia. While the promotion of children's participation appears to be in line with the articles in the UNCRC, the meaning of participation, as defined by the Indonesian government, is argued in this chapter to be very problematic.

The first part of this argument is predicated on the neoliberal discourse, which intersects with an economic model of education. As education in Indonesia is seen as merely a set of economic activities, a child within this model is only perceived as a vehicle to achieve the country's economic progress. A child is hence seen as a means rather than an end. Instead of children becoming the primary beneficiaries, children become the objects of the policies. Second, the ways that the notion of participation policy is translated into everyday practices in an ECE classroom are problematic. The fact that all ECE policies in Indonesia are adult-centric policies means that they give no space for children's voices to be heard, and that no benefits from their perspective are able to be considered.

This chapter calls for reconceptualising the notion of children's participation in ECE in Indonesia. For children's participation to be in line with the notion of children's rights and the UNCRC, it has to include children's voices, perspectives and feelings. Children need to be treated as subjects, not objects, of policies and major global funders of educational initiatives in Indonesia. Children are the primary beneficiaries and stakeholders, rather than passive objects that need to be saved or corrected. Therefore, participation needs to be reframed as a UNCRC claim, and an initiative that should be participatory and empowering to children (Ruiz-Casares, Collins, Tisdal and Grover, 2017).

Notes

1 Regulated by the Presidential Regulation No. 60 Year 2013.
2 Since 2009, the teachers' reform programme has also been introduced to non-formal teachers. Non-formal teachers are encouraged to undergo a non-degree training that consists of three levels: basic, intermediate and advanced (Ministry of Education and Culture Republic of Indonesia, 2014).

References

Adriany, Vina. 2013. *Gendered Power Relations Within Child-centred Discourse: An Ethnographic Study in a Kindergarten in Bandung, Indonesia* (Unpublished doctoral dissertation). Lancaster University, UK.

Adriany, Vina, and Kurniawan Saefullah. 2015. "Deconstructing human capital discourse in early childhood education in Indonesia." In *Global Perspectives on Human Capital in Early Childhood Education: Reconceptualizing Theory, Policy, and Practice*, edited by Theodora Lightfoot-Rueda, Ruth Lynn Peach, and Nigel Leask, 159–179. New York, NY: Palgrave Macmillan US.

Adriany, Vina, and Jo Warin. 2014. "Preschool teachers' approaches to gender differences within a child-centered pedagogy: Findings from an Indonesian kindergarten." *International Journal of Early Years Education*, 22 (3): 315–386, doi:10.1080/09669760.2014.951601.

Alloway, Nola. 1997. "Early childhood education encounters the postmodern: What do we know? What can we count as 'true'?" *Australian Journal of Early Childhood*, 22 (2): 1–5.

Arndt, Sonja. 2015. "Otherness without ostracism or levelling: Towards fresh orientations to teacher foreigners in early childhood education." *Educational Philosophy and Theory*, 47 (9): 883–893, doi:10.1080/00131857.2015.1035155.

Asian Development Bank. 2016. "Indonesia: Economy." www.adb.org/countries/indonesia/economy

Bae, Berit. 2010. "Realizing children's right to participation in early childhood settings: Some critical issues in a Norwegian context." *Early Years*, 30 (3): 205–218.

Chang, Mae Chu, Sheldon Shaeffer, Samer Al-Samarrai, Andrew B. Ragatz, Joppe De Ree, and Ritchie Stevenson (Eds.). 2014. *Teacher Reform in Indonesia: The Role of Politics and Evidence in Policy Making*. Washington, DC: International Bank for Reconstruction and Development/The World Bank. http://documents.worldbank.org/curated/en/726801468269436434/pdf/831520PUB0Teac00 Box379886B00PUBLIC0.pdf

Denboba, Amina, Amer Hasan, and Quentin Wodon. 2015. *Early Childhood Education and Development in Indonesia: An Assessment of Policies Using SABER*. Washington, DC: The World Bank.

Directorate of Early Childhood and Community Education. 2012. "Dirjen PAUDNI: One village one ECE centre." https://paudni.kemdikbud.go.id/berita/1269.html

Dua, Tarun, Mark Tomlinson, Elizabeth Tablante, Pia Britto, Aisha Yousfzai, Bernadette Daelmans, and Gary L. Darmstadt. 2016. "Global research priorities to accelerate early child development in the sustainable development era." *The Lancet Global Health*, 4 (12): e887–e889, doi:10.1016/S2214-109X(16) 30218-2.

Formen, Ali. 2017. "In human-capital we trust, on developmentalism we act: The case of Indonesian early childhood education policy." In *Contemporary Issues and Challenges in Early Childhood Education in the Asia-Pacific Region*, edited by Minyi Li, Fox Jillian, and Grieshaber Susan, 125–142. Singapore: Springer Singapore.

Geertz, Clifford. 1976. *The Religion of Java*. Chicago, IL: The University of Chicago Press.

Hackman, Heather W. 2005. "Five essential components for social justice education." *Equity and Excellence in Education*, 38: 103–109, doi:10.1080/10665680590935034.

Hasan, Amer, Marilou Hyson, and Mae Chu Chang. (Eds.). 2013. *Early Childhood Education and Development in Poor Villages of Indonesia: Strong Foundations, Later Success*. Washington, DC: International Bank for Reconstruction and Development/The World Bank.

Lansdown, Gerison. 1994. "Children's rights." In *Children's Childhoods: Observed and Experienced*, edited by Berry Mayall, 33–45. London, UK: The Falmer Press.

MacNaughton, Glenda. 2005. *Doing Foucault in Early Childhood Studies*. Abingdon, UK: Routledge.

Mannion, Gregory. 2007. "Going spatial, going relational: Why 'listening to children' and children's participation needs reframing" *Discourse: Studies in the Cultural Politics of Education*, 28 (3): 405–420.

Marsh, Monica Miller. 2003. "Examining the discourses that shape our teacher identities." *Curriculum Inquiry*, 32 (4): 453–469, doi:10.1111/1467-873X.00242.

Ministry of Education and Culture Republic of Indonesia. 2014. *2013 Curriculum of Early Childhood Education* (Vol. 146). Jakarta: Ministry of Education and Culture.

Ministry of Education and Culture Republic of Indonesia. 2018. *Technical Guidance on Special Funding Allocation non Pyhsical Operational Cost for ECE Centres*. Jakarta: Ministry of Education and Culture.

Ministry of National Development Planning/National Development Planning Agencies (BAPPENAS). 2013. *Early Childhood Development Study in Indonesia*. Jakarta: BAPPENAS.

Ministry of Women's Empowerment and Child Protection of the Republic of Indonesia (MoWECP). 2011. *The Ministry Regulation no. 3 year 2011 on the Policy of Children's Participation in the Nation's Development*. Jakarta: MoWECP.

Newberry, Jan. 2012. "Durable assemblage: Early childhood education in Indonesia." Asia Research Institute Working Paper No. 194, December 2012. www.ari.nus.edu.sg/wps/wps12_194.pdf

Newberry, Jan, and Sri Marpinjun. 2018. "Payment in heaven: Can early childhood education policies help women too?" *Policy Futures in Education*, 16 (1): 29–42, doi:10.1177/1478210317739467.

Octarra, Harla Sara. 2014. "The reinvention of the UNCRC in Indonesia." Paper presented at the 25 Years Convention on the Rights of the Child International Conference, 17–19 November, 2014, UNICEF and Leiden Law School, University of Leiden, The Netherlands.

Peach, Ruth Lynn, and Theodora Lightfoot. 2015. *Global Perspectives on Human Capital in Early Childhood Education: Reconceptualizing Theory, Policy and Practice*. New York, NY: Palgrave MacMillan.

Penn, Helen. 2002. "The World Bank's view of early childhood." *Childhood*, 9 (1): 118–132.

Penn, Helen. 2008. "Working on the impossible." *Childhood*, 15 (3): 379–395.

Penn, Helen. 2011. "Travelling policies and global buzzwords: How international non-governmental organizatuon and charities spread the word about early childhood in the global south." *Childhood*, 18 (1): 94–113.

Penn, Helen. 2017. "Anything to divert attention from poverty." In *Construction of Neuroscience in Early Childhood Education*, edited by Michel Vandenbroeck, Jan De Vos, Liselott Mariett Olsson, Helen Penn, Dave Wastell, and Sue White, 53–66. Abingdon and New York: Routledge.

Peters, Michael A., and Marek Tesar. 2017. "Bad research, bad education: The contested evidence for evidence-based research, policy and practice in education." In *Practice theory: Diffractive readings in professional practice and education*, edited by Julianne Lynch, Julie Rowlands, Trevor Gale, and Andrew Skourdoumbis, 231–246. London, UK: Routledge.

Ruiz-Casares, Mónica, Tara M. Collins, E. Kay M. Tisdall, and Sonja Grover. 2017. "Children's rights to participation and protection in international development and humanitarian interventions: Nurturing a dialogue." *International Journal of Human Rights*, 21 (1): 1–13, doi:10.1080/13642987.2016.1262520.

Save the Children. 2010. *Review report the implementation of Convention on the Rights of the Child in Indonesia 1997–2009*. Jakarta: Save the Children.

Schaefer, Tali. 2010. "Saving children or blaming parents-lessons from mandated parenting classes." *Columbia Journal of Gender and Law*, 19 (2): 491–537.

Smith, Anne. 2007. "Children and young people's participation rights in education" *The International Journal of Children's Rights*, 15 (1): 147–164.

Solehuddin, Muhammed, and Vina Adriany. 2017. "Kindergarten teachers' understanding on social justice: Stories from Indonesia." *SAGE Open*, 7 (4), doi:10.1177/2158244017739340.

Te One, Sarah, and Carmen Dalli. 2010. "The status of children's rights in early childhood education policy 2009." *New Zealand Annual Review of Education*, 20: 1–35.

Tesar, Marek. 2014. "Reconceptualising the child: Power and resistance within early childhood settings." *Contemporary Issues in Early Childhood*, 15 (4): 360–367, doi:10.2304/ciec.2014.15.4.360.

Tesar, Marek. 2015a. "Te Whāriki in Aotearoa New Zealand: Witnessing and resisting neoliberal and neo-colonial discourses in early childhood education." In *Unsettling the Colonial Places and Spaces of Early Childhood Education*, edited by Veronica Pacini-Ketchabaw, and Affrica Taylor, 98–113. New York and Abingdon: Routledge.

Tesar, Marek. 2015b. "Power and subjectivities: Foucault and Havel on the complexities of early years classroom." In *Routledge International Handbook of Social Psychology of the Classroom*, edited by Christine Rubie-Davies, Jason M. Stephens, and Penelope Watson, 475–492. Abingdon, UK: Routledge.

Tesar, Marek. 2016. "Timing childhoods: An alternative reading of children's development through philosophy of time, temporality, place and space." *Contemporary Issues in Early Childhood*, 17 (4): 399–408, doi:10.1177/1463949116677924.

Thomas, R. Murray. 1988. "Dividing the labor: Indonesia's government/private early childhood education system." *Early Child Development and Care*, 39 (1): 33–43, doi:10.1080/0300443880390103.

Thomas, R. Murray. 1992. "Early childhood teacher education in Indonesia." *Early Child Development and Care*, 78 (1): 85–94, doi:10.1080/0300443920780107.

Tzuo, Pei Wen. 2007. "The tension between teacher control and children's freedom in a child-centered classroom: Resolving the practical dilemma through a closer look at the related theories." *Early Childhood Education Journal*, 35 (1): 33–39, doi:10.1007/s10643-007-0166-7.

UNESCO Bangkok. 2016. "Putrajaya declaration on early childhood care and education in Asia-Pacific." www.unescobkk.org/news/article/putrajaya-declaration-on-early-childhood-care-and-education-in-asia-pacific/

United Nations (UN). 1989. *Convention on the Rights of the Child*. Geneva: United Nations.

United Nations Children's Fund (UNICEF). 2014. "Indonesia and UNCRC: 25 years of progress and challenges." http://unicefindonesia.blogspot.com/2014/11/indonesia-and-uncrc-25-years-of.html

Van Bruinessen, Martin. 2011. "What happened to the smiling face of Indonesia Islam? Muslim intellectualism and the conservative on post-Suharto Indonesia." *RSIS Working Papers*. Singapore: Nanyang Technological University. http://hdl.handle.net/10220/7533

World Bank. 2007. "Implementation completion and results report on a loan in the amount of $21.5 million to the Republic of Indonesia for an early childhood development project. Human development sector unit, East Asian and Pacific Region." wwwwds.worldbank.org/external/default/WDSContentServer/WDSP/IB/2007/08/29/000020439_20070829111054/Rendered/INDEX/ICR0000560.txt

World Bank. 2012a. "Early childhood education and development in Indonesia: Strong foundations, later success - A preview." Jakarta: World Bank. https://openknowledge.worldbank.org/handle/10986/12122

World Bank. 2012b. "The Indonesia ECED Project findings and policy recommendations." http://documents.worldbank.org/curated/en/330141468044650822/The-Indonesia-Early-Childhood-Education-and-Development-ECED-Project-findings-and-policy-recommendations

World Bank. n.d. "Early childhood education and development in Indonesia. An investment for a better life." http://documents.worldbank.org/curated/en/750451468268182766/Early-childhood-education-and-development-in-Indonesia-an-investment-for-a-better-life

World Population Review. 2018. "Indonesia population 2018." http://worldpopulationreview.com/countries/indonesia-population/

Yulindrasari, Hani 2014. "Neoliberal early childhood education policy and women's volunteerism." Paper presented at the Negotiating Practices of Early Childhood Education, 18–19 November 2014. Universitas Pendidikan Indonesia Bandung.

Yusuf, Arief Anshory, Andy Sumner, and Irlan Adiyatma Rum. 2014. "Twenty years of expenditure inequality in Indonesia, 1993–2013." *Bulletin of Indonesian Economic Studies*, 50 (2): 243–254.

PART 2

Young children's rights to protection

7

INTRODUCTION

Young children's rights to protection

Jane Murray

Introduction

This short chapter introduces the section of the handbook concerning young children's rights to protection. UNICEF (2006) suggests that children may need protection from exploitation, violence and abuse. The United Nations High Commissioner for Refugees (UNHCR) (2001) defines child exploitation as:

> abuse of a child where some form of remuneration is involved or whereby the perpetrators benefit in some manner – monetarily, socially, politically, etc. Exploitation constitutes a form of coercion and violence, detrimental to the child's physical and mental health, development, and education.
>
> *(p. 7)*

Examples of child exploitation might include child labour, sexual exploitation, abduction, sale or trafficking of children, as well as child soldiers. 'Child abuse' is regarded as 'an act of commission that is outside of accepted cultural norms' (physical abuse, sexual abuse or emotional abuse) or an act of 'omission, the failure to provide for the child's basic needs' (neglect) (UNHCR, 2001, pp. 6–7). Child abuse and exploitation are incorporated into definitions of violence against children. The United Nations Convention on the Rights of the Child (UNCRC) (United Nations (UN), 1989) (Article 19) identifies violence against children as 'all forms of physical or mental violence, injury or abuse, neglect or negligent treatment, maltreatment or exploitation, including sexual abuse' (p. 7). The World Health Organization (WHO) and International Society for Prevention of Child Abuse and Neglect (ISPCAN) (2006) define child maltreatment as:

> all forms of physical and/or emotional ill-treatment, sexual abuse, neglect or negligent treatment or commercial or other exploitation, resulting in actual or potential harm to the child's health, survival, development or dignity in the context of a relationship of responsibility, trust or power.
>
> *(p. 9)*

Violent acts against children are quite simply identified as physical abuse, psychological or emotional abuse, sexual abuse, or neglect experienced by those up to 18 years (World

Health Organization (WHO), 2017). One person may perpetrate violence on another, it can be self-inflicted, or a large group may act violently as a collective (WHO and ISPCAN, 2006). Data and research findings about violence against children are limited (UNICEF Child Protection and Monitoring Group, 2014), but, according to available data, violence against children is endemic across the world: globally, one in four adults was abused physically as a child (WHO, 2017). However, children's right to protection from all forms of violence is enshrined in the UNCRC (Article 19) (UN, 1989) and bolstered by the United Nations Committee on the Rights of the Child (UNComRC) in its General Comment No. 13 (2011). The chapter opens by drawing together data that highlight the prevalence of violence against children. It then discusses some of the causes and effects of violence against children and what is being done by global organisations to address the situation, with consideration of what more might be done. This introductory chapter leads into the section with an overview of its other chapters.

What is the extent of violence against children?

It is recognised that much violence perpetrated against children goes unreported (UN, 2006). Nevertheless, in 2017, children informed the World Health Organization that in the previous year, 23 per cent of them had been physically abused, 36 per cent had been emotionally abused, 16 per cent had suffered physical neglect, and 18 per cent of girls and 8 per cent of boys (26 per cent) had experienced sexual abuse (WHO, 2017). While some children are victims of violence by strangers, generally the people who are violent to children tend to be people they know well, including family members, teachers and neighbours (UNICEF, 2015). Children are victims of violence in a range of environments, many of which are familiar to them, including their homes and schools (UNICEF, 2015). Increasingly, the Internet is a medium used to abuse children, including infants and toddlers (NSPCC, 2019; We Protect Global Alliance, 2018).

In a systematic review, Moody, Cannings-John, Hood, Kemp and Robling (2018) compiled evidence from studies where adult participants over 18 years or child participants under 18 years had self-reported experiences of maltreatment before reaching the age of 18 years. Their results revealed the international prevalence of self-reported child abuse as follows:

- *Physical abuse (200 studies)*: Africa: 18.9%, Asia: 13.9%, Australia: 6.7%, Europe: 22.2%, South America: 9.7%, North America: 18.1%
- *Sexual abuse (287 studies)*: Africa: 15.4%, Asia: 16.4%, Australia: 10.1%, Europe: 13.2%, South America: 2.6%, North America: 18.2%.
- *Emotional abuse (105 studies)*: Africa: 26.9%, Asia: 33.4%, Australia: 9.2%, Europe: 21.7%, South America: no data, North America: 23.9%.
- *Neglect (72 studies)*: Africa: 44.8%, Asia: 47.2%, Australia: 14.4%, Europe: 27%, South America: 6.6%, North America: 30.1%.

These data were mirrored in the results of the United Nations General Assembly (UNGA) (2006) global study concerning violence against children, which concluded that commitments to protect children from violence made by countries that had ratified the UNCRC were not being honoured. The report observed that 'all violence against children is preventable' (UN, 2006, p. 24).

Causes and effects of violence against children

Numerous underlying causes have been identified for people committing violence against children and risk factors present at individual, family and community levels. They include – but are not limited to – low self-esteem, difficulty bonding with a baby following birth, poverty, poor housing, cultural norms that accept physical punishment, unemployment, children aged 0–4 years, disability, mental or physical illness, substance abuse, family history of neglect or abuse, young parents, adults other than the child's parents living in the home, social isolation, and lack of knowledge about child development (Centers for Disease Control and Prevention, 2019; WHO and ISPCAN, 2006).

Children's experiences of the effects of violence are diverse. Violence against children can result in fatal and non-fatal injury, physical health problems and disability, psychological, emotional and mental health problems, including trauma, anxiety, depression and insecurity, as well as cognitive impairment. It may also result in school exclusion, antisocial behaviour and aggression: violence leads to violence (UNComRC, 2011). War and conflict in the early part of the twenty-first century have affected children in their millions: in 2017, 347 million children in Africa and Asia and 20 per cent of children in the Middle East were living in a conflict zone (Save the Children, 2019). Children younger than 5 years are twice as likely to be victims of homicide as children aged 5–14 years, because of their 'dependency, vulnerability and relative social invisibility' (WHO and ISPCAN, 2006, p. 11). Children who experience violence are often not only deeply affected in the short term, but also throughout their lives, and the trauma they experience can affect subsequent generations (Lumsden, 2018). Because of the brain's architecture and development, this impact tends to be magnified when infants and younger children are the victims of violence (WHO and ISPCAN, 2006, pp. 10–11).

What is being done at global level to address violence against children?

In recent years, global non-governmental organisations (NGOs), including UNGA (2006) and the United Nations Educational, Scientific and Cultural Organization (UNESCO) (2017), have conducted large studies to attempt to establish the extent and reach of violence against children. They report that much of the issue is hidden from view, yet they also report figures indicating that violence against children is widespread across the world.

The UNCRC (UN, 1989) is explicit in outlining children's rights to protection as well as optional protocols. Children have rights to be protected from kidnapping (Article 11) and any type of violence (Article 19). They have rights to protection if their parents cannot care for them, if they are adopted or in foster care, or if they are refugees (Articles 20, 21, 22). Children also have the right to be protected from any work that may endanger their health or education (Article 32), as well as rights to be protected from drug abuse, sexual exploitation, abduction, sale or trafficking, detention or cruel punishment (Articles 33, 34, 35, 36, 37). Children affected by war and armed conflict have the right to be protected (Article 38), children who have experienced abuse, neglect or exploitation have the right to rehabilitation (Article 39), and children accused of breaking the law have the right to fair treatment and legal help (Article 40). In 2000, optional protocols were added to the UNCRC (UN, 1989); these provided additional protections to children in the case of armed conflict, and in respect of the child pornography and prostitution and the sale of children (UNICEF, 2014). Two further protection articles focus on protecting children's rights: 'If the laws of a country provide better protection of children's rights than the articles in this Convention, those laws should apply' (UN, 1989, Article 41), and an explicit statement that 'Governments have a responsibility to take all available measures to make sure children's rights are respected, protected and fulfilled' (UN, 1989, Article 4). In principle, every country except the United States of America is a signatory to child protection rights – along with child provision and child participation rights – but the evidence, discussed above, suggests that many children find their protection rights are not respected in practice. The United Nations General Assembly agrees with this analysis (UNGA, 2006).

New perspectives on young children's rights to protection

As discussed above, the youngest children are the group of children who are most susceptible to experiencing violence, exploitation and abuse against them; their 'vulnerabilities, and ... requirements for protection, guidance and support in the exercise of their rights' are recognised by the United Nations Committee for the Rights of the Child (2005, p. 2). Nevertheless, young children are also considered 'social actors from the beginning of life, with particular interests (and) capacities' (United Nations Committee for the Rights of the Child, 2005, p. 2). The chapters in this section provide new perspectives on many – though not all – of their rights to protection. An underlying theme running though all the chapters is governments' 'responsibility to take all available measures to make sure children's rights are respected, protected and fulfilled' (UN, 1989, Article 4). All 'articles' alluded to below refer to the UNCRC (UN, 1989).

The section opens with Philip Garner's examination of policy and practice for young children with special educational needs and disabilities (SEND). In Chapter 8 – 'Rhetoric and realities: macro-policy as an instrument of deflection in meeting the needs of young children marginalised by SEND' – Garner argues powerfully that governments are not translating policy into practice for young children with SEND, so they are failing in respect of Article 4 by not protecting their rights in respect of discrimination (Article 2), living with their parents (Article 9), good-quality healthcare (Article 24), and education that develops their personality, talents and abilities to the fullest (Article 29) (UN, 1989). Zoi Nikiforidou argues in Chapter 9 – 'Risk and safety in Western society' – that many children living in Westernised countries are subject to too much protection from potential risks such as violence (Article 19), kidnapping (Article 11) and abduction (Article 35), and that paradoxically this means their parents and carers deny them other rights, so that, for example, they do not protect their right to play (Articles 4 and 31). Nikiforidou's argument focuses in part on who decides the 'best interests of the child' (Article 3).

In Chapter 10 – 'The (in)visibility of infants and young children in child protection' – Eunice Lumsden highlights that violence and abuse against children may be hidden. With particular focus on the English context, she critiques how child protection procedures may or may not help adults to protect the rights of young children (Article 4), particularly their rights to protection from violence (Article 19) and to rehabilitation if they have been neglected, exploited or abused (Article 39). Peter Moss critiques 'Childcare and standardisation: threats to young children's rights to education' in Chapter 11. While his chapter touches on the best interests of the child and who decides (Article 3), the main thrust of his argument is that by linking young children's early education and care to economic imperatives, some governments are failing to protect young children's rights to an education that develops their personality, talents and abilities to the fullest (Articles 4, 28, 29).

In Chapter 12 – 'Leave no one behind: young children's rights to education' – Mercy Musomi highlights some of the challenges for government and educators in securing rights to an equitable and fulfilling education, free of discrimination, for young children with disabilities in Kenya (Articles 4, 28, 29, 34). Musomi illustrates ways the Girl Child Network in Kenya is helping to protect these rights in practice. Kristina Konstantoni and Kyriaki Patsianta have further suggestions for how young children's rights in times of crisis might be protected (Article 4). In Chapter 13 – 'Young children's rights in 'tough' times: towards an intersectional children's rights policy agenda in Greece and Scotland' – they argue that the application of intersectionality to the fields of early childhood and young children's rights may support understanding about how to reduce apparently intractable barriers to securing young children's rights to health, education and play (Articles 24, 28, 31). Prospera Tedam's Chapter 14 – 'Achieving rights for young children in Ghana: enablers and barriers' – is a balanced critique of the extent and nature of the protection of particular young children's rights in Ghana (Articles 4, 7, 8, 12, 13).

Cristina Devecchi's Chapter 15 – 'Being a refugee child in Lebanon: implementing young children's rights in a digital world through the blockchain educational passport' – draws our attention to the special protection that member states should secure for refugee children (Article 22), with specific focus on how young refugee children's rights to education might be respected and protected in challenging transient circumstances (Articles 4, 28, 29). Emma Nottingham takes a very different slant to young children's experiences of digital technology in Chapter 16, '"Dad! Cut that part out!" Children's rights to privacy in the age of "generation tagged": sharenting, digital kidnapping and the child micro-celebrity'. She argues that young children's right to privacy is not protected when their images are shared on social media (Articles 4, 16).

My own Chapter 17 with my UNICEF East Caribbean Area colleagues Shelly-Ann Harper, Lisa McLean-Trotman and Heather Stewart highlights the prevalence of violence against children in the East Caribbean, particularly child sexual abuse. In 'Safeguarding the protection rights of children in the Eastern Caribbean', we draw on research and literature to highlight that young children experience violence, abuse and exploitation in the sub-region, which hinders their positive development and indicates that UNCRC rights embedded in Articles 19, 34, 37 and 39 have not been achieved universally. The chapter sets out some of the work of the UNICEF ECA being undertaken to protect these rights for young children living in the Eastern Caribbean (Article 4). In the final chapter in this section on young children's rights to protection, Chapter 18, Vera Lopez examines young children's experiences of domestic violence by adopting a child rights framework. 'Understanding young children's experiences growing up with domestic violence from a children's rights perspective' is concerned predominantly with children's rights to protection from violence (Article 19). By considering young children's own accounts of growing up with domestic violence, Lopez considers how these experiences affect young children's functioning, and concludes that such experiences have an adverse effect on young children, and she offers policy and practice recommendations for supporting young children growing up in homes with domestic violence.

Conclusion

Many children find that their protection rights are not respected in practice (UNGA, 2006), and this is particularly the case for younger children, who are the most likely to be subject to violence perpetrated against them (WHO and ISPCAN, 2006). The chapters in this section highlight both support and barriers in respect of protecting young children's rights (Article 4). A number of protection rights are addressed in detail by the authors. However, several are not addressed in this section's chapters. This omission is an authentic reflection of the hidden nature of abuse, exploitation and violence against children. In particular, it highlights the paucity of research and discourse concerning the lives of children younger than 8 years who experience adoption (Article 21), drug abuse (Article 33), and juvenile justice (Article 40).

References

Centers for Disease Control and Prevention. 2019. "Risk Factors for Victimization." www.cdc.gov/violenceprevention/childabuseandneglect/riskprotectivefactors.html

Lumsden, Eunice. 2018. *Child Protection in the Early Years*. London: Jessica Kingsley.

Moody, Gwenllian, Rebecca Cannings-John, Kerenza Hood, Alison Kemp and Michael Robling. 2018. "Establishing the International Prevalence of Self-reported Child Maltreatment: A Systematic Review by Maltreatment Type and Gender." *BMC Public Health*, 18: 1164, doi: 10.1186/s12889-018-6044-y

NSPCC. 2019. "Online Abuse Facts and Statistics." www.nspcc.org.uk/preventing-abuse/child-abuse-and-neglect/online-abuse/facts-statistics/

Save the Children. 2019. "Stop the War on Children." www.stopwaronchildren.org/report.pdf

UNICEF. 2006. "Child Protection Information Sheets." www.unicef.org/publications/index_34146.html

UNICEF. 2014. "Optional Protocols to the Convention on the Rights of the Child." www.unicef.org/protection/57929_58013.html

UNICEF. 2015. "Violence against Children. Children from All Walks of Life Endure Violence, and Millions More are at Risk." https://data.unicef.org/topic/child-protection/violence/

UNICEF Child Protection Monitoring and Evaluation Reference Group. 2014. "Measuring Violence against Children: Inventory and Assessment of Quantitative Studies." New York: UNICEF Division of Data, Research and Policy. https://data.unicef.org/wp-content/uploads/2014/11/Measuring-Violence-against-Children-%E2%80%93-Inventory-and-assessment-of-quantitative-studies.pdf

United Nations. 1989. *United Nations Convention on the Rights of the Child*. Geneva: United Nations.

United Nations (UN). 2006. "Rights of the Child. Notes by the Secretary General. Report of the Independent Expert for the United Nations Study on Violence against Children. A/61/299." www.unicef.org/violencestudy/reports/SG_violencestudy_en.pdf

United Nations Committee on the Rights of the Child (UNComRC). 2011. "General Comment No. 13 The Right of the Child to Freedom from All Forms of Violence." www.refworld.org/docid/4e6da4922.html

United Nations Educational, Scientific and Cultural Organisation (UNESCO). 2017. "School Violence and Bullying: Global Status Report." https://unesdoc.unesco.org/ark:/48223/pf0000246970

United Nations General Assembly (UNGA). 2006. "Rights of the Child. Notes by the Secretary General. Report of the Independent Expert for the United Nations Study on Violence against Children. A/61/299." www.unicef.org/violencestudy/reports/SG_violencestudy_en.pdf

United Nations High Commissioner for Refugees. 2001. "Action for the Rights of Children. Critical Issues: Abuse and Exploitation." www.unhcr.org/3bb81aea4.pdf

United Nations, UN Committee on the Rights of the Child. 2005. *Implementing Child Rights in Early Childhood General Comment no. 7 (2005) UN/CRC/GC/2005/1*. Geneva: United Nations.

We Protect Global Alliance. 2018. "Global Threat Assessment 2018." https://static1.squarespace.com/static/5630f48de4b00a75476ecf0a/t/5a85acf2f9619a497ceef04f/1518710003669/6.4159_WeProtect+GA+report+%281%29.pdf

World Health Organisation (WHO). 2017. "Child Maltreatment: The Health Sector Responds." www.who.int/violence_injury_prevention/violence/child/Child_maltreatment_infographic_EN.pdf?ua=1

World Health Organisation (WHO) and International Society for Prevention of Child Abuse and Neglect (ISPCAN). 2006. Preventing Child Maltreatment: A Guide to Taking Action and Generating Evidence." www.who.int/violence_injury_prevention/publications/violence/child_maltreatment/en/

8

RHETORIC AND REALITIES

Macro-policy as an instrument of deflection in meeting the needs of young children marginalised by SEND

Philip Garner

Introduction

The absence of contextual sensitivity in national and international policies directed towards supporting the development of children who experience one or multiple factors which result in their marginalisation from educational communities is paradoxically the principal reason why only slow progress has been made in addressing the negative experiences of a significant population of young children. I contend that such generic protocols form a regulatory shield that has no connection with the lived experiences of many professionals working with young children and the resulting practices in which they are engaged. Grandly worded affirmations of 'right' are constructed mainly by those with often only a distal experience of, and direct contact with, children 'at the margins'.

One such group comprises those young children who experience special educational needs and/or disabilities (SEND).[1] These are children for whom question marks and risks consistently abound in respect of equality, access and recognition of their rights. For this group, not very much has altered, notwithstanding the enduring gaze of international commentators, activists and researchers. This chapter examines this thesis, first by challenging the ideological orientation of several recognised, internationally agreed conventions relating either directly or by default to the 'rights' of children. It maintains that these rhetorical devices adopt what Sowell (1995) has referred to as an 'anointed' position which bears little resemblance to the realities of young children and their parents and families who remain excluded from even basic services. A key reason for this is the serial failure of policymakers, and those in schools and settings who are charged with putting policy into practice, to connect with the realities of marginalised groups. Nor are the efforts of those working directly with young children with SEND necessarily supported or validated by all advocacy groups, academic researchers and other stakeholders. This shortcoming is often a result of a singular, ideological dependence on the belief that needs and rights are not explicitly synonymous; in other words, that using the term 'special need' explicitly denies the rights of any child to whom the term is directed (Gernsbacher, Raimond, Balinghasay and Boston, 2016). What is often omitted, in the discussion and policymaking, is the incorporation of the wishes and expectations of these children. Often using parents as advocates, there are indications of more subtle and nuanced interpretations and use of what is available for SEND populations. Illustrating this, Nind and Flewitt (2006) also amplify parent perspectives expressed elsewhere in Europe, commenting that:

> It is significant for the development of inclusive education that parents who opt for a mixture of special and inclusive education see this as the 'best of both worlds' – the 'specialist' input and the 'inclusive' social interaction and community belonging. Inclusive education is intended to offer these dual benefits but the data indicate that many parents may be unconvinced that one setting can meet all of their child's needs. Inclusive education providers, it seems, need to build trust in their capacity to meet children's specialist as well as general learning needs and be alert to dangers in relation to both the reality and perception regarding this capacity.
>
> *(Nind and Flewitt, 2006)*

Ongoing misunderstanding, misinterpretation and definitional cul-de-sacs have resulted in a systemic failure to address fundamental questions concerning the dispensation of power and opportunity – with little recognition also given to the voices of practitioners. This coincides with a growing fear of negative judgement on the part of those working in those parts of education that are viewed by inclusion fundamentalists as 'segregated', as alluded to by Imray and Colley (2017). As such, the current circumstance, even after 30 or more years of commitment to children's rights, remains uncomfortably close to the position described by Barton and Tomlinson (1984), in which those who experience SEND are disadvantaged because of their perceived failure to assimilate within existing social, economic and educational arrangements, with an ideological and conceptual battle deflecting from concrete progress in meeting needs.

This chapter examines the gap between rights-based international conventions and the realities of those working directly with young children. It illustrates the ongoing tension and challenge that inhibits such well-meaning global agreements from having greater direct impact on their life chances. The rights of children are defined by the vision of a small group of influential gatekeepers, many of whom have little exposure to the real lives of children, their parents and those who work to provide support to them. The chapter illustrates the resulting inconsistencies and paradoxes by reference to several national educational contexts; these are representative of dramatically different manifestations of culture, socio-economic status and political orientation. As a collective, they evidence that slow and largely ineffectual progress has been made in addressing the basic needs of SEND populations. I suggest that – even in some advanced post-industrial democracies – early intervention in the first phase of a child's life remains a figment in the fertile but disconnected minds of policymakers and their messengers.

Then, in keeping with a desire to avoid the negative and an inclination to 'gaze at the problem' (Ball, 2008, p. 650), I offer some suggestions that might support a more grounded shift in establishing 'rights' as a professional given, connected fundamentally to the provision made for all young children, demonstrated in the ways that educational systems can embed accepted international understandings while giving it dimension, colour and status in the way that young children's rights are made real. To question the efficacy of the present arrangement is, I contend, a necessary exercise to highlight structural failure on the part of many governments to do this; proposing at least some framework or reorientation is perhaps of greater necessity.

In the present chapter, I explore some aspects of the position outlined above, recognising in so doing that the argument I make is dissonant with the views of many. In the light of this, and as a sensible precaution, I first set out some parameters and restrictions as a baseline context for my version of a pro-rights stance. First, I do not rehearse in detail the implications of key international and national protocols that seek to officially define young children's rights; this is done elsewhere in this collection. Nor am I comprehensive in my reference to the diverse range of agreements and statutes that relate to children's rights or which are tangential to them. Reference is made, nonetheless, to certain parts of certain important and globally accepted conventions and statements. I also restrict my commentary to formal educational provision for those young children experiencing SEND – as made available in schools and other settings – as opposed to the informal, though no less important, arrangements that prevail in homes and in communities. Many of the challenges faced by these children are experienced by others, marginalised by race, gender, religion or culture; in some cases, their position is even more tenuous.

I adopt a personal and therefore partial approach to the question of young children's rights. This is not self-indulgence, but more a vehicle whereby illustrations of the sharp disconnects between rhetorical 'policy' and ground-level practices can be provided. What I present is not an onlooker's account: it is one that has been scarified by the inequalities that prevail even within apparently well-resourced post-industrial democracies. Inevitably, this will result in some parochialism, although I attempt to offset this by calling on my experiences in a diverse range of international settings. Essentially, though, my remarks are those whose predominant experience has been drawn from working in geographic locations that continue to benefit from the product of highly developed economies of the Global North and their historical sociopolitical domination. Fourth, my focus on formal education is exclusively directed to the recent emphasis on 'inclusion', in recognition that this has become the de facto ideological battleground for theorists, activists and practitioners. As such, it captures crucial tensions that exist among educationalists, sometimes to the detriment of those young children with SEND that this admirable approach seeks to support.

Finally, while expressing herein a somewhat combative position that echoes Sowell's withering complaint about those who pontificate at a distance, I nail my colour to the high mast that carries the full recognition and application of dignity, respect and opportunity in the lives of all young people. In attempting to depict the nature of contemporary challenge by highlighting rhetoric–reality tensions, I am guided by my regard for the writing of Janusz Korzcak:

> Children are not the people of tomorrow, but are people of today. They have a right to be taken seriously, and to be treated with tenderness and respect. They should be allowed to grow into whoever they were meant to be. 'The unknown person' inside of them is our hope for the future.
>
> *(quoted in Joseph, 1999, p. 4)*

Young children's rights: current aspirations

Several major international or European protocols help proscribe accepted current understandings of the rights of young children with SEND within education. Each highlights the generic principles that underpin ground-level provision, and in turn each is inhibited by a serial failure to recognise that their practical application requires common assent and individual responses to educational need. Neither is convincingly apparent or widespread in contemporary systems, irrespective of their economic or knowledge capital. Such a condition does not prevent a vociferous expression of opinion that 'inclusive education is a rights-based issue' Jones et al. (2004) (Browne and Millar, 2016). There is a recognition that children with SEND can be best included by attention to a framework that comprises seven components: citizenship and social inclusion; recognition; agency; voice; capabilities; equality; and self-realisation. They are at the heart of current conceptualisations of young children's rights. The struggle to apply each in the practices of formal educational settings highlights the paradoxes between global statements regarding children's rights and the way that these are being adopted in schools and other settings.

For young children with SEND, the overarching international protocol is the United Nations Convention on the Rights of the Child (UNCRC, 1989). The UNCRC 'applies to everyone, whatever their race, religion, abilities; whatever they think or say, whatever type of family they come from' (Article 2). Article 29 of the Convention establishes the child's right to education. The UNRC has become the most widely referenced document when arguments are made when matters relating to educational opportunity and equality are being advanced (Jones, 2008). The UNCRC captures the rationale for formally embedding the rights of children within policy and practice, indicating that children need their own rights because they:

- are separate and unique to adults;
- need special protection because of their vulnerability and developing maturity;
- have special developmental needs and evolving capacities;
- are sometimes less articulate than adults; and
- are less likely to be taken seriously, and have less power.

Its associated United Nations Convention on the Rights of Disabled Persons (2008), hereafter termed UNCRDP, sought 'to promote, protect and ensure the full and equal enjoyment of all human rights and fundamental freedoms by all persons with disabilities, and to promote respect for their inherent dignity' (UNCRDP, 2008). It is perhaps indicative of the slow progress being made to address the rights agenda (and therefore the needs) of disabled persons that nearly 20 years following the formal recognition of UNCRC, it was felt imperative that a separate articulation of rights was needed for those experiencing SEND. Both, however, map the indelible and unquestionable concepts that should inform the way that children should be educated, and as summarised in the seven dimensions recalled by Browne and Millar (2016): citizenship and social inclusion; recognition; agency; voice; capabilities; equality; and self-realisation.

For countries within the European Union and Europe at large, the European Convention on Human Rights (ECHR), established in 1950, gives all people – adults, children and young people – a set of rights (Council of Europe, 1950). Article 9 indicates that this comprises:

> the right to survival; to develop to the fullest; to protection from harmful influences, abuse and exploitation; and to participate fully in family, cultural and social life. It further protects children's rights by setting standards in health care, education and legal, civil and social services.

While predating the subsequent international conventions, the ECHR remains important in the context of the education of young children. Article 2 provides for the right not to be denied an education and the right for parents to have their children educated in accordance with their religious and other views, though it is notable that this wording does not guarantee any specific level of education, or its quality.

Against these three substantive international concordats informing policymakers about their responsibility to secure the rights of children in educational settings, the Millennium Development Goals (MDGs) can be used as a reality check regarding the shortcomings of supranational agreements. The international development goals for 2015 have been significantly enhanced and now specify that by 2030, 'all girls and boys have access to quality early childhood development, care and pre-primary education so that they are ready for primary education' (United Nations, 2017). The associated aim of building and upgrading education facilities that 'are child, disability and gender sensitive and provide safe, nonviolent, inclusive[2] and effective learning environments for all' is emphasised as integral within this process.

The MDG documentation is useful as a reminder of two important contextual matters when considering the rights of young children. First, it emphasises once more how slow progress has been in connecting the rights-based principles defined within the international conventions to their practical operation within educational settings. More especially, it provides a stark illustration of the impact of their uneven application across different geographical regions, or between individual nation states. In some instances, powerfully documented in the literature (Achvarina and Reich, 2006; Kuhlthau, Hill, Yucel and Perrin, 2005), the rights of all young children, and especially those who are marginalised by learning, social or cultural differences, are seriously compromised. The UN itself reported:

> Although significant achievements have been made on many of the MDG targets worldwide, progress has been uneven across regions and countries, leaving significant gaps. Millions of people are being left behind, especially the poorest and those disadvantaged because of their sex, age, disability, ethnicity or geographic location.
>
> *(United Nations, 2015, p. 8)*

Implicated as being among the most at-risk populations, whose rights under existing international agreements are most susceptible to be infringed, are those marginalised populations in diverse regions across the globe. The UN (2015) analysis provides a stark reminder of these inequalities, which themselves are inhibitors of universal application of children's rights:

> According to 2012 estimates, 43 per cent of out-of-school children globally will never go to school. However, regional disparities are large. In Southern Asia, an estimated 57 per cent of out-of-school children will never go to school, while in sub-Saharan Africa the proportion is 50 per cent. Gender is also an important factor. Almost half of out-of-school girls (48 per cent) are unlikely to ever go to school, compared to 37 per cent of boys.
>
> *(United Nations, 2015, p. 26)*

Moreover, the same report confirms that SEND among early years populations remains a barrier to these children securing one of their fundamental rights, common to each existing international convention relating to children – their right to education. Thus, it is reported that 'Disability is another major impediment to accessing education. In India, for instance, more than one third of children and adolescents aged 6 to 13 who live with disabilities are out of school' (United Nations, 2015, p. 26). While recognising these depressing variations in access to marginalised children's rights, as exemplified by their educational needs being met in schools and settings, it is important to ensure that the positive development which has taken place over the past 30 years is fully acknowledged. This has been as apparent in both international contexts as in national. Even so, there is a depressing tendency to deflect attention from these small steps or green-shoots in the early years rights agenda: instances where practitioners demonstrate a ground-level understanding of the challenges they experience and the solutions they suggest in enabling young children's learning to be enriched or, in some locations, take advantage of formal education for the very first time.

This ongoing tendency can be illustrated in several ways. I have already referred to some of the predominating concerns regarding terminology (Gernsbacher et al., 2016). While this is no doubt a preoccupation for academics and researchers who operate some distance away from direct engagement with young children, it is an almost self-fulfilling task that contributes little to the eventual 'rights well-being' of the child. Kauffman (1985) observed that in relation to historical legislation relating to SEND in the USA and its omission of behaviours of socially 'maladjusted' from the then existing categorisation, 'The addition of that clause makes the definition nonsensical by any conventional logic … and is … the kind of ambiguity of language and the frailty of logic that keeps lawyers busy and drives decent people insane' (p. 259).

So, the predilection to 'gaze at the problem' has been a structural feature in SEND (in its various terminological guises) over the last 35 years. And it still remains a staple consideration in those sectors of education where the focus ought to be more properly directed towards equipping new practitioners with the knowledge and skills to enable the right of all children to experience thoughtful, stimulating early years experiences in play, aesthetics, social and emotional skills, and the establishment of engagement and enthusiasm in key curriculum areas. Instead, further effort is directed towards debating the nuances and concepts involved in terminology. In England, Jerome, Emerson, Lundy and Orr (2015) and Robson (2016) illustrate this continued preoccupation. Robson (2016), for example, states, 'I found that practitioners operated a counter-discourse that gave visibility to children's rights without reference to the formal legal or policy frameworks supporting children's rights. In doing so they worked with an incomplete knowledge and theory of rights' (Robson, 2016, p. 10).

While this summation may have merit, little was then connected to the practice-related impact of such a course of action: the principal link is suppositional – that 'practitioners could have been supported by having more knowledge' of the prevailing rights conventions (Robson, 2016, p. 10). An alternative and more persuasively meaningful approach would be to demonstrate what the rights conventions might 'look like' in the learning spaces occupied by these young children and their teachers and other professionals.

Practical challenges and tensions

Making 'rights' a reality within individual schools or settings where early years children are being accommodated presents several challenges, and the resulting tensions can both obscure progressive approaches and deflect professional energies. These have been rehearsed over a considerable period (Doek, 2009), and are suggestive of features within national provision for early years that are almost intractably negative; this is because they are invariably located within a complex ecosystem of contextual factors – including cultural, social, economic and political determinants. If it is acknowledged that an effective promotion of children's rights in education requires political will, resources, professional training and development and leadership (EADSNE, 2017), it must equally be accepted that each of these vital components of growing a 'rights-based culture' should be viewed as major challenges to the workforce in their task of establishing a rights-based culture. Each will impact in a negative fashion on their efforts.

Currently, in England, a depressing scenario is being played out, in which a significantly advantaged nation state is demonstrating studied indifference to the denial of some of the basic rights of young children in its formal educational settings. These have been effectively mapped by the Children's Rights Alliance for England (CRAE, 2017). Although modest in its purposive data capture, this study intimates that, irrespective of the perception of England as a major world influence on educational ideas and social change, all is not well in its systemic response to securing the rights of young children. Importantly, the study suggested that 'only organisations consisting of children's rights experts who had children's rights as part of their core ethos or aims were currently using an explicit children's rights approach to policy' (CRAE, 2017, p. 1).

Moreover, the accompanying suggestion was that a children's rights-based approach was more likely to be apparent in certain charity sectors, implying that its adoption within formal educational settings as a fundamental element in defining policy and practice was less clearly visible. The CRAE study examined eight of the barriers in all settings (health, education and social care), though these were only partly differentiated within the reporting documents. These covered:

- use of inappropriate technical and legal language in the conventions;
- absence of statutory duty in the public sector in respect of the UNCRC;
- efficacy of added value of children's rights;
- expertise within the 'sector';
- querying the shift in the balance of power to children;
- rights are only used for certain groups of children (e.g. LGBTQ children);
- understanding of 'rights' limited to participation; and
- toxic anti-human rights and international rhetoric.

Responses to some of these barriers are discussed in the final section of this chapter. Meanwhile, it is worth commenting on two of these as illustrations of the complexity of the challenges being encountered.

First, I want to briefly comment on the final barrier identified above. It provides the substantive political, social and cultural context within which practitioners operate and which, it seems, generic rights conventions take little account of when their application in practice is being scrutinised. A worrying feature emerging in the data reported was the widespread sense of reluctance to base policy on a rights-footing for fear of being 'labelled a woolly lefty in the current environment' (CRAE, 2017); this was especially the case where organisations were delivering services for children on behalf of government. Potently, the study suggested that 'The toxic anti-human rights rhetoric is also being intensified by Brexit which has further exacerbated anti-international/European feeling including about the ECHR and, by association, the CRC' (CRC, 2017, p. 4).

These sentiments are particularly apposite to marginalised young children, who in the present anti-human rights narrative are often portrayed as recipients of 'freebies' (*sic*). The study points out that 'There was substantial opposition in the media to applying the fundamental principles of human rights to everyone; instead, minority groups were regularly presented as undeserving of human rights protections' (CRC, 2017, p. 4).

It is again worth reiterating the advantaged position from which such oppositional views are emerging. In other less economically favoured or resourced contexts, the position of young children is further substantially compromised by cross-cutting issues of poverty, natural disaster, political instability or armed conflict. In such locations, the right to life is sometimes at stake, and certainly requires a reassessment of the practical application of the existing children's rights conventions – a task that is undoubtedly a significant focus of policymakers in many global regions that are experiencing some of these conditions (e.g. see Drame and Kamphoff, 2014; Majoko, 2018).

The need to have a workforce who are both aware of the core content of international rights agendas and who are empowered to incorporate their principles into practice is fundamental to changing the current orientation (EADSNE, 2017). The role of leaders in schools and settings is crucial in mediating between their theoretical and practical manifestations, as is the case with other vital educational initiatives (Kugelmass and Ainscow, 2003). For marginalised children and young people, the leader performs a critical function. In the case of SEND, for instance, Black and Simon (2014) have noted that the effectiveness of inclusive practices (which, in whatever configuration they assume, are an engagement right for *all* children) is central to the establishment and maintenance of an institutional culture which is positively geared towards ensuring that everyone embeds the rights of learners, as defined in the conventions, in their daily activities (Bishton, 2007).

Sometimes, however, practical interventions encounter unexpected challenges. This is especially the case in respect of the contested themes of SEND and inclusive education. There are recent examples where the use of international conventions relating to children's rights have resulted in the process becoming weaponised. A case in point is a recent government-supported initiative, Leading Learning 4 All (LL4All), to provide ground-level information to school principals relating to SEND in Australia (Leading Learning 4 All, 2017). The stated aim of this was to complement and support already existing resources for school leaders in Australian states and territories; it was formulated as a contributory starting point (the first of its kind) which sought to directly address the doubts that some mainstream school principals were connecting effectively with their responsibilities for SEND under currently obtaining national 'standards'. The launch of an online resource provoked an outcry, principally from stakeholder groups and from academics and activists (Open Letter, 2017). Their claim was that the initiative was flawed, in part because insufficient emphasis was placed on a specific interpretation of Article 24 of the UNCRC – which related to 'inclusive education'. The latter, in a SEND context, is only contested in respect of how the term is operationalised, and various commentators have identified a range of variants (Reindal, 2016). The protest called for the project to be halted, and subjected to 'expert' review, given that, for example, 'some resources did not represent inclusive learning environments or arrangements but illustrate students learning in isolation, away from their classes (and that) This is not consistent with evidence of effective practice in inclusive education' (Open Letter, 2017).

Though the LL4All initiative itself, which was received well by those practitioners to whom it was aimed, did not claim to be a definitive source, its purpose of securing an initial 'SEND threshold', in the mindset of some school leaders, risked being derailed because of others who were operating from considerable distance from the realities of principalship. It thus comprises a further example of a failure to recognise educational change as a process, and that mediating between generic international and national conventions when contested definitions and practices are involved requires an incremental shift rather than a seismic event. Hence the importance of winning the hearts and minds of leaders in schools and settings, recognising that 'the role of the school principal in providing leadership for such processes is crucial' (Riehl, 2000), and that in respect of issues such as children's rights, SEND and inclusive education, this effort is longitudinal and incremental, rather than episodic. Such intentions appeared to be lost, however, in the unedifying social media catcalling that ensued.

Moving towards more inclusive, rights-based practice

I have noted at various points in scoping the challenges in implementing a rights-based approach with marginalised young children that there has been some progress made, both in respect of a wider recognition of the issue within educational contexts and in respect of the support and resources that are sometimes more widely available (Hand, 2003; Paige-Smith and Rix, 2011; UNICEF, 2014a; Zakin, 2012).

The key determinants of effective, impactful change have been articulated by Rodd (2014), among these the development of a 'community of learning', professional capacity (skills and knowledge), collective leadership and collaborative teams. These are significantly underpinned by the generic development of interpersonal 'soft skills', which can help offset the significant contextual challenges described earlier in this chapter, and on which Rodd (2014) notes:

> It is apparent that early years professionals in various countries experience considerable and constant pressure to implement many different initiatives and developments. The pressure for change creates a further challenge, that of equipping the workforce with appropriate competence … However, perhaps because they have experienced years of chronic change and limited training and support, some early years practitioners report that they are weary and wary of embracing yet more demands for change.
>
> *(p. 2)*

Strategies to grow, embed and sustain the rights of young children in educational settings must above all take account of established understandings of the change process in institutions. Well before attention is given to establishing a rights approach to both the formally articulated, externally regulated curriculum, as well as the 'hidden' or social curriculum, all professionals need to have opportunities to engage in reflective dialogue regarding their own beliefs on the rights of children. This process may be time-consuming, but it is an essential cornerstone in establishing a community of practice that actively promotes rights. As discussed elsewhere, Article 29 of the UNCRC asserts the right of children to education. The quality of that educational experience will be largely informed by the extent to which whole settings engage in practical application of the Convention's content. To successfully do this, the starting point is critical self-reflection, in a structured professional development programme. As was noted many years after the inception of the UNCRC:

> there were serious challenges to the implementation of the Convention, the most difficult of which was related to cultural attitudes that disfavour children in many countries. Training and awareness-raising among parents, teachers and professionals were therefore identified as essential tasks.
>
> *(van Leer, 2007, p. 24)*

The process of reformulating a rights-based vision in early childhood education requires that careful selection of change objectives is identified. Auditing existing attitudes and practices often forms a viable basis for action, although sometimes focus and momentum are lost because of a failure to restrict the changes to individual, prioritised actions. Connecting these to a doable timeline is a further desirable action, ensuring that the actions are defined by measurable indicators. This process is a collective endeavour, in which leadership and responsibility are distributed across the setting (Rodd, 2014).

In all these processes, however, professionals need to recognise that children's rights are non-negotiable, and require systematic embedding using overt, whole-setting development. Support for this endeavour is now widely available, notably via such initiatives as UNICEF's *Child Rights Education Toolkit* (UNICEF, 2014b) and Oxfam's *Children's Rights Teachers' Guide* (Oxfam, 2015). The former is of valuable assistance in charting a pathway to more complete rights engagement. These materials, though comprehensive, require careful mediation to ensure that they can be applied in early years settings in an incremental fashion that is sensitive to the capacity of the professional workforce. The Oxfam guide is eminently practical, illustrating the value of providing user-friendly, practical materials that practitioners can adapt for their own context. A further illustration of the mediation so necessary between generic protocols on young children's rights and their application in practice is provided by Dell (n.d.), which seeks to make direct connection between the explicit content of the UNCRC and policy and practice implementation in early years settings.

Conclusion

The purpose of these illustrations is not to offer a compendium of resources for practitioners. Rather, they exemplify that even though there are significant points of tension and several barriers to further progressing the rights agenda in early years settings, there is a sufficiently varied range of models available to be catalysts for refining current practices. I have signalled at various points the importance of resource discrepancy as being a major barrier to introducing measures to advance an understanding and embedding of rights-informed responses to children's early education – and at the time of writing, it is being reported that in London, England, 'Nursery schools that look after some of the capital's most vulnerable children are at risk of closing within the next two years because of a funding crisis' (*Evening Standard*, 17 September 2018). There can be little doubt that one of the principal catalysts to progress will in many respects be cost-neutral – the willingness of stakeholders to acknowledge that in all matters, the child's interests must come first and that the child's voice (or that of an advocate) must be prominent in all decision-making and resulting practices.

Notes

1 I use the term 'special educational needs and disabilities' (SEND) throughout this chapter, recognising that it is interchangeable with other generic descriptors for children with learning difficulties and/or disabilities dependent on national variation (for example, Scotland uses the term 'additional support needs' to describe this group within educational settings).
2 I use the term 'inclusive education' in its widest sense to include all those educational interventions that support children with SEND to learn, thrive and be recognised as individuals so that they can be recognised as part of, and not apart from, wider society. I do not associate 'inclusive education' per se with place or time. I associate it with empowered being.

References

Achvarina, Vera and Simon Reich. 2006. "No place to hide: refugees, displaced persons, and the recruitment of child soldiers," *International Security*, 31: 127–164.
Ball, Stephen. 2008. "Some sociologies of education: a history of problems and places, and segments and gazes," *The Sociological Review*, 56 (4): 650–669.
Barton, Len and Sally Tomlinson (eds.). 1984. *Special Education and Social Interests*. London: Croom Helm.

Bishton, Helen. 2007. *Children's Voice, Children's Rights*. Nottingham: National College for School Leadership.

Black, William and Marsha Simon. 2014. "Leadership for all students: planning for more inclusive school practices," *NCPEA International Journal of Educational Leadership Preparation*, 9 (2): 153–172.

Browne, Michael and Michelle Millar. 2016. "A rights-based conceptual framework for the social inclusion of children and young persons with an intellectual disability," *Disability and Society*, 31 (8): 1064–1080.

Children's Rights Alliance for England. 2017. *Barriers and Solutions to Using Children's Rights Approaches in Policy*. London: CRAE.

Council of Europe. 1950. *The Convention for the Protection of Human Rights and Fundamental Freedoms*. Strasbourg: Council of Europe. www.coe.int/en/web/human-rights-convention/the-convention-in-1950

Dell, C. n.d. "Children's rights in the early years settings." www.centreforglobaleducation.org/includes/documents/ChildrensRightsintheEarlyYearsSetting.pdf

Doek, Jaap. 2009. "The CRC 20 years: an overview of some of the major achievements and remaining challenges," *Child Abuse and Neglect*, 33 (11): 771–782.

Drame, Elizabeth and Kaytie Kamphoff. 2014. "Perceptions of disability and access to inclusive education in West Africa: a comparative case study in Dakar, Senegal," *International Journal of Special Education*, 29 (3): 69–81.

European Agency for Special Needs and Inclusive Education. 2017. *Inclusive Early Childhood Education*. Odense: EADSNE.

Gernsbacher, Morton Ann, Adam R. Raimond, M. Theresa Balinghasay and Jilana Boston. 2016. "'Special needs' is an ineffective euphemism," *Cognitive Research: Principles and Implications*, 1–29. https://cognitiveresearchjournal.springeropen.com/articles/10.1186/s41235-016-0025-4

Hand, Pam. 2003. *First Steps to Rights: Activities for Children Aged 3-7 Years*. London: UNICEF UK.

Imray, Peter and Andrew Colley. 2017. *Inclusion is Dead. Long Live Inclusion*. London: Routledge.

Jerome, Lee, Lesley Emerson, Laura Lundy and Karen Orr. 2015. *Teaching and Learning about Children's Rights*. London: UNICEF. www.unicef.org/crc/files/CHILD_RIGHTS_EDUCATION_STUDY_11May.pdf

Jones, Adele et al. 2004. "Children's Experiences of Separation From Parents as a Consequence of Migration," *Caribbean Journal of Social Work*, 3: 89-109.

Joseph, Sandra. 1999. *A Voice for the Child. The Inspirational Words of Janusz Korczak*. London: Thorsons.

Kauffman, James. 1985. *Educating Children with Behavior Disorders*. New York: Sage.

Kugelmass, Judy and Mel Ainscow. 2003. *Leadership for inclusion: a comparison of international practices*. Paper presented at the meeting of the American Educational Research Association, Chicago, April 21–25, 2003.

Kuhlthau, Karen, Kristen Smith Hill, Recai Yucel and James M. Perrin. 2005. "Financial burden for families of children with special health care needs," *Maternal and Child Health Journal*, 9 (2): 207–218.

Leading Learning 4 All. 2017. *Learning Learning 4 All*. www.leadinglearning4all.edu.au/

Majoko, Tawanda. 2018. "Effectiveness of special and inclusive teaching in early childhood education in Zimbabwe," *Early Child Development and Care*, 188 (6): 785–799.

Nind, Melanie and Rosie Flewitt. 2006. *Parents' choice of education for their young children: lessons for inclusive education*. Paper presented at the European Conference for Educational Research, Geneva, 13–15 September, 2006.

Open Letter. 2017. *Concerns Regarding Leading Learning 4 All Resource*. https://openletterll4all.com/

Oxfam. 2015. *Children's Rights Teachers' Guide*. www.oxfam.org.uk/education/resources/childrens-rights

Paige-Smith, Alice and Jonathan Rix. 2011. "Researching early intervention and young children's perspectives – developing and using a 'listening to children approach'," *British Journal of Special Education*, 38 (1): 28–36.

Reindal, Solveig. 2016. "Discussing inclusive education: an inquiry into different interpretations and a search for ethical aspects of inclusion using the capabilities approach," *European Journal of Special Needs Education*, 31 (1): 1–12.

Riehl, Carolyn. 2000. "The principal's role in creating inclusive schools for diverse students: a review of normative, empirical, and critical literature on the practice of educational administration," *Review of Educational Research*, 70 (1): 55–81.

Robson, Jenny. 2016. "Early years teachers and young children's rights: the need for critical dialogue," *Research in Teacher Education*, 6 (1): 6–11.

Rodd, Jillian. 2014. *Leading Change in the Early Years*. Maidenhead: Open University Press.

Sowell, Thomas. 1995. *The Vision of the Anointed*. New York: Basic Books.

United Nations. 1989. *The Convention on the Rights of the Child*. New York: United Nations.

United Nations. 2015. *The Millennium Development Goals Report 2015*. New York: United Nations. www.un.org/millenniumgoals/2015_MDG_Report/pdf/MDG%202015%20rev%20(July%201).pdf

United Nations. 2017. *Sustainable Development Goals*. New York: United Nations. www.un.org/sustainabledevelopment/development-agenda/

United Nations International Children's Emergency Fund. 2014a. *Child Rights Education Toolkit: Rooting Child Rights in Early Childhood Education, Primary and Secondary Schools*. Geneva: UNICEF.

United Nations International Children's Emergency Fund. 2014b *Child Rights Education Toolkit*. Geneva: UNICEF. www.unicef.org/crc/files/UNICEF_CRE_Toolkit_FINAL_web_version170414.pdf

van Leer, Bernard. 2007. *Early Childhood and Primary Education: Transitions in the Lives of Young Children*. Milton Keynes: The Open University.

Zakin, Andrea. 2012. "Hand to Hand: teaching Tolerance and Social Justice One Child at a Time," *Childhood Education*, 88 (1): 3–13.

9

RISK AND SAFETY IN WESTERN SOCIETY

Zoi Nikiforidou

Introduction

Since the mid-1980s, risk has been a topic of research and policy in Western society. There has been a 'rise of risk' (Garland, 2003) in the sense that there is an explosion of risk discourse and risk literature. Modern society is characterised as 'risk society' in that it is increasingly preoccupied with debates on the prevention and management of risks that it itself has produced (Beck, 2006). Similarly, Giddens (1999) underlines that the idea of 'risk society' does not necessarily suggest a more hazardous world, but instead a society that is increasingly concerned with the future and also with safety. Within the broader risk discourse, Garlen (2019) notes that nowadays, childhood is at risk and childhood innocence is threatened; hence, the rhetoric of protection has been (re-)raised and maintained. The protective practices of adults on behalf of children, from parental monitoring of daily activities to governmental policies, take for granted the naturalness of childhood innocence. Equally, Faulkner (2011) states that 'the value of a child's innocence depends on their capacity to be protected' (p. 6). Within this rhetoric, adults have a responsibility to protect children who are innocent, naive and vulnerable, and can become helpless victims who need protection.

However, Meyer (2007) argues that this discourse of innocence is challenged by a new discourse that has emerged over the last 30 years, that of children's rights. This discourse highlights children's rights instead of children's needs, and addresses rights for children to do things instead of having things done to and for them by adults. Children are conceptualised as active, independent persons with rights, interests and agency (Lansdown, 1994). In children's rights discourse, children's voices are valued and there is rising interest in equipping children from early years to become independent and knowledgeable decision-makers, rather than passive recipients characterised as a 'cotton wool' generation (Nikiforidou, 2017).

Child protection and child welfare service systems aim to keep children safe. These are structured in many countries and function differently around the world as they are 'social configurations rooted in specific visions for children, families, communities and societies' (Cameron and Freymond, 2006, p. 3). Despite the sociocultural variations that characterise policies and orientations, the common interest underpinning child protection is the child's best interests. However, this raises questions about who determines children's 'best interests', who defines the balance between safety, (over-)protection, fear and risk, and where children are positioned in this context.

The United Nations Convention on the Rights of the Child (UNCRC) (Office for the United Nations High Commissioner for Human Rights (OHCHR), 1989) frames children's protection rights as the rights that include protection for children from all forms of child abuse, neglect, exploitation and cruelty, including the right to special protection in times of war and protection from abuse in the criminal justice system. Thus, children's rights that can be violated by risks and threats worldwide include, but are not limited to, Articles 9, 11, 19, 20, 21, 32, 33, 34, 35, 36 and 38, including protection from various forms of exploitation, child labour, violence, war and cases of maltreatment. Along these lines, the aim of this chapter is to explore how societies respond to risk, safeguarding and child protection, and how the risk-aversion culture that portrays Western societies challenges children's rights of protection and play. For the purpose of this chapter, Western society is considered to be mainly geographically aligned to Europe, the USA, Canada, Australia and New Zealand. Initially, the notions of risk and society are explored, then an overview of safeguarding and child protection orientations are discussed, drawing on the example of the UK, followed by critical argument about how the risk-aversion culture is shaped and influences children's experiences of protection and play.

Risk (and) society

Risk is constructed and 'confined by space, time and social limitations' (Beck, 2006, cited in Wimmer and Quandt, 2006, p. 341). Risks change and develop; what is safe today might be unsafe in the future, and vice versa. Risks can be magnified, dramatised or minimised and are open to personal and social definition (Beck, 1992, p. 23). It is the framework in which they evolve that defines their severity and need for action. Furthermore, Giddens (1999) calls for a distinction between risk and hazard, and Adams and Thompson (2002) conclude that risk depends on the different perceivers and management attempts. Sometimes risks are real and at other times they are only anticipated. As such, risks are events that are threatening and gain interest through techniques of visualisation, symbolic forms and mass media (Beck, 2006). Lastly, in attempting to define the complex notion of risk, risks can be calculated based on probabilities and statistics, but they can also underpin an amalgam of subjective emotions, interests and values (Slovic, Finucane, Peters and MacGregor, 2004).

In most cases, risk has a negative connotation and is viewed as a threat, danger or factor that needs elimination. Terms such as a 'good risk' or a 'risk worth taking' are absent in contemporary discourse. Furedi (2007) remarks that risk is not even represented as neutral, but instead is connected to negative outcomes that people are expected to fear. Subsequently, he makes the point that through risk management, fear is institutionalised and culturally affirmed. Wolff (2006) agrees that in considering the 'anatomy of risk', besides probability and magnitude, risk integrates cause, fear and moral concern. Fredrickson (2001) also contemplates how risk prompts fear, a powerful negative emotion that narrows human actions to protection (i.e. fight, flight or freeze).

In response to risk, societies have in place safety and protection policies and strategies. Especially when children are involved, societies have the responsibility and duty to find the best possible ways to ensure safe and secure environments where children can thrive and develop socially, mentally, physically, emotionally and personally. One of the most basic measures of child well-being is the ability of a society to safeguard its children and young people from injury and abuse (Jack and Gill, 2010). Thus, when considering the relationship between risk, young children and safety, there is always a key aspect to account for: Are children being protected from risks in a way that meets their rights?

Safeguarding and child protection welfare systems

There is general consensus that young children are vulnerable to some extent by virtue of their age, immaturity and dependence on adults (Munro, 2011). This means that, on one hand, children's needs and rights (different in some respects from those of adults) are recognised, and, on the other hand, adults have responsibility and accountability for ensuring safety and protection. In this respect, child safeguarding and protection is a matter of both private and public responsibility (Wulczyn et al., 2010). It starts from the children themselves and extends to their families, their communities and wider societal layers. As Article 19 states:

> 1. States Parties shall take all appropriate legislative, administrative, social and educational measures to protect the child from all forms of physical or mental violence, injury or abuse, neglect or negligent treatment, maltreatment or exploitation, including sexual abuse.
>
> (OHCHR, 1989)

Societies have developed different child protection systems that reflect their ideologies, priorities and desired outcomes (Devaney and McGregor, 2017). Cultural, political and institutional contexts that are developing over time frame these systems, and therefore it is hard to expect one country or community to simply adopt the systems and policies from another country. Thereby, child protection approaches are tied to geography, political and social history, religion, wealth, social structure, and a more general sense of purpose that blends cultural beliefs about how to protect children with everyday realities and risks (Wulczyn et al., 2010). Nevertheless, for the countries that have ratified the UNCRC, OHCHR (1989) emphasises: 'The best interests of children must be the primary concern in making decisions that may affect them ... [including] budget, policy and law maker' (Article 3).

In 1997, Gilbert provided a categorisation of child protection and welfare systems: the 'child protective orientation', which prevails in the Anglo-Saxon countries (evident in Australia, the USA, the UK, Canada and New Zealand) and the 'family service orientation', which is represented in both Nordic and continental European countries (such as Denmark, Belgium and Sweden). Under these two categories, the relationship between the family and the state and the position of child abuse differ. In the child protective orientation, child abuse tends to be framed as a problem of individual pathology and is dealt with by legal investigations, whereas in the family service orientation the emphasis is on family dysfunction and is tackled through a therapeutic approach. Furthermore, in the child protective orientation, the family and the state can be described as adversarial, while in the family service orientation they work in partnership.

Nevertheless, Gilbert, Parton and Skivenes (2011) suggest that these two categories no longer account for the complex reality of society's response to child abuse, and they propose a third approach: the 'child-focused orientation'. This emerging orientation focuses on the individual child's rights, development and well-being, and may coexist with more traditional orientations. Instead of simply protecting children from risk, this orientation aims to promote children's welfare and holistic well-being under a present and future perspective. With a child-focused orientation, the state takes on a growing role for itself in providing a range of early intervention and preventive services. Thus, the discourse of children's rights prevails and replaces the discourse of innocence (Meyer, 2007), where children are seen as rights-holders, and not simply victims within a vulnerable position.

Léveillé and Chamberland (2010) argue that the UK has been at the forefront of responding to children in need, and accordingly has developed methods and support systems. In their meta-analysis, they present how these have inspired 15 other countries in 10 years, and how the recognition of the interdependence of the three systems (the child, the parent, the family and social environment) enables gaining a better understanding of children's situations, of the risk and protection factors in their lives, and in the end of the most effective services for their welfare and safety. However, they recognise the legislative, political, administrative and social challenges in aiming at '1) a holistic analysis of children's welfare; 2) a common understanding of the human development of children and adolescents; and 3) parental involvement oriented towards the needs of their children and not according to the logic of reporting' (Léveillé and Chamberland, 2010, p. 942).

Within the British context, child protection refers to the activity that is undertaken to protect specific children who are suffering, or are likely to suffer, significant harm. Safeguarding and promoting welfare is broader and is defined as:

> a. protecting children from maltreatment, b. preventing impairment of children's health or development, c. ensuring that children are growing up in circumstances consistent with the provision of safe and effective care, d. taking action to enable all children to have the best outcomes.
>
> *(Her Majesty's Government, 2018, p. 6)*

It is evident that safeguarding aims at protecting every child, not only the children who suffer violation of their rights or are at immediate risk. Safeguarding is underpinned by implications of proactiveness and early intervention, aiming at a child-centred and coordinated approach. Early intervention is seen as 'a policy approach designed to build the essential social and emotional bedrock in children aged 0–3 and to ensure that children aged 0–18 can become the excellent parents of tomorrow' (Allen, 2011, p. xvii). The aim is to buffer or reduce known risk factors and strengthen protective factors in order to make a difference in children's and families' lives. Parton (2011) agrees that the role of prevention and protection is not only to combat the negatives involved, but also to enhance the positive opportunities for child development through the maximisation of protective factors and processes.

Svevo-Cianci, Hart and Rubinson (2010) propose that child protection measures can be organised into three major child protection areas of focus: '(a) laws, regulations, and policies; (b) education, training, service programs and data management; and (c) the status and progress of the child's well-being, health and development' (p. 46). They argue that child protection infrastructure in coordination with information-based interventions leads to effective child protection. Based on their study, which included expert respondents from 42 countries, they concluded that child protection measures cannot be implemented in isolation, without an informed, strategic approach to policy, infrastructure design and progressive advances. They claim that it is necessary to establish strategies that are most valuable as well as practically instituted, based on local realities, strengths and challenges.

Risk-aversion culture and rights

Risk-aversion culture and overprotection

Besides structural policies and decisions, risk and danger are perceived through attitudes and predispositions. Societies, especially in the Western world, tend to be preoccupied by risk discourse (Garland, 2003), and in many cases protection directs towards overprotection. The overprotective stance leads to a 'no-risk culture', characterised by excessive regulations, risk assessments, and increased adult surveillance and concern. Bundy et al., (2009) highlight that this 'no risk' is itself a risk as it distorts and limits children's experiences. Similarly, Wyver et al., (2010) agree that there is an overload of 'surplus safety' today having long-term consequences on children's well-being. They observe that many parents, concerned mainly about injuries during play, traffic danger and stranger danger, try to remove children from 'risky' areas and activities, resulting in the lessening of important developmental experiences, especially outdoors. Thus, the desire to reduce risks leads to the occurrence of other new and sometimes unnecessary risks. In addition, it limits children's own understanding and perception of dangers and hazards.

In Western societies, a key implication of the dominant risk-averse culture is the formation of so-called 'cotton wool' generations (Nikiforidou, 2017). Adults, whether they are parents, teachers or policymakers, often take excessive safety measures, which in turn limit children's freedom and position them in a vulnerable, dependable position (Meyer, 2007). Health and safety regulations have invaded the contexts in which children grow and interact with while adults take decisions on behalf of children, aiming to keep them safe under the rhetoric of protection (Garlen, 2019). However, as Gill (2007) states, childhood is a journey from dependence to autonomy. At the heart of this journey is a transfer of responsibility from adult to child. Children need to become independent and self-reliant. They need to learn to take risks, to get hurt, and to fail as part of their development and identity formation.

Parents often frame risk narrowly, in terms of their own daily worries and concerns (Alaszewski and Coxon, 2009). This, in turn, has implications on the lifestyle they choose for their children. If parents' perceptions of risk include only their insecurities about keeping children safe and being a 'good' parent, then they may miss the benefits that risk-taking affords children. Hoffman (2010) explains that this reality 'leads parents to micromanage all aspects of their children's lives in an effort to protect the child from adverse experiences' (p. 387). Franklin and Cromby (2009) found in a study in the UK that parents recognised that overprotection causes problems and limitations in children's lives. They also addressed that the long-term effects of over-supervision, lack of risk-taking, and over-assessment of danger warrant further attention. Similarly, parents in Sydney, Australia, expressed that the strategies they were using to protect their children were imposing restrictions on freedom to play, and appreciated that the resilience-building risks they had experienced when young themselves were unlikely to be available to their own children (Little, 2010).

In individualistic societies, the sense of community and joint upbringing of children is fading, according to Furedi (2005). This means that children are predominantly the responsibility of their own parents. He argues that there is underpinning mistrust and suspicion, and adults become less involved in children's lives, especially if it is about other people's children. Intentions can be misinterpreted and adults themselves are viewed as risks to children. This stems from a 'culture of fear'. The 'culture of fear' prevails in contemporary British and American culture and reinforces the mantra 'better safe than sorry', according to Franklin and Cromby (2009). However, this is not the case everywhere in Western societies. In Germany and Scandinavia, for example, children enjoy much higher levels of freedom as parents are more secure in knowing that if their children need guidance from an adult, they will ask for it (Gill, 2007).

Parents' perceptions and reactions to risks are vastly influenced by the media (Franklin and Cromby, 2009). In Western societies, through the Internet and technology, parents experience a wealth of advice from 'experts' and gain increased pressure to keep up to date with the latest dangers, recommendations and safety products. As a matter of fact, the media reproduces anxieties and intensifies fear through the presentation of isolated cases of child maltreatment or abuse, causing moral panics (Piper, 2014). These portray the construct of the innocent child (Meyer, 2007), where children are viewed as victims, and as they are considered immature, adults' wishes, rules and practices dominate.

The role of professionals working with children has also been influenced by the risk discourse. To protect themselves from accusations of negligence, teachers make decisions that exclude opportunities for children's outdoor play, school trips, games with skipping ropes, and other activities that could potentially lead to injury (Thompson, 2005). Teachers sometimes intentionally choose to restrict children's freedom to play, under the pressure of fear of litigation if injuries occur (Bundy et al., 2009). Vyvey, Roose, De Wilde and Roets (2014) agree that the climate of fear affects professionals who work with the children and families who are considered to be at risk, augmenting anxiety, panic and more need for control. Thus, this culture of fear and insecurity affects young children too. According to Beck (2006), this experience has become global; a key, common experience, transcending borders beyond local, regional and national levels.

Risk-aversion culture and the right to play

In an attempt to minimise risk and harm, play – and in particular risky outdoor play – has been affected significantly. Children's opportunities for independent, active, creative and diverse play have been restricted (Bundy et al., 2009). As a consequence, the risk-aversion culture confines children's right to play (OHCHR, 1989, Article 31). Children have the right to relax and play, and to join in a wide range of cultural, artistic and other recreational activities (OHCHR, 1989), but these activities tend to take place in more controlled environments in the twenty-first century, as a matter of child protection. For instance, playgrounds in many urban cities are artificially designed to follow playground safety standards, and therefore provide limited affordances for children's play (Woolley and Lowe, 2013). As Thompson (2005) claims, in an overprotected playground, children cannot experience bumps and bruises that act as trophies of playtime. Thus, their sense of adventure and ingenuity is adversely affected under the premise of adult caution and concern.

In addition, nowadays, children are more likely to be driven or accompanied usually by adults to their play activities (Fotel and Thomsen, 2004) and play is more likely to be indoors and adult-led or supervised (Ginsburg, 2007). Fyhri, Hjorthol, Mackett, Fotel and Kytta (2011) analysed children's active travel and independent mobility in Denmark, Finland, Great Britain and Norway to find a reduction in children's cycling and walking and an increase in car use. Among their justifications, parents referred to traffic danger and fear of assaults as the key reasons for taking children to school by car.

In risk-averse societies, safety becomes a greater concern than age-appropriate risk and adventure, sometimes resulting in 'play deprivation'. Hughes (2003) explains that not playing may deprive children of experiences that are regarded as developmentally essential, resulting in a lack of sensory interaction with the world. Also, play deprivation is interconnected with sedentary lifestyles and disconnection from the natural world (Louv, 2005). This sedentary behaviour has detrimental implications for children's health and is related to body composition, metabolic syndrome, cardiovascular disease risk factors, behavioural conduct, prosocial behaviour, academic achievement, fitness, and self-esteem in children and youth (Carson et al., 2016). Consequently, in the name of protecting children from the risk of injury or accident, new risks have surfaced related to children's physical and psychological well-being. This point resonates with the concept of the 'risk society' (Beck, 2006; Giddens,

1999), where society needs to negotiate, manage and confront the risk of sedentary lifestyles and children's distancing from nature that stems from and is reproduced by adults' own concerns and fears.

It is undeniable that play offers young children experiences that help them broaden and build skills for their present and future (Pellegrini, 2009). Play has been widely acknowledged as an essential part of human development (Ginsburg, 2007) connected with holistic growth. Through accidents, mistakes and challenges, children can learn how to manage their emotions and the consequences of their actions and choices. By playing, children discover themselves and the world around them. They try out new ideas, build independence and confidence, overcome conflicts with themselves and others, and experience both failure and success.

Specifically, risky play enables children to learn to deal with their fears and anxieties in healthy ways (Sandseter and Kennair, 2011) and offers them opportunities to test their limits and decision-making. Risky play is defined as the type of thrilling and exciting play that can include the possibility of physical injury (Sandseter, 2010). It promotes important skills related to persistence, entrepreneurship, self-knowledge and problem-solving (Tovey, 2011). Moreover, in their systematic review, Brussoni et al. (2015) found that the overall positive health effects of increased risky outdoor play provide greater benefits than the health effects associated with avoiding outdoor risky play. They suggest that the quality of play spaces is determined by the presence of natural elements, including trees and plants, and materials that can be manipulated by the children, as well as the freedom to engage in activities of their choice based on their interests. Being daring, experimental and creative encourages a child to evaluate an uncertainty and decide on a course of action. Through risk-taking, children become responsible for themselves and agents of their decisions; they become independent and have a voice and ownership (Lansdown, 1994).

Conclusion

There needs to be a balance between safeguarding and risk. The management of risk, as positioned in Western societies currently, in a climate of surplus safety, impacts negatively on the rights of children and their growth, development and quality of life (Wyver et al., 2010). No matter how much adults try, they can never totally eliminate risks and harm. Of course, it is their duty and responsibility to nurture and protect children as best they can, but encouraging 'cotton wool' generations, increasing supervision or installing rubber surfaces in playgrounds is not the only way forward. As Giddens (1991) underlines, 'living in the "risk society" means living with a calculative attitude to the open possibilities of action, positive and negative, with which, as individuals and globally, we are confronted in a continuous way in our contemporary social existence' (p. 28).

The obsession with the negative risk discourse has led to an overemphasis on structural and policy-based actions, sometimes deviating attention from the real needs and rights of children and their families (Vyvey et al., 2014). If risks are dramatised or minimised, they do not reflect reality, but the anticipation of reality (Beck, 2006). They can be misleading and can enhance the affirmation of fear (Furedi, 2007) as part of daily practice. Therefore, this rise in risk and fear justifies and facilitates the discourse of innocence that promotes a 'needs' and not 'rights' perspective foregrounding children's dependence. According to Meyer (2007), in this case, children's needs are defined by adults and children's agency is constrained in the name of protection. Also, children are rendered incapable of exercising many rights and their demands for equal rights may be undermined.

Children are not always sufficiently protected, according to Wulczyn et al. (2010). Sometimes there are risks present within the family context and parents or carers are either unwilling or unable to protect their children. Other times, risks derive from external economic, societal, environmental or political factors. Equally, at times, the risks are situational, based on both natural and man-made emergencies that disrupt daily routines to such an extent that children are placed in harm's way. In every case, in considering future directions, it is important to implement a child-focused rights-based approach by considering children's own opinions and by raising their awareness on risk and rights.

For example, Uyan-Semerci, Erdoğan, Akkan, Müderrisoğlu and Karatay (2017) found in their study, based on 35,417 responses from children aged 10 to 12 years old from 15 countries, that risk and safety relate to high levels of subjective well-being. Children as citizens admitted that they perceive a happy life when they feel and are safe. This view should be listened to, according to Article 12 of the UNCRC (OHCHR, 1989), and should be the foundation of exploring ways to work together to ensure safety and regulate risk. Another example of valuing children's agency and views relates to UNICEF's Child Friendly Cities Initiative, which demonstrates how children can 'participate in family, community and social life' and 'influence decisions about their city' and the spaces where they spend time (Riggio, 2002, p. 45).

Children have the right to protection, but not to overprotection, and they have the right to play, but not to play deprivation. By positioning them in an innocent, vulnerable or dependant framework, we do not give them enough opportunities to develop their own understanding and consideration of risks, threats, safety and protection. Garlen (2019) proposes that becoming more attentive to the rights of children as human beings is not enough; we need to encourage them to be more attentive to their own rights and the rights of others. In this way, the 'cotton wool' child can be transformed into an agentic child who has a voice and is involved in the decision-making and management on issues of safeguarding, risk and well-being.

References

Adams, John, and Michael Thompson 2002. "Taking Account of Societal Concerns about Risk: Framing the Problem, Health and Safety Executive, Research Report 035." www.hse.gov.uk/research/rrpdf/rr035.pdf

Alaszewski, Andy, and Kirstie Coxon. 2009. "Uncertainty in Everyday Life: Risk, Worry and Trust." *Health, Risk and Society*, 11 (3): 201–207, doi:10.1080/13698570902906454.

Allen, Graham. 2011. *Early Intervention: The Next Steps – An Independent Report to Her Majesty's Government*. London: Her Majesty's Government, Cabinet Office.

Beck, Ulrich. 1992. *The Risk Society: Towards a New Modernity*. London: Sage Publications.

Beck, Ulrich. 2006. "Living in the World Risk Society." *Economy and Society*, 35 (3): 329–345.

Brussoni, Maria, Rebecca Gibbons, Casey Gray, Takuro Ishikawa, Ellen Beate Hansen Sandseter, Adam Bienenstock, Guylaine Chabot, Pamela Fuselli, Susan Herrington, Ian Janssen, William Pickett, Marlene Power, Nick Stanger, Margaret Sampson, and Mark S. Tremblay. 2015. "What Is the Relationship between Risky Outdoor Play and Health in Children? A Systematic Review." *International Journal of Environmental Research and Public Health*, 12: 6423–6454.

Bundy, Anita C., Tim Luckett, Paul J. Tranter, Geraldine A. Naughton, Shirley Wyver, Jo Ragen, and Greta Spies. 2009. "The Risk Is that There Is 'no Risk': A Simple Innovative Intervention to Increase Children's Activity Levels." *International Journal of Food Science and Technology*, 17: 33–45.

Cameron, Gary, and Nancy Freymond. 2006. "Understanding International Comparisons of Child Protection, Family Service, and Community Care Systems in Child and Family Welfare." In *Towards Positive Systems of Child and Family Welfare: International Comparisons of Child Protection, Family Service and Community Care*, edited by Nancy Freymond and Gary Cameron, pp. 3–26. Toronto, Canada: University of Toronto Press.

Carson, Valerie, Stephen Hunter, Nicholas Kuzik, Casey E. Gray, Veronica J. Poitras, Jean-Philippe Chaput, Travis J. Saunders, Peter T. Katzmarzyk, Anthony D. Okely, Sarah Conner Gorber, Michelle E. Kho, Margaret Sampson, Lee Helena, and Mark S. Tremblay. 2016. "Systematic Review of Sedentary Behaviour and Health Indicators in School-aged Children and Youth: An Update." *Applied Physiology, Nutrition and Metabolism*, 41 (6): S240–S265, doi:10.1139/apnm-2015-0630.

Devaney, Carmel, and Caroline McGregor. 2017. "Child Protection and Family Support Practice in Ireland: A Contribution to Present Debates from a Historical Perspective." *Child and Family Social Work*, 22: 1255–1263.

Faulkner, Joanne. 2011. *The Importance of Being Innocent: Why We Worry about Children*. Cambridge: Cambridge University Press.

Fotel, Trina, and Thyra Uth Thomsen. 2004. "The Surveillance of Children's Mobility." *Surveillance and Society*, 1 (4): 535–554.

Franklin, Leanne, and John Cromby. 2009. "Everyday Fear: Parenting and Childhood in a Culture of Fear." In *The Many Forms of Fear, Horror and Terror*, edited by Leanne Franklin and Ravenel Richardson, 162–174. Oxford: Inter-Disciplinary Press.

Fredrickson, Barbara L. 2001. "The Role of Positive Emotions in Positive Psychology: The Broaden-and-build Theory of Positive Emotions." *American Psychologist*, 56: 218–226.

Furedi, Frank. 2005. "Making Sense of Child Safety: Cultivating Suspicion." In *Cotton Wool Kids: Making Sense of Child Safety*, edited by Stuart Waiton and Stuart Baird, pp. 4–6. Glasgow: Generation Youth Issues.

Furedi, Frank. 2007. "The Only Thing We Have to Fear Is the 'Culture of Fear' Itself." *American Journal of Sociology*, 32: 231–234.

Fyhri, Aslak, Randi Hjorthol, Roger L. Mackett, Trine Fotel, and Marketta Kytta. 2011. "Children's Active Travel and Independent Mobility in Four Countries: Development, Social Contributing Trends and Measures." *Transport Policy*, 18 (5): 703–710.

Garland, David. 2003. "The Rise of Risk." In *Risk and Morality*, edited by Richard V. Ericson and Aaron Doyle, 48–86. Toronto, Canada: University of Toronto Press.

Garlen, Julie C. 2019. "Interrogating Innocence: 'Childhood' as Exclusionary Social Practice." *Childhood*, 26 (1): 54–67.

Giddens, Anthony. 1991. *Modernity and Self-Identity*. Stanford, CA: Stanford University Press.

Giddens, Anthony. 1999. "Risk and Responsibility." *The Modern Law Review*, 62 (1): 1–10.

Gilbert, Neil. 1997. *Combatting Child Abuse: International Perspectives and Trends*. New York, NY: Oxford University Press.

Gilbert, Neil, Nigel Parton, and Marit Skivenes. (Eds.). 2011. *Child Protection Systems: International Trends and Orientations*. New York, NY: Oxford University Press.

Gill, Tim. 2007. *No Fear: Growing Up in a Risk Averse Society*. London: Calouste Gulbenkian Foundation.

Ginsburg, Kenneth R. 2007. "The Importance of Play in Promoting Healthy Child Development and Maintaining Strong Parent–Child Bonds." *Pediatrics*, 119: 182–188.

Her Majesty's Government. 2018. *Working Together to Safeguard Children a Guide to Inter-Agency Working to Safeguard and Promote the Welfare of Children*. London: Department for Education.

Hoffman, Diane M. 2010. "Risky Investments: Parenting and the Production of the 'Resilient Child'." *Health Risk and Society*, 12: 385–394.

Hughes, Bob. 2003. "Play Deprivation, Play Bias and Playwork Practice." In *Playwork Theory and Practice*, edited by Fraser Brown, 66–80. Milton Keynes: Open University Press.

Jack, Gordon, and Owen Gill. 2010. "The Role of Communities in Safeguarding Children and Young People." *Child Abuse Review*, 19: 82–96, doi:10.1002/car.1077.

Lansdown, Gerison. 1994. "Children's Rights." In *Children's Childhoods: Observed and Experienced*, edited by Berry Mayall, 33–44. London: Falmer Press.

Léveillé, Sophie, and Claire Chamberland. 2010. "Toward a General Model for Child Welfare and Protection Services: A Meta-Evaluation of International Experiences regarding the Adoption of the Framework for the Assessment of Children in Need and Their Families (FACNF)." *Children and Youth Services Review*, 32 (7): 929–944.

Little, Helen. 2010. "Relationship between Parents' Beliefs and Their Responses to Children's Risk-Taking Behaviour during Outdoor Play." *Journal of Early Childhood Research*, 8 (3): 315–330.

Louv, Richard. 2005. *Last Child in the Woods: Saving Our Children from Nature-Deficit Disorder*. Chapel Hill, NC: Algonquin Books of Chapel Hill.

Meyer, Anneke. 2007. "The Moral Rhetoric of Childhood." *Childhood*, 14 (1): 85–104.

Munro, Eileen. 2011. *The Munro Review of Child Protection: Final Report. A Child-Centred System.* London: Department for Education.

Nikiforidou, Zoi. 2017. "The Cotton Wool Child." In *Childhood Today*, edited by Alex Owen, pp. 11–22. London: Sage Publications.

Office for the United Nations High Commissioner for Human Rights (OHCHR). 1989. "United Nations Convention on the Rights of the Child." www.ohchr.org/en/professionalinterest/pages/crc.aspx

Parton, Nigel. 2011. "Child Protection and Safeguarding in England: Changing and Competing Conceptions of Risk and Their Implications for Social Work." *British Journal of Social Work*, 41 (5): 854–875.

Pellegrini, Anthony D. 2009. "Research and Policy on Children's Play." *Child Development Perspectives*, 3 (2): 131–136, doi:10.1111/j.1750-8606.2009.00092.x.

Piper, Heather. 2014. "Touch, Fear, and Child Protection – Immoral Panic and Crusade." *Power and Education*, 6: 229–240.

Riggio, Eliana. 2002. "Child Friendly Cities: Good Governance in the Best Interests of the Child." *Environment and Urbanization*, 14 (2): 45–58, doi:10.1177/095624780201400204.

Sandseter, Ellen Beate Hansen. 2010. "'It Tickles in My Tummy!' Understanding Children's Risk Taking in Play through Reversal Theory." *Journal of Early Childhood Research*, 8 (1): 67–88, doi:10.1177/1476718X09345393.

Sandseter, Ellen Beate Hansen, and Leif Edward Ottesen Kennair. 2011. "Children's Risky Play from an Evolutionary Perspective: The Anti-phobic Effects of Thrilling Experiences." *Evolutionary Psychology*, 9: 257–284.

Slovic, Paul, Melissa Finucane, Ellen Peters, and Donald MacGregor. 2004. "Risk as Analysis and Risk as Feelings: Some Thoughts about Affect, Reason, Risk, and Rationality." *Risk Analysis*, 24 (2): 311–322.

Svevo-Cianci, Kimberley A., Stuart N. Hart, and Claude Rubinson. 2010. "Protecting Children from Violence and Maltreatment: A Qualitative Comparative Analysis Assessing the Implementation of U. N. CRC Article 19." *Child Abuse and Neglect: The International Journal*, 34 (1): 45–56.

Thompson, Sarah. 2005. "Risky Play." In *Cotton Wool Kids: Making Sense of Child Safety*, edited by Stuart Waiton and Stuart Baird, p. 12. Glasgow: Generation Youth Issues.

Tovey, Helen. 2011. "Achieving the Balance: Challenge, Risk and Safety." In *Outdoor Provision in the Early Years*, edited by Jan White, 86–94. London: Sage Publications.

Uyan-Semerci, Pinar, Emre Erdoğan, Basak Akkan, Serra Müderrisoğlu, and Abdullah Karatay. 2017. "Contextualizing Subjective Well-being of Children in Different Domains: Does Higher Safety Provide Higher Subjective Well-being for Child Citizens?" *Children and Youth Services Review*, 80: 52–62.

Vyvey, Eline, Rudi Roose, Liselot De Wilde, and Griet Roets. 2014. "Dealing with Risk in Child and Family Social Work: From an Anxious to a Reflexive Professional?" *Social Sciences*, 3: 758–770, doi:10.3390/socsci3040758.

Wimmer, Jeffrey, and Thorsten Quandt. 2006. "Living in the Risk Society: An Interview with Ulrich Beck." *Journalism Studies*, 7 (2): 336–347, doi:10.1080/14616700600645461.

Wolff, Jonathan. 2006. "Risk, Fear, Blame, Shame and the Regulation of Public Safety." *Economics and Philosophy*, 22: 409–427, doi:10.1017/S0266267106001040.

Woolley, Helen, and Alison Lowe. 2013. "Exploring the Relationship between Design Approach and Play Value of Outdoor Play Spaces." *Landscape Research*, 38: 53–74.

Wulczyn, Fred, Deborah Daro, John Fluke, Sara Feldman, Christin Glodek, and Kate Lifanda. 2010. *Adapting a Systems Approach to Child Protection: Key Concepts and Considerations.* New York, NY: UNICEF.

Wyver, Shirley, Paul Tranter, Geraldine Naughton, Helen Little, Ellen Beate Hansen Sandseter, and Anita Bundy. 2010. "Ten Ways to Restrict Children's Freedom to Play: The Problem of Surplus Safety." *Contemporary Issues in Early Childhood*, 11 (3): 263–277.

10

THE (IN)VISIBILITY OF INFANTS AND YOUNG CHILDREN IN CHILD PROTECTION

Eunice Lumsden

Introduction

This chapter is concerned with the inherent challenges of child protection (CP) in early childhood (conception to the age of 8) that can render the 'voices' of infants and young children invisible to others. Even when they are heard, they are not always listened to, or acted upon, by protection services. While there have been substantial improvements globally since the United Nations Convention on the Rights of the Child (UNCRC) was introduced (United Nations (UN), 1989), our youngest global citizens continue to face adversity. Their everyday lives, well-being and lifetime outcomes continue to be affected by physical, emotional and sexual violence and neglect. However, protecting children globally is complex, with legislation, policy and procedures specific to each country. This chapter critiques these global challenges, with specific focus on the English CP system. England is one of four countries comprising the United Kingdom (UK) and has been chosen because it has a well-developed CP system, yet even when children are 'visible' in legislation, policy and procedures in England, they can be 'invisible', exemplified in this chapter by the case study of Daniel Pelka.

In this chapter, I argue that 30 years after the UNCRC was adopted, the lived experiences of infants and young children suggest we can and must do better in addressing their rights to protection. The chapter draws on UNCRC Articles 19 and 39 (UN, 1989), which focus specifically on the protection of children and ensuring that intervention services are available to those who have faced adversity. These articles are strengthened and amplified by General Comments 8 and 13 (United Nations Committee on the Rights of the Child (UNCRC), 2006, 2011). However, these articles cannot be seen in isolation from global policy initiatives. Discussion also focuses on children's rights to protection, what they need to be protected from, exploration of the prevalence of abuse, and why intervening in the early childhood period is crucial for improving long-term outcomes. There will be consideration of how CP procedures facilitate (or not) the rights of the youngest citizens to be protected by their parents or caregivers, as well as the other adults and environments they interact with. The chapter starts by introducing you to the case of Daniel Pelka, who died in England of abuse and starvation in 2012 aged 4 years and 8 months (Table 10.1).

Table 10.1 Case study of Daniel Pelka, with Articles 19 and 39 (UN, 1989)

Article 19

States Parties shall take all appropriate legislative, administrative, social and educational measures to protect the child from all forms of physical or mental violence, injury or abuse, neglect or negligent treatment, maltreatment or exploitation, including sexual abuse, while in the care of parent(s), legal guardian(s) or any other person who has the care of the child.Such protective measures should, as appropriate, include effective procedures for the establishment of social programmes to provide necessary support for the child and for those who have the care of the child, as well as for other forms of prevention and for identification, reporting, referral, investigation, treatment and follow-up of instances of child maltreatment described heretofore, and, as appropriate, for judicial involvement.

(UNICEF, 1989, p. 7)

Article 39

States Parties shall take all appropriate measures to promote physical and psychological recovery and social reintegration of a child victim of: any form of neglect, exploitation, or abuse; torture or any other form of cruel, inhuman or degrading treatment or punishment; or armed conflicts. Such recovery and reintegration shall take place in an environment which fosters the health, self-respect and dignity of the child.

(UNICEF, 1989, p. 11)

Case study

Daniel Pelka
Born: 15 July 2007
Died: 3 March 2012 aged 4 years 8 months

Family information
Daniel's mother came to live in England from Poland in 2005 and had several different partners. He was the middle of three children; his elder sibling was 7 years old and the other was 1 year old at the time of his death.

Cause of death
The Serious Case Review (Coventry Local Safeguarding Children Board, 2013) stated that:

> The circumstances of Daniel's death suggested that he had been suffering abuse and neglect over a prolonged period. He was found to be malnourished at the time of his death and also had an acute subdural haematoma1 to the right side of his head, as well as other bruises on his body. The subsequent pathological examination also identified older mild subdural haematoma of several months or years duration.
>
> (p. 3)

His mother and stepfather were convicted of his murder in August 2013, and his short life is a profound example of how infants and young children can be 'invisible' even when they are 'visible' to health and education professionals, social services and the police. In fact, the police had responded

(Continued)

Table 10.1 (Cont).

___

to 27 domestic abuse reports. The inquiry into his death found that Daniel had lived in adverse circumstances typified by alcohol abuse and domestic violence, and his mother and stepfather had starved, assaulted, neglected and abused him (Coventry Local Safeguarding Children Board, 2013). Furthermore, a child protection inquiry following a broken arm, where abuse was suspected but there was no medical evidence, was closed as no further involvement was believed necessary.

When he started school, he had limited English, his attendance was erratic, and he was always hungry and scavenged rubbish bins for food. He also had bruises and other marks, but safeguarding procedures were not followed. The inquiry suggested that he was 'invisible' as a child in need because of his language skills and mother's controlling behaviour. They also recorded following missed opportunities:

> at the time of his broken arm in January 2011, which was too readily accepted by professionals as accidentally caused, when the school began to see a pattern of injuries and marks on Daniel during the four months prior to his death, and these were not acted upon, and at the paediatric appointment in February 2012 when Daniel's weight loss was not recognised, and child abuse was not considered as a likely differential diagnosis for Daniel's presenting problems.
>
> (Coventry Local Safeguarding Children Board, 2013, p. 6)

This brief outline of the circumstances in which Daniel died captures the essence of this chapter; that young children may have rights to be protected, but even in societies where there are robust procedures in place, there are real barriers that prevent the professionals involved in families acting on what they actually see, rather than accepting the explanations provided by the caregivers.

___

Protection rights

UNCRC Articles 19 and 39 (UN, 1989) focus on the rights of children to have safe caregivers and environments that meet their physical and emotional needs and provide appropriate interventions if they experience maltreatment (Table 10.1). Although these articles underpin this chapter, they are intertwined with other UNCRC articles and global policy. For example, there is a global campaign to eradicate violence against children (Lenzer, 2018) and a commitment to provide all children with the best possible start to life has permeated the Millennium Development Goals (MDGs) (United Nations (UN), 2000) and the Sustainable Development Goals (SDGs) (United Nations (UN), 2015). SDGs 5 and 16 call for an end to violence against women and children by 2030.

While the UNCRC aspirations and development plans are laudable, achieving them globally is challenging and may remain a work in progress. Violence against women, children and young people occurs in every society (United Nations Children's Fund (UNICEF), 2017). Increasing refugee and migrant movement as a result of conflict, natural disasters and open borders presents further protection issues, including 'lack of access to services, detention and family separation' (United Nations Children's Fund (UNICEF), 2018, p. 6). The wider issues that present protection issues lead to violence being embedded into the structure of societies; Galtung (1969) refers to them as 'structural violence' (p. 171). This situation is then manifested through inequalities of life chances and power at macro and micro levels, in different societies and by global organisations. To secure visibility of infants and young children and ensure their voices are heard requires proactive action at every stratum of society. Daniel Pelka's case exemplifies this issue. His mother was a migrant from Poland to England. Despite well-established CP systems in England, and professionals from a range of services being actively engaged with his family, Daniel Pelka was invisible and was not heard and was not protected (Table 10.1).

The urgent need for action to end structural and localised violence is reinforced further by neurodevelopmental and epigenetic research that reinforces how the impact of adversity in early childhood can last for life (Burke Harris, 2018; Black et al., 2017; Center of the Developing Child, 2016; Shonkoff and Garner, 2012). Violence not only has an immediate effect on well-being, but also has intergenerational consequences (United Nations Children's Fund (UNICEF), 2006). Young children require enhanced levels of protection because of their vulnerability, and governments that have ratified the UNCRC have a responsibility to protect and safeguard them (UN, 1989; UNCRC, 2006, 2011). These international direct-ives are especially important in early childhood when our youngest citizens are most vulner-able to adverse experiences impacting on their holistic development. However, protection issues in early childhood can often go undetected, especially as most abuse takes place in the home environment and infants and young children are reliant on adults around them. More-over, while the UNCRC clearly identifies that children have the right to be heard (UN, 1989, Article 12), the world's youngest citizens are either preverbal, do not have the lan-guage to explain what is happening to them, or indeed know that it is wrong. Even before birth, the developing fetus can be impacted upon by the experiences of its mother (Wave Trust, 2013), and the case of Daniel Pelka illustrates this point (Table 10.1).

CP concerns can be identified by other family members, practitioners and professionals who may be engaged with the family. However, if infants and young children are not seen consistently outside the family context, their situation will remain invisible to services that could protect them. Even when CP issues are identified, intervening in family life and pro-viding appropriate support and protection services is complex and challenging. In England, for example, where abuse is recognised and protection procedures have been activated, ser-ious case reviews publishing the results of inquiries into cases where children have died or there has been serious abuse have evidenced that children can and do become invisible to the professionals involved (Sidebotham et al., 2016) (Table 10.1). A range of factors affect the extent to which infants and young children are visible, including different political view-points about the role of the state in family life (Parton and Reid, 2014), cultural and reli-gious beliefs (Tedam and Adjoa, 2017), and different perceptions about how children should be disciplined (Banahene Adjei and Minka, 2018). These issues are discussed further later in the chapter.

Prevalence of violence against infants and young children

Across the world, infants and young children usually reside with their families. The family home should be a place of safety for infants and young children where they are nurtured and cared for as they develop from dependency to independence. Babies need reliable, nurt-uring caregivers to develop secure attachments; initially, this is usually their mother, though others can fulfil this role (Center on the Developing Child, 2017). Attachment is a popular area of research, and assessing attachment patterns requires an interdisciplinary approach (Balbernie, 2013; Lumsden, 2018). Secure attachment occurs when primary caregivers understand and respond appropriately to cues given by the baby. Usually, attachment behav-iours are triggered when the baby is distressed because they feel threatened or anxious and are not comforted successfully. Some caregivers are unable to respond, and in some situations the safe, nurturing family environment is a place of adversity, where babies and young children are harmed physically, emotionally, sexually or through neglect by adults who are meant to care for them. As Landers, Paula and Kibane (2013) observe, 'The first year is the single most dangerous period in a child's life with respect to the risks to survival, not only from infectious disease but also due to abuse and neglect' (p. 244). Moreover, the risks remain high for the first five years of life.

The private nature of the family home means that babies and young children's protection needs can remain invisible to CP services and their holistic development can be negatively impacted by violence in their environments and directed towards them. Some babies and young children live in volatile family environments that reflect the 'toxic three' of drugs, alcohol and violence (Bellis, Lowey, Leckenby, Hughes and Harrison, 2014; Children's Commissioner, 2018). Some young children's experiences of adversity and abuse are not only within the family. Schools, church and other organisations and institutions they attend, including early childhood settings, can be places where they experience harm perpetrated by adults, other children and young people, including their siblings (Department for Education (DfE), 2018; World Health Organization (WHO), 2006).

War and conflict also bring new risks from which infants and young children need protection, as well as the need for services that foster their recovery from traumatic experiences (UNICEF, 2018; WHO 2006, 2018). When our youngest global citizens experience violence, they are positioned as victims, not rights-holders, and if they survive the conflict, they will carry the impact of their experiences to future generations (Wagner et al., 2018). However, regardless of the focus on children's rights and the need for protection and support services, 30 years and more after the UNCRC was adopted, it is difficult to obtain exact data about the lived experiences of children globally (UNICEF, 2017). Furthermore, despite thousands of early interventions, detection and treatment, there are insufficient 'evidence-based solutions for CP' (Svevo-Cianci, Herczog, Krappmann and Cook, 2011, p. 979). In its presentation of contemporary data about the prevalence of violence experienced by children across the World, UNICEF (2017) reveals that even with Articles 19 and 39 and General Comments 8 and 13, only 60 countries have instigated 'full legal protection from corporal punishment in the home' (p.2 1) and very few countries have banned smacking children. UNICEF's (2017) findings reinforce the work of WHO (2006) and the British Medical Association (BMA) (2013), suggesting that CP is a serious social, legal and human rights issue that requires a public health approach. This position is reinforced by the research into adverse childhood experiences (ACEs) considered later in the chapter.

Drawing on data from 30 countries, the UNICEF (2017) report identifies that almost 50 per cent of 12–23-month-old children are exposed to corporal punishment or verbal abuse, and that:

> Three-quarters of children aged 2–4 worldwide – close to 300 million – are regularly subjected to violent discipline ... by their parents or other caregivers at home, and around 6 in 10 (250 million) are subjected to physical punishment ... Worldwide 1 in 4 children (176 million) live with a mother who has been a victim of intimate partner violence.
>
> *(p. 7)*

Such abuse in childhood can have lifelong implications (Burke Harris, 2018; Lyons-Ruth et al., 2017).

Obtaining data about abuse in any country can be hindered by the barriers to detecting abuse. In England, for example, which has a long history of implementing legislation and policy to protect children, the National Society for the Prevention of Cruelty to Children

(NSPCC) suggest the number of children in need of protection is eight times the number that are known about (Bentley et al., 2016; Harker et al., 2013). Bentley et al. (2016) identify the challenges in recording information and processes of how information is recorded. They also highlight the lack of the children's 'voice' about their perceptions of how safe they feel. Nevertheless, most children in England who need intervention and protection services rightly remain in their families. Only a small percentage of children are removed permanently through a court order and placed in adoptive families (Lumsden, 2018). This situation is mirrored globally, reinforcing the importance of a strengths approach to engaging with families and providing appropriate support services that foster proactive factors to reduce violence against children in the family. These factors include stable caring relationships, knowledge of the parenting tasks and how children develop, parental resilience, support for parents, and social networks (Landers et al., 2013).

Defining child abuse

The global definition of what constitutes situations when a child may need protection is outlined in General Comment 8 and was reaffirmed and strengthened in General Comment 13 (UNCRC, 2006, 2011), which emphasises that violence against children is not acceptable and is preventable (Table 10.2).

Table 10.2 Definitions

Definitions
Internationally, the CRC and subsequent General Comments and reports have defined what children need protection from, both within families and other institutions. As society progresses at a pace, definitions have been expanded to incorporate new forms of abuse, such as those presented by the growth of social media and sexual exploitation, as well as addressing the broader issues of protection and intervention. General Comment 8 states that:

> The Committee defines 'corporal' or 'physical' punishment as any punishment in which physical force is used and intended to cause some degree of pain or discomfort, however light. Most involves hitting ('smacking', 'slapping', 'spanking') children, with the hand or with an implement – a whip, stick, belt, shoe, wooden spoon, etc. But it can also involve, for example, kicking, shaking or throwing children, scratching, pinching, biting, pulling hair or boxing ears, forcing children to stay in uncomfortable positions, burning, scalding or forced ingestion (for example, washing children's mouths out with soap or forcing them to swallow hot spices). In the view of the Committee, corporal punishment is invariably degrading. In addition, there are other non-physical forms of punishment that are also cruel and degrading and thus incompatible with the Convention. These include, for example, a punishment which belittles, humiliates, denigrates, scapegoats, threatens, scares or ridicules the child.

(United Nations, 2008, p. 19)

UNICEF (2017) provides the following definitions of what constitutes particular areas of abuse:

(Continued)

Table 10.2 (Cont).

Physical punishment: Shaking, hitting or slapping a child on the hand/arm/leg, hitting on the bottom or elsewhere on the body with a hard object, spanking or hitting on the bottom with a bare hand, hitting or slapping on the face, head or ears, and hitting or beating hard and repeatedly.

Severe physical punishment: Hitting or slapping a child on the face, head or ears, and hitting or beating a child hard and repeatedly.

Psychological aggression: Shouting, yelling or screaming at a child, as well as calling a child offensive names such as 'dumb' or 'lazy'.

Violent discipline: Any physical punishment and/or psychological aggression.

(p.20)

The international definitions inform national CP legal and policy frameworks; however, this is not implemented in a uniform way. Countries take different approaches that are influenced by political ideologies and interpretations of the rights of the child (Moss, 2018; Svevo-Cianci, Herczog, Krappmann and Cook, 2011). In the UK, for example, all four nations approach CP differently. Scotland and Northern Ireland have different legislation, statutory guidance and policies, and while England and Wales share the same legislation, their statutory guidance and procedures differ. The document for England (DfE, 2018) provides guidance about professional roles and procedures and is updated regularly, outlining how the state defines abusive situations and how agencies and professionals should work together to protect children, as well as the process for early intervention.

Definitions of child abuse used in England change as English society evolves. They have recently been broadened to include sexual exploitation, Internet abuse and the impact of domestic violence. In England, however, safeguarding is seen consistently as 'everyone's business' (Department for Education (DfE), 2015) and 'safeguarding and promoting the welfare of children' is adopted as the umbrella term embracing:

- protecting children from maltreatment;
- preventing impairment of children's health or development;
- ensuring that children are growing up in circumstances consistent with the provision of safe and effective care; and
- taking action to enable all children to have the best life chances.

(DfE, 2018, p. 103)

However, despite clear, shared definitions of what children need protection from, identifying, intervening and supporting families is complex. Sometimes this complexity leads to the centrality of the child in the CP process being lost and their 'voice' going unheard. Even in countries that actively address CP, where infants and young children are visible to services, challenges of prevention, detection and intervention mean their individual experiences of adversity remain invisible. At a time of austerity, this situation is heightened (Kelly, Lee, Sibieta and Waters, 2018). For example, in England, the case study of Daniel Pelka and other serious case reviews have continually found that lack of professional communication and information-sharing contributes to child deaths because of abuse (Sidebotham et al.,

2016), despite clear guidance for how agencies should work together (DfE, 2018). Enquires into CP issues concerning sexual abuse in early childhood settings in England have also found that poor leadership and management, lack of safeguarding training, poor qualification levels, and blurred boundaries between staff and parents were contributing factors (Plymouth Safeguarding Children's Board, 2010; Wonnacott, 2013).

Variations in how countries view their role in intervening in family life are not static and are influenced by the ruling political party's ideologies (Parton and Reid, 2014). These differences have become more visible in contexts where numbers of migrants and refugees have increased. Migrants and refugees bring both benefits and challenges to the societies they join in relation to child-rearing practices and diverse views about what constitutes appropriate discipline for children. This can lead to challenges for CP and support services as, following migration, what may have been acceptable parental behaviour in their home country is not in their new country, such as physical punishment (Africans Unite Against Child Abuse (AFRUCA), 2012, p. 4). Furthermore, some migrant families may also face problems in their new countries that are factors that can lead to child abuse, including poverty, poor housing, social exclusion, unemployment and low pay (BMA, 2013).

While child abuse is a global issue, most of the research into child abuse has been conducted in affluent societies (Landers et al., 2013). If research into violence against children is to deepen our understanding about its multiple causal factors, it must explore cultural contexts and acknowledge the previous experiences of families and different parenting styles (Barn and Kirton, 2016). Since black children appear overrepresented in care systems in Western countries, these issues are pertinent in respect of the UNCRC and the child's visibility in CP systems. Banahene Adjei and Minka (2018) suggest that perceptions of parenting styles during investigations may have contributed to the high percentage of black children in the Canadian child welfare system. Similarly, in the UK, reporting of physical abuse of black children is higher than for children from white or mixed cultural backgrounds, and they are overrepresented in serious case reviews (Barn and Kirton, 2016).

Understanding parenting styles and what may influence them is reinforced by Tedam and Adjoa (2017) in their exploration of witchcraft, which raises questions about how societies intellectualise issues concerning parenting in migrant families, including 'faith and beliefs, as well as family dynamics' (p. 3). For many communities across the world, faith and belief are strong components of family life, and the situation for black children in the UK is complicated further by the fact that child abuse occurs 'in a societal context that stigmatises their identities, marginalises their experiences, and fosters a racialised deficit perspective on their families' (Bernard and Harris, 2016, p. 271).

These factors can contribute to CP decision-making processes being complex and challenging, though this need not be the case. Clarification guidance from the United Nations (UN) (2008) indicates clearly that across the world, however difficult the parenting task, there is a distinction between 'punitive' and 'non-punitive' interventions with children. Children should not experience 'deliberate and punitive use of force to cause some degree of pain, discomfort or humiliation' (UN, 2008, p. 25). In other words, our youngest citizens' boundaries should enable them to flourish and develop resilience rather than increase their vulnerability through neglect and/or physical, emotional or sexual abuse.

Consequences of abuse

Evidence about the personal and economic impact of abuse reinforces the importance of a child's right to protection. The early childhood period, especially 'from conception to two years' (Norman, 2019; Wave Trust, 2013), is a period of exceptional, physical, emotional and brain development. The impact of abuse, neglect or adverse environments is well documented (Burke Harris, 2018; Center on the Developing Child, 2016; Wave Trust, 2018). However, those working in CP with children, young people and adults have always known that adverse experiences can impact negatively, and the intergenerational cycle of disadvantage is difficult to break. For example, in England, Pringle and Naidoo (1975) called for action to break the 'vicious cycle of the emotionally and intellectually deprived children of today becoming tomorrow's parents of yet another generation of deprived children' (p. 169). They were writing nearly 45 years ago, before the UNCRC was published (UN, 1989) and before the Children Act 1989 (Department of Health (DoH), 1989) came into force in England to shift parents' rights over their children to responsibilities. The UNCRC (UN, 1989) and the Children Act (DoH, 1989) made children rights-holders whose individual needs were paramount in decision-making processes affecting them.

Decades later, ongoing research in neuroscience and molecular biology are shedding greater light on to child development, especially how the brain develops and responds to environmental factors. Stress experienced by living in adverse, toxic environments impacts negatively on the development of resilience: although some level of stress is needed to develop resilience, prolonged, unpredictable and severe exposure promotes vulnerability that can lead to long term physical and mental health problems (Perry and Szalavitz, 2017; Wave Trust, 2018). Recent research into epigenetics provides valuable new insights into childhood adversity leaving a biological, lifelong impact and how this can be mediated (Champagne, 2018). This deeper understanding reinforces the vital role of prevention: if infants and young children are to be visible and their UNCRC rights upheld, parental support and appropriate family services that facilitate protective behaviours need to be prioritised. This must be done in conjunction with policies that address the structural inequalities that perpetuate the role of social injustice, identified by Galtung (1969), that lead to violence and the abuse of power at all levels of society.

Making the invisible visible

Ensuring the visibility of infants and young children is not just about the violence directed towards them. It is also about the structural inequality and the power imbalances of the societies they live in and the wider adversity they experience, even before they are born. CP not only relies on legislation, policy and procedures, but on ensuring those working alongside children and families have appropriate knowledge, skills, attributes and the continual desire for professional development. The case study of Daniel Pelka (Table 10.1) raises challenging issues about the role of services involved with families and barriers that prevent CP and render specific children invisible in complex family situations. In his short life, there were numerous opportunities when intervention could have led to less tragic outcomes for this family.

Working to combat adversity is challenging, personally and professionally. Not only is direct work with children and families complex, but so also is the task of addressing incongruity that often exists between political rhetoric, policy development, research evidence and services for families. For example, in England, at the start of the new millennium, following consultation with children, government recognised in law and policy that 'Every Child Matters' and adopted an integrated approach to working with children and families (Department for Education and Skills (DfES), 2004a, 2004b). In 2010, the new coalition government between the Conservative and Liberal Democrat political parties made sweeping changes and removed the language of 'Every Child Matters' from common usage

(Fitzgerald, Kay and Baldock, 2016). Although early childhood has continued to be a focus of policy development in England, since 2010 the context has been a very different policy direction. While children helped to develop the 'Every Child Matters' agenda, in accordance with UNCRC Article 12 (UN, 1989), they were not consulted about its removal, so their voices were rendered invisible.

Participation by our youngest citizens involves us listening to their non-verbal as well as verbal communication. Those who work alongside them need to be 'safe practitioners' who understand their role in supporting young children and their parents, as well as the importance of ongoing training in CP that provides a confident workforce (Lumsden, 2018; Norman, 2019). Those working in the early childhood education and care (ECEC) sector also need a strengths approach to young children's holistic development. They cannot be responsible for the home environments of those in their care, but they are responsible for the environments they provide. This includes the quality and training of staff, how they listen to and promote the voice of the child, and how they ensure young children's participation in the services they are using.

Parents, family and community need to be proactively nurtured through policy, procedures and practice, and there are examples across the globe where parenting programmes are making a difference (Landers et al., 2013). Parents and caregivers need to be enabled in their role, with services to enhance their parenting skills and practitioners and professionals who have the appropriate knowledge, skills and qualifications to support them. If infants and young children are to become more visible, parents and those working with them need to understand the intergenerational consequences and structural influences that perpetuate the need to protect them from violence and exploitation.

Conclusion

This chapter has addressed issues that suggest that we can and must do better in addressing the rights to protection of infants and young children, decades on from the adoption of the UNCRC (UN, 1989). As UNICEF (2018) and WHO (2018) have reported, millions of infants are born into adverse environments globally. Not only are infants and young children abused within their families, but ongoing global violence and structural inequalities create toxic environments that adversely affect their immediate and lifelong development. Adverse childhood experiences have lifelong and intergenerational consequences not only for the individual, but for society (Burke Harris, 2018). We also have global jurisprudence and political rhetoric about the importance of the early childhood period and the vital role of protection services (Leadsom, Field, Burstow and Lucas, 2013; Wave Trust, 2013). However, although almost every country has ratified the UNCRC (UN, 1989), we still do have a sustained global approach that has placed children's rights at the centre of all we do. At every milestone since 1989, the same issues about the importance of ending violence against the youngest global citizens have been addressed. Yet while the experiences of some are visible, the work of UNICEF (2017) and the case study of Daniel Pelka reinforce much that is unknown about the violence experienced by infants and young children: they are often invisible.

This chapter therefore ends with more questions than answers about how we can protect children effectively from violence and its lifelong consequences at every level of society. Millions of infants and young children continue to live with structural inequality and violence. They are neglected and physically, emotionally and sexually abused by their parents, caregivers or in institutions they attend. Thousands die each year as a result or are impaired for life. The violence they experience often occurs in the privacy of their home environments, places where they should be safe and receive nurturing care. Solutions at a political level are possible, if policies for children and families are developed across political divides and funding is allocated for longer than specific financial cycles. Sustained services for families are vital for providing a highly trained, ambitious and tenacious workforce that is maintained even in times of austerity. Infants and young children are rights-holders and should be protected from abuse and need access to services that enhance the quality of their lives. Up to this point, many of their 'voices' have remained invisible at every level of society.

References

Africans Unite Against Child Abuse (AFRUCA). 2012. *What Is Physical Abuse?* London: AFRUCA.

Balbernie, Robin. 2013. "The Importance of Secure Attachment for Infant Mental Health." *Journal of Health Visiting*, 1: 210–217. doi: 10.12968/johv.2013.1.4.210

Banahene Adjei, Paul and Eric Minka. 2018. "Black Parents ask for a Second Look: Parenting under 'White' CP Rules in Canada." *Children and Youth Services Review*, 94: 511–524. doi: 10.1016/j.childyouth.2018.08.030

Barn, Ravinder and Derek Kirton. 2016. "Safeguarding Black Children." In *Safeguarding Black Children: Good Practice in Child Protection*, edited by Claudia Bernard and Perlita Harris, 111–127. London: Jessica Kingsley.

Bellis, A. Mark, Helen Lowey, Nicola Leckenby, Karen Hughes, and Dominic Harrison. 2014. "Adverse Childhood Experiences: Retrospective Study to Determine Their Impact on Adult Health Behaviours and Health Outcomes in a UK Population." *Journal of Public Health*, 36 (1): 81–91. doi: 10.1093/pubmed/fdt038

Bentley, Holly, Andy Burrows, Laura Clarke, Abbie Gillgan, Jazmin Glen, Maria Hafizi, Fiona Letendrie, Pam Miller, Orla O'Hagan, Priya Patel, Jessica Peppiate, Kate Stanley, Emily Starr, Nikki Vasco, and Janaya Walker. 2016. *How Safe are Our Children?* London: NSPCC.

Bernard, Claudia and Perlita Harris. 2016. "Concluding Remarks." In *Safeguarding Black Children: Good Practice in Child Protection*, edited by Claudia Bernard and Perlita Harris, 271–273. London: Jessica Kingsley.

Black, Maureen, Susan Walker, Lia C.H. Fernald, Christopher Andersen, Ann Digirolamo, Li Chunling, Dana Charles Mccoy, Gunther Fink, Yusra Shawar, Jeremy Shiffman, Amanda Devercelli, Quentin Wodon, Emily Vargas Baron, and Sally Grantham-Mcgregor. 2017. "Advancing Early Childhood Development: from Science to Scale 1 Early Childhood Development Coming of Age: Science through the Life Course." *Lancet*, 389 (10064): 77–90. doi: 10.1016/S0140-6736(16)31389-7

British Medical Association Board of Science (BMA). 2013. *Growing up in the UK: Ensuring a Healthy Future for Our Children*. London: British Medical Association Board of Science.

Burke Harris, Nadine. 2018. *The Deepest Well: Healing the Long-term Effects of Childhood Adversity*. London: Bluebird.

Center on the Developing Child. 2016. *From Best Practices to Breakthrough Impacts: A Science-based Approach to Building A More Promising Future for Young Children and Families*. Cambridge, MA: Centre on the Developing Child.

Center on the Developing Child. 2017. "8 Things to Remember about Child Development." Cambridge: Centre on the Developing Child. https://developingchild.harvard.edu/resources/8-things-remember-child-development/

Champagne, Frances A. 2018. "Epigenetic and Multigenerational Impact of Adversity." In *Violence Against Children: Making Human Rights Real*, edited by Gertrud Lenzer, 193–209. Abingdon: Routledge.

Children's Commissioner. 2018. "Estimating the Number of Vulnerable Babies." London: Office of the Children's Commissioner for England. www.childrenscommissioner.gov.uk/wp-content/uploads/2018/10/Estimating-the-number-of-vulnerable-infants.pdf

Coventry Local Safeguarding Children Board. 2013. "Serious Case Review RE: Daniel Pelka." https://cscb-new.co.uk/downloads/Serious%20Case%20Reviews%20-%20exec.%20summaries/SCR_Archive/Coventry%20SCR%20-%20Daniel%20Pelka%20(2013).pdf

Department for Education (DfE). 2015. "What to Do if You're Worried a Child Is Being Abused Advice for Practitioners." London: HMSO.

Department for Education (DfE). 2018. "Working Together to Safeguard Children." https://assets.pub lishing.service.gov.uk/government/uploads/system/uploads/attachment_data/file/729914/Working_ Together_to_Safeguard_Children-2018.pdf

Department for Education and Skills (DfES). 2004a. *Children Act 2004*. London: HMSO.

Department for Education and Skills (DfES). 2004b. *Every Child Matters: Change for Children*. London: HMSO.

Department of Health (DoH). 1989. *Children Act 1989*. London: HMSO.

Fitzgerald, Damien, Janet Kay, and Peter Baldock. 2016. *Understanding Early Years Policy*. 4th ed. London: Sage Publications Ltd.

Galtung, Johan. 1969. "Violence, Peace and Peace Research." *Journal of Peace Research*, 6 (3): 167–191. doi: 10.1177/002234336900600301

Harker, Lisa, Sonja Jütte, Tom Murphy, Holly Bentley, Pam Miller, and Kate Fitch. 2013. "How Safe are Our Children?" www.nspcc.org.uk/globalassets/documents/research-reports/how-safe-children-2013-report.pdf

Kelly, Elaine, Tom Lee, Luke Sibieta, and Tom Waters. 2018. "Public Spending on Children in England Institute for Fiscal Studies." www.childrenscommissioner.gov.uk/wp-content/uploads/2018/06/Public-Spending-on-Children-in-England-CCO-JUNE-2018.pdf

Landers, Cassie, Clarice Da Silva E. Paula, and Theresa Kilbane. 2013. "Preventing Violence against Young Children." In *Handbook of Early Childhood Development Research and Its Impact on Global Policy*, edited by Pia Rebello Britto, Patrice L. Engle and Charles M. Super, 242–259. New York: Oxford Press Limited.

Leadsom, Andrea, Frank Field, Paul Burstow, and Caroline Lucas. 2013. *The 1001 Critical Days: The Importance of Conception to the Age of Two Period*. London: APPG Conception to the Age of Two.

Lenzer, Gertrud. (Ed.). 2018. *Violence Against Children: Making Human Rights Real*. Abingdon: Routledge.

Lumsden, Eunice. 2018. *Child Protection in the Early Years: A Practical Guide*. London: Jessica Kingsley Publications.

Lyons-Ruth, Karlen, Jody Todd Manly, Tuula Tamminen, Robert Emde, Hiram Fitzgerald, Campbell Paul, Miri Keren, Astrid Berg, Maree Foley, and Hisako Watanabe. 2017. "The Worldwide Burden of Infant Mental Health and Emotional Disorder Report of the Task Force of the World Association for Infant Mental Health." *Infant Mental Health Journal*, 38 (4): 1–9. doi: 10.1002/imhj.21674

Moss, Peter. 2018. *Alternative Narratives in Early Childhood: An Introduction for Students and Practitioners*. Abington: Routledge.

Norman, Amanda. 2019. *From Conception to Two Years: Development, Policy and Practice*. Abington: Routledge.

Parton, Nigel and James Reid. 2014. "The Recent History of Central Government Guidance about CP." In *Safeguarding and Protecting Children in the Early Years*, edited by James Reid and Steven Burton, 13–34. Abington: Routledge.

Perry, Bruce and Maia Szalavitz. 2017. *The Boy Who Was Raised as a Dog*. 3rd ed. New York: Basic Books.

Plymouth Safeguarding Children's Board. 2010. *Serious Case Review into the Abuse at Little Ted's Nursery*. Plymouth: Plymouth Safeguarding Children's Board.

Pringle, Mia and Sandhya Naidoo. 1975. *Early Child Care in Britain*. London: Gordon and Breach.

Shonkoff, Jack and Andrew Garner. 2012. "The Lifelong Effects of Early Childhood Adversity and Toxic Stress." *American Academy of Paediatrics*, 129: 232–246. doi: 10.1542/peds.2011-2663

Sidebotham, Peter, Marion Brandon, Sue Bailey, Pippa Belderson, Jane Dodsworth, Jo Garstang, Elizabeth Harrison, Ameeta Retzer, and Penny Sorensen. 2016. "Pathways to Harm, Pathways to Protection: A Triennial Analysis of Serious Case Reviews 2011 to 2014 Final Report." www.gov.uk/gov ernment/uploads/system/uploads/attachment_data/file/533826/Triennial_Analysis_of_SCRs_2011-2014_-__Pathways_to_harm_and_protection.pdf

Svevo-Cianci, Kimberly A., Maria Herczog, Lothar Krappmann, and Philip Cook. 2011. "The New UN C+-RC General Comment 13: "The Right of the Child to Freedom from All Forms of Violence"—Changing How the World Conceptualizes CP." *Child Abuse and Neglect*, 35 (12): 979–989. doi: 10.1016/j.chiabu.2011.09.006

Tedam, Prospera and Awura Adjoa. 2017. *The W Word: Witchcraft Labelling and Child Safeguarding in Social Work Practice*. St Albans: Critical Publishing.

United Nations (UN). 1989. *UN Convention on the Rights of the Child*. Geneva: United Nations.

United Nations (UN). 2000. "Millennium Development Goals." www.un.org/en/mdg/summit2010/pdf/List%20of%20MDGs%20English.pdf

United Nations. 2008. *Report on the Committee on the Rights of the Child*. New York: United Nations. www.iom.int/jahia/webdav/shared/shared/mainsite/policy_and_research/un/63/A_63_41.pdf

United Nations (UN). 2015. "Sustainable Development Goals." https://sustainabledevelopment.un.org/?menu=1300

United Nations Children's Fund (UNICEF) (1989). "The Uniited ~Nations Convention of Rights on the Child". https://www.unicef.org.uk/rights-respecting-schools/wp-content/uploads/sites/4/2017/01/UNCRC-in-full.pdf

United Nations Children's Fund (UNICEF). 2017. "A Familiar Face: Violence in the Lives of Children and Adolescents." www.unicef.org/publications/files/Violence_in_the_lives_of_children_and_adolescents.pdf

United Nations Children's Fund (UNICEF). 2018. "UNICEF Humanitarian Action for Children." https://unicef.at/fileadmin/media/Infos_und_Medien/Aktuelle_Studien_und_Berichte/2018/UNICEF_Humanitarian_Action_for_Children_2018_Overview_ENG.PDF

United Nations Committee on the Rights of the Child (UNCRC). 2006. "General Comment No. 8: The Right of the Child to Protection from Corporal Punishment and Other Cruel or Degrading Forms of Punishment. CRC/C/GC/8." www.refworld.org/docid/460bc7772.html

United Nations Committee on the Rights of the Child (UNCRC). 2011. "General Comment No. 13: The Right of the Child to Freedom from All Forms of Violence. CRC/C/GC/13." www.refworld.org/docid/4e6da4922.html

Wagner, Zachary, Sam Heft-Neal, Zuliqar A. Bhutta, Robert E. Black, Marshall Burke, and Eran Bendavid. 2018. "Armed Conflict and Child Mortality in Africa: A Geospatial Analysis." *The Lancet*, 392 (10150): 857–865.

Wave Trust. 2013. "Conception to the Age of 2: The Age of Opportunity." London: Wave Trust.

Wave Trust. 2018. "Age 2 to 18: Systems to Protect Children from Severe Disadvantage." London: Wave Trust.

Wonnacott, Jane. 2013. *Serious Case Review under Chapter VIII Working Together to Safeguard Children in Respect of the Serious Injury of Case No.2010-11/3*. Birmingham: Birmingham Safeguarding Children Board.

World Health Organization (WHO). 2006. "Preventing Child Maltreatment: A Guide to Taking Action and Generating Evidence." www.who.int/violence_injury_prevention

World Health Organization (WHO). 2018. "Violence against Children." www.who.int/mediacentre/factsheets/violence-against-children/en/

11

CHILDCARE AND STANDARDISATION

Threats to young children's right to education

Peter Moss

Introduction

In 2005, the United Nations Committee on the Rights of the Child published General Comment No. 7 (United Nations Committee on the Rights of the Child, 2005) as part of its ongoing role of monitoring the implementation of the United Nations Convention on the Rights of the Child (UNCRC) (UN, 1989). This seventh report by the Committee was on 'implementing child rights in early childhood', and paragraphs 28 to 32 are devoted to the subject of 'early childhood education'. A central conclusion of this review of the UNCRC is that 'the Committee interprets the right to education during early childhood as beginning at birth and closely linked to young children's right to maximum development (UNCRC Art. 6.2)' (para. 28). This is a strong claim, and one that I will explore further in this chapter, both descriptively and critically. I will also argue that the intentions of the Committee in their General Comment are at risk of being undermined by two features of early childhood services: the failure of many countries to get beyond childcare as a focus of these services and a tendency towards standardising early childhood education through imposing universal norms of performance.

The UN Committee's conclusions

Having stated that the right to education begins at birth, the Committee elaborates on this conclusion by emphasising a number of other conclusions about early childhood education. It advocates a broad approach to education, drawing on the Committee's General Comment No. 1 to define the aims of education as being to 'empower the child by developing his or her skills, learning and other capacities, human dignity, self-esteem and self-confidence' (para. 28). Governments should therefore 'ensure that all young children receive education in the broadest sense' (para. 30). The education that the Committee supports should be 'child-centred, child-friendly and reflect the rights and inherent dignity of the child' (para. 28; see also para. 29), and acknowledge a partnership between parental and public responsibilities built

120

upon the principle that 'parents (and other primary caregivers) are children's first caregivers', a principle that should be 'a starting point for planning early education' (para. 29). This means that governments, in planning early childhood education, should 'aim to provide programmes that complement the parents' role and are developed as far as possible in partnership with parents' (para. 29b), and that 'empowerment and education of parents (and other caregivers) are main features' of publicly supported early childhood programmes (para. 31). But not only should parents and the state have a key role in education; there should also be a key role for 'wider family and community' and 'the community and civil society institutions' (para. 30).

What should be provided for young children? Governments are 'encouraged to construct high-quality, developmentally appropriate and culturally relevant programmes … [avoiding] a standardized approach' (para. 31), and which recognise 'the need for a coordinated, holistic, multisectoral approach to early childhood', one that gets beyond the 'traditional divisions between "care" and "education"' (para. 30). In pursuit of this aim, governments have a major role to play by 'providing a legislative framework for the provision of quality, adequately resourced services, and for ensuring that standards are tailored to the circumstances of particular groups and individuals and to the developmental priorities of particular age groups' (para. 31). When it comes to the early childhood workforce, they should be 'provided with thorough preparation, ongoing training and adequate remuneration' (para. 32).

The General Comment's section on early childhood education ends with a section headed 'The private sector as service provider', in which the Committee recommends that governments 'support the activities of the non-governmental sector as a channel for programme implementation … [and] further calls on all non-State service providers ("for profit" as well as "non-profit" providers) to respect the principles and provisions of the Convention' (para. 32). However, the Committee emphasises, the primary responsibility for implementing the Convention resides with governments:

> the role of civil society should be complementary to – not a substitute for – the role of the State … [which has] an obligation to monitor and regulate the quality of provision to ensure that children's rights are protected and their best interests served.
>
> *(para. 32)*

Some critical reflections

The Committee's General Comment No. 7 makes a number of important points about early childhood education, starting with its recognition that the right to education begins at birth. However, the conclusions that the Committee draws are not beyond critique, and in this section I will offer some critical comments. In particular, I will draw on the words and work of the Italian educator Loris Malaguzzi (1920–1994), an important figure in the creation of the world-famous early childhood education in the Italian city of Reggio Emilia, situated 60 kilometres east of Bologna. Apart from his educational achievements, including his contribution to the creation and evolution of one of the most extensive and long-lasting example of progressive education, Malaguzzi is relevant because his pedagogical thinking was built on a belief in children's rights, a position held well before the passing of the UNCRC.

This belief was part of his image of the child, the starting point for his educational work. He argued that a 'declaration [about the image of the child] is not only a necessary act of clarity and correctness, it is the necessary premise for any pedagogical theory, and any pedagogical project' (Cagliari et al., 2016, p. 374). His declaration was explicit and clear: the image of what he termed the 'rich child':

[A] powerful image: there are rich children and poor children. We [in Reggio Emilia] say all children are rich, there are no poor children. All children whatever their culture, whatever their lives are rich, better equipped, more talented, stronger and more intelligent than we can suppose.

(p. 397)

This 'rich' child is born with a hundred languages and an avid desire to learn, to make meaning of the world. This child is an active subject, a 'protagonist', to use a term Malaguzzi frequently employed, 'active in constructing the self and knowledge through social interactions and inter-dependencies' (p. 377). Last but not least, such a child was to be seen as a citizen and 'bearer of rights', not, he insisted, a 'bearer of needs'. Pursuing this theme, he further insisted that children with disabilities should be seen as having 'special rights' rather than 'special needs', and such children received priority admission to Reggio Emilia's municipal schools from the 1960s, exemplifying the General Committee's later conclusion that 'It is a priority to ensure that they [young children with disabilities] have equal opportunities to participate fully in education' (para. 36d).

Malaguzzi was at one with the General Committee in his view that a fundamental right of young children was 'to education during early childhood', given expression in the network of municipal schools for young children, from a few months of age up to 6 years, opened by the *commune* of Reggio Emilia from the early 1960s onwards. The rationale for these schools was rooted in the explicit image of the rich child, a born learner and meaning-maker, a child full of potential that could so easily be wasted if not nurtured, a potential that was unknowable and unpredictable, a source of constant wonder and surprise: 'every other week, every other fortnight, every month, something unexpected, something that surprised us or made us marvel, something that disappointed us, something that humiliated us, would burst out in a child or in the children' (Cagliari et al., 2016, p. 392).

However, Malaguzzi, especially as he got older, eschewed the language of development, which is widely used by the Committee in its General Comment, seeing in 'development' and the idea of developmental stages a means of governing the child. Speaking in 1991, Malaguzzi said that:

now we come to the problem of stages. Let us take them and throw them out of the window. Perhaps we do not have time to speak ill of stages today, but there are several aspects here to convince us that breaking flow into stages means submitting to the rules of the municipal police. But we will not be subjected. We [want to] create the kind of encounter that is continuous in a way, and yet also highly discontinuous, and discontinuing of its own accord.

(Cagliari et al., 2016, p. 409)

Malaguzzi is not alone in questioning the discourse of child development, and its potential regulatory role; such critiques have developed since the 1980s (e.g. see the discussion in Dahlberg, Moss and Pence, 2013). Of course, others would refute these criticisms and adopt a developmental perspective and 'developmentally appropriate practice'. So, while the Committee can legitimately choose to adopt this perspective, it might also have acknowledged that this was neither self-evident nor uncontentious.

Malaguzzi shared with the Committee a strong commitment to the role of parents in children's early education and the need for the schools to create a close working partnership with them. Underpinning this commitment, providing a rationale for Reggio

Emilia's relationship with parents, was an equally strong commitment to democracy as a fundamental educational value, a concept completely missing from the Committee's General Comment. This democratic impulse found expression in the system of social management of the municipal schools, involving committees of democratically-elected parent representatives (as well as representatives of other groups such as teachers) participating in all aspects of decision-making, educational as well as administrative: families, he argued, 'must be taken from a passive position as pure consumers of a service and brought to an active, direct presence and collaboration' (Cagliari et al., 2016, p. 113), while the school:

> must be capable of living out processes and issues of participation and democracy in its inter-personal relations, in the procedures of its *progettazione* [project work] and curriculum design, in the conception and examination of its work plans, and in operations of organisational updating.
>
> *(Cagliari et al., 2016, p. 354)*

Parents, wider family and community are all important participants in early childhood education: on this, Malaguzzi and the Committee agree. But for Malaguzzi, there was another important participant: other children. From the earliest days of Reggio Emilia's educational project, Malaguzzi insisted that '[g]roups should be conceptualised not merely as an organisational and disciplinary tool but a situation that is necessary to satisfy the needs of individuals to be educated and mature' (Cagliari et al., 2016, p. 112). Education, Malaguzzi believed, was a process of co-constructing identity and knowledge, and the 'co-' part of this involved meaning-making in relationship with others, not only adults, but other children. Education, therefore, was the creation of individual understandings and subjectivity, personal identity, 'the self', yet this, so Malaguzzi thought, could only be done 'through social interactions and inter-dependencies' (Cagliari et al., 2016, p. 377). This key dimension, with the importance attached to the group of children in the process, is missing from the Committee's General Comment.

The Committee endorses a 'coordinated, holistic' approach to early childhood and questions the 'traditional divisions between "care" and "education"', which 'have not always been in the child's best interests' (para. 30). But it fails to offer a deeper analysis of the relationship between 'care' and 'education' or the meaning of truly 'integrated services'. Instead, it offers 'the concept of "educare"', a recent invention of the anglophone world, a concept with no theoretical underpinning that reflects a struggle to bring together concepts – 'education' and 'care' – that arguably should never have been divided (para. 30). I always remember a Danish colleague saying she could not understand how the anglophone world could ever have imagined that education and care were separable, an implausible idea in social pedagogy, a holistic approach informing early childhood services in Denmark, as well as other services for children and young people in many continental European countries (Cameron and Moss, 2011).

Integrated early childhood services should, I would argue, be based on 'education', with care retaining an important role but understood as a relational ethic, drawing on the work of feminist scholars in developing the concept of an 'ethic of care' (e.g. Carol Gilligan, Nel Noddings, Joan Tronto, Virginia Held, Selma Sevenhuijsen). This argument is based partly on a holistic concept of education – 'education in its broadest sense' – but also on the problems that arise when defining and identifying a service in terms of 'care' – be it 'childcare', 'day care' or 'social care'.

Typically, the meaning of 'care' in such 'care services' is rarely articulated, and becomes by default understood as a package of practical activities applied to dependent others, children or adults, and as a commodity that needs to be delivered to and paid for by customers, in the case of England's 'childcare services' meaning parents purchasing care in a private market. Not only is 'care' in this context far too narrow to ensure a holistic approach to working with children, or anyone else, but 'care' as a descriptor applied to services and workers invariably becomes synonymous with work that has low status, qualifications and pay.

For conceptualising services in terms of care is a recipe for low quality employment and low valued work. Perhaps it should not be, but in reality it is, most likely because it expresses a particular understanding of the work: as something akin to what is done 'naturally' by women in the home, especially as mothers, and as such assumed to require little in the way of education, reflection or judgement when transferred to the public arena (Cameron and Moss, 2007). Even when this quasi-maternal image shifts, with an acknowledgement of the need for a better qualified care workforce, it moves up only a notch to the image of a low skilled technician, with basic training in how to apply technologies to children consistently and without much need for thought and analysis of practice.

To say that services should not be defined or described in terms of 'care' does not mean that care is unimportant and irrelevant. Quite the reverse: 'care' is vital and highly relevant to early childhood services – and indeed to schools, universities, hospitals or virtually any other public service or institution that you care to name. But not 'care' understood simply as a commodity, as a package of activities, something done to 'poor' children or adults, who are understood to be dependent and deficient. Rather 'care' understood as an ethic that should pervade all relationships, and not just in early childhood services.

(Moss, 2018, 265)

Malaguzzi also insisted on Reggio Emilia's early childhood services having a clear educational identity. This did not mean, however, that they ignored the needs of employed parents. The municipal schools, he made clear, 'must adapt to factory hours', but this was an organisational matter, not a defining feature, a necessary but not very interesting condition for services in close relationship with families. It is inconceivable that he would have used a term such as 'educare', which seems to put 'education' and 'childcare' on an equal footing, without giving thought to the meaning of either term or their actual relationship. Would we, after all, refer to primary or secondary schools as providing 'educare' when in fact we understand them as primarily educative, while at the same time recognising that they provide safe and secure care for children (though not, in practice, always adapted to factory or office hours)?

Just as the Committee's General Comment skirts around a substantive discussion of the relationship between education and care, it refers to a 'coordinated, holistic, multisectoral approach to early childhood' without any discussion of what such an approach might imply (para. 30). To move from what the Committee refers to as the 'traditional divisions between "care" and "education" services' towards such an approach requires not only the adoption of an integrative concept (e.g. 'education in its broadest sense'), but also major structural change, across a wide range of dimensions: policy, regulation (including curriculum), access, funding, workforce and provision (Kaga, Bennett and Moss, 2010, para. 30). Globally, very few countries have achieved such change, the Nordic states being notable exceptions; the obstacles are substantial (including greatly increased costs), and a number of countries that have started the integration process (e.g. England, New Zealand, Scotland, Spain) have stalled well short of completion (for England and Scotland as examples of stalled integration, see Cohen, Moss, Petrie and Wallace, 2004, 2018).

A final observation can be offered on the Committee's reference to a 'multisectoral approach to early childhood' (para. 30). One of the Committee's stated aims is to 'contribute to the realization of rights for all young children through formulation and promotion of comprehensive policies, laws, programmes, practices, professional training and research specifically focused on rights in early childhood' (para. 2g), and it does indeed highlight a number of important policy areas besides early childhood education, including birth registration, standard of living and social security, healthcare, and the right to rest, leisure and play. Yet the Committee has nothing to say about policy measures to support parents combine employment and child upbringing, in particular leave policies, a measure that not only affects children's well-being, but which, it has been argued (Haas and Hwang, 1999), involves the right of young children to be cared for by both mothers and fathers. This is a major omission, given the large numbers of young children with employed parents, the increasing attention given in many countries to work–family policies, and the widespread failure to develop an integrated approach to leave and early childhood services (notable exceptions being, again, the Nordic countries). The result in most countries is a substantial gap between the end of well-paid maternity or parental leave and the start of an entitlement for children to attend early childhood services, a major failure in creating a 'coordinated, holistic and multisectoral approach to early childhood' (for a cross-national comparison of the relationship between leave and early childhood services, see Blum, Koslowski, Macht and Moss, 2018).

Undermining the committee's intent

The Committee's General Comment, like any document, can and should be treated critically, its concepts and assumptions deconstructed and questioned. Yet whatever the results of this necessary process, General Comment No. 7 remains an important statement of principle: that the right to education, a child's right, begins at birth; that this education should be broadly conceived, culturally relevant and avoid a standardised approach; that it should also be in partnership with parents and others; and that it should benefit from a coordinated and holistic approach. But stating and implementing are two different things, and implementation faces a number of challenges that can and do undermine the good intentions of the Committee. There are, for instance, many obstacles that impede the creation of fully integrated early childhood services, including the different traditions, cultures and perspectives of 'childcare' and 'education', deeply embedded beliefs that 'childcare' rather than education is the main requirement for very young children, and, as already noted, the extra funding involved in moving from low-cost 'childcare' (based, as these services invariably are, on a low-qualified and low-paid workforce) to an integrated system of early childhood education. The type of early childhood services that the UN Committee envisages will cost considerably more than most countries are currently prepared to lay out – nearer the 1.6 per cent of GDP spent by Sweden on its fully integrated and universal early childhood services than the 0.7 per cent that is the average for the 34 higher-income countries that are members of the Organisation for Economic Co-operation and Development (OECD, 2018a, PF3.1). But I want to look in more detail at two other obstacles to attaining the Committee's goals, both undermining the good intent of General Comment No. 7: the continuing hold of 'childcare' on early childhood services and growing pressures for a standardised approach to early childhood education.

The right to education: getting beyond 'childcare'

The UN Committee highlights the 'traditional divisions between "care" and "education" services' for young children, which militate against an integrated, coordinated and holistic approach; such divisions create, instead, early childhood services that are dysfunctional, divisive and unequal (Kaga et al., 2010). But this split also militates against young children's right to early childhood education. Most countries in the world today, even those with higher incomes and more developed early childhood services, still have split systems, divided between 'childcare' and 'early education' (Bennett, 2011). In some countries, for example Anglophone states, the former is dominant due to less developed early education services; while in other countries (e.g. Belgium, France, Italy, Spain), 'early education' is dominant, with at least three years of such provision long established.

Either way, though, the 'childcare' sector is generally treated as a targeted service for children deemed to be in need (e.g. because of some perceived family problem), or more commonly as a service for employed parents, a necessary condition for participating in employment. As such, 'childcare' is seen either as a welfare service, based on meeting eligibility conditions of need, or else primarily as a private parental responsibility. It is not considered a universal right for children. In contrast, 'early education' is viewed in this light, with children increasingly entitled to two or three years of attendance (for a fuller discussion of split systems and some of their consequences, see Kaga et al., 2010; OECD, 2001, 2006).

The contrast can be illustrated by taking two recent national experiences (Cohen et al., 2004, 2018). In Sweden, early childhood services received policy attention and steadily increasing resources from the 1960s, in response to the economy's growing demand for women's labour and a commitment to gender equality. But this growth in provision was matched by movement over time from previously separate day-care and kindergarten systems to a fully integrated system, with one type of provision, centres for 1–6-year-olds called 'preschools' (children under 1 year old are almost all cared for at home by parents taking well-paid parental leave), a common workforce based on a graduate preschool teacher, a common system of tax-based funding, and a strong emphasis on a holistic approach, which views 'care' and 'education' as inseparable. By the 1990s, an entitlement existed to a preschool place for children from 1 year old, if their parents were employed or studying.

All this was achieved while early childhood services were located in the welfare sector, the responsibility of the Ministry of Social Affairs. But in 1996, the decision was taken to move national responsibility for these services from welfare to education, in so doing following a movement that had already been widely made at the local level by municipalities. A main consequence of this move was that preschools were absorbed increasingly into the education system; a curriculum was introduced, preschools were defined as a type of school, their heads were accorded the same status as school heads, and a period of free attendance was introduced for 3–5-year-olds along with capping parental fees at a low level for additional attendance, as well as for children under 3 years – the *maxtaxa*. In addition, access to early childhood education, as it now was, became a universal child-based right from 12 months, independent of parental employment or student status.

England also moved all responsibility for early childhood services into education, soon after Sweden in 1998; previously, 'day-care' or 'childcare' provision had been the responsibility of the health ministry. After decades of policy neglect and under-resourcing, these services became a policy priority and public funding increased, including to support a new entitlement to early education for all 3- and 4-year-olds, which by 2010 had been extended to 570 hours a year. But having integrated early childhood policy in one ministry, education, followed by the introduction of an integrated curriculum and system of regulation, further integration stalled; England today still has a system split between 'childcare' and 'early education', with different workforces ('childcare workers' and 'teachers'), different funding (parental fees subsidised by tax credits for 'childcare', direct funding for 'early education'), and provision ('childcare' mainly provided by day nurseries and childminders', 'early education' mainly provided by schools, though 'childcare services' can provide the education entitlement if they meet certain conditions).

England therefore has never escaped the 'childcare'/'education' split, either structurally or conceptually; governments, organisations and individuals still talk and think in terms of 'childcare'; indeed, the focus on 'childcare' has become more marked in recent years, expressed, for example, in the titles given to two recent government policy papers: 'More Great Childcare' and 'More Affordable Childcare' (Department for Education, 2013a, 2013b). Moreover, further extensions of entitlement have reverted to a targeted welfare approach: a right to part-time 'early education' for 2-year-olds is limited to children from lower-income families, and an increase to 30 hours a week of free provision for 3- and 4-year-olds (1,140 hours a year) is offered as 'childcare', rather than 'early education', and restricted to children of employed parents – a parental benefit, not a child's entitlement. Thus, while Sweden has moved from an entitlement limited to employed parents to a universal entitlement, England has moved away from extending universal entitlement towards a more restricted approach applied to children deemed in need and children of working parents. Sweden has established a right to education from birth (through parental leave and preschools); England has moved away from this goal, enmeshed in a discourse increasingly dominated by 'childcare'. Put another way, Sweden has escaped the restrictive clutch of 'childcare' into a fully educational early childhood service and its regime of universality, while England has failed, conceptually and structurally, to get beyond 'childcare' and its regime of conditionality (for a fuller comparison of England and Sweden, see Cohen et al., 2004, 2018).

Culturally relevant programmes or a standardised approach

The UN Committee encourages governments to opt for 'culturally relevant programmes', achieved by 'working with local communities', rather than 'imposing a standardized approach' (para. 31). There are important examples of the former, a striking example being *Te Whāriki* (New Zealand Ministry of Education, 2017), the New Zealand early childhood curriculum, which recognises the diversity of New Zealand society and early childhood provision, and which was created through a partnership of Māori and non-Māori drawing on important Māori concepts and perspectives. In the words of an OECD report:

> [r]ather than employing a one-world view of human development emptied of context, or articulating a curriculum with the subject-based learning areas and essential skills of the school, Te Whariki chooses a socio-cultural approach to curriculum based on a desire to nurture learning dispositions, promote bi-culturalism and to reflect the realities of the young children in the services.
>
> *(Organisation for Economic Co-operation and Development, 2004, p. 17)*

But elsewhere, there are also clear signs of increasing standardisation being exerted through the influence of powerful international organisations and the application of standardised assessment measures, whether of children or the services they attend, assessment measures that claim to be of universal applicability, at the expense of a 'sociocultural approach'. Towards the end of his life, Malaguzzi was noticing this trend, referring to 'Anglo-Saxon testology' with:

> [i]ts rush to categorise ... where it is enough to do some tests on an individual and immediately the individual has been defined and measured in some way ... which is nothing but a ridiculous simplification of knowledge, and a robbing of meaning from individual histories.
>
> *(Cagliari et al., 2016, pp. 331, 378)*

As Malaguzzi's comments imply, such testology is perhaps for the moment most prevalent in the anglophone world, reflecting a strong cultural and political attachment to a positivist paradigm and technical, managerial and instrumental approaches to education. But it is likely to be spread more widely through the influence of international organisations, especially the OECD and its International Early Learning and Child Well-Being Study (IELS) (OECD, 2018b). The IELS is a cross-national assessment of early learning outcomes involving the standardised testing of samples of 5-year-old children in participating countries on a range of cognitive, social and emotional skills. First mooted by the OECD back in 2012, the initial round of IELS went into the field in 2018 in England, Estonia and the US; despite this small number of countries initially participating, the OECD presumably hopes that more can be recruited for subsequent rounds, until the IELS has the global reach of the OECD's Programme for International Student Assessment, better known as PISA, the well-established and well-known international assessment of 15-year-olds now spanning over 70 countries and regions.

The IELS adopts and applies a uniform approach to the study and comparison of early childhood education in different countries, an approach that finds no room for cultural and other contextual diversity; all are subjected to the same universal measures. As such, it should be seen as yet another strand in a universal web of standardised measurement, spun by the OECD and encompassing a broad swathe of education:

> At the centre of the web is PISA ... [which] has in turn spawned the 'Pisa-based Test for Schools', 'a student assessment tool, used by [individual] schools to support research, benchmarking and school improvement' (http://www.oecd.org/pisa/pisa-basedtestforschools/), and PISA for Development, 'which further develops and differentiates the PISA data-collection instruments to produce results that better support evidence-based policy making in middle- and low-income countries' (http://www.oecd.org/pisa/aboutpisa/pisa-for-development-background.htm).
>
> Then moving up the education age range, there is the 'Assessment of Higher Education Learning Outcomes', 'a feasibility study for assessment of higher education outcomes that will allow comparison between higher education institutions across countries' (http://www.oecd.org/education/imhe/theassessmentofhighereducationlearningoutcomes.htm). Nor does OECD stop at higher education. There is also a 'Survey of Adult Skills', conducted in more than 40 countries, and which 'measures adults' proficiency in key information-processing skills – literacy, numeracy and problem solving in technology-rich environments – and gathers information and data on how adults

use their skills at home, at work and in the wider community' (http://www.oecd.org/skills/piaac/).

And finally, at least for the moment, coming down the road is 'The Study on Social and Emotional Skills', another international survey that 'assesses 10 and 15-year-old students in a number of cities and countries around the world, identifying the conditions and practices that foster or hinder the development of these critical skills.

(Moss and Urban, 2018, pp. 4–5)

Such standardised measures are likely to beget standardised approaches to early childhood and other sectors of education, as these measures come to be adopted as national norms by countries wanting to improve their position on league tables displaying their performance on these comparative assessments. Such homogenising tendencies are further reinforced by educational advice on improving performance issuing from the OECD, which treats educational policymaking 'as a technocratic exercise, to be undertaken by an elite band of experts who are immune to the influence of politics and ideology' (Morris, 2016, p. 9); immune, too, one might add to diversity of context and perspective.

What is particularly worrying about this spreading web of measurement is the lack of information, consultation and dialogue surrounding this vast and consequential enterprise, epitomised by the history of the IELS. The early childhood community was neither informed nor consulted about the IELS, with deliberations confined to the OECD and member state governments. Even today, when the IELS is actually being implemented, many in this community are unaware of its existence. As information about the IELS has leaked out, it has generated an increasing body of criticism, yet the OECD has made no effort to engage with its critics, choosing simply to ignore them. Despite the large and potentially adverse implications of the IELS (and other OECD standardised assessments) for diversity in early childhood education, and the enormous power wielded by the OECD, the organisation has eschewed any attempt at democratic accountability (for some of the criticisms levelled at the OECD and the IELS, see Carr, Mitchell and Rameka, 2016; Moss et al., 2016; Moss and Urban, 2017, 2018; Urban and Swadener, 2016).

Conclusion

The French philosopher Michel Foucault once observed that '[m]y point is not that everything is bad, but that everything is dangerous' (Foucault, 1984, p. 343). I have been a long-standing advocate of early childhood education and concur with the UN Committee that it should be a right that begins at birth. Yet at the same time, it is important to recognise that such a public good has the potential to be dangerous, a means of governing young children more effectively by applying to them a wide array of what Nikolas Rose describes as 'human technologies': '[t]echnologies of government … for the shaping of conduct in the hope of producing certain desired effects and averting certain undesired events' (Rose, 1999, p. 52). There are plenty of such technologies available to early childhood education that are widely deployed today, including child development concepts and knowledge, developmental and learning goals, prescriptive curricula, pedagogical programmes (e.g. developmentally appropriate practice), child observation techniques, inspection regimes, standardised assessment, and 'datafication'.

The right defined by the UN Committee, the right to education beginning at birth, is then only a starting point. For those who support this right, it is necessary to subject it to constant critical thinking, to contest its potential dangers and to develop understandings of what it might mean (e.g. an education commensurate with the image of a rich child and with values of democracy and wonder). It is also important to continually question under what conditions these understandings might be enacted. Last but not least, we need to ask how a universal concept such as a right can be realised in a way that eschews a universal, standardising approach in favour of welcoming diversity and complexity.

References

Bennett, John. 2011. "Early Childhood Education and Care Systems: Issue of Tradition and Governance." In *Encyclopaedia on Early Childhood Development*. www.child-encyclopedia.com/child-care-early-childhood-education-and-care/according-experts/early-childhood-education-and-care.

Blum, Sonia, Alison Koslowski, Alexandra Macht, and Peter Moss, (eds.). 2018. "International Review of Leave Policies and Related Research 2018." www.leavenetwork.org/leave-policies-research/

Cagliari, Paula, Marina Castegnetti, Claudia Giudici, Carlina Rinaldi, Vea Vecchi, and Peter Moss, (eds.). 2016. *Loris Malaguzzi and the Schools of Reggio Emilia: A Selection of His Writings and Speeches 1945–1993*. London: Routledge.

Cameron, Claire and Peter Moss. 2007. *Care Work in Europe: Current Understandings and Future Directions*. London: Routledge.

Cameron, Claire and Peter Moss, (eds.). 2011. *Social Pedagogy and Working with Children and Young People*. London: Jessica Kingsley Publishing.

Carr, Margaret, Linda Mitchell, and Lesley Rameka. 2016. "Some Thoughts about the Value of an OECD International Assessment Framework for Early Childhood Services in Aotearoa New Zealand." *Contemporary Issues in Early Childhood*, 17 (4): 450–454.

Cohen, Bronwen, Peter Moss, Pat Petrie, and Jennifer Wallace. 2004. *A New Deal for Children? Reforming Education and Care in England, Scotland and Sweden*. Bristol: Policy Press.

Cohen, Bronwen, Peter Moss, Pat Petrie, and Jennifer Wallace. 2018. "'A New Deal for Children?' – What Happened Next: A Cross-national Study of Transferring Early Childhood Services into Education." *Early Years*, doi:10.1080/09575146.2018.1504753.

Dahlberg, Gunilla, Peter Moss, and Alan Pence. 2013. *Beyond Quality in Early Childhood Education and Care: Postmodern Perspectives on the Problem with Quality*. 3rd ed. London: Routledge.

Department for Education. 2013a. "More Great Childcare: Raising Quality and Giving Parents More Choice." https://assets.publishing.service.gov.uk/government/uploads/system/uploads/attachment_data/file/219660/More_20Great_20Childcare_20v2.pdf

Department for Education. 2013b. "More Affordable Childcare." www.gov.uk/government/publications/more-affordable-childcare

Foucault, Michel. 1984. "On the Genealogy of Ethics: An Overview of Work in Progress." In *The Foucault Reader*, edited by Paul Rabinow, 340–372. New York, NY: Pantheon.

Haas, Linda and Philip Hwang. 1999. "Parental Leave in Sweden." In *Parental Leave: Progress or Pitfall?*, edited by Freddy Deven and Peter Moss, 45–68. Brussels: NIDI CBGS Publications.

Kaga, Yoshie, John Bennett, and Peter Moss. 2010. *Caring and Learning Together: A Cross-national Study of Integration of Early Childhood Care and Education within Education*. Paris: UNESCO.

Morris, Paul. 2016. *Education Policy, Cross-national Tests of Pupil Achievement, and the Pursuit of World-class Schooling*. London: UCL Institute of Education Press.

Moss, Peter. 2018. "What Place for 'Care' in Early Childhood Policy?" In *The SAGE Handbook of Early Childhood Policy*, edited by Linda Miller, Claire Cameron, Carmen Dalli, and Nancy Barbour, 256–267. London: Sage.

Moss, Peter, Gunilla Dahlberg, Susan Grieshaber, Susanna Mantovani, Helen May, Alan Pence, Sylvia Rayna, Beth Blue Swadener, and Michel Vandenbroeck. 2016. "The Organisation for Economic Co-operation and Development's International Early Learning Study: Opening for Debate and Contestation." *Contemporary Issues in Early Childhood*, 17 (3): 343–351.

Moss, Peter and Mathias Urban. 2017. "The Organisation for Economic Co-operation and Development's International Early Learning Study: What Happened Next?" *Contemporary Issues in Early Childhood*, 18 (2): 250–258.

Moss, Peter and Mathias Urban. 2018. "The Organisation for Economic Co-operation and Development's International Early Learning Study: What's Going On." *Contemporary Issues in Early Childhood*, doi:10.1177/1463949118803269.

New Zealand Ministry of Education. 2017. "Te Whāriki: Early Childhood Curriculum." www.education.govt.nz/assets/Documents/Early-Childhood/Te-Whariki-Early-Childhood-Curriculum-ENG-Web.pdf

Organisation for Economic Co-operation and Development (OECD). 2001. *Starting Strong I*. Paris: OECD.

Organisation for Economic Co-operation and Development (OECD). 2004. *Starting Strong: Curricula and Pedagogies in Early Childhood Education and Care – Five Curriculum Outlines*. Paris: OECD.

Organisation for Economic Co-operation and Development (OECD). 2006. *Starting Strong II*. Paris: OECD.

Organisation for Economic Co-operation and Development (OECD). 2018a. "OECD Family Database." www.oecd.org/els/family/database.htm

Organisation for Economic Co-operation and Development (OECD). 2018b. "International Early Learning and Child Well-being Study." www.oecd.org/education/school/international-early-learning-and-child-well-being-study.htm

Rose, Nikolas. 1999. *Powers of Freedom: Reframing Political Thought*. Cambridge: Cambridge University Press.

United Nations. 1989. *United Nations Convention on the Rights of the Child*. https://www.unicef.org.uk/rights-respecting-schools/wp-content/uploads/sites/4/2017/01/UNCRC-in-full.pdf

United Nations Committee on the Rights of the Child. 2005. *General Comment No. 7 (2005): Implementing Child Rights in Early Childhood*. Geneva: United Nations.

Urban, Mathias and Beth Blue Swadener. 2016. "Democratic Accountability and Contextualised Systemic Evaluation." *International Critical Childhood Policy Studies*, 5 (1): 6–18.

12

LEAVE NO ONE BEHIND

Young children's rights to education

Mercy Musomi

Introduction

Inclusive education is a widely accepted international right and practice, supported by international human rights instruments and national legislations globally (Haug, 2015). Inclusive education is an educational approach that states that all children learn within the general education system of a country irrespective of their differences and diversities (Nederlof and Van der Kroft, 2006, p. 2). This model thrives to ensure full participation of children with disabilities (CWDs) in age-appropriate general education levels without any restriction or discrimination (World Health Organization (WHO), 2013). Disability-inclusive education is one of the main thrusts of current global development policy and practice (Armstrong, Armstrong and Spandagou, 2010; WHO, 2013). The United Nations Convention on the Rights of the Child (UNCRC) articulates provision rights of all children to education that develops their 'personality, talents and abilities to the fullest' (Articles 28 and 29), but importantly it requires governments to do all they can to protect all children's rights to education, alongside other rights (Article 4) (United Nations (UN), 1989).

In all countries in the world, there are young children living in difficult conditions, which can include physical, cognitive, mental, social and emotional difficulties (WHO, 2013). Because of these challenges, they may be regarded as a burden, as non-responsive or as non-productive people of the society. This attitude leads to exclusion and discrimination in respect of young CWDs receiving care, protection, rights and services, at family, community and state levels. As a result, a significant number of people do not progress as fully as they might in their development. This exclusion from education and rehabilitation services for CWDs denies them the opportunity to create a sustainable future for themselves and their families (Rohwerder, 2015; Saebones, 2015; WHO, 2013). To attempt to address this problem and improve the living conditions of young CWDs, the international community and national governments have articulated disability-inclusive development policies and practice. Inclusive education lies at the heart of these policies and practices across the world (Peters, 2004; Republic of Kenya, 2018; WHO, 2013).

This chapter addresses ways that rights to education and inclusion of young CWDs in Kenya may be protected and promoted. It opens by describing features of the country of Kenya. The chapter then discusses inclusive education for children below 8 years before setting out international policy concerning universal inclusive education, then national legislation concerning universal inclusive education in Kenya. The latter part of the chapter presents and discusses interventions adopted by Girl Child Network. The interventions illustrate the experiences, challenges and lessons learned by workers at Girl Child Network as they have attempted to protect the rights of young CWDs to education in Kenya.

Background on Kenya

Kenya is a lower middle-income country with an estimated population of 43 million (Republic of Kenya, 2014). Arid and semi-arid lands (ASALs) occupy 80 per cent of Kenya's land, with 21 of the 47 counties forming the ASALs. An estimated 80 per cent of all individuals living with disabilities live in isolated areas of developing countries, with 94 million being children aged 14 and below.

Education in Kenya is governed by the Constitution of Kenya 2010 (Republic of Kenya, 2010), which provides for free and compulsory education for all. Article 53 affirms the right to free and compulsory basic education and is supported by other national legal frameworks. The Basic Education Act (Republic of Kenya, 2013) affirms the right to basic-quality education and provides for the two years of pre-primary education. Pre-primary 1 serves children aged 4 years while pre-primary 2 serves children aged 5 years. Article 28a provides for the provision of pre-primary within reasonable distances within the county. Article 34(1) affirms that children should not be discriminated against on the basis of race, colour, sex, disability, age, religion or culture. However, the Act advocates for establishment of special and integrated schools for CWDs (Republic of Kenya, 2013, Article 28b). Through the recently launched Sector Policy for Learners and Trainees with Disabilities (Republic of Kenya, 2018), the country sought to move from establishment of integrated schools for CWDs to implementing an inclusive education where these children are mainstreamed in the regular schools. The policy affirms the Constitution's right to education for all, including full access to lifelong opportunities for learners with disabilities, and provides for inclusive quality education and training at all levels of learning.

According to the National Survey for Persons with Disabilities 2008, 4.6 per cent of Kenyans, approximately 1.7 million (based on the 2009 census) have disabilities. Of this, only 39 per cent have gone through the primary education level. Despite the introduction of free primary education (FPE) in 2003 (Republic of Kenya, 2003a), more than a million children are not in schools, with a child in an ASAL region being three times more likely to be out of school than a child in a non-ASAL region (Ndichu, 2013). Some of the notable obstacles to education for young children in ASAL regions include lack of school supplies, long distances between home and school, poor learning environment, negative sociocultural norms, and attitudes among others. The bulk of ASAL regions form the marginalised counties where development lagged behind due to discrimination.

Inclusive education for children below 8 years

Many communities in Kenya believe that disability is retribution for past wrong deeds by ancestors; parents of CWDs may feel ashamed and tend to hide their children from the rest of society, denying them their right to education (Mukuria and Korir, 2006; United Nations Educational, Scientific and Cultural Organization (UNESCO), 1974). However, recently, this pattern has been changing as parents in Kenya increasingly enrol their children in special units as well as regular schools to access education.

In countries whose governments have ratified the UNCRC, education is been established as every child's right (UN, 1989; United Nations Educational, Social and Cultural Organization (UNESCO), 2005), and the Salamanca Statement and Framework for Action on Special Needs Education (United Nations Educational, Social and Cultural Organization (UNESCO), 1994) recognised the right to education for every child. The World Conference on Education for All (EFA) in Jomtien, Thailand (1990) affirmed the significance of early childhood education when it positioned it as the first goal, aiming to expand and improve comprehensive early childhood care and education for the most vulnerable and disadvantaged children (United Nations Educational, Social and Cultural Organization (UNESCO), 1990). The importance of early childhood development and education (ECDE) for all children has been further established by research evidence suggesting that ECDE can contribute to brain development, health outcomes, future academic successes and the overall economic development of nations (Piper, Merseth and Ngaruiya, 2018; Smith and Douglas, 2014). The recent concerted focus by policy makers on early childhood education is emphasised in Sustainable Development Goals Target 4.2, which calls for access and quality early childhood education care and pre-primary education by 2030 (United Nations, 2015).

The Constitution of Kenya 2010 (Republic of Kenya, 2010) provides for the rights of every child, including the right to education as enshrined in the Bill of Rights (Article 53 (1b)). Article 54(1b) guarantees CWDs the right to access educational facilities.

International policies supporting children younger than 8 years with disabilities

The Universal Declaration of Human Rights (United Nations, 1948) sets out fundamental human rights for CWDs as enshrined in the Bill of Rights: 'Everyone has the right to education. Education shall be free, at least in the elementary and fundamental stages. Elementary education shall be compulsory' (Article 26). In 2006, the United Nations adopted the Convention on the Rights of Persons with Disabilities (UNCRPD). Article 24(2a) of the UNCRPD states that 'CWD are not excluded from the general education system on the basis of disability, and that CWD are not excluded from free and compulsory primary education, or secondary education on the basis of disability'. Kenya assimilated the UNCRPD into its domestic law with the Disability Act 2003 (Republic of Kenya, 2003b). This right to education for CDWs is also anchored in the UNCRC (UN, 1989). Article 23(3) states that 'education shall be provided free of charge and that CWDs will have effective access to and will receive education to help the child in achieving the fullest possible social integration and individual development'. General Comment No. 9 (United Nations Committee on the Rights of the Child, 2006) deals specifically with the rights of CWDs. These two conventions bear witness to the growing global movement geared to inclusion of CWDs in education. Concern for inclusion is rooted in the belief that all children are full members of the society: that each child is a unique individual and has skills and aspirations worth nurturing, who is entitled to be consulted and respected, and whose contributions are to be valued and encouraged.

The World Declaration on Education for All, adopted in Thailand (UNESCO, 1990), sets out the vision for universal access to education for all to promote equity. The Salamanca Statement and Framework for Action (UNESCO, 1994) recognised the right to education for every child, and declared that 'every child has a fundamental right to education' and 'those with special needs must access regular schools which should accommodate them within child centered pedagogy capable of meeting their needs' (p. viii). Other key international policies that promote the protection of rights to education for all children include the Dakar Framework for Action (United Nations, 2000) and Target 4.2 of the Sustainable Development Goals (UN, 2015) on early childhood development and universal pre-primary education.

The first world report on disability (World Health Organization (WHO) and World Bank, 2011) suggested that more than a billion (15 per cent based on 2010 global population estimates) people in the world experience disability, of whom 95 million (5.1 per cent) are children aged 0–14 years (World Health Organization, 2004). The report further indicates that CWDs experience lower educational outcomes than those without disabilities, often because their access to services is comparatively inhibited. CWDs are left behind by global efforts to improve education opportunities for all, as gaps between children with and without disabilities have increased significantly in Majority World countries; primary school completion rates for CWDs are only 48 per cent, since as many as three in ten have never been in school and only six in ten can read and write (Male and Wodon, 2017).

Governments, the international community, civil society organisations and the private sector have a joint responsibility to create enabling environments, ensure adequate social protection, create inclusive policies and programmes, and enforce new and existing legislation to the benefit of CWDs.

Kenya's policies on inclusive education for children below 8 years

In response to international legal obligations, Kenya has made strides to ensure CWDs are provided with education in an inclusive learning environment. The Constitution of Kenya 2010 Article 27(4) prohibits discrimination on the basis of disability, and Article 53 sets out the requirement for free and compulsory basic education to all children, as well as basic nutrition, shelter and healthcare, parental care and protection from abuse, neglect, harmful cultural practices, all forms of violence, inhuman treatment and punishment, and hazardous or exploitative labour. Article 56 obliges the state to put in place affirmative action programmes for minorities and marginalised groups, including CWDs, to have special opportunities in education (Republic of Kenya, 2010).

Kenya domesticated the CRC and ACRWC through the Children Act to protect the rights of children (Republic of Kenya, 2001). The Act protects every child's entitlement to education, the provision of which shall be the responsibility of the government and the parents, and that the education shall be compulsory in accordance with Article 28 of the CRC. The Basic Education Act seeks to increase access and retention and improve learning outcomes for all children. Article 46(1) requires the government in Kenya to establish education assessment resource centres (EARCs) to strengthen early identification, assessment and placement for CWDs (Republic of Kenya, 2013). Equally, Kenya's Vision 2030 recognises the importance of education and training for all Kenyans as fundamental to the development of human capital for the country's economic development (International Labour Organization (ILO), 2009; Republic of Kenya, n.d.).

The CWD Act in Kenya acknowledges that CWDs face various forms of discrimination (Republic of Kenya, 2003b). Article 18 requires learning institutions to admit CWDs without discriminating on the basis of their disability and that learning institutions shall take into account the special needs of CWDs with respect to the entry requirements, pass marks, curriculum, examinations, auxiliary services, physical education requirements, class schedules and other similar considerations. Nevertheless, while approximately 1.7 million people in Kenya live with some form of disability, only 39 per cent of this group has had a primary education (Republic of Kenya, 2008). In Kenya, special needs education (SNE) is provided in special schools, integrated units and in inclusive settings in regular schools. However, the majority of CWDs are not in schools. The Ministry of Education (MoE) in Kenya reported that in 1999, only 22,000 learners with special educational needs (SEN) enrolled in schools, with the number increasing to 26,885 in 2003 and 45,000 in 2008 (Republic of Kenya, 2009). This figure compares poorly with the proportion of their regular peers, given that the total population of pupils in 2008 was 8,563,821. Njoka et al. (2012) note that despite the reintroduction of FPE in 2003, about 1 million children of school age were still out of school in 2012. The high number of CWDs out of school suggests that children's rights to education may not be protected in Kenya. Protection and promotion of the rights of *all* children are anchored on the understanding that any disability, restriction, obstacle or lack of ability to participate effectively on an equal basis to others should mean only that one is differently abled.

Historically, CWDs in Kenya have been placed in 'special schools' away from their families. Some of the special schools are residential institutions, where the children would spend long periods of time, isolated from the community (Adoyo and Odeny, 2015). CWDs have very low rates of initial enrolment, and even if they do attend school, CWDs are more likely to drop out and leave school early without transitioning to secondary school and beyond (Global Campaign for Education/Handicap International, 2014). CWDs in Kenya are also at risk of school violence and bullying, preventing the safe enjoyment of their right to education (United Nations Educational, Scientific and Cultural Organization (UNESCO), 2016). [[AC]] In Kenya, other barriers that CWDs face in accessing education alongside their peers include infrastructural and environmental barriers, lack of learning resources and assistive devices, and discrimination and prejudices.

Nevertheless, the government of Kenya is committed to implementing its international, regional and national commitments, and has adopted laws and policies pertaining to CWDs, including their right to productive and decent work and basic services. Kenya has ratified treaties that guarantee the right to education, and is therefore obligated to respect, protect and fulfil these rights for children in Kenya. In addition to incorporating the UNCRPD through the Persons with Disabilities Act (Republic of Kenya, 2003b), Kenya has established the National Council for Persons with Disabilities, which is responsible for formulating and developing measures and policies to achieve equal opportunities for CWDs in respect of education and employment, sporting, recreational and cultural activities, full access to community and social services, and measures to prevent discrimination against CWDs.

Based on this policy framework, the Kenyan government launched the Sector Policy for Learners and Trainees with Disabilities in May 2018 (Ministry of Education (MoE), 2018) to realise education as a basic human right for all Kenyans, including full access to lifelong educational opportunities for CWDs. The policy recognises the importance of inclusive education, emphasising the need for all learners to learn together in an inclusive environment. The policy came into effect following revision of the Special Needs Education (SNE) Policy Framework (Ministry of Education (MoE), 2009), which guided the provision of special needs education in Kenya. Prior to the SNE policy, the government of Kenya relied on circulars developed after several commissions were appointed by the government in Kenya to conduct research and give recommendations on the implementation of the various international and regional policies.

In 2001, Kenya enacted the Children's Act (Republic of Kenya, 2001), followed by the Persons with Disability Act 2003 (Republic of Kenya, 2003b), among other legal and policy frameworks. Over time, these have been implemented, reviewed with subsequent laws, and policies enacted to ensure all children have the right to quality and compulsory basic education with the adequate legal and policy framework to protect children from all forms of abuse. These efforts have provided a framework whereby CWDs are enrolled and access quality education in Kenya.

Girl Child Network

Girl Child Network (GCN) is a rights-based organisation whose mission is to protect and promote the rights of children, youth and women in Africa. To achieve this, GCN implements interventions that seek to eliminate barriers that prevent girls, boys and youth from marginalised communities in arid and semi-arid lands (ASALs) and informal settlements from attaining inclusive quality education.

For GCN, education is fundamental in empowering girls and boys towards self-realisation and promoting their well-being. It considers the school a safe place, with the understanding that every single day a girl or boy spends in school reduces exposure and vulnerability to risks, including gender-based violence. Education is therefore a catalyst for development and is at the heart of the organisation's strategic objectives. Under the education programme, the interventions aim to enhance access, enrolment, retention and completion of school by girls, boys and CWDs from marginalised and hard-to-reach communities. These interventions address social, cultural, institutional and environmental barriers that limit participation of CWDs as full and equal members of the society.

As an advocacy organisation, GCN has, over the last 23 years, endeavoured to lobby for a society that upholds and respects the rights of all children, especially girls and CWDs. One way of doing this has been through advocating for inclusive education for all. This means children with and without disabilities participate and learn together in the same classes, just as they are served by the same teaching and non-teaching staff among other stakeholders at the school level. As a result, all learners are enrolled and attend schools at an age-appropriate regular class, supported to learn, contribute and participate in all aspects of the school curriculum. Thus, all children attend schools with their peers and are provided with adequate support to succeed socially and academically. The peers are able to appreciate and support CWDs. This reduces barriers and prejudice to disability.

Girl Child Network's inclusive education interventions

On the basis of international and national legal frameworks, GCN has been implementing inclusive education projects since 2015. The projects have sought to enhance provision of education services to learners with disabilities in inclusive school settings. Some of the interventions implemented to accommodate learners with disabilities in regular schools have included: partnership with EARCs to carry out functional assessment of CWDs; environmental and infrastructural modifications to improve accessibility of learning and recreational areas; classroom adaptation and management; provision of learning resources; capacity-building and awareness creation; and advocacy for inclusion. All the GCN interventions are geared towards improving access to education and fulfilment of the right to education by learners with disabilities through inclusive education.

Background of the No One Out (NOO) project

Universal primary education is intended to ensure all children who are eligible for primary school, including pre-primary, have the opportunity to enrol, remain in school and acquire quality basic education. However, CWDs in this category remain excluded, exposing them to abject poverty. Inclusive education is a model that allows CWDs to learn in the same schools with their peers without disabilities through an integration approach. Inclusion is an integration approach that involves a process of reform and restructuring to ensure all children have access to educational and social opportunities offered in schools.

Despite efforts the government has put in place to support inclusive education for CWD, challenges have persisted in its implementation. According to MoE (2009, reviewed 2018), inappropriate infrastructure, inadequate capacity of teachers to manage learners with disabilities in regular schools, inadequate and expensive learning and teaching materials, negative attitudes and sociocultural norms, and inadequate monitoring of schools have been impediments to inclusive education.

The role of non-governmental organisations (NGOs) in support of inclusive education has been important. In collaboration with government, they have made immense contributions in the implementation of inclusive education. Since April 2017, GCN has implemented the No One Out (NOO) project in 16 schools from five informal settlements of Nairobi. The project aims to improve learning outcomes for CWDs through interventions geared towards increased enrolment, retention and progression. The project takes cognisance of the challenges facing inclusive education in Kenya, which include a lack of disability-friendly school infrastructure, negative attitude and sociocultural norms towards CWDs, and poor policy implementation.

In responding to these challenges, the project engaged strategies such as early identification of CWDs, infrastructure modification to improve accessibility of learners and recreational areas, provision of assistive devices and learning resources to schools and learners with disabilities, child-led initiatives ('rights of the child' clubs), and advocacy and awareness creation for inclusive education as discussed.

Early identification and interventions for CWDs

Research has shown that children's capacity for learning and development is optimal in preschool years (Center on the Developing Child, 2016). CWDs miss out on education due to conditions noticed at birth, but miss out on early interventions to enhance their learning outcomes. Early identification is critical in facilitating timely interventions and averting or reducing the impact of impairment in the quality of life of CWDs. Early identification paves the way for timely assessment, placement, and referral for medical, educational and social support, leading to better health, social and educational outcomes for CWDs. Early interventions, on the other hand, help CWDs on the path to making the most of their abilities and skills, leading to improved learning outcomes, better employment, participation in decision-making spaces and better economic outcomes. The services also support parents and siblings who, due to cultural norms, face acute stigma and experience frustration, disappointments and helplessness. It positively impacts the well-being of the entire family.

Collaboration and teamwork are also essential aspects of inclusive practice (Lindsay, 2007). Parents also have a contribution to make in the inclusion process. The project conducts community outreaches with support from a multisectoral team, including community health volunteers (CHVs), child protection volunteers, parents and community members to help in identification of CWDs in the community for assessment.

Kenya established education assessment and resource centres (EARCs) in 1984 to ensure early identification, assessment, intervention and placement of learners with disabilities.

However, there is low capacity of teachers to manage the centres. This GCN project supports building the capacity of teachers to manage the EARC centres and, through their support, conduct screening and functional assessment of CWDs to inform interventions.

The assessments are conducted using a comprehensive tool that collects background information about the child, with the aim of identifying potential causes and informing supportive interventions. After assessment, children are provided with direct early interventions, including medical assessment provided by professionals, planning and preparation of activities at home and in the communities, and therapy services and psychosocial support services for both the child and their families and caregivers.

Placement decisions are also informed by functional assessment results where the officers recommend assessed CWDs for enrolment in inclusive schools, together with the necessary accommodations that should be made for the learner. Recommendations are given to both the school and parents for provision of support to ensure that the learner with disabilities receives the best support and learning outcomes.

However, the strategy has faced challenges in its implementation, including the acute understaffing of teachers, lack of acoustic rooms for assessment of children with hearing impairment, and the prohibitive costs of devices for assessment.

Enhancing referrals for social economic services for young CWDs

The burden of care in households caring for CWDs is higher due to the extra costs for clinic visits, treatment, medication and costs for assistive devices, among others. The assessment of children through EARCs also paves the way for their registration with the National Council for Persons with Disabilities, where they can access government-run social protection schemes such as bursaries, cash transfers and medical cover, among others. Children supported by the project have all been registered with the National Council for Persons with Disabilities and access social protection schemes from the government and non-governmental organisations.

Case study on enhancing referrals for social economic services for young CWDs

For Ian's parents, having a child with a physical disability meant that their already tight budget was always stretched thinner than they could afford. Ian has spina bifida and needs constant medical attention and permanent care, meaning that his parents must make regular trips to hospital to seek support. Ian also needed physiotherapy and dressing of persistent bedsores, which kept him out of school most times. Ian was reached during an outreach event at his school in Kariobangi, Nairobi, and referred for medical assessment. He was also supported to register with the National Council for Persons with Disabilities (NCPWD), making him eligible for the cash transfer programme for persons with disabilities. The registration also gives him access to the National Fund for the Disabled of Kenya, which gives assistive devices and cash grants to schools where CWDs are enrolled, among other benefits, and with this social protection scheme Ian's life is much improved.

Improved accessibility of learning and recreational areas

Article 2 of the UNCRPD defines 'Discrimination on the basis of disability' as 'any distinction, exclusion or restriction on the basis of disability which has the purpose or effect of impairing or nullifying the recognition, enjoyment or exercise, on an equal basis with others, of all human rights and fundamental freedoms in the political, economic, social, cultural, civil or any other field' (United Nations, 2006). This includes all forms of discrimination, including denial of reasonable accommodation.

Kenya's education policies identify measures to promote a barrier-free environment for learners with disabilities and inclusion in all learning institutions. However, challenges abound, with a lack of facilities, services, assistive devices, equipment, teaching and learning materials in schools. GCN recognises that school and classroom environment adaptation and management is critical for optimising learners' access to education. Adaptations to the environment are therefore necessary to help learners with disabilities access, move around and function safely and efficiently.

GCN commissioned a disability audit to determine the readiness of schools to accommodate learners with disabilities. The audit assesses:

- teachers' awareness of the concept of inclusive education and adequacy of teaching and learning materials;
- awareness levels of children and non-teaching staff on disability and inclusive education;
- awareness levels and participation of the boards of management and the community in disability and inclusive education; and
- the school's accessibility.

A report of the assessment is then prepared, which informs the interventions that are put in place by the organisation to promote inclusive education. Where GCN projects are implemented, the school environments have tended to be characterised by sharp stairs, unpaved pathways and walkways, unlevelled playing fields/recreation areas and potholed compounds. One of the interventions is modification of the school's physical environment to accommodate learners with various categories of disabilities. Access to school amenities, including classrooms, offices, washrooms and play areas, has been made easy and safe for all learners, but these modifications and other interventions have led to an increase in the enrolment of learners with disabilities in schools. This has been a successful intervention because more children are willing to enrol in these schools and parents approve of the services their CWD can access.

Case study on infrastructural modifications

Valley Bridge Primary School is in Kiamaikon, Huruma, in the eastern part of Nairobi. The school is a public primary school, with 1,132 pupils (568 boys and 564 girls), of whom 63 are CWDs, and is surrounded by low-income residential housing and temporary shanties.

A disability audit conducted by GCN in February 2018 to determine the readiness of the school for inclusive education revealed that the school's facilities were not accessible by learners with disabilities. The school lacked access ramps all through the school compound, adaptive toilet facilities for CWDs, learning and interactive/play resource materials, and trained teachers, and the playing field was unpaved and uneven. Through the No One Out project, GCN carried out modifications of the school's infrastructure by constructing ramps and an accessible toilet. The project also procured learning and interactive/play materials that are used for instruction and participation in extracurricular activities by CWDs. Prior to the modifications, the school only enrolled children with mild visual impairment and learning difficulties. Since the modifications, the school has enrolled learners with cerebral palsy, physical disabilities, intellectual disabilities, and speech and communication disorders in an inclusive setting. The demand is continuing to rise, with numbers expected to increase as the school adopts the concept of inclusive education.

Provision of assistive devices and learning resources

Since the introduction of free primary education in 2003 (Republic of Kenya, 2003a), parents, especially those from resource-constrained settings, have not been willing to financially support schools by paying levies and school development fees. Public schools, which form 25 per cent of the project-supported schools, receive capitation of approximately US$10 for regular students and US$20 for CWDs, which is used for purchasing textbooks, stationery and basic maintenance of school facilities. The allocated funds are not adequate to support procurement of specialised devices, resources and materials for learners with disabilities.

Lack of assistive devices for CWDs hinders their participation in learning and social activities. There is a gap in production and provision of specialised learning resources that respond to various categories of disabilities, and there is need for interventions to complement the efforts of families, schools and the government in provision of specialised learning resources and assistive devices for learners with disabilities and schools.

The NOO project responded to this gap by conducting a needs assessment in schools to determine the requirements for materials, appliances, resources and devices to promote learning and ensure learners with disabilities are able to operate with minimal support. The teachers are supported by aides to help them teach the curriculum content using inclusive pedagogy. In schools where CWDs were previously dependent on their peers for mobility assistance, learners who have been supported with assistive devices have reduced the need for support from others. This has enhanced their self-esteem, supported their integration into social environments and ultimately improved their learning outcomes.

Advocacy and awareness creation for inclusive education

There is noted evidence of increased advocacy in inclusive education in Kenya, demonstrated by the increase in enactment of legal frameworks. However, there is little evidence of the implementation of these (Donohue and Bornman, 2014). GCN has taken the lead in efforts to lobby for and influence the development and review of policies that translate them into special needs education provision. GCN supported the review of the Special Needs Education Policy Framework (MoE, 2009) to align the sector policy to the Kenya Vision 2030 (Republic of Kenya, n.d.), the Constitution of Kenya (Republic of Kenya, 2010), the Sustainable Development Goals (Goal 4) (UN, 2015), and the national curriculum reform. These efforts culminated in the Sector Policy for Learners and Trainees with Disabilities (MoE, 2018), launched by the President of Kenya in May 2018. The goal of the policy is to promote educational provision and training for CWDs.

Challenges and opportunities

Despite numerous efforts by the government of Kenya for the successful implementation of inclusive education, children aged 8 years and younger continue to face challenges in accessing education and early education. CWDs find it difficult to exercise their right to education due to their condition, and distances to schools remain challenging for CWDs to navigate. The school environment makes it difficult for these children to fit in and participate in education. An ingrained negative perception on disabilities exposes CWDs to discrimination and neglect as parents struggle to align community norms and the right to education for CWDs, especially for those under the age of 8 who depend more on their parents. There is a positive attitude among the duty-bearers, including the government, civil society organisations and communities, to accord the right to education to all children irrespective of their status. The current Sector Policy for Learners and Trainees with Disabilities (Republic of Kenya, 2018) mandates the government to achieve this.

Conclusion

Education for all should just mean that, opportunities for every child to have access to an inclusive quality basic education without discrimination on the basis of race, colour, geographical location, language, sex or disability. Education can break the cycle of poverty, contribute to healthier and more stable communities, and lead to greater economic growth of nations. However, CWDs are at risk of not fulfilling their educational potential and are more vulnerable to poverty and gender-based violence. This exclusion is likely to have a long-term impact on their lives unless services are adapted to promote their inclusion in the public spaces, particularly if children's right to education is not protected fully. With the introduction of Sustainable Development Goals Target 4.2 (United Nations, 2015), there is a new imperative to protect early education for children younger than 8 years.

Disability is strongly associated with poor educational outcomes and poverty, and disabilities have both educational and medical implications. The cost associated with provision of assistive devices and making accommodations for CWDs can be high, but it is necessary if children's rights to education are to be protected. It is the responsibility of governments, civil society organisations and the private sector to support CWDs to access education and early education by providing appropriate resources.

References

Adoyo, Peter O. and Michael L. Odeny. 2015. "Emergent Inclusive Education Practice in Kenya: Challenges and Suggestions." *International Journal of Research in Humanities and Social Studies*, 2 (6): 47–52.

Armstrong, Ann, Derrick Armstrong, and Ilektra Spandagou. 2010. *Inclusive Education. International Policy and Practice*. London: Sage Publications Ltd.

Center on the Developing Child. 2016. *From Best Practices to Breakthrough Impacts: A Science-based Approach to Building a More Promising Future for Young Children and Families*. Cambridge, MA: Centre on the Developing Child.

Donohue, Dana K. and Juan Bornman. 2014. "The Challenges of Realizing Inclusive Education in South Africa." *South African Journal of Education*, 34 (2): 1–14.

Global Campaign for Education/Handicap International. 2014. "Equal Right, Equal Opportunity: Education and Disability." www.right-to-education.org/resource/gce-report-equal-right-equal-opportunity-education-and-disability

Haug, Peder. 2015. "Understanding Inclusive Education: Ideals and Reality." *Scandinavian Journal of Disability Research*, 19 (3): 206–217, doi: http://doi.org/10.1080/15017419.2016.1224778

International Labour Organisation (ILO). 2009. "Decent Work for People with Disabilities. Inclusion of People with Disabilities in Kenya." www.ilo.org/wcmsp5/groups/public/@ed_emp/@ifp_skills/documents/publication/wcms_115097.pdf

Lindsay, Geoff. 2007. "Educational Psychology and Effectiveness of Inclusive Education." *British Journal of Educational Psychology*, 77: 1–24.

Male, Chata and Quentin T. Wodon. 2017. "Disability Gaps in Educational Attainment and Literacy (English). The Price of Exclusion: Disability and Education." Washington, DC: World Bank Group.

http://documents.worldbank.org/curated/en/396291511988894028/Disability-gaps-in-educational-attainment-and-literacy

Ministry of Education (MoE). 2009."The National Special Needs Education Policy Framework." www.unesco.org/education/edurights/media/docs/446808882707702aafc616d3a2cec918bfc186fc.pdf

Ministry of Education (MoE). 2018. "Sector Plan for Learners and Trainees with Disabilities." http://planipolis.iiep.unesco.org/sites/planipolis/files/ressources/kenya_sector_policy_learners_trainees_disabilities.pdf

Mukuria, Gathogo and Julie Korir. 2006. "Education for Children with Emotional and Behavioral Disorders in Kenya: Problems and Prospects." *Education News*, 26 March, 2006. www.redorbit.com/news/education/436674/education_for_children_with_emotional_and_behavioral_disorders_in_kenya/

Ndichu, Gitau David. 2013. "Impact of Drought in Primary School Learning." https://ir-library.ku.ac.ke/bitstream/handle/123456789/9019/Gitau%20David%20Ndichu.pdf;sequence=1

Nederlof, Corinne and Marlies Van der Kroft. 2006. *Disabilities and Development: All Equal, All Different.* Utrecht: DCDD.

Njoka, Evangeline, Andrew Riechi, Charles Obiero, Everlyn Kemunto, Daniel Muraya, Joel Ongoto, and Donvan Amenya. 2012. "Towards Inclusive and Equitable Basic Education System: Kenya's Experience." *Trienniale on Education and Training in Africa. Ouagadougou, Burkina Fasu,* February 12–17, 2012. www.yumpu.com/en/document/read/40105634/towards-inclusive-and-equitable-basic-education-system-adea

Peters, Susan J. 2004. "Inclusive Eduaction. An EFA Strategy for All Children." http://siteresources.worldbank.org/EDUCATION/Resources/278200-1099079877269/547664-1099079993288/InclusiveEdu_efa_strategy_for_children.pdf

Piper, Benjamin, Katherine Merseth, and Samuel Ngaruiya. 2018. "Scaling up Early Childhood Development and Education in a Devolved Setting: Policy Making, Resource Allocations, and Impact of the Tayari School Readiness Program in Kenya." *Global Education Review*, 5 (2): 47–68.

Republic of Kenya. 2001. *The Children's Act. No8 of 2001.* Nairobi: Government Printers.

Republic of Kenya. 2003a. *Free Primary Education Policy.* Nairobi: Government Printers.

Republic of Kenya. 2003b. *Persons with Disabilities Act.* Nairobi: Government Printers.

Republic of Kenya. 2008. "Kenya National Survey for Persons with Disabilities." www.ncpd.go.ke/wp-content/uploads/2017/09/2007-Kenya-National-Survey-on-Persons-with-Disabilities.pdf

Republic of Kenya. 2009. *The National Special Needs Education Policy Framework.* Nairobi: Government Printers.

Republic of Kenya. 2010 "The Kenya Constitution 2010." www.kenyalaw.org/lex/actview.xql?actid=Const2010

Republic of Kenya. 2013. "Basic Education Act. No 14 of 2013." http://kenyalaw.org/lex/rest//db/kenyalex/Kenya/Legislation/English/Acts%20and%20Regulations/B/Basic%20Education%20Act%20No.%2014%20of%202013/docs/BasicEducationActNo14of2013.pdf

Republic of Kenya. 2014. "Kenya Demographic and Health Survey." https://dhsprogram.com/pubs/pdf/fr308/fr308.pdf

Republic of Kenya. 2018. "Sector Policy for Learners and Trainees with Disabilities." http://planipolis.iiep.unesco.org/sites/planipolis/files/ressources/kenya_sector_policy_learners_trainees_disabilities.pdf

Republic of Kenya. n.d. "Kenya Vision 2030." https://vision2030.go.ke/publication/kenya-a-frontier-of-great-opportunity/

Rohwerder, Brigitte. 2015. *Disability Inclusion: Topic Guide.* Birmingham, UK: GSDRC, University of Birmingham.

Saebones, Ann-Marit. 2015. "Towards a Disability Inclusive Education. Background Paper for Oslo Summit on Education for Development, 7th July 2015." http://atlas-alliansen.no/publication/towards-a-disability-inclusive-education-2/

Smith, Emma and Graeme Douglas. 2014. "Special Education Needs, Disability and School Accountability: An International Perspective." *International Journal of Inclusive Education*, 18 (5): 443–458, doi: 10.1080/13603116.2013.788222

United Nations. 1948. "Universal Declaration of Human Rights." www.un.org/en/universal-declaration-human-rights/

United Nations (UN). 1989. *United Nations Convention on the Rights of the Child.* Geneva: United Nations.

United Nations. 2006. "United Nations Convention on the Rights of Persons with Disabilities (UNCRPD)." www.un.org/development/desa/disabilities/convention-on-the-rights-of-persons-with-disabilities.html

United Nations (UN). 2015. "Sustainable Development Goals." https://sustainabledevelopment.un.org/?menu=1300

United Nations Committee on the Rights of the Child. 2006. "General Comment No. 9. The Rights of Children with Disabilities." www.refworld.org/docid/461b93f72.html

United Nations Educational, Scientific and Cultural Organisation (UNESCO). 1974. "Record of the General Conference, 18th Session, Paris 17 October to 23 November 1974. Vol. 1: Resolutions." https://unesdoc.unesco.org/ark:/48223/pf0000114040

United Nations Educational, Scientific and Cultural Organisation (UNESCO). 1990. "World Declaration on Education for All and Framework for Action to Meet Basic Learning Needs." https://unesdoc.unesco.org/ark:/48223/pf0000127583

United Nations Educational, Scientific and Cultural Organisation (UNESCO). 1994. *The Salamanca Statement and Framework for Action on Special Needs Education. Adopted by the World Conference on Special Needs Education: Access and Equity*. Paris: UNESCO.

United Nations Educational, Scientific and Cultural Organisation (UNESCO). 2000. "The Dakar Framework for Action." https://unesdoc.unesco.org/ark:/48223/pf0000198641?posInSet=4&queryId=2f614d4b-101a-4f63-b537-3f4ba770ecc3

United Nations Educational, Scientific and Cultural Organisation (UNESCO). 2005. "Guidelines for Inclusion: Ensuring Access to Education for All." https://unesdoc.unesco.org/ark:/48223/pf0000140224

United Nations Educational, Scientific and Cultural Organisation. 2016. "Global Status Report. School Violence and Bullying." https://unesdoc.unesco.org/ark:/48223/pf0000246970

World Health Organisation (WHO). 2013. "Disability Weights in the Global Burden of Disease. Unclear Meaning and Overstatement of International Agreement." *Health Policy*, 111 (1): 99–104, doi: 10.1016/j.healthpol

World Health Organisation (WHO) and World Bank. 2011. "World Report on Disability." www.who.int/disabilities/world_report/2011/report.pdf

13

YOUNG CHILDREN'S RIGHTS IN 'TOUGH' TIMES

Towards an intersectional children's rights policy agenda in Greece and Scotland

Kristina Konstantoni and Kyriaki Patsianta

Introduction

On 20 November 1989, the United Nations General Assembly adopted the United Nations Convention on the Rights of the Child (UNCRC) (United Nations (UN), 1989), drawing academic, policy and practice attention to children's rights (CR). Progress has been made by many countries in incorporating the UNCRC into national laws and policies, but differences between countries exist regarding the state and progress of CR in respect of policy discourses and implementation (Gadda, Harris, Tisdall and Millership, 2019), and securing recognition of CR for children younger than 8 years remains challenging (Liwski, 2006; United Nations Committee on the Rights of the Child (UNCRC), 2005). This situation contravenes the UNCRC (UN, 1989), which states that country governments that have ratified UNCRC 'have a responsibility to take all available measures to make sure children's rights are respected, protected and fulfilled' (Article 4). This chapter engages with the politics of childhood, particularly in respect of early childhood up to 8 years, to showcase differences in CR policy and rhetoric between two 'Minority World' states: Greece and Scotland.

The term 'Majority World' refers to 'the majority of the world's population, poverty, land mass and lifestyles [which are] located in Africa, Asia and Latin America' (Punch, 2016, p. 353). In Majority World countries, children tend to combine work, school and play, whereas children in the Minority World are less likely to work (Punch, 2019, p. 1). While concepts of Majority and Minority World states may lead to homogeneous perceptions of dissimilar contexts (Konstantoni, 2012), they can also be helpful for understanding diverse childhood experiences (Hanson, Abebe, Aitken, Balagopalan and Punch, 2018; Punch, 2016; Punch and Tisdall, 2012). Cross-cultural learning opportunities may emerge from consideration of features of two or more countries in either the Majority World or the Minority World, or in one of these. The focus of this chapter is on the latter: two countries from the Minority World.

In recent years, people in both Scotland and Greece have experienced austerity and the arrival of many refugees and migrants; at the time of writing, young children are subject to complex inequalities in both countries. This chapter explores the current policy agenda and implementation of CR in the two countries to critique these 'wicked problems': complex challenges that lie at the juncture of multiple disciplines and synergies and cannot be solved easily (Grint, 2008). In the chapter, we argue that addressing such 'wicked problems' requires an intersectional approach to CR policy to facilitate 'a strengthening and deepening of the current rights framework' (Wall, 2008, p. 537) and we propose an intersectional approach to young children's rights policy and practice. By 'intersectional approach' to CR policy, we mean a policy approach that responds to complex childhood inequalities by addressing 'the simultaneous and interacting effects of gender, race, class, sexual orientation, and national origin (and others) as categories of difference' in children's lives (Bassel and Emejulu, 2010, p. 518).

We open the chapter by explaining in detail why Greece and Scotland are worthy cases for focus and comparison concerning an intersectional CR policy agenda. We then engage with key debates in the childhood studies (CS) field, looking first at how CS may link with the fields of intersectionality and early childhood, then at the emerging field of CR studies, with particular emphasis on younger children. Next, the chapter focuses on Scotland, analysing its CR policy landscape, before critiquing how CR policy there influences young children's rights (YCR) in practice, especially in respect of early childhood education and care (ECEC) provision for young children living in Scotland. In the following section, we analyse the CR policy landscape in Greece, then we discuss critically some ways that policy affects YCR in practice in Greece, particularly in ECEC provision for young children. We then propose an intersectional approach to young children's rights policy and practice in Scotland and Greece, before concluding the chapter.

The rationale for Greece and Scotland

Greece and Scotland are diverse European countries, challenged to varying degrees in the early part of the twenty-first century by austerity, the European refugee and migrant crisis, and the implementation of CR, including YCR.

Since 2009, Greece has experienced exceptional levels of austerity and reduction of its welfare state (Child Rights International Network (CRIN), 2016). Greece is also at the forefront of the European refugee and migrant crisis (United Nations Children's Fund (UNICEF), 2018), having further played a key role in the EU–Turkey agreement 2016, with border controls that have trapped refugees in the country. Children have been especially affected by this situation; in 2016, for example, 37 per cent of refugees and migrants arriving in Greece by sea were children (United Nations High Commissioner for Refugees (UNHCR), 2016). Yet Greece only published its first National Action Plan for Children's Rights as recently as 2018 (Hellenic Government, 2018), and early educational philosophies and pedagogies inspired by CR principles are not yet widespread in Greek ECEC provision.

Scotland has also been affected by austerity in the early years of the twenty-first century, with one in four children officially recognised as living in poverty, a percentage higher than many other European countries (Child Poverty Action Group, 2018). Compared with Greece, Scotland has received fewer refugee and migrant children via the Vulnerable Persons Resettlement Scheme (UK Government, 2018). Unlike Greece, Scotland has a strong policy rhetoric concerning CR; early learning and childcare are high on its policy agenda and are regarded as tools to address social inequalities in Scotland (Dunlop, 2016).

These two country cases are interesting to compare for two reasons. First, they are both European countries, but their geographical, political, cultural and socio-economic differences have led to diversity in their experiences, needs and responses to the 2008 global financial crisis and the European refugee and migrant crisis. For example, Greece is considered a country of transit for many migrants, whereas Scotland is a destination. Second, both countries have ratified the UNCRC but their current implementation of CR in policy and practice is divergent, with Scotland at a more advanced stage than Greece in respect of CR, at least in terms of policy. However, Greece has many CR grassroots initiatives that are building momentum for CR change (e.g. the Network for Children's Rights in Athens) (Patsianta, 2016).

Links between the fields of childhood studies, early childhood and intersectionality

Intersectionality theory derives from black feminist thought and grassroots activism, political and legal sociology (Crenshaw, 1989). It has received attention across various social science disciplines as a way to understand difference and complexity in social and political life. Intersectionality is defined as 'the interaction between gender, race and other categories of difference ... and the outcomes of these interactions in terms of power' (Davis, 2008, p. 68; see also Crenshaw, 1989). As a theoretical and practical framework, intersectionality seeks the transformation of institutions towards social justice aims (Konstantoni and Emejulu, 2017). Cho, Crenshaw and McCall (2013) refer to three ways in which intersectionality studies have been used: the first applies intersectional frames of analysis to research; the second draws attention to intersectionality as theory and methodology; and the third explores intersectionality as praxis beyond academia. Cho et al. (2013) state that 'further elaboration of intersectionality's theoretical and practical content can be advanced through collaborative efforts across and within disciplines, sectors, and national contexts' (p. 807).

Childhood studies (CS) is a field characterised by participation and rights, critical understandings of the social construction of childhood, children positioned as subjects, not objects of research, and children as agentic social actors in their communities (Tisdall and Punch, 2012). CS has focused on diversity, social inequalities and identities in different socio-spatial and cultural contexts, and advocates of CS have long advocated for the importance of CR. However, Punch (2019) argues that the CS field is hindered by a persistent gap between academic discourse, on the one hand, and policy and practice, on the other. Alongside this tension, a call to develop deeper intersectional understandings of CR within CS has emerged (Konstantoni and Emejulu, 2017). Konstantoni and Emejulu (2017) recently provided the first explicit theoretical attempt to develop critically an analytical, theoretical and practical framework for applying the concept of intersectionality in the interdisciplinary field of childhood studies. Prior to this, there had been no wide critical and analytical debate about the theories, methods, practices and politics of intersectionality in the field of childhood studies (Alanen, 2016).

The field of early childhood is multidisciplinary and has attracted much attention from different disciplines, including psychology, sociology, history, human geography, philosophy, design and architecture, which aim to investigate young children's lives and experiences and how early childhood is constructed. Evidence shows that early childhood experiences impact on children's present and future development, well-being, economic security and lifetime outcomes (Organisation for Economic Co-operation and Development (OECD), 2012, 2017; United Nations Children's Fund (UNICEF), 2014). The strength of this evidence has resulted in significant financial and political investment on children and children's services globally (Davis et al., 2016). However, there is also increasing evidence to suggest that younger children face deeper inequalities than others, including poverty, and are often deprived of their rights (O'Kane, 2016). Children have faced particularly deep intersectional inequalities as a result of the severity of the global austerity and European refugee and migrant crises of the early twenty-first century – the 'double crisis' (Ruxton, 2012). However, research in the CS field that has adopted intersectional analysis of inequalities has tended to focus on older children, so young children are further excluded and disadvantaged (Kustatscher, Konstantoni and Emejulu, 2015).

Links between the fields of childhood studies and children's rights

Since the inception of the UNCRC (UN, 1989), the field of CR studies has begun to emerge. CR studies shares similar interests with the fields of childhood studies, including positioning children as agentic social actors and children as subjects rather than objects. The emerging field of CR studies has also highlighted intersectionality's 'potential to contribute to a strengthening and deepening of the current rights framework' (Wall, 2008, p. 537), responding in this way to the diversity of children and the interacting oppressions they experience (De Graeve, 2015). In the CR field, a shift 'from a top-down understanding towards a bottom-up approach of children's rights' and the importance of a contextual understanding of these rights has recently been conceptualised as living rights (Vandenhole, Desmet, Reynaert and Lembrechts, 2015, p. xv). Living rights highlight that children, 'while making use of notions of rights, shape what these rights are – and become – in the social world', challenging in this way that children's rights are 'exclusively … defined by international institutions or states' (Hanson and Nieuwenhuys, 2012, p. 6).

Within the austerity regime of the early twenty-first century, early intervention has become a key driver internationally for shaping early childhood policies and practices to address inequalities (Farrell, Kagan and Tisdall, 2016). For example, high-quality early childhood education and care (ECEC) can act as a protective factor for children against negative effects of poverty and other intersectional inequalities and improve long-term developmental and employment outcomes (García, Heckman, Leaf and Prados, 2017; Organisation for Economic Co-operation and Development (OECD), 2018). Therefore, increasing access to high-quality ECEC has become an international imperative (OECD 2018; United Nations, 2015).

The effects of the 'double crisis' on children and their experiences of living rights in such 'tough times' reveal interacting experiences of childhood inequalities and rights from a bottom-up perspective. Literature concerning CR and participation has 'concentrated on older children and young people' (Tisdall, 2016, p. 13), despite General Comment 7, which emphasised the explicit recognition of 'Implementing Child Rights in Early Childhood' (UNCRC, 2005). Therefore, understanding living rights as experienced by young children, including babies, while challenging, is intellectually exciting.

The case of early childhood rights in Scotland

The children's rights policy landscape in Scotland

Scotland is a devolved nation of the UK. Following the 1997 devolution referendum, the Scotland Act 1998 enacted the current parliament as a devolved legislator. Education and training, health and social services, law, and local government are matters devolved to the

Scottish Government. The UK ratified the UNCRC (UN, 1989) in 1991, but although bound by international law, the UNCRC has not yet been fully incorporated into domestic law. This means that although the UNCRC gives children in the UK a comprehensive set of economic, cultural, social and political rights, they cannot rely on them in court, and complaints cannot be brought to court solely on the basis of a potential breach of the UNCRC (UN, 1989).

Nevertheless, as a devolved nation of the UK, Scotland has certain obligations regarding implementation of the UNCRC, and Scotland has an official national commitment to 'making rights real', with policy and strategies in place to embed children's rights legally and in practice (Gadda et al., 2019). A significant piece of legislation in Scotland is the Children and Young People Act that came into force in 2014 (Scottish Government, 2014a). The Scottish Government has taken positive steps to implement children's rights. The Scottish Government submits a report to the Scottish Parliament every three years about steps taken to implement the UNCRC and planned actions. The UNCRC (UN, 1989) is explicitly mentioned in Scottish domestic legislation, providing 'a platform for systemic change' (Gadda et al., 2019, p. 3). However, the duties that comprise that platform have been considered 'vague and weak legally', with stronger accountability needed to implement CR (Gadda et al., 2019, p. 3).

The Scottish Government is making stronger commitments to rights-based approaches, including the establishment of 'an expert advisory group to lead a participatory process to make recommendations on how Scotland can continue to lead by example in human rights' (Scottish Government, 2017, p. 22). Gadda et al. (2019) stress the importance of 'involving children and young people in the implementation, monitoring and evaluation of embedding children's rights into legislation and practical experience' (p. 10). Scotland has an official national commitment to 'making rights real' with policy strategies in place with an aim to embed children's rights legally and in practice (Gadda et al., 2019), and it follows a national approach for supporting children: 'Getting It Right for Every Child' (Scottish Government, 2012). The Scottish Government has also 'integrated non-legislative measures into legislation and policy', including child rights and well-being impact assessments (Gadda et al., 2019, p. 10); 2018 was the Scottish Government's Year of Young People, and the Scottish Cabinet held its first official meeting with children and young people in March 2016, with a commitment to make this an annual event to ensure that their views are taken into account in high-level decision-making: 'children and young people's involvement in governance is growing' in Scotland (Gadda et al., 2019, p. 3). However, there remain gaps in the recognition and implementation of CR in Scotland (Scottish Alliance for Children's Rights, 2016).

Young children's rights in Scotland: early learning and childcare provision

Scotland's early learning and childcare (ELC) offers young children 'entitlements, opportunities, expectations and aspirations' (Dunlop, 2016, p. 1). Within ELC, there are policies and strategies in place and practice guidance linked to early years and children's rights. For example, the *Early Years Framework* (Scottish Government, 2008) sets out a vision for early years services in Scotland to ensure that children get 'the best start in life'. Equally, *Building the Ambition* (Scottish Government, 2014b) provides national practice guidance for all those working in early learning and childcare for babies and young children. *Pre-Birth to Three: Positive Outcomes for Scotland's Children and Families* (Learning and Teaching Scotland, 2010) is national guidance to support practitioners and students working with babies and children

(0–3) and their families, and the *Curriculum for Excellence* (Scottish Government, 2004), builds on foundations developed in the period pre-birth to 3 years, providing a broad general education for all children in Scotland from 3 to 18 years. Evaluation methodologies are also available, including *How Good Is Our Early Learning and Childcare* (Education Scotland, 2016). Alongside these documents, the Scottish Government emphasises skills development and professional registering bodies to provide a fully qualified workforce in children's services. For example, the *Standard for Childhood Practice Revised* (Scottish Social Services Council, 2015) governs the practice of childhood practitioners.

In Scotland, care has been taken to link policies to social justice aims. Key debates in Scottish early years policy align with aspirations to combat inequalities by prioritising high-quality early learning and childcare provision and closing the attainment gap between socio-economically disadvantaged and affluent children (Dunlop, 2016). Providing flexible, high-quality, accessible, affordable, integrated early learning and childcare, supporting parents/carers to work, train or study, and a skilled children's workforce to improve ELS quality are integral to these aspirations. The Children and Young People (Scotland) Act 2014 (Scottish Government, 2014a) made 600 hours of free ELC available for all children aged 3 and 4 years old, as well as eligible 2-year-olds, in Scotland. The Scottish Government has committed to expanding early years provision and increasing the hours of free ELC to 1,140 hours per year by 2020.

Given its range of policies in place linked to children's rights and early childhood, Scotland may be described as progressive. However, the key issue within the Scottish context is that the policy has not smoothly translated into practice (Dunlop, 2016). Without that translation, policy cannot address the complex and intersecting inequalities that young children face in Scotland. For example, there is a tendency in policy rhetoric to focus on combatting poverty (Dunlop, 2016) without addressing the complex causes and effects of poverty. Equally, little work has been done concerning children's rights to non-discrimination and intersectional inequalities (Harris, 2014), yet there is a growing body of work showing that young children are experiencing complex inequalities (Konstantoni and Emejulu, 2017).

The case of early childhood rights in Greece

The children's rights policy landscape in Greece

The UNCRC defines a child as 'every human being below the age of eighteen years unless under the law applicable to the child, majority is attained earlier' (Article 1) (UN, 1989), while the United Nations Committee on the Rights of the Child (UNCRC) (2005) defines early childhood as 'the period below the age of 8 years' (p. 2), but observes that YCR do not receive adequate attention in national legislation and policies. The UNCRC (2005) specifies that children of all ages are 'holders of all the rights enshrined in the Convention' (p. 2), including the right to the enjoyment of the highest attainable standard of health (Article 24), the right to education (Article 28) and the right to play (Article 31) (UN, 1989). However, in Greece, babies and toddlers are not considered 'persons in their own right' or 'active members' of their family and community who need 'physical nurturance, emotional care and sensitive guidance' to exercise their rights successfully (UNCRC, 2005, p. 3). There is no organised system in Greece to protect and nurture CR, so the effective exercise of the youngest children's rights depends on the goodwill of their family and carers.

Despite ratification by Greece of the UNCRC in 1992 (UN, 1989) (Law 2101/1992), by 2012 there was still no clear legal framework in Greece for safeguarding CR and no comprehensive system to coordinate implementing and protecting CR in the country (UNCRC, 2012, pp. 3, 5). The Children's Rights Department of the Independent Authority of the Greek Ombudsman monitors the fulfilment of CR in Greece (UNCRC, 2012, p. 4), but its activities cannot fully guarantee CR. Moreover, the economic crisis of the early twenty-first century made the situation worse, reducing social investment in CR, public spending (education, healthcare) and subsistence costs for families (UNCRC, 2012, pp. 2, 4). Finally, in 2017, the Ministry of Justice (MoJ) established a body to develop, monitor and evaluate national plans of action for CR (Article 8, Law 4491/2017) on the basis of Articles 8–12 of Law 4491/2017. This body consults stakeholders, including children (Articles 10 and 12 of Law 4491/2017), but its responsibilities are vague and its activities are not subject to external scrutiny. Nevertheless, in 2018, the MoJ developed a national plan of action for CR, consisting of a lengthy list of programmes on CR funded by different ministries and entities, mostly based in Athens, the country's capital. However, the 2018 National Action Plan lacked strategic, time-bound and measurable goals to monitor progress and failed to uphold a key UNCRC principle (Article 12): the right of the child to express his or her views freely in all matters that affect him or her (UN, 1989; UNCRC, 2003, pp. 3–4).

In the 2018 Greek National Action Plan, few actions concerned young children. For example, the Ministry of Health aimed to raise awareness of the importance of breastfeeding but provided no plan of action to achieve this aim. Despite the lack of policies and legislation for young children in Greece, an attempt has been made to build an ECEC system that underpins children's physical, emotional, mental and social development (Ministry of Education, Research and Religious Affairs (MERRA), 2003). In theory, the kindergarten curriculum takes into consideration children's individualities, their interests and needs, Greek cultural products and social values, as well as the need to provide children with knowledge, skills and values in order to enable them to live a happy and creative life (MERRA, 2003). Although children's interests are supposedly taken into consideration, there is a tendency to view adults as the ones who transmit knowledge and values, rather than emphasise a more participatory and child-led pedagogical approach. This will be further discussed in the following section.

Young children's rights in Greece: early learning and childcare provision

Until recently, school attendance in Greece was compulsory from 5 years onwards, but in September 2018 school attendance became compulsory for children reaching 4 years old in 184 municipalities of the country, with the rest of Greece following suit. MERRA (2003) established guidelines for designing kindergarten curricula that acknowledge the important contribution of ECE to young children's holistic development and prioritise that young children's learning should be shaped by children themselves. The importance of evaluating and updating the full range of educational work, to improve its impact on the lives of children and their families, is explicitly underlined in the guidelines, which also emphasise that children's assessments should be compatible with their age, daily, continuous and tailored to each child. The guidelines state that educational progress should be assessed in relation to children's potential and capabilities, and not in comparison to their classmates, and collaboration between teachers and parents regarding children's progress should be cultivated. The Ministry of Education, Research and Religious Affairs (MERRA, 2018, p. 4) affords teachers flexibility to adjust children's daily schedule according to their needs. MERRA (2018, pp. 8–9) also underlines that ECE teachers should attend regular mandatory training.

Although the MERRA (2003) kindergarten curriculum guidelines do not refer explicitly to YCR, they influence the realisation of YCR in Greece. For example, they underline the importance of quality education for young children, linking early education to child development (UN, 1989, Article 29)[1] and they promote 'child-centered', 'child-friendly' ECE (UNCRC, 2001, p. 2; 2005, p. 13). They also recognise 'the value of creative play and exploratory learning' and the right of young children to express their views and feelings, according to their 'levels of understanding and preferred ways of communicating' (UNCRC, 2005, pp. 6–7, 15).

Nevertheless, the Greek kindergarten guidelines present some serious shortcomings, elucidating why the UNCRC (2012) urged Greece to 'intensify its efforts to incorporate child rights issues into all curricula of different levels of education' (p. 5). First, the guidelines do not refer explicitly to the UNCRC (UN, 1989) and they do not identify young children as rights-holders. Moreover, they do not advocate for education that empowers children by 'providing them with practical opportunities to exercise their rights and responsibilities in ways adapted to their interests, concerns and evolving capacities' (UNCRC, 2005, p. 15). The guidelines seem to disregard young children as 'persons in their own right' (UNCRC, 2005, p. 3) by emphasising that parents' expectations should be considered when shaping kindergarten curricula (MERRA, 2003, p. 586), which disregards young children as people with their own views and thoughts (Sandberg, 2014, p. 3). Equally, while MERRA (2018, p. 10) makes brief reference to marginalised young children's groups (Roma and refugee children), regarding school enrolment requirements, the guidelines seem to pay little attention overall to children that face intersectional inequalities, and while they state that each child's individual needs should be taken into consideration in ECE, they do not emphasise the specific needs of children who are marginalised because of their status, such as refugee or homeless children.

Due to limited financial resources, the Greek ECE guidelines (MERRA, 2003) have not yet been fully implemented (Tsalagiorgou and Avgitidou, 2017; UNCRC, 2012, pp. 2, 4). Indeed, the Greek educational system as a whole has weaknesses that affect the quality of ECE: education is not regulated (Pios, 2013), teacher attrition is high (Tsalagiorgou and Avgitidou, 2017, p. 255), and teachers' professional development is inconsistent and does not focus on CR (Filokosta, 2010; UNCRC, 2012, pp. 5–6). Additionally – and of particular concern for YCR – child-initiated learning and free play are very limited in ECE (Tsalagiorgou and Avgitidou, 2017, p. 256).

Towards an intersectional approach to young children's rights policy and practice in Scotland and Greece

Policy plays a significant role in creating socially just societies (Hankivsky, Grace, Hunting and Ferlatte, 2012), yet the world of public policy is in a constant state of flux, due to political, economic, environmental and health crises 'creating new kinds of policy problems and challenges at international and national levels' (Hankivsky et al., 2012, p. 7; Orsini and Smith, 2007). In the light of the 'double crisis' and its effects, the usefulness of existing policies for responding to 'wicked problems' may benefit from examination. Intersectionality has the potential to advance equity in public policy and practice, by supporting the 'development of appropriate equality objectives and equality outcomes' (Christoffersen, 2017, p. 2; Hankivsky et al., 2012, p. 7). However, as we have indicated, intersectionality applied to early childhood policy and practice has yet to fulfil its promise in securing high-quality early childhood services and CR for all children in the country cases of Scotland and Greece.

Adopting intersectionality as a model enables those who use it to question who is benefiting and who is excluded from policy goals, agendas and priorities, taking into account the 'multi-level interacting social locations, forces, factors and power structures that shape and influence human life' (Hankivsky et al., 2012, p. 8). Therefore, intersectional analysis can support new understandings of children's lived experiences of complex inequalities and in turn allow for the development of effective strategies to address them.

Ferree (2009, cited in Hankivsky et al., 2012) warns of:

> policies that, by privileging the treatment of some inequities and ignoring the fact that inequalities are often mutually constitutive, end up marginalizing some people, reproducing power mechanisms among groups, and failing to address the creation of categories that are at the root of the constitution of inequities. Applying intersectionality in the context of policy can thus be considered a political action, as it demonstrates a commitment to ameliorating inequitable relations of power that maintain inequity – relations that often remain unquestioned in dominant policy approaches.
>
> *(p. 18)*

New empirical examples are needed to help us to understand how intersectionality can be operationalised in policy concerning early childhood and children's rights and what that could mean in practice for all children.

Bacchi and Eveline (2010) argue that 'policies do not simply "impact" on people; they "create" people' (p. 52), including their social positionings and access to power and resources. However, this stand undermines the complexity of people's agency and lived experiences, which are themselves constructed in intersectional contexts and draw on intersectional resources. For example, although Greek social policy has neither an explicit CR policy agenda nor framework, unlike Scotland, significant work is being undertaken by third sector organisations in Greece in respect of advocacy and practical implementation of CR (Patsianta, 2016). Moreover, irrespective of wider social policy, young children shape and make use of their rights through their everyday lived experiences. For example, although young children's participation does not feature explicitly in the Greek National Action Plan for the implementation of CR, a recent study undertaken in Greece found that children claimed their right to be listened to and to participate within private–family and public–community spaces on an everyday basis, albeit with varying degrees of success (Konstantoni, 2019).

These points suggest that applying intersectionality to the concept of living rights is a useful option for understanding and implementing young children's rights, shaped by institutions and also by children and their advocates in the social world. Manuel (2006) argues that 'intersectionality theory represents an incredibly useful analytical lens for policy scholars who wish to strengthen the explanatory power of policy models that evaluate policy impacts and outcomes' (p. 175). Understanding living rights through the lens of intersectionality offers new possibilities for advancing our knowledge and understanding about the policies and practices concerning young children's rights.

Conclusion

In this chapter, we have engaged with the politics of childhoods. We have compared policy and practice landscapes concerning young children's rights in two Minority World countries – Scotland and Greece – to reveal striking differences in children's rights policy, rhetoric and practice. Scotland has an official national commitment to 'making rights real', with strategies in place to embed children's rights legally and practically in their lives (Gadda et al., 2019), whereas Greece has only just published its first National Action Plan for CR (Hellenic Government, 2018). However, irrespective of either country's policy progress in relation to children's rights, both countries face challenges in implementing CR in practice. This is problematic, since both governments have ratified the UNCRC, and as such are responsible for protecting CR (UN, 1989, Article 4). Finally, drawing on theoretical perspectives and recognising that CR are shaped not only by institutions, but also by children operating in the social world, we have argued that engaging with the concepts of living rights and intersectionality may offer new possibilities for advancing our knowledge and understanding the policies and practices concerning young children's rights.

Note

1 Article 29(a) of the CRC: 'States Parties agree that the education of the child shall be directed to:
(a) The development of the child's personality, talents and mental and physical abilities to their fullest potential.'

References

Alanen, Leena. 2016. "'Intersectionality' and Other Challenges to Theorizing Childhood." *Childhood*, 23 (2): 157–161, doi: 10.1177/0907568216631055.

Bacchi, Carol, and Joan Eveline. 2010. "Mainstreaming and Neoliberalism: A Contested Relationship." In *Mainstreaming Politics: Gendering Practices and Feminist Theory*, edited by Carol Bacchi and Joan Eveline, 39–60. Adelaide: University of Adelaide Press.

Bassel, Leah, and Akwugo Emejulu. 2010. "Struggles for Institutional Space in France and the United Kingdom: Intersectionality and the Politics of Policy." *Politics & Gender*, 6 (4): 517–544, doi: 10.1017/S1743923X10000358.

Child Poverty Action Group. 2018. "Child Poverty in Scotland." www.cpag.org.uk/scotland/child-poverty-facts-and-figures

Child Rights International Network (CRIN). 2016. "Greece: Children's Rights References in the Universal Periodic Review." https://archive.crin.org/en/library/publications/greece-childrens-rights-references-universal-periodic-review.html

Cho, Sumi, Kimberlé Crenshaw, and Leslie McCall. 2013. "Toward a Field of Intersectionality Studies: Theory, Applications, and Praxis." *Signs*, 38 (4): 785–810, doi: 10.1086/669608.

Christoffersen, Ashlee. 2017. "Intersectional Approaches to Equality Research and Data. Research and Data Briefing." *Equality Challenge Unit*. www.ecu.ac.uk/wp-content/uploads/2017/04/Research_and_data_briefing_2_Intersectional_approaches_to_equality_research_and_data.pdf

Crenshaw, Kimberlé W. 1989. "Demarginalizing the Intersection of Race and Sex: A Black Feminist Critique of Antidiscrimination Doctrine, Feminist Theory and Antiracist Politics." *The University of Chicago Legal Forum*, 140: 139–167. https://chicagounbound.uchicago.edu/uclf/vol1989/iss1/8

Davis, John, Rona MacNicol, Lynn McNair, Jamie Mann, Melissa O'Neill, and Ben Wray. 2016. *An Equal Start: A Plan for Equality in Early Learning and Care in Scotland*. Biggar. https://pureportal.strath.ac.uk/en/publications/an-equal-start-a-plan-for-equality-in-early-learning-and-care-in-

Davis, Kathy. 2008. "Intersectionality as Buzzword: A Sociology of Science Perspective on What Makes a Feminist Theory Successful." *Feminist Theory*, 9 (1): 67–85, doi: 10.1177/1464700108086364

De Graeve, Katrien. 2015. "Children's Rights from a Gender Studies Perspective: Gender, Intersectionality and Ethics of Care." In *The Routledge International Handbook of Children's Rights Studies*, edited by Wouter Vandenhole, Ellen Desmet, Didier Reynaert and Sarah Lembrechts, 147–163. London: Routledge.

Dunlop, Aline-Wendy. 2016. "A View from Scotland: Early Years Policy in the Four Nations: Common Challenges, Diverse Solutions." *Early Education Journal*, 78 (10–12): 15.

Education Scotland. 2016. "How Good Is Our Early Learning and Childcare." https://education.gov.scot/improvement/documents/frameworks_selfevaluation/frwk1_niheditself-evaluationhgielc/hgioelc020316revised.pdf

Farrell, Ann, Sharon Lynn Kagan, and E. Kay M. Tisdall (Eds). 2016. *The Sage Handbook of Early Childhood Research*. London: Sage.

Ferree, Myra Marx. 2009. "Inequality, Intersectionality and the Politics of Discourse: Framing Feminist Alliances." In *The Discursive Politics of Gender Equality: Stretching, Bending and Policy-making*, edited by Emanuela Lombardo, Petra Meier and Meike Verloo, 86–104. London: Routledge.

Filokosta, Theodora. 2010. "Αντιλήψεις των εκπαιδευτικών για την επιμόρφωσή τους [Teachers' point of view on their professional education]." Master's Dissertation, University of Thessaly. http://ir.lib.uth.gr/handle/11615/14334?locale-attribute=en.

Gadda, Andressa, M. Juliet Harris, E. Kay M. Tisdall, and Elizabeth Millership. 2019. "'Making Children's Rights Real': Lessons from Policy Networks and Contribution Analysis." *International Journal of Human Rights*, 1–16. doi: 10.1080/13642987.2018.1558988

García, Jorge Luis, James J. Heckman, Duncan Ermini Leaf, and Maria Jose Prados. 2017. *Quantifying the Life-cycle Benefits of a Prototypical Early Childhood Program*. Cambridge, MA: National Bureau of Economic Research. doi: 10.3386/w23479

Grint, Keith. 2008. "Wicked Problems and Clumsy Solutions: The Role of Leadership." *Clinical Leader*, 1 (2): 54–68, doi: 10.1057/9780230277953_11

Hankivsky, Olena, Daniel Grace, Gemma Hunting, and Olivier Ferlatte. 2012. "Why Intersectionality Matters for Health Equity and Policy Analysis." In *An Intersectionality-Based Policy Analysis Framework*, edited by Olena Hankivsky, 7–30. Vancouver, BC: Institute for Intersectionality Research and Policy, Simon Fraser University.

Hanson, Karl, Tatek Abebe, Stuart C. Aitken, Sarada Balagopalan, and Samantha Punch. 2018. "Global/Local' Research on Children and Childhood in a 'global Society'." *Childhood*, 25 (3): 272–296, doi: 10.1177/0907568218779480

Hanson, Karl, and Olga Nieuwenhuys. 2012. "Living Rights, Social Justice, Translations." In *Reconceptualizing Children's Rights in International Development: Living Rights, Social Justice, Translations*, edited by Karl Hanson and Olga Nieuwenhuys, 3–26. Cambridge: Cambridge University Press.

Harris, Juliet. 2014. "Using the UNCRC to Consider Intersectionality in Policy and Practice." Spotlight Presentation at Scottish Universities Insight Institute Seminar Series, *Children's Rights, Social Justice and Social Identities in Scotland. Seminar 4. Intersectional childhoods: Practical applications across Practice, Policy and Research'*, 2 October 2014, Glasgow.

Hellenic Government. 2018. *National Action Plan for Children's Rights*. https://government.gov.gr/eth niko-schedio-drasis-gia-ta-dikeomata-tou-pediou/

Konstantoni, Kristina. 2012. "Children's Peer Relationships and Social Identities: Exploring Cases of Young Children's Agency and Complex Interdependencies from the Minority World." *Children's Geographies*, 10 (3): 337–346, doi: 10.1080/14733285.2012.693382

Konstantoni, Kristina. 2019. "Towards Intersectional Childhood Studies: Beyond Diverse Childhoods." Invited Keynote at Bergische University Wuppertal, Germany, 22 January 2019.

Konstantoni, Kristina, and Akwugo Emejulu. 2017. "When Intersectionality Met Childhood Studies: The Dilemmas of a Travelling Concept." *Children's Geographies*, 15 (1): 6–22, doi: 10.1080/14733285.2016.1249824.

Kustatscher, Marlies, Kristina Konstantoni, and Akwugo Emejulu. 2015. "Hybridity, Hyphens and Intersectionality-Relational Understandings of Children and Young People's Social Identities." In *Families, Intergenerationality, and Peer Group Relations*, edited by Samantha Punch, Robert M. Vanderbeck and Tracey Skelton, 1–19. Singapore: Springer.

Learning and Teaching Scotland. 2010. *Pre-Birth to Three: Positive Outcomes for Scotland's Children and Families*. Glasgow: Learning and Teaching Scotland. https://education.gov.scot/improvement/docu ments/elc/elc2_prebirthtothree/elc2_prebirthtothreebooklet.pdf.

Liwski, Norberto I. 2006. "Implementing Child Rights in Early Childhood." In *A Guide to General Comment 7: Implementing Child Rights in Early Childhood*, edited by United Nations Committee on the Rights of the Child United Nations Children's Fund and Bernard van Leer Foundation, 8–10. The Hague: Bernard van Leer Foundation. https://issuu.com/bernardvanleer foundation/docs/a_guide_to_general_comment_7_implementing_child_ri.

Manuel, Tiffany. 2006. "Envisioning the Possibilities for a Good Life: Exploring the Public Policy Implications of Intersectionality Theory." *Journal of Women, Politics and Policy*, 28 (3–4): 173–203, doi: 10.1300/J501v28n03_08.

Ministry of Education, Research and Religious Affairs (MERRA). 2003. *Διαθεματικό Ενιαίο Πλαίσιο Προγραμμάτων Σπουδών (Δ.Ε.Π.Π.Σ.) και Αναλυτικό Πρόγραμμα Σπουδών (Α.Π.Σ.) για το*

Νηπιαγωγείο [Cross-Thematic Comprehensive Curriculum Framework and Detailed Curriculum for Kindergarten]. www.pi-schools.gr/programs/depps/

Ministry of Education, Research and Religious Affairs (MERRA). 2018. *Λειτουργία Νηπιαγωγείων για το σχολικό έτος 2018–2019* [Operation of Kindergartners for the School Year 2018–2019]. www.alfa vita.gr/ekpaideysi/266440_egkyklios-leitoyrgia-nipiagogeion-gia-sholiko-etos-2018-2019

O'Kane, Claire. 2016. "Children in Conflict Situations: Applying Childhood Research with a Focus on the Early Years." In *The Sage Handbook of Early Childhood Research*, edited by Ann Farrell, Sharon Lynn Kagan and E. Kay M. Tisdall, 345–362. London: Sage.

Organisation for Economic and Cooperation and Development (OECD). 2012. "Starting Strong III: A Quality Toolbox for Early Childhood Education and Care." www.oecd.org/edu/school/49325825.pdf

Organisation for Economic and Cooperation and Development (OECD). 2017. "Starting Strong 2017. Key OECD Indicators on Early Childhood Education and Care." www.oecd-ilibrary.org/education/starting-strong-2017_9789264276116-en

Organisation for Economic and Cooperation and Development (OECD). 2018. *Engaging Young Children-Lessons from Research about Quality in Early Childhood Education and Care*. www.oecd.org/educa tion/engaging-young-children-9789264085145-en.htm

Orsini, Michael, and Miriam Smith. 2007. "Critical Policy Studies." In *Critical Policy Studies*, edited by Michael Orsini and Miriam Smith, 1–16. Vancouver: University of British Columbia Press.

Patsianta, Kyriaki. 2016. *Μίνι οδηγός για τα δικαιώματα των νεογέννητων [Mini Guide: Newborns' Rights]*. Athens: Network for children's rights. https://kpatsianta.wordpress.com/page/

Pios, Stefanos. 2013. "Self-assessment of the Teaching Process in 1st Grade Schools: Schoolteachers' Views and Suggestions." *International Conference in Open & Distance Learning*, 7 (B): 1–21, doi: 10.12681/icodl.629

Punch, Samantha. 2016. "Cross-world and Cross-disciplinary Dialogue: A More Integrated, Global Approach to Childhood Studies." *Global Studies of Childhood*, 6 (3): 352–364, doi: 10.1177/2043610616665033

Punch, Samantha. 2019. (Forthcoming). "Why Have Generational Orderings Been Marginalised in the Social Sciences Including Childhood Studies?" *Children's Geographies*.

Punch, Samantha, and E. Kay M. Tisdall. 2012. "Exploring Children and Young People's Relationships across Majority and Minority Worlds." *Children's Geographies*, 10 (3): 241–248, doi: 10.1080/14733285.2012.693375

Ruxton, Sandy. 2012. *How the Economic and Financial Crisis Is Affecting Children and Young People in Europe*. Brussels: Eurochild.

Sandberg, Kirsten. 2014. *25 Years of the Convention on the Rights of the Child: The Genesis and Spirit of the Convention on the Rights of the Child*. New York: UNICEF. www.unicef.org/crc/files/03_CRC_25_Years_Sandberg.pdf

Scottish Alliance for Children's Rights. 2016. "State of Children's Rights Report 2016." www.togethers cotland.org.uk/pdfs/TogetherReport2016.pdf

Scottish Government. 2004. "A Curriculum for Excellence: The Curriculum Review Group." www.scotland.gov.uk/Publications/2004/11/20178/45862

Scottish Government. 2008. *The Early Years Framework I*. Edinburgh: Scottish Government. www.gov.scot/Publications/2009/01/13095148/0

Scottish Government. 2012. "Getting It Right for Every Child." www.gov.scot/policies/girfec/

Scottish Government. 2014a. "Children and Young Peoples (Scotland) Act. 2014." www.legislation.gov.uk/asp/2014/8/contents/enacted

Scottish Government. 2014b. *Building the Ambition: National Practice Guidance on Early Learning and Child-care: Children and Young People (Scotland) Act 2014*. Edinburgh: The Scottish Government.

Scottish Government. 2017. "A Nation with Ambition: The Government's Programme for Scotland 2017–2018." www.gov.scot/Publications/2017/09/8468

Scottish Social Services Council. 2015. "Standard for Childhood Practice Revised." www.sssc.uk.com/knowledgebase/article/KA-01548/en-us

Tisdall, E. Kay M. 2016. "Participation, Rights and 'participatory' Methods'." In *The Sage Handbook of Early Childhood Research*, edited by Ann Farrell, Sharon Lynn Kagan and E. Kay M. Tisdall, 73–88. London: Sage.

Tisdall, E. Kay M., and Samantha Punch. 2012. "Not So 'New'? Looking Critically at Childhood Studies." *Children's Geographies*, 10 (3): 249–264, doi: 10.1080/14733285.2012.693376

Tsalagiorgou, Eleni, and Sofia Avgitidou. 2017. "An Exploration of Early Childhood Teachers' Needs: An Effort to Document the Context of Early Childhood Education." *Hellenic Journal of Research in Education*, 6 (1): 255–273, doi: 10.12681/hjre.14764

UK Government. 2018. "Over 10,500 Refugees Resettled in the UK under Flagship Scheme." www. gov.uk/government/news/over-10000-refugees-resettled-in-the-uk-under-flagship-scheme

United Nations. 1989. *United Nations Convention on the Rights of the Child.*

United Nations (UN). 2015. "Sustainable Development Goal 4." https://sustainabledevelopment.un. org/sdg4

United Nations Children's Fund (UNICEF). 2014. "The Formative Years: UNICEF's Work on Measuring Early Childhood Development." https://data.unicef.org/resources/the-formative-years-unicefs-work-on-measuring-ecd/

United Nations Children's Fund (UNICEF). 2018. "Refugee and Migrant Crisis in Europe Humanitarian Situation Report #30". www.unicef.org/eca/sites/unicef.org.eca/files/2019-02/Refugee% 20Migrant%20Crisis%20Europe%2030%20Dec%202018_0.pdf

United Nations Committee on the Rights of the Child (UNCRC). 2001. *General Comment N°1: Article 29 (1): The Aims of Education.* CRC/GC/2001/1.

United Nations Committee on the Rights of the Child (UNCRC). 2003. *General Comment N°5: General Measures of Implementation of the Convention on the Rights of the Child (Arts. 4, 42 and 44, Para. 6).* CRC/ GC/2003/5.

United Nations Committee on the Rights of the Child (UNCRC). 2005. *General Comment N°7: Implementing Child Rights in Early Childhood.* CRC/C/GC/7/Rev.1.

United Nations Committee on the Rights of the Child (UNCRC). 2012. *Consideration of Reports Submitted by States Parties under Article 44 of the Convention: Concluding Observations: Greece.* CRC/C/GRC/ CO/2-3. www2.ohchr.org/english/bodies/crc/docs/co/crc_c_grc_co_2-3.pdf

United Nations High Commissioner for Refugees (UNHCR). 2016. "Refugees and Migrants Sea Arrivals in Europe." https://data2.unhcr.org/en/documents/download/53447

Vandenhole, Wouter, Ellen Desmet, Didier Reynaert, and Sarah Lembrechts (Eds). 2015. *The Routledge International Handbook of Children's Rights Studies.* London: Routledge.

Wall, John. 2008. "Human Rights in Light of Childhood." *International Journal of Children's Rights*, 16: 523–543, doi:10.1163/157181808X312122.

14

ACHIEVING RIGHTS FOR YOUNG CHILDREN IN GHANA

Enablers and barriers

Prospera Tedam

Introduction

There has been considerable attention given to children and children's welfare by researchers, policymakers, professionals and ordinary citizens of the world. This attention has emanated from a growing understanding of the need to change the way in which children are understood and positioned in contemporary discourse. There is continual reference to children as 'the future', with little or no consideration about what kind of future we are preparing children for if we do not engage them at an early age in matters that affect them. The idea of children as rights-bearers can be at odds with many traditional communities and societies, who cite the dilution of cultural norms as the reason why rights for children is difficult to realise in Africa. This view is challenged by Ekundayo (2015), who argues that culture is fluid and can be changed by perceptions of individuals and communities. For this reason, adults must ensure that children are adequately protected from harm and exploitation, are provided opportunities to be educated with access to good healthcare, and can participate in decision-making in matters that affect them (Wyness, 2013).

In Ghana, harmful cultural and traditional practices, child labour, child domestic servitude, absence of birth registration, street children, poverty and socio-economic disadvantage have meant that rights have not been protected for all children in Ghana (United Nations (UN), 1989, Article 4). While there have been developments in the understanding of young people's rights, the same cannot be said for younger children. This chapter draws on research evidence to examine the enablers and barriers to achieving and protecting rights for young children in Ghana. Legislative and policy frameworks underpinning children's rights are examined, and practice in early childhood education and care (ECEC) is explored. The impact of gender on young children's rights is also discussed. As celebrities and artists are increasingly promoting children's rights across Ghana, the impact of this growing phenomenon is discussed, alongside the role of government and non-governmental organisations (NGOs) in advocating for the rights of young children to be given the attention and commitment they deserve. The chapter opens by providing context about the country of Ghana and children's rights there.

History and location of Ghana

Ghana, a country in West Africa, was the first sub-Saharan African country to gain its independence from Britain on 6 March 1957, and has been recognised internationally for its move from a military dictatorship to a democracy in 1992, two years after it ratified the UNCRC (Obeng-Odoom, 2010). Prior to this, Ghana had experienced five *coups d'état*, interspersed with periods of civilian rule. Ghana, known as the Gold Coast before independence, is famous for its cocoa, coffee, gold, timber, bauxite, tuna and more recently for petroleum products. Ghana shares its borders with Togo, Côte d'Ivoire and Burkina Faso, and has a population of 29.46 million people, of whom 57 per cent are estimated to be under the age of 25 years (World Population Review, 2018).

Children's rights in Ghana

Children's rights have been welcomed globally as affirming and confirming a nation's progress and development (Alston and Tobin, 2005). However, this has not meant that these rights are always respected or actively supported as a global standard. Understanding children's rights involves recognising and respecting children's integrity, dignity and worth. The UNCRC was heralded as one of the most progressive and forward-thinking conventions, ratified by many; however, according to Cowden (2016), children's rights has become a sham because countries that were quick to ratify it appear to be the ones who are unable to commit to its tenets and are violating it. In the case of Ghana and many African countries, the need for an Africa-specific set of rights for children resulted in the drafting of the African Charter on the Rights and Welfare of the Child (ACRWC) (Organisation of African Unity, 1990) as a means of Afrocentrising what has been perceived as a Western concept. Leaders of African countries claimed not to have been consulted during the drafting of the UNCRC and argued that only Algeria, Morocco, Senegal and Egypt participated meaningfully in the drafting process. Initially, the Declaration on the Rights and Welfare of the African Child (DRWAC) was adopted in Liberia in July 1979, well before the UNCRC, with the recognition that the African child needed to be protected from harm, maltreatment and exploitation, and their well-being and welfare promoted with due regard not only to their African heritage and culture, but also to the specificity or their experiences linked to poverty, hunger, war, armed conflict and ethnicity. The ACRWC recognised the nuanced context of African children's lives and in many other ways confirmed and complemented the various articles contained in the UNCRC. For example, both the UNCRC and the ACRWC regard a child to be any person who has not yet reached their 18th birthday. With regard to children's participation rights specifically, Article 7 states that freedom of expression where 'every child who is capable of communicating his or her own views shall be assured the rights to express his opinions freely in all matters and to disseminate his opinions subject to such restrictions as are prescribed by laws' (Organisation of African Unity, 1990).

The Declaration adds in Article 4 that children should be allowed to express their view in judicial and administrative proceedings. In terms of participation in relation to freedom of association and assembly, the Declaration is clear in Article 8 that children should be afforded these rights and in Article 12 that a child should be able to participate freely in cultural life. This reaffirms children's rights generally and participation rights specifically (Organisation of African Unity, 1990, p. 4); however, African societies expect African children to act in accordance with their parents' wishes and family needs (Adu-Gyamfi, 2013). In many African societies, the dominant view is that allowing children to exercise agency, autonomy and free will threatens parental control and authority.

Twum-Danso (2009, p. 423) has argued that in Ghana, children's rights can be understood within the context of what she refers to as the three Rs (respect, responsibility and reciprocity). She found that the concept of respect was operationalised by parents demanding that their children respect them by being obedient and not questioning them in any way. Children who questioned their parents were seen to be disrespectful, a trait that is shunned in homes and communities. Children in Ghana were also required to be responsible both within their homes and in the wider community. Often these responsibilities were gendered, with girls overseeing cooking and collecting water, while boys would be expected to sweep, clean their fathers' shoes and support the family trade where one existed. The value of reciprocity was seen as a culmination of being respectful and responsible in that parents would reward children with affection, time and resources. Participants in the Twum-Danso (2009) study suggested that children who were respectful and responsible could be rewarded with education and a home, and that 'if you do not respect your mother, she will take you out of school or kick you out of the house' (p. 428). This view reflects the weight given to the concept of respect within Ghanaian families and communities, and underscores sociocultural family dynamics as an important component of family life in Ghana. It is useful to recognise this as it can assist any discussion about the place of children's rights, at least in the context of the family.

Children's participation rights

Article 12 of the UNCRC is the first article about children's participation, and stipulates that:

> States Parties shall assure to the child who is capable of forming his or her own views the right to express those views freely in all matters affecting the child, the views of the child being given due weight in accordance with the age and maturity of the child.
>
> *(UN, 1989)*

In this chapter, children are acknowledged as individuals, although the decisions about what the criteria is for decision-making is mediated by the various sociopolitical and other contexts. It has been suggested that the concept of children's rights is culturally relative in that cultural differences exist in the interpretation and understanding of rights for children (Cherney, Greteman and Travers, 2008). In Ghana, these cultural differences are exacerbated by the existence of around eight major tribal and ethnic groups, each with their own set of values, beliefs and practices (World Population Review, 2018). Indeed, this cultural diversity within Ghana further adds to the complexity of realising children's rights in Ghana.

The United Nations Convention on the Rights of the Child (UNCRC), the international instrument promoting the rights of children globally, has been widely ratified; however, with its focus on individual children as opposed to children within families, it is at odds with some cultures that are family-focused and see the child as functioning within their family (Cherney et al., 2008).

Children's participation rights in Ghana

Participating in matters that affect them should be every child's right; however, this is often inconsistently applied in Ghana, with evidence that many adults find it difficult to accept that children have rights. Within the family, parents and adult relatives tend to view young children as dependent and devoid of agency (Adonteng-Kissi, 2018). In the professional spheres, teachers and other education staff have been found to violate children's rights on a regular basis in schools and education establishments (Dzang-Tedam and Gaisie-Ahiabu, 2017).

Research by Ansell (2005) and Adu-Gyamfi (2013) found that children's participation holds immense benefits for children themselves and their societies at large. Ansell (2005) argued that children's participation increased their sense of self-worth, competence and confidence. In addition, children develop a deeper understanding of democratic processes, which can enhance their future potential. These benefits also enable adults to respect and recognise children as capable of making meaningful contributions in the many spheres of life affecting them. However, as emphasised by Ruiz-Casares, Collins, Tisdall and Grover (2017), it is important that contextual factors are carefully contemplated as they determine the way in which children and young people's participation occurs.

Research by Manful and Manful (2014) revealed that at strategic government and policy levels, as well as operational levels where practical strategies are implemented, participation rights for children in Ghana would be difficult to achieve and sustain due to cultural practices and socialisation that are incompatible with children's participation rights. The view that Ghanaian children should not argue, disagree or contribute to discussions being held by adults means that there is an unspoken rule about children's participation, at least in the Ghanaian context (Twum-Danso, 2009). The UNCRC contains several provisions in relation to participation rights for children. Article 12 stipulates the right of children to participate in matters concerning them. This means that their views and contributions should be listened to, valued and respected.

Twum-Danso (2009), referring to Articles 12 and 13 of the UNCRC, concludes that there appears to be what she calls a hierarchy of rights, beginning with the right to life, shelter and food, with rights to participate being low on the list of priorities. This, she argues, in addition to children themselves not feeling the need to express their opinions or participate in decisions about matters affecting them, has resulted in children appearing to be disinterested in opportunities to participate in matters affecting them. Children in her study felt that decision-making should be something parents did on their behalf. This idea is in direct contrast to research by Björnsdóttir and Einarsdóttir (2018), who found that children and youth in Ghana 'believed participation could increase their future opportunities' (p. 288).

It has been found that, depending on the gender of the child, they are provided with different opportunities and face different expectations, opportunities and choices throughout childhood (Abane, 2004). The discrimination of girls is a global problem, recognised in international human rights instruments, policy documents, action plans, reports and similar texts. Child participation recognises children as actors in their own development, progress and protection. Participation involves children's right to freedom to express opinions and to have a say in matters affecting their social, economic, religious, cultural and political life, all of which will prepare children for playing active roles in their societies.

Elsewhere, Twum-Danso (2010) has also recognised that there are two categories of children's participation: negative and positive. By 'negative' participation, she is referring to the use of children in situations such as armed conflict, as opposed to 'positive' participation, which is characterised by children thinking for themselves, forming and expressing their views, and contributing to decisions within their families, communities and wider society.

Enablers of children's rights

As has already been mentioned, realising rights for children is no mean feat, and it has been established that goodwill alone is insufficient to achieve this. In this regard, the enablers of this process appear to be a helpful starting point to making this possible. These are:

- family values and support;
- participatory projects;
- childcare professional status and visibility;
- government and ministerial backing via Ministry of Gender, Children and Social Protection;
- Sustainable Development Goals (SDGs), international pressure and monitoring;
- media and social networking; and
- improved birth registration

Family values and support

Families are the first point of socialisation for children, and in Ghana the family often includes wider extended family. Respect, honour, commitment, honesty, loyalty and belonging are among the values expected by families, and these values have been found to exist in many religious teachings. For this reason, it is important to recognise the impact of family values on not only the interpretation of children's rights, but also the ways in which these rights are either undermined or promoted. For example, the interpretation of the biblical scripture 'spare the rod and spoil the child' is one that is often used to justify child physical abuse under the guise of discipline. In addition, the gendered roles within the family focus on respect for males, and this patriarchal leaning, which does not always promote children's rights, is discussed further in this chapter.

Participatory projects

Björnsdóttir (2011) found that participatory projects existed in Ghana and that these have been sponsored and supported by local and international organisations as well as central government. Examples of these participatory projects included Child Rights Clubs, located mostly in schools, national events such as Ghana Water Forum and Global Handwashing Day, and radio programmes such as 'Curious Minds', which all create platforms aimed at promoting participation of children at all levels in Ghana. The 'Curious Minds' project, founded in Ghana in 1996, aims to 'ensure that all children and youth are well informed and meaningfully participate in decision-making that affects their lives by advocating, generating knowledge, sharing information, building partnerships and training young activists at local, national and international levels' (Curious Minds, 2018).

Initiatives such as this could enable the realisation of children's rights in Ghana and continue to provide unique opportunities for children of different ages, genders and life experiences. In a study by Adu-Gyamfi (2013), however, young people did not feel that their voices and opinion through the 'Curious Minds' project were listened to or respected.

Goodwill and intentions are not sufficient to ensure children's rights become a reality for all children in Ghana and younger children specifically; however, there are certain conditions and circumstances that enable the realisation of children's rights, and these are discussed below.

Childcare professional status and visibility

Over the last 20 years, there has been a consistent rise in the number of professional bodies and organisations working to ensure an improved application of children's rights in Ghana. These organisations include NGOs such as World Vision, Plan International and Action Aid, as well as international organisations such as UNICEF. Professional children's rights advocates, social workers, teachers and welfare officers have also widely publicised their commitment to children's rights in Ghana.

Government and ministerial backing

The mandate of the Ministry of Gender, Children and Social Protection (MoGCSP), created in 2010, was to ensure that women, children, persons with disabilities and older people are empowered to participate fully in national development. In establishing this ministry, the government of Ghana has also made visible its loyalty to ensuring that children's rights take their rightful place in policy and practice. The issue of the right to participation by children with disabilities is perhaps one that requires a depth of analysis that this chapter is unable to provide; however, it has been found that such children in Ghana experience disproportionate levels of inequality in the areas of access to education and health services, as well as within the family and other social spaces.

The Ministry is mandated to 'coordinate and ensure gender equality and equity, promote the survival, social protection and development of children, vulnerable, excluded and persons with disability and integrate fulfilment of their rights, empowerment and full participation into National development' (Ministry of Gender, Children and Social Protection (MGCSP), 2018). If functioning optimally, this strategy should enable the realisation of children's rights in Ghana from a broader policy perspective.

SDGs, international pressure and monitoring

The Sustainable Development Goals (SDGs) are a universal call to action to end poverty, protect the planet and ensure that all people enjoy peace and prosperity by 2030. They have been adopted by 193 countries, including Ghana, aiming to foster economic growth, ensure social inclusion and protect the environment. The annual UN political forum plays a central role in reviewing progress made with regard to the SDGs at a global level. Such monitoring brings pressure to bear on countries to comply and report on any areas of concern or tensions. As a country, Ghana will need to ensure that it has met the monitoring requirements and that any areas in need of further work will be acknowledged and improved towards subsequent review and monitoring (United Nations Development Group, 2017).

Media and social networking

Social media is a more recent and youth-friendly form of communication that is cheap, fast and effective in many respects. It has provided unprecedented ways of free expression and social activism around the world. While not being oblivious to the dangers and risks involved with social networking, it is important to examine the ways in which the media and social networking might facilitate and enable children's rights to be operationalised in Ghana. There are a number of artists, such as Noella Wiyaala, a renowned musician, who is also using her stage and position to galvanise support of Ghanaians against child abuse. Her Twitter handle @GACA is proving a popular platform for discussing child abuse in an open and honest way and also for challenging practices that infringe on children's rights. She tweets about a range of activities and policies, and by so doing is involved in community education about issues affecting children in Ghana. She also highlights issues that have been reported in the mainstream media about children's rights infringements and abuse such as the effects of child marriage. While not specifically targeting child participation rights, the point being made here is that social media and networking can be effective mediums through which children's participation rights could be enhanced and promoted and could afford children the opportunity to have their voices heard on a range of issues that concern them.

Improved birth registration

Ghana has made significant progress in improving its rate of birth registration, which increased from 17 per cent in 2000 to a high of 62 per cent in 2007 (Dake and Fuseini, 2018). Registration of newborn babies has also increased since 2003, the reason for this being the introduction of free registration within the first 12 months of delivery. Indeed, the right to a name and nationality are fundamental rights every child should have, and the improvement of birth registration processes in Ghana is one example of the strides made in the area of children's rights. According to Plan International, the rights perspective with regard to birth registration in Ghana is that:

> A birth certificate is the first official acknowledgement of a child's existence by the State and is essential if they are to access other rights. Where births remain unregistered, there is an implication that children are not recognised as persons before the law ... access to fundamental rights and freedoms may be compromised.
>
> *(Amo-Adjei and Annim, 2015, p. 1)*

This emphasises the legal responsibility and duty of the state to ensure that all child births are recorded because 'where existence has never been recorded, there is no guarantee that their disappearance will be either ... as they will not be included in statistical information about children, their situation cannot be monitored' (p. 1).

A strong birth registration process, therefore, is the first step to recognising and respecting children and their rights to participation in the future. The ACWRC specifically notes that a child is a national of the state in which he or she is born, and in addition children must be registered immediately after the birth. This specific provision for birth registration was considered important particularly because many children born in rural areas with limited or no health facilities could be born at home and unlikely to be registered until their parent took them to larger towns where the provision existed. where they could register the birth. Arguably, children cannot be protected if their existence is unknown. This process is different from the practice in the UK, for example, where parents are required to register their child's birth within 42 days and there is a penalty for parents who are non-compliant with this requirement.

Barriers to achieving children's rights

There are many barriers to achieving children's rights in Ghana, and these include:

- cultural beliefs about childhood and children;
- harmful traditional and cultural practices;
- child labour and modern-day slavery;
- challenges in law and policy enforcement; and
- perceived power and powerlessness.

Cultural beliefs about childhood and children

It has already been argued that traditional beliefs and cultural practices go some way to preventing the realisation of children's rights. One of the main barriers to achieving children's rights in Ghana comes from the way in which children and childhood are viewed and constructed by adults. Constructs about children and childhood (e.g. the saying that 'children should be seen and not heard') is one sure way of ensuring that children's rights as a concept is questioned and efforts to achieve it undermined. In many cultures and family traditions, children are not encouraged to speak up or share their views, or else they run the risk of being labelled rude, arrogant or with bad manners. Indeed, this places children and young people in an unenviable position of having to watch as their right to participation is taken away from them. Children who live in extended family circumstances have also been found to be vulnerable to a range of abusive and neglectful practices that strip them of their right to participate in decisions and matters affecting them, owing to large numbers of adult decision-makers within the extended family set-up.

In a study of children's rights in children's residential care homes in Ghana, Darkwah et al. (2018) identified that adults in the parenting role within the children's care home found it frustrating that children were given priority in their settings and suggested that children's rights were in some way a barrier to parenting. One participant, a 58-year-old mother, expressed it thus: 'I came here to be a parent, but I can't confidently say I am parenting these children … the child rights rules just tie your hands (p. 6).

Indeed, views and sentiments of this nature are unhelpful and portray children's rights as unable to coexist with parenting practices within a children's home. It should be noted that, on the contrary, children's rights provide a framework from which effective parenting strategies can be developed and sustained. The female caregiver or 'mother' implies that children's rights principles are a barrier to effective parenting, a view that is corroborated by another caregiver in a different study who suggests that she would not raise her own biological children with the principles of children's rights in mind; however, she has had to utilise a rights-informed approach with children in the children's home where she works (Darkwah et al., 2016). The role of parenting children in care homes in Ghana is important if we are to understand the broader context of adherence to children's rights in the various parenting roles. While Ghana does not have disproportionate numbers of children in care homes, it could be argued that children in these environments are not cushioned from the unhelpful perceptions and beliefs held by adult caregivers that undermine children, children's rights and childhood in Ghana. A report by Hickman and Adams (2018) found that in 1997, there were only 10 residential homes for children in Ghana; however, by 2006, the number had increased to an estimated 138 residential homes for children. By the end of 2016, there were approximately 2,900 children in 95 residential children's homes (RCHs), representing a decrease from 2015, when 4,520 children were being looked after in residential care homes. This reduction in the number of children in RCHs was found to be the result of the withdrawal of licences to operate these kinds of provisions, in favour of family-based care.

Harmful traditional and cultural practices

It has been argued that the sociocultural context of child-rearing in Ghana is complex and often at odds with children's rights principles and the UNCRC. Children cannot consent to their own exploitation or abuse; consequently, any cultural or traditional practice that is harmful cannot claim to have children as active participants. Female genital mutilation (FGM), witchcraft labelling and abuse, child and early marriages, child exploitation, and other forms of harm, maltreatment and neglectful parenting cannot coexist in an environment claiming to be working in support of children's rights. According to Amoakohene (2004), existing legislation in Ghana prohibits alleged cultural practices that cause harm to the physical, mental and emotional well-being of people; however, they continue to exist due to weak and ineffective monitoring and reporting structures. It is now widely known that FGM is an example of gender-based violence, practised in some communities in Ghana, which Sakeah et al. (2006) suggest is done because FGM is used as selection criteria by some men seeking wives. This is an example of the way in which patriarchy continues to influence the outcomes for female children in some parts of Ghana.

Child labour and modern-day slavery

A report by UNICEF (2017) found that in Ghana, 39 per cent of children between the ages of 5 and 17 years were engaged in some form of economic activity, mainly as unpaid family workers, apprentices or in low-paid work, primarily in the agriculture and fishing industries. It is estimated that nearly 20 per cent of children (1.27 million) were engaged in child labour, which included *kayayee* (head porters) and the *trokosi* system of ritual servitude. This *trokosi* label, according to Asomah (2015), turns virgin girls usually between the ages of 6 and 8 into slaves of the 'gods' to atone for crimes allegedly committed by their family members. The girls are often held under harsh restrictive conditions and subjected to sexual exploitation and other forms of abuse by a male 'priest'. It has been suggested that up to 20,000 young girls have been victim to this form of modern-day slavery; however, it is impossible to verify these numbers as it is believed that many go unreported. It is also unfortunate that in relation to trafficking in persons, Ghana has been identified as a 'source, transit and destination country' for human trafficking (UNICEF, 2017, p. 1).

According to Lansdown (2001), by failing to consult children about the nature and reality of their lives as working children, national and international campaigns to end child labour do not appear to have improved their lives or their circumstances. Alongside being made to work, children experience a range of other harmful and abusive treatment, such as verbal and physical abuse, neglect and sexual harassment and abuse (Ghana Statistical Service, 2014).

Hamenoo et al. (2018) concluded that children were directed by their parents and other adults to work, and all proceeds from child labour contributed to the family's overall income. Children engaged in hazardous work, such as in the fishing, mining and agricultural sectors, often worked harder and longer hours, and were found not to benefit from income generated from their work (Hamenoo and Sottie, 2015). This is another example where children are not consulted with regard to their participation in labour, nor paid directly for their work.

Challenges in law and policy enforcement

While there are various policy and legislative frameworks to promote and enforce children's rights in Ghana, enforcing these can be difficult if not impossible. It could be argued that this is not due to a lack of will, but rather due to weak and inconsistent law enforcement practice in Ghana. For example, the Domestic Violence and Victim Support Unit (DOVVSU) of the Ghana Police Service deals with issues of domestic abuse, including neglect and child abuse issues; however, research suggests that it is often difficult to access support for victims and survivors of abuse (Anyemadu et al., 2017). Some have argued that financial constraints, coupled with a lack of understanding about the process of reporting domestic abuse, has resulted in the law being unable to be enforced. For example, victims are expected to pay for their medical examination, which also forms part of the investigation process, and Mitchell (2011) concluded that this financial constraint resulted in about 70 per cent of victims failing to progress their grievances. In addition, it was found that three in five women in Ghana have experienced domestic abuse; however, very few cases are fully investigated or prosecuted (Mitchell, 2011).

Perceived power and powerlessness

It has been suggested that stability and quality of relationships are an important component of developmental outcomes for children in later life. With this in mind, it is crucial that adults' behaviour towards children is nurturing and caring and consistent with children's rights principles and practices. Any meaningful participation for children must consider how participation becomes embedded as an integral part of adults' relationship with children in that parental attitudes must enable the participation of children in matters affecting them. McNeish and Newman (2002), writing more generally about children, have proposed that affording children the opportunity to be involved in individual decision-making, in research, in communities and influencing policy, in creating public awareness and in-service development and delivery, are the different contexts in which children's participation can be actualised. In order to achieve this, there will need to be a reconsideration about power and powerlessness; however, as has already been intimated, the idea of children as powerless and adults as powerful has contributed to the way in which rights for young children in Ghana are viewed generally. In addition, there is a gendered powerlessness associated with being female or a child. Adomako Ampofo and Prah (1999) concluded that 'Women and children are expected to show respect and deference to men. To obey them and accept their authority in decision making, all the while being modest in their behaviour' (cited in Cussack and Manuh, 2009, p. 206). The point being made here is that decision-making in families is perceived as a male prerogative; consequently, the views of women and children are often marginalised or completely ignored.

This account is an uncomfortable revelation in that it addresses the complexities of children's rights generally and participation rights specifically in relation to gender relations and the implied powerlessness of female adults and children. There is a danger that male adults are replacing – and will continue to replace – children's voices with their own, and in so doing continue to misunderstand the ways in which children's capacity is evolving in Ghana. The patriarchal family context that exists in most Ghanaian homes relies on the male head of the family being the final decision-maker, thereby obscuring the voices of women and children. By obscuring these important voices, the rights of children to participate will be continually undermined and dismissed.

Conclusion

This chapter has outlined the enablers and barriers to achieving rights for young children in Ghana. While some literature alludes to adults as encountering day-to-day frustrations in adhering to child rights in Ghana, other findings bear out the need and relevance of children's rights in contemporary child-rearing and parenting practices. It has not been possible to extrapolate the experiences of participation among specific groups of children in Ghana. For example, children with disabilities, children living in extended family situations and those with other special needs have not been specifically addressed. Instead, the broader category of children has been examined. It can, however, be concluded that the experiences of children in Ghana in terms of access to rights is fairly standard and difficult. While there has been some improvement in this area, it is clear that there is still some way to go in ensuring that children in Ghana are progressing towards a situation where their rights are more visible in the many spheres of Ghanaian life. In schools and education establishments, teachers need to create safe spaces in which children can participate in deciding, for example, curriculum-related matters, play activities and ideas that are appropriate for their age and understanding. As the world approaches the 30th anniversary of the formulation of the UNCRC, it is even more critical that claims to liberty rights for children are regarded with similar high concern as those of protection and provision rights.

Björnsdóttir and Einarsdóttir (2018) have argued that further research on child participation is needed in Ghana focusing specifically on the benefits and barriers of enabling such a strategy. This chapter has only scratched the surface of this very important area of concern.

The situation in most African countries, including Ghana, is such that the socio-economic circumstances, exploitation, war and conflict, and hunger all impact on the well-being, development and growth of children, which then impacts on their ability to effectively participate. If Maslow's hierarchy of needs theory is to be applied, it is crucial that they should have their most basic needs met first; however, this does not devalue the need for participation. Years before the CRC was adopted, Hillary Clinton (1973) pointed out that children's rights appeared to be 'a slogan in search of a definition', and nearly 30 years later her sentiments ring true in many countries, communities and families (p. 487). Children's true capacity and competence can only be assessed by providing opportunities for participation in various contexts.

References

Abane, Henrietta. 2004. "The girls do not learn hard enough so they cannot do certain types of work. Experiences from an NGO sponsored gender sensitization workshop in a southern Ghanaian community." *Community Development Journal*, 39 (1): 49–61.

Adomako Ampofo, A. and M. Prah. 1999. "You may beat your wife, but not too much: The cultural context of violence against women in Ghana." *In The architecture for violence against women in Ghana*, edited by Kathy Cusack and Takyiwaa Manuh, pp. 93–105. Accra, Ghana: Gender Studies and Human Rights Documentation Centre.

Adonteng-Kissi, Obed. 2018. "Parental perceptions of child labour and human rights: A comparative study of rural and urban Ghana." *Child Abuse and Neglect*, 84: 34–44.

Adu-Gyamfi, Jones. 2013. "Can children and young people be empowered in participatory initiatives? Perspectives from young people's participation in policy formulation and implementation in Ghana." *Children and Youth Services Review*, 35 (10): 1766–1772.

Alston, Philip and John Tobin. 2005. "Laying the foundations for children's rights: An independent study of some key legal and institutional aspects of the impact of the convention on the rights of the child." www.unicef-irc.org/publications/pdf/ii_layingthefoundations.pdf

Amo-Adjei, Joshua and Samuel K. Annim. 2015. "Socio-economic determinants of birth registration in Ghana." *BMC International Health and Human Rights*, 15: 14.

Amoakohene, M. I. 2004. "Violence against women in Ghana: A look at women's perceptions and review of policy and social responses." *Social Science and Medicine*, 59: 2373–2385.

Ansell, Nicola. 2005. *Children, Youth and Development*. Abingdon: Routledge.

Anyemadu, Akua, Eric Y. Tenkorang, and Patricia Dold. 2017. "Ghanaian women's knowledge and perceptions of services available to victims of intimate partner violence." *Journal of Interpersonal Violence*, 1–25. doi:10.1177/0886260517689886

Asomah, Joseph Y. 2015. "Cultural rights versus human rights: A critical analysis of the trokosi practice in Ghana and the role of civil society." *African Human Rights Law Journal*, 15 (1): 129–149.

Björnsdóttir, Þóra. 2011. "Children are agents of change: Participation of children in Ghana." https://skemman.is/bitstream/1946/8023/3/%C3%9E%C3%B3ra%20Bj%C3%B6rnsd%C3%B3ttir.pdf

Björnsdóttir, Þóra and J. Einarsdóttir. 2018. "Child participation in Ghana: Responsibilities and rights." In *What Politics? Youth and Political Engagment in Africa*, edited by Elina Oinas, Henri Onodera and Leena Suurpää, 285–299. Leiden: Brill.

Cherney, Isabelle D., Adam J. Greteman, and Brittany G. Travers. 2008. "A cross-cultural view of adults' perceptions of children's rights." *Social Justice Research*, 21 (4): 432–456.

Cowden, Mhairi. 2016. *Children's Rights: From Philosophy to Public Policy*. Basingstoke: Palgrave Macmillan.

Curious Minds. 2018. "What we do." http://cmghana.org/what-we-do

Cussack, Kathy and Takyiwaa Manuh (Eds) 2009. *The Architecture of Violence against Women in Ghana*. Accra-North, Ghana: Gender Studies and Human Rights Documentation Centre.

Dake, Fidelia A.A. and Kamil Fuseini. 2018. "Registered or unregistered? Levels and differentials in registration and certifications of births in Ghana." *BMC International Health and Human Rights*, 18: 25.

Darkwah, Erenest, Marguerite Daniel, and Joana S. Yendork. 2018. "Care-'less': Exploring the interface between child care and parental control in the context of child rights for workers in children's homes in Ghana." *British Medical Journal of International Health and Human Rights*, 18: 13.

Darkwah, Ernest, M. Marguerite Daniel, and Maxwell Asumeng. 2016. "Caregiver perceptions of children in their care and motivations for the care work in children's homes in Ghana: Children of god or children of white men?" *Children and Youth Services Review*, 66: 161–169.

Dzang-Tedam, Prospera and Elsie Gaisie-Ahiabu. 2017. *Child Protection in Boarding Schools in Ghana: Contemporary Issues, Challenges and Opportunities*. Litchfield: Kirwin Maclean.

Ekundayo, Osifunke. 2015. "Does the African Charter on the Rights and Welfare of the Child (ACRWC) only underlines and repeats the Convention on the Rights of the Child (CRC)'s provisions? Examining the similarities and the differences between the ACRWC and the CRC." *International Journal of Humanities and Social Science*, 5 (7): 143–158.

Ghana Statistical Service. 2014. "Child labour report." www.statsghana.gov.gh/docfiles/glss6/GLSS6_Child%20Labour%20Report.pdf

Hamenoo, E.S., E.A. Dwomoh, and M. Dako-gyekye. 2018. "Child labour in Ghana: Implications for children's education and health." *Children and Youth Services Review*, 93: 248–254.

Hamenoo, Emma Seyram and Cynthia Akorfa Sottie. 2015. "Stories from Lake Volta: Lived experiences of trafficked children in Ghana." *Child Abuse and Neglect*, doi:10.1016/j.chiabu.2014.06.007.

Hickman, Mari and Bashiru Adams. 2018. "Assessing alternative care for children in Ghana." www.measureevaluation.org/resources/publications/tr-18-251

Lansdown Gerison. 2001. *Promoting Children's Participation in Democratic Decision-Making*. Italy: UNICEF Innocenti Research Centre.

Manful, Esmeranda and Saka E. Manful. 2014. "Child welfare in Ghana: The relevance of children's rights in practice." *Journal of Social Work*, 14 (3): 313–328.

McNeish, Diana and Tony Newman. 2002. "Involving children and young people in decision making." In *What Works for Children? Effective Services for Children and Families*, edited by Diana McNeish, Tony Newman and Helen Roberts, 186–204. Buckingham: Open University Press.

Ministry of Gender, Children and Social Protection (MGCSP). 2018. "About us." http://mogcsp.gov.gh/

Mitchell, Laura. 2011. "Service users' perceptions of the domestic violence and victims' support unit, Ghana Police Service." https://static1.squarespace.com/static/536c4ee8e4b0b60bc6ca7c74/t/5437f188e4b05ef245bd6a2a/1412952456336/Perceptions+of+the+Domestic+Violence+and+Victim%27s+Support+Unit+Ghana+Police+Service+2012+Laura+Mitchelll+June+2012.pdf

Obeng-Odoom, Franklin. 2010. "An urban twist to politics in Ghana." *Habitat International*, 34 (4): 392–399.

Organisation of African Unity. 1990. "African charter on the rights and welfare of the child." www.achpr.org/files/instruments/child/achpr_instr_charterchild_eng.pdf

Rodham, Hilary. 1973. "Children under the law." *Harvard Educational Review*, 43 (4): 487–514.

Ruiz-Casares, Monica, Tara M. Collins, E. Kay M. Tisdall, and Sonja Grover. 2017. "Children's rights to participation and protection in international development and humanitarian interventions: Nurturing a dialogue." *International Journal of Human Rights*, 21 (1): 1–13.

Sakeah, Evelyn, Andy Beke, Henry Doctor, and Abraham Hodgson. 2006. "Males' preference for circumcised women in northern Ghana." *African Journal of Reproductive Health*, 10 (2): 37–47.

Twum-Danso, Afua. 2009. "Reciprocity, respect and responsibility: The 3 R's underlying parent-child relationships in Ghana and the implications for children's rights." *International Journal of Children's Rights*, 17 (3): 415–432.

Twum-Danso, Afua. 2010. "The construction of children and socialisation in Ghana." In *A Handbook of Children's and Young People's Participation: Perspectives from Theory and Practice*, edited by Barry Percy-Smith and Nigel Thomas, 133–140. London: Sage.

UNICEF. 2017. "National plan of action for the elimination of human trafficking in Ghana." www.unicef.org/ghana/Human_Traficking_NPA_-_9.11.17(2).pdf

United Nations. 1989. *UN Convention on the Rights of the Child*. Geneva: United Nations.

United Nations Development Group. 2017. "Guidelines to support country reporting on the sustainable development goals." https://undg.org/wp-content/uploads/2017/03/Guidelines-to-Support-Country-Reporting-on-SDGs-1.pdf

World Population Review. 2018. "Ghana population 2018." http://worldpopulationreview.com/countries/ghana-population/

Wyness, Michael. 2013. "Children's participation and intergenerational dialogue: Bringing adults back into the analysis." *Childhood*, 20 (4): 429–442.

15

BEING A REFUGEE CHILD IN LEBANON

Implementing young children's rights in a digital world through the Blockchain Educational Passport

Cristina Devecchi

Introduction

> Every day, every day in Lebanon there is a family coming from Syria.
> (Teacher and field officer, Ana Aqra non-governmental organisation, Lebanon)

The road from Beirut to the Bekaa Valley winds through the cacophony of building styles of noisy Beirut all the way up to the peaceful and majestic sights at the top of Mount Lebanon to then descend onto the Bekaa Valley. Encrusted between the Mount Lebanon and the Anti-Lebanon ranges, the Bekaa Valley is a green jewel that becomes progressively more arid and a semi-desert as we drive north-east to Hermel and towards the border with Syria and Homs.

Scattered along the main highway are tents, their blinding whiteness a sharp contrast with the ochre reddish colour of the soil onto which they have settled. As we drive along, there are pools of humanity, a scattering of people in the distance surrounded by goats making the most of the meagre grass on the stony ground. Some people huddle together by the side of the road, waiting to be chosen for a day's work. Others, women, stand and sit in open trucks ferried along the fields. This is a precarious existence, a hand-to-mouth economy that tracks the passing of the days while all around them others decide their fate, while they long to go back home.

Home is not the white tents with the light blue 'UN' logo on them. Home is not Lebanon. Home is Syria, a stone's throw away on the other side of the low mountains. Home, in some cases, is no more. It has been wiped out, destroyed in the bombardments. For those who might still have bricks and mortars to go back to, entire families have been decimated. Home is, for many, just an indelible memory.

The Syrian refugees settled in the Bekaa Valley are, however, only the most visible of the 1 million who have moved to Lebanon due to the war in Syria. According to UNICEF

(2017), one in six residents in Lebanon were, at the time of the survey, a Syrian refugee. According to the UNHCR (2016), the count is even larger since 'Lebanon hosted the largest number of refugees in relation to its national population, with 183 refugees per 1,000 inhabitants' (p. 2). However, this is *not the reality*, since:

- some refugees do not choose to register for fear of future reprisal by the Syrian government;
- some might have worked in Lebanon before, due to bilateral agreements between Syria and Lebanon, and might be working illegally; and
- refugees keep arriving every day.

The numbers are even more staggering for what matters in this chapter: the children. Of the 1 million registered refugees in Lebanon, half a million are children. Of these, a quarter of a million are not in school. Despite Sustainable Development Goal (SDG) 4 to 'ensure inclusive and equitable quality education and promote lifelong learning opportunities for all', including its target that 'by 2030, all girls and boys have access to quality early childhood development, care and pre-primary education' (UN, 2015), children in Lebanon are working, begging on the streets of Beirut, engaged in sexual exploitation, and many younger children cannot access nurseries because these tend to be the privilege of the wealthy in Lebanon. However, recently, the Lebanese government has funded school preparation classes for 24,000 refugee children aged 5 and 6 years, through its Reaching All Children with Education (RACE) programme (Watt, 2019), and NGOs are also working to protect young children's right to education in Lebanon by providing formal, informal and non-formal early childhood education programmes. These NGOs include the large international NGOs (e.g. Save the Children and the UN), but smaller, local NGOs are also contributing to the effort. The Ana Aqra Association is an example. Ana Aqra aims to 'make learning accessible to all children by fostering an equitable and sustainable learning environment' in the Lebanon (Ana Aqra Association, 2018), and it provides several programmes for young refugee children, often in partnership with other NGOs. Ana Aqra developed the Community Based Early Childhood Education (CBECE) programme, a non-formal early childhood education programme that supports refugee children aged 3–6 years to develop social-emotional, language, cognitive and motor skills through structured activities and play. Its Just Right Start programme supports refugee children aged 4–6 years old in Akkar, Bekaa and Mount Lebanon to be ready for school, enhancing their chances of integration and retention at school. Additionally, Ana Aqra has created spaces for young children's early learning, collaborating with the Al Madad Foundation to develop the Children's Learning Center in the Bekaa Valley, which provides early childhood education for refugee children, and run the Classroom in a Bus, which travels to remote areas to enable refugee and other disadvantaged children to gain literacy and numeracy skills from 4 years old.

While Lebanon is the focus of this chapter, the challenges of providing educational opportunities to refugee children are similar across the world, and the scale of the challenge is overwhelmingly large. In this context, basic education provision is prioritised, and although many refugee families own mobile phones, mobile data and Wi-Fi access tend to be limited in refugee settlements (Schwartz, 2017). However, advances in digital technologies are surging ahead globally (UBI Global, 2019), and without access to these, refugee children are digitally disadvantaged. To that end, international technology and education corporations have started to provide online learning opportunities for some refugee children (Menashy and Zakharia, 2017). Attention has also begun to turn to ways that refugee children's learning can be recorded, accredited and evidenced for their future lives, notwithstanding their current unsettled status.

Within the timely and highly contested field of the appropriate use of technology in general, and the use of technology for and by children, this chapter puts forward the argument that the right to a secure digital identity is a fundamental right of all people, but most importantly of our children as they will work and live in a much-changed society. In doing so, it argues that current debates about the use of technology as enshrined in legislation and academic research are mainly focused on the use and impact of social media and the Internet, rather than on what technologies such as artificial intelligence (AI) and blockchain can do, and on the benefits and challenges that ensue.

In developing this argument, the chapter draws from the UN UNITE Global Challenge #BlockchainEducationalPassport. The challenge made use of an open-source platform, hosted by the UN UNITE team, to bring together computer scientists, software engineers, blockchain experts, educationalists and teachers working for an NGO in Lebanon to solve the challenge of ensuring that refugee children have their learning credentials securely kept. Blockchain was chosen as an innovative and secure technology that makes use of an immutable ledger, which is tamper-proof. Creating such a record as early as possible for each refugee child, beginning with their early childhood education, has the potential to optimise the benefit of their formal, non-formal and informal learning for their lifetime outcomes.

The chapter starts with an introduction of the state of refugee children and their rights to then focus on the particular challenges of Syrian refugee children with regard to their education. It will then describe the use of blockchain and the specifications of the Blockchain Educational Passport. Drawing from the lessons learned, the chapter will then conclude by developing the case for a revision of the Convention on the Rights of the Child (CRC) to include the right to a secure digital and educational identity.

In between states: being a refugee learner

In the age of instant information and big data, it is not only their volume, velocity and variety as their three key features (Kitchin and McArdle, 2016), but also their accuracy, that matters the most. The issue of accuracy is key in determining both the refugee children's actual numbers and their learning achievement and attainment, and consequently the intervention needed to support them in compliance with current international legislation. Both are major enterprises fraught with many real and practical challenges that technology can help to solve. As gathered through interviews with teachers on the ground, in Lebanon, the first challenge is to determine whether the focus of attention should be only on those children who are formally registered as refugees, or if humanitarian aid and concern should include all those children who are temporarily or indefinitely displaced. The terminology used is important because it determines the support nation states would be obliged to offer in line with international treaties and legislations. A second and related challenge is to develop systems using current technology that can maintain and protect personal data once proof of identity has been obtained. The third challenge is to manage the gap between the post hoc nature of available data and the ever-changing situation on the ground, which has to deal with a population whose settled status is fluid and always in movement. The fourth, and no less important, challenge is to explore how, once individual needs and achievement have been identified and certified, technology can help to make them portable across the learner's lifetime. All four challenges are more acute and important for children who might not be in a position to provide the information, but who are the ones to benefit the most from a long-term approach to their development and future.

These challenges are all the more pressing, since the data available paint a concerning picture whose trend shows increasing numbers of displacement. The latest United Nations High Commissioner for Refugees' (UNHCR, 2017) report, *Global Trends: Forced Displacement in 2017*, reports the following:

- 68.5 million people are currently displaced worldwide;
- 16.2 million were newly displaced in 2017, 11.8 million within their own country;
- 44,400 are displaced every day;
- 3.1 million are asylum seekers;
- only 5 million returned to their own country; and
- only 102,800 were resettled.

With regard to refugee children, the same report identifies the following:

- 35.6 million, or 52 per cent, are children below the age of 18; and
- 173,800 are unaccompanied or separated children

Current international legislation addresses the issues by obliging UN signatory countries to fulfil a number of rights. For example, Article 22 of the Convention Relating to the Status of Refugees (UN, 1951) and Articles 28 and 29 of the UN Convention on the Rights of the Child (UNCRC) (UN, 1989) state the rights of all children, including refugees, to health, safety, and meaningful and successful education. Aimed primarily at protecting children and providing the necessary measures to deal with the crisis, the education-focused rights include favourable treatment, the right to free primary education, and the recognition of diplomas and certificates. While the ideals and aspirations behind such rights are admirable, the UNHCR (2017) report also acknowledges the strain on some of the hosting countries, highlighting that 'Developing regions hosted 85 per cent of the world's refugees under UNHCR's mandate, about 16.9 million people. The least developed countries provided asylum to a growing proportion, amounting to one-third of the global total (6.7 million refugees)' (p. 2).

The education of refugee and displaced children in poor host countries, therefore, presents a number of challenges. Specifically concerning Syrian refugee children, Culbertson and Constant's (2015) report highlights access, management, society and quality as four key areas of focus. With respect to Lebanon, Watkins (2013) claims that 'The enrolment rate among primary school age refugee children (aged 6–14) is around 12 per cent – less than half the level in South Sudan. For secondary school age children it is probably below 5 per cent' (p. 8). First of all, it is a matter of system capacity, since countries that are already facing internal challenges in providing education for all children are asked to stretch their limited capacity to provide schooling and education for refugees and displaced children. In many cases, NGOs provide the human and infrastructure resources necessary, but, as testified by conversations with NGOs, this leads to a second challenge: that of recognition and portability of the learning achievements acquired through an informal or non-formal parallel system. As Culbertson and Constant (2015) suggest, depending on the size and financial means of the NGO itself, the quality of the education they can provide may be variable and inconsistent over time. As Watkins and Zyck (2014) attest, Syrian refugee children in Lebanon were and still are 'living in hope, hoping for education' (p. 1). Within this context, a third, and no less important, challenge is to ensure record-keeping of children's learning through certificates and qualifications acquired through formal, informal or non-formal education (Culbertson and Constant, 2015). Current paper-based approaches have limited use for a refugee and displaced population that is on the move or settled in refugee camps. In addition, such documents tend to be the property of the issuing institution, and therefore their portability across time and space remains limited and precarious.

While the fundamental right to education is therefore necessary, how we ensure its realisation and lifelong impact raises the need for a revision, especially in the light of how new technologies can help. However, to do this requires a reconsideration of the Convention, which was written in a time when the world was still based on paper, where education meant formal schooling, and where the digital revolution had not raised the issue of personal data and digital identity. The section that follows offers a base for this discussion, starting from a consideration about the changing notion of children's rights.

The changing rights of children: from protection to participation

The road towards the recognition that children have rights is relatively recent. Stemming from changes about the conception of childhood in the nineteenth century, a notion of childhood as different from adulthood has resulted in the need to protect children from adults first. Grounded in a notion equating childhood with innocence and vulnerability, international legislation has developed to include increasing examples of adult practices detrimental to children (Table 15.1).

In addition to the list in Table 15.1, measures to protect children from harm and exploitation include a number of multilateral instruments focusing on a range of issues, including child labour, slavery, marriage and health. The Convention (United Nations, 1989) was the culmination of such efforts and the first piece of international legislation to focus solely on children's rights.

Table 15.1 Timeline of key international legislation specifically referring to the rights of children prior to the UNCRC

Legislation	Notes
Geneva Declaration of the Rights of the Child (League of Nations, 1924)	Adopted by the League of Nations, mainly addressing children during conflict and generally aspirational
Universal Declaration of Human Rights (UN, 1948)	Article 25 (special protection for children) and Article 26 (right to education)
International Covenant on Civil and Political Rights (OHCHR, 1966)	Article 6 (barring death penalty for minors), Article 14 (judicial procedures for juveniles), Article 23 (protection regarding divorce), Article 24 (right to a name and nationality)
International Covenant on Economic, Social and Cultural Rights (OHCHR, 1966)	Article 10 (protection for family and children), Article 12 (right to health care), Article 13 (right to education)
Declaration of the Rights of the Child (1959)	The first document to focus specifically on the topic of children's rights

Yet childhood is a contested term, and, as Livingstone, Lansdown and Third (2017) argue, 'the child invites recognition of human possibility and yet, by the same token, represents a site of necessary containment, and her proper socialization must be secured in order to preserve the future' (p. 660). Within the complex debate about the nature and necessity of children's rights, a number of criticisms have been raised concerning the CRC (UN, 1989). From a legal perspective, Bennett (1987), for example, warned against the shortcoming of what he called the 'legislative impulse' (p. 35), which can create a situation where ideals, aspirations and social policy are defined as rights, and which can lead to vagueness, overbreadth, lack of comprehensive planning and dilution of already established rights. Sen (2009) further argues that rights have two key shortcomings: their universalist approach does not take into account the specific cultural norms and, above all, the language of rights tends to focus on freedom 'from' rather than the freedom 'to' pursue what one has reason to value. Conversely, Nussbaum (2007) advocates the need to have rights enshrined in national and international legislation as the only way to bring nation states to fulfil their obligations.

Despite these and other criticism, the Convention draws attention to and requires the signatory states to implement three fundamental types of rights:

- the right to protection;
- the right to provision; and
- the right to participation.

While the first was already part of earlier legislations, the right to provision is fraught with practical challenges in the case of refugee children. However, it is the last right, the right of children to participate in decisions that would impact on their lives, that is the most innovative, and no doubt most challenging and controversial. Lundy (2007), for example, argues that in practice, children's voice, and the extent to which they can use it, is dependent on the cooperation of adults who might not share the same interests. Additionally, allowing children to assert their voice is still framed within a view of the child as innocent and ignorant, and therefore lacking the 'rational' capacity to choose. Asserting one's voice can also be seen as undermining adults' authority (Brighouse, 2003).

In the specific case of using technological innovation to keep a record of learning, the issues of protection from, provision for, and participation in are key. In all three cases, children and adults are confronted with making choices on topics for which they are ill-prepared and, in the majority of cases, still lacking the basic knowledge to understand the affordances and perils of the new technology.

The world to come: enabling protection, provision and participation for the digital child

The challenge of dealing with the digital world is a recent development that could not have been envisaged in the original Convention, which was adopted the same year Sir Tim Berners-Lee released the code at the base of the World Wide Web (Livingstone and Third, 2017). Since then, technology has developed at a rate of innovation that has changed how we live our lives, how we work and how we study. It has, somehow paradoxically, and not without unintended consequences, increased our participation in a socially and virtually created world, enhancing our knowledge and reach while at the same time making us dependent and passive consumers. Most interestingly, the latest developments in artificial intelligence, the Internet of things, and blockchain are still out of the grasp of everyday people, while contemporaneously, behind back doors, shaping our behaviours, learning, and current and future work.

The debate about how to ensure that the Convention can be applied to the digital environment has gained pace as the speed of change has increased, yet government and international bodies are still catching up. The state of affairs regarding children's rights in the digital age is well captured by Livingstone et al.'s (2017) report, *The Case for a UNCRC General Comment on Children's Rights and Digital Media*. In acknowledging that 'Digital media are no longer luxuries, but are rapidly becoming essentials of modern existence' (p. 2), they draw attention to the need for an 'urgent and compelling' (p. 2) case for reform, because:

- digital media raise risks such as sexual exploitation, violence and online bullying, but they also afford opportunities that can benefit children;
- access to the digital affordances is uneven, thus preventing some children from taking advantage of the opportunities; and
- transformation has so far been led by corporate interests that do not have children's rights at their core.

In the final analysis, they recommend 'not taking an overly protectionist approach' (p. 4), but instead reframing the digital into the already existing CRC's rights with regard to protection, provision and participation (Livingstone and Bulger, 2014). With regard to protection, they suggest preventing the creation, use and distribution of online material of child abuse, grooming, sexual exploitation, bullying and trafficking, but also protection of children's privacy and the misuse of personal data. As a consequence, they suggest more provision in relation to educational technology and the promotion of digital skills. Finally, protection and provision can be achieved through a process of participation, inviting children to be consulted on matters of education and ICT governance.

Livingstone and Bulger's (2014) recommendations are now part of a more consistent and systematic approach to the inclusion of new technologies and the online environment as part of a reformed understanding of the rights of the digital child (Council for Europe, 2016). Of particular interest is the UNICEF (2017) report *Children in a Digital World*, which is entirely dedicated to the topic and which stresses the concerns and recommendations already highlighted by Livingstone and her colleagues.

Although there are clearly mounting efforts at the international level to address the issue of children's digital rights, there is still a fundamental gap that remains unaddressed (i.e. the risks and opportunities of using new technologies). All documents cited conceive the 'digital' child in terms of their online activities, and thus frame the discourse as one related to the Internet and social media. No direct mention is made of the use of the Internet of things, artificial intelligence and blockchain, and the way in which the development of the big data society is already applied to our online identity. There is still little mention or awareness of how this same technology can actually impact positively on the lives of children, and refugee children in particular, by:

- providing permanent proof of certification of learning for life; and,
- ensuring and protecting the right to ownership of personal data, including data referring to one's educational and professional qualification or data that prove one's skills, competences and capabilities.

If these official documents do not extend their remit to new technologies, more recent research and debates have started querying how technologies can simultaneously protect and support the child, while at the same time impinging on their rights, identity and privacy. These concerns are raised by Lupton and Williamson (2017), who explore the concept of the 'datafied child' and how dataveillance impacts, negatively or positively, on the child's rights. As they argue, 'There remains little evidence that specific instruments to safeguard children's rights in relation to dataveillance have been developed or implemented, and further attention needs to be paid to these issues' (p.780).

Building the future by investing in the present: enabling the digitally poor

This section starts to answer Lupton and Williamson's call for further attention by arguing that new technologies, how we develop them and implement them, is becoming a pivotal and urgent matter within a changing economic and social context. The issues in this regard are many. For what matters to this chapter, it is the educational rights of children that is at the centre of attention. This is in view of the needs to take into account not only the present, but, above all, the future the refugee children would inhabit. That future is already here. In a mobile, globalised, uncertain future world, one of the greatest challenges as we move steadily into a knowledge economy is to make visible and tangible the knowledge that each one of us has acquired through a lifetime of learning and experience. Even more challenging is to keep a permanent record that each individual can own as his or her intellectual property and capital. If this is a challenge for children and adults living in more developed and technologically advanced countries, creating a permanent record of learning achievements for refugee children is, at present, an insurmountable challenge.

I contend that the young refugee children I met in the Bekaa Valley and across Lebanon are and will be digitally poor. Their identity has been shattered and they are aliens in the hosting country, if they have managed to find one who welcomes them. Their primary need is to be safe, and being in school can help them to stay safe, rebuild a sense of self, and forge new hopes and aspirations. But while the right 'to' education is necessary, access to schooling is not sufficient to ensure long-term educational outcomes. Another two fundamental rights need to be pursued, enabled and, above all, documented.

In doing so, we need to take into account the right 'in' education (i.e. supporting the development of the child's sense of identity, well-being and sense of self through active participation in one's learning and the life of the school and the community) (Ainscow, 1999). However, access, well-being and participation are foundation rights that refer to the quality of education while the child is 'at' school. The third essential right is the right 'through' education, which stresses the need to empower and enable the child to achieve while in school what he or she needs to develop into adulthood. It refers to the ability of decision-making, but it also puts the onus on the education system to assess, document and safely keep the learning achievements of the child.

The impossibility to keep a permanent, portable and personal record of one's learning can lead to the inability of the person to contribute to a society that will increasingly be more reliant on new skills and on lifelong learning (WEF, 2018). Without a portable, permanent, transparent and certified proof of one's learning achievement, an individual can be considered poor. And those who cannot claim ownership through the affordances of technology would be the future 'digitally poor' (i.e. deprived of the opportunity to succeed in a much-changed future landscape).

The Blockchain Educational Passport: a decentralised and permanent proof of learning

'You left with no papers; you left with your mind only'
'What we need is to give them a certificate'

This chapter started with the account of a visit to an NGO-supported school in the Bekaa Valley in Lebanon. Despite the burgeoning number of Syrian refugee children, and the fact that Lebanon is not a signatory to the 1951 Refugee Convention (UNHCR, 1951), the country has provided educational opportunities within its already stretched schools in collaboration with the UNHRC and NGOs. Based on first-hand encounters with young refugee children, their parents, teachers and NGOs in various parts of Lebanon, it became clear that providing access to school was only one of the many challenges. From a purely pedagogical point of view, the key challenge was assessing the level of education, if any, many of the children had experienced and the learning they had achieved. It was the lack of 'papers' that hampered teachers' ability to provide the children with the education they needed. Further down the years, when the children progressed in their education, the lack of a system to permanently record qualifications and development further hampered the children's progress through the schooling system.

Teachers were keen to point out that what the children knew already was difficult to assess because of language barriers, trauma, or because they never had the opportunity to go to school and learn. In the case of older children who might be working, the skills and competences they had gained were unaccounted for and difficult to certify. In almost all cases, refugee children were not responsible for what papers and certifications their parents managed to take with them. The Syrian refugee children are not unique. Disempowered, dispossessed, displaced and misinformed, many refugee children are denied their entitlement to education, and through education to do (i.e. to become empowered and enabled to participate as learners and as future adults).

Neither the Convention nor more recent legislation stress the fact that despite much emphasis on education being the engine of innovation and the fundamental pillar to building a better future, the schooling system we rely upon was created for an industrial age that is no more. More importantly, the current education system is still built on settled learners, which is ill-equipped to deal with the 'intellectual migrant' of the future in a globalised, interconnected, mobile and fast-changing world. Additionally, the current system is built on single institutions to be the repository and guardians of educational paperwork and certification. If the economy of the future will depend more and more on each person's ability to acquire, use and, above all, prove one's skills, competences and intellectual capabilities, then to do this will require changing the way in which we assess learning, validate and certify achievements, and prove skills and competences. It will also require creating a portable, validated and permanent proof of one's learning equal to and protected by the right to ownership.

As a way to solve this challenge, a group of colleagues at the University of Northampton and colleagues at the Ana Aqra NGO in Lebanon revised a more generic Decentralised Learning Ledger proof of concept (Devecchi et al., 2017) to develop a Blockchain Educational Passport (BEP) (Devecchi, 2018) to address the specific requirements of educating refugee children. The BEP was then chosen as one of the United Nations' UNITE Ideas Sustainable Development Goals Global Challenges, which ran from January to June 2018, when Path Foundation was awarded the prize for the best solution. Based on blockchain technology, the passport makes use of processes of decentralisation and distributed information to create a permanent record of learning achievements that is envisaged to remain the personal property of the learner. Not unlike a passport, the BEP is a digital document that uses algorithmic encryption to provide a secure pathway to the certification of the acquisition of learning achievements in the form of permanent 'personal learning data'. Blockchain technology will be used to create a Decentralised Learning Ledger onto which, through smart contracts and predefined algorithms, the following information will be permanently available:

- Learning achieved through *informal education*, such as that provided by NGOs.
- *Non-formal learning achievements*, such as those gained through volunteering activities and, later, employment.
- *Formal education and certification* (diplomas, degrees).

Blockchain is increasingly seen as a way to create secure ways of accounting for matters related to proof of identity, provenance and ownership (Swan, 2015). At least in theory, it has the potential to address the need of schools, employers and, above all, individuals to securely certify learning, identity and records (Cresitello-Dittmar, 2016). In the case of refugee children, developing a fully operational BEP can equip them with the proof they need to prove their qualifications independently from where they happen to be or where they would move to in future. It will also help preschools, schools and teachers to develop a personalised learning response. Additionally, it will help international bodies and national institutions to collect data in real time and develop provisions and in-time responses when and where needed.

In practice, however, blockchain, like other newer technologies, has its limitations and risks, which can be organised under four broad categories: pedagogical, technical, operational and legal-normative. The pedagogical challenges can be summarised as follows:

- A current lack of agreed framework for assessing children's learning that would be accepted across different educational systems.
- Overcoming the accepted view of formal education as the only acceptable proof of learning, and thus devising an assessment framework to take into account competences, skills and knowledge acquired through informal and non-formal education and work-based learning.
- Finding a balance between the transactional and the transformational assessment of learning, the former required for certifying learning and the latter for determining further learning opportunities.

Technical challenges are related to the technology itself, and would include:

- Blockchain reliance on the use of cryptocurrencies as incentives to process the data.
- Current high cost of mining due to the energy requirement to provide proof of transaction.
- Lack of digital infrastructure to support the use of the BEP on a large scale.

Operational challenges, on the other hand, relate to the practical application of the technology and would include the following:

- The technology's affordances and limitations.
- Cost and length of time required to input the necessary data.

- Current gap in technology-skilled workforce.
- Provision to educate parents, teachers and children about ICT in general and new technologies in particular.

Conclusion

To conclude, the moral-normative challenges are those that have more immediate implications for the key argument put forward in this chapter (i.e. the need to review children's digital rights by broadening our concerns to technological tools beyond the Internet). Such moral and normative challenges would include:

- the inalterability of the blockchain infrastructure, which can clash with other legislation allowing individuals the right to be forgotten;
- disputes over data protection and data ownership, especially in the case of minors; and
- still ill-defined legal response, especially in the field of contract law and identity rights.

The Blockchain Educational Passport is one of many ways in which new technologies can contribute positively to the lives of children, and refugee children in particular. Creating a BEP for each refugee child as early as possible, beginning with their early childhood education, has the potential to optimise the benefit of their early formal, non-formal and informal learning for life. New technologies have, as Livingstone et al. (2017) argued, the capacity to help us protect children, develop educational provision, and enhance their present and future participation. Yet they can be misused and misapplied. The lack of specific considerations in current national and international legislation on matters related to new technologies such as blockchain, artificial intelligence and the Internet of things is a serious gap that should be addressed as a matter of urgency. This chapter has highlighted the need to develop the technology, alongside starting a broader and multidisciplinary debate on how best we can create technology-enhanced tools that are of benefit to all children, safeguarding children's freedoms from exploitation by technological advances and ensuring children's freedom to exploit what the technology can afford them to do and achieve throughout their lives.

References

Ainscow, Mel. 1999. *Understanding the Development of Inclusive Schools*. London: Falmer Press.

Ana Aqra Association. 2018. Ana Aqra Association. https://ana-aqra.org/

Bennett, Walter J., Jr. 1987. A critique of the emerging convention on the rights of the child. *Cornell International Law Journal*, 20 (1): 1–52. scholarship.law.cornell.edu/cgi/viewcontent.cgi?referer=www .google.co.uk/&httpsredir=1&Articleicle=1168&context=cilj

Brighouse, Harry. 2003. How should children be heard? *Arizona Law Review*, 45 (3). http://arizonalawre view.org/pdf/45-3/45arizlrev691.pdf

Council of Europe. 2016. *Council of Europe Strategy for the Rights of the Child (2016–2021)*. Brussels: Council of Europe. https://rm.coe.int/168066cff8

Cresitello-Dittmar, Ben. 2016. *Application of the Blockchain for Authenticationand Verification of Identity*. www.cs.tufts.edu/comp/116/archive/fall2016/bcresitellodittmar.pdf

Culbertson, Shelly and Louay Constant. 2015. *Education of Syrian Refugee Children Managing the Crisis in Turkey, Lebanon, and Jordan*. Santa Monica, CA: RAND Corporation.

Devecchi, Cristina. 2018. *Blockchain Educational Passport: From Concept to Practice*. New York: UniteIdeas. https://github.com/UniteIdeas/BlockchainEducationalPassport/blob/master/BlockchainEducational Passport-%20Specifications.pdf

Devecchi, Cristina, Ali Hadawi, Scott Turner, Ale Armellini, Ian Brooks, Barbara Mellish, Nick Petford, and Olinga Ta'eed. 2017. *Blockchain Educational Passport. The Decentralised Learning Ledger*. https://cpbeu-w2.wpmucdn.com/mypad.northampton.ac.uk/dist/7/7932/files/2017/03/SERATIO-WHITE PAPER-Educational-Passport-Distributed-Learning-Ledger-30-April-2017-v-5.03-2gyqndf.pdf

Kitchin, Rob and Gavin McArdle. 2016. What makes big data, big data? Exploring the ontological characteristics of 26 datasets. *Big Data & Society*, January–June, 1–10. https://doi.org/10.1177/2053951716631130

Livingstone, Sonia and Monica Bulger. 2014. A global research agenda for children's rights in the digital age. *Journal of Children and Media*, 8 (4): 317–335. https://doi.org/10.1080/17482798.2014.961496

Livingstone, Sonia, Gerison Lansdown, and Amanda Third. 2017. *The Case for a UNCRC General Comment on Children's Rights and Digital Media*. London: Children's Commissioner for England. www.childrenscommissioner.gov.uk/wp-content/uploads/2017/06/Case-for-general-comment-on-digital-media.pdf

Livingstone, Sonia and Amanda Third. 2017. Children and young people's rights in the digital age: an emerging agenda. *New Media & Society*, 19 (5): 657–670. https://doi.org/10.1177/1461444816686318

Lundy, Laura. 2007. 'Voice' is not enough: conceptualising articleicle 12 of the United Nations Convention on the Rights of the Child. *British Educational Research Journal*, 33 (6): 927–942. https://doi.org/10.1080/01411920701657033

Lupton, Deborah and Ben Williamson. 2017. The datafied child: the dataveillance of children and implications for their rights. *New Media and Society*, 19 (5): 780–794.

Menashy, Francine and Zeena Zakharia. 2017. *Investing in the Crisis: Private Participation in the Education of Syrian Refugees*. Belgium: Education International.

Nussbaum, Martha. 2007. *Frontiers of Justice. Disability, Nationality, Species Membership*. Cambridge, MA: Harvard University Press.

Schwartz, Sarah. 2017. *Cellphones, Apps Power Learning for Syrian Refugees*. www.edweek.org/ew/articles/2017/09/06/cellphones-apps-power-learning-for-syrian-refugees.html

Sen, Amartya. 2009. *The Idea of Justice*. Cambridge, MA: Allen Lane & Harvard University Press.

Swan, Melanie. 2015. *Blockchain: Blueprint for a New Economy*. Sebastopol, CA: O'Reilly.

UBI Global. 2019. *New Infographic: Innovation Defining Our World 2019*. https://resources.ubi-global.com/technology-infographic-2019

UNICEF. 2017. *Children in a Digital World*. Paris: UNICEF.

United Nations. 1948. *Universal Declaration of Human Rights*. New York: United Nations.

United Nations. 1989. *Convention on the Rights of the Child*. New York: United Nations.

United Nations. 2015. *Sustainable Development Goals: 4 Education*. New York: United Nations. [Available from: https://www.un.org/sustainabledevelopment/education/, accessed August 2019].

United Nations High Commissioner for Refugees. 1951. *1951 Refugee Convention*. New York: The UN Refugee Agency.

United Nations High Commissioner for Refugees. 2016. *Global Trends. Forced Displacement in 2015*. New York: The UN Refugee Agency.

United Nations High Commissioner for Refugees. 2017. *Global Trends. Forced Displacement in 2017*. New York: The UN Refugee Agency.

Watkins, Kevin. 2013. *Education without Borders: A Summary*. London: A World at School.

Watkins, Kevin and Stephen A. Zyck. 2014. *Living on Hope, Hoping for Education. The Failed Response to the Syrian Refugee Crisis*. London: Overseas Development Institute.

Watt, Ewan. 2019. *How Lebanon Is Giving Very Young Syrian Refugees the Skills They Need for School*. https://theirworld.org/news/syrian-refugee-children-get-early-education-skills-for-lebanon-schools

World Economic Forum (WEF). 2018. *The Future of Jobs Report 2018*. Geneva: World Economic Forum.

16

'DAD! CUT THAT PART OUT!'

Children's rights to privacy in the age of 'generation tagged': sharenting, digital kidnapping and the child micro-celebrity

Emma Nottingham

Introduction

This chapter argues that children who are exposed on social media or broadcast as a result of the actions of their parents are in need of greater protection. It suggests that the risks involved need to be made clear, and that law and policy changes are needed so that risks to children can be guarded against. Accordingly, this research highlights some of the risks that may occur when 'generation tagged' have been exposed by their parents. The term 'generation tagged' refers to children who have been exposed on social media as a result of the actions of adults (Oswald, James and Nottingham, 2016). The risks to these children include infringement of the privacy rights of the child, the risk of both present and future harm, and concerns about 'digital kidnapping' (Whigham, 2015). Different examples of children appearing on social media as a result of the actions of their parents are explored in this chapter, and the associated risks are considered. The examples include: when children appear on the social media channels of 'micro-celebrities'; when children appear on parent blogs or family vlogs, such as on a YouTube channel; and when children appear on fly-on-the-wall documentaries as a result of the actions of their parents.

Moreover, this chapter outlines some of the existing recommendations that have been made in order to safeguard children. It highlights that some recommendations, if implemented, will offer children some protection. However, it suggests that there is still much to be done if children who appear on social media as a result of the actions of their parents are to be better protected. Therefore, this chapter argues that more adequate safeguards for 'generation tagged' need to be developed, and that parents, and society as a whole, need to be better educated of the impact of their online behaviour, especially the impact on their children.

What is 'sharenting'?

The term 'sharenting' refers to the practice of parents oversharing information related to their children on social media (Bessant, 2018; Blum-Ross, 2015; Steinberg, 2016). The 'always-online' culture, encouraged by the popularity of social media, sees many parents regularly share details of their day-to-day lives online. Social media sites such as Twitter, Facebook, YouTube, Snapchat and Instagram have given both celebrities and non-celebrities a platform to distribute information, images and videos to large audiences. The term 'sharenting' is derived from the words 'share' and 'parenting', and refers to the practice of parents uploading images, videos and information about their children on social media. The term is usually used to refer to when parents do this frequently or excessively. This is sometimes referred to as 'over-sharenting'.

Kumar (2019) has suggested that 'sharenting' is not a new practice. She has identified that people have been recording their daily lives for centuries, using diaries, scrapbooks and baby logbooks. Humphreys (2018) has suggested that when parents share information about their children, it is simply a form of 'media accounting', where individuals use media to document their everyday lives. He emphasises that 'media accounting' is important for an individual's sense of self and identity. Furthermore, posting on social media has become a cultural norm. Thus, even in spite of the dangers outlined below, entirely stopping parents from posting images and information regarding their children on social media is not a realistic demand. Recommendations for greater protection must therefore find a balance by permitting parents to use social media as a form of 'media accounting' but ensuring that the risks and dangers are eliminated or minimised.

'Sharenting' and the older child

Children of all ages can be subjected to 'sharenting'. Older children are at risk but are in a better position to voice their concerns to their parents and ask them not to post information, images or videos on social media. Moreover, a child who is considered to be legally competent could be in a position to initiate court proceedings against their parents (Bessant, 2017a; Oswald et al., 2016). In English law, a child is considered 'Gillick-competent' and able to give valid consent if they have reached 'sufficient understanding and intelligence to understand the nature and implications of the proposed treatment' (*Gillick v West Norfolk and Wisbech Area Health Authority* [1985] AC 112). The 'Gillick-competent' child whose parents have engaged in 'sharenting' without their child's consent might be able to seek leave to apply for a specific issue order or a prohibited steps order (Children Act, 1989, section 8), or by using the inherent jurisdiction of the court (Oswald et al., 2016). This would have the effect of stopping the parents posting information online or restricting how much and where they post this information. However, these types of court orders are yet to be used in this context. Furthermore, legal proceedings brought by a child are rare, given that the support of a third-party adult is normally needed at some stage, not least to help with accessing financial support for legal costs.

'Sharenting' and the young child

Young children are likely to be the most vulnerable. If a child is too young to speak, then they will not be able to express or effectively articulate concerns to their parents in the way that an older child might. Moreover, a young child might not even be aware that their parents have shared information about them online. In contrast to an older child, a young child is extremely unlikely to be considered legally competent, and will therefore be unable to initiate legal proceedings. Young children are entirely reliant on an interested third party to act on their behalf. For example, if a parent posts information online about a child, the other parent could theoretically seek a court order to prohibit this (Children Act, 1989, section 8). It has been questioned whether 'generation tagged', once they become adults, might be able to bring legal action against their parents for their past 'sharenting' activity (Kobie, 2016).

Pre-birth 'sharenting'

'Sharenting' can even begin in the womb, when expectant parents upload images from their ultrasound scan or reveal their due dates (Taylor, 2008). Some parents have created social media 'handles' and usernames for their unborn children. For instance, a mother, who is known as 'bongqiuqiu' on Instagram, created a dedicated hashtag, #MereGoRound, and Instagram account, @MereGoRound, for her unborn child when she was three months pregnant. The account amassed over 5,500 followers prior to her child's birth (Abidin, 2015). Similarly, Halston Blake Fisher, born in March 2019, had 112,000 Instagram followers while still in the womb (Morse, 2019).

The dangers of 'sharenting'

Parents might have positive motivations for 'sharenting' (e.g. for seeking and sharing parenting advice, for finding a support network or for keeping in touch with relatives and friends) (Bessant, 2017b). 'Sharenting' can be relatively low-risk, such as when parents ensure that children are not identifiable. For example, Holly Willoughby, a famous television presenter in the UK, ensures that only photographs of the back of her children are posted on her social media profiles, their faces never being visible (BBC Newsround, 2019). Similarly, ex-footballer Rio Ferdinand ensures that his children's faces cannot be seen on his social media profiles, either by making sure he only uses pictures taken from behind or by pixelating his children's faces (BBC Newsround, 2019). However, 'sharenting' can be a dangerous practice when parents reveal too much information, especially inappropriate or identifying information (Children's Commissioner, 2018).

Digital kidnapping

In a 2010 report by AVG, a digital security company, it was found that 92 per cent of 2-year-olds in the USA had a digital footprint (Magid, 2010). The Children's Commissioner for England stated in her 2018 report, 'Who Knows About Me?', that '[o]n average, by the age of 13, parents have posted 1300 photos and videos of their child to social media' (Children's Commissioner, 2018, p. 2). 'Sharenting' can result in the identification of a child's home or school, reveal what a child looks like, their birthday, and their likes and dislikes (Kumar, 2019). Exposure of identifying information could put a child at risk of 'digital kidnapping' (Whigham, 2015). In a UK report, Barclays suggested that by 2030, 'sharenting' will account for two-thirds of identity fraud (Coughlan, 2018). Information exposed about a child when they are young might be recorded and stored until the child is an adult, when fraudsters could open accounts using the details they have collected (Coughlan, 2018).

Information about children could also be collected by data-brokers, who collect and sell information to companies, often for marketing purposes.

Emotional harm

'Sharenting' can also lead to a child being emotionally harmed (e.g. when a child becomes older and unexpectedly discovers that an archive of their childhood is available on social media). A baby or young child is unlikely to have been aware that 'sharenting' was taking place, but emotional harm could ensue when a child is old enough to understand, perhaps wishing that their parents had not exposed them online. Therefore, the negative effects of 'sharenting' will not necessarily be immediately apparent at the time that images or information are posted on social media. Problems might materialise in the future.

Emotional harm might also occur if a parent engages in 'Internet child shaming' (Kinghorn, 2018). 'Internet child shaming' is the term used to describe situations where parents post on social media (usually in the form of a video) to embarrass and humiliate their child in order to punish them. Some 'Internet child shaming' videos have amassed a high number of views. For example, a mother in Devour, USA, published a video in which she humiliated her daughter for lying about her age on Facebook (Henderson, 2015). This practice has attracted both positive and negative responses, but has raised questions regarding whether such a public punishment is in the child's best interests (Apostolides and Harvey, 2018; Knight, 2015; Turner, 2014).

Privacy

Article 16 of the United Nations Convention on the Rights of the Child 1989 states that:

> (1) No child shall be subject to arbitrary or unlawful interference with his or her privacy, family, home or correspondence, nor to unlawful attacks on his or her honour and reputation; (2) The child has the right to the protection of the law against such interference or attacks.

In addition, Article 8 of the European Convention on Human Rights and Fundamental Freedoms offers protection of privacy rights to individuals. Although this makes no explicit mention of children, they are entitled to the protection offered by the Convention. Therefore, in light of both of the aforementioned conventions, the practice of 'sharenting' can be considered to infringe a child's right to privacy. As Hancock (2016) has stated, '[p]otentially the greatest threat to a child's privacy can come from their own parents, who are in a position to sacrifice the rights of their children'. Oswald et al. (2016) have argued that children should be entitled to a reasonable expectation of privacy, distinct from that of their parents, and have suggested that 'society is at risk of embedding a new privacy-intrusive norm' (p. 199).

Exploitation

Social media platforms have become a forum for the 'attention economy', where individuals compete for media attention. The inclusion of a child in social media posts can be imperative for some parents for increasing online popularity (e.g. by posting 'selfies' with children or uploading family videos). This behaviour can be common among parents who are 'micro-celebrities', who might use their children to gain an increased audience.

The term 'micro-celebrity' refers to individuals who use technology such as webcams, blogs and social networks to seek to increase their own popularity (Senft, 2008). Marwick (2016) has referred to micro-celebrity as 'a self-presentation technique in which people view themselves as a public persona to be consumed by others, use strategic intimacy to appeal to followers, and regard their audience as fans' (p. 331). Accordingly, Marwick (2016) has identified 'micro-celebrity' as 'something one does, rather than something one is' (p. 331).

The role of a micro-celebrity is a full-time job for some, which can be very lucrative. Companies pay individuals to act as brand ambassadors or for product endorsement. Organisations such as Walmart, Staples and Mattel are said to be arranging product endorsement deals for children who have large followings on YouTube and Instagram (Maheshwari, 2019). It has also been reported that children with smaller social media followings are approached by organisations. For example, in 2018, a toy company launched an influencer campaign in which they offered payments and free toys to parents in return for weekly Instagram posts of their children playing with their toys (Maheshwari, 2019).

When 'micro-celebrity' parents post images, videos or information about their child on social media, they might be doing this for their own selfish interests; to make money or to use their children to elevate their celebrity status or to increase the amount of followers they have. Children of 'micro-celebrities' are therefore particularly vulnerable to being exposed on social media. Abidin (2015, 2017) has used the term 'micro micro-celebrities' to refer to the children of 'micro-celebrity' parents who have been exposed online and become 'celebrified' in order to support or augment their parent's own celebrity status. She has identified that such exposure is primarily by 'influencer mothers'. Moreover, she has suggested that 'influencer mothers are more prolific, deliberate and commercial' (Abidin, 2017). In 2018, social media influencer Clemmie Hooper deactivated her Instagram account, allegedly after she was criticised for exploiting her children by having them appear on her profile to help advertise products (Dixon and Horton, 2018).

Parent blogging

Parent blogs are an example of 'media accounting', where parents document their everyday lives in their role as a parent. 'Mummy blogs' in particular have become increasingly popular, with mothers using blogs to establish an online community of parents perhaps for discussion or support. Parent blogs, by their nature, involve individuals discussing their lives as parents, and this could inevitably be intertwined with information about their children. Blum-Ross and Livingstone (2017) have suggested that parent bloggers face an ethical dilemma, 'representing their identities as parents inevitably makes public aspects of their children's lives, introducing risks that they are, paradoxically, responsible for safeguarding against' (p. 110). Accordingly, they have argued that the 'boundaries between parent and child are difficult, if not impossible, to maintain' (p. 115).

Vlogging and YouTube families

The trend of family vlogging has resulted in some children living their daily lives in the public eye from their own home. Some YouTube families gain a large following, with millions of viewers watching each day. Children who appear in family vlogs can end up becoming 'Internet famous'. YouTube families make money through advertising and can be provided with free products to help boost sales. Successful vloggers can do this as a full-time job. Children who appear in vlogs are therefore at risk of being pressurised or manipulated by their parents in order to ensure continued followers and financial gain. In a vlog by 'The Shaytards', the 9-year-old daughter repeatedly pleads, 'Dad! Cut that part out!' when she tells her dad about a boy she has a crush on. The vlog shows scenes of the child running away from her dad and hiding under the bed. Her father follows her with the camera and can be heard saying, 'This is good footage' (The Shaytards, 2014).

YouTube families are entirely unregulated (Abidin, 2015; Oswald, James, Nottingham, Hendry and Woodman, 2017). Therefore, children who are part of a YouTube family may have to endure long hours of filming every day. The lack of regulation also means that there is no limit on the amount of footage uploaded. In contrast to child actors and child performers, who have to have a licence and have limits to the amount of hours they can work, children who appear in YouTube family vlogs do not benefit from any legal protection (Tate, 2015). No guidelines are in place to protect the psychological well-being of these children (Tate, 2015). In the UK, the government passed up the opportunity to address the problems for children in YouTube families when updating their licensing legislation relating to child performance and activities. It states, 'Note that this does not extend to used-generated content, e.g. where young people or a family record themselves and share it on a website or social media' (Department for Education, 2015, p. 7). Regulation is essential as children are unable to escape.

Fly-on the-wall documentaries

The rise in popularity of fly-on-the-wall documentaries has led to similar concerns about children's privacy and future well-being. Fly-on-the-wall documentaries can feature children being filmed in their day-to-day lives or in manufactured environments with hidden cameras. A Twitter hashtag can appear on screen while programmes are being shown, to encourage discussion on social media. Comments made via a hashtag are not always positive and can lead to children being branded in a negative way. Once comments are posted on social media, they might be difficult to remove, as they will have already spread into the echo chamber as a result of being retweeted or shared. Therefore, even if comments are only displayed for a short period of time before being removed, damage to the child might have already been done.

Research by Oswald et al. (2016) expressed concerns about children who have appeared in the British fly-on-the-wall documentaries *The Secret Life of 4 Year Olds*, *The Secret Life of 5 Year Olds* and *The Secret Life of 6 Year Olds*. These documentaries feature children being filmed together in a pretend school. It films their interactions and behaviour, and includes interjections where psychologists provide their own commentary about the children. Channel 4, who broadcast the series, describes it as 'eavesdropping on the children's "secret world"' (Oswald et al., 2016). Twitter hashtags appeared on screen, which resulted in extensive comments about the children, both positive and negative. The negative comments can easily be discovered long after the original broadcast through the hashtag. Oswald et al. (2016) argued that children who appeared in these programmes are at risk of harm in the future. They identified that the current legal framework is not sufficient to protect a child's right to privacy in these circumstances. Although parents provide consent for their children to be involved in these types of shows, it is not clear how much information they are given about the potential risks and harms, including future harms (Oswald et al., 2016). The editing process also raised concerns, as these types of television series typically capture children misbehaving more than children being well behaved. Furthermore, interaction with the programme makers highlighted that they badge the series as a form of 'science entertainment', and that they did not consider that there was a need for research ethics approval (Oswald et al., 2016, pp. 201, 207, 219).

Recommendations

Some scholars and organisations have made recommendations to better protect children from the risks associated with 'sharenting'. Suggestions have been made as to how parents could alter their online behaviour to better protect their children. For instance, Kumar (2019) has suggested that parents could use a pseudonym for their child and give their child veto power over content. Moreover, the Children's Commissioner (2018) has recommended that parents should not 'post photos and videos which reveal personal information about your children online' (p. 23). However, Barassi (2019) has suggested that the problem that needs to tackled is not parents. She has stated that 'we need to abandon the very notion of sharenting, because by focusing on parents' digital practices alone and the narrative of blame, we are blaming parents for something that is really a societal problem'. Therefore, she has maintained that the problem is with society at large (Barassi, 2019).

It has been argued that social media companies need to take greater responsibility. Oswald et al. (2017) have argued that social media sites should owe children a duty of care. Similarly, in England, the Children's Commissioner (2018) has argued that a statutory duty of care should be imposed on social media companies. However, her published proposals are not sufficient to protect 'generation tagged'; the proposals appear to offer protection only to child users of social media, rather than those who appear on social media as a result of the actions of others, including their parents.

A call for more research has been made by scholars. Abidin (2017) has suggested that '[f]uture research should look into safeguards for micro-microcelebrities for whom commercial work and personal documentation are not always distinct, but in fact deliberately intertwined in order to better engage with followers for relatability'. Further, Oswald et al. (2017, p. 5) have argued that 'More open discussion is needed around the digital social norm that accepts the objectification of young children, the posting of negative comments and images' (p. 5). In addition, they suggest that further research should be done to consider how older children can identify and control images and data that had been posted about them in the past. Recommendations have also been made by Oswald et al. (2017, p. 29) in regard to the need for more education for both children and parents about the impact of 'sharenting', especially regarding the level of personal information that parents are potentially exposing by doing this. Furthermore, they suggested that there should be 'a limitation on the extent to which information and images relating to a young child can be copied, re-contextualised and re-shown in a different context to the original post' (p. 29).

Conclusion

Parents are the gatekeepers of their children's privacy. When parents infringe their children's privacy through 'sharenting', parent blogs or family vlogging, children lose the protectors of their privacy, since they cannot easily assert their own rights. This is especially the case for young children who might not be aware of what is happening until they are older and who are not in a position to discuss their concerns with their parents. Children in this situation are also at risk of harms developing in the future, including emotional harm, once they discover that images, videos or information about themselves have been posted on social media by their parents. Information about a child could also be stolen by fraudsters who will open up accounts in a child's name, having accumulated and stored information about a child throughout their entire life up until adulthood. Parents who use social media, blogs and vlogs for financial gain to increase their own celebrity status can be considered to be exploiting their children.

Law and society need to find a balance. The current social climate indicates that parents will continue to use social media as a form of 'media accounting', and it is important to acknowledge the benefits of social media. For example, parents can more easily reach out and share parenting advice through parent support networks and online communities. Social media also makes it easier for parents to keep in touch with relatives and friends and provide them with updates about their child (Bessant, 2017b). However, in an age where digital wellness is becoming highly important, more needs to be done to ensure the rights, welfare, dignity and privacy of children. The recommendations identified earlier in this chapter, if implemented, could provide better protection for children of the social media age.

References

Abidin, Crystal. 2015. "Micromicrocelebrity: Branding babies on the Internet." *M/C Journal*, 18 (5). www.ojphi.org/ojs/index.php/fm/article/view/6401/5529

Abidin, Crystal. 2017. "Micro-microcelebrity: Famous babies and business on the Internet." *Parenting for a Digital Future*. https://blogs.lse.ac.uk/parenting4digitalfuture/2017/01/20/micro-microcelebrity-famous-babies-and-business-on-the-internet/

Acts of Parliament. 1989. *Children Act 1989*. London: The Stationery Office.

Apostolides, Zoe and Phil Harvey. 2018. "A crying shame: The shocking rise of Internet 'child shaming': How parents are taking to social media to humiliate and punish their kids on camera." *The Sun*, 9th April 2018. www.thesun.co.uk/news/6006140/internet-child-shaming-parents/

Barassi, Veronica. 2019. "Against sharenting." http://childdatacitizen.com/against-sharenting/

BBC Newsround. 2019. "Sharenting: Holly Willoughby and Robbie Williams against the Idea." *BBC Newsround*, 12th February 2019. www.bbc.co.uk/newsround/47199356

Bessant, Claire. 2017a. "Could a child sue their parents for sharenting?" *Parenting for a Digital Future*, 10th November 2017. https://blogs.lse.ac.uk/parenting4digitalfuture/2017/10/11/could-a-child-sue-their-parents-for-sharenting/

Bessant, Claire. 2017b. "Too much information? More than 80% of children have an online presence by the age of two." *The Conversation*, 20th September, 2017. https://theconversation.com/too-much-information-more-than-80-of-children-have-an-online-presence-by-the-age-of-two-83251

Bessant, Claire. 2018. "Sharenting: Balancing the conflicting rights of parents and children." *Communications Law*, 23 (1): 7–24.

Blum-Ross, Alicia. 2015. "'Sharenting': Parent bloggers and managing children's digital footprints." *Parenting for a Digital Future*. http://blogs.lse.ac.uk/parenting4digitalfuture/2015/06/17/managing-your-childs-digital-footprint-and-or-parent-bloggers-ahead-of-brit-mums-on-the-20th-of-june/

Blum-Ross, Alicia, and Sonia Livingstone. 2017. "Sharenting: Parent blogging and the boundaries of the digital self." *Popular Communication*, 15 (2): 110–125.

Children's Commissioner. 2018. "Who knows about me?" www.childrenscommissioner.gov.uk/wp-content/uploads/2018/11/who-knows-what-about-me.pdf

Coughlan, Sean. 2018. "'Sharenting' puts young at risk of online fraud," BBC News, 21 May 2018. www.bbc.co.uk/news/education-44153754

Department of Education. 2015. "Child performance and activated licensing legislation in England." https://assets.publishing.service.gov.uk/government/uploads/system/uploads/attachment_data/file/401345/Child_performance_and_activities_licensing_legislation_in_England_-_departmental_advice_-_final.pdf

Dixon, Hayley and Helena Horton. 2018. "Instagram mega mum quits app after claims she exploits her children." *The Telegraph*, 24 May 2018. www.telegraph.co.uk/news/2018/05/22/instagram-mega-mum-takes-account-accusations-used-children-advertising/

Gillick v. West Norfolk and Wisbech Area Health Authority and Department of Health and Social Security (1985) 3 AER 402.

Hancock, Holly. 2016. "Weller & Ors V Associated Newspapers Ltd [2015] EWCA Civ 1176: Weller case highlights need for guidance on photography, privacy and the press." *Journal of Media Law*, 8 (1): 17, 29.

Henderson, Hannah. 2015. "The mother who 'outed' her daughter's Facebook lie." *BBC News*, 21 May 2015. www.bbc.co.uk/news/blogs-trending-32828014

Humphreys, Lee. 2018. *The Qualified Self: Social Media and the Accounting of Everyday Life*. Cambridge, MA: MIT Press.

Kinghorn, Brian Edward. 2018. "Why shaming your children on social media may make things worse." *The Conversation*, 13 December, 2018. https://theconversation.com/why-shaming-your-children-on-social-media-may-make-things-worse-108471

Knight, Susan, A. 2015. "Technology trends: Social media shaming – Parenting strategy failure." *Social Work Today*, 15 (8): 6. www.socialworktoday.com/archive/111715p8.shtml

Kobie, Nicole. 2016. "Could children one day sue parents for posting baby pics on Facebook?" *The Guardian*, 8th May 2016. www.theguardian.com/sustainable-business/2016/may/08/children-sue-parents-facebook-post-baby-photos-privacy

Kumar, Priya C. 2019. "The real problem with posting about your kids online." *The Conversation*, 4 February 2019. https://theconversation.com/the-real-problem-with-posting-about-your-kids-online-110131

Magid, Larry. 2010. "Study: 92% of U.S. 2-year-olds Have Online Record." www.cnet.com/news/study-92-of-u-s-2-year-olds-have-online-record/

Maheshwari, Sapna. 2019. "Online and making thousands, at age 4: Meet the kidfluencers." *The New York Times*, 1 March, 2019. www.nytimes.com/2019/03/01/business/media/social-media-influencers-kids.html

Marwick, Alice. 2016. "You may know me from YouTube: (Micro)-celebrity in social media." In *A Companion to Celebrity*, edited by P. David Marshall and Sean Redmond, 333–350. Oxford: John Wiley and Sons.

Morse, Jack. 2019. "So it's come to this: An unborn baby 'kidfluencer' has 112,000 Instagram followers." https://mashable.com/article/unborn-kidfluencer/?europe=true#yPsTNMsD1iqS

Oswald, Marian, Helen James, Emma Nottingham, Rachael Hendry, and Sophie Woodman. 2017. "Have 'generation tagged' lost their privacy? A report on the consultation workshop to discuss the legislative, regulatory and ethical framework surrounding the depiction of young children on digital, online and broadcast media." 7th June 2017. https://docplayer.net/89293640-Have-generation-tagged-lost-their-privacy.html

Oswald, Marion, Helen James, and Emma Nottingham. 2016. "The not-so-secret life of five-year-olds: Legal and ethical issues relating to disclosure of information and the depiction of children on broadcast and social media." *Journal of Media Law*, 8 (2): 198–228.

Senft, Terri. 2008. *Camgirls: Celebrity and Community in the Age of Social Networks*. New York: Peter Lang.

Steinberg, Stacey. 2016. "Sharenting: Children's privacy in the age of social media' (March 8, 2016)." *Emory Law Journal* 66: 839 (2017); *University of Florida Levin College of Law Research Paper*, 16–41.

Tate, Amelia. 2015. "Is it safe to turn your children into YouTube stars?" *The Guardian*, 16 September 2015. www.theguardian.com/technology/2015/sep/16/youtube-stars-vlogging-child-safety-saccone-joly-katie-and-baby

Taylor, Janelle S. 2008. *The Public Life of the Fetal Sonogram: Technology, Consumption, and the Politics of Reproduction*. New Brunswick, NJ: Rutgers University Press.

The Shaytards. 2014. "Dad! Cut that part out!" (3 April 2014). www.youtube.com/watch?v=JdboPfhrXBg

Turner, Beverley. 2014. "Kid shaming: Should we really publicly humiliate our children on the internet?" *The Telegraph*, 21 May 2014. www.telegraph.co.uk/women/mother-tongue/10845797/Kid-Shaming-Should-we-really-publicly-humiliate-our-children.html;

Whigham, Nick. 2015. "Digital kidnapping will make you think twice about what you post to social media." *News.com.au*, 21 July 2015. www.news.com.au/lifestyle/real-life/digital-kidnapping-will-make-you-think-twice-about-what-you-post-to-social-media/story-fnq2oad4-1227449635495

17

SAFEGUARDING THE PROTECTION RIGHTS OF CHILDREN IN THE EASTERN CARIBBEAN

Jane Murray, Shelly-Ann Harper, Lisa McClean-Trotman and Heather Stewart

Introduction

The Eastern Caribbean Area (ECA) is a relatively wealthy subregion of four overseas territories and eight independent states where the positive development of many young children is hindered because they are disproportionately affected by experiences of violence, including child sexual abuse (CSA) (Meeks-Gardner et al., 2007). This situation continues to prevail despite ECA island states' policy commitments and considerable social progress towards child protection, which means that ECA states are not meeting their commitments as signatories to the United Nations Convention on the Rights of the Child (UNCRC) (United Nations (UN), 1989), particularly in respect of Articles 19, 34, 37 and 39. This situation contributes to the global situation for which children's rights are not secured universally.

Violence against children (VAC) is considered both a violation of human rights and an international public health issue. CSA is regarded as a form of VAC (Wirtz et al., 2016) that has been acknowledged as a social problem since the 1970s (Rock Letnie, 2013). Joseph (2013) notes that CSA in the Caribbean countries is not only a social issue, but also an issue that infiltrates health, education and economic domains. The World Health Organization (WHO) and the International Society for the Prevention of Child Abuse and Neglect (ISPCAN) (2006) define CSA as:

> the involvement of a child in sexual activity that he or she does not fully comprehend, is unable to give informed consent to, or for which the child is not developmentally prepared, or else that violates the laws or social taboos of society. Children can be sexually abused by both adults and other children who are – by virtue of their age or stage of development – in a position of responsibility, trust or power over the victim.
>
> *(p. 10)*

Infants and young children may be particularly vulnerable to CSA since they tend to be physically smaller and less strong than adults and older children, and they are especially reliant on adults to provide for many of their care needs. Child abuse is most often perpetrated by family members at home (United Nations General Assembly, 2006), and young children do not have contacts outside the home or the verbal lexicon that may enable them to tell others about their abuse.

In their study of CSA in the ECA, Jones and Trotman-Jemmott (2009) identified the following behaviours as CSA:

- rape;
- 'consensual' sexual intercourse with a minor;
- incest;
- children used as sexual objects in videos, photos or as pimps;
- exposure to sexual material through different media (e.g. radio, photos, movies, text, mobile telephone, Internet, parent/adult sexual toys, sexual DVDs);
- exposing the child to the sexual act deliberately or unknowingly; and
- uncomfortable or intrusive touching of child.

(p. 9)

It is acknowledged that CSA requires 'a consolidated response from several levels' to be tackled effectively in Caribbean states (Howe, 2013; Joseph, 2013, p. 4). As part of their rights-based work, the United Nations Children's Fund (UNICEF) has recognised that a multilevel response is required to address the specific CSA challenges in ECA states (Howe, 2013, pp. 50–52). In this chapter, we examine the prevalence of VAC, including CSA, in ECA states, we identify ways that UNICEF is attempting to address this in the subregion, and we discuss some of the challenges in respect of that work. We open the chapter with an overview of UNICEF's global work since its inception. Discussion follows concerning the ECA island states and their issues of VAC, including CSA. We then chart ways that the UNICEF Eastern Caribbean Area Office (UNICEF ECA) collaborates with governments and non-governmental and civil society organisations across health, education and social development sectors to address the issue of VAC, including CSA, as well as the prevention and responsive protection strategies implemented by the UNICEF ECA with its partners. We argue that the paramount challenges to the implementation of those strategies reside in the Eastern Caribbean states' recognition of the multidimensional nature of the issue of CSA as a form of VAC and their realisation of multifaceted, integrated solutions.

UNICEF's work in the world

The United Nations Children's Fund (UNICEF) is an international non-governmental organisation (NGO) that was first set up in 1946 by the United Nations General Assembly as the United Nations Children's International Emergency Fund to help countries emerging from World War II conflict to 'mend the lives of their children' (Black, 1986, p. 16). An executive board is responsible for UNICEF's governance; it is funded by voluntary contributions, and its 8,000 employees work out of its headquarters as well as regional and field-based offices (MOPAN, 2016). UNICEF builds partnerships towards reifying 'the vision of peace and social progress enshrined in the Charter of the United Nations' (United Nations Children's Fund (UNICEF), 2003). UNICEF 'works in 190 countries and territories to save children's lives, to defend their rights, and to help them fulfil their potential, from early childhood through adolescence' (United Nations Children's Fund (UNICEF), 2019a). It identifies that it partners governments and NGOs to secure child survival, education, child protection and inclusion, providing supplies, logistics and support in emergencies, addressing gender inequalities, innovation, and research and analysis (UNICEF, 2019a). According to its mission statement, the United Nations General Assembly mandates that UNICEF 'advocate(s) for the protection of children's rights, to help meet their basic needs and to expand their opportunities to reach their full potential' (UNICEF, 2003). The United Nations Convention on the Rights of the Child (UN, 1989) guides its work, and UNICEF is committed to establishing children's rights internationally, alongside universal recognition that children's survival, protection and development underpin human progress. UNICEF is particularly committed to making sure disadvantaged children, including those who have experienced violence and exploitation, receive 'special protection'. The United Nations Children's Fund (UNICEF) (2019b) position statement is clear that the organisation 'has zero tolerance for sexual exploitation and abuse'.

An assessment of UNICEF's work in 2014–2016 by MOPAN (2016) found much to commend, in particular the organisation's focus on the future, its organisational transparency and its commitment to realising child rights and gender equality, as well as its governance, equity, human rights, performance management, agility in operations, advocacy, fundraising and communications. UNICEF also produces many of its own reports about its work, among which its Annual Results Reports identify many successes: the 2017 Annual Results Report highlights the organisation's achievements in 'health; HIV and AIDS; water, sanitation and hygiene (WASH); nutrition; education; child protection; social inclusion; humanitarian action; and gender' (United Nations Children's Fund (UNICEF), 2018a).

However, UNICEF's work is not universally condoned. In a challenge to its reputation, for example, its industry partnership with the confectionary company Cadbury Adams Canada was criticised (Collier, 2010): in return for being allowed to display UNICEF's logo on its confectionary packaging, the company donated $500,000 to UNICEF. Critics noted that this agreement had the potential to compromise UNICEF's nutrition programme (Collier, 2010). Furthermore, although MOPAN (2016) identified strengths in UNICEF's operation, as indicated above, it also reported several aspects of UNICEF's work requiring development. These areas for organisational improvement included results-based management and budgeting, clearer role differentiation, robust evaluative evidence on UNICEF programming, a more systematic approach to knowledge generation, use of country systems, and enhanced environmental sustainability. Equally, UNICEF is self-critical: in 2013, its Innovation Unit Co-Lead highlighted the value it places on identifying and critiquing its failures to leverage improvements for its future work (Fabian, 2013). Moreover, McVeigh (2018) reported that UNICEF acknowledged its failure to support children in the Central African Republic who claimed they were victims of sexual abuse and rape by French peacekeepers.

Violence against children in the Eastern Caribbean states

In this section, we describe briefly the situation for children in the Eastern Caribbean Area, before considering issues of violence against children (VAC), including child sexual abuse (CSA), that prevail in that subregion.

The situation for children in the Eastern Caribbean Area

Children constitute about a third of the population in the 12 countries under the UNICEF ECA Multi-Country Programme of Co-operation, which comprises four overseas territories – Anguilla, Montserrat, Turks and Caicos Islands, and the Virgin Islands – and eight independent states – Antigua and Barbuda, Barbados, the Commonwealth of Dominica, Grenada, St. Kitts and Nevis, Saint Lucia, St. Vincent and the Grenadines, and Trinidad and Tobago. The ECA population is eclectic in terms of faith, culture and ethnicity (United Nations Educational, Scientific and Cultural Organisation (UNESCO), 2010); the ECA small island states, which are categorised as high or upper middle-income category, score well on the Human Development Index overall and have high levels of universal primary and secondary education (United Nations Children's Fund (UNICEF), 2016). However, ECA island states are vulnerable to climate change and natural disasters, including tropical storms and hurricanes and their effects, which can be devastating for the population as a whole (Organisation of Eastern Caribbean States (OECS), 2016; UN News, 2018). Reduced public expenditure and unemployment that tend to follow natural disasters often impact negatively on children's lives (Meeks-Gardner et al., 2007). When Hurricanes Irma and Maria caused children and their families to lose their homes in 2017, social protection services were disrupted, the sanitation infrastructure was compromised, and children's pre-school and school buildings were destroyed; children's needs for psychosocial and health support in the ECA increased at the very time services were lost (United Nations Children's Fund (UNICEF), 2018b). A few weeks before this book was published, Hurricane Dorian caused further turmoil in the ECA.

Economic growth has been comparatively low in the ECA since the 2008–2009 financial crisis (UNICEF, 2016). There is increasing inequality among the subregion's population, with deprivation disproportionately affecting children, unequal access to social services, high unemployment among the young, and significant VAC, particularly in Trinidad and Tobago (Meeks-Gardner et al., 2007; UNICEF, 2016). Human Development Index scores in the subregion have declined in recent years (World Bank Group, 2018). Many fathers are absent from children's lives in ECA states, and children in the region whose fathers are absent tend to experience marginalisation (UNICEF, 2016; United Nations Children's Fund Office for the Eastern Caribbean Area (UNICEF ECA), 2017a, 2017b). Child health issues in the ECA include a relatively high incidence of nutritional deficiencies, disadvantaged children lost from the health system (as well as education and protection systems) and childhood obesity linked to diseases later in life (UNESCO, 2010; UNICEF, 2016).

Equally, despite high levels of universal primary and secondary education in the ECA, educational outcomes are disproportionately low, with poor quality of education in schools and early childhood education (ECE) settings. Less than 20 per cent of ECE provision is state-maintained, with the rest run by the private and voluntary sectors (Harvard, 2017; UNICEF, 2016). Many disadvantaged young children do not access structured early childhood development (ECD) programmes in ECA states, with 10 to 20 per cent of children aged 3 to 5 years not attending preschool. Differences are prominent between the richest and the poorest households. In Trinidad and Tobago, for example, 93 per cent of children living in the richest households were estimated to be receiving ECD services, compared with 72 per cent of children from the poorest households (UNICEF ECA, 2017a). Limited data suggest that fewer than 50 per cent of the children under 3 years old are accessing structured ECD programmes and services of the United Nations Children's Fund Office for the Eastern Caribbean Area (UNICEF ECA, 2017c), which is an alert to potential problems that poor – or no – ECE provision may be storing up for the subregion's future: 'Failure to invest in early childhood education (ECE) means that children in the 0–5 age group are robbed of their potential for optimal development in the physical, cognitive, linguistic and socio-emotional areas' (p. 49). This position taken by UNICEF ECA (2017c) is based on robust scientific findings suggesting that experiences in the earliest years of life have the greatest effect on cognitive development, mental and physical health, and lifetime outcomes (Shonkoff and Richter, 2013).

Violence against children in the Eastern Caribbean Area

Inequality, unemployment, poverty, absent fathers and parental conflict are recognised as risk factors for neglect and VAC (UNICEF, 2016; Wilkinson, 2004). Physical, emotional and sexual VAC is a significant issue in education settings and homes in the ECA: up to 70 per cent of children told UNICEF that they had experienced either physical or emotional abuse in the previous month (UNICEF, 2016). VAC is identified as a legacy of the British colonial history of some ECA states: neither childhood nor children were protected when children and adults worked together as slaves on Caribbean plantations in the seventeenth and eighteenth centuries, and the prevalence of physical punishment of children in ECA homes and schools is recognised as a vestige of colonialism in the subregion (Burns, 2013; Meeks-Gardner et al., 2007). Boduszek et al. (2017) found that 52 per cent of children from Barbados and 60 per cent of children from Grenada said they had experienced verbal violence at home, while 30 per cent of children from Barbados and 40 per cent of children from Grenada said they had experienced physical violence at home. Boduszek et al. (2017) also found that boys from both countries were more likely than girls to accept – and engage in – violent behaviour. In their study of violence in the home in Caribbean countries, Sutton and Álvarez (2016) report that 66 per cent of Caribbean respondents thought corporal punishment should be administered to children if they misbehave, and 91 per cent of them said they had experienced physical punishment as children. UNICEF (2016) found that younger children and boys are most likely to be physically punished; Sutton and Álvarez (2016) also report that neglect of younger children is not uncommon in the ECA region. For example, in Barbados, 29 per cent of reports of neglect concern children up to 36 months, while children younger than 9 years are involved in 69 per cent of reports. Among a population of 1.3 million, the Children's Authority of Trinidad and Tobago (2015, 2016) identified 5,809 cases of child abuse in 2015–2016, most of which were physical or sexual abuse, and they found children younger than 9 years engaged in illegal activities.

CSA occurs through threat, intimidation, manipulation and force (Collin-Vézina, Daigneault and Hébert, 2013) and its victims present with trauma, disease, relationship problems and psychopathology (Reid, Reddock and Nickenig, 2014). Jones, Trotman-Jemmott, Maharaj and Da Breo (2014) noted that CSA and exploitation were common in the ECA, no comprehensive CSA data systems were in place, and CSA incidents tended to be subject to secrecy. Howe (2013) identifies that securing reliable statistics on the extent of CSA is difficult. Nevertheless, UNICEF (2016) found that 40 per cent of women in ECA states said they had experienced sexual VAC, while trafficking of girls (and women) for sexual exploitation has been identified as a 'serious problem' in the ECA, with economic, social and racial inequality identified as the root cause (Jones et al., 2014).

Based on data from a major mixed methods study conducted with 1,400 participants from six ECA states, Jones and Trotman-Jemmott (2009) identified CSA in the ECA as:

an alarming picture of a social problem that is escalating, has increasingly severe consequences for Caribbean societies, has multiple layers and is perpetuated not only by adults who carry out harmful sexual practices with children but also by non-abusing adults through complicity, silence, denial and failure to take appropriate action.

(p. 9)

The men (37.9 per cent) and women (62.1 per cent) who took part in Jones and Trotman-Jemmott's (2009) study were practitioners, clinicians and policymakers from various disciplines who work with CSA victims, as well as adults who had experienced CSA. Participants reported that CSA was more prevalent in family homes than elsewhere; they identified that most child sex abusers are men, but some women are also abusers, and they thought most victims were girls, although some practitioners said they had recently noticed more boys becoming victims of CSA. Some participants reported the CSA of babies. Twenty-five per cent of respondents agreed that sex between adults and children is considered normal in some families, 22 per cent agreed that sex between brothers and sisters is considered normal in some families, and more than 70 per cent agreed that 'women sometimes turn a "blind eye" when their partners have sex with children in their families' (Jones and Trotman-Jemmott, 2009, p. 238). Participants thought that a number of factors resulted in CSA in the home, including lack of parental supervision, single-parent families, stepfathers, multiple partners, complex family structures, mothers failing to protect their children, and secrecy. Although participants in Jones and Trotman-Jemmott's study identified home as the principle site for CSA in ECA island states, they also noted that CSA happens outside the home. Sixty-seven per cent of participants agreed that adults children trust – including bus drivers, priests, teachers and coaches – are more likely than strangers to engage in CSA. They also noted that others in positions of authority sometimes knew about incidences of CSA but did nothing. Transactional CSA between minors and adult men, for which money or other commodities are exchanged for sex, was identified by participants as an increasing problem in the ECA.

In a review conducted by the UNICEF ECA concerning sexual violence against children in the Caribbean, Howe (2013) identified challenges and weaknesses in respect of prevention, response and service delivery for children who have experienced CSA and their families. These included, but were not limited to:

- insufficient services and allocation of resources;
- inadequate staff training;
- inadequate and variable service accessibility, coverage and response;
- inadequate provision for reporting and referral pathways;
- variable waiting times for initial assessment;
- insufficient focus on gender aspects of CSA prevention and treatment;
- inadequate data collection and use of data to inform service provision;
- inconsistent information-sharing among agencies;
- weak or non-existent monitoring and evaluation;
- lack of child-friendly procedures;
- fear and confusion concerning disclosure;
- insufficient programmes to prevent and raise awareness of CSA;
- silence, shame and stigma among children who have experienced CSA and their families;

- insufficient school, family and community-based resources and services; and
- inadequate involvement of children in decisions affecting them.

Based on the report findings, Howe (2013) made 14 recommendations for how CSA in the Eastern Caribbean Area could be addressed.

How is UNICEF addressing child sexual abuse in the Eastern Caribbean?

The research findings set out in the previous section provide evidence that some children's rights (UN, 1989) are not respected by all in ECA island states. Specifically, children's UNCRC rights (UN, 1989) to be protected from all forms of violence (Article 19), to be protected by governments from sexual exploitation and abuse (Article 34) and cruel or harmful punishment (Article 37) have been ignored in many cases. As we indicated earlier in the chapter, this may be especially the case for younger children and infants: because of their relative lack of size and strength, their need to depend on adults, and their reliance on non-verbal communication, they are, as noted in UNCRC General Comment No. 7, particularly vulnerable to 'poverty, discrimination, family breakdown and multiple other adversities that violate their rights and undermine their well-being' (United Nations (UN), UN Committee on the Rights of the Child (UNCRC), 2005).

Ideas on to tackle CSA in the ECA

Rafferty (2013) recommends that measures to address violence internationally should include social protection, awareness-raising, community involvement, provision of resources, and funding to support gender equality, communication and collaboration. In respect of addressing CSA in the ECA, Howe (2013) proposes that:

> A more determined and coordinated effort is… needed to prevent and respond to child sex abuse in the region. The obstacles facing child sexual abuse prevention and responses in the region are many but none are insurmountable. The paramount challenge for states is to recognize the multidimensional nature of the child sexual abuse problem and therefore conceive solutions which are multifaceted, focused and integrated.
>
> *(p. 50)*

Jones et al. (2014) concur and identify there may be value in adopting an integrated systems approach. An integrated systems approach 'assumes that any desired outcome may be dependent on services provided by multiple organizations' (Teske, 2011, p. 92). In respect of CSA in the ECA, the model may translate to:

> a synergistic approach to analysing the ways in which the multi-layered facets of abuse interact to reinforce each other (to) generate multi-level activities (conceptual, material, structural) that together might produce effects that are greater than their individual components. For example, a sex offender treatment programme that is developed alongside a public health-oriented education and prevention programme, and in which both address the status of children and gender socialization, may be more effective in combination than as separate interventions.
>
> *(Jones and Trotman-Jemmott, 2016, p. 836)*

What is UNICEF doing?

In recognition of work that needs to be done to address VAC and CSA, and related issues of poverty and inequalities, with the ultimate goal to realise all children's rights in the Eastern Caribbean Area, UNICEF allocated a budget of $24,100,000 for 2017–2021, subject to available funds. The intention of the funding was to develop and implement 'national legislation to prevent, mitigate and address violence and other childhood abuses and (ensure that) the justice, education, public health, security and other sectors observe children's rights to this protection' (UNICEF, 2016, p. 7). As well as directly focusing on VAC and CSA, the programme addresses a range of issues that are risk factors for VAC, including CSA (World Health Organization (WHO), 2019).

As a result of the programme funding, UNICEF ECA is committed to supporting countries to implement new prevention and responsive protection strategies with its partners, including governments, as part of a large-scale programme. The programme builds on previous work; for example, the *Breaking the Silence Gender and Community Empowerment Model*, a community-based intervention that was part-funded by UNICEF and which increased knowledge of CSA in agricultural and fishing villages (Reid et al., 2014). The office has identified 2017–2021 programme goals for its Eastern Caribbean Multi Country Programme (MCP) across the ECA countries and territories; the UNICEF ECA MCP is aligned with UNICEF's Strategic Plan 2018–2021 goals related to learning, protection and equitable chance in life (United Nations Children's Fund (UNICEF), 2018c). Its goals focus principally on supporting 'the most vulnerable girls and boys … at risk of violence, abuse, exploitation and discrimination' (United Nations Children's Fund (UNICEF) Eastern Caribbean, 2019). A key challenge to programme implementation resides in Eastern Caribbean states recognising the multidimensional nature of the issue of child sexual abuse and their realisation of multifaceted, integrated solutions so the UNICEF ECA team will work with country governments and other partners 'to fulfil their commitments to the UNCRC so that every child can grow and develop to reach his or her full potential' (United Nations Children's Fund (UNICEF) Eastern Caribbean, 2019). The programme focuses on three 'pillars': (i) lifelong learning; (ii) 'safety and justice for children'; and (iii) 'social protection and child rights' (UNICEF Eastern Caribbean, 2019). In respect of:

(i) Lifelong learning …
All children in the EC subregion will 'have every opportunity to improve their education and developmental outcomes and access equitable and inclusive learning environments across the life cycle, including in emergencies', through:

- equitable and inclusive early childhood services;
- promoting positive learning and inclusive environments;
- strengthening institutional capacity for planning, monitoring and disaster risk reduction.

(ii) Safety and justice for children …
'National legislation will be implemented to prevent, mitigate and address violence and other childhood abuses and the justice, education, public health, security and other sectors observe children's rights to this protection', by:

- supporting national justice and systems to develop so that violence, abuse, exploitation and neglect are prevented and treated;

- fostering political commitment to legislate and budget for strengthening interventions that prevent and respond to violence, abuse, exploitation; and
- building adults' and children's capacity to protect children from violence and abuse.

(iii) Social protection and child rights ...
Sufficient funding provided by national systems and policies for rights-based quality social policies and social investments, based on disaggregated data on children, to address multiple deprivations affecting the most vulnerable children, and build their resilience. This will be achieved by:

- facilitating exchanges and technical support; and
- supporting national governments to strengthen their capacities to:

    ➢ plan, develop and deliver inclusive child-focused social protection systems that reduce social vulnerabilities;
    ➢ strengthen resilience against shocks and crises affecting food, fuel, finance and environment; and
    ➢ protect children from poverty and social exclusion.

(UNICEF 2016; UNICEF Eastern Caribbean, 2019)

UNICEF Eastern Caribbean (2019) also identifies that throughout the 2017–2021 programme, its team will also reduce disaster risk reduction, monitor child rights, strengthen data systems, and promote gender equality.

With whom is UNICEF working?

The UNICEF ECA has adopted an integrated systems approach to optimise the effectiveness of its 2017–2021 programme. Its 'Country Programme Document' (UNICEF, 2016) sets out its intention to work with ECA governments, NGOs and civil society organisations across health, education and social development sectors to address problems in the ECA, including CSA. For the *lifelong learning* element of its programme, it identifies as its partners the ECA Ministries of Education, Health and Social Development, statistical departments, the OECS Commission, and the Caribbean Community (CARICOM). To achieve the second element of the programme, which is arguably the pillar most directly linked to CSA – *safety and justice for children* – the UNICEF ECA states its intention to build partnerships with the Ministry of Social Development, Offices of Attorneys General, the OECS, the Eastern Caribbean Supreme Court, statistical departments, regional faith-based organisations, and the West Indies Cricket Board. In respect of securing the third element – *social protection and child rights* – identified partners are ECA Ministries of Finance, Planning, Social Development, Health and Education, central statistics offices, the OECS, World Bank, the Caribbean Regional Technical Assistance Centre, and the International Monetary Fund.

What progress has UNICEF ECA made in achieving the Multi-Country Programme goals?

At the time of writing, the most recent published progress towards achieving the UNICEF ECA MCP goals was available in the 'UNICEF Annual Report 2017 Eastern Caribbean Multi-Country Programme' (UNICEF, 2018c). The sections below exemplify selected aspects of progress drawn from that report of work achieved in 2017: the first year of the UNICEF ECA MCP programme. In 2017, the ECA suffered two hurricanes across five of its countries and overseas territories, debts in excess of 75 per cent, and low economic growth, all of which increased the vulnerabilities of children and families (UNICEF, 2018c). Consequently, UNICEF adapted strategies, built new partnerships and recruited new staff to support children and families.

(i) Progress towards lifelong learning

The UNICEF ECA MCP provides for enhanced focus on early childhood development, and the pace of work was increased to allow enhancement of development potential in young children. The UNICEF early child development (ECD) programme has focused on provision of equitable access to high-quality, holistic, inclusive ECD provision and responsive care for boys and girls up to 8 years, in safe, interactive environments. Additionally, UNICEF ECA supported collaboration between stakeholders from health, education and social development sectors to enhance provision for young children's ECE and holistic development. Partnership between UNICEF and the OECS Commission resulted in the OECS integrated operational framework that affords practical guidance to ECE service providers and enhances provision and coordination of ECA ECE services. It is also notable that 900 stakeholders attended capacity-building and training supported by UNICEF with the potential to reach more than 7,000 children aged 0–5 years, including opportunities to learn more about positive child development, protecting children from child sexual abuse, and improving their skills in creating safe and stimulating ECD spaces for children in ECA states and territories. In addition, UNICEF ECA has worked in partnership with the Child Care Board in Barbados, the Barbados Red Cross, and the Office of the Prime Minister in Trinidad to enhance children's knowledge about violence and disaster risk reduction and violence.

(ii) Progress towards safety and justice for children

To prevent VAC, UNICEF ECA has promoted cross-sectoral collaboration between government departments focused on the promotion of positive behaviours, and it has worked in partnership with ministries responsible for child protection and ministries of education in Antigua and Saint Lucia to enhance educators' knowledge and skills for preventing and responding to VAC.

UNICEF generated evidence to build new knowledge about the situation of children in the ECA to address information gaps. Five ECA countries developed action plans, five countries completed and shared and situation analyses about children and women, and the ECA overseas territories developed national action plans for child safeguarding, as well as completing a study on migration and children. Child poverty analysis was conducted across the ECA, and financial studies were completed in Montserrat and the British Virgin Islands. This new knowledge has led to the identification of policy issues so that they can be addressed.

UNICEF ECA conducted an assessment of child protection systems which identified that all OECS countries have ratified the Convention on the Rights of the Child (CRC) and some have developed child protection policies, action plans and programmes. The assessment identified problems with implementation and service delivery, as well as significant gaps in coordination of institutional arrangements and lack of interaction between community-level structures and national systems for child protection. UNICEF ECA supported peer-to-peer opportunities for children to act as change agents to address CSA. By working with key partners, UNICEF ECA supported teachers in three ECA states to implement positive behaviour management practices in their classrooms and enhance the capacity of more than 3,000 professionals across five countries to identify, prevent and respond to child sexual abuse.

(iii) Progress towards social protection and child rights

UNICEF has supported ministries responsible for child protection in all ECA countries and linked ministries of education and child protection departments to enable them to work together to implement stronger child protection programmes. Social surveys in ECA overseas territories in 2017 provided data on child sexual abuse, corporal punishment and bullying that were used to advocate for child protection strategies with stakeholders in Anguilla, BVI and TCI. UNICEF ECA provided or supported participatory interventions that increased knowledge and skills to keep children safe from violence; for example, by enabling 50 per cent of early childhood supervisors in Saint Lucia to teach young children about sexual abuse in culturally and age-appropriate ways, and by providing children with opportunities to sensitise their peers about child protection issues.

In the five countries and overseas territories that were affected by Hurricanes Irma and Maria, UNICEF provided for more than 13,000 children to receive psychosocial support, enabled in excess of 12,000 children to access safe community spaces, and messaged two-thirds of children about how to protect themselves from harm during and after the hurricanes. UNICEF also ensured that children had access to safe water and arranged for over 1,000 pre-school children and over 19,000 school-aged children to access ECD and education services.

A collaborative report by UNICEF ECA and the OECS Commission provided disaggregated poverty data on children, informed by datasets from ECA country poverty assessments. These data are important because poverty is recognised as a risk factor for child abuse (WHO, 2019). The data revealed that child poverty varies considerably across ECA countries, though one in every three children in the ECA is poor, children in ECA are disproportionately represented among the poor, and child poverty concentrated among children living in households with four children or more. The report provides the basis for new awareness-raising activities in ECA country states on issues related to child poverty, as well as policy and programme development to address child poverty now and prevent it in the future.

What constraints has UNICEF ECA encountered in programme implementation?

Alongside successful aspects of progress in the 'UNICEF Annual Report 2017 Eastern Caribbean Multi-Country Programme', UNICEF (2018c) identifies constraints that have hindered efforts so far towards achieving the UNICEF ECA MCP. First, UNICEF (2018c) identifies gaps in the capacity of partners, including limited resources to improve ECE accessibility, poor-quality education, weak prioritisation of child protection system reforms, and poor focus on disaster risk reduction in sector plans. Second, it notes delays in several countries concerning policy development and programmes that need approval. Delays in finalising surveys and studies are the third constraint to making progress, alongside ongoing inadequacies in data and systematic use of data to provide evidence for decision-making and allocation of resources. The fourth and final constraint UNICEF (2018c) identifies to progress is mobilisation of resources for areas that are unaffected by emergencies.

Conclusion

In this chapter, we have considered issues concerning certain protection rights of children in the Eastern Caribbean and ways these may be safeguarded. To set this issue in context, we have explored UNICEF's global work and we have discussed the prevalence of VAC, particularly CSA, in the context of multiple inequalities in the ECA island states. We have noted that this situation indicates that children's rights specified in UNCRC Articles 19, 34, 37 and 39 (UN, 1989) are not respected by all in ECA island states. We have also argued that this situation may affect younger children and infants especially, who, for a variety of reasons, are particularly vulnerable to 'poverty, discrimination, family breakdown and multiple other adversities that violate their rights and undermine their well-being' (UN UNCRC, 2005, p. 2). In our chapter, we have shown how UNICEF has drawn on evidence to recognise that a multilevel, 'consolidated response from several levels' is needed to tackle the complex issues underpinning VAC and CSA (Howe, 2013; Joseph, 2013, p. 4). We have discussed UNICEF's launch of the UNICEF ECA 'Multi-Country Programme' (UNICEF, 2016), with funding of $24,100,000 allocated for the period 2017–2021. By launching the ECA MCP, UNICEF has indicated its commitment to implementing prevention and responsive protection strategies in partnership with governments and non-governmental and civil society organisations across health, education and social development sectors. We have charted ways that the UNICEF ECA has worked with partners since the launch of the MCP to begin to implement prevention and responsive protection strategies with the potential to address VAC, CSA and related issues. We have also highlighted constraints UNICEF has identified that will need to be addressed if the ECA MCP goals are to be achieved by 2021. The implementation of the MCP strategies and the successful achievement of the ECA MCP goals are dependent on UNICEF's partners – including ECA governments – joining with UNICEF to recognise the multidimensional nature of VAC and CSA and working with UNICEF in strong partnership to realise multifaceted, integrated solutions for all children in the ECA.

References

Black, Maggie. 1986. *The Children and the Nations: The Story of UNICEF.* New York: UNICEF.

Boduszek, Daniel, Agata Debowska, Ena Trotman Jemmott, Hazel Da Breo, Dominic Willmott, Nicole Sherretts, and Adele D. Jones. 2017. *Victimisation, Violence Perpetration, and Attitudes towards Violence among Boys and Girls from Barbados and Grenada.* Huddersfield, UK: University of Huddersfield Press.

Burns, Sheron C. 2013. "The ontology and social construction of childhood in the Caribbean." In *Understanding Child Abuse: Perspectives from the Caribbean*, edited by Adele D. Jones, 26–37. Basingstoke: Palgrave Macmillan Ltd.

Children's Authority of Trinidad and Tobago. 2015. *Annual Report for the Period Ending September 30, 2015.* Port of Spain: Children's Authority of Trinidad and Tobago.

Children's Authority of Trinidad and Tobago. 2016. *Statistical Bulletin, Nine Months and Counting … May 18, 2015 – February 17, 2016.* Port of Spain: Children's Authority of Trinidad and Tobago.

Collier, Roger. 2010. "Critics say UNICEF-Cadbury partnership is mere sugarwashing." *Canadian Medical Association Journal.* 182 (18): E813–E814. DOI:10.1503/cmaj.109-3720

Collin-Vézina, Delphine, Isabella Daigneault, and Martine Hébert. 2013. "Lessons learned from child sexual abuse research: Prevalence, outcomes, and preventive strategies." *Child and Adolescent Psychiatry and Mental Health.* 7, Article ID 22. DOI:10.1186/1753-2000-7-22

Fabian, Chris. 2013. "Institutionalizing risk taking (UNICEF + Failure)." *UNICEF Stories*, 18th December. http://unicefstories.org/2013/12/18/institutionalizing-risk-taking-unicef-failure/

Harvard. 2017. "The situation of children in the Eastern Caribbean area and UNICEF response." https://canvas.harvard.edu/courses/5175/files/1505148/download? verifier=cDwJvND04TSKUkhzRxmzRz2EeYy8H4nKpE43UFtr&wrap=1.

Henry-Lee, Aldrie, and Julie Meeks-Gardner (eds.). 2007. *Promoting Child Rights through Research: Proceedings of the Caribbean Child Research Conference 2006*. Kingston, Jamaica: SALISES, UWI.

Howe, Glenford. 2013. *Sexual Violence against Children in the Caribbean: Report 2012*. Barbados: UNICEF Office for the Eastern Caribbean Area.

Jones, Adele D., and Ena Trotman-Jemmott. 2009. Child sexual abuse in the Eastern Caribbean. www.unicef.org/media/files/Child_Sexual_Abuse_in_the_Eastern_Caribbean_Final_9_Nov.pdf

Jones, Adele D., and Ena Trotman-Jemmott. 2016. "Status, privilege and gender inequality: Cultures of male impunity and entitlement in the sexual abuse of children: Perspectives from a Caribbean study." *International Social Work*. 59 (6): 836–849. DOI:10.1177/0020872814537853

Jones, Adele D., Ena Trotman-Jemmott, Priya E. Maharaj, and Hazel Da Breo. 2014. *An Integrated Systems Model for Preventing Child Sexual Abuse: Perspectives from the Caribbean*. Basingstoke: Palgrave Macmillan Ltd.

Joseph, Lorita. 2013. "Introduction." In *Understanding Child Sexual Abuse: Perspectives from the Caribbean*, edited by Adele D. Jones, 1–8. Basingstoke: Palgrave MacMillan Ltd.

McVeigh, Karen. 2018 "UNICEF admits failings with child victims of alleged sex abuse by peacekeepers." *The Guardian*, 13th February.

Meeks-Gardner, Julie, Aldrie Henry-Lee, Pauletta Chevannes, Joan Thomas, Helen Baker-Henningham, and Charlene Coore. 2007. "Violence against children in the Caribbean: A desk review." In *Promoting Child Rights through Research: Proceedings of the Caribbean Child Research Conference 2006*, edited by Aldrie Henry-Lee and Julie Meeks-Gardner, 3–19. Kingston, Jamaica: SALISES, UWI.

MOPAN. 2016. "MOPAN 2015–2016 Assessments: United Nations Children's Fund (UNICEF) institutional assessment report." www.mopanonline.org/assessments/unicef2015-16/

Organisation of Eastern Caribbean States (OECS). 2016. "The climate change and disaster risk management unit." www.oecs.org/ccu-about

Rafferty, Yvonne 2013. "International dimensions of discrimination and violence against girls: A human rights perspective." *Journal of International Women's Studies*. 14 (1): 1–23.

Reid, Sandra D., Rhoda Reddock, and And Tisha Nickenig. 2014. "Breaking the silence of child sexual abuse in the Caribbean: A community-based action research intervention model." *Journal of Child Sexual Abuse*. 23: 256–277. DOI:10.1080/10538712.2014.888118

Rock Letnie, F. 2013. "Research on child sex abuse: Caribbean and international perspectives." In *Understanding Child Sexual Abuse: Perspectives from the Caribbean*, edited by Jones, A., 145–167. Basingstoke: Palgrave MacMillan Ltd.

Shonkoff, Jack P., and Linda Richter. 2013. "The powerful reach of early childhood development." In *Early Childhood Development Research and Its Impact on Global Policy*, edited by Britto, Pia Rebello, Patrice L. Engel, and Charles M. Super, 24–34. Oxford: Oxford University Press.

Sutton, Heather, and Lucciana Álvarez. 2016. *How Safe Are Caribbean Homes for Women and Children? Attitudes toward Intimate Partner Violence and Corporal Punishment*. Policy Brief No. IDP-PB-258. Washington, DC: Inter-American Development Bank.

Teske, Steven C. 2011. "A study of zero tolerance policies in schools: A multi-integrated systems approach to improve outcomes for adolescents." *Journal of Child and Adolescent Psychiatric Nursing*. 24 (2011): 88–97. DOI:10.1111/j.1744-6171.2011.00273.x

UN News. 2018. "In the eye of the Caribbean storm: One year on from Irma and Maria". *UN News*, 5th September. https://news.un.org/en/story/2018/09/1018372

United Nations (UN). 1989. *UN Convention on the Rights of the Child*. Geneva: United Nations.

United Nations (UN), UN Committee on the Rights of the Child. 2005. *Implementing Child Rights in Early Childhood General Comment No. 7 (2005) UN/CRC/GC/2005/1*. Geneva: United Nations.

United Nations Children's Fund (UNICEF). 2003. "UNICEF's mission statement." www.unicef.org/about/who/index_mission.html

United Nations Children's Fund (UNICEF). 2016. "Country programme document: Eastern Caribbean multi-country programme." E/ICEF/2016/P/L.24. https://data2.unhcr.org/en/documents/details/50028

United Nations Children's Fund (UNICEF). 2018a. "2017 annual results report." www.unicef.org/reports/2017-annual-results-reports

United Nations Children's Fund (UNICEF). 2018b. "Eastern Caribbean humanitarian situation report no. 15." https://reliefweb.int/sites/reliefweb.int/files/resources/UNICEF%20ECA%20Humanitarian%20Situation%20Report%20No.%2015%2C%2017%20January%202018.pdf

United Nations Children's Fund (UNICEF). 2018c. "UNICEF annual report 2017. Eastern Caribbean multi-country programme." www.unicef.org/about/annualreport/files/Eastern_Caribbean_Multi-Country_Program_2017_COAR.pdf

United Nations Children's Fund (UNICEF). 2019a. "UNICEF: What we do." www.unicef.org/what-we-do

United Nations Children's Fund (UNICEF). 2019b. "UNICEF's position on sexual exploitation and abuse and sexual harassment." www.unicef.org/press-releases/unicefs-position-sexual-exploitation-and-abuse-and-sexual-harassment

United Nations Children's Fund (UNICEF) Eastern Caribbean. 2019. "Our 2017–2021 programme goals." www.unicef.org/easterncaribbean/who-we-are_36222.html

United Nations Children's Fund Office for the Eastern Caribbean Area (UNICEF ECA). 2017a. *Situation Analysis of Children in Trinidad and Tobago*. Barbados: UNICEF ECA.

United Nations Children's Fund Office for the Eastern Caribbean Area (UNICEF ECA). 2017b. *Situation Analysis of Children in St Kitts and Nevis*. Barbados: UNICEF ECA.

United Nations Children's Fund Office for the Eastern Caribbean Area (UNICEF ECA). 2017c. *Situation Analysis of Children in Antigua & Barbuda*. Barbados: UNICEF ECA.

United Nations Educational, Scientific and Cultural Organisation (UNESCO) 2010. "Early childhood care and education regional report: Latin America and the Caribbean. 2010/ED/BAS/ECCE/RP/4." Presented at the *World Conference on Early Childhood Care and Education*, Moscow, 22–24 September 2010.

United Nations General Assembly. 2006. "Rights of the child: Report of the independent expert for the United Nations study on violence against children. A/61/299." https://documents-dds-ny.un.org/doc/UNDOC/GEN/N06/491/05/PDF/N0649105.pdf?OpenElement

Wilkinson, Richard. 2004. "Why is violence more common where inequality is greater?" *Annals of the New York Academy of Sciences*. 1036: 1–12. DOI:10.1196/annals.1330.001

Wirtz, Andrea L., Alessadra C. Carmen Alvarez, Luisa Brumana Guedes, Cecilie Modvar, and Nancy Glass. 2016. "Violence against children in Latin America and Caribbean countries: A comprehensive review of national health sector efforts in prevention and response." *BioMed Central Public Health*. 16 (1006): 1–16. DOI:10.1186/s12889-016-3562-3

World Bank Group. 2018. "Organisation of Eastern Caribbean States Systematic Regional Diagnostic." Report Number: 127046-LAC. https://openknowledge.worldbank.org/bitstream/handle/10986/30054/OECS-Systematic-Regional-Diagnostic-P165001-1-06292018.pdf?sequence=1&isAllowed=y.

World Health Organisation (WHO). 2019. "Child maltreatment." www.who.int/news-room/fact-sheets/detail/child-maltreatment

World Health Organization (WHO) and International Society for the Prevention of Child Abuse and Neglect. (2006). *Preventing Child Maltreatment: A Guide to Taking Action and Generating Evidence*. Geneva: WHO.

18

UNDERSTANDING YOUNG CHILDREN'S EXPERIENCES GROWING UP WITH DOMESTIC VIOLENCE FROM A CHILDREN'S RIGHTS PERSPECTIVE

Vera Lopez

Almost one-third of women worldwide have experienced either physical or sexual intimate partner violence in their lifetime (WHO, 2017). Rates of intimate partner violence against women are high even in countries with higher levels of gender equality (Gracia and Merlo, 2016). A 2014 survey of 28 European Union states, for example, found that some of the countries with the highest levels of gender equality (e.g., Denmark, Sweden, Finland) also had the highest rates of intimate partner violence (European Union Agency for Fundamental Rights, 2014). In the United States,[1] approximately 37 percent of women experience sexual violence, physical violence, and/or stalking victimization during their lifetime.[2] For approximately one-fourth of American women, this violence is severe (Smith et al., 2017). Many women experience violence at the hands of intimate partners. The National Institute of Justice (NIJ) defines intimate partner violence (IPV) as "physical, sexual, or psychological harm by a current or former intimate partner or spouse" (National Institute of Justice, 2018).[3] Examples of physical harm include shoving, kicking, and hitting the victim; examples of sexual harm include unwanted sexual contact and rape; and examples of psychological harm include threatening to harm, humiliating, and controlling the victim (National Institute of Justice, 2018).

Intimate partner violence not only impacts women, but children as well. Although global data on children's exposure to intimate partner violence are scarce, data from the United States indicates that 6.1 percent of children between the ages of 1 month and 17 years had witnessed a parent assaulting another parent in the past year, while approximately 17 percent had witnessed a parent–parent assault in their lifetime (Finkelhor, Turner, Shattuck, Hamby, and Kracke, 2015).[4] Since most surveys only ask about children's exposure to physical violence between parents, and not other forms of IPV such as psychological aggression, the percent of children exposed to domestic violence is even higher than those commonly reported. Young children are more likely than older children and adolescents to directly witness domestic violence (Carpenter and Stacks, 2009).

Contrary to popular misconceptions, young children are sensitive to IPV within their homes even if they may not fully understand what is going on (Carpenter and Stacks, 2009; Herman-Smith, 2013). This chapter adopts a children's rights framework to make the case that exposure to IPV represents a significant harm to children, particularly those between 0 and 8 years of age. Every member of the United Nations except the United States has ratified the UN Convention on the Rights of the Child (CRC). The CRC is a valuable document because it informs how practitioners and policymakers respond to children's issues globally. With respect to children's exposure to IPV, it is necessary to highlight Article 19 of the CRC, which mandates that all states should have laws and procedures in place to protect children under the age of 18 from abuse and neglect. Specifically, Article 19 states:

> States Parties shall take all appropriate legislative, administrative, social and educational measures to protect the child from all forms of physical or mental violence, injury or abuse, neglect or negligent treatment, maltreatment or exploitation, including sexual abuse, while in the care of parent(s), legal guardian(s) or any other person who has the care of the child.
>
> *(Child Rights International Network, 2018)*

Based on this definition, the issue that must be addressed when arguing that children's exposure to IPV is a children's rights violation is whether such exposure (both directly witnessing and indirectly experiencing) constitutes physical or mental violence, abuse, or neglect. If exposure to domestic violence in the home does constitute a children's rights violation, then the second question that must be addressed is: How should states handle such instances and protect children from further harm?

This chapter addresses these questions. The first section of the chapter briefly discusses the short-term and long-term impact of exposure to domestic violence on young children. The second section builds upon the first section by reviewing the qualitative literature on young children's perceptions of and lived experiences related to domestic violence, and argues that including children's voices is critical to developing a fuller understanding of how exposure to IPV impacts their lives. Based on the reviews presented in the first two sections, the third section of the chapter answers the question: Does exposure to IPIV constitute a form of neglect or abuse? The chapter concludes with practice and policy recommendations that take the "child's best interest" into account while also making sure both children and mothers have a voice in the process.

Effects of IPV on young children's development

Children growing up in homes characterized by IPV suffer both short-term and long-term neurological/physiological, cognitive, and social/emotional effects (Artz et al., 2014; Carpenter and Stacks, 2009; Holt, Buckley, and Whelan, 2008; McTavish, Mac-Gregor, Wathen, and MacMillan, 2016). Young children in particular are at increased risk for experiencing detrimental effects (Carpenter and Stacks, 2009; Herman-Smith, 2013). In a review of the impact of intimate violence exposure on infants' development, Carpenter and Stacks (2009) found evidence to suggest that exposure to IPV could change the development of an infant's brain. Infants require exposure to sights, sounds, and care for normal brain development. Without these expected experiences, they are at risk for experiencing later delays in cognitive, verbal, and emotional development. Unexpected experiences such as neglect can also impact infants' brain development by altering how they respond to stress via the release or inhibition of certain hormones and neurotransmitters related to stress and emotional regulation. Carpenter and Stacks (2009) concluded that exposure to IPV among infants negatively impacts stress response systems, emotional regulation processes, and abilities to develop secure attachments with caregivers.

Exposure to domestic violence during the toddler and preschool years also appears to be associated with impaired cognitive and behavioral functioning (Graham-Bermann, Howell, Miller, Kwek, and Lilly, 2010; Ybarra, Wilkens, and Lieberman, 2007). In one study of preschool children, Ybarra et al. (2007) compared 31 children who had been exposed to IPV with 31 children who had not been exposed to IPV. All children were between the ages of 3 and 5. Results indicated that children exposed to IVP exhibited lower verbal functioning and increased internalizing symptoms relative to their matched counterparts. Although Ybarra et al. (2007) did not find a relationship between IPV exposure and externalizing behaviors, other research on preschool children has found support for such a relationship. Based on their analysis of data from the U.S. National Survey of Child and Adolescent Wellbeing, Holmes, Voith, and Gromoske (2015) found that exposure to IPV at time 1 when the child participants were between the ages of 3 and 4 was associated with increased externalizing problems at time 2 when the children were between the ages of 5 and 7.

Exposure to IPV exerts an indirect effect on young children's health and well-being via its influence on mothers' mental health and parenting (Holmes, 2013; Huang, Wang, and Warrener, 2010). Using the first four waves of the Fragile Families and Child Wellbeing study, Huang et al. (2010) found that domestic violence at year 1 influenced mothers' depression at year 3, which in turn impacted preschool children's internalizing behaviors at year 5. Domestic violence at year 1 also exerted a direct effect on mothers' negative parenting behaviors and spanking, which in turn were related to preschool children's internalizing and externalizing behaviors at year 5. Similarly, an analysis of National Survey of Child and Adolescent Wellbeing survey data from the United States revealed that IPV was indirectly associated with young children's (ages 3–8) aggressive behavior via decreased maternal warmth and increased child emotional abuse (Holmes, 2013). Letourneau, Fedick, and Willms (2007) also examined the impact of domestic violence on mothers' parenting of young children (who were between the ages of 24 and 47 months). Analysis revealed that, at baseline, mothers exposed to domestic violence demonstrated lower levels of three types of parenting behaviors: parental discipline, warmth and nurturance, and consistency in parenting. They further found that mothers' levels of warm and nurturing behaviors decreased over time while parental discipline and consistent parenting behaviors increased over time, but these changes occurred for both groups of mothers.[5] Taken together, these studies indicate that intimate partner violence exerts an indirect influence on young children's social-emotional functioning via maternal mental health and parenting behaviors.

Not surprisingly, child abuse and intimate partner violence often co-occur in the same families (Hamby, Finkelhor, Turner, and Ormrod, 2010; Herrenkohl, Sousa, Tajima, Herrenkohl, and Moylan, 2008; Kohl, Edleson, English, and Barth, 2005). Hamby et al. (2010) examined the relationship between witnessing partner violence and child maltreatment among a nationally representative sample of children (ages 0–17) in the United

States who completed (or had their parent complete) the National Survey of Children's Exposure to Violence (NatSCEV). They found that more than a third of the youth who had witnessed partner violence in the past year had also experienced some type of maltreatment. Approximately 57 per cent of youth who had witnessed partner violence at some point in their lifetime had also been mistreated. The past year rate for physical abuse for children who had witnessed partner violence was 17.6 per cent and the lifetime rate was about one-third. More than 60 per cent of child neglect victims and 70 per cent of child victims of sexual abuse had also witnessed partner violence.

Together, the aforementioned studies indicate that exposure to IPV harms children, and this is especially true for younger children who are more likely than older children to directly witness such violence (Carpenter and Stacks, 2009). While these studies are informative, they fail to consider children's voices and lived experiences growing up in households characterized by domestic violence. The next section presents children's experiences as shared by children themselves (or their mothers for infants and toddlers).

How young children experience intimate partner violence

This section focuses on qualitative studies published between 2000 and 2018, and draws upon two published literature reviews related to children's experiences growing up in homes characterized by domestic violence (see Table 18.1; for reviews, see Gorin, 2004; Hines, 2015). Due to the limited research in this area, most of the cited studies were conducted in the US, the UK, and in Nordic countries (for more information on where the studies were conducted, see Table 18.1). Nevertheless, as indicated in the beginning of this chapter, rates of intimate partner violence are high even among countries with higher levels of gender equity (Gracia and Merlo, 2016). Still, it should be emphasized that the children's experiences presented in the reviewed studies are not representative of all children or even children within the countries where the research was conducted, primarily because most of the studies reviewed in this section relied on small samples of children and their mothers.

Given the dearth of research on young children's experiences, narratives that reflect early childhood experiences across three main areas are highlighted: (1) how children experience IPV in early childhood; (2) how they cope with IPV; and (3) what they want from adults whose job it is to protect them. Given that so few studies have focused exclusively on young children's lived experiences, most of the narratives presented in this section are based on older children's and adolescents' retrospective accounts as well as mothers' accounts. Although limitations exist with retrospective accounts as well as "child-friendly" methods for obtaining information from very young children (Punch, 2002), the presented narratives are generally consistent with the quantitative research: children between the ages of 0 and 8 are sensitive to domestic violence in their homes and suffer as a result (Carpenter and Stacks, 2009; Herman-Smith, 2013).

Young children are aware of domestic violence

As indicated by the quantitative studies presented in the previous section, young children, even infants, are sensitive to domestic violence in their homes (Carpenter and Stacks, 2009; Herman-Smith, 2013). Maternal reports corroborate this link between exposure to domestic violence and young children's distress, as indicated by the following quote from a mother:

Table 18.1 Qualitative studies of children's exposure to domestic violence

Authors	Study aims	Data collection/sample size	Themes
Buckley, Holt, and Whelan (2007)	Examine the impact of DV on children and identify their needs	Focus groups, 22 children, ages 8–17 in Ireland	• Anxiety, fear, and dread • Loss of confidence and self-esteem • Stigma and being different • Relationships with parents and peers • Educational experiences • Sense of lost childhood • What children and young people want from services

Callaghan, Alexander, Sixsmith, and Fellin (2018)	Explores how children experience domestic violence and abuse, specifically focusing on their experiences of coercive control in the family, its impact, and their capacity for agentic and resistant action in these situations.	Semi-structured interviews, 20 children (12 girls, 9 boys) ages 8–18 in the UK.	• Children's awareness of abusive control—children know what's going on (cognitive understanding)
			• Constraint—children's experiences with abusive control (behavioral strategies)
			  • Seeking safe spaces in home
			  • Try to avoid being noticed by abuser
			• Children as agents
			  • Diverting and de-escalating tension
			  • Disclosure and help-seeking
			  • Resisting father's controlling actions/supporting mothers

De Board-Lucas and Grych (2011)	Explored how children thought and felt about domestic violence encounters that children described	Semi-structured interviews with 34 children ages 7–12, U.S. sample	CognitionsFelt threatened/worried about parent's well-being Worried about uncertain outcomesBlamed one or both parentsThought about interveningBehavioral responsesWithdrewObservedAttempted to directly interveneSought support/companionshipAttempted to indirectly intervene (e.g., calling 911)Withdrew to observeEmoted

Study	Purpose/Research Question	Sample/Method	Findings/Themes
Humphreys (2001)	Examined the lived experiences of growing up in homes characterized by domestic violence	Life history interviews with 10 resilient adult women between the ages of 20 and 40 in the United States about their experiencing growing up in households characterized by domestic violence	Initially thought families were normalLater thought families were not normalSecrecy—keeping abuse a secretFeeling confused, fearful, being on guard
Joseph, Govender, and Bhagwanjee (2006)	Understand the lived experiences of children growing up with domestic violence	Interviews with five children between the ages of 8 and 12 in South Africa	Behavioral responsesCrying, expressing fear (girls, ages 8 and 10)Wanting to hit abuser (boys)Cognitive responsesEscapist/wishful thinkingReframing the abuseDenialMinimizing abuseRationalizing abuseBlaming the victimAffective responsesDepression/anxietyHelplessness/powerlessnessAnger/disapproval of abuserAmbivalence toward the abuser
Lopez (2017)	Explored the early childhood experiences system—involved adolescent girls who grew up in homes characterized by domestic violence and parental substance abuse	65 girls in juvenile justice system	Taking care of mom and younger siblingsServing as mom's relationship advisorProtecting mom from violencePerforming "normality" in front of social service providers
McGee (2000)	How can we best support children when there is domestic violence? What do children and mothers themselves have to say about support services they have wanted or received? Whom do children and mothers most often approach for help?	Interviews with 54 children between the ages of 5 and 17 and 48 mothers in England and Wales	Effects of domestic violence (fear, sadness, anger, effect on identity, effects on relationship with mother/extended family/friendships)Children's awareness and memories of violenceChildren's awareness of the atmosphere in the homeChildren's coping strategies (safety, long-term, psychological)Children's powerlessnessChildren's perception of social services

(Continued)

Table 18.1 (Cont.)

Authors	Study aims	Data collection/sample size	Themes
Mullender et al. (2002)	How do children make sense of the experience of living with domestic violence? What coping strategies do they use? What help do they consider would meet their needs and build on their coping strategies? What help do they currently get? How do children and young people consider it could be improved?	Interviews and focus groups with 54 children between the ages of 8 and 16 who lived in homes where their mothers were abused. Study took place in England.	Children are aware of abuseMaking sense of the abuseDecision to interveneSeeking and getting support from othersWhat children need (safety, someone to talk to)Leaving and lossTaking a tollWhat children wantListening to what children have to sayInvolving children in making decisionsCoping—immediate strategiesReframing domestic violence incidentsSafety and help-seeking strategiesProtecting mothers/intervening in violent situations
Överlien and Hydén (2009)	Explored how children experienced domestic violence	Methodology included observing group therapy sessions with 15 children, ages 12 to 15, and conducting ten qualitative interviews with children to determine how they responded to violence during and after actual domestic violence incidents between their caregivers. Study took place in Sweden.	Actions during an event: turning on music, reading a book, and closing one's earsRescuing the mother, playing along with dad, and calling the police
Swanston, Bowyer, and Vetere (2014)	Examined children's experiences growing up with domestic violence	Semi-structured interviews with five children, ages 8–13, in the UK	Domestic violence through the eyes of childrenChildren are awarePervasive sense of threat and fearTrying to predict the unpredictableLoss of a normal childhoodLearning from children's experiencesDiminished trust in adultsChildren learned to rely on themselvesServices and support
Thornton (2014)			

Eight children between the ages of 5 and 9. The researchers gleaned young children's views via projective play and drawing assessments, which were then compared to themes that emerged from interviews with their mothers. Study took place in the UK. Each child selected eight stories from the Story Stem Assessment Profile (SSAP). These story stems were then used to provide structured play prompts for each child. Each child also completed two drawing assessments: the Kinetic Family Drawing and the Human Figure Drawing.	Qualities of domestic violenceCauses painPowerfulBeyond controlImpact on children's feelingsUnhappiness, anger, anxiety, confusionImpact on family dynamicsCare available for childrenCommunication and collaborationDivided loyaltyRoutine and predictabilityContainment and securityChildren's coping responsesKeeping adults safeAcceptance and safe relianceTaking responsibilityChildren's capacity to process emotions

There was always an atmosphere, you know, you could cut it with a knife some-times. Even as babies they can sense, sense it. 'Cause I always thought it was colic to be honest and I'm giving them Infacol and took 'em to the doctor's and the doctor's saying "No there's nothing wrong with them." And I thought, "Well why the hell do they scream, you know? And they used to scream like they were in pain."

(Gorin, 2004, p. 11)

Research with mothers of young children also indicates that children are aware of domestic violence, even when mothers try to shield them from directly witnessing the violence, as indicated by the following quote:

You always try and kid yourself that you think yeah I'm protecting them and then, you know, that they don't really hear the arguments cos I'd go out the room or whatever. And you forget your children are like miniature radar devices, you know. Like to earwig absolutely everything to then draw their own conclusion.

(Swanston et al., 2014, p. 192)

In another instance, a mother told a story about how her partner had given her a black eye and how she lied to her young son about what happened. Looking back, this mother surmised that her son, though only 5 at the time, had understood what had really happened:

They knew because they used to walk along to the school and I used to put my head down and Padraig used to go "Mum where did you get your black eye from?" and I used to [say] "Oh I was rubbing it too much, I had something in my eye," and he used to go "Oh all right." Just the look on his face! He wouldn't say anything else, but he'd be ashamed for me, I could see so on his little face … And I used to walk off and think to myself, he's 5 years old and he knows.

(McGee, 2000, p. 96)

Although maternal accounts provide important insight into children's functioning, it should be noted that such accounts could be subject to recall, social desirability, and other interpretation biases. Thus, whenever possible, researchers should rely on multiple meas-ures and accounts to better understand how young children experience intimate partner violence.

Anxiety, fear, dread

Not surprisingly, the awareness of being exposed to domestic violence can be stressful for young children. Retrospective accounts of older children, adolescents, and adults indicate that they most often felt *anxiety, fear, and dread* during domestic violence encounters experi-enced as young children (Buckley et al., 2007; Callaghan et al., 2018; De Board-Lucas and Grych, 2011; Humphreys, 2001; Joseph et al., 2006; Mullender et al., 2002; Swanston et al., 2014; Thornton, 2014). Recognizing the importance of obtaining information directly from young children, Thornton (2014) used task-based methods to gain insight into how children experience domestic violence. She tasked each of the eight children (ages 5–9) in her study with selecting eight stories from the Story Stem Assessment Profile (SSAP). These story stems were then used to provide structured play prompts for each child. Each child also completed two drawing assessments: the kinetic family drawing and the human figure drawing. Based on these assessments, Thornton (2014) concluded that young children often view domestic violence as powerful, causing pain, and beyond their control. She further noted that children exposed to domestic violence often feel unhappy, anxious, angry, and confused —a finding that is consistent with the retrospective accounts of older children, adolescents, and adults who grew up with domestic violence (Buckley et al., 2007; McGee, 2000; Mullender et al., 2002; Överlien and Hydén, 2009; Swanston et al., 2014). What makes Thorton's study notable is her reliance on task-based methods to directly assess young children's experiences with domestic violence rather than relying on maternal reports or retrospective accounts. Still, more research is needed to determine the validity of such assessment methods with young children (Punch, 2002).

Seeking security and safety

Not surprisingly, children develop behavioral strategies for dealing with domestic violence. These involve *seeking security and safety*. Of course, these strategies are constrained by children's age. While older children can physically withdraw by leaving the house, younger children's options are more limited. Yet even young children have reported hiding as a strategy. One child in Buckley et al.'s (2007) study of children growing up with domestic violence said, "I used to hide under my bed all week. I used to make a little place out of it with all my teddies" (p. 300).

Young children growing up in homes characterized by domestic violence also learn to distinguish between "risky" and "safe" places in their homes (Callaghan et al., 2018). Generally, they describe shared family spaces as risky, as indicated by the following quote from a young girl:

> I went straight upstairs to my bedroom, I'd sort of like sneak downstairs and check that no one was arguing or anything and if it was all OK, I'd come downstairs and sit down and watch TV with my brother but if there was an argument I'd run downstairs, grab my brother and take him upstairs.
>
> *(Callaghan et al., 2018, p. 1565)*

Directly intervening

Half of the 45 children interviewed by Mullender et al. (2002) said they had intervened on behalf of a mother who was being physically assaulted by a male partner. Although older children were more likely to directly intervene, there were also instances of younger children intervening. The most common strategy reported was yelling at the abuser to stop. In the narrative below, a 13-year-old girl describes how as a younger child, she would plead with her father to not be bothered by her mother:

> No that was the thing. I was so little and had so many feelings sometimes I could say to daddy that please dad please be quiet (in a pleading voice) don't be bothered by what mummy says. I played along with him for a while and played along with him and thought this will help and pretended that mummy was the one who was sick, so I said that if you could only be quiet don't be

bothered by what she is saying you know she is wrong (pause) so be quiet and
go outside and be angry.

(Överlien and Hydén, 2009, p. 486)

Although not as common, young children sometimes directly intervened by using their
bodies to block fathers from attacking their mothers (McGee, 2000). One 6-year-old boy
from McGee's (2000) study shared what happened when he tried to intervene on behalf of
his mother: "I tried to stop him and he pushed me away" (p. 101). Similarly, a teen girl
described how as a young child, she tried to help her mom:

> Yeah, one time ... oh, my God. We went to my mom's friend's house and we
> got home by 9:13. And my mom went in the room, and I heard her crying, and
> I opened the door. And it was locked, but that was not gonna stop me. And
> I opened it, and he had her like a little kid bent over his knees, like spanking her.
> I'm like, "No!" That's not cool you know. I jumped on top of her, I'm like, I'm
> a little girl still, but I jumped on my mom to protect her.

(Lopez, 2017, p. 55)

Although rare, even toddlers sometimes try to intervene on behalf of their mothers, as
indicated by this quote from one of the mothers interviewed by Mullender et al. (2002):

> She was always the one that told him off and shouted at him, even from two-
> years-old, she'd go and say "Don't." I'd always give excuses and she'd see
> through them. Sometimes it got me into trouble, but she didn't realize it—
> because she was saying things that an adult would say and he'd presume I'd put
> the words in her mouth ... Even at three or four, she could tell him that. He'd
> say, "You are putting words in their mouths again," but children are innocent
> and they are honest.

(p. 99)

Thornton (2014) found that young children's stories and drawings reflected the need to
keep adults close, becoming self-reliant, taking responsibility for the violence and their
mothers. For example, Mandy (age 8) indicated "a strong desire to keep her mother close to
her by ending the majority of her stories with the mother and daughter characters spending
time alone together and all of the other story characters disappearing" (p. 97). An 8-year-old
child from the Mullender et al. (2002) study also described how he wished he could help his
mother:

> I'm doing everything I can to help her get more courageous. We could change it
> around to take out all the terrible memories for her. We've got all our friends
> there to help. We could get a guard dog. That's what I'd like to do—help her be
> stronger ... I want to make an effort to help her.

(p. 117)

Younger children sometimes try to help their mothers by seeking help from adults, as indicated by this narrative from a 14-year-old girl talking about calling the police on her father
when she was younger: "Yeah, I went to the neighbors and asked them to ring the police
and, yeah, I was only about 7 so" (Callaghan et al., 2018, p. 1567). This strategy is less
common among younger children due to their limited mobility. Furthermore, even when
this strategy is used, it is rarely effective (Mullender et al., 2002).

What children want from helping professionals

Very few studies have explicitly asked children what they think about social services designed to help them, or, even more rarely, what types of support and services they would like. Of those studies that have asked children these questions, the focus has been on older children. These studies generally reveal that some children do not want to talk to anyone about their problems for several reasons, including being afraid of the abuser, being afraid of the consequences to their parents if they tell, and being afraid they will be removed from their parents' care if domestic violence is disclosed (Gorin, 2007). Unfortunately, when children do talk with adults, they often feel as if they are not being listened to, nor do they have any input into decisions that impact them (Gorin, 2007; McGee, 2000). What children want, according to Mullender et al. (2002), is to be safe and secure, followed by having someone to talk to that they can trust. They also want to be involved in decision-making processes that impact their families (Gorin, 2007; McGee, 2000). Although most of the limited research on what children want from helping professionals focuses on older children and teens, developmentally appropriate techniques can be used to gauge younger children's wants and needs as well (Thornton, 2014). Task-oriented methods, for example, can be useful in establishing rapport with younger children and gaining insight into their experiences; however, more traditional assessment methods (i.e., interviewing, observations) should be used to complement such approaches (Punch, 2002).

Does exposure to IPIV constitute a form of neglect or abuse?

The first part of this chapter discussed Article 19 of the CRC, which stipulates that States Parties should "protect the child from all forms of physical or mental violence, injury or abuse, neglect or negligent treatment, maltreatment or exploitation." The question posed was: Does exposure to IPV constitute a form of neglect or abuse? A brief review of the research indicates that such exposure is a form of neglect or abuse because it directly and indirectly (via its impact on the quality of the mother–child relationship) harms children, especially younger children (Holmes, 2013; Huang et al., 2010). Further, as the children's narratives so vividly demonstrated in the second part of the chapter, children are aware of violence in the homes even when mothers attempt to shield them from its pervasive effects (see Table 18.1 ; for reviews, see Gorin, 2004; Hines, 2015).

As illustrated throughout this chapter, children are not just bystanders to domestic violence. They experience it on many levels, and these experiences negatively impact many areas of their lives (Överlien and Hydén, 2009). In accordance with Article 19 of the CRC, States Parties must protect children from such harm (Child Rights International Network, 2018). Yet the ways in which this goal should be accomplished are not clear-cut. Some scholars argue that exposure to IPV is a form of child maltreatment and that victimized mothers should be held legally uncountable for not protecting their children under child abuse and failure to protect statutes. Kintner (2005), for example, in her article "The Other Victims: Can We Hold Parents Liable for Failing to Protect their Children from Harms of Domestic Violence?" argues that victims of domestic violence can report their abuse, seek out restraining orders against their partners, and/or physically remove children from the home. She further argues that holding victims of domestic violence liable for exposing their children to domestic violence:

sends a message to society-at-large, including domestic violence perpetrators, that exposing a child to domestic violence is not acceptable parental conduct. It underscores that the battering victim is not the only person harmed by domestic violence, and that even in the absence of physical scars, children's psychological well-being may be seriously compromised.

(p. 288)

Such views are based on a conception of children, irrespective of age, as incompetent, dependent on adults, and in need of special safeguards and protections (Hanson, 2012). Children's perspectives or desires are not taken into account. Even more disturbing, such views present parents—especially mothers, who are most often the victims of IPV—as "bad" parents who should be held legally accountable for failing to protect their children from the harms caused by domestic violence exposure. According to this view, the state has a responsibility to ensure that children exposed to domestic violence in their homes are safe and secure, even if it means punishing mothers and taking their children away from them.

Such stances fail to take the full complexity of the mother–child relationship into account within the context of domestic violence. Many children growing up in households characterized by intimate partner violence are deeply attached to their mothers and want to live with them, as long as they feel safe and secure in their homes (Mullender et al., 2002). As this chapter has demonstrated, mothers who are victims of domestic violence are often stressed with few support systems. They also experience many other barriers related to seeking help, such as failure to recognize events as IPV, self-doubt and low self-esteem, fear of losing their children, and fear of their perpetrator (Nixon, Tutty, Weaver-Dunlop, and Walsh, 2007; Petersen, Morocco, Goldstein, and Clark, 2005). Despite these challenges, many mothers do attempt to shield their children from exposure to domestic violence (Mullender et al., 2002).

Children are also hesitant to disclose domestic violence out of fear of repercussions. Like their mothers, children do not want their families split apart. Generally, they do not want to be removed from their mothers' care, nor do they want to be forced to leave their homes, schools, and communities (Mullender et al., 2002). Thus, while the answer to the question "Does exposure to IPIV constitute a form of neglect or abuse?" is an unequivocal "yes," blame should not be placed on already victimized mothers, nor should children be taken away from their mothers unless their safety and security requires such a drastic measure. The issue then becomes: How can States Parties best support mothers and children? The answer to this question is not simple.

Practice and policy recommendations

As indicated at the beginning of this chapter, violence against women is a worldwide phenomenon that knows no borders. In fact, gendered violence continues to be a problem even in countries and regions with relatively high levels of gender equality, such as the countries where most of the research presented in this review was carried out (Gracia and Merlo, 2016). Thus, evidence-based multilevel interventions are necessary to address both the macro and micro causes and correlates of domestic violence.

At the macro level, various agencies charged with supporting families impacted by intimate partner violence should develop plans to foster collaboration. In the United States, the U.S. Office of Juvenile Justice and Delinquency Prevention (OJJDP) funded 11 Stay Safe community demonstration programs that focused on influencing change at the macro or systems level to reduce the impact of exposure to domestic violence on young children (Kaufman, Ortega, Schewe, Kracke, and Safe Start Demonstration Project Communities, 2011; Safe Start Center, 2013). One such program, located in Chicago, Illinois, convened an implementation advisory board (IAB) consisting of stakeholders from the community, city and state agencies, and community organizations that served children 6 and younger and their families (Staggs, Schewe, White, Davis, and Dill, 2007). The IAB created eight work teams (e.g., Direct Service Implementation Team, the Training Collaborative, Evaluation and Data Collection Implementation Team) to enhance various agencies and systems' capacity to respond to the needs of young children (age 0–6) who had been exposed to violence. More information on other promising system-level interventions that were funded under the OJJDP Stay Safe initiative can be found in their 2013 report, "Safe Start: Promising Approaches Communities: Improving Outcomes for Children Exposed to Violence" (Safe Start Center, 2013).

While the Stay Safe programs implemented in the United States focus on interagency and cross-systems collaborations, other research has highlighted the types of strategies that individual agencies can implement to better address the various needs of mothers and children impacted by intimate partner violence. Chibber and Krishnan (2011), for example, argue that reproductive health clinics are an ideal venue for reaching victims of intimate partner violence, because the rate of women accessing services at such clinics has been increasing globally, "whereas their use of other institutional services (e.g., police, social services) in response to intimate partner violence continues to be limited" (p. 452). Chibber and Krishnan (2011) recommend several actions that reproductive health clinics can take to implement such changes, including:

> (1) creating a supportive environment within the clinic for clients to discuss IPV, (2) displaying informational materials in the clinics, (3) focused training for all health care providers with mechanisms for continuous feedback and evaluation of their new skills, (4) on-site referral services, (5) strong linkage between the health and community agencies, (6) commissioning an independent task force within the organization to develop and promote an integrated IPV response, and (7) ensuring interdepartmental collaboration.
>
> *(p. 453)*

Such comprehensive approaches have been found to be effective both in the United States and globally (see Chibber and Krishnan, 2011).

At the micro level, social service professionals working with families impacted by intimate partner violence should make sure that both mothers and children are safe and secure (Mullender et al., 2002). Ideally, this means developing a safety plan for mothers and children that involves both legal and social support buttresses against the abuser. Children, even younger ones, can be involved in the development of such a plan. Indeed, children want to help, as indicated by their narratives related to directly and indirectly intervening on behalf of their mothers and siblings. Mullender et al. (2002) suggest that practitioners build upon children's desires to help by incorporating them into the decision-making process. Involving children in such a way:

> encourages them to follow a plan designed to keep themselves and younger siblings safe, and to summon help where possible. It is not a "do nothing" approach but it could be framed in a less negative way, building not just on children's knowledge

of their own situation but also on their desire to help, rather than just presented as adults knowing best, abstracted from the real contexts in which children have to construct their own survival strategies.

(Mullender et al., 2002, p. 216)

Children and mothers should also be provided with the opportunity to participate in evidence-based programs targeting families affected by domestic violence. Such programs should focus on supporting mothers and strengthening the mother–child relationship by focusing on positive parenting behaviors and healthy child development. Unfortunately, as indicated by a 2016 meta-analysis of programs targeting children affected by domestic violence, relatively few programs focus on younger children (see Howarth et al., 2016). Nevertheless, some promising programs do exist. One example is the child–parent psychotherapy (CPP) program, which targets preschoolers and their mothers who have been impacted by domestic violence (Lieberman, Ippen, and Van Horn, 2006). The goal of this program is to strengthen the mother–child relationship by focusing on "safety, affect regulation, the joint construction of a trauma narrative, and engagement in developmentally appropriate goals and activities" (Lieberman et al., 2006, p. 914). Results of a randomized control trial indicate that participation in CPP resulted in improved maternal stress symptoms and children's behaviors at six months post-treatment relative to mothers and children in the control group. The strengths of programs such as CPP is that they focus on promoting healthy attachments between mothers and young children by enhancing mothers' ability to care and nurture their children.

Children should also have a safe place to discuss their experiences with trusted adults (Mullender et al., 2002). Unfortunately, as indicated in this chapter, children rarely feel listened to and understood by adults (Gorin, 2004; Mullender et al., 2002). Thus, state organizations charged with supporting children impacted by domestic violence should invest in training their staff on how to develop rapport and trust with children, and this is especially true for those working with young children. In such instances, as indicated by Thornton (2014), task-oriented strategies such as projective play, storytelling, and drawing can potentially help younger children feel listened to and safe. Adults working with children should, whenever possible, seek children's feedback about decisions directly impacting their well-being.

Finally, policies should be developed and strengthened that focus on the well-being of children and mothers as opposed to punitive policies that further stigmatize mothers. The overall goal should be to support mothers so that they can better support their children. In doing so, States Parties will go a long way toward ensuring that children are safe and protected from the harms of growing up in homes characterized by domestic violence.

Notes

1 The National Intimate Partner and Sexual Violence Survey is an ongoing national telephone-based survey of intimate partner violence administered to women and men in the United States.

2 One in 15 women reported experiencing one of these types of violence by an intimate partner in the 12 months prior to taking the survey.

3 In this chapter, the terms 'intimate partner violence' and 'domestic violence' are used interchangeably.

4 For children under 10, the survey was conducted with the caregiver who was most familiar with the child's experiences and routines.

5 Yet mothers of children exposed to domestic violence demonstrated a greater increase in positive discipline and less of a decrease in warm and nurturing behaviors than mothers of children who were not

exposed to intimate partner violence, leading the researchers to suggest that mothers of children exposed to domestic violence may compensate for this exposure by attempting to be more nurturing and attentive to children.

References

Artz, Sibylle, Margaret A. Jackson, Katherine R. Rossiter, Alicia Nijdam-Jones, István Géczy, and Sheila Porteous. 2014. "A comprehensive review of the literature on the impact of exposure to intimate partner violence on children and youth." *International Journal of Child, Youth and Family Studies*, 5: 493–587.

Buckley, Helen, Stephanie Holt, and Sadhbh Whelan 2007. "Listen to me! Children's experiences of domestic violence." *Child Abuse Review*, 16: 296–310.

Callaghan, Jane E., Joanne H. Alexander, Judith Sixsmith, and Lisa Chiara Fellin. 2018. "Beyond "witnessing": Children's experiences of coercive control in domestic violence and abuse." *Journal of Interpersonal Violence*, 33(10): 1551–1581.

Carpenter, Georgia L., and Ann M. Stacks. 2009. "Developmental effects of exposure to intimate partner violence in early childhood: A review of the literature." *Children and Youth Services Review*, 31(8): 831–839.

Chibber, Karuna S., and Suneeta Krishnan. 2011. "Confronting intimate partner violence: A global health priority." *Mount Sinai Journal of Medicine: A Journal of Translational and Personalized Medicine*, 78: 449–457.

Child Rights International Network. 2018. "Article 19: Protection from abuse and neglect." www.crin.org/en/home/rights/convention/articles/article-19-protection-abuse-and-neglect

De Board-Lucas, Renee L., and John H. Grych. 2011. "Children's perceptions of intimate partner violence: Causes, consequences, and coping." *Journal of Family Violence*, 26(5): 343.

European Union Agency for Fundamental Rights. 2014. *Violence against women: An EU-wide survey.* Luxembourg: Publications Office of the European Union. http://fra.europa.eu/en/publication/2014/vaw-survey-main-results

Finkelhor, David, Heather Turner, Ann Shattuck, Sherry Hamby, and Kirsten Kracke. 2015. *National survey of children's exposure to violence: Children's exposure to violence, crime, and abuse: An update.* Washington, DC: US Department of Justice, Office of Juvenile Justice and Delinquency Prevention. www.ojjdp.gov/pubs/248547.pdf

Gorin, Sarah. 2004. *Understanding what children say: Children's experiences of domestic violence, parental substance misuse and parental health problems.* London: National Children's Bureau.

Gracia, Enrique, and Juan Merlo. 2016. "Intimate partner violence against women and the Nordic paradox." *Social Science and Medicine*, 157: 27–30.

Graham-Bermann, Sandra A., Kathryn H. Howell, Laura E. Miller, Jean Kwek, and Michelle M. Lilly. 2010. "Traumatic events and maternal education as predictors of verbal ability for preschool children exposed to intimate partner violence (IPV)." *Journal of Family Violence*, 25(4): 383–392.

Hamby, Sherry, David Finkelhor, Heather Turner, and Richard Ormrod. 2010. "The overlap of witnessing partner violence with child maltreatment and other victimizations in a nationally representative survey of youth." *Child Abuse and Neglect*, 34(10): 734–741.

Hanson, Karl. 2012. "Schools of thought in children's rights." In *Children's rights from below*, edited by Manfred Liebel, 63–79. London: Palgrave Macmillan.

Herman-Smith, Robert. 2013. "Intimate partner violence exposure in early childhood: An ecobiodevelopmental perspective." *Health and Social Work*, 38(4): 231–239.

Herrenkohl, Todd I., Cynthia Sousa, Emiko A. Tajima, Roy C. Herrenkohl, and Carrie A. Moylan. 2008. "Intersection of child abuse and children's exposure to domestic violence." *Trauma, Violence, and Abuse*, 9(2): 84–99.

Hines, Lisa 2015. "Children's coping with family violence: Policy and service recommendations." *Child and Adolescent Social Work Journal*, 32: 109–119.

Holmes, Megan R. 2013. "Aggressive behaviour of children exposed to intimate partner violence: An examination of maternal mental health, maternal warmth and child maltreatment." *Child Abuse and Neglect*, 37(8): 520–530.

Holmes, Megan R., Laura A. Voith, and Andrea N. Gromoske. 2015. "Lasting effect of intimate partner violence exposure during preschool on aggressive behaviour and prosocial skills." *Journal of Interpersonal Violence*, 30(10): 1651–1670.

Holt, Stephanie, Helen Buckley, and Sadhbh Whelan. 2008. "The impact of exposure to domestic violence on children and young people: A review of the literature." *Child Abuse and Neglect*, 32(8): 797–810.

Howarth, Emma, Theresa H. Moore, Nicky J. Welton, Natalia Lewis, Nicky Stanley, Harriet MacMillan, and Gene Feder. 2016. "Improving outcomes for children exposed to domestic violence (IMPROVE): An evidence synthesis." *Public Health Research*, 4(10): 1–342.

Huang, Chien-Chung, Lih-Rong Wang, and Corinne Warrener. 2010. "Effects of domestic violence on behaviour problems of preschool-aged children: Do maternal mental health and parenting mediate the effects?" *Children and Youth Services Review*, 32(10): 1317–1323.

Humphreys, Janice C. 2001. "Growing up in a violent home: The lived experience of daughters of battered women." *Journal of Family Nursing*, 7(3): 244–260.

Joseph, Safia, Kay Govender, and Anil Bhagwanjee. 2006. "'I can't see him hit her again, I just want to run away … hide and block my ears': A phenomenological analysis of a sample of children's coping responses to exposure to domestic violence." *Journal of Emotional Abuse*, 6(4): 23–45.

Kantor, Glenda Kaufman, and Liza Little. 2003. "Defining the boundaries of child neglect: When does domestic violence equate with parental failure to protect?" *Journal of Interpersonal Violence*, 18(4): 338–355.

Kaufman, Joy S., Sandra Ortega, Paul A. Schewe, Kristen Kracke, and Safe Start Demonstration Project Communities. 2011. "Characteristics of young children exposed to violence: The safe start demonstration project." *Journal of Interpersonal Violence*, 26(10): 2042–2072.

Kintner, Brooke. 2005. "The other victims: Can we hold parents liable for failing to protect their children from harms of domestic violence." *New England Journal on Criminal and Civil Confinement*, 31: 271.

Kohl, Patricia L., Jeffrey L. Edleson, Diana J. English, and Richard P. Barth. 2005. "Domestic violence and pathways into child welfare services: Findings from the national survey of child and adolescent well-being." *Children and Youth Services Review*, 27(11): 1167–1182.

Letourneau, Nicole L., Cara B. Fedick, and J. Douglas Willms. 2007. "Mothering and domestic violence: A longitudinal analysis." *Journal of Family Violence*, 22(8): 649–659.

Lieberman, A. F., C. G. Ippen, and P. Van Horn. 2006. "Child-parent psychotherapy: 6-month follow-up of a randomized controlled trial." *Journal of the American Academy of Child and Adolescent Psychiatry*, 45(8): 913–918.

Lopez, Vera. 2017. *Complicated lives: Girls, parents, drugs, and juvenile justice*. New Brunswick: Rutgers University Press.

McGee, Caroline. 2000. *Childhood experiences of domestic violence*. London: Jessica Kingsley Publishers.

McTavish, Jill R., Jen C. MacGregor, C. Nadine Wathen, and Harriet L. MacMillan. 2016. "Children's exposure to intimate partner violence: An overview." *International Review of Psychiatry*, 28(5): 504–518.

Mullender, Audrey, Gill Hague, Umme Imam, Liz Kelly, Ellen Malos, and Linda Regan. 2002. *Children's Perspectives on Domestic Violence*. London: Sage.

National Institute of Justice. 2018. "Intimate partner violence." www.nij.gov/topics/crime/intimate-partner-violence/Pages/welcome.aspx

Nixon, Kendra L., Leslie M. Tutty, Gillian Weaver-Dunlop, and Christina A. Walsh. 2007. "Do good intentions beget good policy? A review of child protection policies to address intimate partner violence." *Children and Youth Services Review*, 29(12): 1469–1486.

Överlien, Carolina, and Margareta Hydén. 2009. "Children's actions when experiencing domestic violence." *Childhood*, 16(4): 479–496.

Petersen, Ruth, Kathryn E. Moracco, Karen M. Goldstein, and Kathryn Andersen Clark. 2005. "Moving beyond disclosure: Women's perspectives on barriers and motivators to seeking assistance for intimate partner violence." *Women and Health*, 40: 63–76.

Punch, Sarah. 2002. "Research with children—The same or different from research with adults?" *Childhood*, 9: 321–341.

Safe Start Center. 2013. "Safe start: Promising approaches communities: Improving outcomes for children exposed to violence." www.ojjdp.gov/programs/safestart/ImprovingOutcomesforChildrenExposedtoViolence.pdf

Smith, Sharon G., Kathleen C. Basile, Leah K. Gilbert, Melissa T. Merrick, Nimesh Patel, Margie Walling, and Anurag Jain. 2017. "National Intimate Partner and Sexual Violence Survey (NISVS): 2010–2012 state report." www.cdc.gov/violenceprevention/pdf/NISVS-StateReportBook.pdf

Staggs, Susan L., Marlita L. White, Paul A. Schewe, Erica B. Davis, and Ebony M. Dill. 2007. "Changing systems by changing individuals: The incubation approach to systems change." *American Journal of Community Psychology*, 39(3–4): 365–379.

Swanston, Jennifer, Laura Bowyer, and Arlene Vetere. 2014. "Towards a richer understanding of school-age children's experiences of domestic violence: The voices of children and their mothers." *Clinical Child Psychology and Psychiatry*, 19(2): 184–201.

Thornton, Victoria. 2014. "Understanding the emotional impact of domestic violence on young children." *Educational and Child Psychology*, 31(1): 90–100.

World Health Organization (WHO). 2017. "Violence against women." www.who.int/news-room/fact-sheets/detail/violence-against-women

Ybarra, Gabriel J., Susan L. Wilkens, and Alicia F. Lieberman. 2007. "The influence of domestic violence on preschooler behaviour and functioning." *Journal of Family Violence*, 22(1): 33–42.

PART 3

Young children's rights to provision

19

INTRODUCTION

Young children's provision rights

Kylie Smith

Introduction

Provision rights have been part of the children's rights agenda from 1924 when the League of Nations adopted the Geneva Declaration. The Geneva Declaration (1924) recognised adults' responsibility to enact the right of children to be fed, nursed and sheltered. The Declaration of the Rights of the Child (1959) expanded the mandate of provisional rights to account for the child's right to education, nutrition, housing, medical services and recreational activities. This chapter foregrounds the book's section on provision rights under the current United Nations Convention on the Rights of the Child (1989) to bring a critical gaze on the current state of how signatories are enacting children's right to education, housing, healthcare, food and nutrition, places to explore and play, and environments that respect diverse cultural beliefs, rituals and practices. As interest and research has grown over the past 20 years in children's participatory rights and engagement in research and civic life, provision rights have been less popularised. As the distribution of wealth continues to narrow and countries across the Global North and South are having to deal with economic crises due to war, natural and man-made disasters, political corruption, and unemployment, provision rights need greater attention. Layered alongside this is the political shift of many countries (e.g. the UK, Australia, New Zealand and the USA) from a social welfare model, where services and provisions are provided by the state, to a neoliberal policy agenda, where service provision is privatised, deregulated and market driven (Braedley and Luxton, 2010; Moss, 2014; Smith, Tesar and Myers, 2016). As a result, children's rights to provisions such as education, housing, food, clean water and places for play have been eroded, with greater demand on individual families to provide these provisions.

Budgets and finance

Provision rights have direct financial implications for signatories of the Convention as budgetary systems and accountability are required to ensure that resources and services are available to children. Article 4 of the CRC (1989) requires states parties to ensure that:

> all appropriate legislative, administrative and other measures for the implementation
> of the rights recognized in the Convention. With regard to economic, social and

cultural rights, States parties shall undertake such measures to the maximum extent of their available resources and, where needed, within the framework of international cooperation.

(p. 3)

In 2016, General Comment No. 19 on public budgeting for the realisation of children's rights was published to support States Parties to enact this article. Few countries have a children's budget where the financing of services and resources is planned for in a strategic long-term approach and accountability and reporting can occur. For example, in the national budget 2015–2016 in Bangladesh, a child budget was established to show the resources allocated to children and as a way to measure and report on spending for children's health and well-being (Save the Children, 2016). Some governments, such as Australia (Australian Government, 2018), argue that the allocation of funding and resources is through the family and that it is too difficult to separate funds for parents and children. Marshall, Lundy and Orr (2016) undertook a global review of child participatory budgeting in which they argue that not only should governments have children's budgets, but they should be consulting with children to ensure that funding and resources best meet the needs of the children they effect. In a consultation with 2,693 children across 71 countries aged 4–19 years, Lundy, Marshall and Orr (2016) found that children believed that they should be told how their government is spending money to support children's rights and that 'governments should plan well and not waste or misuse public resources' (p. 6). In this consultation, children suggested that technology, play spaces and roads should be prioritised (Lundy et al., 2016, p. 7).

Education

The United Nations General Assembly (UNGA) Sustainable Development Goal (SDG) 4.1, universal primary and secondary education, advocates for governments globally to provide free, equitable and quality schooling for all children by 2030. SDG 4.2 targets early childhood development and universal pre-primary education for all girls and boys to have access to quality early childhood development and pre-primary education by 2030. The importance of the first five years of life for learning, development and well-being has been well documented (Phillips and Shonkoff, 2000; Sylva et al., 2003), yet early childhood care and education continues to be denied to many children globally. Zubairi and Rose (2019) reported that:

> globally 150 million children are still out of pre-primary education, denied this fundamental stage in their learning and development. There is a stark divide between children in the richest nations and those in low-income countries, with more than 80 per cent of children in high-income countries attending pre-primary education, and more than 80 per cent of those in low-income countries denied access.

(p. 6)

Zubairi and Rose (2019) highlighted how some countries, such as Vietnam, have increased their pre-primary enrolment rate to 99 per cent in the last 10 years, an increase of 35 per cent, through a combination of national funding and international donor support. Increasing access and participation in early childhood education and care is one strand for realising educational rights, but the other key component of education provision is services and pedagogy that acknowledge and respect equity and diversity, as well as diverse cultural knowledges. In Chapter 21, Mathias Urban, Diana Paola Gómez Muñoz and Germán Camilo Zárate Pinto explore rights-based policies in Colombia to consider children's rights and issues of education, poverty, malnutrition and displacement. Rebekah Grace, Mere Skerrett, Jenny Ritchie, Margo Greenwood and Michelle Trudgett, in Chapter 26, explore the possibilities of culturally respectful provision of early childhood education and care in New Zealand, Australia and Canada. In this chapter, the authors explore the rights of indigenous children and how early education founded on Western traditions can and should include indigenous ways of knowing to ensure dignity and diversity of their cultures, traditions, lands and histories. In Chapter 28, Amita Gupta brings further critique of colonised spaces and education exploring rights discourses in India through geo-socio-economics and the distribution of educational resources and opportunities effected by classes, castes and geographies.

Housing

A child's right to housing continues to be a global concern regarding both availability and quality of the dwelling. As growing populations of people are crossing borders due to forced migration, war and natural disasters, refugee and asylum seekers are dealing with issues of accommodation during mobility and arrival in countries of resettlement. Article 27 of the CRC requires States Parties to ensure that children have access to adequate housing. Current housing issues being faced by children and their families are availability, affordability, quality, overcrowding, and absences of a home, with families 'couch-surfing' where they move from place to place between family and friends sleeping on sofas/couches (Clair, 2019). All of these issues create stress due to instability and insecurity for children and families, causing issues around well-being and connectedness to community (Clair, 2019). For children crossing borders seeking asylum in receiving countries, institutional housing facilities such as detention centres or refugee camps are not uncommon. Karlsson (2019) researched the lived experiences of rights and policies for children in an asylum centre in Sweden. Children expressed concerns about privacy and space, lack of facilities and freedom to practise family activities such as cooking, as well as issues of safety connected to the people working in the institutions (Karlsson, 2019).

Home and housing conceptualised as sentry continues to marginalise and discriminate communities that historically and culturally choose nomadic lifestyles. Article 14 of the CRC (1989) calls for States Parties to respect and support children and their families' cultural beliefs and practices. However, traveller and Roma communities continue to be restricted through legislative measures from living in mobile homes (Murray, 2013). In Chapter 23, Colette Murray discusses the structural and institutional discrimination and racism towards travellers, and the affects for realising their rights related to culturally appropriate accommodation, education and care, and health services and treatment.

Health, food and nutrition

Article 24 of the CRC (1989) requires States Parties to recognise and facilitate the right of the child to the enjoyment of the highest attainable standard of health. Further, Article 6 (survival and development): children have the right to live requires governments to ensure the adequate provision of food and nutrition, and health services to ensure that children survive and develop healthily. Article 26 (social security): children – either through their guardians or directly – have the right to help from the government if they are poor or in need. This translates into the need for States Parties to ensure that children have access to adequate food (including breastfeeding) and clean water, as well as medical facilities and treatment that include prevention, promotion, treatment, rehabilitation and palliative care services. In 2013, General Comment No. 15 on the right of the child to the enjoyment of the highest attainable standard of health was released. General Comment No. 15 (2013) notes:

> Health-related facilities, goods and services should be scientifically and medically appropriate and of good quality. Ensuring quality requires, inter alia, that (a) treatments, interventions and medicines are based on the best available evidence; (b) medical personnel are skilled and provided with adequate training on maternal and children's health, and the principles and provisions of the Convention; (c) hospital equipment is scientifically approved and appropriate for children; (d) drugs are scientifically approved, have not expired, are child-specific (when necessary) and are monitored for adverse reactions; and (e) regular quality of care assessments of health institutions are conducted.
>
> *(p. 23)*

In Chapter 24, Luigina Mortari, Ludovica De Panfilis and Luca Ghirotto explore children's rights in paediatric palliative care. They raise questions about how children with long-term and often life-threatening health issues are listened to by health practitioners during periods of care, and the balance of parental wishes and children's best interests.

General Comment No. 15 (2013) also discusses nutrition and health development:

> 'Adequate nutrition and growth monitoring in early childhood are particularly important. Where necessary, integrated management of severe acute malnutrition should be expanded through facility and community-based interventions, as well as treatment of moderate acute malnutrition, including therapeutic feeding interventions'
>
> *(p. 12)*.

Fanzo, Cordes, Fox and Bulman (2018) argue that there are at least three ways to understand malnutrition: '(1) undernourishment (hunger, stunting, and wasting), (2) micronutrient deficiencies ('hidden hunger'), and (3) overweight and obesity' (p. 64). In wealthier countries such as Australia, the UK and the USA, there has been growing attention on obesity, fast food, sugary drinks and issues of economic burden due to diabetes, heart disease and high blood pressure, and children's exercise. The 2018 Global Nutrition Report (UNICEF, 2018) stated that 'children under five years of age face multiple burdens: 150.8 million are stunted, 50.5 million are wasted and 38.3 million are overweight. Meanwhile 20 million babies are born of low birth weight each year' (p. 11). George Kent, in Chapter 20, calls on the countries globally to negotiate a new Optional Protocol on Children's Nutrition to ensure children's access to breastmilk and quality, affordable and accessible formula to ensure the healthy growth and development of infants. In Chapter 27, Cathy Nutbrown considers the UK context and children living in poverty. She highlights the effects of this for nutrition and housing, as well as the flow-on effects for children's capacity to engage with learning and play.

Provision of spaces and places to explore and play

Article 31 of the Convention on the Rights of the Child (CRC) recognises the right of every child to rest, leisure, play, recreational activities, and free and full participation in cultural and artistic life. Casey Y. Myers and Rochelle L. Hostler, in Chapter 25, draw on the perspective of relational materiality (Hultman and Lenz Taguchi, 2010) to reconceptualise play pedagogy in early childhood education and care to support risky play and freedom to move and negotiate everyday spaces outside the early childhood classroom. Considering an alternative theoretical lens created opportunities for teachers to consider how children explore education and learning through human and more-than-human encounters. In Chapter 30, Cat Sewell, Jo Smale and I explore how a local municipality undertook a consultation with children to understand how children accessed play spaces and engaged with outdoor environments. The results highlighted the intersection of provision rights (e.g. waterways, parks, playgrounds, sporting facilities), protection rights (safe places and spaces) and participatory rights (children having a say about the resources provided for and future planning, as well as the municipality reporting back to children through play maps).

Conclusion

Countries signing the CRC is not enough. Signatories have financial obligations under the CRC to provide provisions for children to ensure they have 'adequate' and culturally respectful education, nutrition, preventative and intervention health services and resources, 'housing' (home), and places for play and leisure. While there are exciting initiatives that support children's provisional rights, there are growing gaps between who has access to these provisions. More children are living in poverty (including children in wealthy countries), which has direct effects on access to resources and connections with community. Accountability for the development, spending and reporting on budgets for States Parties should be a priority for the United Nations. Byrne and Lundy (2019) argue that:

> Article 4 of the CRC requires that States parties shall undertake such legal, administrative and other measures to the maximum extent of their available resources with respect to economic social and cultural rights. However, all rights, including civil and political rights, require resources in order to be implemented. In recognition of this, public budgeting for children's rights has become an international human rights policy priority.
>
> *(p. 8)*

Without adequate rights-based strategic and financial planning and spending, generational poverty, homelessness, disconnection from education, and infant and child malnutrition and mortality will not only continue, but will grow. In the next 30 years of the CRC, how will we and signatories change the story?

References

Australian Government. 2018. *Australian Government joint fifth and sixth report under the convention on the rights of the child.* https://static1.squarespace.com/static/580025f66b8f5b2dabbe4291/t/5bda4d6a2 b6a285e2ac55a02/1541033328721/CRC_AUS_5-6_6412_E.pdf

Byrne, Bronagh, and Laura Lundy. 2019. "Children's rights-based childhood policy: A six-P framework." *The International Journal of Human Rights* 23, no. 3: 1–17.

Clair, Amy. 2019. "Housing: An under-explored influence on children's well-being and becoming." *Child Indicators Research* 12, no. 2: 609–626.

Fanzo, Jessica, Kaitlin Y. Cordes, Elizabeth Fox, and Anna Bulman. 2018. "Tying the knot: An interdisciplinary approach to understanding the human right to adequate nutrition." *Columbia Journal of Transnational Law* 57: 62.

Hultman, Karin, and Hillevi Lenz Taguchi. 2010. "Challenging anthropocentric analysis of visual data: A relational materialist methodological approach to educational research." *International Journal of Qualitative Studies in Education* 23, no. 5: 525-542.

Karlsson, Sandra. 2019. "'You said "home" but we don't have a house' – Children's lived rights and politics in an asylum centre in Sweden." *Children's Geographies* 17, no. 1: 64–75.

League of Nations. 1924. *Declaration on the rights of the child.* www.unicef.org/vietnam/01_-_Declaration_of_Geneva_1924.PDF

Lundy, Laura, Chelsea Marshall, and Karen Orr. 2016. *Towards better investment in the rights of children: The views of children.* Belfast, Northern Ireland: Save the Children.

Marshall, Chelsea, Laura Lundy, and Karen Orr. 2016. *Child participatory budgeting: A review of global practice.* Belfast, Northern Ireland: Save the Children.

Moss, Peter. 2014. *Transformative change and real utopias in early childhood education.* Milton Park: Routledge.

Murray, Colette. 2013. "Getting an education. How travellers' knowledge and experience shape their engagement with the system" in *Children's rights and education international perspectives*, edited by Swadener, Beth, Laura Lundy, Janette Habashi, and Natasha Cohen, 203–220. New York: Peter Lang.

Office of the High Commissioner for Human Rights (OHCHR). 1989. *Convention on the rights of the child.* www.ohchr.org/EN/ProfessionalInterest/Pages/CRC.aspx

Office of the High Commissioner for Human Rights (OHCHR). 2006. *General Comment No.15. 2013. On the right of the child to the enjoyment of the highest attainable standard of health (art. 24)*★ http://www2.ohchr.org/english/bodies/crc/docs/GC/CRC-C-GC-15_en.doc

Office of the High Commissioner for Human Rights (OHCHR). 2013. *General Comment No.17. On the right of the child to rest, leisure, play, recreational activities, cultural life and the arts (art. 31)*★ https://www.refworld.org/docid/51ef9bcc4.html

Phillips, Deborah A., and Jack P. Shonkoff, eds. 2000. *From neurons to neighborhoods: The science of early childhood development.* Washington DC: National Academies Press.

Smith, Kylie, Marek Tesar, and Casey Y. Myers. 2016. "Edu-capitalism and the governing of early childhood education and care in Australia, New Zealand and the United States." *Global Studies of Childhood* 6, no. 1: 123–135.

Save the Children. 2016. *Child Budget for 2016-17.* https://bangladesh.savethechildren.net/sites/bangladesh.savethechildren.net/files/library/analysis%20child%20budget%20%202016-17.pdf

Sylva, Kathy, Edward Melhuish, Pam Sammons, Iram Siraj-Blatchford, Brenda Taggart, and Karen Elliot. 2003. *The Effective Provision of Pre-school Education (EPPE) project: findings from the pre-school period.* London: Institute of Education, University of London.

UNICEF. 2014. *Convention on the Rights of the Child.* www.unicef.org/crc/

UNICEF. 2018. *Global nutrition report.* https://data.unicef.org/resources/global-nutrition-report-2018/

United Nations. 1959. *The Declaration of the Rights of the Child.* https://www.ohchr.org/EN/Issues/Education/Training/Compilation/Pages/1DeclarationoftheRightsoftheChild(1959).aspx

Zubairi, Asma, and Pauline. Rose 2019. *Leaving the youngest behind: Declining aid to early childhood education.* Their World. https://s3.amazonaws.com/theirworld-site-resources/Reports/Theirworld-Leaving-The-Youngest-Behind-First-Edition-April-2019.pdf

20

YOUNG CHILDREN'S RIGHT TO GOOD NUTRITION

George Kent

Introduction

Human rights should be viewed as dynamic, so need to be interpreted and updated from time to time. This essay reviews the current situation regarding young children's right to good nutrition and suggests steps for further development. There are many issues that demand attention, including some that result from the changing landscape of children's nutrition. To illustrate, since the Convention on the Rights of the Child came into force in 1989, infant formula marketing and use have expanded globally. We can expect sharply increased use and possibly commercialisation of human milk through milk banks and wet-nursing. Questionable innovations, such as highly processed and overly sweetened foods designed for children, can put their health at risk. Positive innovations, such as better nutrition education, can fail to reach families that need them most. To organise a comprehensive approach to addressing the issues, this essay proposes that the countries of the world negotiate a new Optional Protocol on Children's Nutrition, to be linked to the Convention on the Rights of the Child. It opens by discussing rights-based social systems generally, before focusing on the right to food, children's nutrition issues, and how children's right to good nutrition could be strengthened.

Rights-based social systems

Rights-based social systems are described in this section first as an abstract form, and the global human rights system is then described as one concrete manifestation of that form. The human right to food in particular is then discussed in the following section.

As I have argued elsewhere, in any well-developed rights system, there are three major roles to be fulfilled: the *rights-holders*, the *duty-bearers*, and the *agents of accountability* (Kent, 2005, pp. 63–6). The task of the agents of accountability is to make sure that those who have the duties carry out their obligations to those who have the rights. Thus, to describe a rights system, we need to know:

A. The nature of the *rights-holders* and their rights.
B. The nature of the *duty-bearers* and their obligations (duties) corresponding to the rights of the rights-holders.

C. The nature of the *agents of accountability*, and the procedures through which they ensure that the duty-bearers meet their obligations to the rights-holders. The accountability mechanisms include, in particular, the remedies available to the rights-holders themselves.

Rights imply entitlements, which are claims to specific goods or services. Rights are, or are supposed to be, *enforceable* claims. There must be some sort of institutional authority to which rights-holders whose claims are not satisfied can appeal to have the situation corrected. Enforceability means that the duty-bearers, those who are to fulfil the entitlements, must be obligated to do so, and they must be held accountable for their performance. A clear distinction should be made between having a right and having that right realised. If I pay you to paint my garage, I have a right to have it painted. Whether or not that right is in fact realised (fulfilled) is another matter.

Accountability requires institutional arrangements, specific agencies to carry out specific functions. Accountability agencies such as police departments and perhaps departments of health have two distinct phases in their operations. One element is *detection* to determine whether there is deviation from the standard, and if so, in what degree. The second is *correction* through which something is done with the information obtained to restore the behaviour of the duty-bearers to the range of acceptability.

An accountability agency assesses the performance of the duty-bearers against the established standards. It informs the duty-bearers of those assessments in order to guide them toward improving their performance. In some cases, the accountability agency might also have the power to impose sanctions of different types. However, in many cases, they function on the basis of 'constructive dialogue' – persuasion rather than coercion. Sometimes detecting and reporting on the deviation to the duty-bearers may be sufficient to induce them to correct their actions.

While there can be many different mechanisms of accountability, the most fundamental is that available to the rights-holders themselves. Individuals who fail to get what they are entitled to should have means available to them for pressing their claims. Rights-holders must know their rights, and they must have appropriate institutional arrangements available to them for pursuing the realisation of those rights. Parents and other caregivers should know and be enabled to demand fulfilment of their own rights and also the rights of the children under their care. It is through these remedies that claims become enforceable. Where there are no effective remedies, there are no effective rights. Having rights that are enforceable means recognising that people should have specific powers to make claims on the world in which they live. Rights-holders should be able to act to ensure they get what they are supposed to get.

People sometimes use the word *rights* as shorthand for *human rights*. That is unfortunate because there are many different kinds of rights, including property rights, contract rights and consumer rights. A hospital may have a patients' bill of rights, and prisoners may have their own rights, whether established by the local institution, the local government or the national government. The international human rights system is one concrete manifestation of the generic form of rights-based social systems. In settings such as clubs, schools, prisons and hospitals, responsibility for implementation would rest not with a government, but with the institution's administration.

Human rights are described in international human rights agreements. All current agreements are available through the Office of the High Commissioner for Human Rights (OHCHR, 2019a). The International Bill of Human Rights is comprised primarily of the

Universal Declaration of Human Rights, the International Covenant on Civil and Political Rights, the International Covenant on Economic, Social and Cultural Rights, and the Optional Protocols associated with them (OHCHR, 2019b). All major human rights agreements are available through the OHCHR (OHCHR, 2019c).

The term *human rights* is reserved for those rights that are universal and relate to human dignity. Where people have human rights, their governments and other institutions are obligated to do specific things to further human dignity. Human rights are universal, by definition. They are mainly, but not exclusively, about the obligations of national governments to people living under their jurisdictions. While human rights are universal, they do allow some latitude for differing interpretations, depending on local circumstances. Local rights in subnational jurisdictions do not have to involve the national government and are not universal, so they are not *human* rights. They might reflect local interpretations of the global human rights set out in the global treaties. For most human rights, most of the time, the primary duty-bearers are states (countries), represented by their national governments. On signing and ratifying human rights agreements, they accept that duty and commit to modify their national laws as necessary to conform with their duties under the agreement. This means the primary accountability is that of national governments to the rights-holders under their jurisdiction. The primary institution for hearing complaints about alleged violations of one's human rights may be national judicial systems, but there might be other sorts of arrangements as well, such as public hearings.

The right to food

Historically, national and international responses to food supply problems have been based on compassion and the argument that reducing malnutrition can benefit society as a whole. These responses have ranged from small local feeding programmes to large-scale international actions involving the United Nations Children's Fund, the World Bank, the World Food Programme, the Food and Agriculture Organization of the United Nations, and many non-governmental organisations. Now, however, there is increasing recognition that access to food is a human right, and thus there is an obligation under international law to ensure that all people get the food they need.

Soon after the conclusion of World War II, the global effort to establish a strong and widely accepted legal basis for all human rights was formally launched with the agreement on the Universal Declaration of Human Rights in 1948. The right to food was mentioned in the context of the broader human right to an adequate standard of living. Article 25 says:

> Everyone has the right to a standard of living adequate for the health and well-being of himself and of his family, including food, clothing, housing and medical care and necessary social services, and the right to security in the event of unemployment, sickness, disability, widowhood, old age or other lack of livelihood in circumstances beyond his control.
>
> *(para. 1)*

The concept also appeared in the International Covenant on Economic, Social and Cultural Rights, which came into force in 1976, which states in Article 1, 'In no case may a people be deprived of its own means of subsistence' (para. 2). In addition, Article 6 of the International Covenant on Civil and Political Rights states, 'Every human being has the inherent right to life', implying the right to adequate food and other necessities for sustaining life. The right to an adequate standard of living was elaborated in Article 11 of the International Covenant on Economic, Social and Cultural Rights:

> The States Parties to the present Covenant recognise the right of everyone to an adequate standard of living for himself and his family, including adequate food, clothing and housing, and to the continuous improvement of living conditions.
>
> *(para. 1)*

The article is explicit about food, clothing and housing, but it also implies the right to fulfilment of other needs that are addressed in other parts of the covenant and other human rights instruments.

The right to food, asserted by the International Covenant on Economic, Social and Cultural Rights, means, at least in principle, binding obligations on all countries that have signed and ratified the Covenant. However, the meaning of right was not spelled out until May 1999 when the United Nations Committee on Economic, Social and Cultural Rights issued its document on *Substantive Issues Arising in the Implementation of the International Covenant on Economic, Social and Cultural Rights: General Comment 12*, sometimes referred to as General Comment 12 or GC12 (United Nations Economic and Social Council, 1999). It is an authoritative contribution to international jurisprudence.

GC12 presents the core definition:

> The right to adequate food is realised when every man, woman and child, alone or in community with others, has physical and economic access at all times to adequate food or means for its procurement.
>
> *(para. 6)*

GC12 begins by citing the foundation of the legally binding human right to adequate food in Article 11 of the International Covenant on Economic, Social and Cultural Rights. It draws a distinction between the reference in the first paragraph of that article to an adequate standard of living, including adequate food, and the second paragraph of that article, which calls for ensuring 'the fundamental right to freedom from hunger and malnutrition' (para. 1). GC12 says that 'more immediate and urgent steps may be needed to ensure' the fundamental right to freedom from hunger and malnutrition (para. 1). Thus, hunger and malnutrition signify more acute, more urgent problems than are indicated by inadequate food in itself. The distinction is addressed again in GC12's paragraph 6:

> The *right to adequate food* will have to be realised progressively. However, States have a core obligation to take the necessary action to mitigate and alleviate hunger as provided for in paragraph 2 of article 11, even in times of natural or other disasters.
>
> *(emphasis in original)*

Paragraph 14 summarises the obligations of states as follows:

> Every State is obliged to ensure for everyone under its jurisdiction access to the minimum essential food which is sufficient, nutritionally adequate and safe, to ensure their freedom from hunger.

Paragraph 15 draws out the different kinds or levels of obligations of the state that apply to food:

- *Respect*: 'The obligation to respect existing access to adequate food requires States parties not to take any measures that result in preventing such access'.

- *Protect*: 'The obligation to protect requires measures by the State to ensure that enterprises or individuals do not deprive individuals of their access to adequate food'.
- *Fulfil (facilitate)*: 'The obligation to fulfil (facilitate) means the State must proactively engage in activities intended to strengthen people's access to and utilisation of resources and means to ensure their livelihood, including food security'.
- *Fulfil (provide)*: 'Finally, whenever an individual or group is unable, for reasons beyond their control, to enjoy the right to adequate food by the means at their disposal, States have the obligation to fulfil (provide) that right directly. This obligation also applies for persons who are victims of natural or other disasters'.

Or, more simply:

- *Respect* means do no harm to others.
- *Protect* means prevent harm to others by third parties.
- *Facilitate* means help others to meet their own needs.
- *Provide* means meet others' needs when they cannot do that themselves.

General Comment 12 also discusses issues of implementation at the national level, framework legislation, monitoring, remedies and accountability, international obligations, etc.

GC12 highlights the importance of dignity, a key consideration in all human rights work:

> The Committee affirms that the right to adequate food is indivisibly linked to the inherent dignity of the human person and is indispensable for the fulfilment of other human rights enshrined in the International Bill of Human Rights. It is also inseparable from social justice, requiring the adoption of appropriate economic, environmental and social policies, at both the national and international levels, oriented to the eradication of poverty and the fulfilment of all human rights for all.
>
> *(para. 4)*

In addition, GC12 states:

> The *right to adequate food* shall therefore not be interpreted in a narrow or restrictive sense which equates it with a minimum package of calories, proteins and other specific nutrients.
>
> *(para. 6, emphasis in original)*

Simply delivering pre-packaged meals in the way one might deliver feed pellets to livestock cannot fulfil the right. That sort of approach would be incompatible with human dignity. Delivering such meals might be sensible in a short-term emergency, but it cannot be the means for realising the human right to adequate food over the long run.

GC12, published in 1999, was a major step in the articulation of the right to food. Another major step was taken in 2005 when the executive governing body of the Food and Agriculture Organization of the United Nations adopted *Voluntary Guidelines to Support the Progressive Realisation of the Right to Adequate Food in the Context of National Food Security*, on 23 November 2004 (FAO, 2005). The text augments international human rights law relating to the human right to adequate food, showing that there are different ways in which the obligations described in that law might be fulfilled. Human rights law specifies what the parties *must* do, their obligations, while the voluntary guidelines talk about what they *could* do to fulfil those obligations.

As mentioned earlier, for most human rights, the primary duty-bearers are the states, represented by their national governments. When states become parties to international human rights agreements, they are expected to elaborate their understandings of those obligations by spelling them out in their own national law. There is a positive obligation to do this. In the International Covenant on Civil and Political Rights, for example, Article 2 says:

> Where not already provided for by existing legislative or other measures, each State Party to the present Covenant undertakes to take the necessary steps, in accordance with its constitutional processes and with the provisions of the present Covenant, to adopt such legislative or other measures as may be necessary to give effect to the rights recognised in the present Covenant.
>
> *(para. 2)*

Human rights law and principles are intended to be universal. This can be accomplished only by describing the rights in rather abstract form, leaving room for interpretation at national and subnational levels. Specificity is achieved through the adoption of national law designed to support implementation of global human rights at the national level. General Comment 12 speaks about this in terms of the formulation of broad *framework law* on the human right to adequate food:

> States should consider the adoption of a *framework law* as a major instrument in the implementation of the national strategy concerning the right to food. The framework law should include provisions on its purpose; the targets or goals to be achieved and the time-frame to be set for the achievement of those targets; the means by which the purpose could be achieved described in broad terms, in particular the intended collaboration with civil society and the private sector and with international organisations; institutional responsibility for the process; and the national mechanisms for its monitoring, as well as possible recourse procedures. In developing the benchmarks and framework legislation, States parties should actively involve civil society organisations.
>
> *(para. 29, emphasis in original)*

Thus, a new approach to the food issues has emerged, based on the premise that there is a human right to food (Lambek, 2018). It continues to evolve. The FAO website (www.fao.org/right-to-food) tracks the latest developments.

Nutrition in the Convention on the Rights of the Child

In the Convention on the Rights of the Child, which came into force in 1989, two articles address nutrition. Article 24 says that 'States Parties recognise the right of the child to the enjoyment of the highest attainable standard of health' (para. 1) and shall take appropriate measures 'to combat disease and malnutrition … through the provision of adequate nutritious foods, clean drinking water, and health care' (para. 2c). Article 24 also says that States Parties shall take appropriate measures 'To ensure that all segments of society, in particular parents and children, are informed, have access to education and are supported in the use of basic knowledge of child health and nutrition [and] the advantages of breastfeeding' (para. 2e). Article 27 says that States Parties 'shall in case of need provide material assistance and support programmes, particularly with regard to nutrition, clothing, and housing' (para. 3).

Even if the human right to adequate food had not been asserted explicitly in international human rights law, it is strongly implied in provisions such as those asserting the right to life and health, and the requirement in the Convention on the Rights of the Child (in Article 24) that States Parties shall 'take appropriate measures to diminish infant and child mortality' (para. 2a).

As described above, the international community has taken major initiatives to develop agreed understandings with regard to the right to food. Global meetings and non-binding international declarations and resolutions have helped to shape the emerging international consensus on norms regarding the human right to adequate food.

While there have been remarkable advances in development of the right to food, difficulties remain. Some problems are shared with many other rights, such as the weakness of the recourse mechanisms available to rights-holders, and the simple fact that the entire human rights project has not achieved as much as it supporters have hoped. There is also the question of external obligations. Much of the discussion about human rights focuses on the obligations of national governments to people under their jurisdiction. That leaves open the question of what obligations nations have, or should have, to people elsewhere (Kent, 2008). For example, should there be a legal obligation to provide international humanitarian assistance under some conditions (Kent, 2013)?

The International Baby Food Action Network and the Geneva Infant Feeding Association issue periodic reports on developments in the global agencies relating to children's nutrition (IBFAN-GIFA, 2018).

Young children's nutrition issues

The global right to food campaign that emerged in the 1990s has given little attention to the distinctive nutritional needs and the distinctive vulnerabilities of infants and young children. The Convention on the Rights of the Child has little to say about nutrition. Yet there are many issues concerning nutrition that need to be addressed 30 years on, some of which have only recently emerged. This section raises some of the issues and proposes some ways to address them.

Rights to breastfeed and to be breastfed

Discussion of rights to breastfeed and to be breastfed raise many questions. If infants have a right to be breastfed, does that mean their mothers have an obligation to breastfeed? Should governments require reluctant mothers to breastfeed? What does this mean with regard to the parents' rights and obligations? What does it mean with regard to societies' obligations to parents and infants (Bar-Yam, 2003; Kent, 1998, 2001, 2004, 2006, 2007, 2015, 2017a)?

Support for families

New mothers have special needs, which may include infant feeding support services, paid leave from work, and fair information about feeding methods and other aspects of childcare. However, the human rights treaties say little about these things. The International Labour Organization (ILO) has supported the global Maternity Protection Convention (revised) 1952, along with numerous revisions and recommendations over the years (ILO, 2018). The ILO has also undertaken relevant studies and has made strong recommendations (e.g. Addati, Cassirer and Gilchrist, 2014). The ILO's work in this area should be coordinated with the broader development of human rights relating to children's nutrition.

The International Code of Marketing of Breast-Milk Substitutes

The International Code of Marketing of Breast-Milk Substitutes, adopted by the World Health Assembly in 1981, and the subsequent related resolutions are intended to limit the aggressive marketing of infant formula by manufacturers (Barennes, Guenther Slesak, Goyet, Percy Aaron and Srour, 2016). The Code should be updated and placed explicitly into the international human rights framework. In this process, it should be recognised that not only manufacturers and sellers, but also governments, can violate the spirit of the Code (Kent, 2017b, 2017c).

Industry participation in national and global policymaking

There is growing concern about the interference of the food industry in national and global policymaking (Bass, 2018; TRT World, 2018). This issue is especially important with regard to infant formula and other baby foods, which can be highly profitable (Khayatzadeh-Mahani, Ruckert and Labonté, 2018; Koehn, 2018). The pursuit of private wealth leads to aggressive marketing of foods for children, which can compromise their health (UNICEF, 2018; WHA, 2016; WHO, 2017). There is particular concern about the marketing of foods *to* children (Granheim, Vandevjvere and Torhim, 2018; Handsley and Reeve, 2018).

Childhood obesity was not a major concern when the Convention on the Rights of the Child came into force in 1989, but has become an issue in many countries, at every income level. Also, child obesity has become a major factor in the increase of non-communicable diseases (NCDs) during childhood and continuing on into adulthood. It is largely due to the aggressive marketing of foods, especially highly processed foods. The human rights approach could help to bring coherence to the many different approaches to dealing with child obesity and related NCDs (Garde, Gokani and Friant-Perrot, 2018).

Human milk issues

When women provide their milk to be fed to infants of other women, it is commonly referred to as human milk. It is sometimes called donor milk, but often there are payments for it. For this reason, I refer to the women as milk providers, not donors. The exchange of human milk can be arranged through milk banks or through milk-sharing. Sharing is based on direct contact between the woman providing her milk and the caretaker of the infant who is to receive it, with no intermediate banking. The most common form of sharing is wet-nursing, but modern forms of sharing are often arranged in other ways, such as advertising through the Internet.

The awareness of the need to update human rights law to take account of the increasing systematic exchange of human milk is beginning to emerge (Arnold, 2006). Some concerns are about risks to the health of the infants and the women who might be affected. Some are economic. There is the possibility of exploitation of the women who provide their milk, whether as donors or for compensation of some kind. There are debates about what types and what levels of compensation would be appropriate.

Modern human milk-banking has been devoted primarily to serving the needs of critically ill infants, especially those who are born prematurely or are seriously underweight and are being treated in hospital neonatal intensive care units. Some milk banks are also offering their banked milk to other infants (23ABCNews, 2018; LaVenture, 2018). I advocate broadening the reach of milk banks so that more infants can benefit from their services (Kent, 2017a).

Research issues

Parents' rights to good information about the qualities of their infant feeding alternatives should be made explicit and widely shared. More research is needed on how different methods of feeding infants compare in terms of their impacts, primarily on the health of the infant, but also on the health of the mother and the economic situation of the family. There is a need to somehow find adequate funding while at the same time ensuring that the research is reasonably objective. Although there seems to be a great deal of funding for research serving commercial interests, there seems to be comparatively little to support the interests of the children themselves, especially with regard to their health. Often the research supporting commercial interests shows little evidence of interest in health impacts (Tanmay, 2018). The infant formula industry is growing rapidly, based largely on promoting its use in low-income economies (Baker et al., 2016). The economic benefits are closely tracked by the industry, but no global agency is watching the health impacts. There is a need for more systematic monitoring of the health impacts of the use of infant formula and of the special additives to it (Kent, 2015).

Rights to inputs or results?

One issue that remains unsettled is terminology: What exactly is the right to food? How can it be determined if the right is fulfilled? If it is a right to adequate food, what is the meaning of adequate?

The Food and Agriculture Organization of the United Nations publishes regular annual reports on *The State of Food Insecurity in the World*, but beginning in 2017 it changed the title to *The State of Food Security and Nutrition in the World* (FAO, 2018). This reference to nutrition signals an important shift. The focus has been on the right to *food*, but clearly the underlying objective is to achieve good *nutrition status*, the main outcome of interest. Food is the input to the human body, but the important thing is the result, the body's nutrition status. Children's right to food means they should have enough food to live well. Anything less means the child's rights have been violated. More attention should be given to the idea that people, especially children, have a right to good nutrition. The distinction here is that between inputs and outputs of a process, between efforts and results.

There could be a shift toward ensuring rights to particular outcomes. For example, the basis of the right to food could be shifted from specifying what children must be given to eat to instead (or also) establish a right to particular outcomes. To illustrate, children could be given a right to be within the normal weight range for their age and gender, and assured of whatever is needed if they are outside the normal range. Changes in the food and health services that are provided could then be based on assessment of individual cases.

On the basis of the fundamental right to life, all children should be viewed as having a right to the food and services they need to keep alive and well. Anything less means their rights have been violated, and those responsible – including governments – should be held accountable for that. Ideally, there should be legal limits to the extent to which we allow young children to die of malnutrition (Moitra, 2018). That could be arranged, if the will is there (Kent, 2017a).

Strengthening children's right to good nutrition

The global community has done a great deal since the early 1990s to develop the concept of the right to food. However, little attention has been given to the meaning of the right to food for children, despite their distinctive needs and high vulnerability. The major issues relating to children's nutrition could be brought into sharper focus by calling on the countries of the world to negotiate a new Optional Protocol on Children's Nutrition, to be linked to the United Nations Convention on the Rights of the Child (Kent, 2015).

The Optional Protocol on Children's Nutrition could be limited to broad statements of principles and linked to a detailed General Comment on Children's Nutrition. It could be modelled on General Comment 12 on the right to adequate food. General Comments provide authoritative interpretations of the law in human rights treaties. Work toward the drafting of a new Optional Protocol on Children's Nutrition could be coordinated with the relevant work of the International Labour Organization, mentioned above. It should also be coordinated with the development of nutrition-related rights in the Convention on the Elimination of All Forms of Discrimination Against Women (Galtry, 2015a, 2015b). Equally, CEDAW could have a linked Optional Protocol on Infant Feeding that examines the roles of both parents in feeding their young children. Such a Protocol could also describe the types of support parents should have.

That effort at the global level could guide the formulation of stronger rights systems relating to children's nutrition at the national level. The Convention on the Rights of the Child already has two Optional Protocols associated with it, one on the involvement of children in armed conflict, and another on the sale of children, child prostitution and child pornography. Their forms could be used as a basis for drafting a new Optional Protocol on Children's Nutrition. Working under the auspices of the United Nations General Assembly, the nations of the world could negotiate a draft. The drafters could draw from the many sources of sound principles relating to children's nutrition, such as the International Code of Marketing of Breast-Milk Substitutes, the Global Strategy for Infant and Young Child Feeding, the Innocenti Declaration, and the Baby-Friendly Hospital Initiative. Ideas from many other agencies and documents, currently scattered, could be brought together.

When a draft for the Optional Protocol was ready, the General Assembly would vote on it. If a majority agreed, it would be adopted by the General Assembly. The executive branches of the national governments of the world would then be invited to sign the Protocol, and then have their national legislatures or other appropriate bodies ratify it, in the normal procedure used to formalise a nation's agreement to international treaties. Ratification would indicate the nation's acceptance of the Protocol and its commitment to conform its national laws to the Protocol. Following ratification, its broad principles would be given concrete form through the adoption of appropriate national laws. The ratification would signify the nation's willingness to be held accountable with regard to the principles stated, and the new national laws would be the means by which each nation's leaders follow through on their nation's commitment.

Conclusion

A new Optional Protocol on Children's Nutrition linked to the Convention on the Rights of the Child would begin to provide a comprehensive approach to addressing many of the issues that this chapter has highlighted as barriers to good nutrition for young children. The process of introducing the Optional Protocol on Children's Nutrition would not generate quick solutions to the issues relating to the nutrition, but it would launch much-needed systematic examination of the issues. The process could lead to widely agreed guidelines and regulations for ensuring that children everywhere are well nourished, based on the recognition that all children have the right to be well nourished, especially in the earliest years of life.

References

23ABCNews. 2018. "Kern Medical to Offer NICU and Well Babies Donor Breast Milk." 23ABCNews. www.turnto23.com/news/local-news/kern-medical-to-offer-nicu-and-well-babies-donor-breast-milk

Addati, Laura, Naomi Cassirer, and Katherine Gilchrist. 2014. *Maternity and Paternity at Work: Law and Practice across the World*. Geneva: International Labour Office. www.ilo.org/global/publications/ilo-bookstore/order-online/books/WCMS_242615/lang–en/index.htm

Arnold, Lois D.W. 2006. "Global Health Policies that Support the Use of Banked Donor Human Milk: A Human Rights Issue." *Journal of Human Lactation* 12 (1): 26. December. https://internationalbreast feedingjournal.biomedcentral.com/articles/10.1186/1746-4358-1-26

Baker, Phillip, Julie Patricia Smith, Libby Salmon, Sharon Friel, George Kent, Alessandro Iellemo, Jai Prakash Dadhich, and Mary J. Renfrew. 2016. "Global trends and patterns of commercial milk-based formula sales: Is an unprecedented infant and young child feeding transition underway?" *Public Health Nutrition* 19 (14) May: 2540–2550. doi:10.1017/S1368980016001117 or www2.hawaii.edu/~kent/GlobalFormulaTransition.pdf Summary available at http://blogs.plos.org/globalhealth/2016/05/is-an-unprecedented-infant-feeding-transition-underway/

Barennes, Hubert, B. Guenther Slesak, Sophie Goyet, B. Percy Aaron, and Leila M. Srour. 2016. "Enforcing the International Code of Marketing of Breast-milk Substitutes for Better Promotion of Exclusive Breastfeeding: Can Lessons Be Learned?" *Journal of Human Lactation* 32 (1): 20–27. http://journals.sagepub.com/doi/pdf/10.1177/0890334415607816

Bar-Yam, Naomi Bromberg. 2003. "Breastfeeding and Human Rights: Is There a Right to Breastfeed? Is There a Right to be Breastfed?" *Journal of Human Lactation* (19): 357–361. http://journals.sagepub.com/doi/abs/10.1177/0890334403258208?journalCode=jhla

Bass, Frank. 2018. "Infant Formula Makers Sweetened Mother's Milk of Politics With $60 Million in Lobbying Funds." *MapLight*. Accessed July 12. https://maplight.org/story/infant-formula-makers-sweetened-mothers-milk-of-politics-with-60-million-in-lobbying-funds/

FAO 2005. *Voluntary Guidelines to Support the Progressive Realization of the Right to Adequate Food in the Context of National Food Security*. Rome: Food and Agriculture Organization of the United Nations. http://www.fao.org/3/y7937e/y7937e00.htm

FAO. 2018. *The State of Food Security and Nutrition in the World*. Food and Agriculture Organisation of the United Nations. www.fao.org/search/en/?cx=018170620143701104933%3Aqq82jsfba7w&q=state+of+food+security+in+the+world&cof=FORID%3A9&siteurl=www.fao.org%2Fhome%2Fen%2F&ref=&ss=6355j1595315j37

Galtry, Judith. 2015a. "Strengthening the Human Rights Framework to Protect Breastfeeding: A Focus on CEDAW." *International Breastfeeding Journal* 10 (29) November: 1–10.

Galtry, Judith. 2015b. "Breastfeeding as a Human Right for Women." *BMC Blog Network*. http://blogs.biomedcentral.com/on-health/2015/11/19/breastfeeding-human-right-women/

Garde, Amandine, Nikhil Gokani, and Marine Friant-Perrot. 2018. "Child Rights, Childhood Obesity and Health Inequalities." *UNSCN News (United Nations System Standing Committee on Nutrition)* (43): 65–74. www.unscn.org/uploads/web/news/UNSCN-News43.pdf

Granheim, Sabrina Ionata, Stefanie Vandevjvere, and Live Elin Torhim. 2018. "The Potential of a Human Rights Approach for Accelerating the Implementation of Comprehensive Restrictions on the Marketing of Unhealthy Foods and Non-alcoholic Beverages to Children." *Health Promotion International*. January 5. https://academic.oup.com/heapro/advance-article-abstract/doi/10.1093/heapro/dax100/4791426?redirectedFrom=fulltext

Handsley, Elizabeth, and Belinda Reeve. 2018. "Holding Food Companies Responsible for Unhealthy Food Marketing to Children: Can International Human Rights Instruments Provide a New Approach?" *University of New South Wales Law Journal* 41 (2). www.unswlawjournal.unsw.edu.au/article/holding-food-companies-responsible-international-human-rights/

IBFAN-GIFA. 2018. *IBFAN-GIFA Newsletter.* International Baby Food Action Network and Geneva Infant Feeding Association. (12) July. https://mailchi.mp/6ee484e7a8a4/ibfan-gifa-newsletter-12?e=d8073dc1be

ILO. 2018. *C183 – Maternity Protection Convention, 2000 (No.183).* Geneva: International Labour Organisation. www.ilo.org/dyn/normlex/en/f?p=NORMLEXPUB:12100:0::NO::P12100_ILO_CODE:C183

Kent, George. 1998. "Women's Rights to Breastfeed vs. Infants' Rights to be Breastfed." *SCN News (united Nations System Standing Committee on Nutrition)* (17) December: 18–19. www.unscn.org/layout/modules/resources/files/SCNNews17.pdf

Kent, George. 2001. "Breastfeeding: A Human Rights Issue?" *Development* 44 (2) June: 93–98. www2.hawaii.edu/~kent/breastfeedingrights.pdf

Kent, George. 2004. "Human Rights and Infant Nutrition." *WABA Global Forum II-23-27 September 2002-Arusha, Tanzania.* Penang, Malaysia: World Alliance for Breastfeeding Action, 178–186. www2.hawaii.edu/~kent/HUMAN%20RIGHTS%20AND%20INFANT%20NUTRITION.pdf.

Kent, George. 2005. *Freedom from Want: The Human Right to Adequate Food.* Washington, DC: Georgetown University Press, ISBN I-158901 056 6. http://press.georgetown.edu/sites/default/files/978-1-58901-055-0%20w%20CC%20license.pdf

Kent, George. 2006. "Child Feeding and Human Rights." *International Breastfeeding Journal* 18 (1) December: 1–27. www.internationalbreastfeedingjournal.com/content/1/1/27

Kent, George. 2007. *Global Obligations for Children's Rights.* United Nations. Committee on Rights of the Child. Day of General Discussion. September 21. www.crin.org/docs/George_Kent_global_obligations.pdf.

Kent, George. ed. 2008. *Global Obligations for the Right to Food.* Lanham, Maryland: Rowman & Littlefield.

Kent, George. 2013. "Rights and Obligations in International Humanitarian Assistance." *Encyclopedia of Natural Hazards.* Heidelberg, Germany: Springer. 851–855. www2.hawaii.edu/~kent/RightsObligationsinIHA.pdf. Republished in *Disaster Prevention and Management,* 2014, Vol. 23 (3). http://www2.hawaii.edu/~kent/DPMRightsandObligationsinIHA.pdf.

Kent, George. 2015. "Global Infant Formula: Monitoring and Regulating the Impacts to Protect Human Health." *International Breastfeeding Journal* 10 (1): 6. February. www.internationalbreastfeedingjournal.com/content/10/1/6/abstract.

Kent, George. 2017a. "Extending the Reach of Human Milk Banking." *World Nutrition* 8 (2): 232–250. https://worldnutritionjournal.org/index.php/wn/article/view/143/111

Kent, George. 2017b. "Conflicts of Interest in the WIC Program." *World Nutrition* 8 (1). http://worldnutritionjournal.org/index.php/wn/article/view/47

Kent, George. 2017c. *Governments Push Infant Formula.* Sparsnäs, Sweden: Irene Publishing.

Khayatzadeh-Mahani, Akram, Arne Ruckert, and Ronald Labonté. 2018. "Could the WHO's Framework on Engagement with Non-State Actors (FENSA) be a Threat to Tackling Childhood Obesity?" *Global Public Health* 13 (9): 1337–1340. www.tandfonline.com/doi/full/10.1080/17441692.2017.1342852

Koehn, Emma. 2018. "These China-focused Infant Formula Stocks are Averaging 170pc One-year Returns." Stockhead. Accessed July 27. https://stockhead.com.au/health/these-china-focused-infant-formula-stocks-are-averaging-170pc-one-year-returns/

Lambek, Nadia. 2018. "Transformative Potential: How the Right to Food can Help Combat Malnutrition." *UNSCN News* (United Nations System Standing Committee on Nutrition), (43): 75–83. www.unscn.org/uploads/web/news/UNSCN-News43.pdf.

LaVenture, Tom. 2018. "A Mother's Gift: Woman in Cancer Treatment Receives Mother's Milk for Infant." *Jamestown Sun.* Accessed August 6. http://jamestownsun.com/community/people/4481878-mothers-gift-woman-cancer-treatment-receives-mothers-milk-infant

Moitra, Soha. 2018. "Capital Shame: Children are Going Hungry in Delhi Because Govt Schemes are Poorly Implemented." *Daily O.* www.dailyo.in/single-story.php?id=MjYwMTE=

OHCHR. 2019a. Office of the High Commission for Human Rights. www.ohchr.org/EN/pages/home.aspx

OHCHR. 2019b. *Fact Sheet No. 2 =Rev.1), The International Bill of Human Rights.* www.ohchr.org/Documents/Publications/FactSheet2Rev.1en.pdf

OHCHR. 2019c. Issues/Human Rights Instruments. www.ohchr.org/EN/ProfessionalInterest/Pages/UniversalHumanRightsInstruments.aspx

Tanmay. 2018. "Global Infant Formula Oil and Fat Ingredients Market – Volume and Value Analysis by Product Type (Steel Welded & Seamless), By End User, By Region, By Country: Opportunities and

Forecast 2018–2025." *Business Tactics*. Accessed July 16. https://thebusinesstactics.com/235922/global-infant-formula-oil-and-fat-ingredients-market-volume-and-value-analysis-by-product-type-steel-welded-seamless-by-end-user-by-region-by-country-opportunities-and-forecast-2018-2025/

TRT World. 2018. *Infant Formula: An Ethical Industry? YouTube Video.* www.trtworld.com/video/round table/infant-formula-an-ethical-industry/5b59bce90ab8e2110baea623

UNICEF. 2018. *A Child Rights-Based Approach to Food Marketing: A Guide for Policy Makers.* April. United Nations Children's Fund. www.unicef.org/csr/files/A_Child_Rights-Based_Approach_to_Food_Marketing_Report.pdf

United Nations Economic and Social Council. 1999. Substantive Issues Arising in the Implementation of the International Covenant on Economic, Social and Cultural Rights: General Comment 12. (ECOSOC Publication No. E/C.12/1999/5). www.law.umich.edu/facultyhome/drwcasebook/Documents/Documents/Committee%20on%20Economic,%20Social,%20and%20Cultural%20Rights%20General%20Comment%2012.pdf

WHA. 2016. *Ending Inappropriate Promotion of Foods for Infants and Young Children.* Sixty-Ninth World Health Assembly. Resolution WHA69.9. http://apps.who.int/gb/ebwha/pdf_files/WHA69/A69_R9-en.pdf?ua=1

WHO. 2017. *Guidance on Ending the Inappropriate Promotion of Foods for Infants and Young Children: Implementation Manual.* Geneva: World Health Organisation. www.who.int/nutrition/publications/infant feeding/manual-ending-inappropriate-promotion-food/en/

21

LEARNING WITH AND FROM COLOMBIA

Perspectives on Rights-Based Early Childhood Policies

Mathias Urban, Diana Paola Gómez Muñoz and Germán Camilo Zárate Pinto

Introduction

This chapter offers perspectives on young children's rights as policy drivers in two markedly distinct contexts: Colombia and the European Union. Such a set-up inevitably raises a question: Why compare two entities that are so obviously different in terms of their geopolitical location, history and culture? What can possibly be learned from placing a fast-developing Latin American country, in the Global South, in the same frame of reference – young children's rights policies – as one of the most affluent socio-economic regions in the Global North, the EU? Beneath the immediate question of 'Why Colombia and the EU?' lie more fundamental questions of value, purpose, and usefulness of comparison as an approach to understand and develop policy and practice in international contexts. Comparison of countries against sets of indicators has become common practice (e.g. in the context of education). Standardised approaches that 'compare' and, in consequence, rank countries in league tables has become the methodology of choice for the Organisation for Economic Co-operation and Development (OECD), and is probably best known through its flagship Programme for International Student Assessment (PISA). However, PISA is only one element of an array of standardised tests, run by the OECD and others, for the purpose of country comparison across all levels of education. At the time of writing (spring 2019), the OECD is conducting a standardised assessment of 5-year-olds, the International Early Learning and Child Well-Being Study (IELS), for the same purpose (www.oecd.org/education/school/international-early-learning-and-child-well-being-study.htm). Taking a similar approach to PISA, IELS has been dubbed *preschool PISA* and has drawn substantial critique from early childhood scholars and professionals (Carr, Mitchell and Rameka, 2016; Moss and Urban, 2017, 2018; Pence, 2017; Peter et al., 2016; Urban, 2017, 2018; Urban and Swadener, 2016). A central argument of the critique is that standardised tests regularly fail to take into account the complexities of the local, cultural and historical context of education, making one-to-one comparison impossible, consequently resulting in meaningless data (Morris, 2016) and discrimination of minorities (Madaus and Clarke, 2001). Robin Alexander (2012) points out the importance of understanding context as a prerequisite for any comparative approach:

> National education systems are embedded in national culture ... [so that] no educational policy or practice can be properly understood except by reference to the web of inherited ideas and values, habits and customs, institutions and world views, that make one country distinct from another.
>
> *(p. 5)*

Writing in the report of *Starting Strong*, the landmark study on early childhood systems, its lead author John Bennett raises fundamental questions that should orient our approach to understanding the specific and different ways countries have arrived at, and are proceeding to develop, their early childhood systems:

> ECEC policy and the quality of services are deeply influenced by underlying assumptions about childhood and education: what does childhood mean in this society? How should young children be reared and educated? What are the purposes of education and care, of early childhood institutions? What are the functions of early childhood staff?
>
> *(Bennett, 2001, p. 63)*

In this chapter, therefore, we cautiously use the term *comparison* between Colombia and Europe as an opening to interrogate one context through the lens of the other. In both locations, we can trace a long history of policies addressing young children, their rights and their education. The 'underlying assumptions' of these policies are specific to their respective contexts and are not transferable. However, in a globalised world, the 'lived experiences' (van Manen, 1990) of young children, their families and communities don't exist in isolation, and neither does the economic and political rationale that has led to a broad global consensus on the importance of early childhood (Guevara and Cardini, in print; Urban, Cardini and Flórez Romero, 2018). Hence, we offer this chapter as a contribution to *learning with and from each other*, in order to better understand our own policy choices, and to explore possible alternatives.

We begin the chapter with a short overview of the early childhood policy context in the European Union, beginning with the first EU recommendation on childcare, published in 1992, to the most recent EU Quality Framework for Early Childhood Education and Care. In this section, we point out the substantial progress that has been made in the EU's attention to services for young children, but also the persistent lack of trans-sectoral and systemic thinking that underpin the policies in relation to children's rights.

We then move to the second and main part of the chapter, which introduces the context of children's rights policies in Colombia, presents current policy approaches, and discusses challenges arising from the diversity and high levels of inequality in the country. The final section addresses possible implications of the Colombian experiences for the current children's rights policy context in the EU, and we conclude the chapter with a call to necessary *new conversations between the Global South and North*.

Early childhood policy context of the European Union

The evolution of early childhood policies at European Union level can be described as a progress from a purely macroeconomic argument to a recognition of children's rights to high-quality education and care from birth. As early as 1992, the Council of Ministers of the European Communities urged the 15 member states of what was then still the European

Economic Community (EEC) to increase their investment in 'childcare' (Council of the European Communities, 1992). Providing a sufficient number of childcare places was seen as a precondition for realising an ambitious agenda of economic growth. In order to achieve the goal, member states were encouraged to 'take and/or progressively encourage initiatives to enable women and men to reconcile their occupational, family and upbringing responsibilities arising from the care of children' (Council of the European Communities, 1992, Article 1).

This initial document was complemented, 10 years later, by an agreement on quantitative targets for childcare provision in EU member states, the so-called *Barcelona Targets* (Plantenga, 2004). A paradigm shift can be traced back to the publication of the first two OECD studies on early childhood systems, *Starting Strong I+II* (Bennett, 2001; OECD, 2006): in this study of 20 countries, the authors made the case for the recognition of the educational role of early childhood services, and introduced *early childhood education and care* (ECEC) as the overarching term for services for young children from birth to compulsory school age. EU policy documents adopted the term from the mid-2000s, and strongly argued the case for integrated ECEC systems in the 2011 document *Early Childhood Education and Care: Providing All Our Children with the Best Start for the World of Tomorrow* (European Commission, 2011). I (author 1) have analysed the dramatically changed self-perception of the EU in the wake of the global (financial) crisis elsewhere in more detail (Urban, 2012, 2015). It resulted, not least, in early childhood education and care being allocated a central role in addressing the fundamental structural problems of the Union. These problems manifest themselves in unsustainable levels of inequality (of opportunity and outcome), poverty and exclusion that threaten the social contract at the core of European society and the viability of the entire project. Just as the Lisbon Strategy employed 'childcare' as a tool for labour market policies, education is now used to address and alleviate the crisis at a macro-political level. The 'need to increase participation in early childhood education and care' is:

> particularly acute in the case of those from a disadvantaged background, who statistically tend to perform significantly less well against each of the benchmarks. Only by addressing the needs of those at risk of social exclusion can the objectives of the Strategic Framework be properly met.
>
> *(Council of the European Union, 2010, p. 3)*

Unfortunately, the underlying understanding of early education appears to be rather narrow, reducing early childhood services to their function as preschool institutions, and focuses almost exclusively on ensuring school readiness and preventing early school leaving (Dumčius et al., 2012).

One of the core components of the paradigm shift in EU early childhood policies was the recognition that the complexity of the task requires new approaches to policymaking, professionalisation and development of services. The 2011 *Communication* was the first document that called for governments to take *systemic approaches* instead of the prevalent isolated and often uncoordinated policies and programmes. The move was supported by research findings that emphasise the role of a *Competent System* that encompasses all actors in the ECEC system, including practitioners, professional preparation and development, research, and governance (Urban et al., 2011, 2012). Based on this work and previous policy documents, the EU Commission established a working group to develop *Principles of a Quality Framework for Early Childhood Education and Care* (Working Group on Early Childhood Education and Care, 2014). This document, too, emphasises a systemic approach to quality, which it specifies under the five dimensions of *accessibility, workforce, curriculum, monitoring and evaluation*, and *governance and funding*.

The conceptual shift from childcare as a commodity for working parents, serving a purely socio-economic agenda, is welcome, as is the recognition of the link between the right to education and the sustainability of the entire European project. However, the *integration* remains within the confines of the early childhood education and care (ECEC) framework. It does not extend to other aspects and policy arenas that affect young children's rights and the conditions in which they grow up in contemporary Europe. It is quite remarkable that the term 'children's rights' is only mentioned once, in relation to the 'effectiveness' of services for children, in the entire European quality framework for ECEC: 'Research shows that policies based on children's rights rather than their needs are more effective' (Working Group on Early Childhood Education and Care, 2014, p. 63). No implications of these 'research findings' are discussed. We read this, as we will discuss later in this chapter, as an indication of a persistent lack of systemic thinking, despite claims to the opposite.

Children's rights in Colombia

The policy context

Considering levels of access to welfare and social protection systems in many European countries, comparing the European Union with a Latin American country such as Colombia appears futile. In our social imaginary (*imaginario*), the abysses of inequality and precariousness that exist in most countries of the region are difficult to find in Europe. There appears to be a consensus that the United Nations Convention on the Rights of the Child (UNCRC) was introduced to Latin America, omitting both the historical context that shaped its content and the socio-economic, political and cultural realities of the contexts for its implementation. In some respect, the Convention was considered as a text without its context (*un texto sin su contexto*) (Durán-Strauch, 2017a; Pilotti, 2001).

In Latin America, more than 70 million children (more than 40 per cent of Latin American children) live in situations of poverty, which, added to the conditions of inequality in which they live, implies the violation of basic rights such as the right to life and hinders the possibility of breaking the cycle of intergenerational transmission of poverty (González-Contro, Mercer and Minujin, 2016), Guillén-Fernández (2016). The foregoing then has to do with the context of application of the Convention on the Rights of the Child in Latin America and the Caribbean, since, over the 30 years that have passed since it was adopted, compliance with the rights established in it has been affected by various factors that have operated as both obstacles and facilitators; for example, public spending (in percentage of GDP) for childhood and adolescence, advances in social protection systems, poverty and economic inequality, and violence as a multidimensional phenomenon, among others (CEPAL and UNICEF, 2018).

However, according to Durán-Strauch (2017a, p. 39), the Convention meant a turning point for the states regarding the ways in which they address their responsibilities towards childhood and adolescence. In the case of Colombia, the Convention was fundamental because it mobilised the revision of the attitudes of Colombian society towards children, for the visibility it gave to childhood, and because it placed early childhood on the country's policy agenda, which helped mobilise civil society around the issue. This mobilisation began with the formation of the Alliance for Colombian Childhood (*Alianza por la Niñez Colombiana*), which comprised diverse organisations and individuals in the international, national and local context that worked in the defence and guarantee of the rights of the children.

Forums across the country focused on early childhood, and commissions and working groups were formed with the goal of developing a national policy for early childhood (CIPI, 2013; Salazar, 2001; Torrado et al., 2017).

As a result of these and other efforts, in 2007, the National Public Policy on Early Childhood '*Colombia por la primera infancia*' was reviewed by the National Council for Social Economic Policy (*Consejo Nacional de Política Económica Social*). The document was the outcome of social mobilisation, joint work between the health, education and welfare sectors. It responded to the commitments made in the Convention (CIPI, 2013; Departamento Nacional de Planeación, 2007). Its declared purpose was to promote the comprehensive development of girls and boys from their gestation until they reach 6 years of age, respond to their needs and specific characteristics, and contribute to the achievement of equity and social inclusion (CIPI, 2013, p. 81). This document is considered as the initial step that led to the construction of the Early Childhood Comprehensive Care Strategy '*De Cero a Siempre*' (CIPI, 2013), and later of the State Policy for the Early Childhood Comprehensive Development (Law 1804 of 2016), approved in 2016.

De Cero a Siempre: a comprehensive early childhood policy

'*De Cero a Siempre*' is evidence of the transformations of social policies in Colombia. According to Durán-Strauch (2017b), these transformations range from the concept of policies settled on segmented and sectorialised actions, to the construction of policies that have adopted a comprehensive concept. This concept stipulates that the full realisation of any one right depends on the realisation of other rights, including integral protection. Then the indivisibility and interdependence of children's rights becomes a premise to promote the provision of integral services that guarantee the realisation of all their rights. This, in turn, leads to the perspective of comprehensive attention and cross-sectoral coordination – key aspects of the policy framework '*De Cero a Siempre*'.

'*De Cero a Siempre*' postulates some foundations described below, trying to maintain the terms and definitions set out in the law (CIPI, 2013, 2014; Law 1804):

1. The 'realisations' (*realizaciones*) are understood as the result of the exercise of rights by every single child, in terms of their conditions and states, and enable the comprehensive development. The policy sets out seven *realizaciones*, and each one shows evidence that children's rights are exercised in the present time (e.g. the child lives and enjoys the highest attainable standard of health).
2. The 'environments' (*entornos*) are the physical, social and cultural spaces in which children find themselves; in which the exercise of rights takes place. The policy highlights the home environment, the health environment, the educational environment, the public space, and others specific to each cultural and ethnic context.
3. In relation to the management of the policy, reference is made to 'comprehensive care' (*atención integral*) as the set of cross-sectoral, intentional, relational and effective actions aimed at guaranteeing rights and comprehensive protection. Such actions must occur at the national and territorial levels. The policy establishes that comprehensive care must be relevant, timely, flexible, differential, continuous and complementary.
4. The 'comprehensive care roadmap' (*Ruta integral de atenciones*) is the instrument that orients the management of comprehensive care at local and regional (territory) level. The function of the *Ruta* is a cross-sectoral management tool that brings together all the actors of the National Family Welfare System SNBF (*Sistema Nacional de Bienestar Familiar*) with presence, competencies and functions in the territories.

Challenges and tensions in the context of diversity

Despite the administrative and legislative measures to meet the rights recognised in the Convention, and efforts to reduce poverty and inequality in the country, a debt is maintained with respect to the effective guarantee of the rights of children under the age of 5, especially those belonging to historically excluded regions and population groups (Torrado, Durán and Casanova, 2016, p. 260). Especially national policies that address early childhood in indigenous communities remain a critical case in Colombia: they show significant advances in their conceptualisation and orientations, but the debate remains with the communities around ensuring early childhood rights and the rights of indigenous peoples.

Guaranteeing the rights of early childhood in Colombia under the premise of a comprehensive and cross-sectorial care policy has implied the recognition, at first instance, of the social and cultural diversity of the country. In Colombia, there are more than 100 native peoples, 65 languages and almost 1.5 million people who consider themselves indigenous, who have their own systems of beliefs and worldviews (Ministerio de Cultura, Instituto Colombiano de Bienestar Familiar, Fundalectura, 2016). At second instance, it has implied the recognition of collective rights for indigenous peoples to live with dignity, to maintain and strengthen their own institutions, cultures and traditions, and to seek their own development, determined freely in accordance with their own needs and interests (United Nations, 2007a).

'*De Cero a Siempre*' encompasses *Lenguas nativas y primera infancia. Derechos y orientaciones culturales para la primera infancia*[1] (Ministerio de Cultura, Instituto Colombiano de Bienestar Familiar, Fundalectura, 2016). It states that the strategy is grounded on fundamental principles: the *development of children*, the *enfoque diferencial*, the vitality of the native languages of Colombia and early childhood, and the *semillas de vida* concept. The *development of children* proposes a universal comprehension of the life of indigenous children, grounded on the premise that every child at the age of 6 or 7 should have reached the linguistic capability to communicate, providing each individual (child) with the basic skills to shape his or her identity within any social group.

The *enfoque diferencial* approach targets ways of discrimination against minority groups in order to provide adequate care and protection based on both public policies and the rights of indigenous peoples. Within '*De Cero a Siempre*', this means recognition of the voice of communities, their systems of beliefs and knowledges, based on the trust in the capacity of communities and families to rear their children in appropriate conditions to participate in a local and global society. According to the *enfoque diferencial* approach, the implementation starts with self-diagnosis processes to identify the real situation of indigenous children in their cultural contexts, followed by the inclusion of different strategies of care and education proposed by the communities.

Vitality of the native languages of Colombia and early childhood has the purpose to identify and revitalise those languages that are under threat of disappearance. Early childhood education has the capacity to foster and encourage processes of linguistic revitalisation based on the communities and families that still preserve native languages, such as *wasóna (pisamira), taiwano o eduría, cabiyarí, cofán, andoque, kamentŝa, bora, ette ettaara (chimila)*, and *sáliba y awá*.

Finally, *semillas de vida* ('seeds of life') refers to children from gestation to the age of 6, according to the worldview of each community. It reflects the relevance of this stage in the life project of the indigenous peoples: children are seen on their way to an individual and collective identity as the future of the peoples.

Developing public policies towards the guarantee of young children's rights in Colombia has initiated a local debate and comprehension of such rights, opening opportunities for finding new meanings and understandings of the adoption of the United Nations Declaration on the Rights of Indigenous Peoples (United Nations, 2007a), of policies, and of the challenge of meaningful dialogue with 87 identified indigenous peoples, who speak 64 Amerindian languages, who live in 710 settlements (*resguardos*) (ACNUR, 2011). Established policymaking processes are challenged by communities that display their own worldviews, people's knowledge, and traditional ways of livelihood. Taken-for-granted conceptualisations of universal child development become questionable, for instance, from the perspective of the Nasa people, an indigenous community that states 'we (indigenous peoples) are seeds (*semillas*) all the time, from birth until we return to the bosom of Mother Earth' (Consejo Regional Indígena del Cauca – CRIC, 2019).

Another example comes from the Kamëntšá people, who do not have a word for early childhood. Instead, they have their own representations for growth. *Ngomamana* means the conception and preparation of the parents for the birth of the child. *Onynama* means the moment of birth to 3 months connecting the boy or girl with the earth through the performance of rituals such as the burial of the placenta in the *Shinÿak* (stove). Childhood, for the Kamëntšá, is related to elements of interconnected knowledges and own skills. The entire community affirms no to have age, according to the voice of one community leader:

> we do not have age, because there are some children who walk at year of age, other children who will walk at two years, I think I walked at two years. My daughter walked at one year and eight months, 'as late' anyone would say, but like that. Then it depends on each child.
>
> *(Camacho Muete, Remicio and Cristina, 2017, p. 81)*

These conceptions show how complex it is to subsume, equate, overlap or juxtapose given and accepted conceptions within other worldviews, or only to recognise one indigenous community's views over others. Even the conceptualisation of *enfoque diferencial* can be problematic in the communities despite the benefits aspired by policymakers. The *Consejo Regional Indígena del Cauca* (CRIC, 2019) deliberates

> we must not state a differential education, a differential health, a differential government, because the differential is not ours, the differential is an aspect of another policy [...] We are today resisting a model of economic exploitation, ideological and cultural disappearance.

Colombia exemplifies the encounter of worlds of identities, communities, peoples and subjects that are not easily defined by opposition, but entwined with other and wider situations that characterise Colombian indigenous early childhood. It is not enough to display the natural contradictions between policymakers and the native communities' beliefs. Colombian early childhood can be defined neither by a universal developmental approach nor localised understandings or a simple combination of terms along the policies around children's rights.

Young indigenous children in Colombia are at the core of a more complex society that deserves deeper comprehension. Indigenous communities are affected by more than 500 years of colonisation, 200 of which have been part of Colombia as an independent republic. Today, communities are affected by the ongoing tension between persistent violence and the construction of peace in Colombia. Indigenous communities are not only facing the questioning of their own ways of care and education of their children. They have become entangled in a general situation of infringement of rights of Colombian children.

Violence and displacement

Guaranteeing the rights of young children in Colombia under the premise of a comprehensive and cross-sectorial care policy implies that Colombian children, and specifically indigenous children, are affected by, and must be understood in the context of, more than 50 years of inner armed conflict. Thousands of families and children have suffered from the presence of legal and illegal armed groups, who have encroached on lands and territories of peasants and indigenous peoples. Most affected by the armed conflict are the indigenous communities, particularly women and children (Centro Nacional de Memoria Histórica, 2013, 2017; Fajardo, n.d.). Experiences of displacement, for instance, overshadow the education and care of indigenous children, with severe consequences (Centro Nacional de Memoria Histórica, 2015):

- Demographic weakness of most of the peoples and the resulting political subordination to the majority culture.
- Abrupt changes in the forms of government and internal representation.
- Alteration of the relationships with peasant and Afro-Colombian communities in the historical context of territorial reordering of common areas, making intercultural consolidation difficult, if not impossible.
- Substantial lack of power of social and territorial control by the indigenous authorities.
- General deterioration of living conditions: malnutrition, nutritional deficiencies, the suspension of own education initiatives.
- Disruption of housing patterns and spatial configuration of the settlements, the persistence of terror and fear, and the abrupt separation from the habitat.
- Increasing external influence on communities' traditional economies, resulting in dependency (food, technology, medicine, etc.), destruction of community resources, and disappearance of sustainable cultural practices of reciprocity and exchange.
- Internal tensions and fractures between displaced peoples or communities and those who remain in the territory.

Children and young people are most affected by these disruptive processes as they are not yet fully inducted to the traditional systems of exchange and their community involvement is still evolving. Cultural resilience and resistance are stronger with the older generation, which leads to intergenerational conflicts and undermines the legitimacy of cultural autonomy.

In short, indigenous children in situations of displacement *live* the separation of their traditional practices, sacred places, their language, and their community. The consequences are individual and collective uprooting, acculturation and the rejection of their own indigenous identity (Centro Nacional de Memoria Histórica, 2015; Gaitán, 2014).

Implications for young children's rights

The reality of the social conditions of the indigenous communities in which Colombian children live, both in their worldviews and in the broad context of armed conflict, has implications for the realisation of children's rights policies in Colombia. Policies have to recognise the multiplicity of (often contradictory) elements that shape the identities of indigenous communities that extend beyond the limits of the geographical and traditional worldviews. Instead of the simplistic overgeneralisation of Colombian childhood and the denial of diverse communities, we argue for an encounter of different and diverse narratives that interact with others. The voice of indigenous communities is one of many voices and perspectives that merge with others. Anzaldúa (1987) argues for the necessity to fade the boundaries between 'us' and 'them', and to strengthen the bridges between different cultures. This offers us an alternative to open new critical conversations among all actors committed to early childhood. Indigenous communities along with Afro-Colombian communities, people with disabilities, urban communities, peasant communities, gender view groups, and migrants contribute knowledges, practices and values around their early childhood rights. This necessarily brings, as Anzaldúa (1987) and Cannella and Viruru (2004) affirm, 'tolerance for ambiguity and reconciling contradictory points of view into a whole' (Anzaldúa, 1987, p. 22). Thus, the ambivalence becomes a position of strength from which Colombia (*la mestiza*) creates new consciousness and new realities.

The situation of children's rights for indigenous peoples sheds light on the process of the adoption of the UNCRC in Colombia, from its initial ratification to the development of public policies, and the recognition of the early childhood as a critical period in human life (Woodhead, 1996) that deserves its own strategies and programmes. The conceptualisation of rights and of public policies for early childhood faces great challenges within the social, cultural, political and economic realities of the communities that inhabit the entire national territory. Policies, although showing great advances in their focus on integrality and institutional cross-sectoriality, are weakest in those territories where the presence of the state is weak.

Durán-Strauch and Torrado-Pacheco (2017) point out the centralist, authoritarian and sectorial tradition in programme and service delivery in Colombia, despite now being framed by the comprehensive perspective of the '*De Cero a Siempre*' policy framework. National policies still tend to homogenise problems and solutions without appropriate consultation and participation of the isolated territories. Indigenous communities also exemplify how human rights or children's rights are not abstract ideals or facts already created, but a permanent reconstruction and reconceptualisation and processes of struggle for the creation of material conditions that allow for the fulfilment of rights (De Sousa, 2002).

Colombia today lives the natural contradictions and tensions of establishing policies for different ways of being, doing and valuing in relation to young children's rights. There is, we believe, a unique opportunity to bring policymaking and implementation together in local dialogue. That, in consequence, necessarily implies reconceptualising human rights as concrete, discursive and situated, rather than abstract and decontextualised, and a mere technical matter (Durán-Strauch, 2017a).

Realising young children's rights through '*De Cero a Siempre*' in Colombia, as a local conceptualisation based on the integrality and cross-sectoriality among institutions at regional and national levels, opens a window of opportunities for finding bridges among the multiple identities, communities, peoples, subjects and worldviews (*cosmovisiones*). It invites continuous reconceptualisation and debate of the fundamentals of early childhood education and care policies and rights. In other words, it opens a pathway to integrality beyond official institutionality, and to institutions grounded in communities. This becomes an opportunity to embrace children's rights as an unfinished and necessarily preliminary project.

Two perspectives on children's rights: policy choices, implications and the need for *new global conversations*

An emerging systemic turn: different concepts of integration

The two perspectives on early childhood policies outlined in the previous sections (EU and Colombia) are both manifestations of a growing international consensus on the importance of robust policy frameworks that address services for young children and their families from a more holistic perspective (Urban et al., 2018). In that sense, they can both be read as contributing to an emerging *systemic turn* – a response to the recognition that early childhood programmes and services do not exist in a vacuum but rather in complex social, cultural, economic and political contexts (Powers and Paulsell, 2018). This has prompted countries and international organisations and bodies, including the EU, to works towards greater *integration* of policies and services for young children. However, the level of integration varies widely, as do the conceptualisations that underpin the policies. The European Union has made substantial efforts to overcome the persistent divide between *childcare* and *early education* at both policy and practice levels, and has now adopted the concept *early childhood education and care* (ECEC) as the overarching integrated concept, and consequently advocates a multidimensional approach to developing services to its member states.

The recent EU Quality Framework for Early Childhood Education and Care recognises five dimensions to *quality*: accessibility, workforce, curriculum, monitoring and evaluation, and governance and funding (Working Group on Early Childhood Education and Care, 2014). However, the question arises whether, in the process of defining *integrated* early childhood services through the lens of childcare and education, the EU has effectively excluded other policy areas that impact young children's lives from the framework (e.g. health and well-being, housing, poverty, inequality, exclusion). Despite these aspects being named in the early childhood policy documents, they are only seen through the frame of reference of integrated early childhood education and care under the auspices of the Directorate General (i.e. Department) for Education and Culture. This is the same Directorate General that deals with school education. No cross-references are made, or measures taken, to coordinate policies concerning young children across other Directorates General of the European Commission (e.g. DG Justice, DG Employment, Social Affairs and Inclusion, DG Health, DG Environment). This might explain why, as mentioned in the section on EU policies at the beginning of this chapter, children's rights feature only marginally in the EU Quality Framework for Early Childhood Education and Care, and only with reference to 'effective' education. It might also explain why the document makes not one single reference to the Charter of Fundamental Rights of the European Union (European Union, 2000), despite the charter explicitly listing children's rights as one of the fundamental principles of the Union (Article 24).

The Colombian case illustrates that other vantage points are possible. Whatever the difficulties, complexities and contradictions in relation to implementation, it is clear that concern about children's rights has been a central driver of Colombian early childhood policies for some time. This has led to a conceptualisation of *integrated services* that is markedly different from the one found in EU discourses. *Atención Integral*, in the context of the Colombian policy framework '*De Cero a Siempre*', refers to an intersectoral approach at all levels of policy and practice, oriented by a common goal to realise young children's rights across five interconnected dimensions: care, health, education, recreation, and citizenship (CIPI, 2013), aiming at furthering social cohesion and equality. At the policy level, this has prompted a radical new approach to high-level coordination in order to overcome departmental silo mentality, while service delivery at the local level is the remit of integrated *child development centres* (Centros de Desarrollo Infantil, CDI) as an emerging first step toward integrated services, where education is one (albeit important) aspect among other elements that support children's rights to development and to fulfilling their full potential.

Policy choices

Our point in this chapter is not to state whether or not one approach might be superior to the other. We are acutely aware of the pitfalls of naive comparison that fails to take into account the complex cultural and historical roots and *embeddedness* (Alexander, 2012; Bennett, 2001) of societies' approaches to early childhood policy and practice. Our argument is that no policy – ever – is self-evident. Policy documents, and in consequence practices, are the result of policy choices that are fundamentally based on values and judgements. The question we want to draw attention to is *whose values* and *whose judgements* are part of the policymaking process, and whose are ignored, deemed irrelevant or persistently silenced in the process.

Integration, we argue, has to gain reality – *historical concreteness*, as Paulo Freire (2004, p. 2) writes – beyond policy strategies, documents and occasional consultation. It has to embrace communities' active participation in the construction of public policies for early childhood.

Conclusion

There is a further conclusion we (the authors) draw from our experiences of working with early childhood policy and practice at various levels and in various global locations. It is that instead of league table-style comparison and ranking, we should systematically engage in meaningful, carefully contextualised *learning with and from each other*, in order to better understand our own policy and practice choices, and the possible alternatives at our disposition. The need for *new global conversations* (Urban, 2019) has become even more urgent as simplistic distinctions between so-called *developing* and so-called *developed* countries are no longer tenable in a globalised world. Children in the Global South and North, including the most affluent regions of the world such as the European Union, are growing up under conditions that some once might have called (arrogantly, we would like to add) *Third World conditions*: hunger and malnutrition, forced migration and displacement, violence, poverty, exclusion and marginalisation. We need to learn with and from initiatives aimed at addressing these crises, regardless of where in the world they are located.

Acknowledgements

We wish to express our gratitude to María Cristina Torrado and Ernesto Durán Strauch, from the Observatory on Childhood at the National University of Colombia, for their reflections and contributions to the development of the section on children's rights in Colombia.

Note

1 *Native Languages and Early Childhood: Cultural Rights and Orientations in Early Childhood.*

References

ACNUR. 2011. *Colombia Situation (Colombia, Costa Rica, Ecuador, Panamá y Venezuela) Indígenas* [pdf]. Accessed January 8 2019 www.acnur.org/fileadmin/Documentos/RefugiadosAmericas/Colombia/Situacion_Colombia_-_Pueblos_indigenas_2011.pdf.

Alexander, Robin John. 2012. Moral Panic, Miracle Cures and Education Policy: What can We Really Learn From International Comparisons? *Scottish Education Review, 44* (1): 4–21.

Anzaldúa, Gloria. 1987. *Borderlands. La Frontera. La Nueva Mestiza.* España: Capitán Swing.

Bennett. 2001. *Starting Strong. Early Childhood Education and Care.* Paris: OECD.

Camacho Muete, Lorena, Remicio, Escobar, and Cristina, Maria. 2017. *Niños y Niñas indígenas. Dos visiones de una realidad (tesis de maestría) [pdf].* Bogotá: Universidad Pedagógica Nacional. Accessed January 8, 2019. https://repository.cinde.org.co/handle/20.500.11907/1777.

Cannella, Gaile and Viruru, Radhika. 2004. *Childhood and Postcolonization, Power, Education, and Contemporary Practice.* New York: RoutledgeFalmer.

Carr, Margaret, Mitchell, Linda, and Rameka, Lesley. 2016. Some Thoughts about the Value of an OECD International Assessment Framework for Early Childhood Services in Aotearoa New Zealand. *Contemporary Issues in Early Childhood, 17* (4): 450–454.

Centro Nacional de Memoria Histórica. 2013. *¡basta Ya! Colombia: Memorias de guerra y dignidad.* Bogotá: CNMH. Accessed January 8, 2019. www.centrodememoriahistorica.gov.co/descargas/informes2013/bastaYa/basta-ya-memorias-guerra-dignidad-new-9-agosto.pdf.

Centro Nacional de Memoria Histórica. 2015. *Una nación desplazada: informe nacional del desplazamiento forzado en Colombia.* Bogotá: CNMH - UARIV. Accessed January 8, 2019. www.centrodememoriahistorica.gov.co/descargas/informes2015/nacion-desplazada/una-nacion-desplazada.pdf.

Centro Nacional de Memoria Histórica. 2017. *Una guerra sin edad. informe nacional de reclutamiento y utilización de niños, niñas y adolescentes en el conflicto armado Colombiano.* Bogotá, DC: CNMH. Accessed January 8, 2019. www.centrodememoriahistorica.gov.co/descargas/informes2018/una_guerra-sin-edad.pdf.

Comisión Económica para América Latina y el Caribe -CEPAL- and Fondo de las Naciones Unidas para la Infancia -UNICEF-. 2018. América Latina y el Caribe a 30 años de la aprobación de la Convención sobre los Derechos del Niño (LC/PUB.2018/21), Santiago. Accessed January 27, 2019. https://reposi torio.cepal.org/bitstream/handle/11362/44271/1/S1800977_es.pdf>.

Comisión Intersectorial para la Atención Integral de la Primera infancia -CIPI-. 2013. *Fundamentos políticos técnicos y de gestión.* Bogotá, DC: CIPI.

Comisión Intersectorial para la Atención Integral de la Primera infancia -CIPI-. 2014. *Estrategia de atención integral a la primera infancia. un modo de concebir, comprender y actuar. Cartilla sobre los fundamentos políticos, técnicos y de gestión.* Bogotá, DC: CIPI.

Consejo Regional Indígena del Cauca –CRIC-. 2019. *Semillas de vida desde los tres componentes del SEIP.* Accessed February 1, 2019. www.cric-colombia.org/portal/semillas-de-vida-desde-los-tres-compo nentes-del-seip/.

Council of the European Communities. 1992. *Council Recommendation of 31 March 1992 on Child Care. (92/241 EEC).* Brussels: Council of the European Communities. http://eur-lex.europa.eu/LexUri Serv/LexUriServ.do?uri=OJ:L:1992:123:0016:0018:EN:PDF.

Council of the European Union. 2010. *Council Conclusions of 11 May 2010 on the Social Dimension of Education and Training.* Brussels: Official Journal of the European Union.

De Sousa, Boaventura. 2002. Hacia una concepción multicultural de los derechos humanos. *El otro derecho,* número 28. Julio de 2002: 59–84. www.uba.ar/archivos_ddhh/image/Sousa%20-%20Concepci%C3%B3n%20multicultural%20de%20DDHH.pdf.

Departamento Nacional de Planeación -DNP-. 2007. *Política Pública Nacional de Primera Infancia "colombia por la Primera Infancia". Documento Conpes Social 109.* Colombia: Ministerio de la Protección Social, Ministerio de Educación Nacional, Instituto Colombiano de Bienestar Familiar. DNP. www.sipi.siteal. iipe.unesco.org/sites/default/files/sipi_normativa/colombia_documento_conpes_social_nro_109_2007. pdf.

Dumčius, Rimantas, Peeters, Jan, Hayes, Nóirín, Van Landeghem, Georges, Siarova, Hanna, Peciukonytė, Laura, Cenerić, Ivana, and Hulpia, Hester. 2012. *Study on the Effective Use of Early Childhood Education and Care in Preventing Early School Leaving. Final Report.* Brussels: European Commission.

Durán-Strauch, Ernesto and Torrado-Pacheco, MariaCristina. eds. 2017. *Políticas de infancia y adolescencia ¿camino a la equidad?* Bogotá, DC: Colección Centro de Estudios Sociales -CES-, Universidad Nacional de Colombia.

Durán-Strauch, Ernesto. 2017a. Derechos del niño y políticas públicas: del dicho al hecho hay un buen trecho. In Ernesto Durán-Strauch and MariaCristina Torrado-Pachecoeds, eds. *Políticas de infancia y adolescencia ¿camino a la equidad?* Bogotá, DC: Colección Centro de Estudios Sociales -CES-, Universidad Nacional de Colombia, 13–49.

Durán-Strauch, Ernesto. 2017b. Integralidad y políticas locales de infancia y adolescencia. In Ernesto Durán-Strauch and Maria Cristina Torrado-Pachecoeds, eds. *Políticas de infancia y adolescencia ¿camino a la equidad?* Bogotá, DC: Colección Centro de Estudios Sociales -CES-, Universidad Nacional de Colombia, 221–252.

European Commission. 2011. *Early Childhood Education and Care: Providing All Our Children with the Best Start for the World of Tomorrow.* Brussels: European Commission, Directorate General for Education and Culture.

European Union. 2000. *Charter of Fundamental Rights of the European Union.* Brussels: Official Journal of the European Communities.

Fajardo, Dario. n.d. *Estudio sobre los orígenes del conflicto social armado, razones de su persistencia y sus efectos más profundos en la sociedad colombiana. Comisión Histórica Del Conflicto Y Sus Víctimas.* Bogotá, DC: Universidad Externado de Colombia. Accessed March 8, 2019. www.altocomisionadoparalapaz.gov.co/mesadeconversaciones/PDF/estudio-sobre-los-origenes-del-conflicto-social-armado-razones-de-su-persistencia-y-sus-efectos-mas-profundos-en-la-sociedad.pdf.

Freire, Paulo. 2004. *Pedagogy of Hope. Reliving Pedagogy of the Opressed.* London: Continuum.

Gaitán, Olga Lucia. 2014. *La Construcción de Sentencias de Justicia y Paz y de la "parapolitica".* Colombia: Centro Internacional de Justicia. Accessed March 9, 2019. www.ictj.org/sites/default/files/ICTJ-Informe-Colombia-Sentencias-JyP-2014.pdf.

González-Contro, Monica, Mercer, Raul and Minujin, Alberto. eds. 2016. *Lo esencial no puede ser invisible a los ojos: pobreza e infancia en américa latina.* México: UNAM, Instituto de investigaciones jurídicas, FLACSO México, CROP, Equidad para la Infancia.

Guevara, Jennifer and Cardini, Alejandra. 2019, in print. El Lugar del Currículum en la Primera Infancia: Aportes de una Mirada Comparada. *Profesorado, Revista de Currículum y Formación del Profesorado, 23* (3).

Guillén-Fernández, Yedith. 2016. Derechos del niño: Un marco para la construcción de políticas sociales y erradicación de la pobreza en América Latina y el Caribe. In Monica González-Contro, Raul Mercer, and Alberto Minujin, eds. *Lo esencial no puede ser invisible a los ojos: pobreza e infancia en américa latina.* México: UNAM, Instituto de investigaciones jurídicas, FLACSO México, CROP, Equidad para la Infancia, 133–158.

Madaus, George F., and Clarke, Marguerite. 2001. The Adverse Impact of High-Stakes Testing on Minority Students: Evidence from One Hundred Years of Test Data. In Gary Orfield and Mindy L. Kornhaber, eds. *Raising Standards or Raising Barriers? Inequality and High-stakes Testing in Public Education.* New York: The Century Foundation Press, 85–106.

Ministerio de Cultura, Instituto Colombiano de Bienestar Familiar, Fundalectura. 2016. *Lenguas nativas y primera infancia. Derechos y orientaciones culturales para la primera infancia.* Bogotá, DC: Ministerio de Cultura - Instituto Colombiano de Bienestar Familiar-Fundalectura.

Morris, Paul. 2016. *Education Policy, Cross-National Tests of Pupil Achievement, and the Pursuit of World-Class Schooling.* London: UCL Institute of Education Press.

Moss, Peter, and Mathias. Urban. 2017. The Organisation for Economic Co-operation and Development's International Early Learning Study: What happened next. *Contemporary Issues in Early Childhood, 18* (2): 250–258. doi:10.1177/1463949117714086.

Moss, Peter, and Urban, Mathias. 2018. The Organisation for Economic Co-operation and Development's International Early Learning Study: What's Going on. *Contemporary Issues in Early Childhood, 20* (2): 207–212. doi:10.1177/1463949118803269.

OECD. 2006. *Starting Strong II. Early Childhood Education and Care.* Paris: OECD.

Pence, Alan. 2017. Baby PISA: Dangers that can Arise when Foundations Shift. *Journal of Childhood Studies, 41* (3): 54–58.

Peter, Moss, Dahlberg, Gunila, Grieshaber, Susan, Mantovani, Susanna, May, Helen, Pence, Alan, and Vandenbroeck, Michel. 2016. The Organisation for Economic Co-operation and Development's International Early Learning Study: Opening for Debate and Contestation. *Contemporary Issues in Early Childhood, 17* (3): 343–351. doi:10.1177/1463949116661126.

Pilotti, Francisco J. 2001. *Globalización y Convención de los Derechos del niño: El contexto del texto.* Santiago de Chile: CEPAL. Accessed January 24, 2019. https://repositorio.cepal.org/bitstream/handle/11362/5998/1/S01040321_es.pdf.

Plantenga, Janneke. 2004. Investing in Childcare. The Barcelona childcare targets and the European social model. Paper presented at the Child Care in a Changing World-Conference, Groningen.

Powers, Shawn, and Paulsell, Diane 2018. *Strengthening Early Learning with a Systems Approach: Diagnostic Strategies with an Application to Over-Age Enrollment.* Paper presented at the Comparative and International Education Society annual conference, Mexico City.

Salazar, Maria Cristina. 2001. El derecho a la supervivencia y a la participación de niños, niñas y jóvenes en la construcción de la democracia In Fondo de las Naciones Unidas para la Infancia – UNICEF-2001. In UNICEF eds. *Memorias Primer encuentro Interuniversitario. Derechos de la niñez y la juventud.* Colombia: Área de Políticas Públicas UNICEF, 104–112.

Torrado, Maria Cristina, Durán, Ernesto, and Casanova, Tatiana. 2016. ¿Perpetúan las políticas de primera infancia las desigualdades históricas entre las niñas y niños colombianos? In Monica González-Contro, Raul Mercer, and Alberto Minujin, eds. *Lo esencial no puede ser invisible a los ojos: pobreza e infancia en américa latina.* México: UNAM, Instituto de investigaciones jurídicas, FLACSO México, CROP, Equidad para la Infancia, 259–280.

Torrado, Maria Cristina, Gaitán, María Consuelo, Bejarano, Diana, and Torrado, Marta. 2017. La política pública para la primera infancia frente a la desigualdad social en Colombia. In Ernesto Durán-Strauch and Maria Cristina Torrado-Pacheco, eds. *Políticas de infancia y adolescencia ¿camino a la equidad?* Bogotá, DC: Colección Centro de Estudios Sociales -CES-, Universidad Nacional de Colombia, 87–116.

United Nations. 2007. *United Nations Declaration of the Rights of Indigenous Peoples.* New York: United Nations, https://www.un.org/development/desa/indigenouspeoples/declaration-on-the-rights-of-indigenous-peoples.html

Urban, Mathias. 2012. Researching Early Childhood Policy and Practice. A Critical Ecology. *European Journal of Education,* 47 (4): 494–507. doi:10.1111/ejed.12012.

Urban, Mathias. 2015. From 'Closing the Gap' to an Ethics of Affirmation. Reconceptualising the Role of Early Childhood Services in Times of Uncertainty. *European Journal of Education, 50* (3): 293–306. doi:10.1111/ejed.12131.

Urban, Mathias. 2017. We Need Meaningful, Systemic Evaluation, Not a Preschool PISA. *Global Education Review, 4* (2): 18–24.

Urban, Mathias. 2018. (D)evaluation of Early Childhood Education and Care? A Critique of the OECD's International Early Learning Study. In Michiel Matthes, Lea Pulkkinen, Luis Manuel Pinto, and Clouder Clouder, eds. *Improving the Quality of Childhood in Europe,* Vol. 8. Brussels: Alliance for Childhood European Network Foundation, 90–99.

Urban, Mathias. 2019. Early Childhood in Troubled Times: Competent Systems and New Global Conversations. Paper presented at the Japan Education Forum for Sustainable Development, Tokyo.

Urban, Mathias, Cardini, Alejandra, and Flórez Romero, Rita. 2018. It Takes More Than a Village. Effective Early Childhood Development, Education and Care Services Require Competent Systems/Los servicios efectivos de desarrollo, educación y cuidado de la primera infancia requieren sistemas competentes. In A. Cardini, ed. *Bridges to the Future of Education: Policy Recommendations for the Digital age/Puentes Al Futuro De La Educación: Recomendaciones De Política Para La Era Digital.* Buenos Aires: Fundacion Santillana, 25–42.

Urban, Mathias, and Swadener, Beth Blue. 2016. Democratic accountability and contextualised systemic evaluation. *A Comment on the OECD Initiative to Launch an International Early Learning Study (IELS). International Critical Childhood Policy Studies, 5* (1): 6–18.

Urban, Mathias, Vandenbroeck, Michel, Van Laere, Katrien, Lazzari, Arianna, and Peeters, Jan. 2011. *Competence Requirements in Early Childhood Education and Care. Final Report.* Brussels: European Commission. Directorate General for Education and Culture.

Urban, Mathias, Vandenbroeck, Michel, Van Laere, Katrien, Lazzari, Arianna, and Peeters, Jan. 2012. Towards Competent Systems in Early Childhood Education and Care. Implications for Policy and Practice. *European Journal of Education, 47* (4): 508–526. doi:10.1111/ejed.12010.

van Manen, Max. 1990. *Researching Lived Experience: Human Science for an Action Sensitive Pedagogy.* Albany, NY: State University of New York Press.

Woodhead, Martin. 1996. *In Search of the Rainbow. Pathways to Quality in Large-Scale Programmes for Young Disadvantaged Children.* The Hague: Bernhard van Leer Foundation.

Working Group on Early Childhood Education and Care. 2014. *Proposal for Principles of a Quality Framework for Early Childhood Education and Care.* Brussels: European Commission. http://ec.europa.eu/education/policy/strategic-framework/archive/documents/ecec-quality-framework_en.pdf.

22

ENABLING CHILDREN'S RIGHTS IN WALES WITH EARLY YEARS PROFESSIONALS

Policy and practice

Nichola Welton, Glenda Tinney and Sioned Saer

Introduction

This chapter will critically discuss and outline the Welsh Government's funded training on the implementation of the United Nations Convention on the Rights of the Child (UNCRC) with early years/childcare practitioners. It will explore how such training has the potential to aid the development of praxis and contribute to debates on the social construction of children's rights. Children's rights provision, it is suggested, could be enhanced through personal development opportunities that include reflection and application in practice. The Welsh Government (WG) is committed to making the principles of the UNCRC a reality for all children and young people in Wales (Welsh Government, 2015a). The Convention was formally adopted by the National Assembly for Wales in 2004. From this point, it became the basis of all policymaking (Welsh Government, 2017) and is summarised in the seven core aims for children and young people (Welsh Government, 2015a). Provision rights and provision of rights are central to these core aims:

1 Have a flying start in life.
2 Have a comprehensive range of education and learning opportunities.
3 Enjoy the best possible health and are free from abuse, victimisation and exploitation.
4 Have access to play, leisure, sporting and cultural activities.
5 Are listened to, treated with respect, and have their race and cultural identity recognised.
6 Have a safe home and a community which supports physical and emotional well-being.
7 Are not disadvantaged by poverty.

(Welsh Government, 2015a, p. 4)

The commitment to promoting children's rights is further embedded in its duty as outlined by the Rights of Children and Young Persons (Wales) Measure 2011: 'Duty to promote knowledge of the Convention the Welsh Ministers must take such steps as are appropriate to promote knowledge and understanding among the public (including children) of the Convention and the Protocols' (p. 4). It is recognised that while governments have made such a commitment, the reality of putting children's rights into practice often lies in the hands of individual practitioners (Nutbrown, 2019). Practitioners are thus central to embedding children's rights; this supports the requirement to provide professional development in early years contexts to enable and support praxis for the effective provision of children's rights.

One of the mechanisms for the WG to meet its duty on the enactment of the Convention and the Protocols is to provide training for key children and young people workforce sectors within Wales. Between 2015 and 2018, the WG funded the University of Wales Trinity Saint David (UWTSD) to deliver training to nine workforce sectors, including early years/childcare, education, social care, health, police, local authorities, youth justice, sport and the media. This chapter will focus on the training that was delivered and evaluated with early years practitioners. The aim of the WG-funded training was 'to enable those who work with children and young people to have the knowledge and understanding required to ensure that the principles of the UNCRC are integrated into their practices' (UWTSD (University of Wales Trinity Saint David), 2019, para. 1).

The objectives of the training were for participants to demonstrate awareness of the UNCRC and children's rights in Wales; understand how their own workforce sector impacts on children's rights; and evaluate their workforce sector's importance in enabling children and young people to access their rights, and subsequently take ownership and integrate the training into own workforce planning. A further aim of the training was to ensure that it was pertinent and relevant to each individual workforce sector; thus, engagement with key stakeholders was undertaken to develop the content for the training resources, including animated videos. The training sessions on the UNCRC were underpinned by a theory of praxis (Ormrod, 2008; Smith, 2011), and thus designed to be participatory and reflective as well as engage a range of resources. It allowed debate and discussion around the principles of the UNCRC and how they can be embedded into practice.

The UNCRC is understood within the training as being socially constructed (Hanson, 2012; Reynaert, Bouverne-de-Bie and Vandevelde, 2009) and that rights need to be contextualised within the contexts in which they are embedded, given it is often practitioners who implement children's rights (CR) (Nutbrown, 2019). It is recognised that there are tensions in relation to the efficiency or 'technicalisation' (Reynaert et al., 2009) agendas of implementing CR; this is central to considering how CR training is designed and delivered. The training was therefore purposefully designed within a pedagogical framework of praxis (Ormrod, 2008; Smith, 2011), which resulted in the adoption of participatory methods of delivery that enabled reflection and application. The participatory methods adopted (Durham University-Centre for Social Justice and Community Action, 2012; Save the Children, 2011a, 2011b; UNICEF, 2014a) produced research and evaluation data on the barriers and opportunities of implementing the UNCRC in practice and the process of reflection and implementation. A significant amount of data was collected in relation to implementing CR, alongside evaluation questionnaires. The chapter outlines provision of children's rights within early years settings within Wales through professional development, which is reinforced within a comprehensive policy framework.

Children's rights policy: Wales

Since devolution in Wales from the Westminster Government in 1999 (Williams, 2013), the new Welsh Assembly Government was given significant powers to create legislation on specific policy areas, including health, education and social services. Children and young people therefore have been a significant focus for creating post-devolution legislation and policy that is distinct to Wales (Butler and Drakeford, 2013; National Assembly Wales, 2000a), and in the context of CR is following a different approach to the UK context (Williams, 2013). As noted by Lewis, Sarwar, Tyrie and Waters (2017), the 'UNCRC has been vigorously taken up in post-devolution policy and law in Wales. The Assembly's stance on children's rights distinguishes Welsh policy from the rest of the UK and children's rights have been described as 'emblematic' of Welsh devolution' (p. 1).

The emblematic nature of Wales's commitment to adopting the UNCRC in its policy and legislation is evidenced from a significant number of unique policy and strategy developments. Wales was the first of the UK home nations (the UK constitutes Wales, England, Scotland and Northern Ireland) to instate a Children's Commissioner, an office subsequently appointed in the other home nations. The Commissioner role is an independent champion who can hold the WG to account (Butler and Drakeford, 2013), and the primary aim of the Commissioner is 'to safeguard and promote the rights and welfare of children' and the 'Commissioner must have regard to the United Nations Convention on the Rights of the Child' (Children's Commissioners for Wales, 2018, p. 1). Furthermore, *Extending Entitlement* (National Assembly for Wales, 2000b), which is a policy document produced in 2000, set out a 'series of rights to support services and opportunities that are as far as possible free at the point of delivery' (Butler and Drakeford, 2013, p. 11). This represented a distinct Welsh model of 'unconditional and universal rights, rooted only in citizenship', and 'an inseparable relationship between welfare and rights, with rights being the guarantor of welfare, and participation the key to good governance' (Butler and Drakeford, 2013, p. 12).

In 2004, the Welsh Assembly passed a resolution formally adopting the UNCRC as the basis of policymaking in relation to 'safeguarding and promoting the rights and welfare of children and young people in Wales, particularly those who are vulnerable' (Butler and Drakeford, 2013). This resulted in the commitment to promoting rights through the Welsh Governments Strategy (2004) Children and Young People: Rights to Action, where the core aims (as discussed earlier) remain the focal point of the current *Programme for Children and Young People* (Welsh Government, 2015a) and are directly linked to the UNCRC. The Rights of Children and Young Persons (Wales) Measure 2011 embeds consideration of the UNCRC and the Optional Protocols into Welsh law and required Welsh Government ministers to have due regard for the UNCRC across all their work (Lyle, 2015; Williams, 2013). This was the first time that any government in the UK had been under a duty to have due regard to CR (Welsh Government, 2014b; Williams, 2013). A Children's Rights Scheme made under section 2 of the measure states that ministers must set out the arrangements they have in place to ensure they comply with their duty to have due regard to the UNCRC. This includes a duty to raise awareness and provide training on CR, which has directly resulted in the funding of the training discussed in this chapter.

The Children's Rights Impact Assessment (CRIA) has also been implemented in Wales, and sets out the process for providing the evidence that CR are being analysed and considered with appropriate rigour in the work of Welsh Government ministers. UNCEF (2017) noted that WG is the leader when it comes to CRIA in the UK. The recent

Wellbeing of Future Generations (Wales) Act 2015 (Welsh Government, 2015b) re-emphasises the central importance of rights to a prosperous and heathy Wales, and highlights the continued significance of rights and well-being across all areas of Welsh life.

Early years policy context in Wales

In the context of early years, there have been several developments in Wales that have dovetailed with the ethos of CR and the UNCRC. *The Learning Country* (National Assembly Wales, 2001) was a significant overhaul of education in Wales and included a refocus of early years education, leading to the development of the Foundation Phase Framework for 3–7-year-olds. The Foundation Phase Framework is a play-oriented, holistic curriculum for young children of 3–7 years emphasising the development of skills and knowledge and building on a child's previous experiences (DCELLS, 2008a; Welsh Government, 2015a). It supports WG's seven core aims for children and young people. As noted by Lewis et al. (2017), the Foundation Phase is often described as a radical departure from formal, traditional methods of teaching young children. The emphasis on independence, reflection and activity, and self-worth and confidence are again consistent with the principles of the UNCRC (DCELLS, 2008a, 2008b, 2008c).

Beyond formal education, the right to play is outlined in the 'local authority duties in respect of play opportunities for children', noted in the Children and Families (Wales) Measure 2010; however, safe areas and equity of access to recreational facilities has been critiqued (Bevan Foundation, 2011), especially in the context of children with disabilities and additional needs.

The Social Services and Well-Being (Wales) Act 2014 outlines changes to the delivery of social services and an emphasis on holistic well-being that will have implications for young children's care, safeguarding and support with additional needs, and is also underpinned by the core aims of children's rights. The UNCRC has been included in the National Minimum Standards for Regulated Childcare for children up to the age of 12 years (Care Inspectorate Wales, 2016) and childcare inspection frameworks (Care Inspectorate Wales, 2018a), as well as being taken account of in the primary school inspectorate frameworks (Estyn, 2018). The UNCRC is therefore informing much of the early years sector and is also a basis for recent health and maternity policy (Welsh Government, 2015a).

In Wales, poverty and inequality have been a driving force in the context of early years policy and make direct links to the principles of the UNCRC: 'All possible means should be employed, including "material assistance and support programmes" for children and families (art. 27.3), in order to assure to young children a basic standard of living consistent with rights' (United Nations Committee on the Rights of the Child, 2005, p. 12). The WG policy framework reflects its commitment to assure young children a basic standard of living through a range of legislation and action plans (Welsh Government, 2011, 2013a, 2014a, 2014b, 2015a, 2015b). However, combating childhood poverty remains a significant challenge (Croke and Williams, 2015) due to the complex and interwoven economic, political, social and environmental causes and implications. For example, Flying Start is the Welsh Government's flagship targeted early years programme for families with children less than 4 years of age in specific areas of the most deprived parts of Wales based on the multiple deprivation index, free school meals, and proportion of under-fours entitled to state benefits (Welsh Government, 2013b). This targeted approach, however, may not meet the needs of all children, and this has been recognised by the Welsh Government: 'Members are mindful that the majority of children living in poverty fall outside defined Flying Start areas' (National Assembly for Wales, 2018, p. 26).

Adverse childhood experiences are a current focus in Wales in terms of the implications for children's long-term well-being (Welsh Government, 2017, p. 3), and Families First is a more recent government development that places an emphasis on early intervention, prevention and providing support for whole families, rather than individuals, and is also underpinned in the principles of the UNCRC. Butler and Drakeford (2013) describe free breakfasts for primary school children as a policy that is linked directly to the general principles of the UNCRC and was developed on the principle of a universal service since 2007 to support health and the implications of food poverty. However, not all schools request to provide a free breakfast, and approximately one-third of children nationally may not receive this service (BBC, 2014).

In March 2019, the Welsh Government proposed a Bill to end physical punishment against children and to remove the defence of 'reasonable punishment' from current legislation linked to assault and battery (Welsh Government, 2019). This new Bill indicates the government's commitment to respecting and protecting CR and the duty to fulfil Article 19 of the UNCRC in relation to protecting children from violence. If the Bill is passed into legislation, children in Wales would be offered the same protection from physical punishment as adults (Welsh Government, 2019).

Participation

The Children's Commissioner, with a view to advocate and support CR and participation, has instituted numerous practical initiatives, including school councils (Welsh Assembly Government, 2009) and other forums where school-aged children are given responsibility for developing school initiatives. Estyn (2014) highlighted that in many schools, school councils had a positive effect on influencing decisions that have an impact on the life and work of children (Estyn, 2014). However, Croke and Williams (2015) suggest that the impact on school procedures and policies or teaching and learning methods is not significant. In terms of early years education, the School Council Processes states that school councils do not require participation of young children under the age of 7 (Lewis et al., 2017).

A small-scale study by Tinney (2013) asked 17 Foundation Phase teachers from different settings about the age of children involved in school democratic fora. The teachers questioned highlighted the age policy for joining school councils or other democratic fora, with eight (50 per cent) indicating representation in Year 2 or above, two (12.5 per cent) in Year 3 or above, three (18.8 per cent) in Year 1 or above, and three (18.8 per cent) from Reception class upwards. Merriman et al. (2014) also noted that of 30 primary schools questioned, 40 per cent did not have representation from 3–6-year-olds on the school Eco Committee, which is part of the Eco Schools programme engagement processes (see www.eco-schools.org.uk/). Pupil participation and action is underpinned by the Welsh Assembly Government (2009) school council guidance. However, to involve younger children in the democratic processes that decide school action may require other mechanisms, alongside school councils, to ensure their participation.

The Children and Families (Wales) Measure 2011 refers to participation of children in local authority decision-making. Previously, the Funky Dragon (the Children and Young People's Assembly for Wales) and the recent establishment of a Youth Parliament in Wales through Cymru Ifanc/Young Wales (2018) have supported older children and young people's democratic participation. However, the inclusion of younger children may require different methods that support the particular communication needs of the early years, such as observation and appropriate participatory approaches (Clark and Moss, 2017) or collaborators with young children advancing citizenship (MacNaughton, Hughes and Smith, 2007).

The Children and Families (Wales) Measure 2010 also promotes the need for children and adults to be aware of the UNCRC. Croke and Crowley (2007) and Lewis et al. (2017) suggest that awareness of rights may be poor, with the Welsh Government (2018) UNCRC compliance report noting significant numbers of children questioned across Wales were not aware of CR or the UNCRC. They also noted in their evaluation of enacting rights in an educational context that 'Most of the evidence was related to children aged over seven years, thus indicating that the experiences of the young child are largely unreported' (Lewis et al., 2017, p. 42). This may suggest a need to support the UNCRC agenda in the context of early years in particular (the focus of later sections in this chapter).

Policy and programmes provide aims and objectives, but their fulfilment and interpretation is more complex and challenging. In the context of policy and rights, Fitzpatrick (2013) asks:

> what is the value of a right if it is never afforded, suggesting that we must give them the tools by which outcomes can be achieved, where those rights become reality in the lived experience of the individuals covered by our laws and institutions and in our ways of life, so that everyone can participate.
>
> *(p. 65)*

The next sections will explore the practical implications of supporting the interpretation and enabling of rights, and 'the opportunity for engagement between governmental and non-governmental actors, civil society and children and young people themselves in the development of an informed and shared understanding of, and commitment to, rights-based approaches to governance' (Williams, 2013, pp. 53–4).

Construction of a training framework

CR can be understood as being socially constructed (Hanson, 2012; Reynaert et al., 2009) and as political constructions, as illustrated in the example of Welsh policy, and compared to policy globally (Quennerstedt, 2011; Sullivan and Jones, 2013). This conceptualisation of CR has, it is argued in this chapter, implications for the provision of CR; thus, it underpins the framework for the design and delivery of the training being discussed. The intentional contextualisation of CR and the pedagogical approach of praxis was thus adopted to enable professional development in early years contexts and provide effective provision of CR, in so doing recognising and embedding the importance of provision of rights in such contexts.

Reynaert et al. (2009) argue in their review of academic literature on CR between 1989–2007 'that children's rights is a social phenomenon, arising from constitutive human action' (Cotterrell, 2005; Stammers, 1995, 1999; Tarulli and Skott-Myhre, 2006, as quoted in Reynaert et al., p. 518). Hanson (2012) suggests that 'A consensus on the extent, priorities or even precise content of children's rights is not readily available: children's rights are a morally sensitive domain having to deal with strong, and often competing, normative and ideological perspectives' (p. 63).

If rights are to be viewed as socially situated, then it would be expected that training and provision of rights should reflect the social context and expect to deal with potentially competing normative and ideological perspectives. The need to develop a contextualised critique and reflection of CR is further discussed by Reynaert et al. (2009), illustrating that CR are presented as the new norm in policy and practice without questioning or problematising this new norm, and thus viewed as a discourse of 'technicalisation':

> The debate on children's rights has become a technical debate on the most effective and efficient way to implement children's rights, how best to monitor this implementation and how this can be organized. This is pre-eminently a positivistic representation of children's rights. The consensus-thinking in children's rights that lies at the heart of this 'technicalization' has 'closed' the debate on children's rights. What the children's rights discourse lacks is critique (Evans, 2005), meaning reflection on the legitimacy and relevance of children's rights as the new norm in dealing with children.
>
> *(Reynaert et al., 2009, p. 528)*

It is argued that linked to the 'technicalisation' of children's rights is a decontextualised discourse that does not take into account the living conditions, the social, economic and historical contexts in which children grow up, which can be very diverse, and which are the environments in which children's rights are to be realised (Reynaert et al., 2009, p. 528).

Both the 'technicalisation' and 'decontextualised' discourse are, it would seem, essential to consider in the design and delivery of children's rights training and provision. In this context, the training is meeting the Welsh Governments duty 'to promote knowledge and understanding amongst the public (including children) of the Convention and the Protocols' (Rights of Children and Young Persons (Wales) Measure, 2011, p. 4). The recent publication *The Right Way* by the Children's Commissioner for Wales (2017), it could be argued, promotes an effective and efficient way of embedding CR. It provides a framework for enabling CR: 'It is about placing the UNCRC at the core of planning and service delivery and integrating children's rights into every aspect of decision-making, policy and practice' (p. 3). The document provides guidance for organisations to make an operational and strategic commitment to embedding CR. Its framework was useful in communicating a rights approach within the training outlined here. However, the need to ensure an understanding of the contextual nature of CR and the role of practitioners in enabling rights needs to be considered further. This is supported by Veerman and Levine (2000, as quoted in Reynaert et al., 2009), who highlight the need to shift the discussion from the 'Geneva scene' to the grassroots level, where CR have to be realised in their actual context, and a call for 'Research that provides empirical evidence on the impact that the rhetoric of children's rights has in daily practice assumes a shift from analysing the text of the UNCRC towards examining the contexts in which the UNCRC is applied' (Reynaert et al., 2009, p. 529).

The recognition of the context in which the UNCRC is applied is, we argue, central to the design of training and provision of CR, particularly if we are to have an informed and shared understanding of rights based approaches (Williams, 2013) and if rights are to become a reality (Fitzpatrick, 2013). This is also evident from the data collected from the training (summarised below) that enabled practitioners to relate and reflect on CR in relation to their own contexts; the role of praxis in enabling reflection on practice is therefore key to such professional development and the provision of rights.

In adopting the view that the UNCRC and CR are socially constructed phenomena, the design and delivery of the training was aimed at developing praxis and contextualised understanding of UNCRC principles in practice. For the design of the training, the definition of praxis adopted is one outlined by Smith (2011):

It is not simply action based on reflection. It is action which embodies certain qualities. These include a commitment to human wellbeing and the search for truth, and respect for others. It is the action of people who are free, who are able to act for themselves. Moreover, *praxis* is always risky. It requires that a person 'makes a wise and prudent practical judgement about how to act in this situation'.

(Carr and Kemmis, 1986, p. 190, as quoted in Smith, 2011, para. 12)

While raising awareness and understanding was an important aim of the training expectations of the Welsh Government, enabling reflection on practitioners' own lived experiences as early years practitioners was essential to meet the objective of increasing an understanding of how the early years 'sector can impact on children's rights' (UWTSD (University of Wales Trinity Saint David), 2019, para. 2). Recognising that to integrate a children's rights approach into daily practice requires that the process 'involves interpretation, understanding and application in one unified process' (Gadamer, 1979, p. 275). As within praxis, Smith (2011) argues, 'there can be no prior knowledge of the right means by which we realize the end in a particular situation. For the end itself is only specified in deliberating about the means appropriate to a particular situation' (Bernstein, 1983, p. 147, quoted in Smith, 2011, para. 11). Application of knowledge and reflection is therefore situational. This aligns with Nutbrown's (2019) arguments that the reality of the provision of rights often lies in the hands of individual practitioner's and is supported by Hanson's (2012) and Reynaert et al.'s (2009) view of rights being socially situated.

CR training often adopts appropriate participatory approaches (e.g. Save the Children, 2011a, 2011b). The adoption of participatory methodologies (Durham University-Centre for Social Justice and Community Action, 2012; UNICEF, 2014a) that reflect participation and allow interpretation, understanding, reflection and application was thus adopted as a framework for the design and delivery of the provision of rights within the training, and thus aiming to promote praxis. Training sessions were therefore designed to be participatory and reflective; it engaged a range of resources, including multimedia, to encourage debate and discussion around the principles of the UNCRC and how they can be embedded into practice to enable children to access their rights, as well as raise awareness of the importance of provision rights in this context. The next section will outline how the training was delivered.

Delivery

Training on CR for the early years sector was based upon sessions of 3.5 hours and delivered across Wales. Training sessions were delivered to a wide range of participants, from organisations such as the Care Inspectorate Wales, Flying Start, Action for Children, and higher education and further education institutions, to individuals across the early years workforce, such as head teachers, schoolteachers, school nurses, playgroup leaders and practitioners, *cylchoedd meithrin* leaders and practitioners (*cylchoedd meithrin* is the name for Welsh medium part-time provision; see Mudiad Meithrin, 2018), day nursery practitioners, managers and owners, childminders, and officers from various childcare teams. It is important to note that the training was also delivered bilingually, with all resources and multimedia supporting materials being available in both English and Welsh. These materials have since been made available on the UWTSD website (www.uwtsd.ac.uk/rights), and all participants were signposted to this site at the end of each training session. Facilitators provided ideas for further use of these resources (e.g. as a training tool for parent evenings, early years professionals/school team meetings and as a refresher resource for all participants).

The training programme was designed to enable flexibility in terms of delivery and opportunities for spontaneous responses and reflection, providing a variety and wealth of discussion based upon the range and experiences of early years professions in attendance. The experience for participants during this training also varied due to the number of participants attending each session. Smaller training sessions (15–20 participants) allowed for longer periods of time for discussion, while training sessions with a higher number of participants (over 40 participants) proved more challenging in ensuring that all participants were given opportunities to contribute and offer their views. Within the feedback provided by participants following the training sessions, many noted their appreciation for the time that was provided for views to be heard and that facilitators took the time to listen. Facilitators identified this as an effective model for good practice enabling this style to link to specific rights, particularly Articles 3 and 12.

Training sessions were delivered by two facilitators. Training began with clear introductions, with the session's objectives being explained carefully before inviting participants to share information regarding their professions, their knowledge and understanding of CR, and their expectations from attending the training. This was followed by the opportunity to view short multimedia clips summarising the history and background to the UNCRC developments in Wales since devolution.

The content of the training session was based upon the importance of participatory activities (Save the Children, 2011a). The first activity, for example, invited participants to work in groups to consider Articles 1–42 of the 54 articles of the Convention. Each participant was provided with a summary of the UNCRC (Welsh Government, 2015c). This activity required participants to work in groups to choose nine rights that they felt were relevant to their day-to-day work and to their roles and responsibilities in relation to their professions. With groups being made up of a range of early years professionals, this became an effective icebreaker and led to powerful debate in terms of placing the final nine chosen rights on a diamond ranking chart. This was followed by an opportunity for each group to provide open feedback on their chosen rights. This activity brought about unexpected responses, with participants across all groups collaborating and sharing their thoughts and experiences. Time for this feedback varied within each training session, with previous personal experiences, individual interpretation and barriers all becoming evident in the mix of feedback and debate being provided. For example, the majority of early years practitioners placed Article 31, 'the right to relax and play', as one of the key rights, while teachers' views focused on Article 28, 'the right to education' and Article 29, 'education should develop each child's personality'. It was through this feedback and open discussion that participants' diverse understanding and interpretation of the specific rights became evident.

Facilitators quickly became aware, through initial evaluation feedback, of the value of allowing this style of open discussion and debate. This activity has since been equally as effective within training sessions for other children and young people workforce sectors within Wales. While very different articles were selected, the activity maintained a direct focus on the importance of CR being central to their roles and responsibilities.

The ranking activity was followed by a video on Article 12, 'children having the right to say what they think should happen when adults are making decisions that affect them and to have their opinions taken into account' (Welsh Government, 2015c). A further group activity called the 'The Voice of the Child – Llais y Plentyn' was presented; groups were asked to consider their own roles and experiences in relation to examples where a child's voice had been heard and when a child's voice had not been respected. Again, the open and very honest feedback that was shared was often overwhelming and created an environment within the training room where participants demonstrated deep respect for one another. Participants shared powerful examples of the challenges of respecting the child's voice, and in particular when parents are not always aware of or fail to recognise their children's rights, highlighting Article 12, 'children having their opinions taken into account', and Article 42, 'the government should make the Convention known to all parents', as obstacles in maintaining Article 3, 'all organisations concerned with children should work towards what is best for each child'. Many of the training sessions raised similar concerns from early years professionals regarding the importance of being able to recognise or identify the voice of the child with very young babies and children who are non-verbal, as well as children with additional needs, with ideas, suggestions and examples of good practice being shared openly across training groups.

A further activity adopted later in the training to illustrate the inequalities within society, and one which visualises those who have a voice and those who do not have a voice, was a 'power walk' (Save the Children, 2011a). In this role-play activity, participants were given specific individual roles that they did not disclose to other participants (e.g. head teacher, policeman aged 35, businesswoman aged 40, 3-year-old girl, 16-year-old homeless boy, 12-year-old girl on a school council, a local councillor, etc). They were asked to stand in a straight line and listen carefully to a series of statements. If they could answer positively, they responded by stepping forward. By the end of the activity, those with more powerful roles had been able to move across the room, while those with roles who were more vulnerable and had less support were left behind. The visual impact of this exercise proved to be a very powerful activity, resulting in wider discussion and reflection, in particular on the roles and responsibilities of participants in enabling and supporting the rights of those without a voice.

Following final multimedia clips on Wales's current position in terms of the most recent legislative changes enshrining CR, together with links to the significant role and responsibilities of the Children's Commissioner for Wales, the final task for participants was to complete personal action plans and pledges where key messages were considered for their future practice. Participants were then invited to complete evaluation sheets. Two specific multimedia clips based upon childcare services and the roles and responsibilities of the early years sector followed these activities. These included further links to government policies and inspectorate bodies such as the Care Inspectorate Wales (2018b), as well as further legislative documents, providing links for participants to be able to research. These led to a final activity, 'bricks in the wall', where participants were provided with cards and asked to discuss reasons why they believed children and young people were stopped from having their rights upheld. Having decided on a set of barriers, participants were asked to write their responses on cards and proceed to build a 'wall of bricks' on an empty wall within the training room. This final activity resulted in a powerful visual impact, demonstrating a set of obstacles where participants listed what they believed to be concerns and barriers to their professional roles in being able to implement a CR approach across the early years sector (see Figure 22.1). Participants, in their groups, were then asked to remove bricks from the wall and, together, to consider possible solutions (see Figure 22.2). The interactive training along with opportunities for collaboration and debate led to professionals from across the early years sector working together to share new ideas for future practice.

Following final multimedia clips on Wales's current position in terms of the most recent legislative changes enshrining CR, together with links to the significant role and responsibilities of the Children's Commissioner for Wales, the final task for participants was to

Figure 22.1 Barriers: themes identified by early years and education practitioners in training sessions

Figure 22.2 Opportunities identified by early years and education practitioners in training sessions

complete personal action plans and pledges where key messages were considered for their future practice. Participants were then invited to complete evaluation sheets.

For the facilitators of this training, the completion of each session resulted in a broader understanding of the diverse range of professions and responsibilities across the early years sector in Wales. In addition to this was an appreciation of the daily challenges faced in current practice, the complex barriers, the depth of knowledge and understanding, and the interpretation of the UNCRC already being implemented across Wales. Final reflections allowed for the identification of powerful examples, highlighting the regard and respect for children's rights and evidence of participants' determination to make a difference to the lives of children in Wales.

Evaluation of training

The training session, as noted in the description of activities, provided a considerable amount of data based on the process of reflection and implementation of CR. End-of-session evaluation questionnaires (summative and formative) were also utilised. In total,

14 sessions to early years practitioners were delivered, with over 250 participants. A post-training evaluation questionnaire was administrated three to six months post-training; however, there was a very small response rate (15 per cent). British Educational Research Association (BERA) (2011), community-based participatory research (Durham University-Centre for Social Justice and Community Action, 2012) and UWTSD ethical guidelines were followed.

Figure 22.1 outlines the themes identified from participants on the barriers they face in implementing CR, and Figure 22.2 outlines the opportunities – how they can overcome these barriers. Both figures illustrate how practitioners considered the implications in relation to their practice, and suggests that both reflection and situational application is evident as a result of the training session.

It is recognised that many of the 'barriers' outlined in Figure 22.1 are structural in nature (e.g. may require government/policy/institutional funding or support). It may not therefore be within the power of the practitioners to address these. However, as Figure 22.2 illustrates, the training also focused on solutions that could be addressed by practitioners themselves, while recognising the role of their institutions and the Welsh Government in taking further action. Discussions thus often focused on the issue of current austerity measures and budget cuts in many front-line services, which raises further questions in relation to the seven core aims (Welsh Government, 2015a) and provision rights. Further research is required to explore the challenges faced by early years practitioners in enabling provision rights. All gaps in provision rights highlighted from the evaluation data were, however, reported on a regular (quarterly and yearly) basis to the division responsible for promoting CR in the Welsh Government. The limits of funding of such projects do not necessarily facilitate further exploration of changes, an issue that requires consideration in any future training.

The structural issues faced by practitioners in relation to their own provision of CR further demonstrate the need to consider the tensions in relation to the efficiency or 'technicalisation' (Reynaert et al., 2009) agendas of implementing CR, and recognising the importance of practitioners contextualising CR. Therefore, the consideration of both may be necessary to effectively embed and enable the provision of rights.

The immediate post-session evaluation data, as outlined in Figure 22.3, demonstrate the majority of practitioners' knowledge and understanding of the UNCRC was raised as a result of the training, and all noted the intention to implement and consider it further in their practice. These data were consistent with the view that the interactive activities and group discussion was valued highly as part of the training, again suggesting that the opportunities for reflection and application to own contexts was viewed as positive and allowed contextualisation of knowledge and understanding. The design and delivery of the training enabled co-construction of knowledge (Ormrod, 2008) for both practitioners and facilitators.

As the post-evaluation data collection had a limited response rate, it is difficult to draw assertions on the impact on children's provision rights, as discussed earlier. The training was aimed at informing practitioners' practice and further in-depth analysis of impact is required. The discussions and reflections captured during and at the end of the training did, however, demonstrate the raised awareness and understanding of the importance of the provision of rights in line with the project's objectives.

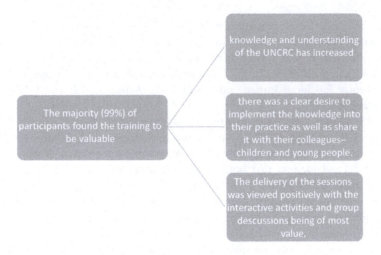

Figure 22.3 Evaluation data

Conclusion

It is evident that children's and young people's policy context in Wales is underpinned by 'unconditional and universal rights' (Butler and Drakeford, 2013, p. 12). The WG commitment to meeting its duty in promoting and provisioning the UNCRC is further demonstrated in the funding of the training outlined in this chapter. However, it has also been recognised that while policy provides aims and objectives, their fulfilment and interpretation is complex and challenging (Fitzpatrick, 2013). Within the context of this training, the UNCRC is understood as being socially constructed (Hanson, 2012; Reynaert et al., 2009); therefore, the provision of the UNCRC training with early years practitioners focused on the contextualisation of CR (Fitzpatrick, 2013; Reynaert et al., 2009), which attempted to challenge to some degree a 'technocentric' model of interpretation and implementation.

Participants engaged in a process of interpretation, understanding, reflection and application, therefore suggesting that the process of praxis was engaged in (Smith, 2011), as suggested by the description of the training and evaluation data. It is hoped that as a result of the training, the embedding of knowledge and understanding will result in a practitioner who 'makes a wise and prudent practical judgement about how to act in *this* situation' (Carr and Kemmis, 1986, p. 190, emphasis in original), and thus apply CR in an appropriate and context-specific way. It is recognised that further follow-up case studies of practice will demonstrate this.

The potential impacts for practice are: first, the need to consider the importance of how CR are recognised and understood in any given context and how that context may influence the interpretation of rights; and second, the importance of the socially constructed knowledge of CR or the development of 'shared understanding' (Williams, 2013) and shared lived experiences (Fitzpatrick, 2013) between practitioners. The co-construction of knowledge was one positive outcome of the training/provision of rights and the process of raising awareness of the importance of the provision of rights in this context.

The call for further research that explores the contexts in which the UNCRC is applied (Veerman and Levine, 2000, quoted in Reynaert et al., 2009) is particularly relevant for the early years sector given that younger children's voices/experiences appear largely unreported

(Lewis et al., 2017; Merriman et al., 2014; Tinney, 2013). A critical analysis of the political context of training (Hanson, 2012) would appear central in relation to examining whether a technocentric or more context-specific model is adopted. The importance of reflection on/in practice when enabling the development of praxis, it is suggested by the authors, is central to encompassing the social and political situatedness of practitioners on the front line of enabling children's rights.

Data availability statement

The data supporting the results and analyses presented in this chapter can be found in the evaluation reports of the research project, available from: www.uwtsd.ac.uk/

Disclosure statement

The project and research data presented in this chapter were funded by the Welsh Government. The chapter does not necessarily reflect the views of the Welsh Government.

References

Clark, Alison, and Peter Moss 2017. *Listening to Young Children: The Mosaic Approach*. 3rd edition London: National Children's Bureau.

Butler, Ian and Mark Drakeford 2013. "Children's Rights as a Policy Framework in Wales." In *The United Nations Convention on the Rights of the Child in Wales*. Edited by Jane Williams, 9–20. Cardiff: University of Wales Press.

BBC (British Broadcasting Corporation). 2014. "Free School Breakfasts 'Must Change', Say Conservatives." BBC News. Accessed August 5 2018. www.bbc.co.uk/news/uk-wales-30234019.

BERA (British Educational Research Association). 2011. *Ethical Guidelines for Educational Research*. London: BERA.

Bevan Foundation. 2011. *Fair Play for Disabled Children and Young People in Wales*. Ebbw Vale: Bevan Foundation.

Children's Commissioner for Wales. 2017. *The Right Way: A Children's Rights Approach in Wales*. Swansea: Children's Commissioner for Wales.

Children's Commissioners for Wales. 2018. "Children's Commissioners for Wales." Accessed July 7 2018. www.childcomwales.org.uk/.

Care Inspectorate Wales (CIW). 2016. *National Minimum Standards for Regulated Childcare for Children up to the Age of 12 Years*. Cardiff: CIW.

Care Inspectorate Wales (CIW). 2018a. *Regulation and Inspection of Social Care (wales) Act 2016 Code of Practice for Inspection*. Cardiff: CIW.

Care Inpectorate Wales (CIW). 2018b. "Online Services." Accessed August 15, 2018. http://careinspectorate.wales/online-services.

Carr, Wilfred and Stephen Kemmis 1986. *Becoming Critical. Education, Knowledge and Action Research*. Lewes: Falmer.

Croke, Rhian and Anne Crowley. 2007. *Stop, Look, Listen: The Road to Realising Children's Rights in Wales*. Cardiff: Save the Children.

Croke, Rhian and Jane Williams 2015. *Wales UNCRC Monitoring Group Report to the United Nations Committee on the Rights of the Child*. Cardiff: Wales UNCRC Monitoring Group.

Cymru Ifanc/Young Wales. 2018. "Cymru Ifanc/Young Wales" Accessed 15 May 2018. www.youngwales.wales/.

Durham University—Centre for Social Justice and Community Action. 2012. *Community-based Participatory Research: A Guide to Ethical Principles and Practice*. Durham: Durham University.

DCELLS. 2008a. *Framework for Children's Learning for 3 to 7-year-olds in Wales*. Cardiff: Welsh Assembly Government.

DCELLS. 2008b. *Learning and Teaching Pedagogy*. Cardiff: Welsh Assembly Government.

DCELLS. 2008c. *Personal and Social Development, Wellbeing and Cultural Diversity*. Cardiff: Welsh Assembly Government.

Estyn. 2014. *ESDGC Progress in Education for Sustainable Development and Global Citizenship*. Cardiff: Estyn.

Estyn. 2018. *Guidance Handbook for the Inspection of Primary Schools from September 2018*. Cardiff: Estyn.

Evans, T. (2005) "International Human Rights Law as Power/Knowledge." *Human Rights Quarterly* 27 (3): 1046–1068.

Fitzpatrick, Kevin. 2013. "What is the Value of a Right if it is Never Afforded?" In *The United Nations Convention on the Rights of the Child in Wales*. Edited by Jane Williams, 65–78. Cardiff: University of Wales Press.

Hanson, Karl. 2012. "Schools of Thought in Children's Right." In *Children's Rights from Below: CrossCultural Perspectices (studies in Childhood and Youth)*. Edited by Manfred Liebe, 63–79. London: Palgrave Macmillan.

Gadamer, Hans-Georg. 1979. *Truth and Method*. London: Sheed and Ward Ltd.

Lewis, Alyson, Sian Sarwar, Jackie Tyrie, and Jane Waters 2017. "Exploring the Extent of Enactment of Young Children's Rights in the Education System in Wales." *Cylchgrawn Addysg Cymru/Wales Journal of Education* 19 (2) November: 27–50.

Lyle, Sue. 2015. "Embedding the UNCRC in Wales (UK): Policy, Pedagogy and Prejudices." *Journal of Educational Studies* 40 (2): 215–232.

MacNaughton, Glenda, Patrick Hughes, and Kylie Smith 2007. "Early Childhood Professionals and Children's Rights: Tensions and Possibilities Around the United Nations General Comment, Number 7 on Children's Rights." *International Journal of Early Years Education* 15 (2): 161–170.

Merriman, Eileen, Rekers-Power Angela, Glenda Tinney, and Anne MacGarry 2014. *An Evaluation of the Eco-Schools Programme in Wales; Final Report June 2014*. Carmarthen: University of Wales Trinity Saint David.

Mudiad Meithrin 2018. "Croeso i Wefan Mudiad Meithrin" Accessed 21 August 2018. www.meithrin.cymru

National Assembly for Wales. 2000a. *Extending Entitlement: Supporting Young People in Wales*. Cardiff: Policy Unit, National Assembly of Wales.

National Assembly for Wales. 2000b. *Children and Young People: A Framework for Partnership*. Cardiff: National Assembly of Wales.

National Assembly for Wales. 2001. *The Learning Country: A Paving Document: A Comprehensive Education and Lifelong Learning Programme to 2010 in Wales*. Cardiff: National Assembly for Wales.

National Assembly for Wales. 2018. *Flying Start Outreach*. Cardiff: National Assembly for Wales.

Nutbrown, C. 2019. "Children's rights, adults' responsibilities." Teach Early Years. Accessed January 2018. www.teachearlyyears.com/a-unique-child/view/childrens-rights-adults-responsibilities

Ormrod, Jeanne Ellis. 2008. *Educational Psychology: Developing Learners*, 6th edition. *Upper Saddle River*, New Jersey: Prentice Hall/Pearson Education Incorprated.

Quennerstedt, Ann. 2011. "The Political Construction of Children's Rights in Education – A Comparative Analysis of Sweden and New Zealand." *Education Inquiry* 2 (3): 453–471.

Reynaert, Didier, Maria Bouverne-de-Bie, and Stijn Vandevelde 2009. "A Review of Children's Rights Literature Since the Adoption of the United Nations Convention on the Rights of the Child." *Childhood* 16 (4): 518–534.

Rights of Children and Young Persons (Wales) Measure. 2011. Accessed March 2019. www.legislation.gov.uk/mwa/2011/2/introduction

Sullivan, Michael, and Helen Mary Jones 2013. "Made to Measure: Cooperation and Conflict in the Making of a Policy." In *The United Nations Convention on the Rights of the Child in Wales*. Edited by Jane Williams, 21–34. Cardiff: University of Wales Press.

Smith, Mark K. 2011. "What is praxis?" Encyclopedia of Informal Education (infed). Accessed June 12 2018 http://infed.org/mobi/what-is-praxis/

Save the Children. 2011a. *Activities from Children's Rights Spice'em Up*. Cardiff: Save the Children.

Save the Children. 2011b. *Bricks in the Wall*. Cardiff: Save the Children.

Tinney, Glenda. 2013. *Perceptions and Understanding of Education for Sustainable Development and Global Citizenship (ESDGC) by Teachers and Teacher Trainees and the Opportunities and Challenges of Integrating ESDGC into Early Childhood Learning within the Foundation Phase*. MA Early Childhood Research Thesis. Carmarthen: UWTSD.

Welsh Assembly Government. 2009. *Sitting on Their Council. Standing up for Their Rights. School Councils in Wales.* Cardiff: Welsh Assembly Government. Accessed 18 2013. http://wales.gov.uk/docs/dcells/publications/090925schoolcouncilbestpracticeguideen.pdf.

Welsh Government. 2004. *Children and Young People: Rights to Action.* Cardiff: Welsh Assembly Government.

Welsh Government. 2007. *Rights in Action. Implementing Children and Young People's Rights in Wales.* Cardiff: Welsh Assembly Government.

Welsh Government. 2010. *Children and Families (Wales) Measure 2010.* Cardiff: Welsh Assembly Government.

Welsh Government. 2011. *Rights of Children and Young Persons (wales) Measure 2011.* Cardiff: Welsh Government.

Welsh Government. 2013a. *Building a Brighter Future: Early Years and Child Care Plan.* Cardiff: Welsh Government.

Welsh Government. 2013b. *National Evaluation of Flying Start: Impact Report. Social Research Paper No.74/2013.* Cardiff: Welsh Government.

Welsh Government. 2014a. *Building Resilient Communities: Taking Forward the Tackling Poverty Action Plan.* Cardiff: Welsh Government.

Welsh Government. 2014b. *Children's Rights Scheme 2014.* Cardiff: Welsh Government.

Welsh Government. 2014c. *Rewriting the Future: Raising Ambition and Attainment in Welsh Schools.* Cardiff: Welsh Government.

Welsh Government. 2014d. *Children's Rights Scheme. Arrangement for Having Due Regard to the United Nations Convention on the Rights of the Child (UNCRC) When Welsh Ministers Exercise Any of Their Functions.* Cardiff: Welsh Government.

Welsh Government. 2015a. *Programme for Children and Young People Comprehensive Version Core Aims 1-7.* Cardiff: Welsh Government.

Welsh Government. 2015b. *The Wellbeing of Future Generations (wales) Act 2015.* Cardiff: Welsh Government.

Welsh Government. 2015c. *A Summary of the United Nations Convention on the Rights of the Child.* Cardiff: Welsh Government.

Welsh Government. 2015d. *Report on the Compliance with the Duty under Section 1 of the Rights of Children and Young Persons (wales) Measure 2011.* Cardiff: Welsh Government.

Welsh Government. 2017. *Families First Programme Guidance.* Cardiff: Welsh Government.

Welsh Government. 2018. *Report on the Compliance with the Duty under Section 1 of the Rights of Children and Young Persons (wales) Measure 2011.* Cardiff: Welsh Government.

Welsh Government. 2019. "Children (Abolition of Defence of Reasonable Punishment) (Wales) Bill." Accessed March 30, 2019. https://gov.wales/children-abolition-defence-reasonable-punishment-wales-bill

Williams, Jane. 2013. "The Rights of Children and Young People's Measure 2011 in the Context of the International Obligations of the UK." In *The United Nations Convention on the Rights of the Child in Wales.* Edited by Jane Williams, 49–62. Cardiff: University of Wales Press.

UNICEF. 2014a. *Methodological Brief No.10: Overview: Data Collection and Analysis Methods in Impact Evaluation.* Italy: UNICEF Office of Research.

UNICEF. 2014b. "Convention on the Rights of the Child: Advancing Children's Rights." Accessed January 6, 2019. www.unicef.org/crc/index_protocols.html

United Nations Committee on the Rights of the Child. 2005. Report of the Committee on the Rights of the Child General Assembly Official Records Fifty-fifth Session Supplement No. 41 (A/55/41). Accessed August 5 2018. www.un.org/documents/ga/docs/55/a5541.pdf

UNICEF. 2017. "Briefing Strengthening Children's Assessment in Wales." Accessed August 5 2018. https://downloads.unicef.org.uk/wp-content/uploads/2017/09/Unicef-UK-Briefing_Child-Rights-Impact-Assessment_Wales_September-2017.pdf?_ga=2.244757509.1076388301.1535801115-437609297.1535382526

UWTSD (University of Wales Trinity Saint David). 2019. "Training Overview" Accessed August 5 2018 www.uwtsd.ac.uk/uncrc/training-overview/

Veerman, P. and H. Levine. 2000. "Implementing Children's Rights on a Local Level: Narrowing the Gap between Geneva and the Grassroots." *International Journal of Children's Rights* 8 (4): 373–384.

23

BEYOND RECOGNITION

Persistent neglect of young Traveller children's rights in Ireland

Colette Murray

Introduction

With the unequivocal recognition of a distinct culture and identity, we can better anticipate and respond to the needs of the Traveller community living in Ireland.
(Irish Human Rights and Equality Commission, 2017)

When Traveller children are born in Ireland, they face considerable challenges to have their rights upheld and to reach their full potential. In the case of Travellers, the added layers of racism and discrimination at institutional and individual levels inhibit and complicate policy implementation, budget allocation and robust actions to address exclusion. This chapter focuses on Traveller children's access to provision rights. I begin with four examples of Traveller children's realities. In 2018, a young Traveller mother and six of her children aged from 1 to 11 years sleep in a Dublin Garda (police) station because she is homeless and there is no suitable emergency accommodation (*Irish Times*, 10 August 2018). The consequences of poor and inadequate accommodation have consistently led to health inequalities, documented by the national *All Ireland Traveller Health Study* (Kelleher, 2010), which found that Traveller infant mortality is 3.6 times higher than the general population. A European research report, *Speak Up* (Eurochild, 2012), found that Traveller children demonstrated considerable understanding of their provision rights. However, they 'did not feel that they could do anything to change their situation at local or at political level and that they see the same powerlessness from their parents' (Eurochild, 2012, p. 45). The principles of the National Early Childhood Curriculum Framework *Aistear* (National Council for Curriculum and Assessment, 2009) includes an equality and diversity principle that states 'support me to feel equal to everyone else and do not let me be excluded because of my ethnicity' (p. 8). While delivering diversity, equality and inclusion training (National Preschool Education Initiative for Children from Minority Groups 2011–2013), early childhood educators related a story about a 3-year-old Traveller child attending their service who was the only child not invited to a birthday party. Heart-wrenching for me personally and equally for the educators, they suggested that there should be a mandatory focus on social justice and children's rights in early childhood pre- and in-service training, which explicitly addresses and fractures entrenched bias against Travellers.

Three decades after the ratification of the United Nations Convention on the Rights of the Child (UNCRC) in Ireland, and after numerous European and national reports and recommendations, Traveller children's rights continue to be routinely neglected and violated. This chapter explores, from a children's rights perspective, whether and how Traveller children's provision rights have progressed in Ireland. Drawing on specific articles of the UNCRC as guiding principles, I explore the current policy discourse regarding Traveller children. I focus on UNCRC Article 27: *adequate standard of living and specifically accommodation*; UN General Comment No. 7: *implementing child rights in early education*; UNCRC Articles 28 and 29: *education*; and UNCRC Articles 6 and 24: *health*. I include UNCRC Articles 2 and 30, which address institutional and structural discrimination, because of their significance to the provision rights for Travellers.

This chapter begins with an outline of who Travellers are and then provides an analysis of the historical context for Travellers. Second, it offers a brief glimpse at Traveller children's lives followed by an examination of the policy context considering new strategies, including the National Traveller and Roma Inclusion Strategy (NTRIS) (DJE, 2017) and the recently published *First 5: A Whole-of-Government Strategy for Babies, Young Children and their Families 2019–2028* (DCYA, 2018). Finally, the chapter deconstructs how provision articles for Traveller children are or are not being implemented and supported in the Irish context. I underpin my argument with the voices of Traveller Elders. While areas of concern for the Roma community are similar and significant, they require a separate focus; hence, Roma issues are not examined here.

Who are the Travellers?

Irish Travellers are a small indigenous ethnic group (30,000) with a nomadic tradition whose presence in Irish society was first officially recorded in the twelfth century. Sixty per cent of Travellers are under age 25, compared with 33.4 per cent of the general population (Central Statistics Office (CSO), 2016). Recent genome research has shown that biologically, Travellers have been a separate population to the general Irish population for at least 1,000 years (Kenny, 2011). There are large communities of Travellers in England, the US and Australia. It is well documented that Travellers experience high levels of marginalisation, oppression, racism and disrespect (Hammarberg, 2012; McGinnity et al., 2017; Murray, 2012, 2013): 'Travellers inhabit two worlds, the hostile settled world and their own Traveller world' (Kenny and Binchy, 2009, p. 123). The community has a long-shared history with common cultural characteristics and traditions evident in the organisation of family, values, language, and social and economic life (Murray, 2002, 2012). The extended family is the embodiment of community for Travellers, and not a specific geographical location:

> The extended family would be very important. I always had my Grannie or my Aunts and they were there. Where I'm living myself now I have nearly all my family around me. I would be seen as very important.
>
> *(Traveller Elder, cited in Murray, 2017)*

In the past decade, the Traveller nomadic lifestyle has been constrained through Irish legislation – the Housing (Miscellaneous Provisions) Act 2002 (the Trespass Law). This law (discussed under 'Traveller accommodation' later in the chapter), since its enactment, has had major implications for Traveller lifestyle and well-being.

Historical context

Since the 1980s, a central premise of Traveller advocacy organisations has been to recognise the Traveller community in Ireland as a minority ethnic group experiencing discrimination and racism. As a 'white' and 'Irish' minority, this construct has been continually contested at state level and in Irish society generally. Historically, the dominant discourse situated Travellers as a subculture of poverty with a negative 'way of life' such as nomadism, living in trailers (caravans) and the Traveller economy or occupations (Helleiner, 2000; Mac Gréil, 2010). The anti-Traveller discourse dismissed this way of life and maintained a narrative of the inferior 'other' rather than acknowledging or addressing systemic marginalisation, discrimination and racism by the state (EU FRA, 2010; Helleiner, 2000; McGinnity et al., 2017). Following years of lobbying, Travellers were formally recognised as a minority ethnic group on 1 March 2017. Pressure from the European Union and the Irish Human Rights and Equality Commission contributed to this historic recognition (Irish Human Rights and Equality Commission, 2016).

Acknowledged as a major step for Travellers and Traveller representative organisations, recognition came in name only with a proviso that Traveller ethnicity would 'create no new individual, constitution or financial rights' (Kenny. Dáil Éireann (Irish Parliament), 1 March 2017). This means that Travellers have no legal right to resources to address Traveller-specific issues as an ethnic group. While exciting for some, the cycle of years of disappointment leaves many Travellers sceptical, as Missy Collins acknowledges:

> Earlier this year we were recognised as an ethnic group. People always say what will it do for us Missy. For me, I said, it gave me respect within my heart that they did recognise us as an ethnic group.
>
> *(Traveller Elder, cited in Murray, 2017)*

The policy patterns for the past 40 years have focused on forced assimilation, prioritising mainstream settlement and education (Commission on Itinerancy, 1963; Report of the Traveller People Review Body, 1983). The foundations of assimilation have been built on the non-recognition of Traveller ethnicity and a 'way of life' deemed inferior. Constructing the Traveller child as 'at risk' and in need of 'saving' also reinforces the 'othering' process and undermines Traveller culture and ways of being. The discourse of 'risk' and 'social deprivation' is continually repeated. In 1984, the Minister for Education stated that Traveller children 'are similar in any respect to other educationally retarded children … aggravated by their social disabilities and other consequences of their unsettled way of life' (Dáil. Faulkener, 24 May 1984, cited in Helleiner, 2000, p. 204). In 2005, the Department of Education and Science (DES) placed blame on parental neglect and 'the negative attitude of some Traveller parents, who have low expectations of schools and of their own children's ability to benefit from the education system' (DES, 2005, cited in Kilkelly, 2017, p. 29). Traveller parents are regularly framed as 'lacking in care' for neglecting their children (Helleiner, 2000), keeping their children in inadequate living conditions and depriving them of education (Oireachtas Report, 2011). This reflects a neoliberal discourse where one's condition in life is seen as the responsibility of the individual, where the social narrative implies that if you work hard enough and exercise your free choice, you will profit in life (Campbell et al., 2017; Moss et al., 2017). Neoliberalism, a policy model based on the free market that positions citizens as consumers, fuels structural, institutional and economic inequality in society. As such, it constrains and inhibits many from achieving or even imagining opportunities beyond their immediate experience and circumstances. The state, in this paradigm, tends not to take responsibility for structural inequality (e.g. poverty).

Traveller children

Each Traveller child should be viewed within the context of their world. If we are to profile the many factors that affect Traveller children in the political, sociocultural and economic spheres, it is necessary to consider the child from inside their own cultural context and the impact of the 'dominant' hegemonic neoliberal discourse on their lives (Giroux, 2003; Murray, 2002). While Traveller children's ethnic status has now been recognised, the restricted range of opportunities available to Travellers remains. In 2002, I highlighted the need for data on Traveller children, stating what is 'particularly obvious is the almost total lack of information about Traveller children' (Murray, 2002, p. 45). This is congruent with the concluding observation for Ireland from the UNCRC committee, which states, 'the committee is concerned at the lack of disaggregated data on Traveller ... children, including their socio-economic situation' (UNCRC, 2016, p. 4).

Traveller children's rights are not indistinguishable from their families' rights because they live with the consequences of their community being deprived of human rights. However, rights are 'key resources for those who lack power' and have no voice or choice (Swadener et al., 2013, p. 6). As a minority within a minority (Murray, 2012), Traveller children are especially vulnerable to the changing policy contexts for their community generally and specifically. The lack of recognition of their cultural practices, lack of data, and the persistent and endemic ignorance about how stereotyping, prejudice, discrimination and racism have contributed to the marginalisation and oppression of Travellers has been a stumbling block in understanding Traveller children and their life experience. It has also contributed to the persistent lack of development and delivery of appropriate services for Traveller children (Baker et al., 2004; Mac Gréil, 2011; Murray, 2013).

Policy analysis

Following the ratification of the UNCRC in 1992, government policy in relation to children became situated within a rights discourse. The six-year strategy Better Outcomes, Brighter Futures (BOBF) (DCYA, 2014), the Irish national policy framework for children and young people 2014–2020, acknowledges that there are obstacles and challenges facing Travellers. The BOBF strategy commits to implementing and monitoring the original National Traveller Roma Integration Strategy (NTRIS) (DJE, 2011), with a specific focus on accommodation, reduction of discrimination, inequality in health, to reinvigorate efforts to improve educational outcomes, and to strengthen inclusion for Travellers (DCYA, 2014). More recently, the NTRIS (DJE, 2011) was extensively amended, and, following consultation with Traveller organisations, the National Traveller and Roma Inclusion Strategy (DJE, 2017) was relaunched. The NTRIS 2011 was never implemented despite the government's commitment. The NTRIS 2017 (DJE, 2017) was welcomed and is considered a positive starting point to address Traveller discrimination comprehensively. However, two years into the strategy, no implementation, targeted monitoring or budget plan has been put forward (Pavee Point, 2018).

Dr Sindy Joyce, a human rights activist, sociologist and the first Traveller in Ireland to obtain a doctorate, expressed the frustration of the community:

Today is the 2nd anniversary of the symbolic recognition of our ethnicity, in those 2 years nothing has changed for my people, things have (*sic*) actually gotten worse. Now we need legal recognition asap.

(Dr Sindy Joyce, Twitter, 1 March 2019)

In a recent Dáil debate (5 July 2018) Minister Stanton, who is responsible for the implementation of the NTRIS, stated that 'to date, work has begun on approximately 130 of the 149 actions included in the Strategy'. While some key areas have been initiated (not implemented), the Civil Society Monitoring Report on the Implementation of the National Roma Integration Strategy 11 (Pavee Point, 2018) states that there was little evidence of progress:

> Across the four domains of employment, education, accommodation, and health, the situation and experience of Travellers and Roma has not seen any tangible improvement and the inequality gap between Travellers and Roma, and the majority population remains entrenched.
>
> *(p. 7)*

For decades, no real effort has been made toward implementing appropriate interventions; broken promises and significant dragging of feet has led to unacceptably slow progress for Traveller children. The historically dominant discourse of cultural assimilation, where the aim is to eliminate difference, cannot be denied when we look at the ongoing lack of implementation of these critical actions (Mac Gréil, 2011; Murray and Urban, 2012). When you consider the passage of a child's life, choosing to do little or nothing over consecutive years amounts to serious neglect of Traveller children's right to a supported childhood under harsh and inadequate conditions.

First 5 states that it is 'a strategy that places children at the centre' (DCYA, 2018, p. 57). As a whole-of-government strategy, NTRIS 2017 is referenced in First 5 to provide a fuller picture of the broader commitments to Travellers. While First 5 is underpinned by rights principles, the challenge remains: How will young Traveller children's rights be comprehensively and holistically met within the strategy. First 5 promotes 'progressive universalism' as a mechanism to ensure all children benefit (DCYA, 2018, p. 27). It acknowledges that not all children have the same needs and need extra supports. 'Some children have additional needs and are at risk of disadvantage, due to individual circumstance or because they … belong to marginalised groups' (DCYA, 2018, p. 26), such as Travellers. The 'progressive universalism' approach in the early childhood care and education (ECCE) (free preschool) two-year scheme appears to be based on an assumption that it will meet Traveller children's needs and rights. Traveller children's identity development and sense of belonging is as important as having their learning needs supported. The discourse of needs over rights has been used in education to support individual children's learning needs in primary school rather than the historic practice of placing all Traveller children in segregated classes or taking them out of class for special supports. This practice of supporting individual needs is welcome. However, a rights focus would rather acknowledge Traveller children's collective rights to recognition, respect and non-discrimination. As Freeman (2000) states:

> The value of a rights-based, as opposed to a needs-or welfare-based approach, lies not just in its universality or legitimacy, but also in the inherent 'oral coinage' of rights, which allows rights holders to make claims for treatment that are not dependent on the good will or charity [or misguided policies] of those who can provide that help.
>
> *(cited in Swadener et al., 2013, p. 3)*

Acknowledging, respecting and proactively working with Traveller children's sense of iden-tity and belonging is key to meeting children's individual and collective rights in universal service provision. We know anecdotally and from research (DCYA, 2016d) that Traveller children experience discrimination in service provision, including primary, secondary school and ECEC services:

> Brigid Nevin [Traveller] Primary Health Care coordinator of TravAct in Coolock said that bullying in schools had become a serious issue and a tailored advice ser-vice needed to be made available to Travellers.
>
> *(The Journal, 25 July 2013)*

The national longitudinal study on children in Ireland titled *Growing Up in Ireland* (GUI) (Economic and Social Research Institute (ESRI), 2008) has been tracking the development of two nationally representative cohorts of children (BOBF, 2014, p. 125). A cohort of Traveller families is included in the study; however, the central statistics office (CSO) has approved the data in such a way as to avoid disclosure. The Traveller numbers in the study are too small to allow for disaggregated data. This is a recurring theme (Watson et al., 2017), yet there is no recommendation in BOBF (DCYA, 2014), NTRIS (DJE, 2018) or First 5 (DCYA, 2018) for a dedicated research study on Travel-ler children. The lack of baseline data for Traveller children and the development of any impact indicators across policy is a concern and raises questions about the govern-ment's commitment to develop service provision based on research evidence. The NTRIS acknowledges that disaggregated data and indicators allow for improved evi-dence-based policymaking, implementation and monitoring, and in delivery of services (DJE, 2018, p. 132). First 5 also affirms the state's responsibility to vindicate the rights of the child through policy and legislation. The state is monitored by the UNCRC committee, which provides guidance on the necessity to monitor and systematically col-lect data on the availability and accessibility of quality services for young children (DCYA, 2018).

The revised NTRIS (DJE, 2017) and First 5 (DCYA, 2018) have the potential to make a difference for Traveller children. These strategies have cross-referenced actions for Travel-ler children to enhance deliverability of services. The UNCRC (2016) and Pavee Point (2018) clearly stated their concerns about the pronounced reductions in budget allocations for Traveller children. The UN Committee also expressed its deep concern about 'structural discrimination against Traveller ... children in Ireland, including their access to education, health and an adequate standard of living' (Children's Rights Alliance (CRA), 2019). The Committee on the Elimination of all Forms of Racial Discrimination (CERD) similarly expressed its regret that 'efforts made to improve the welfare of Travellers have not substan-tially improved their situation' (CERD, 2011).

Who is responsible for ensuring implementation?

> Travellers and Roma are among the most disadvantaged and marginalised people in Ireland. During the years of the financial crisis from which Ireland is emerging, those at the margins of our society frequently – and regrettably – suffered dispro-portionately from the effects of financial adjustments. Now that Ireland's economy is back on a firmer footing, it is a moral and societal imperative that we work together to address the real needs of these communities.
>
> *(Mr David Stanton TD, cited in DJE, 2017, p. 3)*

The CRA publishes an annual Report Card that looks at the progress government has made in living up to its promise to children's rights. It uses a grading system (A–F) to assess what has been done. The grade for Traveller and Roma children's rights over the past nine years was a consistent E. In 2018, a grade D+ was awarded, and was based on the official recognition of Travellers as an ethnic minority. The disconnect and lack of accountability between policy commitments and implementation of concrete actions for Traveller children's rights is deeply shocking. The neglect of Traveller children's rights in the persistent context of discrimination is most manifest in the areas of accommodation, housing, health and education.

Traveller accommodation: an ongoing crisis

Right to a standard of living, UNCRC Article 27

States Parties recognise the right of every child to a standard of living adequate for the child's physical, mental, spiritual, moral and social development. Traveller accommodation is in an ongoing crisis, as reported in the *Irish Independent*:

> Ten people from two families, including a mother, father and a five-month-old baby, have been killed in a fire. Five children under 10 are believed to be among the dead after the blaze broke out at a halting site [official or unofficial space to park caravans] for Travellers in Carrickmines, South Dublin.
>
> *(Irish Independent, 6 April 2015)*

Accommodation is central to a child's right to an appropriate standard of living. For decades, Traveller children have lived in conditions that go against international human and children's rights (CERD, 2011; UNCRC, 2016) despite robust policy frameworks, as Dr Sindy Joyce makes clear:

> Year on year we hear the same thing 'accommodation budget unspent', targets never reached, and yet still today my community are living in the same horrendous condition.
>
> *(Dr Sindy Joyce, Twitter, 14 February 2019)*

Local authorities in Ireland have a statutory responsibility to develop and provide accommodation based on the Traveller Accommodation Programme 2014–2018 (Department of Housing). Many have failed to spend their allocated budgets to provide culturally appropriate accommodation. The CRA concurs, in their Report Card 2019, that there are 'serious concerns regarding the continued underspend of local authorities on Traveller specific accommodation' (CRA, 2019, p. 120).

Traveller children have the right to be supported in their lived context in keeping with UNCRC Article 27, to be with their extended family in culturally appropriate and safe accommodation, and to experience nomadism (if chosen) as part of their cultural life. Nomadism is currently denied to Travellers due to draconian legislation. The Housing (Miscellaneous Provisions) Act 2002 criminalises nomadism and has forced Travellers to live in overcrowded and unsafe Traveller-specific accommodation on halting sites or forced many families into mainstream housing, including apartments. Most Traveller children born in the last 15 years have never had the experience of nomadism. They are losing an important element of their Traveller identity. The UNCRC (2016) has expressed concern about the 'criminalisation of nomadism, pursuant to the Housing

(Miscellaneous Provisions) Act 2002 combined with the inadequate provision of transient halting sites, resulting in forced evictions and the suppression of nomadism as a cultural practice' (p. 16). Consequently, Travellers are travelling less; they are constrained by the law resultant in less places to stop and park up (Community Foundation in Ireland (CFI), 2017; Pavee Point, 2018).

> To put a family into the settled community [non-Traveller community], they don't want to be there, or into apartments, because they have children and there's no freedom for the children is one and the other part … on a halting site or housing scheme … the older generation of Travellers keeps an eye to the children.
>
> *(Traveller Elder, cited in Murray, 2017)*

Despite the state's commitment to NTRIS (DJE, 2011, 2017), the allocated budget for Traveller accommodation was reduced in 2014–2018. This is at a time when Ireland is in the grip of a homelessness crisis. Travellers are especially vulnerable to homelessness because of societal discrimination and Traveller exclusion, as Tessa Collins (2019) stated at the 7th International Roma Women's Conference 2019:

> the overcrowding and poor and dangerous accommodation conditions of Travellers puts them at risk in terms of health and other issues – and is used as basis of evictions by local authorities. Sanctions on local authorities must also be put in place when they fail to spend Traveller accommodation budgets allocated to them.

First 5 (DCYA, 2018) states that it will 'make specific recommendations on access to appropriate accommodation for Traveller families with babies and young children with regard to the NTRIS Expert Working Group' (p. 130). It will be important to monitor the work of First 5 and DCYA in relation to this action, being cognisant of the upcoming UN Committees Concluding Observation 2020 report. Poor and inadequate accommodation has a knock-on effect on all provision rights for Traveller children. The accumulated stress from the uncertainty of Traveller accommodation manifests in poor health and has consequences for Traveller children's life chances.

Traveller health: a characteristic of disadvantage and discrimination

Right to healthcare, UNCRC Articles 6 and 24

> State Parties recognize the right of the child to the enjoyment of the highest attainable standard of health … and … States Parties shall strive to ensure that no child is deprived of his or her right of access to such health care services.
>
> *(Children's Rights Alliance, 2013)*

When asked about their rights, 'the Irish Traveller children found that the right to health care was a top priority for them "it just seems like a very important one"' (Eurochild, 2012, p. 35). Their insight matches the UNCRC concluding observations for Ireland 2016, where they state their deep concern 'about the state of health of … children in poverty, as well as Traveller children being significantly lower than the national average' (p. 11). In the *Social Portrait of Travellers in Ireland* report, Watson et al. (2017) found that the health gap in childhood between Travellers and non-Travellers was relatively small (p. 61), while *Our Geels: All Ireland Traveller Health Study* found infant mortality rates high compared to non-Traveller (Kelleher, 2010, p. 87). However, the health gap for Travellers increases significantly after the age of 35, signifying cumulative disadvantage as the life course progresses (Watson et al., 2017). A behaviour and attitudes survey conducted with Travellers in 2017 by the Community Foundation for Ireland (CFI) suggests that many Travellers feel that their situation has declined in the past five years (p. 14). The suicide rate of Traveller males is 6.6 times higher than the non-Traveller community, accounting for 11 per cent of Traveller deaths (Kelleher, 2010; Watson et al., 2017). Sixty-seven per cent of the CIF survey respondents had been affected by suicide either in their immediate or wider family. The depression, grief and chaos following suicide can have a crushing effect on some children's lives. Much can be attributed to the accommodation crisis, isolation of families, lack of employment, damaging influences of alcohol and drugs in the community, and exclusion and discrimination (DJE, 2017; Watson et al., 2017):

> To me, the houses and moving into other (settled) communities for Travellers is after putting so much on their mental health. So, you have this house and you've it all done up but they're not happy, they're still hungry for something.
>
> *(Traveller Elder, cited in Murray, 2017)*

For some Travellers, relief comes with the opportunity to return to living with extended family on a halting site:

> Fifteen years spent in a house, she could be a week and didn't even see one of your own. It left me sick, it made me sick, she says. But I'm here now [on a site] and it's not much, but the fire is lighting. It's like a healing for me.
>
> *(Traveller Elder, cited in Murray, 2017)*

For others, they despair at the lack of opportunities, employment and the loss of Traveller culture for young Traveller children growing up:

> But I think young people are just hungry for something. They're hanging around, I won't curse over the drugs, but the drugs it's just after taking a toll on the mental health.
>
> *(Traveller Elder, cited in Murray, 2017)*

The 'mainstreaming approach' that the department of health takes to Traveller health ignores the disparities in health outcomes for Travellers (Pavee Point, 2018, p. 15). Despite *Our Geels* and recommendation 73 of the National Traveller and Roma Inclusion Strategy 2017–2021 to develop a National Traveller Health Action Plan, Traveller organisations continue to lobby for an action plan that will address the considerable health inequalities of Traveller families and children.

Education: the struggle for equality of respect, recognition and learning

Education, UNCRC Articles 28 and 29

> The child has a right to education. Education should be directed at developing the child's personality and talents; preparing the child for active life as an adult; fostering respect for basic human rights; developing respect for the child's own cultural and national values and those of others; and developing respect for the natural environment.
>
> *(Children's Rights Alliance, 2013)*

The gap between Traveller children and non-Traveller children in education is very large. While there has been improvement for some Traveller children, the pace of change is unacceptably slow. While 92 per cent of non-Traveller children complete second-level education, just 13 per cent of Traveller children do, and just 1 per cent of Travellers make it to the third level (DJE, 2017). Children in primary school continue to face high levels of discrimination and bullying. Maria Joyce (National Traveller Women's Forum) outlined at the Oireachtas Committee Debate on Education (Oireachtas, 2019) that there are 'Traveller children in the education system who experience racism and discrimination, that's the reality'. Some ongoing issues include the absence of respect for Traveller cultural rights and positive representation of their culture, both historically and currently, in the school curriculum and in ECEC. This also means not shying away from the critical issues of oppression and discrimination.

In 2011, 87 per cent of resourcing for Traveller education under Ireland's austerity measures (2008–2018) was cut, disproportionally affecting Traveller children's engagement with the system. DJE (2017) has 31 education-related actions. More resources and a dedicated budget are needed to ensure the actions are implemented. As Ian McDonagh (young Traveller representative) discussed at the 2019 Oireachtas Debate, there is a need for more after-school schemes, because when Traveller children 'got knocked down' there is often 'no one there to bring them back up'. One promising action under DJE (2017) initiated by Tusla, the Child and Family Agency, comprises four national pilot projects to improve school attendance, participation, and the retention of children and young people in the Traveller community.

Many Traveller children report bullying and some hide their identity to avoid discrimination and exclusion (DCYA, 2016d; Eurochild, 2012; Murray, 2013). Many children disengage and leave education early because of stigmatising and their lack of a sense of belonging. There have been ongoing calls for an intercultural, anti-bias, anti-racist focus in pre- and in-service training for teachers and early childhood educators (Harmon, 2015; Kitching, 2019; Murray, 2013). Intercultural guidelines for primary and secondary schools (NCCA, n.d.) have never been comprehensively implemented. There is a commitment to revise these guidelines based on Traveller recognition, and to change legislation to include Traveller culture and history into the curriculum (*Irish Times*, 27 September 2018). All proactive measures to address the deficit in education attainment for Traveller children are very welcome. However, the struggle continues; anecdotal reports suggest that there may be a disproportionate number of Traveller children on reduced timetables, which means children are sent home early from school (Pavee Point 2018, p. 8). Traveller representative organisations have relentlessly requested the Department of Education and Skills to produce an implementation plan for the *Report and Recommendations for a Traveller Education Strategy* (2006). More than ten years on, very few recommendations have been initiated or implemented. Martin Collins, Co-Director of Pavee Point, recently called for the Traveller education consultative forum, or equivalent, to be re-established: 'we do not have forums to feed into policy development with regard to education for Travellers' (Oireachtas Debate, Tuesday 29 March 2019).

Early childhood education and care: explicitly addressing diversity in ECEC matters

Out of 31 education actions in NTRIS 2017, only Article 12 refers to early childhood education. It states:

> that all relevant Departments and agencies will promote the Early Childcare and Education (ECCE) pre-school scheme, as well as the Access and Inclusion Model

(AIM, http://aim.gov.ie/) for Children with a Disability, within the Traveller and Roma communities in order to facilitate access for every child to free pre-school from the age of three until they start school .

(DJE, 2017, p. 25)

Two recent DCYA initiatives support inclusion under the access and inclusion model: the Leadership for Inclusion programme (LINC) (DCYA, 2016c), accredited with extra capitation in ECCE settings, and Diversity, Equality and Inclusion Training to implement the Diversity, Equality and Inclusion (DEI) Charter and Guidelines (DCYA, 2016b) (15 hours, no extra capitation). The main aim of LINC is to provide professional development for ECEC educators to support the inclusion of children with additional needs in ECEC. While the DEI Charter and Guidelines focuses on all areas of diversity and includes a section on Travellers, the training does not adequately address Traveller exclusion or inclusion because of the short timeframe of the training. First 5 (DCYA, 2018) refers to Traveller accommodation and culturally appropriate service provision. However, neither NTRIS nor First 5 specifically mention the need for culturally appropriate training for the inclusion of Travellers to enhance appropriate representation and anti-discriminatory practice. Because of the embedded anti-Traveller discourse in Irish society and what we know about young children's development in terms of learning positive and negative attitudes to difference, including stereotypes and prejudice (Derman-Sparks, 1989; Lane, 2008; Murray and Urban, 2012), more explicit actions are needed.

One service engaging in high-quality practice around Traveller inclusion is *Curious Minds* early childhood service in Castlebar, Co Mayo. The service operates out of an anti-bias approach and proactively promotes Traveller culture in the setting. One resource they use is persona dolls (www.edenn.org). Working in collaboration with Traveller parents, they build a persona for their Traveller doll. The Traveller parent introduces the doll to the children using photographs from their home to link with the doll's story. This prompts the Traveller children to talk about their lives and the non-Traveller children to get involved, asking questions and making connections with their lives. All the parents, Traveller and non-Traveller, are invited in to explore and talk about Traveller traditions, including, for example, paper flower-making. If they have the opportunity, they extend into the community (e.g. with a visit to an exhibition about Traveller culture). The richness of this experience supports Traveller children's identity and offers the non-Traveller community an opportunity to learn more about the lives of Travellers. Their aim is to increase knowledge, build bridges and support the unlearning of bias and prejudice against the Traveller community (personal communication). Practices such as this do not require substantial resources, but they do require comprehensive diversity, equality and inclusion training and a commitment and ability to put critical knowledge into practice.

Traveller parents are often reluctant to send their young children to ECEC for fear of discrimination, neglect or exclusion (Murray, 1997). Just under half of Traveller children in early childhood services availed of the ECCE scheme (47 per cent) (DCYA, 2018). Another innovative project initiated in 2017 by Galway Childcare Committee (GCC) titled 'ECCE Participation Initiative' is working closely with the Galway Traveller movement: a community development organisation, families from the Traveller community and early childhood settings to increasing participation in the universal ECCE preschool scheme. GCC began this programme because of their concern about the underrepresentation in ECCE of families living in Traveller-specific accommodation. A number of actions have been undertaken in consultation with families, to support Traveller families to begin to trust that ECCE settings are welcoming and inclusive. Initial findings have shown that parents who were consulted place a high value on early learning and care but will only avail of the ECCE scheme in settings where they are confident that their children will have a positive experience. As the initiative progresses, further work will be carried out to deepen and develop shared understandings between families and settings (personal communication with Galway County Childcare Committee). The practice of working collaboratively at the local level with Traveller organisations to support change and the inclusion of Traveller children in ECCE services is a model worth investing in nationally.

Discrimination: layers and layers of prejudice run deep

Right to non-discrimination, UNCRC Articles 2 and 30

All rights in the Convention apply to all children without exception, and the State has an obligation to protect children from any and all forms of discrimination including that resulting from their parents or guardian's status.

(Children's Rights Alliance, 2013)

In a report on his visit to Ireland, Thomas Hammarberg, Council of Europe Commissioner for Human Rights, stated that 'Travellers have been subjected to discrimination and racism in the fields of education, employment, housing, healthcare, media reporting and participation in decision making' (Council of Europe, 2007, p. 28). The UN Committee for Children's Rights, in their concluding observations, stated that Ireland needs to 'strengthen its efforts to combat discrimination against and stigmatisation and social exclusion of Traveller children' (UNCRC, 2016, p. 6).

First 5 (DCYA, 2018) mentions that the state promotes principles of inclusion and non-discrimination in the best interests of the child (p. 24). In NTRIS, there are 19 actions under anti-discrimination and equality (DCYA, 2018, p. 39), but none specifically name Traveller children. Fanning asserts that Travellers' legacy in Ireland is 'characterised by the persistence of institutional racism in many areas of social policy … and denial of anti-Traveller racism' (Fanning, 2002 cited in Kitching, 2019, p. 152). Mac Gréil (2011), inter alia, makes the case for 'an immediate and positive response from those with power and influence' to address the 'unacceptable and negative prejudice and behaviour' towards the Traveller community (p. 598). It remains to be seen what actions will be put in place to comprehensively address discrimination and racism at all levels. Despite tragedies such as Carrickmines, and the lack of accommodation for Travellers, a recent 'decision to abandon a long-term commitment to provide Traveller accommodation in one of the wealthiest parts of Dublin has been made by the Local Authority' (*Irish Times*, 2019). This follows decades of local opposition to the building of a halting site in this area. The UNCRC Committee is concerned about the structural discrimination against Traveller and Roma children and their families, including alleged impunity for publicly expressed discriminatory remarks by public representatives (UNCRC, 2016, p. 6). The negative effects of discrimination and oppression begin early in life. Lessons learned when children are young have harsh consequences for life chances and relationships within society. Oppression and marginalisation have detrimental effects on Traveller children's outcomes. Paulo Freire (1993) argued that 'to surmount the situation of oppression, people must first critically recognise its causes, so that through transformation they can create a new situation, one which makes possible the pursuit of a fuller humanity' (p. 29).

Conclusion

Despite robust policy frameworks and strategies over many decades, Traveller children's lives continue to be negatively affected by the lack of policy resourcing and implementation. There is an opportunity to create change through a focused whole-of-government engagement with the new strategies, First 5 (DCYA, 2018) and NTRIS (DJE, 2017), both of which point in the right direction. Institutional racism persists at all levels of the system and needs to be comprehensively addressed as we struggle against the mindset of assimilationist policies, which continue to demand a uniformity in the provision of accommodation, health and education. Progressive universalism, or 'mainstreaming', falls short of meeting the specific provision rights of Traveller children. It is a profound concern and calls for a radical change in our approach to Travellers in our society. Some of this change has already begun as individuals and organisations delivering state and community services are engaging in real partnership with Traveller children and families. Some are also proactively challenging racism and discrimination, working within the system to try to remove unnecessary barriers and obstacles to Traveller empowerment and emancipation. What is needed is more robust systemic and committed leadership along with resourcing to proactively implement and monitor the actions in the strategies to vindicate Traveller children's rights in Irish society.

References

Baker, John, Kathleen Lynch, Sara Cantillon, and Judy Walsh. 2004. *Equality: From Theory to Action*. New York: Palgrave Macmillan.

Burns, S. 2018. Retrived Februrary 20th 2019. https://www.irishtimes.com/news/social-affairs/home less-mother-criticises-horrible-reaction-to-family-sleeping-at-garda-station-1.3592442

Campbell, Sheralyn, Kate Alexander, and Kylie Smith. 2017. *Feminism in Early Childhood: Using Feminist Theories in Research and Practice*. Singapore: Springer.

Central Statistics Office. 2016. *Census Summary Results*. www.cso.ie/en/csolatestnews/presspages/2017/census2016summaryresults-part1/

Children's Rights Alliance. 2019. *Report Card 2019: Is Government Keeping Its Promises to Children*. Dublin: Children's Rights Alliance.

Children's Rights Alliance. 2013. Summary of the UN Convention on the Rights of the Child.https://www.childrensrights.ie/sites/default/files/information_sheets/files/SummaryUNCRC.pdf

Collins, Tessa. 2019. www.paveepoint.ie/pavee-point-at-the-7th-international-roma-womensconfer ence/?fbclid=IwAR0Lr05UYf2yE8t3lbzjkrug6nWXHFvJ8axkqOv8xRTTPUEGD-qXcyCC_oQ

Commission on Itinerancy. 1963. *Report of the Commission on Itinerancy*. Dublin: The Stationery Office.

Community Foundation Ireland. 2017. National Traveller Survey. Retrieved 20th January 2019. https://www.communityfoundation.ie/insights/news/national-traveller-survey-funded-by-the-community-foundation-for-ireland

Council of Europe. 2007. *Report by the Commissioner for Human Rights, Mr. Thomas Hammarberg on His Visit to Ireland, November 2007*. www.dfa.ie/uploads/documents/Political%20Division/final%20report%20ireland.pdf

Department of Children and Youth Affairs. 2014. *Better Outcomes, Brighter Futures: The National Policy Framework for Children and Young People 2014–2020*. Dublin: Government Publications.

Department of Children and Youth Affairs. 2016a. *Access and Inclusion Model (AIM)*. Dublin. http://aim.gov.ie

Department of Children and Youth Affairs. 2016b. *Diversity Equality and Inclusion Charter and Guidelines*. Dublin: DCYA.

Department of Children and Youth Affairs. 2016c. *Leadership for Inclusion Programme (LINC)*. https://linc programme.ie

Department of Children and Youth Affairs. 2016d. *The State of the Nation's Children*. Dublin: Government Publications.

Department of Children and Youth Affairs. 2018. *First 5: A Whole-of-Government Strategy for Babies, Young Children and Their Families 2019–2018*. Dublin: Government Publications.

Department of Education and Science. 2005. Chief Inspectors Report 2001–2004. www.itm.ie

Department of Education and Skills. 2006. *Report and Recommendations for a Traveller Education Strategy*. Dublin: Stationary Office.

Department of Housing. Planning and Local Government. Local Authority Traveller Accommodation Programmes 2014–2018. https://www.housing.gov.ie/housing/policy/traveller-accommodation/traveller-accommodation

Department of Justice and Equality. 2011. *Ireland's National Traveller/Roma Integration Strategy*. Dublin: Stationary Office.

Department of Justice and Equality. 2017. *National Traveller and Roma Inclusion Strategy 2017–2021*. Dublin: Stationary Office.

Derman-Sparks, Louise. the A.B.C. Task Force. 1989. *Anti-bias Curriculum: Tools for Empowering Young Children*. Washington, DC: National Association for the Education of Young Children.

Economic and Social Research Institute (ESRI) 2008. *Growing Up in Ireland Study*. www.growingup.ie

Eurochild. 2012. *Speak Up*. Brussels: Eurochild.

European Union Fundamental Rights Agency. 2010. *EU-MIDIS: European Union Minorities and Discrimination Survey*. Vienna: FRA.

Fanning, B. 2002. *Racism and Social Change in the Republic of Ireland*. Manchester: Manchester University Press.

Freeman, M. 2000. "The Future of Children's Rights." *Chidren and Society* 14 (4): 277–293.

Freire, Paulo. 1993. *Pedagogy of the Oppressed*. England: Clays Ltd. St Ives plc.

Giroux, Henry. 2003. "Utopian Thinking under the Sign of Neoliberalism: Towards a Critical Pedagogy of Educated Hope". *Democracy and Nature* 9 (1): 91–105.

Hammarberg, Thomas. 2012. *Human Rights of Roma and Travellers in Europe*. Brussels: Council of Europe.

Harmon, Hillary. 2015. *Irish Traveller and Roma Children: A Response to Ireland's Consolidated Third and Fourth Report to the UN Committee on the Rights of the Child*. Dublin: Pavee Point Traveller and Roma Centre.

Helleiner, Jane. 2000. *Racism and the Politics of Culture: Irish Travellers*. Toronto: University of Toronto Press.

Hosford, P. 2013. "A 12-year-old Traveller boy attempted suicide because he was being bullied at school". Retrieved January 20 2019. https://www.thejournal.ie/travellers-groups-launch-two-new-leaflets-1007632-Jul2013/

Houses of the Oireachtas. 2018. National Traveller-Roma Integration Strategy. Dáil Éireann Debate, Thursday-5 July 2018. Retrieved January 20th 2018.https://www.oireachtas.ie/en/debates/question/2018-07-05/25/

Houses of the Oireachtas. 2019. Joint Committee on Education and Skills Debate - Tuesday, 26 Mar 2019. https://www.oireachtas.ie/en/debates/debate/joint_committee_on_education_and_skills/2019-03-26/2/

Independent Newspaper. 2015. Retrieved January 20th 2019. https://www.independent.ie/breaking-news/irish-news/ten-people-including-baby-killed-in-fire-at-travellers-halting-site-31598818.html

Irish Human Rights and Equality Commission. 2016. Retrived October 2018. https://www.ihrec.ie/ihrec-challenges-government-recognise-traveller-ethnicity/

Irish Human Rights and Equality Commission. 2017. https://www.ihrec.ie/historic-step-traveller-ethnicity-recognised-state/

Kelleher, Cecily. 2010. *Our Geels: All Ireland Traveller Health Study*. Dublin: University College Dublin and Department of Health and Children.

Kenny, Máirín. 2011. *An Integrated Approach to Conflict among Travellers, at Family, Community and Structural Context Levels*. Dublin: Pavee Point.

Kenny, Máirín, and Alice Binchy. 2009. "Irish Travellers, Identity and the Education System". In *Traveller, Nomadic and Migrant Education*, edited by Danaher, Patrick Alan, Máirín Kenny, and Judith Remy Leder, 117–131. London: Routledge.

Kilkelly, Ursula. 2017. *Barriers to the Realisation of Children's Rights in Ireland*. Dublin: Ombudsman for Children.

Kitching, Karl. 2019. *Racism and Education*. Dublin: European Network Against Racism (ENAR). http://enarireland.org/racism-and-education/

Lane, Jane. 2008. *Young Children and Racial Justice: Taking Action for Racial Equality in the Early Years – Understanding the Past, Thinking about the Present, Planning for the Future.* London: National Children's Bureau.

Mac Gréil, Micheál. 2010. *Emancipation of the Travelling People.* Kildare: The Survey and Research Unit. Department of Social Studies, NUI Maynooth.

Mac Gréil, Micheál. 2011. *Pluralism and Diversity in Ireland.* Dublin: Columba Press.

McGinnity, Frances, Raaele Grotti, Oona Kenny, and Helen Russell. 2017. *Who Experiences Discrimination in Ireland.* Dublin: Irish Human Rights and Equality Commission and Economic and Social Research Institute.

Merrion Street: Irish Government News Service. 2017. Retrieved: November 20th 2018. https://merrion street.ie/MerrionStreet/en/News-Room/Speeches/Statement_by_An_Taoiseach_Enda_Kenny_T D_On_the_recognition_of_Travellers_as_an_ethnic_group.html

Moss, Peter, Gunilla Dahlberg, Liselotte M. Olsson, and Michel Vandenbroeck. 2017. *Why Contest Early Childhood.* Routledge. www.book2look.com/book/CGQqJCANOX? utm_source=Routledge&utm_medium=cms&utm_campaign=160701429

Murray, Colette. 1997. *Pavee Children. A Study on Childcare Issues for Travellers.* Dublin: Pavee Point Publication.

Murray, Colette. 2002. "The Traveller Child: A Holistic Perspective". In *Diversity in Early Childhood: A Collection of Essays*, edited by Barnardos, 44–63. Dublin: Barnardos.

Murray, Colette. 2012. "A Minority within a Minority? Social Justice for Traveller and Roma Children in Early Childhood Education and Care". *European Journal of Education* 47 (4): 569–583.

Murray, Colette. 2013. "Getting an Education. How Travellers' Knowledge and Experience Shape Their Engagement with the System". In *Children's Rights and Education International Perspectives*, edited by Swadener, Beth, Laura Lundy, Janette Habashi, and Natasha Cohen, 203–220. New York: Peter Lang.

Murray, Colette. 2017. "Heart(h)less: Negative-Visibility and Positive-Invisibility the Irish Travellers' Tale". Paper presented at the 25th International Reconceptualising Early Childhood Education Conference, Toronto, October 24–27.

Murray, Colette, and Mathias Urban. 2012. *Diversity and Equality in Early Childhood an Irish Perspective.* Dublin: Gill and Macmillan.

National Council for Curriculum and Assessment (NCCA). 2009. *Aistear.* Dublin: NCCA.

National Council for Curriculum and Assessment (NCCA). n.d. *Intercultural Education in Post-Primary Schools Guidelines: Enabling Children to Respect and Celebrate Diversity, to Promote Equality and to Challenge Unfair Discrimination.* Dublin: NCCA.

O'Brien, C. 2018. Traveller Culture and History Set to Feature on School Curriculum. Retrieved February 15th 2019. https://www.irishtimes.com/news/education/traveller-culture-and-history-set-to-feature-on-school-curriculum-1.3643924

Oireachtas Report. Joint Committee on Jobs, Social Protection and Education, October 18, 2011.

Pavee Point. 2018. *Civil Society Monitoring Report on the Implementation of the National Roma Integration Strategy 11.* Dublin: Pavee Point.

Raidió Teilifís Éireann (RTÉ). News Groups Call for Initiative for Traveller Children in Education. https://www.rte.ie/news/ireland/2019/0326/1038788-traveller-address-to-committee/

Sindy Joyce. 2019. Retrieved March 1st 2019. https://twitter.com/SindyLJoyce/status/1101477205597663232

Sindy Joyce 2019. 14th Feb Twitter. https://twitter.com/SindyLJoyce/status/1096037424994631680

Swadener, Beth, Laura Lundy, Janette Habashi, and Natasha Blanchet-Cohen. 2013. *Children's Rights and Education: International Perspectives.* New York: Peter Lang.

Travelling People Review Body. 1983. *Report of the Travelling People Review Body.* Dublin: Stationary Office.

United Nations Convention on the Rights of the Child. 1989. www.ohchr.org/EN/ProfessionalInter est/Pages/CRC.aspx

United Nations Convention on the Rights of the Child. 2016. *Concluding Observation on the Combined Third and Fourth Periodic Reports of Ireland.* UN Doc CRC/CRC.IRL/CO/3-4.

United Nations Human Rights Office of the High Commission, International Convention on the Elimination of All Forms of Racial Discrimination (CERD). 2011. https://tbinternet.ohchr.org/_layouts/treatybodyexternal/Download.aspx?symbolno=CERD/C/IRL/CO/3-4&Lang=En.

Watson, Dorothy, Oona Kenny, and Frances McGinnity. 2017. *A Social Portrait of Travellers in Ireland. Research Series No. 56.* Dublin: Economic and Social Research Institute.

24

LISTENING AND DECIDING

Children's rights in paediatric palliative care

Luigina Mortari, Ludovica De Panfilis and Luca Ghirotto

Introduction

In 2002, paediatric palliative care (PPC) was defined by the World Health Organization (WHO, 2002) as 'total care' that addresses the child's body, mind and spirit:

> Palliative care seeks to enhance quality of life in the face of an ultimately terminal condition. Palliative treatments focus on the relief of symptoms (e.g., pain, dyspnea) and conditions (e.g., loneliness) that cause distress and detract from the child's enjoyment of life ... Palliative care includes the control of pain and other symptoms and addresses the psychological, social, or spiritual problems of children (and their families) living with life-threatening or terminal conditions. The goal of palliative care is the achievement of the best quality of life for patients and their families, consistent with their values.
>
> *(American Academy of Pediatrics, Committee on Bioethics and Committee on Hospital Care, 2000, p. 351)*

In general practice, PPC is recommended by paediatricians 'when no treatment has been shown to alter substantially the expected progression toward death' (American Academy of Pediatrics, Committee on Bioethics and Committee on Hospital Care, 2000, p. 351). PPC should be 'offered at diagnosis and continued throughout the course of illness, whether the outcome ends in cure or death' (p. 352), for all children with life-limiting illness.

Indeed, PPC addresses a broad range of aspects, as patients present innumerable issues, from pain, to feeding, respiration, seizures and other symptoms (Hunt, 1990; Hunt and Burne, 1995) caused by progressive deterioration of congenital or chronic diseases (Hynson et al., 2003) alternating between moments of stability and sudden decline (Hynson et al., 2003; Mack and Wolfe, 2006). The standards for PPC were developed in 2007 by the European Association of Palliative Care (EAPC) (2007) Task Force on Palliative Care for Children and Adolescents, acknowledging the importance of the evaluation of symptoms based on elicitation of knowledge.

However, as stressed by the EAPC, the decision to provide PPC should not overlook the patient's voice, which is one of the most important sources of information in this context. In accordance with Article 12 of the United Nations Convention on the Rights of the Child (UNCRC), a child has the right to have his or her opinion heard in all matters affecting him or her. As Article 12 states:

1. States Parties shall assure to the child who is capable of forming his or her own views the right to express those views freely in all matters affecting the child, the views of the child being given due weight in accordance with the age and maturity of the child.
2. For this purpose, the child shall in particular be provided the opportunity to be heard in any judicial and administrative proceedings affecting the child, either directly, or through a representative or an appropriate body, in a manner consistent with the procedural rules of national law.

Nonetheless, newborns, infants, toddlers, and often children and young adults in PPC could not verbally express themselves or provide carers with words to make evident what they are experiencing, as well as their preferences and perspectives. Of note, Article 12 makes reference to the views expressed by the child or 'a representative or an appropriate body to be given due weight in accordance with the age and maturity of the child'. The aspect of the child's point of view is actually a key aspect and has broad meaning. Although parents or others may try their best to speak for the children and communicate on their behalf, they may ignore other non-verbal messages from children that express other wishes. Yet when listening to a child's voice, one must also try to read their non-verbal expressions and 'attention to detail persistence and imagination in seeking solutions, willingness to ask advice' (Hunt and Burne, 1995, p. 26).

Thus, in an ethical discourse on how to best carry out palliative care in children, we must ask ourselves: What type of information do children provide us, and in what form? What are they experiencing as they are provided PC? How can we promote their right to PC in the best manner? With this chapter, we would like to contribute to the debate about children's participation in their healthcare, discussing what listening to children with verbal capacity aged 3–8 in PPC discloses, and how children, even those without verbal capacity, can be involved in the decision-making process. To try to answer the first couple of questions, we will present the results of a systematic review of studies involving children, aged 3–8, who experienced PPC. We then suggest a way to include all children in PPC, by discussing the advance care planning (ACP) tool and the child's assent as means for an effective children's participation within PPC-related decision-making. Our argument is: children's right to have involving, participatory care in PPC is radically based on listening, in all its manifestations, because it makes the children's perspective acknowledgeable and contributes to guaranteeing, formally and ethically, the right itself.

Listening in paediatric palliative care

In 2017, children in the 'E. Balducci' preschool of the municipality of Reggio Emilia visited the brand new wards of haematology and oncology of the Arcispedale Santa Maria Nuova city research hospital. As part of the project called 'The hospital through the eyes of children', promoted by Istituzione Scuole e Nidi d'Infanzia, Reggio Children Foundation, and the hospital, the children were prompted to reflect about hospitals, healthcare and well-being. Later, a selection of their thoughts became an installation along the corridors and on the windows so that patients, healthcare professionals (HPs), parents, relatives and visitors could read them upon accessing the wards and reflect on how the hospital is seen through the eyes of children. For example, Carlotta, 5 years old, said:

> At the beginning, when I was sick, I was a little scared of the doctors, but then the fear went away because my mother was holding my hand, and when I was there, I learned more about the 'sensations' of the hospital.
>
> *(Reggio Emilia Approach, n.d.)*

Listening to the children and recording their impressions provides important information on the way children live and what they need for their healthcare, thus permitting adults to shape a child-centred and child-participatory care environment (Field and Behrman, 2003). Yet achieving the ability to grasp the meanings and the experience of children in physical pain remains greatly challenging for HPs (Weaver et al., 2016).

Current empirical research in PPC lacks information from children and mainly discusses the points of view of other stakeholders. Moreover, in the scientific literature, contributions are few. Despite the studies being single-site and involving small numbers of children, we were able to use them to perform a systematic review, a meta-summary and a meta-synthesis that could provide a greater picture of children's experience of PPC. The meta-summary, which is published elsewhere (Ghirotto et al., 2018), was aimed at highlighting the thematic areas (Thorne et al., 2004) addressed by available qualitative research on PPC. Here, we will draw on findings from our meta-synthesis to attempt to answer a different review question: What does experiencing PPC look like from children's perspective? We discuss the results of the meta-synthesis aggregated for children aged 3–8 years. We acknowledge this is a limit for a comprehensive understanding of children's perspective in PPC as many children living palliative care situations can't verbalise or tell what they are experiencing. Nonetheless, gathering the 'voice' of children, listening to it and analysing it may contribute to improve both participation and the quality of healthcare for all the children in PPC (Stevens et al., 2010).

As the objective here is about understanding meanings and experiences, meta-synthesis allows us to synthesise and re-elaborate qualitative research findings through interpretation rather than mere aggregation. Conducting a meta-synthesis allowed us to recombine qualitative findings on children's experiences in PPC in a transformed whole (Sandelowski and Barroso, 2007).

To collect studies for the meta-synthesis, we searched for qualitative research articles on PPC involving children from 3 to 18 years old in the following electronic databases: MEDLINE, CINAHL, EMBASE, PsycINFO, PsycARTICLES and ERIC, with either publication date or language limits. A total of 1,240 articles were retrieved from the databases and from checking these articles' references. After the removal of duplicates and checking title/abstract/full text, we first included 16 qualitative research articles reporting on 14 unique studies. We then performed an update of the database search (up to March 2018) and we included four more articles. Here, our analysis will focus on the findings of qualitative research involving children younger than 8 years of age alone ($n = 10$).

Analysis led us to found four main categories that highlight the perspectives of children experiencing PPC: recognising pain and its effects from the child's perspective, providing fair communication, surrounding the child with significant others, and letting the child be a decision-maker.

Children can recognise pain and its effects

As gathered from the qualitative research available involving children speaking about their condition, we find that children with life-threatening conditions keep and develop specific competences. First, children are competent in expressing and dealing with pain (Kortesluoma and Nikkonen, 2004, 2006; Kortesluoma, Nikkonen and Serlo, 2008). As an 8-year-old boy said, 'Oh, I was in a quite bad way … I felt it all over my whole body as if I couldn't do anything; it felt like I didn't have strength enough to do anything' (Kortesluoma and Nikkonen, 2006, p. 217).

Such responses show that children are capable of discriminating the nature of pain and linking its physiological sensation to psychological aspects. In the research by Kortesluoma et al. (2008), all the participating children were able to remember different pain experiences and to share those experiences with the researcher. An 8-year-old girl who had acute lymphatic leukaemia stated, 'Some pain makes you feel like crying, others do not. It depends on how much it aches' (Kortesluoma and Nikkonen, 2006, p. 217). A 5-year-old girl affirmed, 'Oh, somehow you feel sort of anxious. Like, you don't know what to do' (Kortesluoma and Nikkonen, 2006, p. 217).

Disease and pain are also frequently linked to their limitations on social activities. Often children in PPC cannot attend school or participate in free-time activities. These children can recognise these limitations as consequences of disease-related pain and suffering. A 5-year-old girl stated, '[It's] quite terrible because you can't move or really do anything at all' (Kortesluoma and Nikkonen, 2006, p. 217). A 7-year-old boy stated, 'When you're in pain, you won't run too much. It is best not to' (Kortesluoma and Nikkonen, 2006, p. 217).

This in turn affects these children's social life, leading to the risk of social isolation and exclusion. Kortesluoma and Nikkonen (2006) found that sometimes pain helps children to avoid harmful situations. An 8-year-old boy commented, 'When you're ill, you don't have to go to school, where someone often might bully you' (Kortesluoma and Nikkonen, 2006, p. 221). Barney, aged 6, suffering from epidermolysis bullosa, reported, 'One day, a boy asked me if my fingers were glued because I had put glue on them. I was angry with this friend from school' (Borghi et al., 2014, p. 71).

Children request fair communication

A main category emerging from the analysis of the included articles is communication. As reported by several studies (Borghi et al., 2014; Coad et al., 2015; Davies et al., 2005; Hinds et al., 2005; Kortesluoma and Nikkonen, 2004, 2006; Kortesluoma et al., 2008), children appeared eager to talk about their situations and their feelings. Some children spoke about 'a special place', describing it as a place where they can 'meet new people who take time to play and talk' (Davies et al., 2005, p. 256). They also enjoyed sharing their experiences with other children, both ill ones and not (Borghi et al., 2014), and recognised communication as emotional support: communicating with family members alleviated anxiety and fear about the future (Davies et al., 2005; Jalmsell et al., 2016).

Regarding communication between children and HPs, Coad et al. (2015) reinforced that children have a need to voice their views. According to children, one of the essential professional skills in HPs was 'excellent communication and listening' (Coad et al., 2015, p. 49). Participants appreciated when HPs contributed to listening and their holistic care.

Surprisingly, the one aspect emerging across all the studies included in the meta-synthesis was the children's request for honest communication about their conditions. The children wanted HPs to speak sincerely, without hiding any information involving them. 'When one seven-year-old child was asked whether the physician should withhold bad news from a young child in some cases, he said: "You should tell the truth" as if anything else was unthinkable' (Jalmsell et al., 2016, p. 1096). 'It would just be better if they told you', another patient said (Spalding and Yardley, 2016, p. 461), and asked to be treated as the protagonist of the situation: 'Some people ... actually just talk to the mum instead of ... talking to the person who has actually got the condition' (p. 461). Children even suggested the way they want to receive this information: first, information should be provided in terms understandable to children and in a child-centred manner: 'All the big words that they use, it was like, can you repeat that again in English, please' (p. 461). Second, it must be conveyed in a compassionate and sensitive manner: 'They need to choose their words carefully ... How they say it [matters] because it can be pretty hurtful stuff, but they don't mean it' (p. 461). In Jalmsell et al. (2016), children commented that the easiest way to communicate bad news was 'just to do it calmly, and in unmistakable terms, but with respect' (p. 1096).

Additionally, communication included non-verbal aspects that children were capable of reading: 'Doctors are standing over you, and you feel intimidated, but [not] if they come down [to this child's level – meaning both physically and metaphorically]' (Spalding and Yardley, 2016, p. 461). Posture, language and even someone's clothing conveyed something to children about the meanings inherent in communication: 'They [doctors] need a new outfit; they do. They scare you with their outfit' (p. 462).

Being surrounded by significant others

Another competence expressed by children in PPC relates to defining the type of relationship being established with their HPs, and their ability to read and discriminate postures and attitudes of their care providers. A sensitive and empathetic relationship established by the HP can help the child receive upsetting or bad news (Davies et al., 2005; Jalmsell et al., 2016). In the Kortesluoma et al. (2008) study:

> some of the children did not trust the nurses' help, because they were not close enough to the child to provide individualised help as needed. Theoretic explanations from nurses who think that they understand the child's experience and try to explain things from their own perspective do not help. On the other hand, the children appreciated the nurses who could empathize.
>
> *(p. 146)*

Moreover, these children were grateful when adults took them seriously (Kortesluoma and Nikkonen, 2004). According to children, being close meant becoming a significant other, which was helpful during daily routines and difficult moments: '[She is] funny, kind, happy, loves us, nice. She couldn't help us anymore' (Carter, Edwards and Hunt, 2015, p. 312). Kortesluoma et al. (2008) found that:

> According to the children's experiences, the presence of family members during pain episodes and pain-provoking procedures puts the child's mind at rest. The significant others can hug the child, hold his/her hand, or nestle and comfort the child and thereby offer emotional support. Some nurses might have the same effect, but not all of them.
>
> *(p. 147)*

The child as decision-maker

Research indicated that children have several vital competences that are the prelude to being a decision-maker in PPC. In Hinds et al. (2005), in fact, it emerged that children were: (1) 'able to accurately identify their treatment options and understood that their death would be one of the outcomes of their decision' (p. 9153); and (2) capable of participating 'in end-of-life decisions on their own behalf' (p. 9153). Of course, this participation was possible due to honest, comprehensible communication, as requested by the children. As noted by Jalmsell et al. (2016):

> addressing the children in words that they understand shows respect for the individual and allows the child to be an active participant in his or her own care, something that is threatened if parts of the information are withheld from the child.
>
> *(p. 1097)*

Jalmsell et al. (2016) again reported, 'The two-seven-year-old children who took part said that receiving understandable information allowed them to prepare for what was to come, which they could not have done if the physician had used words they did not understand' (p. 1096). In particular, patients wanted to be part of the decision process and wanted to receive news the same time it was given to their parents:

> Six children said that they did not want their parents to receive information without them and that they wanted bad news to be shared with them at the same time as their parents. Doing this shows respect for the child as an individual and a patient and, as one-seven-year-old girl said, ensured 'that everyone knows'.
>
> *(p. 1096)*

It is important to note that children made decisions according to the relationship they have with the people surrounding them. As Hinds et al. (2005) observed:

> nearly universal report of the patients that their decision making was relationship-based is a particularly striking finding. Although patients absorbed the factual information about their treatment options, concern and care about family, friends, health care providers, and even unknown others influenced the patients' decision making.
>
> *(p. 9153)*

Communication and relationships could make the difference in children's decisions since they played the pivotal role of entitling children as rights-holders: they said they have the right to be informed, involved and part of the decision-making process.

Spalding and Yardley (2016) stressed that children participating in their research emphasised the importance of 'talking to them (not at them), with a focus on explaining and engaging them in decision-making' (p. 461).

Playtime: nowhere to be found

Interestingly, an important concept that was absent within the health literature we reviewed is play. Despite play being an important activity for children, we did not find many articles addressing the function of play in PPC. Only a few articles addressed the role play had in distracting children from their painful daily life (Borghi et al., 2014; Kortesluoma et al., 2008) and in enhancing and strengthening the developing bond between children and carers (Carter et al., 2015).

Generally, play is recognised for its vital importance for childhood development as it offers physical, emotional, cognitive and social benefits for both healthy children and children with chronic diseases (Nijhof et al., 2018). Children in PPC often experience many social restrictions and it is fundamental that the healthcare providers afford care environments which allow social activities participations (i.e. by facilitating playing activities in hospitals among peers, family members, etc.). Further investigations demonstrating the positive effects of play on children with medical complexities are needed (Nijhof et al., 2018). However, in this meta-synthesis, play emerged as an important part of life for most children in PPC.

The advance care planning for an effective children's participation

This meta-synthesis gave an interpretation of what is important for children experiencing PPC. In particular, we found that children can recognise pain and its effects, they prefer fair communication from HPs and family members, they enjoy being surrounded by significant others, and they should be treated as protagonists of the decision-making process.

While we discuss the practical implications of the first three categories later in the chapter regarding the idea of the child as decision-maker, we will briefly introduce two important topics currently on debate: the child's assent and the ACP, along with the concept of child's best interest. The meta-synthesis results highlighted what is important for children with PPC needs who are capable of expressing their point of view. Nonetheless, we are aware that many children in PPC could not do that: often children with life-limiting conditions cannot express or be involved in decisions that directly affect them. For both situations, we suggest ACP and the child's best interest to inform the right of every child's participation in healthcare. Feudtner and Nathanson (2014) observed that:

> We struggle as a society to envision the ideal care of dying individuals, to engage each other in formulating plans to assure such care, and to enact these care plans. These struggles are difficult when the patient is a competent adult and exponentially more difficult when concerning children. PPC engages in this struggle, patient by patient. Such efforts require [...] grappling with [...] the pursuit of a path of care that is in the child's best interest while respecting the child's emerging capacity to make reasonable decisions [...].
>
> *(S3–S4)*

During the care pathway, children and their parents must make difficult decisions that have an impact on their quality of life and that of their family. When the illness compromises cognitive and communicative abilities, adults (parents and HPs) make important decisions on behalf of children. In fact, children with many of the conditions requiring PPC typically lose, or have never had, mobility and have severely impaired communication (Hunt, 1990; Hunt and Burne, 1995), which makes them very dependent on their family members. It is different when children can understand the situation and express their preferences, as in the studies we reported above.

'Children make very special patients' (Benini et al., 2008, p. 4), both because they are in continuous physical, emotional and cognitive evolution and because they have a very particular ethical and social position in our society: 'When the patient is a child, it is not always easy to speak of freedom of choice, respect for the patients' wishes, and their right to honest communications' (p. 4).

According to the traditional bioethics literature, the ability to make a decision reasonably characterises the principle of self-determination. In other words, those who can justify choices made first logically, then psychologically and morally (Beauchamp and Childress, 2013), can self-determine. The principle of self-determination is the execution of the most abstract principle of autonomy, which has been analysed in depth from different ethical theories. The aim was to define a broad concept of autonomy, taking into account several conditions in which 'vulnerable' subjects cannot be heard. Ethical theories, such as principlism, consider the autonomy of the patient in its classical version of self-government and the freedom to choose without external constraints (Beauchamp and Childress, 2013). In contrast, relational ethics, such as the ethics of care, considers autonomy concerning the understanding of the person's frailty, the vulnerability of the health condition, and the maintenance of personal dignity (Giblin, 2002). According to those theories, the active participation of the patient (one of his or her representatives) in the care relationship does not sacrifice autonomy, but strengthens it (Nedelsky, 1989).

In the field of medical ethics, self-determination has an application in the practice of informed consent to medical procedures and treatments: this tool can guarantee respect for autonomy. Informed consent is based on the assumption that the human subject is entirely rational and autonomous and can act independently. We believe it is necessary to problematise this assumption: ignoring the patient's background, the institutional power of relationships and, moreover, the social context can be misleading since all these factors can affect decisions and freedom of choice (Dodds, 2000).

What happens to the concepts of autonomy and self-determination and to informed consent when decisions involve a child? Do these concepts lose their meaning because of the children's decisions having no legal validity or because the notion of assent can complete and redefine the notion of informed consent? The bioethical principle of 'respect for person' requires that children provide their assent to the degree that they are deemed capable of providing it, taking into account the child's age, maturity and psychological state (U.S. Department of Health and Human Services, 2018). As in the case of informed consent, assent requires, to an even greater extent, a shared definition and uniform procedures to collect it. A Delphi study on the definition of child assent for research (Tait and Geisser, 2017) identified elements to generate four constructs within the definition of assent: assessment of child capacity; information for younger children (7–11 years); information for older children (12–17 years); and requirements for meaningful assent. We report two of these constructs regarding information for younger children (7–11 years) and requirements for meaningful assent:

> If assent is deemed appropriate, younger children should, at the minimum, be told what procedures will be done and how the child might experience them … Children should understand the basic study-specific information, should have a developmentally appropriate awareness of their condition … Children should be free to decide whether or not to participate in a study and articulate their choice absent of any undue influence or coercion.
>
> *(Tait and Geisser, 2017, p. 4)*

We firmly believe that these definitions can be applied in the field of PPC, with particular attention to the clinical and ethical issues of end-of-life care. Child assent has no legal validity, but it has an ethical one, and it is a part of the decision-making process. For this reason, we argue that ACP can represent a tool to valorise the child's assent. ACP is a suitable tool for agreeing with a shared care plan. Through ACP, a patient (or the person identified to represent the will and best interest of an incompetent person or minor) expresses his or her choices regarding treatments that are considered futile or not responsive to his or her concept of quality of life. Furthermore, ACP allows the patient and/or his or her substitute decision-maker to be involved in the step-by-step treatment process: ACP is in progress throughout the illness trajectory. ACP can be defined as 'the formal decision-making process' (Mullick, Martin and Sallnow, 2013, p. 1), and it has not only a clinical but also an ethical value. Implementing ACP helps to preserve the patient's voice (or that of the person who represents him or her); it is also a tool to construct the care relationship properly. In addition, ACP can contribute to dealing with difficult communications: many studies (Buiting et al., 2011; Hillman and Cardona-Morrell, 2015; Mack et al., 2012; Nelson et al., 2006) have shown that inappropriate decisions regarding the prolongation of life or the administration of futile therapies are caused by the difficulty of HPs in communicating bad news.

The opportunity to choose after having been adequately informed is one of the ways to protect the right to health as the WHO defines it: 'a state of complete physical, mental and social well-being and not merely the absence of disease or infirmity' (WHO, 1946). Last but not least, these are choices made within a shared and co-constructed decision-making process. According to this care framework, HPs provide clinical, scientific and relational knowledge to share the planning of the best care in every single case. This approach should ensure the balance between the role of HPs and the personal philosophy of the patient, or substitute, involved. In the case of a child, ACP can help both in respecting the assent given or denied from the perspective of his or her best interest and in listening to the child's voice and respecting his or her right to be a co-decision-maker. As regarding the concept of 'best interest', it has been used as a legal and ethical international standard for more than 200 years, but, as Shah, Rosenberg and Diekema (2017) argued, it primarily 'provides a starting point for clinicians' (p. 937). The concept of best interest is, inter alia, limited by subjective interpretations and relative to an individual case. Nonetheless, best interest represents a decisive criterion if used in a balanced way. Best interest should, in fact, be balanced with the interests, values and beliefs of both the patient and the persons involved.

Withholding or withdrawing treatments, experimental therapies, and end-of-life decisions are key concepts of the ethical and legal debate; above all, they are decisions that are made by the patients or, if the PPC patients cannot speak for themselves, whomever takes their place. However, adults must always question whether what the child wants is good for the child. The more mature a child is and able to deal with these problems, the more adults will have to take his or her opinion into account.

Fulfilling the children's right to participate

If children in PPC are heard, adults can obtain significant information to comprehend psychosocial needs and for child-centred care. Moreover, we maintained that there are ways to involve children in the decision-making process to fulfil their rights. Children's assent and ACP materialise children's right to participate in their healthcare. This chapter is making it clear how negotiating choices and facilitating comprehension and engagement are possible through listening in its fullest meaning. When a child with PPC needs can indicate verbally or non-verbally his or her perspective, listening to children plays a pivotal role in symptom control and comprehending psychological, social and spiritual needs (WHO, 1998). This is also the way for improving PPC, and consequently children's' quality of life (Huang et al., 2010; O'Quinn and Giambra, 2014).

The voice of children in PPC that we gathered through the meta-synthesis, revealed that: (1) Children can recognise pain and its effect. Consequently, participation for children with PPC needs requires adults who understand how the children live (e.g. how they do experience pain in the body). HPs can rely on many scales to recognise symptoms and pain (Crellin et al., 2017). Nonetheless, recognising pain and symptoms is not enough for allowing children to participate in their PPC. Other important questions to answer by adults arise: How do children interpret this pain? What is the emotional mood that connotes children's way of experiencing the disease? To offer the best possible care, adults should search for answers to these questions as well.

(2) Children request fair communication, which is co-dependent with (3) being surrounded by significant others. Children attributed great value to communication and listening. Usually, communication in paediatrics is triadic (parent–child–HPs), and creates unique situations for both parents and children. Understanding how communication in PPC works is essential to improve the HPs' communication skills (Sisk et al., 2018). Besides, our findings confirmed how children perceive an honest, accurate, clear and understandable language from HPs being a beneficial communication intervention (Weaver et al., 2016). This can be the first level of a relationship from which children do not feel excluded (Wangmo et al., 2017) and valuable to capture PPC patients' preferences. Moreover, from a phenomenological analysis in a therapeutic context, Mortari and Saiani (2014) found that the essence of care practising includes paying attention and dedicating time to the other, searching for an understanding of the other, cultivating a good relationship with the other, and having and showing respect. Among these examples of being there, paying attention and dedicating time were the most cited by the research participants. The conditions of children in PPC call for adults to assume the demanding dual responsibilities of of caring for and listening to them. As the rationale for PPC regards the emotional, social and spiritual consequences associated with life-threatening, life-limiting conditions, disability and facing the end of life, all these require adequate support, communication and care (Higginson and Costantini, 2008) from adults and HPs. Children are not always in the position to express what they feel because they are so young that it is difficult to speak or because the experience of suffering is such that it is difficult to find the strength to speak. Listening, in all the aspects discussed, is essential.

Finally, according to the meta-synthesis results, we found that (4) being actively involved is one of the wishes of children with PPC needs. Children's active involvement in the decision-making process can be seen as an ethical imperative. In particular, ACP can be defined as a *process* whereby a child with PPC needs, in consultation with HPs, family members and important others, takes decisions or is taken into account about his or her present and future healthcare. ACP offers a framework not only to planning about end-of life care, but also to personalise the approach to the disease *in progress*, including the children's best interest and their expectations and needs. While adolescents are willing to have these conversations about difficult decisions (Pousset et al., 2009), having ACP at a younger age, in the standard paediatric setting, is still a matter of discussion but is the way to guarantee the right to participate. We assume that implementing ACP in the paediatric setting would help children, family members, healthcare professionals and important others to share decisions that take into account the child's best interests and rights.

Conclusion

UNCRC Article 12 provides for the right of children to be heard even in the PPC context. This means that, beyond the PPC-related clinical and physical symptoms' management, for PPC patients the fulfilment of psychological, emotional, spiritual needs and their wishes and preferences depend upon listening. Of course, to address psychosocial needs, HPs and family members must consider the child's developmental level and clinical condition. For example, infants and children with limited verbal ability depend upon sensations and a physical relationship to their surroundings, while children in the primary school age group may begin to understand their condition and HPs let the child have control when possible, allowing the child to participate in medical decisions when appropriate (Michelson and Steinhorn, 2007). We argued in this chapter that listening to the children reveals the contents and the qualities of the right: the categories of honest communication, being a significant carer, and the children as decision-makers unveil the centrality of relationships as children in PPC are involved and make decisions according to the relationship they have with surrounding persons. Listening to children, in its full implementation, entitles children as right-holders, and hopefully more and more protagonists of their healthcare with the ACP, through which children are involved. Consequently, the right to participate in PPC requires adults to understand what children think and feel, to perform honest and still respectful communication, and to comprehend their wishes. When a child is in a situation of utmost suffering, when his or her usual way of life is interrupted and is in a suspended context (as in the hospital) in which he or she does not have access to the things of his or her daily life, living the experience of someone dedicating time to him or her, listening to him or her and trying to meet his or her desires is essential for that child to know he or she has value, that his or her life matters, and that his or her right is guaranteed by competent adults who listen.

Acknowledgements

We wish to express our gratitude to Manuella Walker for her kind assistance (and prompt help) in editing this chapter.

References

American Academy of Pediatrics, Committee on Bioethics and Committee on Hospital Care. 2000. "Palliative care for children." *Pediatrics* 106 (2): 351–357. doi:10.1542/peds.106.2.351.

Beauchamp, Tom L., and James F. Childress. 2013. *Principles of biomedical ethics*. New York: Oxford University Press.

Benini, Franca, Marco Spizzichino, Manuela Trapanotto, and Anna Ferrante. 2008. "Pediatric palliative care." *Italian Journal of Pediatrics* 34 (1): 4. doi:10.1186/1824-7288-34-4.

Borghi, Camila Amaral, Lisabelle Mariano Rossato, Elaine Buchhorn Cintra Damião, Danila Maria Batista Guedes, Ellen Maria Reimberg Da Silva, Silvia Maria de Macedo Barbosa, and Rita Tiziana Polastrini. 2014. "Living with pain: the experience of children and adolescents in palliative care." *Revista da Escola de Enfermagem USP* 48: 59–66. doi:10.1590/S0080-623420140000600010.

Buiting, Hilde M., Mette L. Rurup, Henri Wijsbek, Lia van Zuylen, and Govert den Hartogh. 2011. "Understanding provision of chemotherapy to patients with end stage cancer: qualitative interview study." *BMJ* 342: d1933. doi:10.1136/bmj.d1933.

Carter, Bernie, Maria Edwards, and Anne Hunt. 2015. "'Being a presence': The way in which family support workers encompass, embrace, befriend, accompany and endure with families of life-limited children." *Journal of Child Health Care* 19 (3): 304–319. doi:10.1177/1367493513516391.

Coad, Jane, Jasveer Kaur, Nicky Ashley, Christopher Owens, Anne Hunt, Lizzie Chambers, and Erica Brown. 2015. "Exploring the perceived met and unmet need of life-limited children, young people and families." *Journal of Pediatric Nursing* 30 (1): 45–53. doi:10.1016/j.pedn.2014.09.007

Crellin, Dianne J., Denise Harrison, Adrian Hutchinson, Tibor Schuster, Nick Santamaria, and Franz E. Babl. 2017. "Procedural Pain Scale Evaluation (PROPoSE) study: protocol for an evaluation of the psychometric properties of behavioural pain scales for the assessment of procedural pain in infants and children aged 6-42 months." *BMJ Open* 7 (9): e016225. doi:10.1136/bmjopen-2017-016225.

Davies, Betty, John B. Collins, Rose Steele, Karen Cook, Amy Brenner, and Stephany Smith. 2005. "Children's perspectives of a pediatric hospice program." *Journal of Palliative Care* 21 (4): 252–261.

Dodds, Susan. 2000. "Choice and control in feminist bioethics." In *Relational autonomy: Feminist perspectives on autonomy, agency, and the social self*, edited by Catriona Mackenzie and Natalie Stoljar, 213–235. New York: Oxford University Press.

European Association of Palliative Care (EAPC) Taskforce. 2007. "IMPaCCT: standards for paediatric palliative care in Europe." *European Journal of Palliative Care* 14: 2–7.

Feudtner, Chris, and Pamela G. Nathanson. 2014. "Pediatric palliative care and pediatric medical ethics: Opportunities and challenges." *Pediatrics* 133 (Suppl. 1): S1–S7. doi:10.1542/peds.2013-3608B.

Field, Marilyn J., and Richard E. Behrman. 2003. *When children die: Improving palliative and end-of-life care for children and their families*. Washington, DC: National Academies Press.

Ghirotto, Luca, Elena Busani, Michela Salvati, Valeria Di Marco, Valeria Caldarelli, and Giovanna Artioli. 2018. "Researching children's perspectives in pediatric palliative care: A systematic review and meta-summary of qualitative research." *Palliative and Supportive Care*. Advance online publication. doi:10.1017/S1478951518000172.

Giblin, Marie J. 2002. "Beyond principles: virtue ethics in hospice and palliative care." *American Journal of Hospice and Palliative Medicine* 19 (4):235–239. doi:10.1177/104990910201900407.

Higginson, Irene J., and Massimo Costantini. 2008. "Dying with cancer, living well with advanced cancer". *European Journal of Cancer* 44 (10): 1414–1424. doi:10.1016/j.ejca.2008.02.024.

Hillman, Ken M., and Magnolia Cardona-Morrell. 2015. "The ten barriers to appropriate management of patients at the end of their life." *Intensive Care Medicine* 41 (9): 1700–1702. doi: 10.1007/s00134-015-3712-6.

Hinds, Pamela S., Donna Drew, Linda L. Oakes, Maryam Fouladi, Sheri L. Spunt, Christopher Church, and Wayne L. Furman. 2005. "End-of-life care preferences of pediatric patients with cancer." *Journal of Clinical Oncology* 23 (36): 9146–9154. doi:10.1200/JCO.2005.10.538.

Huang, I-Chan, Elizabeth A. Shenkman, Vanessa L. Madden, Susan Vadaparampil, Gwendolyn Quinn, and Caprice A. Knap. 2010. "Measuring quality of life in pediatric palliative care: challenges and potential solutions." *Palliative Medicine* 24 (2): 175–182. doi: 10.1177/0269216309352418.

Hunt, Anne M. 1990. "A survey of signs, symptoms and symptom control in 30 terminally ill children." *Developmental Medicine & Child Neurology* 32 (4): 341–346. doi: 10.1111/j.1469-8749.1990.tb16946.x.

Hunt, Anne M., and Roger Burne. 1995. "Medical and nursing problems of children with neurodegenerative disease". *Palliative Medicine* 9 (1): 19–26. doi: 10.1177/026921639500900104.

Hynson, Jenny L., Jonathon Gillis, John J. Collins, Helen Irving, and Susan J. Trethewie. 2003. "The dying child: How is care different?" *Medical Journal of Australia* 179 (Suppl. 6): S20–S22.

Jalmsell, Li, Malin Lövgren, Ulrika Kreicbergs, Jan-Inge Henter, and Britt-Marie Frost. 2016. "Children with cancer share their views: tell the truth but leave room for hope." *Acta Pædiatrica* 105 (9): 1094–1099. doi: 10.1111/apa.13496.

Kortesluoma, Riitta Liisa, and Merja Nikkonen. 2004. "'I had this horrible pain': the sources and causes of pain experiences in 4- to 11-year-old hospitalized children." *Journal of Child Health Care* 8 (3): 210–231. doi: 10.1177/1367493504045822.

Kortesluoma, Riitta Liisa, and Merja Nikkonen. 2006. "'The most disgusting ever': children's pain descriptions and views of the purpose of pain." *Journal of Child Health Care* 10 (3): 213–227. doi: 10.1177/1367493506066482.

Kortesluoma, Riitta Liisa, Merja Nikkonen, and Willy Serlo. 2008. "'You just have to make the pain go away' - Children's experiences of pain management." *Pain Management Nursing* 9 (4): 143–149. doi: 10.1016/j.pmn.2008.07.002.

Mack, Jennifer W., Angel Cronin, Nancy L. Keating, Nathan Taback, Haiden A. Huskamp, Jennifer L. Malin, Craig C. Earle, and Jane C. Weeks. 2012. "Associations between end-of-life discussion characteristics and care received near death: A Prospective Cohort Study." *Journal of Clinical Oncology* 30 (35): 4387–4395.

Mack, Jennifer W., and Joanne Wolfe. 2006. "Early integration of pediatric palliative care: for some children, palliative care starts at diagnosis." *Current Opinion in Pediatrics* 18 (1): 10–14. doi: 10.1097/01.mop.0000193266.86129.47.

Michelson, Kelly Nicole, and David M. Steinhorn. 2007. "Pediatric end-of-life issues and palliative care." *Clinical pediatric emergency medicine* 8 (3): 212–219. doi:10.1016/j.cpem.2007.06.006.

Mortari, Luigina, and Luisa Saiani. 2014. *Gestures and thoughts of caring. A theory of caring from the voices of nurses*. New York: McGraw-Hill Education.

Mullick, Anjali, Jonathan Martin, and Libby Sallnow. 2013. "An introduction to advance care planning in practice." *British Medical Journal* 347: f6064. doi: 10.1136/bmj.f6064.

Nedelsky, Jannifer. 1989. "Reconceiving autonomy: Sources, thoughts and possibilities." *Yale Journal of Law & Feminism* 1 (1): Article 5.

Nelson, Judith E., Derek C. Angus, Lisa A. Weissfeld, Kathleen A. Puntillo, Marion Danis, David Deal, Mitchell M. Levy, Deborah J. Cook, and Critical Care Peer Workgroup of the Promoting Excellence in End-of-Life Care Project. 2006. "End-of-life care for the critically ill: a national intensive care unit survey." *Critical Care Medicine* 34: 2547–2553.

Nijhof Sanne L., Christiaan H. Vinkers, Stefan M. van Geelen, Sasja N. Duijff, E. J. Marijke Achterberg, Janjaap van der Net, Remco C. Veltkamp, Martha A. Grootenhuis, Elise M. van de Putte, Manon H. J. Hillegers, Anneke W. van der Brug, Corette J. Wierenga, Manon J. N. L. Benders, Rutger C. M. E. Engels, C. Kors van der Ent, Louk J. M. Vanderschuren, and Heidi M. B. Lesscher. 2018. "Healthy play, better coping: The importance of play for the development of children in health and disease." *Neuroscience Biobehavioural Reviews* 95: 421–429. doi:10.1016/j.neubiorev.2018.09.024.

O'Quinn, Lucy P., and Barbara K. Giambra. 2014. "Evidence of improved quality of life with pediatric palliative care." *Pediatric Nursing* 40 (6): 284–288.

Pousset, Geert, Johan Bilsen, Joke De Wilde, Yves Benoit, Joris Verlooy, An Bomans, Luc Deliens, and Freddy Mortier. 2009. "Attitudes of adolescent cancer survivors toward end-of-life decisions for minors." *Pediatrics* 124 (6): e1142–e1148. doi: 10.1542/peds.2009-0621.

Reggio Emilia Approach. n.d. "L'ospedale con gli occhi dei bambini". Accessed April 25 2019. www.reggiochildren.it/2017/04/12031/lospedale-con-gli-occhi-dei-bambini/.

Sandelowski, Margarete, and Julie Barroso. 2007. *Handbook for synthesizing qualitative research.* New York: Springer.

Shah, Seema K., Abby R. Rosenberg, and Douglas S. Diekema. 2017. "Charlie Gard and the limits of best interest." *JAMA Pediatrics* 171 (10): 937–938. doi:10.1001/jamapediatrics.2017.3076.

Sisk, Bryan A., Annie B. Friedrich, Jessica Mozersky, Heidi Walsh, and James DuBois. 2018. "Core functions of communication in pediatric medicine: an exploratory analysis of parent and patient narratives." *Journal of Cancer Education* December: 1–8. doi: 10.1007/s13187-018-1458-x

Spalding, Jessica, and Sarah Yardley. 2016. "'The nice thing about doctors is that you can sometimes get a day off school': an action research study to bring lived experiences from children, parents and hospice staff into medical students' preparation for practice." *BMJ Supportive & Palliative Care* 6 (4): 459–464. doi:10.1136/bmjspcare-2015-001080.

Stevens, Michael M., Bruce A. Lord, Marie-Therese Proctor, Sue Nagy, and Elizabeth O'Riordan. 2010. "Research with vulnerable families caring for children with life-limiting conditions." *Qualitative Health Research* 20 (4): 496–505. doi: 10.1177/1049732309356097.

Tait, Alan R., and Michael E. Geisser. 2017. "Development of a consensus operational definition of child assent for research." *BMC Medical Ethics* 18: 41. doi: 10.1186/s12910-017-0199-4.

Thorne, Sally, Louise Jensen, Margaret H. Kearney, George Noblit, and Margarete Sandelowski. 2004. "Qualitative metasynthesis: Reflections on methodological orientation and ideological agenda." *Qualitative Health Research* 14 (10): 1342–1365.

U.S. Department of Health and Human Services. 2018. "Code of federal regulations title 45: public welfare part 46: protection of human subjects." *Government Publishing Office.* Accessed August 20 2018. www.hhs.gov/ohrp/regulations-and-policy/regulations/45-cfr-46/index.html

Wangmo, Tenzin, Eva De Clercq, Katharina M. Ruhe, Maja Beck-Popovic, Johannes Rischewski, Regula Angst, Marc Ansari, and Bernice Elger. 2017. "Better to know than to imagine: Including children in their health care." *AJOB Empirical Bioethics* 8 (1): 11–20. doi: 10.1080/23294515.2016.1207724.

Weaver, Meaghann S., Katherine E. Heinze, Cynthia J. Bell, Lori Wiener, Amy M. Garee, Katherine P. Kelly, Robert L. Casey, Anne Watson, Pamela S. Hinds, and Pediatric Palliative Care Special Interest Group at Children's National Health System. 2016. "Establishing psychosocial palliative care standards for children and adolescents with cancer and their families: an integrative review". *Palliative Medicine* 30 (3): 212–223. doi: 10.1177/0269216315583446.

World Health Organization. 1946. "Constitution of the World Health Organization." Accessed July 25 2018. http://apps.who.int/gb/bd/PDF/bd47/EN/constitution-en.pdf?ua=1

World Health Organization. 1998. *Cancer pain relief and palliative care in children.* Geneva: WHO.

World Health Organization. 2002. "WHO definition of palliative care." Accessed July 25 2018. www.who.int/cancer/palliative/definition/en.

25

YOUNG CHILDREN'S EDUCATION AND CARE BEYOND THE SCHOOL WALLS

The right to adventure, away

Casey Y. Myers and Rochelle L. Hostler

Introduction

In recent years, there has been growing interest around young children's education and care that occurs *beyond* the physical boundaries of the early years center, with much attention being paid to how children emerge through outdoor educational spaces, such as those of forest schools (Maynard, 2007), and through other non-traditional educational settings, such as museums (Hackett, Procter and Kummerfeld, 2018). From a rights perspective, these settings may offer children increased and varied opportunities that a traditional classroom may not – opportunities for risk-taking, freedom of choice and movement, participation, and engagement (Nimmo, 2008; Prout, 2005). Despite this interest in the affordances of non-traditional learning spaces, there is currently limited literature on the ways in which early childhood education and care might emerge through other acts of leaving the school grounds. Rather than focusing on schooling within a specific non-traditional context (e.g., the forest or the museum) or on school trips with a particular instructional focus (e.g., a field trip connected to a curricular unit), this chapter examines the possibilities inherent in being *away* from school during the school day in spaces that allowed for collectively improvised events. Through several vignettes of visual ethnographic data generated with 4-year-olds, this chapter will examine the varied ways in which early years care and education emerged during a weekly improvised day away from school that the children would come to call Adventure Group. Although adults' perspectives on and reactions to Adventure Group were varied, we contend that taking up a perspective of *relational materiality* (Hultman and Lenz Taguchi, 2010) was key to our ability to come to complex understandings of the ways in which spaces, places, humans, and non-humans emerged uniquely from intersecting the enactments of *adventuring* and being *away*. A concluding argument is made for how an attentiveness to more complex notions of how children's emergence with/in their surroundings might better enable adults to support children's rights within their school settings.

Doing adventure, being away

The members of Adventure Group were five children, between the ages of 4 and 5 years old, who were enrolled in a full-time mixed-age preschool classroom at a laboratory school in the Midwestern United States. These children were the five oldest in their cohort and their classroom teacher suggested that a small group experience that offered physical and social challenge/provocation might enrich their school day. The authors (the school's Studio Arts Specialist and Curriculum Coordinator/Pedagogue, respectively) volunteered to lead the group each week. Our first foray away from school, one child described what we did as "an adventure" and the children soon identified as Adventure Group, and we, as their adult teachers, took up their language. Adventure Group met every Monday morning between September and May.

Adventure Group differed from more well-researched out-of-classroom or out-of-doors educational experiences in that there was no specific physical location/setting and no pre-planned curricular focus or theme. The activities of Adventure Group were marked by characteristics of collective improvisation (Gershon, 2006). The children negotiated where to go (e.g., the library or the coffee shop) and how to get there (e.g., walking or taking the bus) among themselves, typically just a few minutes before we departed the school. What would happen once we left the school (i.e., the events that would come to comprise "the adventure") emerged intra-actively between all human and non-human elements we would encounter. Other people and animals figured heavily in our adventures, as did the multiple, interconnected public places within a suburban university campus – buildings, public transportation, shops, micro-parks, pathways, stairwells, art installations, sidewalks, streets, hallways, and furniture. None of these were explicitly created for use by children, but rather for adult students and faculty attending the university (i.e., we didn't visit sanctioned playgrounds, children's museums, play centers, etc.). Our adventures emerged differently each time, although the children developed an ease and familiarity with the ritual of leaving school together as we continued our practices of Adventure Group throughout the year.

We, as their teachers, had no pre-planned lessons to teach them or predetermined goals for the outings. Our main responsibilities during our time adventuring were tasks of management or "keeping track." For example, we had a responsibility to keep children reasonably safe (e.g., we would remind children to stay together in a group so as not to become lost), to keep time so that adventuring lasted about 2.5 hours to ensure children returned to school for their lunch and rest period, and to carry the supplies (snacks and water, children's sketchbooks and markers, and the state-required first aid kit).

Documenting and analyzing Adventure Group

As teacher-researchers, we were provoked to attend to the complex workings of the people and places of Adventure Group. Throughout the year, there were multiple ways in which children and surroundings emerged differently together. In any given moment, there were multiple actors in play. To be a "child" in these spaces was to be *multiple* and dependent upon myriad forces – from weather to environmental design to children's imaginings to our own responsibilities as their teachers to strangers' perceptions of our group.

Like many others who work at the intersections of critical geographies and childhood studies, we attended to what was produced as "the social and the spatial are inextricably realised one in another" (Pile and Keith, 1993, p. 6). By taking up a perspective of relational materiality on the doings of children-in-context (Hultman and Lenz Taguchi, 2010), we acknowledged that more-than-human forces, bodies, actors, things, stuff, etc. are in play within an emergent field, and thus central to a politics of childhood must be the intra-active engagements between children, adults, and "non-human" elements wherein all are responsible for mutually constituting each other. We asked ourselves: How are the children and places/spaces we encounter engaged in acts of simultaneous coproduction? How do children and spaces remake each other in different ways through the adventure encounter? What does adventuring do? What does it do to be away from school? As a function of our wonderings, we constructed images (photos and video recordings), as well as transcribed children's dialogue and memoed other adults' encounters with our group and continued to engage with these photos, videos, and writings as constructed cuts of data within a diffractive mode of analysis (Lenz Taguchi, 2012; Mazzei 2014). A diffractive mode takes into account "that knowing is never done in isolation but is always effected by different forces coming together" (Mazzei, 2014, p. 743).

In a diffractive analytic mode, we seek *multiplicity, ambiguity,* and *incoherence* (Barad, 2007; Haraway, 1997) rather than any singular understanding of what Adventure Group was or did. The following vignettes are reconstructions of events. These combinations of narrative, theoretical concepts, field notes, and photographs are partially constructed cuts of the "differences that made a difference" (Barad, 2012, p. 49) in our own understandings of who/how children were becoming in the spaces and places of adventure group and in our conceptualization of what early care and education could become with/for children.

Stairs and stares

Who/how children were becoming within the public sphere of the university often ruptured when children climbed or played in/on tall stairways. In these events, "child" often emerged somewhere between other adults' notions of children's capabilities, their idea(l)s around uses of public places, the coordinates of our human bodies (e.g., the physical distance between their child bodies and us, their supposedly responsible teachers, the distance between the children and other adults who supposedly "belonged" in these spaces), and the materials with which children engaged. These versions of "child/ren" often shifted quickly. In other words, staircases emerged as a powerful force, rendering the children as delightful or disturbing (see Figures 25.1 and 25.2).

But just as the stairways might dictate to passersby the state of "child" and their "teachers," the children also shaped what stairways might become. When traversing stairways, children continually engaged in processes of *moulding, contracting,* and/or *expanding* – aligning their limbs and trunks to travel on railings, making themselves fit safely within tight boundaries and/or taking up as much space as possible. The physical stairways literally shaped the doings of the children, and simultaneously the children produced a new and different kind of stairway – one that was part slide, part pedestrian roadblock, part deathtrap (see Figures 25.3 and 25.4).

Figure 25.1 and 25.2 While drawing in our books in the 12th floor stairwell of the campus library, a passerby noted that children were "artists!" smiling at the children and asking about their illustrations. As the children stood and moved toward the large glass windows at the foot of the stairs to allow the stranger to pass by, she gave a warning to their teachers, "Be careful! What if they fall?" She covered her eyes with her hands and shook her head, laughing in a nervous way to indicate that nothing was actually funny at all; the children's proximity to the ledge was overwhelming and terrifying to her. Young, capable artists became vulnerable younglings through a minor shifting of bodily coordinates within the emergent field of "the staircase."

Figure 25.3 and 25.4

C: Can I fall through? [pointing to the gaps in the balustrade]

Rochelle: Your body could fit through that space, yes.

C: What if I was 6?

Rochelle: I don't know how big you will be when you are 6. But your 4-year-old body could fall through that space.

C: I'll only touch this side (near the wall).

Finding/founding spaces

Almost every adventure included the use of public transportation – specifically the 53 bus and its associated shelters. We told Adventure Group that *children* had to stay within the walls of the bus kiosk – the entrance was near the busy street. We often explained to the children that although we trusted them to keep themselves safe, we didn't necessarily trust that the motorists would be watching for children. Adult students could wait outside if they wanted to; they were big enough that even a distracted driver would likely see them (see Figures 25.5–25.7).

In analyzing the visual data of child–kiosk events, the notion of *finding space* came to the fore (Woolley, 2015) – a concept frequently used in higher education to describe the ways in which a university might absorb existing community structures when the needs and wants of the university would begin to overrun the physical capacity of the already-established campus. Reading our data *through* the literature on found spaces was as a diffractive provocation for the ways in which the physical structure of the bus shelters and children's embodied desires located spaces where the rules of their teachers no longer applied. Cats could subvert adult discourses by finding spaces.

And yet events also pushed at the notion that children simply subverted "adult" spaces for their own uses. A favorite location for Adventure Group was the Brain Plaza – a sculpture garden that featured high sandstone walls carved to resemble stacks of books. When visiting the brain, children would scale the high walls and then walk along the tops of the books, following the slope of the wall to the ground, and then repeat over and over again (see Figures 25.8 and 25.9).

After climbing up the front of the wall, E and I (Casey) had the following exchange.

Figure 25.5

Figure 25.6

Figure 25.7 The small opening between the bottom of the bus shelter and the ground was large enough for their bodies to crawl through if they became "cats." As we entered the bus kiosk, the children would begin to howl and drop to all fours. The cats came in and out through the cat door over and over again, never veering toward the street as some children might. As C said, beckoning to the other four cats, this was the "only way to get out of jail."

Figure 25.8 and 25.9

E: Can you climb on this?

C: No … it's not made for adults to climb on it. It would break.

E: It's not made for grown-ups? Is this made for kids?

C: It's really not made for anyone to climb on it, actually. You're just small enough that your body won't break it.

E: Are we not allowed to climb here?

C: No one tells us not to.

E: Is it for kids?

C: I don't really know.

This conversation, had with my own feet on the ground and E's dangling from the high wall, ruptured my own thinking about who and what make places. Even with a focus on intra-activity, we continued to say, lazily perhaps, that campus spaces were not "made for children." In one very strict sense, this is true. Designers and engineers did not plan and execute these spaces with children in mind. But in another sense, we have to acknowledge, as Ingold (2015) does, that humans and non-humans alike are caught in a constant flow of (re)making. The intentions of designers and engineers aren't indelible; to claim as much would be to say that the physical environment is securely inscribed with the discourses of its maker. The physical environment is always already an active participant in its own remaking. As such, we have to consider that children may not be simply *finding* space on the margins in spite of adult constraints, but equally implicated in the *founding* of spaces, over and over again, in conjunction with an emergent field of materials and discourses.

Rethinking school with adventure in mind

We acknowledge that it is an impossible task to "fully understand, organise or capture the essence of these material-discursive intra-activities" (Hultman and Lenz Taguchi, 2010, p. 540). Even so, it seems a worthwhile endeavor to seek to highlight the complexities of the spaces and places that matter(ed) to children, to attend to what was happening, and to trace the contours of children's emergences through space and place in order to argue for a more complex way of conceptualising what a school day could become.

The ways in which others encountered these kinds of collective improvisations were shaped by competing means-ends discourses (i.e., who and what should drive the collective experiences of children on any particular school day and for what purposes and outcomes). In conversations with other schoolpeople, we were often pressed to detail the purpose of these outings, specifically to name the focus of our "inquiry," and our refusal to name such a focus was met with suspicion. In these cases, the curricular priority our progressive, inquiry-driven school placed on learners' "meaningful engagement" meant that we should be able to easily articulate children's learning and our own teaching strategies. The same pedagogical priorities that prevented children in our school from ever seeing a worksheet or participating in rote memorisation or even whole-group instruction rendered the spontaneous doings of Adventure Group disorganized, mundane, or invaluable. Our own perspective had afforded us the onto-epistemological space to grapple with the complexity of these events, yet this resistance to reductive thinking meant we couldn't easily locate an origin point and trajectory for a specific line of inquiry for the children. The educational discourse of "meaningful engagement" that we ourselves would have adopted in other situations to argue for high-quality educational experiences for children worked against us here.

In other instances, we found ourselves acquiescing to particular educational discourses in order to make a case for the importance of adventuring, away. In contrast to other schoolpeople, the children's families were overtly enthusiastic about their children's participation in Adventure Group. The children excitedly reported to their families the details of our adventures and Monday mornings became highly anticipated. Families appreciated the extra time and attention their children received from two experienced teachers. During the twice-yearly "curriculum chat" wherein teachers gathered with parents to detail the inquiries of small learning groups, the parents of the adventurers were appreciative and attentive, wanting as much information as possible about our days away from school. While sharing stories, photos, and videos, I (Casey) made a point to name the many complex and difficult-to-measure capacities that adventuring might foster, such as responsible risk-taking, cooperation, and self-control. In reflecting on these engagements with families, perhaps my willingness to name learning objectives stemmed from both my desire to provide reassurance and prove my own capabilities. The spontaneous (and even potentially dangerous) nature of adventuring was ameliorated by way of describing it as a soft skills-building experience.

The fact that the irreducible, improvisational doings of children in the shifting, interconnected spaces away from school could be reduced to something uniformly pointless or purposeful pushes us to question the grand narratives that structure the school days of our youngest children. What are the implications for the field of early childhood care and education when, all at once, Adventure Group was both doing nothing much/going nowhere in particular *and* providing children with an avenue for learning valuable psychosocial dispositions? We need to recognize that the ideals that might liberate us from taking up practices we deem to be ineffective, outmoded, or inappropriate can limit us when our ways of being in (or out) of school overrun the boundaries of those discourses.

Conclusion

In thinking about what the complexity of Adventure Group brings to bear upon conversations of children's rights to educational provision, we argue that those who are given power to make educational decisions on behalf of children – where they go and how they might spend their time during the school day – should advocate and make affordances for improvised adventures and time away, so that children might engage in the finding and founding of spaces and might emerge differently through adventures with a host of more-than-human others. And this may necessitate a radical shift in taken-for-granted beliefs and practices. In the same ways we have come to argue for meaningful engagement as a marker of instructional quality (Keen et al., 2011; McMahon and Portelli, 2004, 2012), we must recognize the rights of children to *disengage* from actions and outcomes that are easily intelligible to others, particularly to the adults that have been deemed responsible for their learning and development. In the same ways in which we have come to expect that high-quality educational environments should be designed with children's developmental capacities in mind (Copple and Bredekamp, 2009; DeVries and Zan, 1994) and that nearly every aspect of the material environment within a school is seen as a purposefully arranged expressive medium, communicating a "nexus of well thought out decisions" on the part of (human) teachers (Gandini, 1998, p. 175), we must acknowledge that children and spaces emerge together in ways that can neither be necessarily *protective* nor *predictive*. To rethink and undo would push us to attend to a fuller entanglement of relations, to contend with the ways in which "children" emerge through thoroughly dependent material-discursive circumstances, and might allow us to imagine better *possibilities*, *pluralities*, and *coexistences* (Massey, 2005) with and for children in their school settings.

References

Barad, Karen. 2007. *Meeting the universe halfway: Quantum physics and the entanglement of matter and meaning.* Durham, NC: Duke University Press.

Barad, Karen. 2012. Interview with Karen Barad. In R. Dolphijn and I. van der Tuin (Eds.) *New Materialism: Interviews & Cartographies,* pp. 48–70. Ann Arbor, MI: Open Humanities Press.

Copple, Carol, and Bredekamp, Susan. 2009. *Developmentally appropriate practice in early childhood programs serving children from birth through age 8.* Washington, DC: NAEYC.

DeVries, Rheta and Zan, Betty. 1994. *Moral classrooms, moral children: Creating a constructivist atmosphere in early childhood.* New York: Teachers College Press.

Gandini, Lella. 1998. Educational and caring spaces. In C. Edwards, L. Gandini, and G. Forman (Eds.) *The hundred languages of children: The Reggio Emilia approach—Advanced reflections,* pp. 161–178, 2nd ed., Westport, CT: Ablex.

Gershon, Walter. 2006. Collevitve improvisation: A theoretical lens for classroom observation. *Journal of Curriculum and Pedagogy,* 3(1), 104-135.

Hackett, Abigail, Procter, Lisa, and Kummerfeld, Rebecca. 2018. Exploring abstract, physical, social and embodied space: Developing an approach for analysing museum spaces for young children. *Children's Geographies,* 2(1), 1–14.

Haraway, Donna. 1997. *Modest_witness@second_millennium. FeMan meets_onco mouse: Feminism and technoscience.* New York: Routledge.

Hultman, Karin and Lenz Taguchi, Hillevi. 2010. Challenging anthropocentric analysis of visual data: A relational materialist methodological approach to educational research. *International Journal of Qualitative Studies in Education,* 23(5), 525–542.

Ingold, Tim. 2015. *Making: Anthropology, archeology, art and architecture.* New York: Routledge.

Keen, Deb, Pennell, Donna, Muspratt, Sandy, and Poed, Shiralee. 2011. Teacher self-report on learner engagement strategies in the early years classroom. *The Australian Association for Research in Education, Inc.,* 38, 293–310. DOI: 10.1007/s13384-011-0029-5

Lenz Taguchi, Hillevi. 2012. A diffractive and Deleuzian approach to analyzing interview data. *Feminist Theory,* 13(3), 265–281.

Massey, Doreen. 2005. *For space.* London: Sage.

Maynard, Trisha. 2007. Forest schools in Great Britain: An initial exploration. *Contemporary Issues in Early Childhood,* 8(4), 320–331.

Mazzei, Lisa. 2014. Beyond an easy sense: A diffractive analysis. *Qualitative Inquiry,* 20(6), 742–746. DOI: 10.1177/1077800414530257

McMahon, Brenda, and Portelli, John Peter. 2004. Engagement for what? Beyond popular discourses of student engagement. *Leadership and Policy in Schools,* 3(1), 59–76.

McMahon, Brenda, and Portelli, John Peter (Eds.). 2012. *Student engagement in urban schools: Beyond neoliberal discourses.* Retrieved from https://ebookcentral.proquest.com.

Nimmo, John. 2008. Young children's access to real life: An examination of the growing boundaries between children in child care and adults in the community. *Contemporary Issues in Early Childhood,* 9 (1), 3–13.

Pile, Steve and Keith, Michael. 1993. *Place and the politics of identity.* London: Rouledge.

Prout, Alan. 2005. *The future of childhood: Towards the interdisciplinary study of children.* New York: RoutledgeFalmer.

Woolley, Helen. 2015. Children and young people's spatial agency. In Julie Seymour, Abigail Hacket, and Lisa Proctor (Eds.) *Children's spatialities: Emotion, embodiment, and agency,* pp. 143–167. Palgrave Macmillan UK: London.

26

EARLY CHILDHOOD EDUCATION AND CARE FOR INDIGENOUS CHILDREN AND THEIR FAMILIES FROM COLONISED NATIONS

Working towards culturally meaningful service provision

Rebekah Grace, Mere Skerrett, Jenny Ritchie, Margo Greenwood and Michelle Trudgett

Introduction

The United Nations Convention on the Rights of the Child (UNCRC) (1989) has been instrumental in bringing attention to the importance of addressing the inequities experienced by Indigenous children who live in their ancestors' countries that were colonised and are now dominated by the cultures, values and political systems of the colonisers. Articles 29 and 30 of the UNCRC call for respect for an Indigenous child's cultural identity, languages and values, including in the curriculum and practices of education settings. The UN Declaration on the Rights of Indigenous Peoples (UNDRIP) (2007) further reinforces this message, with Article 14 outlining the right of Indigenous people to establish and control their own education systems appropriate to their cultural methods of teaching and learning, and Article 15 stressing their right to the dignity and diversity of their cultures, traditions and histories. This chapter explores the ways in which these messages have been understood and have formed the basis for advocacy and change within the field of early childhood.

Indigenous children from Euro-Western colonised nations are frequently positioned in research and government documents as being 'at risk' of poor outcomes or as vulnerable and in need of health, education or socio-economic interventions. From the Indigenous Australians to the Native Americans, from the Indigenous peoples of the West Indies to the Māori people in New Zealand, from the First Nations, Métis and Inuit people of Canada to the people of the Hawaiian islands, such deficit positioning merely masks the dominant discourses and power structures that construct Indigenous peoples as 'needy', as 'helpless victims', as 'deficient' (Kaomea, 2005). While the profound health inequities and gaps in performance on measures of formal educational achievement between Indigenous and non-Indigenous people have been widely documented (e.g. Australian Institute of Health and Welfare, 2017; Romero-Little, 2010), what is not well understood or reflected in the dominant discourse is the destructive legacy of colonisation that lies at the heart of these inequities. The histories and cultures of Indigenous peoples are rich and diverse. Their stories and experiences of colonisation and survival are also diverse. Unfortunately, what so many Indigenous people share is a history of genocide, of displacement from their lands, of the undermining of culture and language, the loss of self-determinism, denial of full and equal access to education and to the rights of citizenship, and the loss of their children to institutions, boarding schools or foster homes to deliberately disrupt their connection to family, community and cultural knowledge (Fournier and Crey, 1997; Franklin, 2014; Human Rights Equal Opportunity Commission, 1997). Internationally, paternalistic policies of assimilation continued into the 1960s and 1970s, directly impacting on the parents and grandparents of today's Indigenous children. These practices have invoked widespread intergenerational trauma, with the impacts of historical trauma continuing to affect current generations (Atkinson, 2013; Bodkin-Andrews and Carlosn, 2016; Brave Heart et al., 2011; Pihama et al., 2014). Such policies and practices continue in the ways in which history is taught, the ways in which many education settings enforce Western cultural expectations (Ritchie and Skerrett, 2014); they continue in targeted child welfare surveillance and the significant over-representation of Indigenous children in out-of-home care (Australian Institute of Health and Welfare, 2017; Hare and Anderson, 2010) and the juvenile justice system (Australian Institute of Health and Welfare, 2017; Pelser, 2008). It is important to acknowledge that while the focus of this chapter is on Euro-Western colonisation, other historically powerful empires, such as Japan, also engaged in imperialistic expansion and the subjugation of Indigenous peoples. The ongoing legacy of colonisation around the world is marked by marginalisation and the struggle for Indigenous voices to be heard (e.g. Clarke, 2001).

Over the last 30 years, across colonised nations, we have seen the resurgence of a vision that has gained strength and voice with time. It is a vision in which Indigenous communities reclaim control over the health, education and social services that are meant to support them, a vision in which culture and language are revitalised, and Indigenous ways of knowing, being and doing are respected and embedded within practice (Ball, 2004; Greenwood, 2006; Martin and Mirraboopa, 2003; Ritchie et al., 2010; Skerrett, 2017). Research and advocacy within the field of early childhood has played a key role in this resurgence. It is in the early childhood years, when the foundations of identity and dispositional orientations are laid, that it is arguably most important for children to experience congruence between their home culture and the cultures of other early learning environments, to feel 'nestled in the bosom of their collective' (Greenwood, 2005, p. 555) and not 'subdivided into competing parts' (Romero-Little, 2010, p. 11).

This chapter will discuss the ongoing impact of colonisation for Indigenous people as this relates to the early childhood years, and particularly early childhood education. The chapter provides three case studies, giving examples of resistance and the changing landscapes of policy and practice in three countries: New Zealand, Australia and Canada. Elements of good practice and guiding principles that can be shared across nations are discussed.

Case study: New Zealand

Socio-historical context

The rights of Māori children need to be understood within their historical context. The sovereign islands of Te Ika a Māui (North Island) and Te Waka a Māui (South Island, commonly known as Aotearoa and Te Waipounamu) were discovered and settled by Māori over 1,000 years ago (Ruru, 2010; Walker, 2004). These islands were renamed by Abel Tasman in the mid-1600s, thinking he was in Central America. Over 100 years later, the British explorer James Cook also got lost in the great ocean of Kiwa. However, he managed to plant a flag and anglicised Tasman's rendition of the name to New Zealand. The planting of a flag was by no means insignificant in the eyes of those British explorers (nor other Catholic-European travellers). The action symbolically represented claiming sovereign, property and commercial rights over Indigenous peoples (Ruru, 2010). These rights are bound up in what has been termed the 'doctrine of discovery', which has several key elements. These include: gaining property rights over lands through occupation and possession within a certain time of planting the flag (or sword, or hanging a plate in a tree or baptising a river mouth); a pre-emption right over lands (claiming title while simultaneously avoiding war with other Christian European nations with competing interests); subjugating Indigenous peoples (seizing their sovereign human rights); imposing the Christian religion (part of a 'civilising' process); and instituting a new system of justice (the rule of law) (Miller et al., 2010). Māori traditional sovereignty rights and social structures of *whānau* (loosely approximating smaller family units), *hapū* (larger units of family groupings) and *iwi* (broader tribal groupings) were systematically dismantled. The collectivism that comes with living connected lives with nature and through *whakapapa* (genealogical links) was seized through instituting individualistic 'rational' autonomy (essentially privileging the god-eyed Euro-male). The sociocultural/linguistic impact for Māori has been, and still is, dire.

Impacts and resistance

The way the doctrine of discovery played out in terms of impacting Indigenous/Māori children's lives is in the most fundamental of ways a shocking aberration, by attacking *whānau*, *hapū* and *iwi* (Māori social structures), *patu wairua* (Māori spirituality) and *te reo Māori* (the Māori language). Legislation criminalised Māori ways of being, formally introduced Christianity through the missionary schools and promoted English monolingualism (formalised in the curriculum) as somehow being a natural law, and therefore 'normal'. Any other language outside of that was deemed unnatural and abnormal. That formed the status quo, the nation state of New Zealand, still extant today. Despite our colonial history, *te reo Māori* is a vibrant, living language luxuriant in expression. Those of our young children who have been steeped in this language have blossomed into the leadership and orientations that position them in touch with this land that is Aotearoa, as is the intent of Te Tiriti o Waitangi.

The 1840 Te Tiriti o Waitangi assured Māori that they were to be treated as equal citizens with their own *tino rangatiratanga* (self-determination), although the commitments to Māori contained in the treaty were largely ignored for 145 years (Walker, 2004). In keeping with the Māori philosophy of *whanaungatanga* and *kotahitanga* (inclusivity of relationships and collectivity), Māori children have been included as *whānau* (extended family) members actively participating within their respective collectives as these engage in expressions of *rangatiratanga*, such as the ongoing Māori activism for promised self-determination and return of stolen lands (Walker, 2004). Perhaps the most iconic example of this is the image of Dame Whina Cooper, who at the age of 80 led a protest march for the entire length of Te Ika a Māui, the North Island of Aotearoa, hand in hand with her *mokopuna* (grandchild) (Hopa, 2017; Turia, 2007).

Elements of practice

The *tino rangatiratanga* guaranteed to Māori in Te Tiriti o Waitangi has seen expression in the Māori early childhood education and *whānau* development initiative Te Kōhanga Reo. Skerrett (2007) has articulated the pedagogical application of *tino rangatiratanga* in Kōhanga Reo as 'praxis and resistance (practice, reflection and a will to do things our way)' (p. 8). She explains that 'Applied educationally as a framework, tino rangatiratanga has an active component and is about the affirmation and reformation of Māori identity, indigeneity, self-definition and self-decision by Māori, in Māori, for Māori, for the nation' (p. 8).

In a study in Te Amokura Kōhanga Reo (see Skerrett-White, 2003), it was argued that the notion of *tino rangatiratanga* is about socialising and conscientising children into a commitment to a Māori way of living and a Māori way of speaking. The interrelatedness of those two aspects of socialisation and politicisation in Māori children's self-identification as Māori is part of their growing up experience – a blossoming recognition rather than a traumatising reality. Children are important allies in the *rangatiratanga* aims of regenerating communities of Māori language speakers. More than that, they must be at the centre of these aims. We realise the conscientisation, resistance and transformative roles of reversing language shift efforts in Kōhanga Reo. Most people do not spend their lives as language planners or language activists, but they are going to spend their lives as speakers of something and as members of communities. For those of us dedicated to Māori language reclamation with young children, the joys of being Māori, speaking Māori and maintaining our unique cultural activities and connections is interwoven so that the children lead rich, meaningful, creative lives without too much pressure or tension. Being a Māori/English bilingual, of course, in a predominantly monolingual English-speaking society (colonised by Britain) is often tension-creating as two sets of lives (Māori and Pākehā) are to be maintained. The challenge is how we go about working out a way of enabling our children to live as Māori, to participate as citizens of the world, and to enjoy good health and well-being (Durie, 2001) without becoming ideologues merely theorising about Māori ways of being rather than living Māori ways of being, while mediating rapidly changing Māori worlds (see Figure 26.1).

Te Whāriki, He Whāriki Mātauranga mō ngā Mokopuna o Aotearoa (New Zealand Ministry of Education, 1996), the first early childhood curriculum for Aotearoa New Zealand, has been described by one of its writers as being 'grounded in the rights of children' as well as acknowledging 'the rightful place of indigenous Māori knowledge', with its 'foundation principle being the "empowerment" of children and families' (May, 2005, p. 23). According

Figure 26.1 Photograph taken during a *hikoi* (march) protesting linguicist government policies

to May, *Te Whāriki* positioned 'the consideration of rights, interests and culture as a crucial foundation for delivering "quality outcomes"' (p. 23). The recently 'refreshed' version of *Te Whāriki* reflects a Māori worldview related to 'rights' in stating that 'Viewed from a Māori perspective, all children are born with mana inherited from their tīpuna. Mana is the power of being and must be upheld and enhanced' (New Zealand Ministry of Education, 2017, p. 18). *Tīpuna* are ancestors.

In a recent study, teachers in a public kindergarten in a culturally diverse urban community in Aotearoa New Zealand intentionally fostered *rangatiranga* (self-determination, leadership) within their play-based programme (Adair et al., 2016). Planning and learning stories written by teachers highlighted children's *rangatiratanga* (i.e. their leadership, confidence, collaboration and self-governance and support for others). They supported their teaching and pedagogical documentation with reference to both the early childhood curriculum *Te Whāriki* (New Zealand Ministry of Education, 1996) and *Te Whatu Pōkeka, Kaupapa Māori Assessment for Learning, Early Childhood Exemplars* (New Zealand Ministry of Education, 2009). As part of their planning process, teachers researched the construct of *rangatiratanga* and leadership and reflected on challenges and strategies for supporting children to demonstrate this disposition. Their reflections on this literature included consideration of ways that they might ensure that children's voices were not only heard, but were responded to in their teaching approaches. Jared, one of the teachers, described one example of how the teachers proactively extended children's understandings of *rangatiratanga*. While implementing their teaching focus on *rangatiratanga* over one school term, the teachers conducted several evaluations with separate focuses, such as on children's voice and on parents' voice. In their reflection on children's voice, the teachers considered children's demonstration of leadership in their play and during teacher-facilitated discussions in relation to how they had been framing the concept of *rangatiratanga* with children, and their pedagogical strategies to foster children's understandings and enactment of leadership.

Case study: Australia

Socio-historical context

The socio-historical context that permeates the experiences of Australia's Indigenous peoples is underpinned by past government policies and interventions designed to eradicate cultural knowledge and connection (Menzies and Gilbert, 2013). Captain James Cook claimed the east coast of Australia for Great Britain in 1770, and British colonisation commenced in 1788 with the establishment of New South Wales as a penal colony to relieve overflowing English prisons. The legal doctrine of 'terra nullius' (land belonging to no one) was applied to justify assumed land ownership, despite the presence of Indigenous people who had lived on this land for more than 60,000 years and the establishment of at least 700 different Indigenous language groups. Early on, Australian Indigenous people, particularly those on good farming ground, were displaced from their lands through war and massacres and collected onto 'missions', effectively alienating them from their spiritual traditions, sacred sites and ancestors. The fight by Indigenous Australians to reclaim their sacred lands has been ongoing ever since (Altman, 2003; Loos and Mabo, 2013). It was not until 1962 that all Indigenous people could vote in federal elections, though some were not able to vote in state elections until a few years later. In 1967, Indigenous people were counted in Australian Census figures for the first time, and the Racial Discrimination Act came into force in 1975. Indigenous people are still not acknowledged in the Australian Constitution as the first owners of the land, although there is a strong movement to support Constitutional amendment (Australian Human Rights Commission, n.d.).

From 1910 to 1970, between one in three and one in ten Indigenous children were forcibly removed from their families and communities to live in institutions, serve as unpaid labourers or domestic hands, or adopted into Anglo-Australian families. In some places, the proportion was much higher, with many families having children taken over a number of generations (HREOC, 1997). These children have come to be known as the 'stolen generations'. Despite legislative changes, Indigenous children are currently ten times more likely than non-Indigenous children to be involved with the child protection system (AIHW, 2017). The high ongoing rate of child removal is a legacy of the trauma suffered by earlier generations, the loss of parenting knowledge, and the breakdown of Indigenous families and communities. It also reflects the workings of a paternalistic system that continues to see deficit in parenting practices that vary from those of the Anglo-European mainstream (Grace, Burns and Menzies, 2016).

The history of Indigenous education in Australia broadly took place in three phases (Burridge and Chodkiewicz, 2012). In the mission period (commencing in 1830), if education was provided at all, it was provided by often unqualified teachers from churches and other charitable organisations, with the key objective of teaching Christianity. In the protection era (commencing in the 1880s), Indigenous children could enrol in government schools at the discretion of principals. Many remained at the mission schools, and some who enrolled in government schools were placed in segregated classes. The exclusion of Indigenous children from school was often justified by the 'clean, clad and courteous' policy (Fletcher, 1989), whereby Indigenous children could be sent home if they were judged by school staff to be dirty, inappropriately clothed, or lacking in appropriate manners. In the assimilation period (commencing in 1937), government schools were encouraged to enrol Indigenous children, although they could be excluded if the parents of non-Indigenous children objected, and principals had the right to refuse enrolment. The principal's right to refuse the enrolment of an Indigenous child continued until 1972. Major education policy revision occurred in 1996, when government funding was allocated to support the professional development of teachers on the place of Indigenous culture in the curriculum.

Impacts and resistance

The impact of this difficult history has been profound. In relation to early childhood education and care (ECEC), we know that Indigenous children are less likely to attend ECEC services than non-Indigenous children. Recent figures suggest that 15.9 per cent of Indigenous children do not engage with early childhood services in the year before school, compared to 7 per cent of non-Indigenous children (Goldfeld et al., 2016). This is a marked improvement from 2006, when figures indicated that 49.2 per cent of Indigenous children did not engage with ECEC services. Low levels of engagement are primarily the result of concern that services are not culturally safe. In research interviews, Indigenous parents have described feeling mistrust of services. Parents are fearful that they will be judged and scrutinised, leaving them vulnerable to being reported to child protection authorities. They are fearful that their culture will be undermined or that ECEC staff will not understand cultural practices such as co-sleeping or allowing older siblings to care for younger siblings. They describe being fearful that their children will experience racism, and concern that their children may struggle to form attachments with staff if there are not adults in the centre who are Indigenous and understand local ways of being and communicating (Bowes et al., 2011; Trudgett and Grace, 2011).

Widespread intergenerational trauma, socio-economic disadvantage and lack of access to appropriate early childhood services has impacted on child development (Australian Government, 2013; De Maio et al., 2005). In 2008, the Council of Australian Governments passed a National Indigenous Reform Agreement committing federal, state and territory governments to invest in 'closing the gap' in health, education and employment outcomes between Indigenous and non-Indigenous Australians (COAG, 2008). Three of the six 'Close the Gap' strategies relate to early childhood health and development, built on the understanding that investment in the early years may be most effective in reducing inequities and social disadvantage in the long term (Cunha et al., 2006; Robinson et al., 2011).

There is movement within the Australian education field to cease using phrases such as 'close the gap' because it implies that Indigenous children are lacking and need to catch up. Some argue that it is the education system, and not the children, who are lacking. Dockett, Perry and Kearney (2010) ask us to shift the focus from whether or not children are ready for school to asking whether or not schools are ready and culturally appropriate for the children who will come into their classrooms. Current education policies include strong statements about incorporating Indigenous knowledges and practices in the delivery of education. For example, the Australian Early Years Learning Framework (Australian Government DET, 2009) states the importance of promoting an understanding of Indigenous ways of knowing and being, valuing the knowledge of local Indigenous Elders, and encouraging children in the use of their languages and cultural traditions. Nonetheless, challenges remain in the implementation of policy and in effective engagement between schools and Indigenous families and communities. Many teachers report feeling unprepared and uncertain about how to incorporate Indigenous perspectives and knowledge into the curriculum (Harrison and Greenfield, 2011; Nakata, 2007).

Elements of practice

There have been multiple attempts in Australia to provide culturally appropriate early childhood services. One of the most significant initiatives is the MACS programme (Multifunctional Aboriginal Children's Services). This federally funded scheme supports community-managed ECEC services. MACS centres are largely staffed by local Indigenous people and are designed to play a key role in supporting children and families to engage not only in centre activities, but also with other community services and in community cultural events. It is common, for example, for MACS centres to provide bus transport for children and their families to and from the centre and other community activities. Harrison et al. (2017) describe one MACS centre in rural Queensland that demonstrates culturally meaningful practices. In this centre, adults interact with children as equals and respect the child's right to autonomy and to negotiate their own decisions. They respect family connections, and older siblings or family members are able to come into the centre at any time to spend time with and care for their young children. Older siblings or cousins at the same centre will be called on to comfort a baby who is unsettled or crying. Attachments to staff are demonstrated through the use of familial labels such as 'Nan' or 'Aunty'. Multiple literacies are utilised in the form of stories, music, dance, and non-verbal forms of communication such as sustained eye contact and gestures.

Another example of an important initiative is the Ngroo Education Walking Together Aboriginal Training Model (www.ngrooeducation.org). Ngroo, a programme developed and run by Indigenous trainers and Elders, provides a training and post-training mentoring programme to non-Indigenous early childhood teachers to support their understanding of cultural practices and communication, and to support the building of connection and relationships with their local Aboriginal communities. Their aim is to ensure that Indigenous children in mainstream settings receive strengths-based and culturally meaningful care, and to facilitate positive social change through increased cultural knowledge and understanding.

One example of a particularly innovative approach to supporting young Indigenous children is the 'Parents as Partners' programme being run by a primary school in South West Sydney. This programme is entirely designed and run by older children in Years 5 and 6 (approximately 10–11 years old) for younger children in the year before they commence formal schooling (ages 4–5). It comprises a playgroup and the development of a large resource box (e.g. books, early literacy and numeracy activities, etc.) that is given to every child who is due to start at the school the next year. As part of the playgroup activities, parents are involved in making the resource boxes, guided by the older child facilitators, who also model how to use the activities to support the learning of their young child. This programme has been very successful in building strong community engagement and in supporting the development of pre-academic skills for the children.

Bowes and Grace (2013) summarised the elements of good practice in working with Indigenous communities as falling into three categories: safe people, safe places and safe programmes. 'Safe people' refers to the importance of local community leadership and endorsement from the Elders. It incorporates prioritising the employment and capacity-building of local Indigenous staff and taking great care in the selection of non-Indigenous staff, as well as investing in their cultural awareness. 'Safe places' speaks to the importance of providing ECEC in spaces that are comfortable and encourage a sense of ownership or control for the local people – whether this be in a community hall or under a tree. 'Safe programmes' incorporates the importance of a strengths-based and culturally meaningful approach to learning, flexibility and programme sustainability, willingness to adapt programmes to be appropriate to local cultural contexts, and developing integrated and collaborative approaches to programme delivery.

Case study: Canada

Socio-historical context

Our children are a sacred responsibility. As the cornerstone of our nations, they are the key to our survival and continuity. Formalised early childhood programmes and services and their rationales evolve from and also reflect the social-political contexts of their day. The nation of Canada, like other colonised parts of the world, was founded on colonial violence toward and incursion into Indigenous personhoods, nationhoods, collectives, identities, and territories. Perhaps the most notorious of these incursions in Canada consists of the abuses inflicted by the now infamous system of residential schooling. From 1883 to 1998, the Canadian government and church organisations used the residential school system in attempts to assimilate First Nations, Métis and Inuit children by systematically severing their ties with their languages, cultures, and connections to family and kin.

The Truth and Reconciliation Commission (TRC), a national inquiry into the residential school system that released its final report in 2015, estimated that more than 150,000 Indigenous children were removed from their families and sent to residential schools – a removal of several generations of children in some families and communities. These deeply harmful practices were rooted in racist views of First Nations, Métis and Inuit peoples as 'savage' and in need of 'saving' – a framing that legitimated and justified what the TRC called cultural genocide. Although assimilation policies became less overt over the latter part of the twentieth century, the Canadian government continued to remove First Nations, Métis and Inuit children from their homes and foster or adopt them out to non-Indigenous families at rates wildly incommensurate with other populations. The 'Sixties Scoop', so named for the decade in which child apprehensions from Indigenous communities soared, in reality has never truly ended, with more children now in the care of the state than at the height of residential schools.

Impacts and resistance

Indigenous people in Canada and elsewhere, however, are anything but passive victims of colonisation, and have been advocating for the rights and well-being of their children and communities in many different ways – both through engaging and working with the Canadian government, and, when more conciliatory processes have proved ineffective, by mounting powerful acts of land-based protest and resistance. In the summer of 1990, the so-named Oka Crisis erupted on Mohawk territories in southern Quebec. One year after the 78-day standoff between the Mohawks and Canadian government forces (at one point, more than 4,000 soldiers and 1,000 vehicles were deployed), then-Prime Minister Brian Mulroney announced the formation of the Royal Commission on Aboriginal Peoples (RCAP), with a mandate to examine the issues brought to light by the Oka Crisis. In 1996, RCAP released its final report, urging the Canadian government and the people of Canada to engage in a process of reconciliation for the harms of colonisation.

Although little follow-through on the 20-year roadmap laid out by RCAP took place, mounting pressure on the Canadian government to deal with the devastating legacy of the residential schooling system came to head with a class action lawsuit brought against the government by former residential school students. In 2005, the federal government released the Indian Residential School Settlement Agreement, which included, among other components, financial compensation for victims of abuse and a commitment to engage in a fuller inquiry through the Truth and Reconciliation Commission, which began its work in 2008 and concluded with a lengthy report in 2015, including 94 'Calls to Action' to begin the work of acknowledging and ameliorating the multigenerational harms caused through the residential schooling system. Call #12 speaks directly to early childhood, and calls on 'federal, provincial, territorial, and Aboriginal governments to develop culturally appropriate early childhood education programs for Aboriginal families' (Truth and Reconciliation Commission, 2015, p. 321).

First Nations, Métis and Inuit communities have always worked to preserve the ways of knowing and raising children that are imbedded within their languages and cultures, but the earliest formalised government programmes specifically designed for Indigenous children emerged in the 1990s with the Head Start urban and northern programmes and the First Nations Child Care Initiative (FNCCI). These programmes were adapted from non-Indigenous programmes in the United States, and were funded and regulated by provincial and territorial governments. With the election of a conservative federal government in 2006, Indigenous early childhood programming in Canada entered a period of suspended growth until a change of government in 2015 brought new opportunities for systemic transformation, shifting the responsibility for early childhood care back where it belongs: with First Nations, Métis and Inuit communities. The shift from non-Indigenous early childhood programming to Indigenous, community-based programming that is rooted in Indigenous language and culture is a crucial move towards self-determination.

In 2015, the Prime Minister asked the Minister of Employment and Social Development Canada (ESDC) and the Minister of Indigenous and Northern Affairs to collaborate with Indigenous peoples, provinces, and territories in developing an Indigenous Early Learning and Child Care (IELCC) Framework as a first step towards delivering affordable, high-quality, flexible and fully inclusive childcare. This process began in 2016 with the national Indigenous organisations (e.g. the Assembly of First Nations, Métis National Council, Inuit Tapiriit Kanataéi, Native Women's Association of Canada, Pauktuuit, etc.) tasked to oversee and implement community engagement processes that would identify and confirm key principles, priorities and actions that would guide development of the national IELCC Framework. Respective regional working group members undertook engagement activities in each of their regions while other groups and individuals across Canada were also invited to provide comment on the direction of the framework.

At its broadest sense, the national IELCC Framework is distinction-based, privileges children in the context of family, and focuses on high-level principles, goals and directions designed to stand the test of time. These principles include:

- recognising the right of First Nations, Inuit and Métis to determine the programmes and services that best meet the needs of their children and families;
- creating new and innovative programmes, supports and services that respond to the needs of the children and families being served while recognising existing ELCC programmes;
- committing to capacity development support at all levels; and
- supporting reciprocal accountability.

Elements of practice

Time will tell how these principles are realised and put into practice in the diverse First Nations, Métis and Inuit communities that are following their own path to self-determination. What we know, however, is that Indigenous peoples across the generations have consistently advocated for our right to take responsibility for our own lives and that of our children. We also know that the health and well-being of Indigenous children, families and nations are prerequisites to self-determination in the context of revitalised relationships with all levels of government. Children are inextricably linked to their families, communities and nations. Realising family as the circle of care for children and as the foundational building block of nations is a fundamental consideration in the creation of early childhood services for Indigenous children.

We look to some promising and exciting programmes, such as the language nest programme in in the Splatsin First Nation near Enderby, BC, which brings grandmothers and Elders into an early childcare setting to teach the Splatsin language (http://splatsin.org/). Recognising that the care of our children reaches from the moment of their conception, *Nehiyô* (Plains Cree) from the Kehewin Cree Nation in Alberta vision a Cree birthing centre that will focus on delivering low-risk births in the community and instilling principles of *Nehiyô opikihâwasiwin* (child-rearing; the act of raising up Cree children) for families. These include utilising the *Nehiyô* seven stages of life teachings, encompassing spiritual ceremonies across the life span. The birth centre is the community's way of reclaiming births back into the nation and an assertion of sovereignty and the knowledge that healthy children and families equal healthy communities.

The care and education of children is considered both a sacred and a highly valued responsibility. Children are vital to the survival of Indigenous cultures because they are imbued with the ways of knowing and being of their collectives (Bear, 2000). It is critically important for early childhood programmes and services to include and support connections between Indigenous languages, ways of knowing (epistemology), ways of being (ontology), and the values underlying relational accountability (axiology).

The home of Indigenous children and their knowledge(s) lies with Indigenous individuals, families and communities. The implication of this reality for structural, policy and operational change is the inclusion of Indigenous peoples in all aspects of planning, development and implementation of early childhood programmes and services. This inclusion is not a one-off experience, but one that is ongoing and reciprocal in nature. Additionally, these realities influence what and how children learn and are taught. These teaching and learning actions, anchored in Indigenous knowledges, demand a revitalisation of protocols and processes that focus on language and orality, storytelling, experiential learning, arts, and diverse ways of coming to know, such as dreams and intuition, which can only be done by meaningfully engaging knowledge-holders. Equally important is ensuring consideration for children's developmentally appropriate care.

Conclusion

It is the birthright of every child to learn and be secure in the cultural foundations that link them to their family and to their ancestors. For many generations, the Indigenous children of colonised nations have been raised within political contexts characterised by active efforts to disrupt and undermine their cultural traditions and ways of knowing, being and doing. Efforts to eliminate Indigenous cultures were, and continue to be, underpinned by misunderstanding and racism, and are deeply damaging. Colonised nations have not yet healed from this legacy. Nonetheless, the stories of Indigenous people are not stories of victimhood and defeat. They are stories of resilience, survival and activism in the face of overwhelming adversity and the delegitimising of their cultural identities.

Children, and their rights, are embedded in the discourses of the wider rights of Indigenous peoples and communities. Some colonised nations, such as New Zealand, have a treaty-based framework that has historically and contemporarily been used by the Indigenous people as a source of rights and redress for continued injustices. In New Zealand, the Kōhanga Reo movement and the early childhood curriculum *Te Whāriki* are at the forefront of recognising these rights and seeking redress. It is significant that *te reo Māori* (the Māori language) is used in the curriculum documents. Other colonised nations, such as Australia, are yet to give constitutional or treaty recognition to their Indigenous people. Nonetheless, there are strong movements within the early childhood field internationally to at least begin to shift the discourses that privilege the perspectives of the Anglo-European culture, and to include Indigenous approaches to early learning. While these shifts are manifest within policy documents, and there are examples of exemplary practice as outlined in the case studies above, there is still much to be done to support their appropriate and widespread implementation.

O'Brien and Trudgett (2018) argue it is essential that Indigenous children are able to recognise their own culture within all systems of education. This requires more than scattering within the curriculum an occasional Indigenous song or an Indigenous story. It requires Indigenous leadership, respect for the right of Indigenous people to self-determination, and the establishment of respectful collaborative partnerships between community leaders and educators. It also requires honest and transparent accounts of history from multiple perspectives. Indigenous languages are at the core of Indigeneity, and are therefore fundamental to Indigenous rights. It is essential that Indigenous languages are taught within education settings. In countries such as Canada, Australia and the United States, the inclusion of Indigenous languages in the curriculum is made complicated by the fact that there is not one national Indigenous language. There are many language groups, and sadly many languages that have become extinct. For these reasons, it is not possible in some countries to establish a set national curriculum for Indigenous language. However, the principle of including some Indigenous language could be mandated at the national level, and designed at the community level, with the inclusion of local Indigenous languages taught by local Indigenous leaders to all students.

The United Nations Convention on the Rights of the Child enshrines in legislation the principle of respect for cultural diversity, and the right of all children to have their traditions and languages taught and valued within education settings. This is reinforced by the United Nations Declaration on the Rights of Indigenous Peoples, which requires governments, 'in conjunction with indigenous peoples' to ensure that Indigenous children have access 'to an education in their own culture and provided in their own language' (Article 14.3). The voices of Indigenous people in standing for their rights are strong across the world. While there is much to be done, the momentum for change within the early childhood context is growing. There are learnings to be shared across nations in relation to effective advocacy and embedding new cultural frameworks within early childhood education settings. The responsibility for positive change does not lie exclusively on the shoulders of Indigenous people. It is the responsibility of us all to create learning environments in which all forms of knowledge are honoured, and cultural diversity is valued as part of the richness of human experience and interaction.

References

Adair, Jennifer, Phillips, Louise, Ritchie, Jenny, and Sachdeva, Shubhi. 2016. "Civic action and play: Examples from Maori, Aboriginal Australian and Latino communities." *Early Child Development and Care* 187 (5–6): 799–811.

Altman, Jon. 2003. "People on country, healthy landscapes and sustainable Indigenous economic futures: The Arnhem Land case." *The Drawing Board: An Australian Review of Public Affairs* 4 (2): 65–82.

Atkinson, Judy. 2013. *Trauma informed services and trauma-specific care for Indigenous Australian children. Resource sheet no. 21.* Canberra: Australian Insitute of Health and Welfare Closeing the Gap Clearinghouse. www.aihw.gov.au/uploadedFiles/ClosingTheGap/content/Publications/2013/ctg-rs21.pdf

Australian Government. 2013. *A snapshot of early childhood development in Australia in 2012: Australian Early Development Index (AEDI) national report.* Canberra: Australian Government. www.aedc.gov.au/docs/default-source/public-documents/reports/report_nationalreport_2012.pdf?sfvrsn=2&download=true

Australian Government Department of Education and Training. 2009. *Belonging, being and becoming: the early years learning framework for Australia.* Canberra: Council of Australian Governments. https://docs.education.gov.au/system/files/doc/other/belonging_being_and_becoming_the_early_years_learning_framework_for_australia._v5_docx.pdf

Australian Human Rights Commission. n.d. *About constitutional reform.* www.humanrights.gov.au/publications/about-constitutional-recognition

Australian Institute of Health and Welfare. 2017. *Child protection Australia 2015-16.* Canberra: AIHW. www.aihw.gov.au/publication-detail/?id=60129558626&tab=3

Ball, Jessica. 2004. "As if Indigenous knowledge and communities mattered: Transformative education in First Nations communities in Canada." *The American Indian Quarterly* 28 (3&4): 454–479.

Bear, Leroy Little. 2000. "Jagged worldviews colliding." In Marie Battiste (ed.), *Reclaiming Indigenous voice and vision*, 77–85. Vancouver: University of British Columbia.

Bodkin-Andrews, Gawaian, and Carlosn, Bronwyn. 2016. "The legacy of racism and Indigenous Australian identity within education." *Race, Ethnicity and Education* 19 (4): 784–807.

Bowes, Jennifer, and Grace, Rebekah. 2013. *Closing the gap in the early childhood years: Prevention and early intervention approaches to parenting education, early childhood education and health for Indigenous children and families in Australia.* Canberra: Australian Institute of Health and Welfare. www.aihw.gov.au/getmedia/bf7f4034-cfde-4f80-b07f-043b5304f923/ctgc-ip08.pdf.aspx?inline=true

Bowes, Jennifer, Kitson, Rosalind, Simpson, Tracey, Reid, Jo-Anne, Smith, Melissa, Downey, Belinda, and Pearce, Sophia. 2011. *Child care choices of indigenous families.* Sydney: Department of Community Services. www.community.nsw.gov.au/__data/assets/pdf_file/0006/321585/researchnotes_childcare_choices_atsi.pdf

Brave Heart, Maria Yellow Horse, Chase, Josephine, Elkins, Jennifer, and Altschul, Deborah. 2011. "Historical trauma among Indigenous peoples of the Americas: Concepts, research, and clinical considerations." *Psychoactive Drugs* 43 (4): 285–290.

Burridge, Nina, and Chodkiewicz, Andrew. 2012. "An historical overview of Aboriginal education policies in the Australian context." In *Indigenous education: A learning journey for teachers, schools and communities*, Nina Burridge, Frances Whalan, and Karen Vaughan, edited by, 11–22. Rotterdam, The Netherlands: Sense Publishers.

Clarke, Gerard. 2001. "From ethnocide to ethnodevelopment? Ethnic minorities and indigenous peoples in Southeast Asia." *Third World Quarterly* 22 (3): 413–436.

Council of Australian Governments. 2008. *National indigenous reform agreement (closing the gap)*. Canberra: COAG. www.coag.gov.au/node/145

Cunha, Flavio, Heckman, James, Lochner, Lance, and Masterov, Dimitry. 2006. "Interpreting the evidence on life cycle formation." In *Handbook of the economics of education*, Eric Hanusket and Finis Welch, edited by, 697–812. Amsterdam: North Holland.

De Maio, John, Zubrick, Stephen, Silburn, Sven, Lawrence, David, Mitrou, Francis, Dalby, Robin, Blair, Eve, Griffin, Judith, Milroy, Helen, and Cox, Adele. 2005. *The Western Australian Aboriginal child health survey: Measuring the social and emotional wellbeing of Aboriginal children and intergenerational effects of forced separation*. Perth: Curtin University of Technology and Telethon Institute for Child Health Research.

Dockett, Sue, Perry, Bob, and Kearney, Emma. 2010. *School readiness: What does it mean for Indigenous children, families and communities?* Canberra: Australian Institute of Health and Welfare and the Australian Institute of Family Studies.

Durie, Mason. 2001. *A framework for considering Māori educational advancement*. Opening address to the Ministry of Education. Taupō, New Zealand: Hui taumata mātauranga.

Fletcher, Jim. 1989. *Clean, clad and courteous: A History of Aboriginal Education in New South Wales*. Sydney: Southwood Press.

Fournier, Suzanne, and Crey, Ernie. 1997. *Stolen from our embrace: The abduction of First Nations children and the restoration of Aboriginal communities*. Vancouver: Douglas & McIntyre Ltd.

Franklin, Corrinne. 2014. "Belonging to bad: Ambiguity, parramatta girls and the parramatta girls home." *Geographical Research* 2: 157–167.

Goldfeld, Sharon, O'Connor, Elodie, O'Connor, Meredith, Sayers, May, Moore, Tim, Kvalsvig, Amanda, and Brinkman, Sally. 2016. "The role of preschool in promoting children's healthy development: Evidence from an australian population cohort." *Early Childhood Research Quarterly* 35: 40–48.

Grace, Rebekah, Burns, Kate, and Menzies, Karen. 2016. "Aboriginal and torres strait islander children: The legacy of strong state intervention." In *Children, families and communities*, Rebekah Grace, Kerry Hodge and Cathy McMahon, edited by, 292–317. Melbourne, Victoria: Oxford University Press.

Greenwood, Margo. 2005. "Children as citizens of first nations: Linking indigenous health to early childhood development." *Paediatric Child Health* 10 (9): 553–555.

Greenwood, Margo. 2006. *Children are a gift to us: Aboriginal specific early childhood programs and services in Canada*. Ottawa, ON: Human Resources Development Canada, Government of Canada.

Hare, Jan, and Anderson, Jim. 2010. "Transitions to early childhood education and care for Indigenous children and families in Canada." *Australasian Journal of Early Childhood* 35 (2): 19–27.

Harrison, Linda, Sumsion, Jennifer, Bradley, Ben, Letsch, Karen, and Salamon, Andi. 2017. "Flourishing on the margins: a study of babies and belonging in an Australian Aboriginal community childcare centre." *European Early Childhood Education Research Journal* 25 (2): 189–205.

Harrison, Neil, and Greenfield, Maxine. 2011. "Relationship to place: Positioning Aboriginal knowledge and perspectives in classroom pedagogies." *Critical Studies in Education* 52 (1): 65–76.

Hopa, Ngapare. 2017. "Ngā rōpū – Māori organisations. Whina Cooper and her moko." In *Te Ara - the encyclopedia of New Zealand*. https://teara.govt.nz/en/photograph/29689/whina-cooper-and-her-moko

Human Rights and Equal Opportunity Commission. 1997. *Bringing Them Home: Report of the national inquiry into the separation of Aboriginal and Torres Strait Islander children from their families*. Sydney: HREOC.

Kaomea, Julie. 2005. "Reflections of an 'always already' failing native Hawaiian mother: Deconstructing colonial discourses on Indigenous child-reading and early childhood education." *Hūlili: Multidisciplinary Research on Hawaiian Well-being* 2 (1): 77–95.

Loos, Noel, and Mabo, Eddie. 2013. *Edward Koiki Mabo: His life and struggle for land rights.* Queensland: University of Queensland Press.

Martin, Karen, and Mirraboopa, Booran. 2003. "Ways of knowing, being and doing: A theoretical framework and methods for Indigenous and Indigenist re-search." *Journal of Australian Studies* 27 (76): 203–214.

May, Helen. 2005. "A 'right as citizen to a free [early childhood] education.' 1930s–2000s." *Childrenz Issues* 9 (2): 20–49.

Menzies, Karen, and Gilbert, Stephanie. 2013. "Engaging communities." In *Our voices: Aboriginal and Torres Strait Islander social work*, Bindi Bennet, Sue Green, Stephanie Gilbert, and Dawn Bessarab, edited by, 50–72. South Yarra, Victoria: Palgrave Macmillan.

Miller, Robert, Ruru, Jacinta, Behrendt, Larissa, and Lindberg, Tracey. 2010. *Discovering Indigenous lands: The doctrine of discovery in the English colonies.* London, UK: Oxford University Press.

Nakata, Martin. 2007. *Disciplining the savages, savaging the disciplines.* Canberra: Aboriginal Studies Press.

New Zealand Ministry of Education. 1996. *Te Whāriki. He whāriki mātauranga mō ngā mokopuna o Aotearoa: Early childhood curriculum.* Wellington, NZ: Learning Media. https://education.govt.nz/assets/Documents/Early-Childhood/Te-Whariki-1996.pdf

New Zealand Ministry of Education. 2009. *Te Whatu Pōkeka. Kaupapa Māori assessment for learning. Early childhood exemplars.* Wellington, NZ: NZ Ministry of Education. www.education.govt.nz/early-childhood/teaching-and-learning/assessment-for-learning/te-whatu-pokeka-english/

New Zealand Ministry of Education. 2017. *Te Whāriki. He whāriki mātauranga mō ngā mokopuna o Aotearoa. Early childhood curriculum.* Wellington, NZ: Ministry of Education. www.education.govt.nz/early-childhood/teaching-and-learning/te-whariki/

O'Brien, Grace, and Trudgett, Michelle. 2018. "From school house to big house." *The Australian Journal of Indigenous Education* (online): 1–9. DOI: 10.1017/jie.2018.13.

Pelser, Eric. 2008. "Learning to be lost: Youth crime in South Africa." *Discussion papers for the Human Sciences Research Council Youth Policy Initiative* 1–4. www.cjcp.org.za/uploads/2/7/8/4/27845461/hsrc_youth_crime_discussion_paper2.pdf

Pihama, Leonie, Reynolds, Paul, Smith, Cherryl, Reid, John, Smith, Linda, and Te Nana, Rihi. 2014. "Positioning historical trauma theory within Aotearoa New Zealand." *AlterNative: An International Journal of Indigenous Peoples* 10 (3): 248–262.

Ritchie, Jenny, Duhn, Iris, Rau, Cheryl, and Craw, Jacinta. 2010. *Titiro Whakamuri, Hoki Whakamua. We are the future, the present and the past: caring for self, others and environment in early years' teaching and learning.* unitec.researchbank.ac.zn/bitstream/handle/10652/1771/Ritchie%20-%20Titiro%20whakamuri.pdf?sequence=1

Ritchie, Jenny, and Skerrett, Mere. 2014. *Early childhood education in Aotearoa New Zealand: History, pedagogy, and liberation.* New York: Palgrave MacMillan.

Robinson, Gary, Tyler, William, Jones, Yomei, Silburn, Sven, and Zubrick, Stephen. 2011. "Context, diversity and engagement: Early intervention with Australian Aboriginal families in urban and remote contexts." *Children & Society* 26 (5): 343–355.

Romero-Little, Mary. 2010. "How should young Indigenous children be prepared for learning? A vision of early childhood education for Indigenous children." *Journal of American Indian Education* 49 (1&2): 1–25.

Ruru, Jacinta. 2010. "Asserting the doctrine of discovery in Aotearoa New Zealand: 1840-1960s." In *Discovering Indigenous lands: The doctrine of discovery in the English colonies*, Robert Miller, Jacinta Ruru, Larissa Behrendt and Tracey Lindberg, edited by, 208–227. Oxford: Oxford University Press.

Skerrett, Mere. 2007. "Kia Tu Heipu: Languages frame, focus and colour our worlds." *Childrenz Issues: Journal of the Children's Issues Centre* 11 (1): 6.

Skerrett, Mere. 2017. "Colonialism, Māori early childhood, language and the curriculum." In *Handbook of indigenous education*, Elizabeth Ann McKinley and Linda Tahiwai Smith, edited by, 1–22. Singapore: Springer. DOI: 10.1007/978-981-10-1839-8_17-1.

Skerrett-White, Mere. 2003. *Kia mate rā anō a tama-nui-te-rā: reversing language shift in kōhanga reo.* Unpublished doctoral thesis. Hamilton, New Zealand: Waikato University.

Trudgett, Michelle, and Grace, Rebekah. 2011. "Engaging with early childhood education and care services: The perspectives of Indigenous Australian mothers and their young children." *Kulumun Journal* 1: 15–36.

Truth and Reconciliation Commission. 2015. *Honouring the truth, reconciling for the future: Summary of the final report of the Truth and Reconciliation Commission of Canada*, 321. Canada: Truth and Reconciliation Commission.

Turia, Tariana. 2007. Speech to grandparents raising grandchildren trust. *Scoop Independent News, Parliament.* www.scoop.co.nz/stories/PA0703/S00047.htm

United Nations. 1989. United Nations Convention on the Rights of the Child. http://www.unicef.org/child-rights-convention

United Nations. 2007. United Nations Declaration on the Rights of Indigenous Peoples. A/RES/61/295. www.un.org/development/desa/indigenouspeoples/declaration-on-the-rights-of-indigenous-peoples.html

Walker, Ranginui. 2004. *Ka Whawhai Tonu Matou. Struggle without end.* Auckland: Penguin.

27

RESPECTFUL EDUCATORS, CAPABLE LEARNERS

Then and now

Cathy Nutbrown

Introduction

This chapter picks up on key themes of an edited collection, *Respectful Educators – Capable Learners* (Nutbrown, 1996), the first early education-focused book on the United Nations Convention for the Rights of the Child (UNCRC) to be published in the UK. It asked: 'What does a respectful service for young children look like?' and 'How do respectful educators behave?' Contributors examined UK policy and practice in early childhood education (ECE) in light of the UNCRC. One overarching theme was the responsibilities of policymakers, parents and early years practitioners to work with the UNCRC to respect and realise young children's rights in ECE. At the time of publication of the book in 1996, the term 'educators' was a generally accepted generic term for all who worked with young children. Since then, in England, it has been made an official term for early years practitioners who held a particular level of qualification. Therefore, while maintaining the original title of the 1996 book, I have, throughout the rest of the chapter, mostly used the term 'practitioners', which is now a more widely used generic term to include all roles in early education regardless of status or qualification.

Reflecting on some of the issues raised in the 1996 book, this chapter also identifies new issues and concerns mainly focusing on goals of education, leisure, play and culture, specifically aspects of Article 29:

> Education must develop every child's personality, talents and abilities to the full. It must encourage the child's respect for human rights, as well as respect for their parents, their own and other cultures, and the environment.

And Article 31:

> Every child has the right to relax, play and take part in a wide range of cultural and artistic activities.

Of course, when thinking holistically about children's lives and learning, there is inevitable and necessary overlap with other articles of the Convention, as this chapter will identify.

This chapter begins by considering how young children are viewed by adults, and how differing perceptions of the construct of 'childhood' inform policy and practice in ECE, and

331

how views of 'the child' in education shape policy and presently seem to restrict their leisure, play and culturally appropriate opportunities. The chapter moves from considering notions of childhood to an examination of some of the practices and lessons from the past, and asks what remains to be done.

Views of childhood

The image of 'the child' has continually changed over time, and across cultures, and does not always coincide with the image of the child in the UNCRC. It is important to acknowledge here that there is no single child or childhood, but rather all children are different, and all childhoods are different. However, policy often situates children as a homogeneous group, and thus this use of the term 'the child' is in relation to that concern. Hazareesingh et al. (1989) challenge an image of children as passive recipients, 'adults in waiting', 'adults in the making' or 'unfinished adult', arguing that this perspective 'effectively denies the essential unity of the child' (p. 18).

The changing language of education policy depicts a changing view of 'the child', and the kind of education considered best. Discourses have moved from 'child' to 'pupil', from 'learning' to 'achievement', and what children achieve is ranked in terms of 'targets', 'goals' and 'levels'. Present English policy emphasises the *outcomes* of ECE in terms of what children will *ultimately become or contribute*. The attention is on the future, on excellence, on high achievement and on economic stability. There is little focus on the role early education can play in the *now*, and in particular on 'the right of the child to rest and leisure, to engage in play and recreational activities appropriate to the age of the child and to participate freely in cultural life and the arts' (Article 31). There is heavy emphasis in current policy on preparing children for the next year of schooling, with funding cuts making it increasingly difficult for some settings to create opportunities for children 'to participate fully in cultural and artistic life' with 'equal opportunities for cultural, artistic, recreational and leisure activity' (Article 31). It is important to bear in mind that play is an essential and powerful means for learning that supports young children's evolving capacities, as well as a crucial element of healthy childhoods (Wood, 2014). There is a hurriedness to policy now, which seems to leave little time for children *to be children*.

There is growing emphasis in England on 'school readiness' (Ofsted, 2017), on early teaching of basic skills, which many see as developmentally inappropriate (KEYU, 2018). The emphasis in a report on the first year in school in England (Ofsted, 2017) is on education for the future, early formal teaching, regardless of children's developmental needs at the cost of play for many children who begin formal schooling aged just 4 years. This homogeneous view of 'the child' requires practitioners to 'deliver' a curriculum, some devoid of play, to all children, and to assess according to a narrow view of what is important in ECE. It begs the question as to how respectful early years practitioners are able to be in a constraining context that largely ignores the individuality and 'voice' of young children.

Our view of children influences our expectations of them, the learning environments we create for them, and the value we place on the role of the practitioners who work with them. While the UNCRC views children as vulnerable and in need of protection, it also upholds children as capable of participation in society, and in particular in decisions that affect them, including their rights in terms of education, play, leisure and culture.

English policy in 2019 remains rooted in a view of childhood as a time of preparation for the future (DfE, 2017, 2018; Ofsted, 2017). A 2019 report on tackling disadvantage in the early years gave a clear indication that the government's view of education was to enhance the economy:

> This Government's vision is for world-class education, training and care for every-one, whatever their background. This will help to build an economy that is more productive and fit for the future so that everyone has the chance to reach their potential and live a more fulfilled life.
>
> *(DfE, 2019, p. 5)*

The UNCRC binds ratifying governments and challenges policymakers, practitioners, parents and the general public to do *all they can* to realise children's rights (Article 4, implementation of the Convention). The next section questions whether the English government and its agencies really are doing 'all they can'.

Then and now. For better? For worse?

The authors who contributed to *Respectful Educators – Capable Learners* focused mostly on issues of provision of high-quality ECE in settings. These included play, curriculum, assessment, work with parents, children with specific needs and difficulties, workforce training, language and culture, and inspection of provision. The effects of austerity policies implemented since 2008 were, of course, not a concern in 1996, but poverty has now impacted on the lives of increasing numbers of families with young children. Its effects have impacted on young children's learning (DfE, 2019) and on the practitioners who work with them in ECE settings. Thus, in reflecting on children's rights past and present, we cannot escape the growing impact of poverty on young children's rights to education, leisure, play and culture.

The impact of child poverty on young children's lives and learning

> Inequity imperils millions of children and threatens the future of the world.
>
> *(UNICEF, 2016, p. xi)*

Globally, the inequity of poverty can only be alleviated by the political will to fund health-care, education, housing and other interventions, and to realise responsibilities in relation to children's rights as a whole, and, in terms of the specific concerns of this chapter, early education, play, leisure and culture. Inadequate funding fosters a disrespect for work with young children. The statistics are shocking and for the richest nations a matter of national disgrace for insufficient action:

> Unless the world tackles inequity today, in 2030: 167 million children will live in extreme poverty; 69 million children under age 5 will die between 2016 and 2030; 60 million children of primary school age will be out of school.
>
> *(UNICEF, 2016, p. 3)*

Studies show that poverty is a fundamental factor in educational underachievement (Ayoub et al., 2009; Cooper, 2010; De Feyter and Winsler, 2009; Mistry et al., 2010). Thus, early childhood practitioners shoulder an immense responsibility because high-quality provision can make a positive difference to the life chances of young children. It is a moral and economic responsibility of governments to properly resource their work.

In the UK, in 2018, it was estimated that over 4 million children were living in poverty – 30 per cent of the child population (www.schoolhomesupport.org.uk/why-we-do-it/). The School Meals Act of 1906 was an outcome of Rachael and Margaret McMillan's campaigning, yet over a century later children still go hungry to preschool and school. The McMillans' focus was twofold – they lobbied parliament to act, and worked practically with families in slum housing around the nursery they established in Deptford. Margaret McMillan visited families in their own homes and argued that the teachers in the nursery should know the families and offer practical support as well as advice about health and development. The numbers of families struggling and hungry, some homeless, in 2019 increases, so some 125 years after the pioneering multi-agency work of the McMillans, there remains an urgent need to alleviate poverty and its effects (McMillan, 1925, p. 45).

It often takes philanthropy and charity to drive change before governments act. The charity School-Home Support (www.schoolhomesupport.org.uk) works with schools, early years settings and local authorities to support children and families according to individual needs, with one head teacher in London, for example, funding a practitioner to help families access funding for food, other essentials and advice (Ferguson, 2018). Indeed, many settings actively support families that need food, clothes and beds. The point here is that because some fundamental UNCRC rights are not being realised (in particular Article 24, health and health services; Article 26, social security; and Article 27, adequate standard of living), children's capacity to learn is inhibited as the work of ECE settings increases. Many ECE settings distribute food to families that is donated by local supermarkets (Tickle, 2010), and food banks are now an established part of the national picture. With its network of some 400 food banks, the Trussell Trust (www.trusselltrust.org) gave around 1.3 million three-day emergency food supplies in 2017, and demand grows year on year. End Hunger UK (http://endhungeruk.org/universalcredit/) has called on the UK government to address the benefits system to ease the lives of people affected.

And at the heart of all of this are hungry children and their families who struggle to keep their lives together, and where children or their parents are disabled the struggle is magnified. While ECE settings are playing an increasing part in alleviating poverty, the All Party Parliamentary Group on Hunger found that the loss of free school meals can add £30–40 to weekly food bills during school holidays. Hunger has a critical impact on children's learning (Forsey, 2017, p. 5).

Poverty means more than hunger. An English charity, Beds for Kids (www.buttleuk.org/areas-of-focus/beds-for-kids), provided over 3,000 beds for children living in poverty in 2017 (Bloom, 2017), and according to Buttle UK, 400,000 of the more than 3,500,000 (some 30 per cent) of children in the UK who live in poverty currently have no bed (www.buttleuk.org/news/need-for-beds-by-area). So-called 'bed poverty' sees children sleeping with older and younger siblings or their parents, or on floors. This is not an issue of temporary homelessness, but a peacetime phenomenon in a rich country. And the atrocity is not confined to the UK; the charity Children Without Beds (http://childrenwithoutbeds.com/the-beginning/) has recently been established in Georgia, in the United States. Extensive anti-poverty charity activity is testament to the size and urgency of the problem and need for government action. In two of the richest countries in the world, this situation is surely a matter of national shame? That children, anywhere, have no adequate and culturally appropriate sleeping arrangements without fear or hunger is appalling, and a situation that international political will must solve.

A grossly unequal start to life and learning for many children means that for many, Article 2, on non-discrimination, is being breached where families' economic circumstances mean that, in the context of this chapter, young children cannot fully benefit from their right to education (www.faireducation.org.uk). Early education provision has often been seen as one means of mitigating inequalities and promoting equality, and nursery schools in England have been shown to make the greatest difference to children identified as being 'at risk' of failure in the education system, and therefore more likely to do less well in terms of employment and well-being (Esping-Andersen, 2009; Heckman, 2000). Almost a decade ago the Field Review (2010) on poverty and life chances drew on considerable evidence to argue that 'Even if the money were available to lift all children out of income poverty in the short term, it is far from clear that this move would in itself close the achievement gap' (p. 16). Some ten years later, more children live in poverty and the effects of disadvantage on young children remains a concern (DfE, 2019). Early intervention to offset potential inequalities in achievement can go some way to breaking the cycle of inequalities. Morabito and Vandenbroeck (2015) highlight the need for interventions to reach poor families, arguing for universal access, rather than targeted provision, because studies have shown that enrolment rates of the poorest families are higher in universally targeted provision than those targeted solely at families in most need (Van Lancker, 2013).

The Sure Start initiative in the UK successfully provided non-stigmatised, targeted interventions, but despite its success Sure Start is now history. Established in the late 1990s, Sure Start programmes provided a new one-stop shop community approach to early support for families. The multi-agency Sure Start programme combined health, social services, education and other services to provide local services for young children and their families, some in partnership with departments of housing and children and family (Weinberger, Pickstone and Hannon, 2005). Around 2010, following drastic reductions in funding, the Sure Start programme was all but annihilated, and its children's centres, once neighbourhood hubs for multi-agency support and early learning (Cotton, 2013), have been on the decline in England since 2010. In 2019, even the existence of state-maintained nursery schools, which have been particularly successful in supporting good outcomes for disadvantaged children, has been threatened by insufficient funding for their work.

The key point here is that a national policy of sustained reduction in funding for vital services effectively inhibits education and care provision for young children, and thus dilutes efforts to provide for young children's rights to education and play.

The training and professional development of early childhood practitioners

Practitioner knowledge is crucial to the creation of high-quality learning environments. Curtis (1996) asked, 'Do we train our early childhood educators to respect children?' Her call for effective training prompts the question as to how initial training and continuing professional development instils the importance of respectful working practices with young children. With ongoing concern around variation in qualification level and length of initial training courses now a global concern, workforce preparation and qualifications are generally underfunded, with many practitioners earning a minimal wage. Constrained training budgets often result in minimal preparation for work with young children. In this scenario, opportunities for potential early years practitioners to discuss and experience respectful education practices are low.

The importance of well-trained early years practitioners was made by Charlotte Mason in 1891, and reiterated by Rachael and Margaret McMillan, whose work led to the establishment of the Rachel McMillan Training College in 1930. Three years of training was deemed essential if practitioners were to be adequately prepared to work with the youngest children. Yet despite a long history of training and the establishment of the first local authority-funded nursery schools in 1918, there remains something of a recruitment crisis. Despite several attempts by the UK government to address the issue of qualifications and recruitment (DfE, 2013, 2017; Nutbrown, 2012), it has not solved the problem of recruitment and retention of ECE practitioners.

Well-educated practitioners are essential if children's rights to learning are to be supported. In UNCRC terms, Article 29 established that children should participate in education which focuses on individuals, fully developing each child's personality, talents and abilities. Thus, ECE practitioners need to know when to watch and wait, and when to offer suggestions, ideas, resources and time. They need to know patience and encourage persistence. We are expecting ECE practitioners to be able to engage with these issues at a high level and to appreciate individual strengths and needs if ECE provision is to truly respect children and affirm their right to high-quality learning environments and encounters, to encourage children themselves to respect others' rights, and show respect for their parents, their cultures and the environment. This means including a focus on training to work with the UNCRC in all ECE initial training regardless of the level of that training.

When children learn in the company of well-educated practitioners, whose qualifications attest to their skills, knowledge and understanding, and provide warrant of their fitness to practice, the likelihood that they will be supported to understand their rights and respect others is enhanced. Questions to ask in 2019 are: Do we show sufficient respect to our early childhood educators? Do educators show sufficient respect to child rights? Do training programmes place sufficient emphasis on supporting educators in this endeavour? ECE practitioners should be respected and respect themselves for the job they do; this can be problematic when pay and conditions of service for many are low (Karp, 2005) and where hierarchies of respect related to qualifications and pay exist in many countries (Hargreaves and Hopper, 2006; Van Laere, Peeters and Vandenbroeck, 2012).

Curriculum

A respectful curriculum offered by knowledgeable practitioners can support children as they learn different ways of communicating through talk using a range of media. This relates to the statements in Article 13, freedom of expression, whereby children must be able to express their thoughts and opinions freely and to access all kinds of information. Of course, Article 29, underpinning every child's right to education, which enables them to fully develop personality, talents and abilities, and Article 31, which states that every child has the right to relax, play and take part in a wide range of cultural and artistic activities, are central to any respectful and rights-based early years curriculum. As Scott (1996) argued:

> Teachers and other workers need knowledge about children's capabilities, and respect for both their powers and their rights to growing autonomy: children are able to make choices, develop responsible attitudes, and become independent learners from a very young age provided that adults ensure that an appropriate curriculum is negotiated within a well-planned environment.
>
> *(p. 35)*

A state curriculum for under-fives in England and Wales began in 1995 (SCAA, 1995), and subsequently what children should learn has been increasingly prescribed, with a narrowing of focus and a dominance of key 'basic' skills. There is no space in this chapter to address issues of early assessment of children's learning, but it is important to acknowledge that presently, assessment policy is driving a narrowing of the curriculum with flawed testing of 4-year-olds in England and Wales (Bradbury et al., 2018; Harvey et al., 2018; KEYU, 2018). In terms of children's rights, narrowing of curriculum restricts the UNCRC goal that gives children the opportunity to develop 'to the full' (Article 29).

A former member of Her Majesty's Inspectorate, Jean Ensing, commented in 1996 on inspection of nursery schools and classes, stressing children's rights to quality provision. She wrote:

> Inspection, done properly, matters because its goal is to improve schools: first by informing parents, professionals, public and politicians about the quality of education provided in them and secondly, by promoting school development after the inspection ... Inspection therefore commits the education system and the government to protect and care for children.
>
> *(Ensing, 1996, p. 37)*

A survey by the present government inspectorate of a small sample of selected schools (0.25 per cent of all the primary schools in England) strongly recommends the use of synthetic phonics and formal methods for teaching writing and maths, and learning to sit correctly for longer periods of time (Ofsted, 2017). Scott (2018, p. 79) notes that there is no mention of play in the recommendations, yet 15 to phonics, reading, writing and maths. Reflecting specifically on Article 29, Ensing (1996) suggested that we ask the following questions about inspection regimes: 'has inspection improved children's chances of developing their personality, talents and mental and physical abilities to their fullest potential? Has inspection really worked in the best interests of the children?' (p. 22).

If the best interests of children are to be served, their early education experiences must include space and time to play, relax and create in the company of respectful practitioners. The narrow focus and limited view of play in the Ofsted (2017) report suggest that a response to Ensing's questions from 1996 has to be that 'their fullest' is not the focus of the current English inspection regime and criteria. England's inspectorate, through promotion of a narrow curriculum focused on specific attainments in literacy and numeracy, is restricting the potential of children to fully reach their potential, especially where their potential lies in other areas of achievement.

Equality and diversity

> Respectful educators will strive to afford every child equality of opportunity. Not just those who are easy to work with, obliging, endearing, clean, pretty, articulate, capable, but *every* child – respecting them for who they are, respecting their language, their culture, their history, their family, their abilities, their needs, their name, their ways and their very essence. This means understanding and building on their abilities.
>
> *(Nutbrown, 1996, p. 54, emphasis in original)*

Thinking about the main focus of play and education as they pertain to young children who are disabled, have learning difficulties, or who are otherwise identified as needing additional or different support, Articles 6 and 23 bring us to a stark reality of how little has been achieved over the last 30 years. Herbert and Moir (1996) focused on attitude above all, in striving for inclusion of disabled pupils. Since then, the argument about the cruciality of positive attitudes towards learners with different and less understood needs and disabilities remains, but the fight for funding seems to have worsened, with many parents giving accounts on social media of their battles with schools and local authorities to achieve the provision their children need, and the dismay of many head teachers whose overall resources are reduced.

Hirst (1996) considered parents to be their children's first teachers and stressed the importance of parental partnership in children's learning. This perspective is now taken for granted in many settings, with many successful initiatives to support collaboration with parents (Nutbrown, 2018). However, some families are marginalised by their circumstances, such as those with refugee status, with disabled children, and families affected by parental imprisonment (Steinhoff and Berman, 2012). For them, Articles 9 and 10, about separation from parents and family reunification, are only partially met (Thulstrup and Karlsson, 2017).

In her consideration of language, culture and difference (Article 29), Siraj-Blatchford (1996) suggested languages that children speak are part of their identity, community and belonging. In recent times, while bi- and pluri-lingualism are valued, there seems to exist a hierarchy of languages where some are more valued than others. As Siraj-Blatchford (1996) put it, 'Just as there is a hierarchy of valuing some "racial" groups more than others, there is a similar racism towards languages' (p. 29).

Questions for respectful educators

This chapter has demonstrated that there is still much to do if children are to enjoy respectful rights-based early years education. The following questions relate specifically to Article 29, and form a reflective tool for respectful educators:

- How does the provision foster the development of individuals, their personality, their talents, their thinking, and their actions to the fullest?
- Do educators observe and discuss the personalities and preferences of the children they work with – babies, toddlers and young children?
- Do the children work on challenging self-determined problems?
- Do children confront issues that puzzle and bother them?
- How can a service for children foster healthy hearts and minds?
- Do educators challenge children to stretch themselves or do they train children to conform?
- How well do settings respect the rights of children?
- What does respectful service/provision for children look like and feel like?
- To what extent do educators foster respect for human rights, freedom of choice, and principles of dignity, individualism and mutual respect enshrined in the UNCRC?
- Does the setting teach children about their rights and enable them to talk about what 'rights' and 'having rights' means?
- What does a respectful early childhood education curriculum look like and feel like?
- To what extent are children helped to understand that they have the right to make choices?
- How much respect is shown to parents, and on what basis do practitioners work with parents?
- How are children encouraged to be proud of who they are, what they look like, how they speak, and to respect the differences of others?
- How are the rights of disabled children – and disabled parents – understood and met?
- Does every bit of the setting look as if diversity of language, culture, ability and identity are valued, or does one culture and language dominate?
- Is there a climate of mutual cooperation and equality?
- Do ECE practices value all children and enable them to make choices for themselves?

- Do ECE practitioners value children's rights to challenge, question and assert themselves?
- Are children taught how they might assert themselves without aggression?
- Are children supported to deal with conflicts and resolve disputes?
- How do the outdoor experiences offered to children foster appreciation, understanding and respect for the natural environment?
- Are children able to able to explore the outdoors, in parks, woods, beaches or forests?
- Are children encouraged to help with waste and recycling, care for the outdoors and wildlife, and the protection of their world in ways that they can understand?

Conclusion

Bearing in mind the focus on children's rights to protection, provision and participation, the four guiding principles of the Convention highlight priorities relating to non-discrimination (Article 2), the best interest of the child (Article 3), the right to life survival and development (Article 6), and the right to be heard (Article 12). While the right to free primary education is clearly stated (Article 28), the right to free preschool education is not, and it remains non-statutory in the majority of countries in the world.

Following Margaret McMillan in 1923, Brierley (1980) noted that 'Progress in education and health go hand in hand, for a sick, tired and hungry child will not learn properly' (p. 17). As this chapter has indicated, unmet needs mean far too many children are too tired and hungry to play and learn.

Every generation has at some point cried 'this is urgent', but the slowness in the realisation of children's rights in the context of early childhood education policy has given rise to a sense of urgency that is not quelled by one government or the next. There is a need for stronger political will to bring children's rights to the fore in terms of practical solutions. There persists a real urgency to enact the UNCRC fully and effectively in terms of early childhood education and care. The children born in 1989, when the UNCRC was first published (if they have survived many of the difficulties that the Convention was designed to protect them from), will turn 30 in 2019. For some of them, and their children, many of the rights in the Convention have yet to be realised.

References

Ayoub, Catherine, Erin O'Connor, Gabrielle Rappolt-Schlictmann, Claire Vallotton, Helen Raikes, and Rachel Chazan-Cohen. 2009. Cognitive skill performance among young children living in poverty: Risk, change, and the promotive effects of Early Head Start. *Early Childhood Research Quarterly*, 24(3), 289–305. http://dx.doi.org/10.1016/j.ecresq.2009.04.001.

Bloom, Adi. 2017 Four hundred thousand UK children without a bed, charity warns. *Times Educational Supplement* www.tes.com/news/exclusive-four-hundred-thousand-uk-children-without-bed-charity-warns

Bradbury, Alice, Pam Jarvis, Cathy Nutbrown, Guy Roberts-Holmes, Nancy Stewart, and David Whitebread. 2018. *Baseline assessment: Why it doesn't add up*. London: More than a Score. https://morethanascorecampaign.files.wordpress.com/2018/02/neu352-baseline-a4-16pp-crop.pdf

Brierley, John. 1980. *Children's well-being-growth, development and learning from conception to adolescence*. Slough: NFER.

Cooper, Carey E. 2010. Family poverty, school-based parental involvement, and policy-focused protective factors in kindergarten. *Early Childhood Research Quarterly*, 25, 480–492. http://dx.doi.org/10.1016/j.ecresq.2010.03.005

Cotton, Lizzie. 2013. 'It's just more in the real world really': How can a local project support early years practitioners from different settings in working and learning together? *Early Years: An International Research Journal*, 33(1), 18–32. www.tandfonline.com/doi/abs/10.1080/09575146.2011.642850

Curtis, Audrey. 1996. Do we train our early childhood educators to respect children? In Nutbrown, Cathy Ed. *Respectful educators-capable learners: Children's rights and early education*, 69–80. London: SAGE.

De Feyter, Jessica and Adam Winsler.2009. The early developmental competencies and school readiness of low-income, immigrant children: Influences of generation, race/ethnicity, and national origins. *Early Childhood Research Quarterly*, 24, 411–431.

DfE. 2013. *More great childcare Raising quality and giving parents more choice*. London: Department for Education. https://assets.publishing.service.gov.uk/government/uploads/system/uploads/attachment_data/file/219660/More_20Great_20Childcare_20v2.pdf. Accessed 20th August 2019.

DfE. 2017. *Early years workforce strategy published March 2017*. London: HMSO.

DfE. 2019. *Government response to the Education Select Committee report on tackling disadvantage in the early years*. London: HMSO.

DfE and National Literacy Trust. 2018. *Improving the home learning environment A behaviour change approach*. London: DfE/NLT. https://assets.publishing.service.gov.uk/government/uploads/system/uploads/attachment_data/file/756020/Improving_the_home_learning_environment.pdf

Ensing, Jean. 1996. Inspection of early years in schools. In Nutbrown, Cathy Ed. *Respectful educators-capable learners. Children's rights and early education*, 11–22. London: SAGE.

Esping-Andersen, Gosta. 2009. *The incomplete revolution: Adapting welfare states to women's new roles*. Cambridge: Polity Press.

Ferguson, Donna. 2018. Headteachers turn to charities as families sleep by bins. *The Guardian*. www.theguardian.com/education/2018/may/15/headteachers-turn-charities-families

Field, Frank. 2010. *The Foundation Years: Preventing poor children becoming poor adults the report of the Independent Review on Poverty and Life Chances*. The Cabinet Office. London: HM Government.

Forsey, Andrew. 2017. Hungry Holidays: A report on hunger amongst children during school holidays Report for the All-Party Parliamentary Group on Hunger. www.frankfield.co.uk/upload/docs/Hungry%20Holidays.pdf.

Hannon, Peter, Anne Morgan, and Cathy Nutbrown. 2005. 'Parents' experiences of a family literacy programme⊠. *Journal of Early Childhood Research*, 4, 19.

Hargreaves, Linda and Bev Hopper. 2006. Early years, low status? Early years teachers' perceptions of their occupational status. *Early Years*, 26(2), 171–186. http://dx.doi.org/10.1080/09575140600759971.

Goldstein Harvey, Harvey Goldstein, Gemma Moss, Pamela Sammons, Gwen Sinnott and Gordon Stobart. 2018. *A baseline without basis: The validity and utility of the proposed reception baseline assessment in England*. London: British Educational Research Association. www.bera.ac.uk/researchers-resources/publications/a-baseline-without-basis

Hazareesingh, Sandip, Kelvin Simms, and Patsy Anderson. 1989. *Educating the whole child – A holistic approach to education in the early years*. London: Building Blocks Early Years Project/Save the Children.

Heckman, James J. 2000. Policies to foster human capital. *Research in Economics*, 54, 3–56.

Herbert, Elaine and Jenny Moir. 1996. Children with special educational needs – A Collaborative and inclusive style of working. In Nutbrown, Cathy Ed. *Respectful educators-capable learners: Children's rights and early education*, 56–68. London: SAGE.

Hirst, Kath. 1996. Parents and early childhood educators working together for children's rights. In Nutbrown, Cathy Ed. *Respectful educators-capable learners: Children's rights and early education*, 81–89. London: SAGE.

Karp, N. 2005. Building a New Early Childhood Professional Development System Based on the 3 Rs: Research, Rigor, and Respect. *Journal of Early Childhood Teacher Education*, 26(2), 171–178. http://dx.doi.org/10.1080/10901020590955798.

Keep Early Years Unique. 2018. A recipe for disaster – Custard and alarm bells! Blog Sue Allingham Mar 17, 2018. https://www.keyu.co.uk/keyu-blog/. Accessed 20th August 2019.

McMillan, Margaret. 1925. *Children, culture and class in Britain*. London: George Allen and Unwin.

Mistry, Rasmita S., Aprile D. Benner, Jeremy C. Biesanz, Shaunna L. Clark, and Carollee Howes. 2010. Family and social risk, and parental investments during the early childhood years as predictors of low-income children's school readiness outcomes. *Early Childhood Research Quarterly*, 25, 432–449. http://dx.doi.org/10.1016/j.ecresq.2010.01.002

Morabito, Christian, and Michel Vandenbroeck. 2015. Equality of Opportunities, Divergent Conceptu-alisations and their Implications for Early Childhood Care and Education Policies. *Journal of Philosophy of Education*, 49(3), 456–472.

Nutbrown, Cathy, Ed. 1996. *Respectful educators-capable learners: Children's rights and early education.* London: Sage.

Nutbrown, Cathy. 2012. *Foundations for quality the independent review of early education and childcare qualifications Final Report.* Cheshire: Department for Education. https://www.gov.uk/government/uploads/system/uploads/attachment_data/file/175463/Nutbrown-Review.pdf.

Nutbrown, Cathy. 2018. *Early childhood education research: International perspectives.* London: SAGE.

Ofsted. 2017. *Bold Beginnings*: The Reception curriculum in a sample of good and outstanding primary schools. www.gov.uk/government/publications/reception-curriculum-in-good-and-outstanding-primary-schools-bold-beginnings.

Schools Curriculum and Assessment Authority. 1995. *Pre-school educatoin consultation – Desirable outcomes for children's learning and guidance for providers – Draft proposals.* London: SCAA and Central Office for Information.

Scott, Wendy. 1996. Choices in Learning. In Nutbrown, Cathy. Ed. *Respectful educators-capable learners: Children's rights and early education,* London: SAGE.

Scott, Wendy. 2018. The power of Ofsted over approaches to the teaching of reading in England. In Margaret M. Clark Ed. *Teaching initial literacy: policies, evidence and ideology,* 34–43. Birmingham: Glendale Educational.

Siraj-Blatchford, Iram. 1996. Language, culture and difference: challenging inequality and promoting respect. In Nutbrown, Cathy Ed. *Respectful educators-capable learners: Children's rights and early education,* 23–33. London: SAGE.

Steinhoff, Richard and Anne H. Berman. 2012. Children's experiences of having a parent in prison: 'We look at the moon and then we feel close to each other'. *Scientific Annals of the "Alexandru Ioan Cuza" University, Iaşi. Sociology and Social Work,* 05(2), 77–96.

Thulstrup, Stephanie H. and Leena E. Karlsson. 2017. Children of imprisoned parents and their coping strategies: A systematic review. *Societies,* 7(15), 1–16. http://dx.doi.org/10.3390/soc7020015.

Tickle, Louise. 2010. Food, clothes, a mattress and three funerals. What teachers buy for children. *The Guardian.* www.theguardian.com/education/2018/may/01/teachers-buy-children-food-clothes-mattress-funerals-child-poverty

UNICEF. 2016. *The state of the world's children: A fair chance for every child.* New York: UNICEF.

United Nations. 1989. *Convention on the Rights of the Child United Nations.* New York.

Van Laere, Katrien, Jan Peeters and Michel Vandenbroeck. 2012. The education and care divide: The role of the early childhood workforce in 15 European countries. *European Journal of Education,* 47(4), 527–541.

Van Lancker, Wim. 2013. Putting the child-centred investment strategy to the test: Evidence for the EU27. *CSB Working Paper,* No. 13/01.

Weinberger, Jo, Caroline Pickstone and Peter Hannon. 2005. *Learning from sure start: Working with young children and their families.* Buckingham: Open University Press.

Wood, Elizabeth A. 2014. Free choice and free play in early childhood education: troubling the discourse. *International Journal of Early Years Education,* 22(1), 4–18. http://dx.doi.org/10.1080/09669760.2013.830562.

28

YOUNG CHILDREN AND THEIR EDUCATIONAL RIGHTS

Critical perspectives on policy and practice in India

Amita Gupta

Introduction

Children's educational rights is a multilayered and complex notion, because, as Lake and Pendlebury (2009) assert, 'the right to education is part of a compendium of socio-economic rights, including rights on access to adequate housing, health-care services, sufficient food and water, and social security' (p. 20). For the purpose of this paper, the discussion has been narrowed down to address the specific issue of *access* to *quality education*.

The UN Committee on Economic, Social and Cultural Rights (CESCR) in 1999 suggested that basic education should be *available* for all children; *accessible* to all children; *acceptable* by all children in being relevant, culturally appropriate and of good quality; and *adaptable* to the needs of changing societies and diversities of the children's backgrounds (Lake and Pendlebury, 2009). But there are varied perspectives on the conceptual and contextual understandings of what counts as quality education for young children, and which educational rights need to be prioritised. From a Western perspective, children's quality of education and educational rights not only include the right of access to schooling, but also the right of children to engage and participate in their learning; to have choices in classroom materials; to be allowed to make decisions in the classroom; to be able to closely relate to curricular content; to be respected by their teachers and peers; to ensure their learning goals are meeting national standards; and so forth. Many of these rights are assumed as being fundamental to a Euro-American middle-class educational context. But in countries of the Global South such as India, where there are large numbers of children and a dearth of schools, just basic access to a school becomes the most urgent educational right. Closely following would be children's right to a culturally responsive pedagogy and curriculum so that children are not measured by dominant global standards, but by standards that are a measure of the skills they need in order to flourish in their local cultural context with regard to their social-emotional well-being and academic proficiency. To illustrate, should children be encouraged to learn the skills of autonomy and independence that are more valued in individualistic communities, or should they be encouraged toward interdependence if they live in collectivist societies that prioritise a prolonged adult–child continuum? Cultural worldviews and contextualised realities of children's lives matter greatly in the debates on what constitutes quality education (Nimmo et al., 2017).

Methodology

This paper draws on research findings from a larger study that consisted of a series of interrelated qualitative inquiries conducted by the author within the social-cultural-political context of five countries in Asia (Gupta, 2014). The focus of the study was to examine how changes in national ECCE policies in Asia were reflected, or not, in local early childhood classrooms. The inquiries employed a comparative approach to examining current trends in ECCE policy and practice within specific sociocultural contexts and worldviews. The methodology allowed for: (1) a bibliographic investigation and review of institutional and policy documents to provide an overview of current and proposed recommendations for early education and teacher education in each country; and (2) an empirical investigation comprising: (a) interviews with policymakers, teacher educators and teachers; and (b) non-participatory classroom observations in teacher education colleges and pre-primary schools in each of the countries. Data were collected from a wide range of sources, including policy institutes, research organisations, teacher preparation colleges and institutions, NGOs, and pre-primary /primary schools. Interviews were audiotaped and then transcribed. Data analysis entailed coding and categorising to identify information with regard to the aims of the study. The findings related to the state of early childhood and early elementary education in India form the basis of this paper.

Background of the educational rights discourse in India

The moral imperative that all children, regardless of race, gender, culture, language, religion or ability, have access to formal education has been a long struggle for the Indian government. Following India's independence from British rule in 1947, Article 45 of the newly drafted Indian Constitution included a provision for free and compulsory education for all children 6–14 years of age. The Constitution was adopted in 1950 and ever since the Indian government has attempted to address this goal (Govinda, 2007). But even 70 years later, India's Constitutional goal of free and compulsory education for all children 6–14 years of age has not been realised. Before proceeding, it is important to clarify that most policy discourse in India has historically addressed elementary education and up, but it is still relevant to this discussion since grades K–2 span both elementary education (EE) and early childhood education (ECE).

When the UN proposed the Convention on the Rights of the Child (CRC) in 1989, India ratified it in 1992, and in 2002 the Indian Parliament voted to support the 86th Constitutional Amendment, which declared the right to education to be a fundamental right. It must be noted that although the education of young children has been accorded much importance by several prominent Indian preschool educators, such as Gijubhai Badheka, Tarabai Modak and Anutai Wagh (in the 1920s and 1930s), it was only after the UN established the 2015 deadline for Education For All (EFA 2015) that the Indian government began to pay urgent attention to early childhood education (ECE) nationally, and how it could be made accessible to all young children in the country. Widespread recognition for ECE in India further gained traction due to sociopolitical forces, such as the global children's rights movements that promoted local political action and middle-class aspirations at the local level that recognised its benefits for children's well-being (Aruldoss and Davis, 2014; Pattnaik, 1996). Nevertheless, the field of ECE in India has remained unregulated, having a large workforce that is formally unqualified, and with massive disparities across various ECCE service providers (Prochner, 2002).

The Right to Free and Compulsory Education (RTE) Act was adopted and implemented in 2010 after it was added to the Indian Constitution as Amendment 21A. The RTE Act, approved by the president of India in August 2009, came into force in April 2010. This put the right to education at par with the right to life (Puar, 2012, pp. 27–28), making India one of the 135 countries to recognise education as a fundamental right for its citizens. The hope was that this policy would work toward ensuring more children would have school access. RTE's core principles viewed schools as inclusive spaces, teachers as key change agents, communities as being more empowered in the running of schools, and institutional infrastructure and governance as being strengthened (UNICEF, n.d.).

The RTE Act binds parents, schools, social institutions, and state and central governments as stakeholders in collaborating to provide free and compulsory education to children 6–14 years old. This was seen as a significant step towards the universalisation of elementary education throughout the country. However, nearly 16 years after the right to education was elevated to a fundamental right, a large number of children in India are still out of school, as reflected in the 71st National Sample Survey (NSS) carried out in 2014 (Dubey, Pankaj and Mitra, 2018). The fact remains that more than 85 million children between the ages of 5 and 6 years still don't go to school due to financial constraints (Times of India, 2013). Out-of-school children aged 6–18 years were estimated as being more than 450 million, or 16.1 per cent of all children in this age group, most of them being from rural areas, scheduled class and castes, and girls (Dubey et al., 2018).

RTE's major shortcoming is that it omits all children under the age of 6 years. Historically, the field of ECE in India has been located within the jurisdiction of health and human development rather than within that of education. ECE was framed within an early years provision discourse (to include care and education) rather than an early childhood education discourse. According to the recent National Early Childhood Care and Education Policy, early childhood in India includes children between the ages of 0 and 6 years, and the term 'early childhood provision' combines childcare and early childhood education (Ministry of Women and Child Development, 2013). Within this framework, the government established the Integrated Child Development Services (ICDS) on a national level in 1975. ICDS programmes provide comprehensive health, social and educational services to all children below the age of 6 years, and may be considered India's equivalent to the American Head Start programme. Current robust voices have been urging the Indian government to include the very young in the RTE policies, and both public and private sectors have been rapidly developing and working to professionalise a distinct ECE field.

The next section highlights inequities that exist within early and primary education in India. Factors that influence schooling include student enrolment, quality of public education, quality of private sector schools, public expenditure patterns, household expenditure on schooling, and initiatives by state governments to support access, retention and quality (Mehrotra, 2006).

Inequities in education for young children

Widely diverse school experiences are to be found in a country where approximately 260 million children attend all levels of school, and disparities can be seen across government, non-profit and private sectors. The following examples help illustrate how young children in India experience schools in vastly different ways. The disparities will be discussed in relation to factors such as institutional infrastructure, pedagogy, curriculum, geo-socio-economics, social class, and public and private sectors.

Infrastructure

Bihar is considered to be an educationally backward state, with almost half its population being illiterate. Karan and Pushpendra (2006) ascribe this to the following observations in public education: inadequate number of schools, schools with poor infrastructure, poorly equipped classrooms, very high student-to-teacher ratios exceeding 60:1 in many instances, class and gender discriminations evidencing a privileging of upper-caste and male students, lack of active teaching, high rates of teacher absenteeism, low allocation and low utilisation of public funds, and high costs incurred by families. Majumdar (2006) notes that free education is not really free as families have to pay for school fees, books, school uniforms and stationery, even in government schools. This contributes toward low enrolment numbers.

In rural Madhya Pradesh, another educationally backward state, Panchmukhi (2006) describes elementary schools as having dilapidated buildings, inadequate light and ventilation, waterlogging during the rainy season, and unbearable heat during the summer months. Almost 99 per cent of the schools lacked drinking water facilities and/or toilet facilities, or where available displayed very unhygienic conditions. The findings from this state also revealed a poor educational culture in schools where teachers were not trusted by families, children were beaten in school, there was a lack of teacher commitment, and teachers promoted their private tutoring classes and pressured families to pay for them (pp. 204–205).

A stark contrast in infrastructure may be seen in private or semi-private schools in metropolitan India that cater to more affluent families. In a study on private school early childhood teachers, Gupta (2006) describes one such school that:

> was housed in a large red brick building and ... a fleet of yellow school buses stood parked outside the gates ... The sun shone brightly on the hundreds of potted Chrysanthemum plants that were lined up against the brick walls. There were the yellow, pink, mauve, and white blossoms that are typical of Delhi in the wintertime when one can see them everywhere – full, fragrant, and expensive. The grounds of the school were neatly manicured and very picturesque. Near to where I stood was a rockery decorated with small, white, marble cherubs and a tiny cascading waterfall. In another section of the grounds was a Japanese garden with a small arched bridge and more figurines.

> *(p. 55)*

Byker (2015) describes an equal opportunity school (an EOS is operated by a private school for children from economically weaker sections) in a semi-rural area of Bangalore located in the southern state of Karnataka. The school campus was designed to look like an upscale village school:

> Small fields of ragi, millet, and red sorghum surround three sides of the school campus. Coconut trees tower over the grain fields; these trees form a natural

border between the school and the forest where many of the area's small villages are located … Large murals adorn the five campus buildings; the murals show Hindu gods, people working in fields, and dancing celebrations. Signs explain the meaning of each mural. The signs are written in English and in the Kannada script, the official state language of the State of Karnataka where Bangalore is located.

(p. 236)

Pedagogy and curriculum

In an ethnographic study of an early childhood classroom in Chennai located in the southern Indian state of Tamil Nadu, Aruldoss and Davis (2015) found the curriculum to be formal. The pedagogy was characterised by group instruction, which encouraged passive learning and memorisation, with children expected to learn academic skills under the instruction and supervision of their teachers. The researchers considered this as not meeting quality as defined by active learning and developing skills of reasoning and reflection (Jeffery, 2005). The researchers did not find evidence of participatory learning in their attempt to 'understand how children functioned within a formal pedagogical context and what this might mean for children's rights and well-being, especially their right to participation in everyday practices' (Aruldoss and Davis, 2015, p. 5).

In comparison were accounts of school experiences where teachers seemed more intentional in their practice. In one example of an urban private early childhood classroom, teachers worked with large class sizes but in well-equipped rooms with adequate learning materials and clean facilities. The teachers in the study seemed to recognise the:

> importance of working with the prescribed academic syllabus and helping students develop the skills to succeed in this competitive environment. But they also recognized the importance of teaching the whole child and ensuring the development of social, emotional, and moral development. More importantly, teachers in these private schools seemed to have the freedom and flexibility to individually implement a more informal curriculum parallel to the rigid academic curriculum where issues in values, good attitudes, environmental protection, and diversity were being addressed.
>
> *(Gupta, 2006, p. 177)*

In the EOS studied by Byker (2015) in Bangalore, the administrators attested to delivering a quality education, which they viewed as preparing their primary-aged students to be proficient in the English language and to be able to operate computer applications. The school's mission was to prepare twenty-first-century citizens who hold a global perspective: 'To adopt an integrated approach to learning, with emphasis on empowering students through leadership competencies, proficiency in English, the power of technology, and a strong sense of their communities' (Byker, 2015, p. 242).

Geo-socio-economics

Socio-geographical factors also create inequities within Indian communities, such as the rural–urban and socio-economic divides. School experiences for Indian children across classes, castes and geographies can be vastly different. With a population of over 1.3 billion, India is considered to have the world's largest and most expansive school system. Not surprisingly, vast disparities are seen to exist between urban schools and rural schools, government schools and private schools, and state government schools and local government schools with regard to enrolment numbers, drop-out numbers, male versus female students, accessibility of schools to students, achievement levels, costs borne by parents with reference to school uniforms, textbooks, meals and transportation, teacher attitudes, absenteeism, training, prior experiences and educational qualifications, attitudes of parents toward teachers, and so forth (Mehrotra, 2006).

Mehrotra's (2006) study focused on an overview of the relationship between costs and financing, and highlighted the socio-economic divides in 6–11-year-old elementary school children across India. States were broadly categorised as educationally backward and educationally high-performing: Uttar Pradesh, Bihar, Rajasthan, Madhya Pradesh, Assam and West Bengal have some of the highest poverty levels and the poorest systems of education in the country. These states also have the largest populations and account for nearly three-fourths of the children out of school in India. They are located in approximately the northern half of India, and create a north–south divide not only in low educational averages, but corresponding trends in nutrition, health services, infant mortality and fertility rates. Southern states such as Tamil Nadu and Kerala are examples of high-achieving states, the former known for the remarkable progress it has made in terms of schooling, literacy, nutrition and health services.

Consistent low numbers of active teachers, high teacher absenteeism in government schools, and the low priority given by states to primary education serve as challenges that impede any progress that might be made in early childhood and elementary education in India. There is a contrast between the training and educational backgrounds of teachers in private and government schools, and also between student achievement in both kinds of schools. Schooling costs that are borne by families is an important obstacle in the universalisation of education in India. Although government schools are required to offer free tuition, families must confront expenses for uniforms, meals, textbooks and other school supplies. Distance of schools and accessibility in the rural regions is another major constraint faced by students, and deters families from sending all their children to school.

Social class, caste and language

The centuries-old caste system in India continues to be the source of deep bias and discrimination in Indian society. Bajaj (2018) presents troubling examples of how children from economically and socially disadvantaged communities are often treated by adults in some schools, especially in villages and small towns. Her research focused on Dalits (members of India's scheduled castes) and highlighted several instances of caste discrimination of Dalit children: separation, punishment, forced to perform menial tasks such as cleaning toilets, shunned by many teachers, and even assaulted by a teacher in one case (Bajaj, 2018). Teachers who are posted to schools for Adivasis (India's tribal or original inhabitants) perceive it as a punishment, and in turn view Adivasis with disregard and disrespect. A high incidence of teachers beating Dalit children with brooms, sexually assaulting them, and even appropriating their school meals for themselves and providing students with watered-down meals was found (Bajaj, 2018).

When the RTE policy was implemented, there was a dearth of government schools to accommodate the large population of young children in India. Thus, RTE policy mandated all government and private schools to reserve 25 per cent of their incoming class for children from economically disadvantaged communities (EWS). Alternatively, a private school could construct a separate school building (EOS) earmarked for underprivileged and EWS students living in the neighbourhood (Byker, 2015). In many schools, this mandate led to a juxtaposition of poor and affluent families in one classroom, each side representing very different socio-economic classes and castes, and adhering to different social values. Further, private schools in India mostly utilise English as the language of instruction, and most middle-class and affluent families are familiar with the language, but not so children belonging to EWS families. In-service teachers in private schools were not adequately trained in bilingual education or TESOL, and were challenged by these socio-economic and linguistic divides in their classrooms.

At the time RTE was established, the Indian government also set out the infrastructure provisions that schools were mandated to implement a rights-based approach to primary school education. Ray and Saini (2015) conducted a study on the effectiveness of this approach in the states of Kerala and Bihar (the best- and worst-performing states in India), and examined the levels of performance in these states with regard to the mandates defined by the RTE legislation enacted in 2009. They argued that a rights-based discourse was insufficient because social bias was deeply entrenched in the environment and strongly influenced whether the approach would succeed (Ray and Saini, 2015).

Public and private sectors

In India, a dual system of ECE has existed for decades: (1) programmes that are government-funded as well as those supported by NGOs, which cater to children and families from marginalised and economically weaker sections of society to promote their holistic development; and (2) programmes that are privately sponsored, which cater to children from middle and affluent-class families and focus on academic proficiency (Swaminathan, 1998). A helpful example of this public–private divide in ECE might be seen in the government-sponsored ICDS programmes called *anganwadis* and the private nursery schools. There is a clear distinction between the two with regard to educational objectives and pedagogy. The purpose of ICDS programmes has been to offer children (0–6 years) and young mothers a package of services that would include health and nutrition education, medical exams, immunisation, referral services, supplementary food, and preschool education (Rao, 2005). The goal of ICDS is to empower underprivileged children below the age of 6 years and ensure that they are physically healthy, mentally alert, emotionally secure, socially competent and intellectually ready to learn when they reach primary school age. A report by the National Council of Educational Research and Training (NCERT) in 1999 revealed that more than 70 per cent of *anganwadis* had activities for children that were geared toward rote learning and were teaching the 3Rs, or reading, writing and arithmetic. There has been ongoing concern about the quality of preschool education offered by *anganwadis*, specifically with regard to lack of resources, lack of awareness, lack of indicators, distortions in curriculum, poor training, lack of institutional capacity, and inadequate advocacy about the need and significance of early care and education programmes (NCERT, 2002). Although the purpose and philosophy of these educational initiatives is good, the resources are scarce and the training of staff is inadequate.

Private nursery schools in India, on the other hand, often offer small half-day programmes and an academic curriculum to prepare children to be admitted to larger private schools. More recently, the nursery school sector has been moving toward more clearly defined standards of professionalism. Increasingly, qualified and experienced individuals and organisations are establishing schools for young children with more qualified and experienced teachers, and a curriculum that is carefully planned and well designed. The curriculum is still focused on academic proficiency, but schools are widely claiming the utilisation of a play-way method or child-centred pedagogy.

Policy initiatives such as NCF 2005 have recommended changes in ECE and EE within both the private and government sectors, urging an approach that is less academically rigid, less structured and formal, more child-centred, more activity based, and more experiential and creative. Private schools have been known to hold parent interviews and tests for children, and admission into some of the more elite schools is very competitive. Private nursery schools may be financially supported by high tuitions and/or other private funds, and certainly have the resources to offer better facilities and services, as well as hire teachers who are better qualified and experienced. This can have negative and positive consequences, leading to better learning outcomes but resulting in overcrowding of classrooms and social inequity. Another point to note is that a high percentage of families from low income levels prefer to enrol their children in private schools at the early childhood and primary levels that boast of better learning experiences and instruction in the English language.

Critical frameworks: postcolonialism and neoliberal globalisation

Post-independence education approaches in India saw a continuation of the academically rigorous, textbook-driven, examination-oriented British colonial curriculum in schools and in teacher education colleges while embracing and institutionalising behaviourist and constructivist theories of learning and development from the West (Gupta, 2006; Viruru, 2001). A dissonance existed between such teacher preparation and teacher practice, as described in some private schools in India (Gupta, 2006). Until about 2012, there were no university-based degree-granting ECE programmes, and teachers for the very young were usually trained in diploma-granting institutions, or in Montessori schools, or they received their teaching degree in elementary education. ECE in South Asia in general gained national recognition only within the last 20 years or so due to increased momentum of the children's rights movement globally and nationally, as previously described. The Indian government responded by instituting policies that highlighted the importance of a holistic, learner-centred approach to ECE in documents such as the National Curriculum Framework (2005) and the National Policy on ECCE (Ministry of Women and Child Development, 2013). The conundrum that educators have found themselves in was that classroom teachers were not familiar with the new learner-centred pedagogy, and there was a dearth of teacher educators who had the expertise to prepare teachers accordingly. Many schools and colleges of education began to depend on teacher educators from the Western English-speaking world for guidance in learner-centred approaches. Western early childhood discourse tends to focus strongly on developmental theory and neuroscience. The developmentally appropriate practice discourse that has dictated ECE policy and pedagogy in much of the US exerted a recent hold on ECE in India. This implied the universalisation of child development with a disregard for cultural nuances, and the possibilities of cultural incursions created by a pedagogy that may not be culturally responsive. This instance of globalisation of education in itself posed as a colonising influence. More recently, post-structural theories rooted in social and anthropological contexts of education have supported pedagogical and curricular objectives that are more inclusive and mindful of marginalised groups.

Another colonising instance is seen in the currently popular embrace of the English language by families across socio-economic sectors. Several scholars in India attribute this to the public's perception of English as the medium of the global economy (Advani, 2009; Guha, 2007; Sen, 2005), and it is increasingly being perceived as an essential language for upward social mobility. According to Aula (2014), the socio-economic status of an individual in India is often measured against their fluency in the English language, resulting somewhat in the creation of a new caste system. EWS families in Indian society, in recognising the enormous capital that comes with the English language, are consciously opting to enrol their children in private English-medium schools where they will be taught English proficiency and technical skills. In fact, many state governments in India have tried to make English the medium of instruction for government schools in addition to private schools so as to meet the demands of poor families (Aula, 2014). Much debate has ensued on what the child's right is in this case, and whether children should be taught in English or not.

Pedagogy and curriculum are complex domains situated within the intersecting forces of diverse perspectives, cultural worldviews and power positions (Aruldoss and Davis, 2015). The image of the child within local contexts is key in determining how children's rights are perceived and what pedagogical decisions are made at the local levels. But here, too, are differing notions as to how children may be perceived within their home environments versus within the larger sociopolitical context of society. Several tensions emerge from a desire to remain local and yet feel the need to become global. These tensions are rooted in India's colonial history and are now re-emerging as an instance of neocolonialism brought on by neoliberal globalisation (Gupta, 2014).

Conclusion

Indian government initiatives such as Sarva Shiksha Abhiyaan (SSA) in support of the universalisation of education and the global children's rights movement have sought to alleviate access to primary schools (Iyengar, 2010). Other attempts have included offering programmes in teacher training, establishing resource centres, providing materials and supplies to marginalised children, and constructing new classrooms. But despite these efforts, problems still persist with regard to quality of education, access to schools, and unequal treatment of children within the school systems (Bajaj, 2018). The progress of RTE is constrained by several factors, including the absence of quality physical and social infrastructure, absence of accountability mechanisms, problematic institutional and budgetary processes for fund utilisation, exclusion of children from 0 to 6 years of age, insufficient availability of trained teachers and staff, absence of a complete ban on child labour, and mostly an overall absence of political will (Jha and Parvati, 2014).

Other roadblocks to better-quality education may be summarised in the following points: teachers and students come from very different castes and classes, and teachers need to be well prepared in multicultural, culturally responsive, culturally sensitive teaching practices; teacher preparation is still inadequate with regard to not only deeper cultural awareness of students' backgrounds, but also greater rigor in their knowledge of developmental and learning theory; increased privatisation of educational institutions and market economy forces continue to put profit before child at every level; and since a clear definition of the term 'educational quality' is still lacking, influences from neoliberal globalisation begin to define 'good quality' based mostly on Western parameters.

It would benefit educators to keep in mind that 'Quality is not a universal concept but depends on national curricula and cultural priorities. The outcomes deemed important in children's development will relate in different ways to the many measures of quality' (Sylva, Siraj-Blatchford and Taggart, 2006, p. 51). Sriprakash (2009) found in her study on 'quality of education' conducted in rural Indian primary schools the implications of introducing child-centred pedagogic principles in rural, low-income Indian contexts. Her study examined a programme called 'Joyful Learning' as an example of child-centred pedagogic reform.

Her findings indicated that social control of knowledge acquisition can remain hidden and unchallenged by the rhetoric of child-centred pedagogy (Sriprakash, 2009). Even the understanding of child-centredness differs with context because of the varying cultural worldviews on how the child is located within the child–adult continuum. Quality universal education can only be achieved by a view of pedagogy that is more complex, more nuanced and contextually layered, as opposed to the dichotomous view of pedagogy as being defined by either direct instruction or joyful learning. A unique dynamic between diverse educational and curricular ideas gets enacted within spaces that have experienced intercultural transactions as a result of colonialism or neocolonialism in countries of the Global South. Gupta (2006, 2013) demonstrated how early childhood teachers in urban India were observed to navigate between tradition and modernism, their voices in dialogue with the voice of the dominant discourse of the 'West' (Gupta, 2006). Discourses not only refer to what is said and thought, but also who has the authority to speak and when. Using a 'Western' discourse to describe educational philosophy and pedagogy undoubtedly provides credibility to schools in the developing world, but cultural incursions almost always occur when ideas from one pedagogical discourse get embedded into a culturally different one.

As related to children's rights, much more attention needs to be paid to the impact of globalisation, both positive and negative, on ECE pedagogy and policy in postcolonial societies of the Global South. It is clear that the ground realities in India are still not free of deeply entrenched discrimination toward children based on social class, caste, economics and gender despite national educational policies that mandate otherwise. The momentum has been generated but much work still needs to be done in order to achieve the four core principles of the CRC of non-discrimination, devotion to the best interests of the child, the right to life, survival and development, and respect for the views of the child.

References

Advani, Shalini. 2009. *Schooling and the national imagination: Education, English, and the Indian modern*. New Delhi: Oxford University Press.

Aruldoss, Vinnarasan and Davis, John M. 2015. "Children's rights and early-years provision in India." In *Enhancing Children's Rights. Studies in Childhood and Youth*, edited by A.B. Smith, 95–107. London: Palgrave Macmillan.

Aula, Sahith. 2014. "The problem with the English language in India." *Forbes*, November 6, 2014. www.forbes.com/sites/realspin/2014/11/06/the-problem-with-the-english-language-in-india/#7dde6350403e.

Bajaj, Monisha. 2018. "Children's rights in India: Critical insights on policy and practice." In *Critical human rights, citizenship, and democracy education: Entanglements and regenerations*, edited by Michalinos Zembylas and André Keet, 139–156. London, UK: Bloomsbury.

Byker, Erik Jon. 2015. "Teaching for "global telephony": A case study of a community school for India's 21st century." *Policy Futures in Education* 13 (2): 234–246.

Dubey, Muchkund, Pankaj, Ashok and Mitra, Susmita. 2018. "Still too many children out of school". *The Hindu*. September 4, 2018.

Govinda, Rangachar. 2007. *Education for all in India: Assessing progress towards Dakar goals. Background paper for the Education for All Global Monitoring Report, 2008*. Paris: UNESCO.

Guha, Ramachandra. 2007. *India after Gandhi: The history of the world's largest democracy*. New York: Harper Collins.

Gupta, Amita. 2006. *Early childhood education, postcolonial theory, and teaching practices in India: Balancing Vygotsky and the Veda*. 1st ed. New York: Palgrave Publications.

Gupta, Amita. 2013. *Early childhood education, postcolonial theory, and teaching practices and policies in India: Balancing Vygotsky and the Veda*. 2nd ed. New York: Palgrave Publications.

Gupta, Amita. 2014. *Diverse early childhood education policies and practices: Voices and images from five countries in Asia*. New York: Routledge.

Iyengar, Radhika. 2010. "Different implementation approaches to a common goal: Education for all in the Indian context." *Society of International Education Journal* 7: 1–7.

Jeffery, Patricia. 2005. "Introduction: Hearts, minds and pockets." In *Educational regimes in contemporary India*, edited by Radhika Chopra and Jeffery, Patricia in collaboration with Helmut Reifeld, 13–38. New Delhi: Sage Publications.

Jha, Praveen and Parvati, Parvati. 2014. "Assessing progress on universal elementary education in India." *Economic and Political Weekly* 69 (16): 44–51.

Karan, Anup and Kumar P. 2006. "Bihar: Including the excluded, and addressing the failures of public provision in elementary education." In *The economics of elementary education in India: The challenge of public finance, private provision, and household costs*, edited by Santosh Mehrotra, 106–158. New Delhi: Sage Publications.

Lake, Lori and Pendlebury, Shirley. 2009. "Children's right to basic education." Accessed July 3, 2018. http://open.uct.ac.za/bitstream/handle/11427/4014/CI_chapters_sachildgauge08-09_rightbasiceducation_2009.pdf?sequence=1

Majumdar, Tapas. 2006. "Cost and financing of elementary education in West Bengal." In *The economics of elementary education in India*, edited by Santosh Mehrotra, 106–158. New Delhi: Sage Publications.

Mehrotra, Santosh. Ed. 2006. *The economics of elementary education in India*. New Delhi: Sage Publications.

Ministry of Law and Justice. 2009. *The Right of Children to Free and Compulsory Education Act (RTE). 2009*. New Delhi: The Gazette of India. http://mhrd.gov.in/sites/upload_files/mhrd/files/upload_document/rte.pdf.

Ministry of Women and Child Development. 2013. *National Early Childhood Care and Education (ECCE) Policy*. New Delhi: Ministry of Women and Child Development. Government of India.

Ministry of Women and Children. 2013. *National Policy on ECCE. Resolution* Ministry of Women and Children, Government of India. New Delhi, India.

National Curriculum Framework. 2005. New Delhi, India: NCERT.

NCERT. 2002. *Report published by the National Council of Educational Research and Training*. New Delhi, India.

Nimmo, John, Marcilio, Ana, Fowler, Angela and Goyal, Vashima. 2017. "Voices of children: Intercultural collaborations in understanding and documenting the meaning of children's rights through dialogue and video." In *Collaborative cross-cultural research methodologies in early care and education contexts*, edited by Samara Madrid Akpovo, Mary Jane Moran and Robyn Brookshire, 151–168. New York: Routledge.

Panchmukhi, P.R. 2006. "Universalizing elementary education in Madhya Pradesh: Can the successes of decentralized governance offset the problems of public finance, private provision, and private cost?" In *The economics of elementary education in India*, edited by Santosh Mehrotra, 106–158. New Delhi: Sage Publications.

Pattnaik, Jyotsna. 1996. "Early childhood education in India: History, trends, issues and achievements." *Early Childhood Education Journal* 24 (1): 11–16.

Prochner, Larry. 2002. "Preschool and playway in India." *Childhood* 9 (4): 435–453.

Puar, Surjit Singh. 2012. "Right to Education Act: A critical analysis." *International Journal of Educational and Psychological Research* 1 (2): 27–30.

Rao, Nirmala. 2005. "Children's rights to survival, development, and early education in India: A critical role of the Integrated Child Development Services Program." *International Journal of Early Childhood* 37 (3): 15–31.

Ray, Sharmila and Saini, Sakshi. 2015. "Efficacy of rights-based approach to education: A comparative study of two states of India." *Policy Futures in Education* 14 (2): 274–285.

Sen, Amartya. 2005. *The argumentative India: Writings on Indian culture, history, and identity*. London: Penguin Books.

Sriprakash, Arathi. 2009. "'Joyful learning' in rural Indian primary schools: An analysis of social control in the context of child-centered discourses." *Compare: A Journal of Comparative and International Education* 39 (5): 629–641.

Swaminathan, Mina. 1998. "Introduction." In *The first five years: A critical perspective on early childhood care and education in India*, edited by Mina Swaminathan, 15–20. New Delhi: Sage Publications.

Sylva, Kathy, Siraj-Blatchford, Iram and Taggart, Brenda. 2006. *Assessing quality in the early years: Early Childhood Environment Rating Scale Extension (ECERS-E), four curricular subscales*. rev. ed. Stoke-on-Trent, and Sterling, VA: Trentham Books.

Times of India. 2013. "8 crore Indian children still don't go to school." *Times of India*, January 13, 2019. https://timesofindia.indiatimes.com/home/education/news/8-crore-indian-children-still-dont-go-to-school/articleshow/67515425.cms.

UNICEF. n.d. "India." Accessed February 9, 2018. http://unicef.in/Whatwedo/13/RTE-and-CFSS.

United Nations Committee on Economic, Social and Cultural Rights. 1999. *General Comment No. 13: The Right to Education (Art. 13 of the Covenant), 8 December 1999.* Geneva: Office of the United Nations High Commissioner for Human Rights.

Viruru, Radhika. 2001. *Early childhood education: Postcolonial perspectives from India.* New Delhi: Sage Publications.

29

CHILDREN'S RIGHTS IN HUNGARY IN EARLY CHILDHOOD EDUCATION AND CARE

Sándor Pálfi, Erzsébet Rákó, Anikó Varga Nagy and Eleonóra Teszenyi

Introduction

The introduction of the United Nations Convention on the Rights of the Child (UNICEF, 1989) signifies a change in how children are viewed in today's societies (Teszenyi and Sykes, 2018), and it is no different in Hungary. In the Hungarian early childhood programmes and practice, the image of the child as an individual in his or her own right, an active agent with rights and responsibilities, is beginning to unfold.

In Hungary, kindergarten education has a long tradition. The first kindergarten opened its doors in 1828, while the first crèche opened in 1852. Since September 2015, attendance has been compulsory from the age of 3, the aim of which is to minimise disadvantage and to ensure equal opportunities and life chances for all children. Hungary was one of the first countries to ratify the United Nations Convention on the rights of the child ('the Convention' from here on) (Herczog 2009, 2011). This commitment is enshrined into the Constitutional Act LXIV of 1991. The Constitution Act of Hungary provides the legal foundations for children's rights, which states that every child has the right to protection and care that secures their appropriate physical, mental and moral development.

This chapter discusses some of the key aspects of the implementation of children's rights, with a focus on early childhood care and education in Hungary. The first half of the chapter examines how children's rights are understood in light of underpinning policy and legislation, while the second half focuses on the implementation of children's rights in early years practice. This is where country-specific features are highlighted as relevant aspects of kindergarten practice are examined.

Understanding children's rights in the Hungarian context

Understanding children's rights in light of relevant policy and legislation is crucial because it frames and underpins early years institutional practice. It is this understanding that guides pedagogues' daily work with children and their families and affords a respectful approach to the youngest citizens of our society.

To aid the understanding of children's rights expressed in the 40 articles, Filó-Katonáné (2006) identifies five categories that the articles of the Convention fall into. How children's rights are understood in Hungary is examined in relation to these five distinct categories in this section. They are: (i) political and civil rights (Articles 6–10 and 12–17); (ii) economic, social and cultural rights (Articles 6, 18, 24, 26–29 and 31); (iii) the right to protection for children within their families and society (Articles 11, 19, 32–37 and 39–40); (iv) the right to protection for children with special needs (Articles 20–21, 23, 25 and 30); and (v) the right to protection for children at risk or disadvantage (Articles 22 and 38).

Children's political and civil rights

With a focus on early childhood (0–7 years), this section provides an overview of the specificalities of children's political and civil rights in relation to policy and legislation. We have drawn on the Comprehensive Commentary (number 7) of the Children's Rights Committee (CRC) on the Implementation and Application of Children's Rights in Early Childhood and the National Core Programme for Kindergarten Education ('Core Programme' from here on) (Hungarian Government, 2012). The Core Programme lays down the principles of pedagogical practice in early childhood institutions in Hungary. It views children as developing personalities who are entitled to special protection. In the introductory section of the document, it states that all aspects of care and education must be in accordance with fundamental human rights and with respect for children's rights. Kindergartens must provide equal opportunities for all children to high-quality care and education (Hungarian Government, 2012).

The child's right to healthy development is explicitly expressed in many parts of the Core Programme. It is part of its child-centred approach, and there is a requirement for the physical environment and the pedagogical activities to provide optimal conditions for a child's holistic development, care and education. The document states that:

> The aim of kindergarten care and education is to support children's harmonious and holistic development, the development of their personalities, to reduce disadvantage by taking into consideration children's unique and age-related characteristics as well as the varying pace of development.
>
> *(Hungarian Government, 2012)*

The kindergarten provides a personalised physical and emotional environment necessary for children's development and the educational processes to take (Hungarian Government, 2012)

Economic, social and cultural rights

Article 18 is one of the articles in the category of 'economic, social and cultural' rights. It emphasises parents' responsibilities in the shared duty of bringing up their children, in which the government provides support for parents. The CRC maintains that early childhood cannot be seen as purely a period for socialisation. Children are rightful members of society, and to be able to practise their rights they need to be cared for physically and emotionally, and they also need guidance and protection.

Children's rights to health are enshrined in Article 24, which also belongs to the group of 'economic, social and cultural' rights. Every child must be provided access to health services. The Convention highlights the need to reduce the number of infant and child deaths, access to health services, and pre- and postnatal care for mothers. Early childhood is a particularly important period from a health education point of view. The CRC emphasises in its commentary that participating states have the responsibility to provide clean drinking water, appropriate hygiene, necessary immunisations, nutritious food and medical care, all of which are indispensably necessary for the healthy development of a young child, along with a stress-free environment. Malnutrition and childhood illnesses can have a lifelong impact on children's physical health and development. They negatively impact on their mental state, present obstacles to learning and social participation in society, and reduce children's chances to fulfil their potential. The same applies to obesity and unhealthy lifestyles (CRC, 2005, Comprehensive Commentary No. 7, 27, para. 256).

To ensure children's rights to health, access to free paediatric services from family doctors in local surgeries is provided as part of the National Health Service. Hungary has an over 100-year tradition of health visiting, the primary aim of which is prevention. Health visitors provide pre-, peri- and postnatal care. For example, they advise on family planning, monitor pregnancies and attend to families in their home, advising mothers on the care and upbringing of their babies or young children. Additionally, they fulfil a safeguarding role in reporting any concerns to the local safeguarding boards at the family assistance centre.

A particularly important pedagogical aim of kindergarten education is to help children develop a healthy lifestyle (37/2014 (IV.30.). The Core Programme focuses on meeting children's physical and psychological needs, helping them to learn to safeguard their own health and to make healthy lifestyle choices. When necessary, kindergartens provide specialist support for physical and psychological development, which involves relevant professionals from outside agencies (Hungarian Government, 2012). The Core Programme expects kindergarten pedagogues to help children and their families to develop preventive healthcare practices. This includes, for example, providing children with more fresh fruit, vegetables or dairy products, and less sugar, salt and unsaturated fatty acid, in addition to cleaning their teeth at home and in the kindergarten. In this way, parents are partners in helping children establish healthcare routines for life.

Children's rights to social security are expressed in Article 26, whereas their right to an appropriate standard of living is summarised in Article 27. The right to social security includes access to services and access to financial resources, as well as benefits for those persons who are responsible for the upbringing of children. Growing up in relative poverty undermines children's well-being, self-esteem and acceptance in society, and reduces opportunities for education and progress (Körmöci, 2007). To keep child poverty at bay and to eradicate its negative impact on children's well-being, the Hungarian government allocates significant resources to support families. The Act LXXXIV of 1998 on supporting families establishes eligibility and regulates financial benefits given to families with children. The most common of these is the universal family subsidy or family child benefit given to all families with school-aged children. These different programmes, when provided alongside education, can contribute to breaking the cycle of poverty (Gábos, 2009).

Children's right to education is enshrined in Article 28. There is an ever-growing emphasis placed on early childhood education worldwide and its role in the later life journey of an individual (Campbell-Barr, 2012). Currently, in Hungary, both pre-primary and elementary education are compulsory and free. The introduction of compulsory early childhood education in 2015 for children between the age of 3 and 6 may prove to be a long-term solution to strengthening the role of ECEC provision in early development. The CRC urges participating states to support early childhood development programmes, among them the home- and community-based pre-primary school programmes. It also encourages a harmonised, integrated, cross-sector approach to early childhood services (CRC, 2005, Comprehensive Commentary No. 7, §30).

Article 31 guarantees children's right to play, recreation and cultural activities. Children's main activity in early childhood that reflects their culture is play. The CRC (2005) refers to children's right to play as a 'forgotten' right, even though play provides the optimal opportunity to develop their skills and abilities. The significance of creative play and exploratory learning are widely recognised in the field of early childhood education (Brown, 2010; Pálfi, 2019). Yet the limited opportunities young children currently have in Hungary to play with peers in child-centred, secure and harmonious environments creates obstacles for children's rights to recreation and play to be realised (CRC, 2005, Comprehensive Commentary No. 7, §35).

When considering children's economic rights, compared to other European countries, the systems of family support in Hungary could be seen as generous. The support allocated for families amounts to 1.9 per cent of the annual GDP and, with other, non-financial support included, represents a considerable investment by the government (Makay, 2015). Financial support is provided to mothers in the form of a 'one-off' payment after giving birth, and thereafter 70 per cent of their average annual income pro rata for the first period of the maternity leave, which is 168 days. During the second period of maternity leave, mothers receive an income for providing home care for their children up to the age of 2. In the third period of maternity leave, mothers can draw on what might be called a 'child carer's allowance', which is universal financial support until children reach their third birthday. These systems of support enable mothers to stay at home with their children until they are 3, but they also allow them to work part-time while caring for their children.

With the aim of reducing child poverty, the Hungarian government further supports families by providing meals for children in institutional care for either free or at a 50 per cent reduced rate based on individual circumstances. On the families' prior formal request, local authorities are obliged to ensure that children with free meals continue to receive their daily lunch over a 43 working day period during the summer holidays and on every working day during the autumn, winter and spring school holidays. According to the Public Education Act, from the academic year of 2017/18, all school-aged children in Years 1–9 and children with special educational needs (SEN) and from ethnic minority backgrounds receive their school books package free.

Children's rights to protection within their families and society

The Act CCXI. of 2011 on the Protection of Families states that children have the right to support that: (i) enables them to be brought up in a family; (ii) ensures their personalities can evolve; and (iii) removes threats to their development and ensures they are seen as rightful citizens of society. The law also states that children can only be separated from their parents and relatives in the interest of their healthy physical, mental and psychological development, and only in law-enforced cases and in a lawful manner (Act CCXI. of 2011 on the Protection of Families, 13. §. 2.3.). In the Core Programme, it is clearly stated that bringing up children is the right and responsibility of families, and in this kindergartens have a complementary role. The responsibility of the kindergarten is to establish conditions for cooperation and to develop working partnerships.

There are a number of officers responsible for guaranteeing children's rights in Hungary. It is the responsibility of all legal personnel and early childhood professionals, and currently the Commissioner of Fundamental Rights fulfils the role of protecting children's rights along with dealing with complaints and any breach of legislation (Act CXI of 2011 on Fundamental Rights, §1). An ombudsman to represent children's rights was established as a result of the introduction of Act IX of 2002, which altered child protection law. The role of the Children's Rights Officer is to listen to issues and complaints raised by children, to investigate and remedy them, and to advocate for children by representing their interests. The Children's Rights Officer can inspect institutions of education, including kindergartens and schools, where the implementation of children's rights is examined, and in cases of breach of legislation an investigation can be initiated: 'The Officer monitors safeguarding practices in kindergartens, schools, halls of residence, in pedagogical specialist services and support the implementation of children's rights' (Act XXXI of 1997 on Child Protection and Administration of Guardianship 11/A7).

The right to protection for children with special educational needs (SEN)

The education of children with SEN is regulated by the Government Decree of 32/2012 (X.8), which refers to the educational aims of the National Core Programme. In ECEC, inclusive education must be ensured for children whose pace of development is deviant from the norm. The principles of kindergarten education for children with SEN assert that these children's education must be in harmony with the 'image of the child', as described in the Core Programme. Pedagogues are required to create an environment to meet any special needs by providing necessary resources and by offering help that does not exceed what a child needs to be able to engage in daily activities independently.

The right to protection for children in disadvantage

Early childhood community-based programmes were rare in Hungary until the appearance of Sure Start children centres in the 2000s, and after this they became a more widespread type of service provision. The first Sure Start [*Biztos Kezdet*] children centre was opened in 2009 in one of the most disadvantaged areas in Hungary. The main aim of the programme was to reduce child poverty and extreme poverty. Currently, 112 children centres provide services for local communities (Németh, 2018). With the aim of improving children's well-being, they offer developmental programmes for families with children under 3 as one of the fundamental services. Further aims of the programme are:

- to provide healthy living conditions right from birth;
- to offer programmes and services that help children develop their skills and abilities from an early age;
- to reduce regional and ethnic inequalities;
- to improve parental employment;
- to reduce segregation;
- to improve healthy living conditions; and
- to develop social services provision.

(Rákó, 2017, p. 148)

Ensuring and protecting children's rights is a fundamental role for all institutions of public education. This is supported by the Office of the Ministerial Commissioner for Education Rights and the institution for implementing education rights. The Office offers guidance on the implementation of civil rights (relating to education) for all participants of the educational processes. The Commissioner of Education Rights provides an annual report of the work carried out during the year, in this way supporting the analysis of issues around children's rights in the educational processes.

Having examined how children's rights could be understood in the Hungarian context, the next section of this chapter discusses aspects of practice that provide evidence for the implementation of children's rights in early childhood care and education institutions.

Implementing children's rights in practice

What the future holds for children is greatly influenced by what children are experiencing now. Through ethical, sensitive and respectful care and education practices, children learn to become members of their community and society, learn to take responsibility for themselves and others, and learn to understand about their rights (Teszenyi and Sykes, 2018). Kindergarten pedagogues have an important role in facilitating this by creating a safe, dynamic and respectful environment that embraces children's rights. The CRC (2005) recommends that the direct teaching of children's rights should be part of the early childhood education and care curriculum. Currently, this is not typical in Hungarian early education programmes and there is little pedagogical material to support the education of children about their human rights. The *Kiskompasz Handbook for Educating Children about their Human Rights*, published in 2009, provides much needed guidance for early childhood professionals. Teaching material that is developmentally appropriate for young children was created by Ildikó Boldizsár in 2016 in the form of a picture book entitled *The Lost Bird Feather*. The book aims to help children learn about and become aware of their rights. The pedagogical material uses ten short stories to introduce concepts to children such as the right to property, the right to a healthy life, doing no harm, anti-discrimination, and the right to freedom of speech. There is also detailed practical guidance for early childhood professionals on how they can use the stories to talk to children about each of the rights represented in the stories. In this subsequent section, aspects of rights-respecting practice in Hungarian ECEC institutions are highlighted.

Respecting children's rights in view of the hierarchy of needs (Maslow)

One guarantee for children to be able to practise their rights while in kindergarten care is a child-centred approach where children are able to lead their own learning instead of pedagogues pursuing their own agendas or imposing their authority upon children. Children practising their rights can be detected in everyday activities and relationships. There are natural, biological aspects of children's development and children have unique 'urges' that are evidenced in their expressed emotions, actions and attitudes, which we accept as children's needs. There are ways of categorising these, one of which is in relation to Maslow's (1943) hierarchy of needs and theory of human motivation. With the aims of Hungarian ECEC firmly in mind, the Core Programme asserts that meeting children's physical and emotional needs must be a starting point for all activities planned for children. Table 29.1 offers some examples.

Körmöci (2007) connected meeting the child's physical and physiological needs with the pedagogues' role to help children develop a healthy lifestyle. There are three personal attributes that are expected of kindergarten pedagogues: being accepting, supportive and sensitively responsive. A child has the right to his or her movement needs to be met and his or her health to be protected and maintained. Furthermore, the child has the right to care for

Table 29.1 Alignment between the child's needs and rights in relation to Maslow's hierarchy of needs (adapted by Körmöci, 2007, pp. 193–194)

Needs of a kindergarten-aged child	Children's rights
The need for movement; biological, physiological needs	The child has the right to ample space, a well-balanced diet and an institutional life that follows his or her own biological rhythm.
The need for emotional security	The child has the right to: • joy, peace and a harmonious atmosphere; • the right to respect human dignity; • the protection of his or her own interests; • follow his or her own daily routine; • be treated with respect; • know his or her own opportunities; • be accepted for who he or she is; • trust; and • his or her pace of development to be accepted.
The need for love	The child has the right to: • love; • be loved; • unconditional acceptance; and • have his or her personality be respected.

his or her own body, to keep clean, to a healthy diet and dental hygiene, to rest, and to practices that maintain good health. A child's emotional needs also strongly influence his or her well-balanced development. With regard to the previously mentioned universal rights to play, the Core Programme fiercely protects this right when stating, 'play – a free process that follows the flow of free imagination – is a young child's elementary psychological need, for which the provision must be daily, continuous, and where possible, uninterrupted' (Hungarian Government, 2012). Free play, therefore, is seen as a child's right that protects him or her from an overload of direct teaching. The right to play is also secured by the Core Programme, which limits the presence of the pedagogue in children's play. When the pedagogue joins a child's play, always on the child's request, it is suggested that the pedagogue displays supportive, encouraging and motivating behaviours so that the child's play can be supported indirectly, and therefore more sensitively.

Kindergarten education promotes the child's development together with the nurturing provided by families. For this to succeed, the kindergarten cooperates with families. The forms of cooperation are varied, from establishing personal relationships to organising shared kindergarten events, and include all the opportunities that either the kindergarten or the families initiate. A kindergarten pedagogue serves as a model for young children to identify with. This commences with the emotional relationship between the pedagogue and the child, through which the pedagogue complements the role of the mother in the processes of socialisation (Antal and Zsubrits, 2015, p. 17; Brayfield and Korintus, 2011). The presence of a beloved pedagogue ensures emotional security for children, which is one of the main roles of kindergartens in Hungary. A kindergarten pedagogue offers help personalised to the needs of each family by considering the unique characteristics and customs of families (Hungarian Government, 2012).

The dominance of free play

The Core Programme emphasises that the right conditions for play must be created and applied across the curriculum. It also claims that 'free-play must be in the forefront of kindergarten provision and its primary role must be recognised in the kindergarten's daily routines, schedules and in the planning for play-based activities' (Hungarian Government, 2012, p. 5) Kindergarten pedagogues in Hungary must ensure that there is time for children's unstructured free play both inside and outside during the day, and free play is seen as the 'protected activity' in each early childhood setting (Pálfi, 2019). The Core Programme declares that play, as an unstructured process led by imagination and free association, is a basic psychological need for young children, which they have to satisfy daily in a continuous, sustained and preferably undisturbed manner.

Another guarantee for children's rights to play is when free play is placed in the forefront of all activities in the kindergarten. The Core Programme claims that 'the dominance of free play must prevail' (Hungarian Government, 2012, p. 7). Children's rights to play can also be seen in how conditions for play are created in a kindergarten. The Core Programme expects practitioners to provide for children's need for space and to use flexible materials, tools and play resources that allow for children's imagination and fantasies to unfold (Hungarian Government, 2012).

Furthermore, the child has the right to daily stories, rhymes and poems, which are key to children's mental hygiene. This is a term used in Hungary in relation to both children and adults, and it reflects the processes of mental 'laundering' to maintain emotional, psychological and physical well-being (Körmöci, 2017). It is interesting to note that maintaining mental hygiene is part of the tertiary training for kindergarten pedagogues.

It is also the child's right to have access to 'intimacy during storytelling', which is one of the criteria for sharing stories with children. Kindergarten pedagogues must also consider children's rights when inviting them to engage in work-like activities (e.g. sweeping, mopping, laying the table for meals, tidying up, etc). Children cannot be forced to carry out these tasks and they must be allowed to volunteer. The stipulation of the Core Programme is that work-like tasks are active pursuits that children carry out happily and willingly. It is important to help children develop positive attitudes to work, the necessary skills and abilities to gain experiences and to understand the world around them; these include perseverance, independence, responsibility and determination.

Nurturing tradition and education in children's ethnic language: ways of realising children's rights

The right to cultural activities was mentioned in the 'Understanding children's rights' section of this chapter. One of the key features of Hungarian culture is music and dance. Singing and listening to folk songs, playing traditional ring games, learning folk dance and playing folk games are ways for children to become familiar with and to preserve their tradition. Engaging with folk tradition can be described as one of the processes through which cultural identity is developed. This is also outlined in the curriculum area of 'active exploration of the outside world', which requires pedagogues to plan opportunities for children to get to know their country and its traditions.

Each child is entitled to be educated in their ethnic language or mother tongue in Hungarian kindergartens. Developing language in each child's mother tongue is one of the key aims of Hungarian early childhood programmes. This is achieved holistically (in every aspect of kindergarten education and care) and through the active participation of children. For those children whose mother tongue is not Hungarian, care and education in their 'ethnic minority' kindergartens can be requested in their ethnic language:

> As long as minimum of eight parents of the same ethnicity request kindergarten education to be delivered in an ethnic minority kindergarten, for the academic year in the calendar year after the date of the request, ethnic educational provision must be planned and the provision to be delivered provided a minimum of eight children enrol.
>
> *(Hungarian Government, 2013, 17, (III. 1) Decree 1, §2)*

Flexible daily routines

To ensure children's rights are implemented in children's everyday lives, the organisation of kindergarten care and education is considered from the children's point of view. Hungarian kindergartens accept (contrary to schools) that children within a group tend to choose to engage with a variety of activities running at the same time, which require varying conditions and, most importantly, time. The Core Programme specifies two criteria that guarantee this to happen: one is that 'daily schedules adjust to the various activities and to children's individual needs' (Hungarian Government, 2012, p. 4); the other is that 'an effective daily schedule is characterised by continuity and flexibility' (Hungarian Government, 2012, p. 8) In the organisation of a day, it is the children's interests, not the adults', that take priority.

The implementation of children's rights is also evidenced in that children are not harmed or disadvantaged because of their actual stage of development. Hungarian kindergartens cater for children aged 3–6 years. Those children who, for whatever reason, do not reach the normative developmental stage for their chronological age, which is necessary to start school, can stay in the kindergartens for an additional academic year, even though they have reached the school starting age. The Core Programme states that 'flexible school enrolment allows for entering school according to not only chronological age but also to developmental stage' (Hungarian Government, 2012, p. 12).

Conclusion

It can be concluded that legislative documents and the requirements of Hungarian ECEC provision strive to implement children's rights in everyday practice and to ensure all children have equal access to high-quality care and education. This review of children's rights confirms that explicitly or implicitly children's rights are represented in the Hungarian National Core Programme for Kindergarten Education. Hungarian kindergartens follow the requirements of international regulatory documents, and the National Core Programme reflects an ethos of safeguarding children's interests. This is particularly important because the entire cohort of 3–6-year-olds access institutional care and education in Hungarian ECEC. Kindergarten provision and children's activities could provide more opportunities (than observed) for information-sharing and sharing good practice with regard to children's rights. This would require appropriate pedagogical materials and for these materials to be embedded into kindergarten pedagogue training nationally. In return, those professionals of early childhood who are privileged to work with young children could develop a greater level of awareness and consciousness about children's rights and adults' responsibilities in institutional care.

References

Antal, Bernadett, & Zsubrits, Attila. 2015. "Az óvodapedagógus gyermekszemmel." *Óvodai Nevelés* 4: 16–19.

Boldizsár, Ildikó. 2016. *Az elveszett madártoll. Beszélgetős mesekönyv*, Budapest: Országos Betegjogi, Ellátottjogi, Gyermekjogi és Dokumentációs Központ.

Brayfield, A., & Korintus, M. 2011. "Early childhood socialization: Societal context and childrearing values in Hungary." *Journal of Early Childhood Research* 9 (3): 262–279. doi: 10.1177/1476718X11402444

Brown, Stuart. 2010. *Play: How it shapes the brain, opens the imagination, and invigorates the soul.* New York: Penguin Group.

Campbell-Barr, Verity. 2012. "Early years education and the value for money folklore." *European Early Childhood Education Research Journal* 20 (3): 423–437.

Constitution Act of Hungary (Magyarország Alaptörvénye). 2011. *Netjogtar*, Accessed 4th April, 2019. Április 25. https://net.jogtar.hu/jogszabaly?docid=A1100425.ATV

CRC, 2005. Comprehensive Commentary No. 7, 27, para. 256.

Egészségügyi, szociális és családügyi miniszter. 2004. "ESzCsM rendelet a területi védőnői ellátásról." (49/2004. [IV. 30]) http://njt.hu/cgi_bin/njt_doc.cgi?docid=84519.361892

Emberi erőforrások minisztere. 2012. "EMMI rendelet A Sajátos nevelési igényű gyermekek óvodai nevelésének irányelveiről." (32/2012. [X. 08] EMMI) http://njt.hu/cgi_bin/njt_doc.cgi?docid=154929.229241

Emberi erőforrások minisztere. 2013. "EMMI rendelet a nemzetiség óvodai nevelésének irányelve és a nemzetiség iskolai oktatásának irányelve kiadásáról." (17/2013. [III. 01] EMMI) http://njt.hu/cgi_bin/njt_doc.cgi?docid=159180.353179

Emberi Erőforrások Minisztere. 2014. "EMMI rendelet, a közétkeztetésre vonatkozó táplálkozás- egészségügyi előírásokról." (37/2014 [IV. 30]) EMMI) http://njt.hu/cgi_bin/njt_doc.cgi?docid=169011.361140

"EMMI rendelet, a közétkeztetésre vonatkozó táplálkozás- egészségügyi előírásokról" (37/2014 (IV.30.) *Netjogtar*, Accessed 5th May, 2019, http://njt.hu/cgi_bin/njt_doc.cgi?docid=169011.361140

"EMMI rendelet a nemzetiség óvodai nevelésének irányelve és a nemzetiség iskolai oktatásának irányelve kiadásáról" (17/2013. [III. 01] EMMI). *Netjogtar*, Accessed 21st March, 2019, http://njt.hu/cgi_bin/njt_doc.cgi?docid=159180.353179

EMMI rendelet A Sajátos nevelési igényű gyermekek óvodai nevelésének irányelveiről (32/2012. [X. 08]. *Netjogtar*, Accessed 1st May, 2019, http://njt.hu/cgi_bin/njt_doc.cgi?docid=154929.229241

ESzCsM rendelet a területi védőnői ellátásról 49/2004. [IV. 30]). *Netjogtar*, Accessed 4th April, 2019, http://njt.hu/cgi_bin/njt_doc.cgi?docid=84519.361892

Filó-Katonáné, Erika, & Pehr, Erika. 2006. *Gyermeki jogok, gyermekvédelem*, Budapest: HvgOrac.

Gábos, András. 2009. "A gyermekszegénység csökkentését célzó kormányzati beavatkozások: Irodalom-áttekintés." *Esély* 20 (évf. 5. sz): 48–68.

Gyermekjogi Bizottság, 7. sz. átfogó kommentár. 2005a.edited by Herczog, Mária 2009. *Kézikönyv a gyermekjogi egyezmény alkalmazásához. Család, Gyermek Ifjúság Egyesület*, Budapest: UNICEF.

Gyermekjogi Bizottság, 7. sz. átfogó kommentár. 2005b. edited by Herczog, Mária 2009. *(szerk) kézikönyv a gyermekjogi egyezmény alkalmazásához*, Budapest: Család, Gyermek Ifjúság Egyesület, UNICEF.

Herczog, Mária. 2011. "A gyermekjogi egyezmény érvényesülése." www.okri.hu/images/stories/OKRISzemle2009/OKRISzemle_2011/011_herczog.pdf

Hungarian Government. 2012. "363/2012 (XII.07.) Kormányrendelet Óvodai nevelés országos alapprogramja 2012. [the Hungarian National Core Programme for Kindergarten Education]." Budapest. Accessed March 20, 2019 www.njt.hu/cgi_bin/njt_doc.cgi?docid=157536.23376028223-28231

Körmöci, Katalin. 2007. *A gyermek szükségleteire épített tanulás az óvodában*, Budapest: *Fabula BT*.

Körmöci, Katalin. 2017. "Az óvoda, mint szociális anyaöl – Ismét a személyes bánásmód fontosságáról, a befogadásról." www.kormocikatalin.hu/?menu=33

Magyarország Alaptörvénye (Constitutional Act). *Netjogtar*, Accessed 15th March 2019, http://njt.hu/cgi_bin/njt_doc.cgi?docid=140968.356005

Makay, Zsuzsanna. 2015. "Családtámogatás, gyermeknevelés, munkavállalás." In Monostori, Judit et al. *Demográfiai Portré KSH*, 57–74. Budapest: NKI.

Maslow, Abraham H. 1943. "A theory of human motivation." *Psychological Review* 50 (4): 370–396.

Németh, Szilvia. 2018. *A Biztos kezdet gyerekházak heterogenitása. Esettanulmány.* Budapest: MTA TK.

Office of the Commissioner for Educational Rights. "The commissioner for educational rights." www.oktbiztos.hu/mission/index.html

OM rendelet az Oktatási Jogok Miniszteri Biztosa Hivatalának feladatairól és működésének szabályairól (40/1999. [X. 8.] OM). *Netjogtar*, Accessed 15th March 2019, http://njt.hu/cgi_bin/njt_doc.cgi?docid=40515.274574

Oktatási miniszter. 1999. "OM rendelet az Oktatási Jogok Miniszteri Biztosa Hivatalának feladatairól és működésének szabályairól (40/1999. [X. 8.] OM)." http://njt.hu/cgi_bin/njt_doc.cgi?docid=40515.274574

Országgyűlés. 1991. "Törvény a Gyermekek jogairól szóló New Yorkban 1989. November 20-án kelt Egyezmény kihirdetéséről (1991. évi LXIV)." http://njt.hu/cgi_bin/njt_doc.cgi?docid=15579.284771

Országgyűlés. 1997. "Törvény a gyermekek jogairól és a gyámügyi igazgatásról (1997. évi XXXI)." http://njt.hu/cgi_bin/njt_doc.cgi?docid=29687.366932

Országgyűlés. 1998. "Törvény a családok támogatásáról (1998. évi LXXXIV)." http://njt.hu/cgi_bin/njt_doc.cgi?docid=35344.362729

Országgyűlés. 2003. "Törvény az egyenlő bánásmódról és az esélyegyenlőség előmozdításáról (2003 Évi CXXV)." http://njt.hu/cgi_bin/njt_doc.cgi?docid=76310.366950

Országgyűlés. 2011a. "Törvény a nemzeti köznevelésről (2011. Évi CXC)." http://njt.hu/cgi_bin/njt_doc.cgi?docid=139880.366984

Országgyűlés. 2011b. "Törvény alapvető jogok biztosáról (2011. Évi CXI)." http://njt.hu/cgi_bin/njt_doc.cgi?docid=139247.348563

Országgyűlés. 2011c. "Törvény a családok védelméről (2011. Évi CCXI)." http://njt.hu/cgi_bin/njt_doc.cgi?docid=143096.245265

Pálfi, Sándor. 2019. *Az óvodai játék a gyermekközpontúság mutatója: az óvodai játék jelene és amilyen lehetne.* Budapest: Sprint Kiadó.

Rákó, Erzsébet. 2017. "A gyermekjólét-gyermekvédelem és a gyermek- szegénység aktuális kérdései." In *Kihívások és válaszok. tanulmányok a szociálpedagógia területéről*, edited by Erzsébet, Rákó & Zsolt, Soós, 136–155 Rákó Erzsébet-Soós Zsolt Debrecen: Debreceni Egyetemi Kiadó.

Szebenyi, Mariann. 2009. "Kiskompasz Kézikönyv a gyerekek emberi jogi neveléséhez." https://rm.coe.int/2009-compasito-hu-with-cover/168075abf6

Teszenyi, E., & Sykes, G. 2018. Final thoughts from the editors. In Sykes & Teszenyi *Young children and their communities: Understanding collective social responsibility.* Abingdon: Routledge.

Törvény a családok támogatásáról (1998. évi LXXXIV). *Netjogtar*, Accessed 5th May, 2019, http://njt.hu/cgi_bin/njt_doc.cgi?docid=35344.362729

Törvény a családok védelméről (2011. Évi CCXI). *Netjogtar*, Accessed 11th Apil 2019, http://njt.hu/cgi_bin/njt_doc.cgi?docid=143096.245265

Törvény a gyermekek jogairól és a gyámügyi igazgatásról (1997. évi XXXI). *Netjogtar*, Accessed 11th Apil 2019, http://njt.hu/cgi_bin/njt_doc.cgi?docid=29687.366932

Törvény a Gyermekek jogairól szóló New Yorkban 1989. November 20-án kelt Egyezmény kihirdetéséről (1991. évi LXIV). *Netjogtar*, Accessed 15th March 2019, http://njt.hu/cgi_bin/njt_doc.cgi?docid=15579.284771

Törvény alapvető jogok biztosáról (2011. Évi CXI). *Netjogtar*, Accessed 11th Apil 2019, http://njt.hu/cgi_bin/njt_doc.cgi?docid=139247.348563

Törvény a nemzeti köznevelésről (2011. Évi CXC) *Netjogtar*, Accessed 11th Apil 2019, http://njt.hu/cgi_bin/njt_doc.cgi?docid=139880.366984

Törvény az egyenlő bánásmódról és az esélyegyenlőség előmozdításáról (2003 Évi CXXV). *Netjogtar*, Accessed 5th May, 2019, http://njt.hu/cgi_bin/njt_doc.cgi?docid=76310.366950

United Nations. 1989. "Convention on the rights of the child." www.ohchr.org/EN/ProfessionalInterest/Pages/CRC.aspx

30

PLAY MAPS

Supporting children's provisional rights to play in their local community

Cat Sewell, Jo Smale and Kylie Smith

Introduction

There has been much written about the value of play framed within developmental theories, particularly in relation to cognitive development, gross motor skills, social skills and academic outcomes (Bento and Dias, 2017; Fjørtoft, 2001; Johnson, Sevimli-Celik and AlMansour, 2013; Whitebread et al., 2017). In recent years in Australia and internationally, play has been attached to a health agenda to motivate children to be physically active to combat childhood obesity and diabetes (Danielzik et al., 2002; de Silva-Sanigorski et al., 2010). While there has been critique of the concept of play as a Western middle-class construction that privileges Euro-Western norms of childhood (Richie and Rau, 2010; Viruru, 2001), the provision of play as a 'universal' right has been advocated through the United Nations Convention on the Rights of the Child (CRC) (United Nations, 1989). Article 31 of the CRC states that all children have the right to 'rest, leisure, play, recreational activities, cultural life and the arts' (United Nations, 1989). The United Nations General Comment 17 discusses how these rights should be enacted (UN Committee on the Rights of the Child, 2013) and outlines the obligations of States Parties to provide the provision of spaces and places for children to play within local communities, stating that municipalities should ensure the provision of:

> Availability of inclusive parks, community centres, sports and playgrounds that are safe and accessible to all children; creation of a safe living environment for free play, including design of zones in which players, pedestrians and bikers have priority; public safety measures to protect areas for play and recreation from individuals or groups who threaten children's safety; provision of access to landscaped green areas, large open spaces and nature for play and recreation, with safe, affordable and accessible transport.
>
> *(UN Committee on the Rights of the Child, 2013, p. 21)*

This chapter will report on how the City of Darebin, a local municipality in Victoria, Australia, reviewed their community playspaces and developed Play Maps with children, families and early years teachers to ensure that all children had access to safe and free environments to explore and play in. The aim of the project was to promote and support children's development and healthy lifestyle, and for children to have a sense of belonging and connection to community. Play Maps were designed to be used by children and families to stimulate ideas, give prompts and mark out the local spaces that children love to play in. Fourteen Play Maps have been developed across the municipality.

Background

The City of Darebin is situated between 5 and 15 km north of Melbourne's central business district and has been home to the Wurundjeri people for many thousands of years. It covers 53 km^2 of land, which stretches from Melbourne's inner northern suburbs of Northcote and Fairfield, and out to Reservoir and Bundoora. The city's population is 158,745 (Australian Bureau of Statistics Estimated Resident Population, 2017), and this number is expected to increase to 230,118 by 2041. Darebin is home to one of the largest, most diverse communities in Victoria in terms of culture, language, religion, socio-economic background, employment status, occupation and housing need. There were 48,842 people living in the City of Darebin in 2016 who were born overseas, and 25 per cent arrived in Australia in the five years prior to 2016. The children population aged between 0 and 12 in the City of Darebin in 2016 was 20,959. Darebin has 120 playspaces.

In 2010, Darebin City Council adopted the Darebin Playspace Strategy 2010–2020. The vision of this strategy was to connect all people across the municipality to open spaces, stating that Darebin is 'A well connected network of accessible open spaces that meet the diverse needs of the community and provide a range of social and environmental benefits' (2010, p. 7).

The four principles underpinning the Playspace Strategy ensure the interconnection of participation, protection and provision rights of children living and visiting the community (and adults). The first principle focuses on accessibility and inclusion, committing to 'provide an environment where children, youth, older people and people of all abilities and backgrounds are welcome' (2010, p. 7). The second principle commits to provision rights, endeavouring 'to provide for play within 500 metres of every home' (2010, p. 7). The third principle attends to provision, participation and protection rights, with a focus on creating 'sustainable and safe playspaces that are evolving, dynamic and challenging' (2010, p. 7). Finally, the fourth principle reflects Darebin's commitment to respect for diversity, inclusion and engagement across many areas, including ability, culture, gender and sexuality. The four principles ensure that playspaces are 'developed with and for the community reflecting the diversity of local neighbourhood communities' (2010, p. 7). The Darebin Playspace Strategy 2010–2020 specifically acknowledges Australia as a signatory to the CRC (1989) and notes the relevance of the strategy to Articles 23, 29 and 31:

> Article 23: Recognises that a mentally or physically disabled child should enjoy a full and decent life, in conditions which ensure dignity, promote self-reliance and facilitate the child's active participation in the community.
>
> Article 29: Recognises that education should foster the development of the child's personality, talents and mental and physical abilities to their fullest potential.
>
> Article 31: Recognises the right of the child to rest and leisure, to engage in play and recreational activities appropriate to the age of the child and to participate freely in cultural life and the arts.

The Playspace Strategy is the backdrop to the Play Map consultation with the council's Child Friendly City Framework (2016). The Child Friendly City Framework outlined Darebin's commitment to ensure that the provision of parks, playgrounds and green spaces provided opportunities for children to engage in healthy lifestyles. The framework also acknowledged the need for walking and cycle paths that encouraged children to want to travel using 'active transport' and support children's independent mobility.

In 2017, a representative from Families, Youth & Children at Darebin Council met with a play specialist (and local resident) to brainstorm ways they could collaborate to advocate for and promote play in the early years. They devised a project based on a previous play map concept that Cat Sewell had developed as part of the Department of Education and Early Childhood Development, Linking Learning Project in Thomastown, a nearby suburb. The partnership applied for, and were successful in obtaining, a grant from the Darebin Creative Arts and Cultures Department under their Arts Partnership Initiative. The Kingsbury Play Map project was trialled, children, families and educators were consulted, and the first Play Map was developed. It was also documented with creative output such as photography, video and sound recordings. Due to the success of this pilot, the City of Darebin allocated funds to complete a further six Play Maps in other areas across the municipality. The project gained further traction after it won a Victorian Early Years Award for the Kingsbury Play Map Project, and the final seven Play Maps were committed to by the incoming Manager for Families, Youth & Children and completed by the end of 2018.

Consultation methodology

From the conceptualisation of the consultation methodology, children were recognised as competent meaning-makers with valuable knowledge about their worlds and the places and spaces they explore (Woodhead, 2008). Drawing from a sociological and rights-based perspective, children were understood as active citizens in their world (MacNaughton and Smith, 2008) who have a right under the CRC to have a say in matters affecting them, irrespective of age. The effect of this in practice was that children were at the centre of the consultation. Consultations occurred with children and families in playgroups, childcare centres, kindergartens and primary schools across Darebin to ask them what they enjoyed and when and where they play. In total 1,854 people took part in conversations about the importance and value of play in their community, including 1,407 children aged between 1 and 12 years and 111 adults (families, carers and teachers). For this chapter, data from children birth to 7 years will be the focus, drawing from the 1,053 children who participated in this age category.

In total, there were 24 facilitated sessions with children and adults. A one-hour session facilitated by the first author was undertaken at the primary schools and sessional preschools. In Australia, sessional preschools offer 15 hours of funded education and care programmes for children aged 4 to 5 years in the year before entering school. After an initial group discussion, children were asked to do a drawing that illustrated their responses to any or all of three questions: What is your favourite thing to play? Where do you like to play? Who do you like to play with? When they had finished drawing, the first author or teachers present asked the children to tell them about their drawings so that they could document their response and support the interpretation of the data. Fifty responses also came from services who facilitated their own sessions, rather than being led by the first author. The services including playgroups and long day care centres were provided with posters and prompt questions to assist in leading a discussion with their children. Picture 30.1 provides an example of the poster template provided to services.

ALPHINGTON & FAIRFIELD

What do you like to play?

Where do you like to play?

We are developing a play map in your area.

Please write and draw your responses on this poster.

We would love to hear from **children** and **adults** about their experiences and memories!

Picture 30.1 Example of 'Where do you like to play?' poster

These sheets were then used to support children to draw about what play activities, materials and spaces they engaged in and the people they spent time playing with. The adults who participated in the consultation were asked to draw and respond to memories in relation to *how they played as a child.*

What did children say?

Children discussed the places, spaces and play activities across 11 themes. Figure 30.1 provides an overview of the number of children that talked about or drew their ideas about play across 23 areas. From these 23 areas, the 11 themes were identified.

It is important to note that in many drawings, the areas, people or types of play were interconnected, as illustrated in the drawing in Picture 30.2, which represents the child's engagement with trees, nature, monkey bars and friends.

In some spaces within Darebin, there are a number of playspaces that are co-located. For example, the All Nations Park in the Northcote area has two playgrounds that are suitable for children aged 2 to 15 years of age and sports facilities that include a basketball half court, skate ramp, chess boards, tennis and down ball wall and outdoor gym equipment, as well as two barbeque areas and shade and seating around three picnic spaces, and a rock hill with views across the cityscape. The 11 most prominent themes children drew and talked about were playground equipment, natural environments, ball sports, water, pretend play, taking risks (e.g. going fast, climbing high), private spaces, interacting with animals, sensory exploration and art-making, being with friends, and being with family.

Playground equipment

Playground equipment was identified as the most common place to play and was important to 272 children of birth to 7 years of age, represented in 26 per cent of drawings. The City of Darebin has oversight of the development and maintenance of playgrounds across the municipality. These sites are diverse in size and equipment but generally have a combination of fixed equipment such as slides, swings and climbing structures. Designated playground equipment areas for children has been seen by some to compartmentalise where children play, reducing the child-friendly nature of the city, rather than children being welcomed in all public areas. Playground equipment has also been more recently questioned over its risk-averse nature – being 'too safe' and not providing enough challenge and stimulation for children (Little and Wyver, 2008; McFarland and Laird, 2018). Playground equipment does provide children with physical play development opportunities and is beginning to incorporate more natural spaces and diverse play types, such as adding sensory and sound play elements. The City of Darebin has been working towards upgrading their playspaces and working to maximise the play value they bring to a wide range of children. Picture 30.3 illustrates one of the children's engagement on the monkey bars where they swing upside down.

Nature

Natural elements such as trees, grass and flowers were the second most discussed and drawn feature of spaces for children to play and explore. Natural phenomena such as rainbows, snow or raindrops were also featured. Some 225 children had natural elements in their

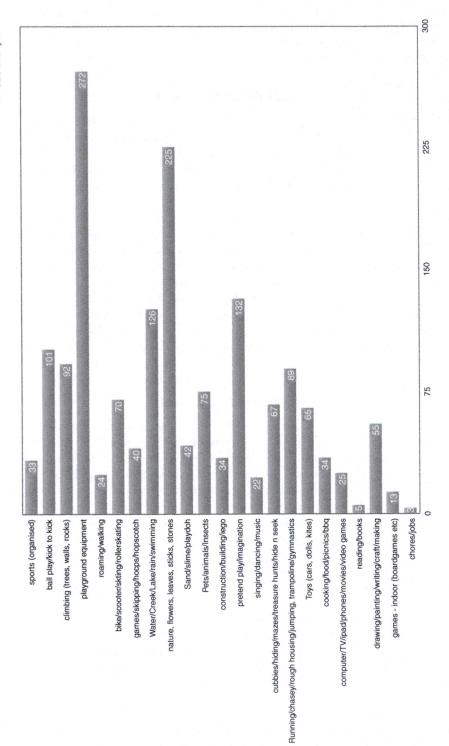

Figure 30.1 Table of play type responses for children 0–7 years

Picture 30.2 The importance of climbing trees, monkey bars, nature and friends

Picture 30.3 Upside down on the monkey bars

drawings, representing 21 per cent of all responses. Much has been written on the benefits for children playing outdoors in natural environment (Bento and Dias, 2017; Clements, 2004; Fjørtoft, 2001). The data from Play Map consultations show it is also something that children value highly themselves. Darebin has been strategically planning and developing green spaces throughout the community. This has been driven by Darebin's Open Space Strategy (2007–2017), a key planning document providing the policy framework for the Playspace Strategy and the Green Streets Strategy (1995). Picture 30.4 illustrates one of the children's drawings depicting playing in spaces with trees.

Picture 30.4 Green spaces

Water

Water featured in many drawings, either as playing in the rain, puddles, along creeks or rivers, or swimming at the pool or beach. Some 126 drawings explicitly mentioned water in their responses, or 12 per cent of responses. Water is a precious resource in Australia, with many communities battling the effects of drought. As an island nation surrounded by sea and waterways threaded through the country, water is also a material for play activities, whether that is swimming at the beach or in a local swimming pool or playing by the local riverbank at Merri Creek. Conservation of water and water as a play material is constantly negotiated within the community and within families. Picture 30.5 illustrates one child's discussion of playing at the swimming pool.

Pretend play

Role play, pretend play and imaginative play featured strongly for 0–7-year-olds, with 13 per cent of drawings including one of these elements. Dressing up as characters, role play with figurines and toys, as well as imagining they were in a movie, book or video game, were all responses in this category. Watching TV or playing games on computers and tablet devices was rarely drawn about; only 25 drawings out of 1,053. In Picture 30.6, a child draws themselves role-playing with a phone ('I like to be a policeman'). Picture 30.7 illustrates an imaginative game of 'the floor is lava' played with a group of friends pretending 'we are in a jungle'.

Ball sports

A range of ball play and sports were included in drawings (although the number was much higher in the 7–12 years age group), such as Australian Football League (AFL), soccer, netball, basketball and cricket. In the 0–7 years age group, only 3 per cent cited organised sports play, while 10 per cent drew about informal ball play, such as kick to kick with a sibling, friend or

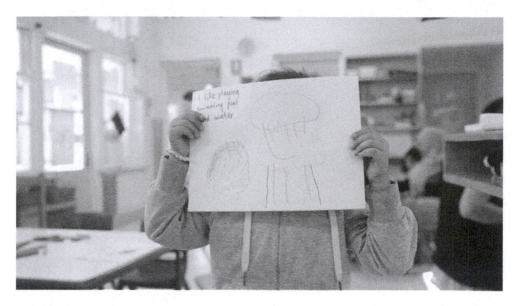

Picture 30.5 I like playing swimming pool and water

Picture 30.6 I like to be a policeman

parent. This is not a surprise in some ways as children have to be 5 years of age in many organised sports organisations such as AFL AUSkick or at junior soccer clubs. In Picture 30.8, we see a drawing showing a child kicking goals with their dad at a park, while in Picture 30.9 the child has drawn about playing basketball in the school grounds.

Picture 30.7 Pretend we are in a jungle

Picture 30.8 Kicking goals with Dad

Risk and challenge

Drawings often described play that had an element of risk and challenge in it, such as a very big slide, going fast on a bike or jumping from a high wall. While some drawings showed a parent helping on playground equipment, some children also described independence as part of their challenge (e.g. climbing to the top 'all by myself'). Nine per cent of drawings showed children enjoying climbing structures other than playground equipment, most

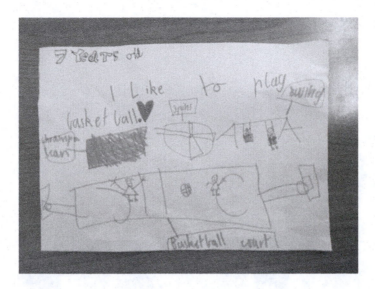

Picture 30.9 I like to play basketball

commonly trees, rocks or walls. In Picture 30.10, a child has drawn themselves jumping on big rocks outside, while Picture 30.11 shows friends climbing *up* a big slide instead of going down it. The risks that children naturally seek out during their play help to develop coordination, muscle strength, balance and the vestibular system, but also develop confidence and an understanding of limitations and boundaries (Canadian Public Health Association, 2019; Little, 2017; Whitebread et al., 2017). Rough housing, 'chasey' and other very active play was represented in 89 drawings, while 70 drawings featured bikes, skateboards and other moving equipment. Children enjoyed going fast, whether going down a slide, 'running really fast' or 'going fast on my skateboard', as described in Picture 30.12.

Picture 30.10 Jumping on big rocks

Picture 30.11 A big slide and you climb up

Picture 30.12 Going fast on the skateboard

Cubby houses/private spaces

Children drew about wanting to find their own spaces and to hide away. Sixty-seven children drew about cubby houses (or dens/forts), treehouses, games of 'hide and seek', treasure hunts or mazes. Playspaces that provide children with privacy are an important way of supporting children's rights to privacy provided under Article 16 of the CRC (United Nations, 1989). From a very early age, children engage in elements of surprise and hiding, such as 'peekaboo' with babies (Whitebread et al., 2017; Yogman et al., 2018). Children explore themes of safety and shelter during this type of play, but also develop their stress response mechanisms and problem-solving skills (Cole-Hamilton, 2011; Gray, 2014). In Picture 30.13, a child draws about hiding in the forest with a friend, while Picture 30.14 shows an 'awesome' treehouse.

Art-making and sensory exploration

Another area that children depicted was playing and creating in tactile ways, in art-making and sensory explanation. These were represented in a number of ways, such as playing with sand, slime or play dough (42 responses) and painting, craft or drawing (55 responses), but when combined form a more significant theme. This group of sensory explorations could also connect with playing with the natural sensory elements such as mud, leaves, sticks or water. The key to this type of play was children describing playing *with* an element, not describing *making a particular thing*, as we see in Picture 30.15 ('I like to do painting'). They are interested in exploring the material, not necessarily creating a 'product'.

Picture 30.13 I like to hide

Picture 30.14 Awesome treehouse

Picture 30.15 I like to do painting

Animals

Animals were a regular addition to drawings of play. Some children spoke explicitly about playing with an animal, such as in Picture 30.16 ('I like playing with my dog and my cat'), while other drawings simply had animals such as butterflies, birds or dogs present in the picture. New materialist theories provide transformative understandings of children's play with animals and nature, suggesting that the relationship between child and animal is more complex than children merely playing *with* animals. Taguchi (2014) proposes that as well as children affecting animals in their play, animals are also capable of influencing children's play.

Picture 30.16 I like playing with my dog and my cat

Picture 30.17 A snail I met in the zoo

Who children play with

Not all drawing responses outlined who they liked to play with, but of the 361 that did, 43 per cent liked to play with members of their family, 39 per cent with friends, 12 per cent with animals and 7 per cent on their own (shown in Figure 30.2). Picture 30.18 illustrates a child who enjoys playing with their friends. In Picture 30.19, the child has drawn about having a dance party with their mum, dad, brother and the dog in the lounge or family room of their house. Many members of families were represented; children drew about siblings, cousins, grandparents, parents, carers and pets. In Picture 30.20, we see that the child drew about their brother ('I like when my brother takes me to the park close to my home when he is not at school') and their mother ('When my mum is (not) too busy she plays with me. We draw together.').

Where children like to play

When looking specifically at where children said they liked to play, we see similarities to the responses about types of play (such as playground equipment being the most common). It also points to areas that are potentially underutilised, such as street play (only 10 children from 1,053 drew about playing on the street). The prevalence of children playing in the street has declined sharply over the last 20 or so years in Australia, as well as elsewhere in the world (Gray, 2014; Hart, 2008. From the responses given, the most common place to play was at the park on the playground equipment (272), followed by playing in park gardens and fields (152), at school/kindergarten/childcare (134) and at home/in their bedroom (128). Trees were important places for play (68), as well as front/backyards to homes (71) (see Figure 30.3).

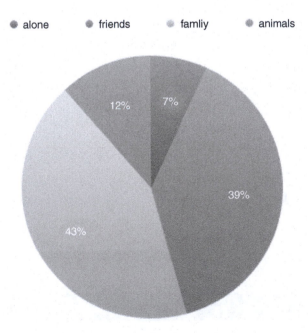

Figure 30.2 Graph of people with whom children 0–7 years like to play

Picture 30.18 Playing with my friends

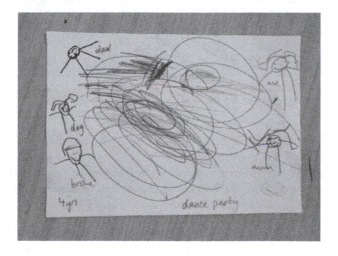

Picture 30.19 Dance party with my family

Creating short videos from consultations

Persons doing audio-recording, photography and videography attended consultation sessions to capture footage of participants drawing and recording their stories. Having quality artists with experience in working with children in these roles allowed participants to feel comfortable. Representing their experiences through drawings and words only, rather than through images of their faces, was a deliberate decision by the project team, both to protect the privacy of participants but also to allow viewers of the films to use their imaginations. Listening to the

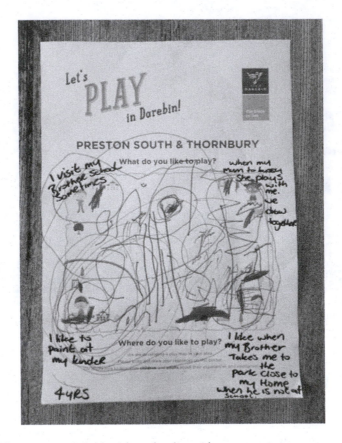

Picture 30.20 When my mum is (not) too busy she plays with me

voices of the children and adults involved adds richness and depth to the consultation data. The footage was edited into 16 one-minute films that were uploaded and posted on websites and social media. These bite-sized videos were edited around the main themes described above, such as focusing on stories of playing with water, or drawings that focused on sport, or nature play, or risk and challenge. Videos can be viewed at the City of Darebin Play Maps playlist on YouTube: www.youtube.com/playlist?list=PL5OVRsbC_lonoPUBUV-29bZsQo8RVSaTu

Creating the Play Maps

The children's ideas with the adults' discussions were collated through photos, drawings and voice memos, and were the foundations of the creation of each Play Map. In addition to consultations with children, the first author also drove around each area, walked around parks and public spaces, and used satellite maps to look for interesting places for play. Play prompts for each of the maps were chosen to encompass a wide range of types of play, and combined specific points of interest as well as play ideas that can be done anywhere. The prompts all begin with action verbs to promote and advocate for active play and involvement (e.g. 'Sing loud and free as you ride your bike', 'Make a magic wand from a stick and leaves', 'Dream of the snow as you sprinkle sand on your hand'). There are a total of 191 different play prompts across the 14 Play Maps. Picture 30.21 provides an example of the Play Map in Preston.

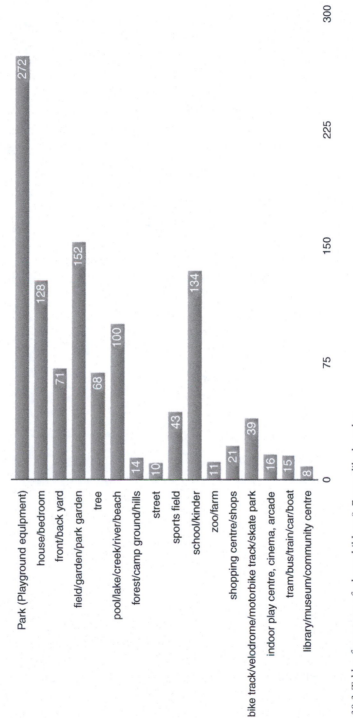

Figure 30.3 Table of responses of where children 0–7 years liked to play

Let's PLAY in Preston!

1. **SPIN** round and round on this clown swing.

2. **BALANCE** along low brick fences as you walk.

3. **CHAT** to a cat, talk to the birds, smile at a dog, the world is yours...

4. **MIX** a magic potion with petals and leaves and water.

5. **HANG** upside down and spin around.

6. **GRAB** a handful of sand and let it slip through your fingers like rain.

7. **BECOME** a superhero, a zombie, a teacher, a bee...

8. **ADD** blocks and rocks to build a tower.

9. **RELAX** in a bean bag with your favourite book.

10. **BEND** your body to make a bridge.

11. **GO** for a mark! Catch that ball.

12. **FLOP** on a cushion and bounce on the bed.

13. **PEEP** out at the view from this egg shaped cubby.

14. **FEEL** your senses open and sing at the fresh food market.

Thanks to: all the children, staff and families of the many Primary Schools, Kindergartens, Childcare Centres and playgroups in Darebin who participated in this project; joining in play sessions, drawing pictures of their favourite places to play and sharing their stories.

Picture 30.21 Preston Play Map

Using the Play Maps

The Play Maps were designed to support children and families to explore their local community. The visual design was intended to support children and families with diverse linguistic skills to be able to engage with the map to choose places and spaces to visit. The maps were also intended as an educational tool to promote awareness and understanding of the importance of play for children and within the primary school setting as a resource to incorporate the map into curriculum studies across subject areas: mathematics, geography, literacy, physical education, and social and emotional learning. The maps may be used as part of transition to preschool and school. The Play Maps also offer families ideas for no-cost activities across the municipality and are a way to welcome new families to the area, and familiarise families, communities and services with each other.

Conclusion

For the City of Darebin, the consultation process provided opportunities to understand how the provision of community places and spaces, such as playgrounds, sports ovals, bike paths and parks, was supporting young children's right to play. The consultation will further support Darebin to consider future planning and budgets to ensure infrastructure is reflective of children's needs, as well as accessible and safe. For example, many children talked about enjoying climbing trees, so councils may change their policy of lopping off low branches to make it easier for children to climb trees at parks. Or future designs might consider the inclusion of sensory play, such as water and natural loose parts, into playground provision. At the launch of the Play Maps, a key take-home message for the councillors who attended was that children value open space, natural materials, unstructured play spaces, trees and waterways.

Children's views align well with Darebin's priorities around providing more and better open space, biodiversity protection and responding to the climate emergency. It also aligns well with emerging practice at the council around community led design, including pilots in the master-planning of local parks and involving children in playspace design.

The consultation will influence future strategic planning such as Darebin's Open Space Strategy, the Climate Emergency Plan, public playground developments, and the development of children's and community centre playgrounds. For the City of Darebin, the enactment of provision rights for and with children is an everyday endeavour that sits alongside children's protection and participation rights. For Darebin, children's rights are an important driver for creating respectful and inclusive communities, where children are active and engaged citizens who have a strong sense of belonging.

References

Australian Bureau of Statistics. 2017. *Estimated resident population.* https://www.abs.gov.au/ausstats/abs@.nsf/cat/3101.0

Bento, Gabriela, and Gisela Dias. 2017. "The importance of outdoor play for young children's healthy development." *Porto biomedical journal* 2 (5): 157–160.

Canadian Public Health Association. 2019. Risk, hazard and play. Accessed February 20, 2019. www.cpha.ca/risk-hazard-and-play-what-are-risks-and-hazards.

City of Darebin. 2012 *Greenstreets streetscape strategy (2012–2020).* http://www.circlesoffood.org/2016/04/19/city-of-darebin-urban-agriculture-framework/

City of Darebin. 2016. *Child friendly city framework.* http://www.darebin.vic.gov.au/Your-Coun cil/How-council-works/Meeting-Agendas-and-Minutes/Council-Meetings? a=D10D6424D18D4F33B654A7F4AC36CB54#2016

Clements, Rhonda. 2004. "An investigation of the status of outdoor play." *Contemporary Issues in Early Childhood* 5 (1): 68–80.

Cole-Hamilton, Issy. 2011. *Getting it right for play. The power of play: An evidence base.* Midlothian: Play Scotland.

Danielzik, Sandra, Kristina Langnäse, Mareike Mast, Carina Spethmann, and Manfred J. Müller. 2002. "Impact of parental BMI on the manifestation of overweight 5–7 year old children." *European Journal of Nutrition* 41 (3): 132–138.

Darebin City Council. 2010. *Darebin playspace strategy 2010–2020.* http://objective.darebin.vic.gov.au/ Page/Page.aspx?Page_Id=10115

de Silva-Sanigorski, Andrea M., A. Colin Bell, Peter Kremer, Melanie Nichols, Maree Crellin, Michael Smith, Sharon Sharp et al. 2010. "Reducing obesity in early childhood: Results from Romp & Chomp, an Australian community-wide intervention program." *The American Journal of Clinical Nutrition* 91 (4): 831–840.

Fjørtoft, Ingunn. 2001. "The natural environment as a playground for children: The impact of outdoor play activities in pre-primary school children." *Early Childhood Education Journal* 29 (2): 111–117.

Gray, Peter. 2014. "Free to learn: Why unleashing the instinct to play will make our children happier, more self-reliant, and better students for life."

Hart, Roger. 2008. "Stepping back from 'The ladder': Reflections on a model of participatory work with children." In *Participation and learning*, 19–31. Springer: dordrecht.

Lenz Taguchi, Hillevi. 2014. "New materialisms and play." In *The SAGE handbook of play and learning in early childhood*, edited by Liz Brooker, Mindy Blaise and Susan Edwards, 79–90. London: SAGE.

Little, Helen. 2017. "Promoting risk-taking and physically challenging play in Australian early childhood settings in a changing regulatory environment." *Journal of Early Childhood Research* 15 (1): 83–98.

Little, Helen, and Shirley Wyver. 2008. "Outdoor play: Does avoiding the risks reduce the benefits?" *Australasian Journal of Early Childhood* 33 (2): 33–40.

MacNaughton, Glenda, and Kylie Smith. 2008. "Engaging ethically with young children: Principles and practices for consulting justly with care." In *Young children as active citizens*, edited by Glenda MacNaughton, Patrick Hughes and Kylie Smith, 31–43.London: Cambridge Scholars Publishing.

McFarland, Laura, and Shelby Gull Laird. 2018. "Parents' and early childhood educators' attitudes and practices in relation to children's outdoor risky play." *Early Childhood Education Journal* 46 (2): 159–168.

Richie, Jenny and Rau Cheryl. 2010. "Kia mau ki te wairuatanga: Countercolonial narratives of early childhood education in aotearoa." In *Childhoods a handbook*, edited by Gaile. S. Cannella and Lourdes Diaz Soto, 355–374. Peter Lang: New York.

UN Committee on the Rights of the Child (CRC). 2013. "General comment No. 17 on the right of the child to rest, leisure, play, recreational activities, cultural life and the arts (art. 31)." www.refworld. org/docid/51ef9bcc4.html.

UNICEF. 2014. "Convention on the rights of the child." www.unicef.org/crc/

United Nations. 1989. "Convention on the rights of the child, 1989." www.ohchr.org/en/professionalin terest/pages/crc.aspx.

Viruru, Radhika. 2001. "Colonized through language: The case of early childhood education." *Contem porary Issues in Early Childhood* 2 (1): 31–47.

Whitebread, David, Dave Neale, Hanne Jensen, Claire Liu, S. Lynneth Solis, Emily Hopkins, Kathy Hirsh-Pasek, and Jennifer Zosh. 2017. *The role of play in children's development: A review of the evidence.* Billund, Denmark: LEGO Fonden.

Woodhead, Martin. 2008. "Childhood studies: Past, present and future." In *An introduction to childhood studies*, edited by MJ Kehily, 17–34. Berkshire: Open University Press.

Yogman, Michael, Andrew Garner, Jeffrey Hutchinson, Kathy Hirsh-Pasek, Roberta Michnick Golinkoff, and Committee on Psychosocial Aspects of Child and Family Health. 2018. "The power of play: A pediatric role in enhancing development in young children." *Pediatrics* 142 (3): e20182058.

Zosh, Jennifer N., Emily J. Hopkins, Hanne Jensen, Claire Liu, Dave Neale, Kathy Hirsh-Pasek, S. Lynneth Solis, and David Whitebread. 2017. *Learning through play: A review of the evidence.* Billund, Denmark: LEGO Fonden.

PART 4

Young children's rights to participation

31

INTRODUCTION

Young children's participation rights

Beth Blue Swadener

Introduction and context

Research and program-planning related to early childhood have increasingly reflected children's participation rights, recognition of competency, and related ethical issues. Disciplines including childhood studies, early childhood education, sociology of childhood, and related "movements," including the European Early Childhood Education Research Association (EECERA) Young Children's Perspectives Special Interest Group and the international Reconceptualizing Early Childhood Education network (Bloch, Swadener & Cannella, 2018), have foregrounded children's views, voices, and embodied experiences, while at the same time complicating universals and reflecting collective as well as individual experiences and cultural contexts (e.g., Una, 2011). These approaches offer ethical frameworks in which children are understood to be active citizens in their world (MacNaugton & Smith, 2008). An array of research methodologies seek to involve children as co-researchers (Lundy & Swadener, 2015), including participatory action research (PAR), arts-based approaches, photo voice and digital storytelling, use of "walking interviews" (Somerville & Green, 2011) and approaches that reflect nature, culture, and "children's common worlding" (Haraway, 2008; Taylor, 2014; Taylor & Pacini-Ketchabaw, 2015) with more-than-human animate and inanimate others (Goebel, 2019).

As Sue Dockett and Bob Perry (Chapter 37) observe, "Respect for children's rights and competences has been a distinctive feature of much early childhood research in recent decades" (Clark & Moss, 2001; Einarsdóttir, 2014; Flewitt, 2005). This section features scholarship from 11 nations, focusing on participation rights, often combined with other rights and early childhood practices. Authors in this section discuss methods they have used to support and build capacity for children's participation in their research. They also discuss logistical and ethical challenges of consulting with children—from infants to lower primary ages.

Participation rights, as specified by the UNCRC (particularly Articles 12 and 13) have reinforced the assertion, first applied in the disability rights movement, "nothing about us without us" (Charlton, 1998). Lundy (2007) and others have clarified that adults are duty-bearers to assist children as rights-bearers develop the capacity to express their views and be consulted in issues affecting them. Article 12 focuses on children's right to express their views and recognizes children's right to be listened to regarding matters that affect them—and have their views be given "due weight." Article 13 states that children have the right to freedom of expression and to impart information and ideas through any means of their choosing, including orally, in writing, and in forms of art or other media. Further, the United Nations Committee's General Comment No. 7, Implementing Child Rights in Early Childhood (United Nations, 2005), addresses the rights of young children under the age of 8. A combination of these articles, General Comment No. 7, and Articles 3.3 and 36 have shaped participatory principles of research with young children.

Other articles that relate directly to children's participation rights include Article 14, which protects freedom of thought, conscience, and religion. This article affirms that children have the right to think and believe what they want and to practice their religion as long as they are not stopping other people from enjoying their rights. The Convention respects the rights and duties of parents in providing religious and moral guidance to their children, while supporting children's right to examine their beliefs. It also states that their right to express their beliefs implies respect for the rights and freedoms of others. Article 15 protects children's right of association. Children have the right to meet and to join groups and organizations. In exercising their rights, children have the responsibility to respect the rights, freedoms, and reputations of others.

Article 16 affirms that children have a right to privacy. The law should protect them from attacks against their way of life, their good name, their families, and their homes. The right to privacy has also come up in child advocacy and research ethics related to childcare settings, where supervision of the group is balanced with respecting children's need for privacy.

Finally, Article 17 focuses on children's access to information and mass media. Children have the right to get information that is important to their health and well-being. This article stipulates that governments should encourage mass media to provide information that children can understand and to not promote materials that could harm children. Mass media should particularly be encouraged to supply information in languages that minority and indigenous children can understand. Children should also have access to children's books.

Lundy and McEvoy (2012) argue that a rights-based ethical framework requires specific criteria in their research designs. These criteria include: (1) research aims informed by the UNCRC; (2) compliance with the UNCRC in the research process; (3) outcomes that build the capacity of children and duty-bearers; and (4) studies that further the realization of children's rights through the research. As Alison Moore reminds us in Chapter 36, Lundy (2007) also argued that "the meaning of individual provisions of the UNCRC can only be understood when they are read and interpreted in conjunction with the other rights protected in the Convention" (p. 932). In her germinal 2007 arguments that "voice is not enough," Lundy further proposed that the successful implementation of Article 12 requires researchers and others working with children to consider the implications of four separate factors:

- *Space*: Children must be given the opportunity to express a view.
- *Voice*: Children must be given the opportunity to express a view.
- *Audience*: The view must be listened to.
- *Influence*: The view must be acted upon, as appropriate.

In Chapter 36, Moore applies these guidelines as a framework for engagement and dialogue with adults, including mothers of young children and early childhood practitioners, and several chapters make reference to these guidelines in their work.

While much of the research and practical application of children's participation rights is found in work with children over age 8, including a myriad of youth involvement in participatory action, research (Bertrand, 2018), activism (Cohen-Blanchet, 2013), and use of social media, this volume and chapters in this section emphasize ways to better understand the views of much younger children, including infants and toddlers, and give them due weight. As stated earlier, participation rights of young children are emphasized in General Comment No. 7, which explicitly addresses children under the age of 8. The recognition of children as younger human beings (Cannella, 1997) and persons in their own right, and not merely "deferred citizens" (Cheney, 2007), has also shaped much of the rights-related scholarship in early childhood and childhood studies. Polakow, Soto, Swadener and others have argued that an existential versus instrumental (e.g., early investment, cost–benefit analysis, deferred citizenship) view of children that respects their being versus becoming is critical. Langsted (1994, p. 29) and later Clark and Moss (2001) have further argued that children are experts on their own lives.

While protection and provision rights are typically well understood and assumed to be universal human and children's rights, participation rights tend to be less well understood and more likely to be culturally contested (Swadener & Ndimande, 2014) and better understood in the context of the good of the community (Cheney, 2017). As Kristen Cheney (2017) observed in her research with children orphaned by HIV/AIDS in Uganda:

> adults must come to see children's rights as beneficial to the entire community rather than as a tool that can either be manipulated or implemented at the expense of adults. Given that childhood is such a naturalized concept, however, that change will likely require a significant shift in both local and global understandings of children as rights bearers.
>
> *(p. 51)*

Various transnational learning groups (e.g., Una, 2010, 2011) and collaborative networks (e.g., Children's Views and Voices) have similarly sought to confront cultural tensions between often Western, individual, and universal human rights discourse and assumptions, and indigenous and Global South perspectives and epistemologies that emphasize more culturally and community-focused assumptions about children, belonging, respect for elders, and learning in silence through observation versus through voice. As we consider the arguments made in the following chapters, these tensions are important to hold in play as dynamic ethical issues when seeking to understand young children's participation rights. These issues were also reflected in the African Charter on the Rights and Welfare of the Child (1990), which frames children's rights in a more communitarian worldview.

Participation rights for young children: issues and possibilities

In foregrounding voice, it is also important to ask questions regarding the language(s) used and implications for children who are not verbal and express their views in embodied ways (e.g., children with diverse abilities who may use sign language or other ways to express their views). Infants and toddlers also present challenges to build capacity in research designs, as discussed by Ioanna Palaiologou in Chapter 38.

We also recognize that, as in other areas of children's rights discussion in previous sections, the gap between rights and reality remains wide—and growing in all too many geopolitical regions. One of the places that children's rights have been grossly violated is in the United States, particularly as it concerns children in immigrant and asylum-seeking families who have been separated from parents, detained, and experience related trauma. Chapter 33 (Angeles Maldonado, Beth Blue Swadener, and Casey Khaleesi) examines the narratives of young children in immigrant families in the Southwest United States, framed in borderlands critical race theory (CRT).

As evident across many chapters in this handbook, other globalized issues in early childhood policy and practice intersect with work to enhance young children's rights. Themes related to globalized neoliberal early childhood education policy and curriculum regimes are analyzed in Chapter 32 and, by counter-example, in Chapters 34 and 35. In Chapter 32, Caralyn Blaisdell, John M. Davis, Vinnarasan Aruldoss, and Lynn McNair draw from research in India, Scotland, and the EU, analyzing examples of children's experience of pedagogies informed by universalist ideals. They argue that "regimes of standardisation and universalism, though claiming to improve the quality of early experiences, do not address the lived, culturally sensitive reality of rights for children, families and caregivers." Going beyond a critique of standardized practices, they advocate for children's rights to be at the fore in early learning contexts, with children understood as being capable and creative beings "who can provide solutions to their own everyday life issues."

Providing examples of children and global citizenship, Jodi Streelasky (Chapter 34) shares findings from a cross-cultural study in which Canadian and Tanzanian children learned about each other's experiences through voice and multimodal meaning-making. This work helped build capacity in children to share their perspectives on what mattered to them as they developed cross-cultural understandings that expanded their worldviews and valuing of diversity. Johanna Einarsdottir and Sara M. Ólafsdóttir (Chapter 35) sought to better understand preschool children's sense of belonging in Iceland, in the broader context of migration, accountability, and globalization, as they affected early childhood education. Using a relational versus individualistic approach to the politics of belonging, this study used a combination of observations, discussions of photos taken by children, and group interviews to identify themes that included friendship, participation, solidarity, and identity. Empathy and children's relationship with the environment were also analyzed.

Several authors (in Chapters 37, 38, 39, and 40) take up several nuanced ethical and methodological concerns regarding rights-based research with young children. In Chapter 37, Sue Dockett and Bob Perry engage the question, "What do children expect out of research participation?" They note that researchers using participatory approaches expect children to be active, competent, and interested in research participation, while little is known about young children's views and expectations about participating in research. Drawing from a project with children entering school, they analyze children's expectations about their participation and ways they convey their views. In Chapter 39, Sonya Gaches and Megan Gallagher reflect on the ethics of researching children through a discussion of their work with a children's research consultation group of lower primary students before pursuing further child-based research in early education settings. Using a consultative approach, as advocated by Lundy (Lundy, 2007; Lundy, McEvoy & Bronagh, 2011; Lundy & Swadener, 2015), they reflect on how children's input is shaping their research with younger children.

In Chapter 38, Ioanna Palaiologou reflects on how participation principles of rights-based research apply to work with children ages birth to 3, arguing that "otherness" or differentiation of infants in research is less about marginalization and more about opening a space for methodological and epistemological awareness and framing needed to develop and sustain ethical praxis in this research. Palaiologou argues that "instead of striving to balance the asymmetry in relationships between researchers and infants, rather we should acknowledge these imbalances and seek for relationships between researchers and infants that, although mostly non-reciprocal, can become an ethical imperative in the participatory ideology that has current credence."

In Chapter 40, Aline Cole-Albäck argues that an ethics framework deeply informed by the UNCRC offers a more comprehensive starting point to doing research with young children—and that viewing the CRC as primarily a legal document misses this opportunity. Using the UNCRC as a frame of reference in research may also challenge adult authority, emphasize the importance of relationships in early childhood research, and promote greater respect for children.

Petra Büker (Chapter 41) continues the discussion of ethics through the example of early childhood practitioners and how results of research projects involving children can be used as stimuli to affect the professionalization processes in kindergarten and primary teachers. Recommendations are made regarding how research settings should be designed so that they reflect children's participation rights while at the same time enhancing the professionalization of educators and teachers. Also emphasizing adult perspectives, Alison Moore (in Chapter 36) utilizes the Lundy model of child participation (Lundy, 2007) to explore practitioner and parent understanding of child voice in children's centres in the UK. The construct of an "open listening climate" is explored through parent narratives, providing understanding, personal perceptions, and a shared dialogue based upon UNCRC Article 12. Application of child participation models to primary caregivers and early educators, particularly in support of increasing children's voice and efficacy, is a powerful new area of research.

The participation section concludes with Chapter 42, in which Daniela S. Jadue-Roa and Matias Knust analyze children's right to play during their transition experiences from early childhood settings to primary school in Chile. Young children's greatest concern about moving to the first grade was the lack of opportunities to play, particularly outdoors. They argue that early childhood and primary teachers should understand this expressed need and find ways to accommodate it. This chapter highlights the intersectional nature of children's rights, given the focus on compliance with young children's UNCRC rights to play and education, as well as their right to be heard and their views given due weight.

References

African Charter on the Rights and Welfare of the Child. 1990. Geneva: UNICEF. www.unicef.org/esaro/African_Charter_articles_in_full.pdf

Bertrand, Melanie. 2018. Youth participatory action research and possibilities for students of color in educational leadership. *Educational Administration Quarterly,* 54(1): 1–30.

Bloch, Marianne N., Beth Blue Swadener, and Gaile S. Cannella. 2018. *Reconceptualizing Early Childhood Care and Education: Critical Question, New Imaginaries and Social Activism – a Reader* (2nd Ed). New York: Peter Lang.

Cannella, Gaile S. 1997. *Deconstructing Early Childhood Education: Social Justice and Revolution.* New York: Peter Lang.

Charlton, James. 1998. *Nothing About Us Without Us.* Oakland, CA: University of California Press.

Cheney, Kristen E. 2007. *Pillars of the Nation: Child Citizens and Ugandan National Development.* Chicago: University of Chicago Press.

Cheney, Kristen E. 2017. *Crying for our Elders: African Orphanhood in the Age of HIV and AIDS.* Chicago: University of Chicago Press.

Clark, Alison & Peter Moss. 2001. *Listening to Young Children: The Mosaic Approach*. London: National Children's Bureau and Joseph Rowntree Foundation.

Cohen-Blanchet, Natasha. 2013. The protaganism of under-18 youth in the quebec student movement: The right to political participation and education. In Beth Blue Swadener, Laura Lundy, Janette Habashi & Natasha Blanchet-Cohen (Eds.), *Children's Rights and Education: International Perspectives*, 63–81. New York: Peter Lang.

Einarsdóttir, Johanna. 2014. Children's perspectives on the role of preschool teachers. *European Journal of Early Childhood Education*, 23(4): 679–697. doi: 10.1080/1350293X.2014.969087

Flewitt, Rosie. 2005. Conducting research with young children: Some ethical considerations. *Early Child Development and Care*, 175, 553–565.

Goebel, Janna. 2019. *What Matter(s) in Education beyond the Human? Tempe*. Arizona: Arizona State University, unpublished essay.

Haraway, Donna J. 2008. *When Species Meet*. Minneapolis: Univeristy of Minnesota Press.

Langsted, Ole. 1994. Looking at quality from the child's perspective. In Peter Moss and Alan Pence (Eds.), *Valuing Quality in Early Childhood Services: New Approaches to Defining Quality*, 28–42. London: Paul Chapman.

Lundy, Laura, & Beth Blue Swadener. 2015. Engaging with young children as co-researchers: A child rights-based approach. In Olivia Saracho (Ed.), *Handbook of Research Methods in Early Childhood Education, Volume II* (pp. 657–676). Charlotte, NC: Information Age Publishing.

Lundy, Laura. 2007. Voice is not enough: Conceptualising Article 12 of the United Nations convention on the rights of the child. *British Education Research Journal*, 33(6), 927–942.

Lundy, Laura, & Lesley McEvoy. 2012. Childhood, the United Nations convention on the rights of the child, and research: What constitutes a 'rights-based' approach? In Michael Freeman (Ed.), *Law and Childhood Studies: Current Legal Issues* (Vol. 14, pp. 75–91, 17). Oxford, UK: Oxford University Press.

Lundy, Laura & Lesley McEvoy, and Bronagh Byrne. 2011. Working with young children as co-researchers: An approach informed by the United Nations convention on the rights of the child. *Early Education and Development*, 22(5), 714–736.

Naugton, Glenda Mac, & Kylie Smith. 2008. Engaging ethically with young children: Principles and practices for consulting justly with care. In Glenda Mac Naughton, Patrick Hughes and Kylie Smith (Eds.), *Young Children as Active Citizens: Principles, Policies and Pedagogies*, 14–35. Newcastle, UK: Cambridge Scholars Publishing.

Somerville, Margaret & Monica Green. 2011. A Pedagogy of "organized chaos": Ecological learning in primary schools. *Children, Youth & Environments*, 21(1), 14–35.

Soto, L.D. 2002. "Young bilingual children's perception of bilingualism and biliteracy: Altruistic possibilities." *Bilingual Research Journal*, 26(3), 599–610.

Swadener, Beth Blue, & Bekisizwe Ndimande. 2014. Community perceptions on children's rights in South Africa. In N. Denzin & M. Giardina (Eds.), *Qualitative Inquiry Outside the Academy* (pp. 128–145). Walnut Creek, CA: Left Coast Press.

Taylor, Affrica. 2014. Situated and entangled childhoods: Imagining and materializing children's common world relations. In M. N. Bloch, B. B. Swadener & G. S. Cannella (Eds.), *Reconceptualizing Early Childhood Care and Education: A Reader* (pp. 121–130). New York, NY: Peter Lang.

Taylor, Affrica & Veronica Pacini-Ketchabaw. 2015. Learning with children, ants, and worms in the Anthropocene: Towards a common world pedagogy of multispecies vulnerability. *Pedagogy, Culture & Society*, 23(4), 507–529.

Una Children's Rights Learning Group. 2010. *Children's Rights in Una and Beyond: Transnational Perspectives. Una Working Paper 7*. Belfast, Northern Ireland: Una (Queens College).

Una Children's Rights Learning Group. 2011. *Children's Rights in Cultural Contexts. Working Paper 8*. Belfast, Northern Ireland: Una (Queens College).

United Nations. 1989. *United Nations Convention on the Rights of the Child*. Geneva: United Nations.

United Nations. 2005. General comments No. 5. & No. 7. www.unicef-irc.org/publications/pdf/crcgen commen.pdf

32

TOWARDS A MORE PARTICIPATORY FULFILMENT OF YOUNG CHILDREN'S RIGHTS IN EARLY LEARNING SETTINGS

Unpacking universalist ideals in India, Scotland and the EU

Caralyn Blaisdell, John M. Davis, Vinnarasan Aruldoss and Lynn McNair

Introduction

A universal path to the fulfilment of rights in early childhood?

The Jomtien Declaration by the World Conference on Education for All (EFA), held at Jomtien, Thailand in 1990, stated that 'learning begins at birth'. This declaration provided an impetus to advocacy for early childhood care and education (ECCE) programmes around the globe that emphasised both care and education (UNESCO, 1990). Advocates argued that the early years are crucial in human life and that investment in early years reaps benefits both at the individual level and the societal level (Arnold, 2004; Evans, 1996). In a normative sense, early years provision is construed as 'the greatest of equalizers' (Bokova, 2010): a powerful mechanism to address various complex and persistent issues such as poverty, malnutrition, morbidity, mortality and inequality.

This view appears to dovetail nicely with a children's rights approach. The UN Convention on the Rights of the Child (1989) enshrines the right to education (Article 28), with the direction of education (Article 29) accentuating the development of the child to their fullest potential (para. 1a). Running through the Convention are its four general principles, which include the right to life, survival and development (Article 6) and protection from discrimination (Article 2). If early learning is framed as a social intervention, from which disadvantaged children benefit the most (e.g. Elango et al., 2015), investment into ECCE contributes significantly to the fulfilment of educational rights. However, as decades of research on children's rights has demonstrated, the translation of international legal standards into lived reality is a complex endeavour (Hanson and Nieuwenhuys, 2012). Claiming that the rights to education, development and non-discrimination have been fulfilled does not tell us much about *how* they have (supposedly) been fulfilled.

This chapter focuses on how global tensions around standardisation, testing, universalism and children's rights are experienced by young children in India and Scotland. Rather than create a false dichotomy between pedagogy in India and Scotland, we analyse the ways that both systems experience the impact of universalist ideas and ask how such ideas impinge on professional thinking concerning pedagogy and practice.

Literature review: universalist ideals in India and Scotland

Moss (2015) argues that because the early years discourse is mainly constructed around economic terms such as 'social investment' and 'human capital' (e.g. Heckman, 2017), there is therefore a need to use technological jargon such as 'evidence-based' and 'high returns' and explain things in a predefined and predetermined manner. The early childhood field seems particularly vulnerable to technical discourses (Dahlberg et al., 2013; MacNaughton, 2003) in which standardisation is thought to ensure 'universal' best practice.

In theory, identifying best practice would lead to better implementation of young children's rights. However, Urban and Swadener (2016) argue that 'comparative studies across complex international and cultural contexts inevitably lose sight of the messy, complex, unique – and therefore crucially important – aspects of educational practices' (p. 5). While public discussions and beliefs about early childhood are multi-stranded and complex (Dahlberg et al., 2013), there is one strand that has come to dominate public discussion: the idea of early childhood experiences as the 'path to the whole person' (Alderson, 2008, p. 114). The complexity of human development is often muted in early childhood policy, in favour of a more simplistic understanding that is easier to digest, as it promises 'simple roadmaps to certain destinations' (MacNaughton, 2004, p. 100). In global policy discourses on early childhood education, attention to young children's rights – particularly their participation rights – has perhaps taken a back seat to the promotion of their development.

Turning to the cases of India and Scotland specifically, both countries have complex developing systems of ECCE in which international trends interact with local practices and histories. Early years provision in India has been strongly influenced by universalist developmental ideals. For example, early years normative discourses in India have become dominated by terms such as 'developmentally appropriate practices' (DAP), 'age-appropriate practices', 'culturally appropriate practices' and 'child-centred education' (Aruldoss, 2011, 2013).

One of the most striking criticisms of approaches to early learning in India came from ethnographic research that argued that dominant minority world childhood discourses were parachuted into Indian early years provision in a manner that specifically set out to reject indigenous knowledge (Viruru, 2001, 2005). In India, the political and ideological influence of British colonial rule strongly convinced the population, particularly the middle class, that science-based education is essential for human progress and prosperity (Nandy, 1988; for a similar critique on civilisational narrative, see Balagopalan, 2014). Thus, there is little surprise that the indigenous educational philosophies found little mention in early years educational discourses. Moreover, the pedagogy of cultural relativism and multiple perspectives was not favoured at all due to fear that a complex pedagogy might sit uncomfortably in a country where there are many languages and subcultures (see Raina, 2011).

In Scotland, there are similar trends around complexity reduction and cultural multiplicity. For example, the influential Siraj and Kingston (2015) review of early years in Scotland urged a greater focus on quality, going on to define 'quality' based on the usual standardised rating scales. Similarly, in seeking to create universal solutions, reviews of early learning provision in Scotland (Commission for Childcare Reform, 2015; Siraj and Kingston, 2015) have tended to treat families as if they are one type. They make little mention of the experiences of ethnic minority or LGBT parents who, for example, may experience discrimination in early learning centres by rarely being invited to take part in social events, seldom being asked to carry out leadership tasks (e.g. during outings), or never being requested to take management roles on parent committees (Davis, 2011; Davis and Hancock, 2007).

What we see, looking at these two contexts, is a complex interweaving of global, regional and local trends, with both acceptance and resistance to universality as 'best practice' in early childhood. In the following sections, we draw on a variety of studies carried out by the authors in order to analyse how universalist ideals affect children's lived experience of their participation rights.

Children's participation rights in early learning settings: are these the rights we are looking for?

Baseline testing in Scotland: classification, alienation, institutionalisation

Children in Scotland go to school between 4.5 and 5.5 years old – one of the earliest starts to compulsory schooling globally. Early in the transition to primary school, McNair (2016) found that children were required to undergo 'baseline testing' in literacy and numeracy. The results were used to classify children into ability groupings, reinforcing stereotypes, power differences and negatively impacting on how children regarded themselves (Donaldson, 1978; Entwistle, 1995). Both children and parents were also found to rank children, whether consciously or subconsciously, into social hierarchical groupings.

Some parents viewed the classification of their child as a sign of success:

> A nice wee positive sign is that he has gone into the top reading group … but aye it is nice to hear … not that we are competitive or anything … but he is slightly better at reading than other children.
>
> *(parent interview, August 2013, Westfield School)*

Yet others noted the perverse nature of this approach when connected to the idea that children who did not do homework would not gain reward, and the ultimate punishment would be a placement in a lower group.

> It is funny, because the teacher actually commented to me the other day about reading groups and who would be in the groups because they [the children] would practise at home and if they don't practise at home they are not doing so great … and I said 'Really?' And that is probably true.
>
> *(parent interview, August 2013, Westfield School)*

Hence, classification occurred at multiple levels. First, children were classified by perceived academic ability and differentiated as pupils who have 'done well' if they achieve the desired results in their tests. Second, parents who support the homework procedure are classified as good parents and as supportive or unsupportive depending on whether they participated or not in homework tasks. Parents who resist these assumptions about homework, ability and testing can find themselves alienated members of the school community in settings where 'blame cultures' prevail over contemporary concepts of creative, enabling and participatory pedagogy (McNair, 2016).

The baseline tests utilised by schools in McNair's study were only one in a sequence of standardised tests that children experienced in their first year of primary school, as explained by one head teacher:

> YARC (York Assessment in Reading and Comprehension) is mandatory. All pupils are presented for this in May of Primary One. PIM (Progress in Maths 5) is mandatory. All pupils are presented for this in May of Primary One. All Primary One and Primary Two pupils in [Name of] council follow the 'Literacy Rich Programme' – each unit concludes with a check-up assessment. I would think that all schools use these – although these are not mandatory. Some schools may buy in additional assessments – GL tests (formerly NFER/Nelson) are popular. However, I would consider that most head teachers feel that the above is enough assessment.
>
> *(head teacher interview, January 2013, Westfield School)*

McNair (2016) concluded, in keeping with other studies, that baseline testing in the early weeks of primary school meets the needs of the educative system, and not necessarily the children (Jeffrey and Woods, 2003). The testing regime served as part of a wider school culture where children's voice, agency and contributions (e.g. Moosa-Mitha, 2005) were not widely valued, and at times were actively denied.

Despite this lack of value placed on children's participation rights, the children in this study also had a remarkable capacity to respond to the authoritative discourse, even when they may not appear to have a voice (White, 2016), as the following example illustrates. Here, the researcher was asked by the teacher to assist with an art project in which children were instructed to assemble a spider with exactly eight legs:

> I began my task. The children came over one by one and put their spider together according to the instructions they were given. Hazel arrived, began her task, looked up at me and smiled and said, 'I am going to add ten legs'. And she meticulously did. In me Hazel knew she had found a benevolent ally, one who would honour her gestures and not disclose her open defiance. I thought her brave.
>
> *(field notes, October 2012, Westfield School)*

Here, one glimpses the subordinated Hazel going up against the perceived power-holder (in the teacher), refusing to abide by the rules. This, according to Moore (2013), counts as resistance. The stakes were high; Hazel asserted herself, despite the potential for ridicule, used at various times by the teacher when a child displayed any purposeful subordination.

In contrast with Hazel's example, many children in McNair's (2016) study did not appear to question the status of the teacher, nor why rules were being imposed. There appeared to be little room in the school system for adults to appreciate that children learn in different ways, or for approaches to pedagogy that value diversity between children (e.g. see Dockett and Perry, 2005; Sanagavarapu and Perry, 2005). McNair (2016) found that participation rights, which at their core are supposed to demonstrate respect for the child's diverse perspectives, were paid lip service to but not meaningfully enacted (for an explanation of issues with participation in Scottish educational settings, see also Brown et al., 2017). It is important to note, however, that while these practices of classification and regulation are linked to global ideals of standardised testing, they are not completely an outside imposition.

They also involve historical links to Scottish Calvinist notions of acceptable behaviour, values unsympathetic to individual 'failure' and productive of a non-child-centred education system (Elsley, 2017).

A clash of ideals? Montessori, moral values and disciplining bodies in Tamil Nadu, India

Aruldoss (2013) carried out his research in three early learning settings: a corporation nursery, a private nursery and an ICDS (Integrated Child Development Services) Anganwadi centre in Chennai in Tamil Nadu, India. In the corporation nursery, which had collaboration with an NGO, teachers followed a combination of formal and Montessori approaches. Although the Montessori curriculum was child-centred, and it valued individuals as unique human beings, at times these ideals seemed to be incompatible with practice, especially when it came to disciplining bodies. Teachers used a variety of techniques to regulate the bodies of children: how to sit, how to walk, how to eat, and how to talk were taught and reiterated during the activities.

As the children in this preschool mainly came from underprivileged communities, the Montessori teacher connected discipline with cultural and ethical responsibility: 'it is our moral responsibility to teach children good behaviours'. Thus, extra emphasis was given to teaching children how to present their bodies in a culturally appropriate manner. Aruldoss (2013) found that the curriculum and pedagogy was very structured and individualised, and there was a high degree of personalised teaching of values on cleanliness and personal hygiene incorporated with the official curriculum. For example:

> The teacher talked about the importance of cleanliness and personal hygiene after Morning Prayer. She advised children to brush their teeth and take a bath every day in the morning before they come to school.
>
> *(field notes, third visit)*

Here, the clash between the ideals of Montessori philosophy and discipline in everyday classroom practice was overt. Although the Montessori curriculum does put an emphasis on 'care of the person' and 'control of the movement' within the classroom (Isaacs, 2010; Montessori, 1912), advising children about cleanliness and personal hygiene was something beyond the scope of the curriculum. Significantly, the moral values and body conditioning that were imparted in the nursery were not only through group instruction; sometimes they were enforced at an individual level:

> The teacher saw a girl squeezing her food with her hand. Considering that an uncultured way of eating, the teacher said to the girl, 'This is not the way you are supposed to eat. Don't squeeze the food too much. Take the food gently with your fingers and eat'.
>
> *(field notes, seventh visit)*

> The teacher noted that Ajith has got long hair and it repeatedly fell down on his face while he was doing the activity. Ajith just kept on adjusting his hair. Seeing this the teacher said, 'Ajith go and tell your father to cut your hair. The hair is falling on your face'.
>
> *(field notes, tenth visit)*

This indicates that the control and regulation of individual bodies in the classroom were imposed on matters beyond the prescribed curriculum. Similar to McNair's (2016) findings, control was extended to the child's parents in an insidious way – in these examples, through the implication that parents were not upholding correct manners and grooming. In the examples above, one can see the resemblance of the monitorial school system where the purpose of schooling was to change the habits of children who were affected by crime or pauperism, by placing them under constant moral regulation through regular supervision and engaging them continuously in activity (Walkerdine, 1998). This type of body civilisation happens in the institution perhaps based on the belief that these young poor children should learn to attune their behaviour in concurrence with the dominant values and culture (Vinovskis, 1996). Thus, the physical body of the child was put under pressure to function according to the expectations of the teacher's imagination of an ideal social body. Much like the Scottish example, children's participation rights – the valuing of their diverse perspectives, richness and capabilities – were pushed to the sidelines, if recognised at all.

When questioned about these practices, the teacher asserted, 'That seems one of the major criticisms in this approach, but I think a certain amount of physical discipline is required for mental discipline'. In the teacher's explanation, there are parallels with Hindu philosophy, which says that mind and body are intrinsically connected to each other and 'discipline is not simply manifest as an objectification of the body but equally as a subjectification of the self' (Alter, 1992, pp. 92–93). It is assumed that the restriction of bodily movements, bodily desires and senses of the body will automatically result in disciplining the functioning of the mental system.

Contrary to teachers' beliefs that child-centred education matches children's choices and interests (and therefore, implicitly, their participation rights), children were sometimes overtly or covertly forced to do activities against their wishes. As a result, children used different forms of resistance to overcome the control exercised in the classroom. For example, one common tactic was to just pretend that they were doing the activity:

> Thyagu was assembling the broken eagle pieces (puzzle). After 5 minutes, he looked disinterested and just looking around what other children were doing. When I asked why he didn't do the activity, he replied it was boring. But whenever the teacher looked at his side he acted as if he was doing something.
>
> *(field notes, seventh visit)*

On other occasions, children simply kept materials in front of them but did not do anything until they received a warning from the teacher; sometimes children used the materials with a completely different purpose. Repetition was also used as a form of resistance in the classroom. Children tended to do the same activity or repeat the same behaviour/action in a way to show their resistance to the power structure. As these examples illustrate, despite child-centred rhetoric, children's right to have their views taken seriously was pushed to the margins, manifesting in the form of creative resistance.

Participatory alternatives: reflexive practice, resistance, flexibility

In the final findings section of this chapter, we look at participatory alternatives, highlighting resistance, reflexivity about power politics, and flexibility as a path toward more participatory fulfilment of young children's rights. For example, Blaisdell (2016) conducted ethnographic fieldwork at Castle Nursery in Scotland, a setting with a strong rights-based and participatory ethos. She found that reflexive practice by practitioners was an essential element of creating a culture of children's participation. Practitioners openly questioned their 'attitudes, thought processes, values, assumptions, prejudices and habitual actions' about their work with young children (e.g. Bolton 2014, p. 3). Dialogue was the mainstay of daily life at the nursery.

Practitioners were also willing to take risks in order to maintain the participatory ethos of the nursery. For example, during the research, the local authority area where Castle Nursery was located introduced new standardised assessments of children's development, to be carried out in nurseries during the school year and then used as transition reports when children went to primary school. The suggested change provoked disgust from practitioners, who described them as 'reductionist', saying that they diminished children's complex identities down to a simplistic list of judgements about their academic abilities, or perceived lack thereof. It would be difficult to incorporate either parents' or children's voices in meaningful ways.

After deliberation, the head of the centre and the nursery teacher informed the local authority that they would not be using the new forms. Instead, the nursery used more open-ended, flexible documents that included the children's own views on their learning and going to school. In this example, fostering space for children's participation rights took precedence over practitioners having an 'easy life' in terms of their relationship with the local authority.

There were similar findings about reflexivity from the FIESTA project (Facilitating Inclusive Education and Supporting the Transition Agenda), which employed mixed-methods – including qualitative interviews with disabled children themselves – to better understand disabled children's transitions related to early learning, schooling, integrated working and inclusion in eight EU countries (Davis et al., 2012, 2014a; Ravenscroft et al., 2017, 2018). Much like Blaisdell's (2016) research at Castle Nursery, the FIESTA team learned that reflexive practice, resistance and flexibility were key for facilitating children's meaningful participation during times of transition. For example, previous research has suggested that the views of disabled pupils are often overlooked in processes of transition (O'Donnell, 2003). Disabled children confirmed this during the FIESTA project, in one case calling on staff to take children's views seriously regarding access issues:

> Well, I also quite often went to my care coordinator about that door, so many times that I am fed up with it, because that door is driving me insane. He keeps saying that he did something about it, but nothing changes so then at some point I was just like; forget it.
>
> *(pupil, the Netherlands)*

This example demonstrates the complex nature of participation and resistance. Here, resistance is both an act of confronting the disablist design features of the door, outwardly bringing it to the attention of professionals, but also subsequently, when there is no change, inward, embodied frustration (e.g. when the door issue is not addressed).

As the above example illustrates, the FIESTA project found that parents, professionals and pupils often held different views of inclusion, participation and integrated working. Professional separation between child development, medical and social model thinking could lead 'professional experts' to disregard children's participation rights, excluding children from the decision-making and planning process:

> A 12 year old is not fully capable of making a well-considered decision ... But I do think that the parents are more capable of making the decision of what is better for the child. A 12 year old does not yet have the overall picture of what is better in the long term.
>
> *(health professional)*

The FIESTA project strongly indicated that parent- and child-led participatory/collaborative approaches to planning, evaluation and change made a substantive and qualitative difference to the way that pupils experienced schooling, yet it also found that only 38.4 per cent of professionals said that children were involved in defining the aims and outcomes of the transition process.

The FIESTA project also found that the most inclusive settings enabled children to lead the process of transition, define outcomes, and provide solutions to their everyday life issues. Inclusion flourished where professionals were able to engage with non-linear, politically nuanced and intersectional approaches to children's services that included practices of minimum intervention, participation, anti-discriminatory working, resource redistribution and self-empowerment (Ball and Sones, 2004; Broadhead et al., 2008; Davis, 2011; Dolan et al., 2006; Hill, 2012; Moore et al., 2005). The project also found that for inclusive practice to flourish, professionals need to be clear about the concepts, structures and relationships of their workplaces (reflexive practice). The project recommended that professionals engage in training with children and parents that is scenario-based, so that they learn to operationalise and work through the complexities of transition and inclusion, including how to locally enable practices of participation, dialogue and flexible pedagogy that are tailored to each family's aspirations.

Conclusion

Rights and early learning as a contested space: the messiness of participatory practice

In this chapter, we have argued that children's right to early education is not a neutral endeavour. Instead, participation rights are lived by children in relational contexts of power, bodily and moral discipline, resistance, and reflexivity. Regimes of standardisation and universalism, though claiming to improve the quality of early experiences, do not address the lived, culturally sensitive reality of rights for children, families and caregivers. In fact, children's participation rights may particularly suffer when standardised solutions are imposed.

Children often give well-reasoned, rational and logical explanations for why they wish to challenge adult orthodoxies and children are able to proactively make decisions about their transition preferences (Davis et al., 2014a). However, as our research illustrates, in Scotland (McNair, 2016), India (Aruldoss, 2013) and several EU countries (Davis et al., 2014a, 2014b), policymakers and apparent 'experts' in positions of power/authority made life-changing decisions to suit their system, not the child's diverse requirements. Far from leading to high-quality outcomes, universalist approaches to learning can contribute to processes of discrimination, act as a barrier to participatory rights fulfilment and negatively impact on children's sense of self.

As recent work in the field of childhood and children's rights studies suggests, rights are fulfilled (or not) in the context of complex relational entanglements; there can be no children's rights in isolation (e.g. Esser et al., 2016; Reynaert et al., 2015). As this chapter has demonstrated, it is not useful to put local practices on a pedestal, as if they were at one time pure and rights-based for children and now have been corrupted by global trends. Instead, the chapter has analysed the complex ways that standardisation, testing and universalist ideals interact with existing histories and cultural beliefs. We hope that by making these tensions and successes visible, others will find inspiration on a journey toward a more participatory fulfilment of children's rights in early learning spaces that perceives children to be leaders of their own learning and creative beings who can provide the solutions to their own everyday life issues.

References

Alderson, Priscilla. 2008. *Young Children's Rights: Exploring Beliefs, Principles and Practice*, 2nd ed. London: Jessica Kingsley Publishers.

Alter, Joseph. 1992. *The Wrestler's Body: Identity and Ideology in North India*. Berkeley: University of California Press.

Arnold, Caroline. 2004. "Positioning ECCD in the 21st century". *Co-ordinators Notebook*, No. 28, The Consultative Group on ECCD.

Aruldoss, Vinnarasan. 2011. "Construction of Early Childhood and ECCD Service Provisioning in India". In *Reinventing Public Management & Development in Emerging Economies*, 298–319, edited by P. Sigamani, N.U. Khan. New Delhi: Macmillan. ISBN 9780230332737.

Aruldoss, Vinnarasan. 2013. *Complexity, Complicity and Fluidity: Early Years Provision in Tamil Nadu (India)*. PhD Thesis, University of Edinburgh, Edinburgh.

Balagopalan, Sarada. 2014. *Inhabiting 'Childhood': Children, Labour and Schooling in Postcolonial India*. Basingstoke: Palgrave Macmillan.

Ball, Jessica and Rose Sones. 2004. "First Nations Early Childhood Care and Development Programs as Hubs for Intersectoral Service Delivery". Paper Presented at The Second International Conference on Local and Regional Health Programmes. Quebec City, October 10.

Blaisdell, Caralyn. 2016. *Young Children's Participation as a Living Right: An Ethnographic Study of an Early Learning and Childcare Setting*. PhD Thesis, University of Edinburgh, Edinburgh.

Bokova, Irina. 2010. "The ECCE global challenge: Setting the stage". Presented at the World Conference on Early Childhood Care and Education. Moscow, 27 September.

Bolton, Gillie. 2014. *Reflective Practice: Writing and Professional Development*, 4th ed. Los Angeles: SAGE.

Broadhead, Pat, Chrissy Meleady and Marco A. Delgado. 2008. *Children, Families and Communities: Creating and Sustaining Integrated Services*. Maidenhead: Open University Press.

Brown, Jane, Linda Croxford and Sarah Minty. 2017. "Pupils as citizens: Participation, responsibility and voice in the transition from primary to secondary school". CREID Briefing 34: www.docs.hss.ed.ac.uk/education/creid/Briefings/Briefing34.pdf

Commission for Childcare Reform. 2015. *Commission for Childcare Reform: Final Report*. www.commissionforchildcarereform.info/.

Dahlberg, Gunilla, Peter Moss and Alan Pence. 2013. *Beyond Quality in Early Childhood Education and Care: Languages of Evaluation*, 3rd ed. Abingdon, Oxon: Routledge.

Davis, John M. 2011. *Integrated Children's Services*. London: Sage.

Davis, John M. and A. Hancock. 2007. *Early Years Services for Black and Ethnic Minority Families: A Strategy for the Children and Families Department*. Edinburgh: University of Edinburgh/City of Edinburgh Council.

Davis, John M., John Ravenscroft and Nik Bizas. 2014a. "FIESTA—Best practice report: Report from the facilitating inclusive education and supporting the transition agenda project". Funded by the Education, Audiovisual and Culture Executive Agency (EACEA) of the European Commission Project Number 517748-LLP-1-2011-IE-COMENIUS-CNW.

Davis, John M., John Ravenscroft and Nik Bizas. 2014b. "Transition, inclusion and partnership: Child, parent and professionals led approaches in a European research project". *Child Care in Practice* 21 no. 1: 3–49. doi:10.1080/13575279.2014.976543

Davis, John M., John Ravenscroft, Lynn McNair and Abby Noble. 2012. "FIESTA: A framework for European collaborative working, inclusive education and transition: analysing concepts, structures and relationships". Report from the Facilitating Inclusive Education and Supporting the Transition Agenda Project Funded by The Education, Audiovisual and Culture Executive Agency (EACEA) of the European Commission. Project Number 517748-LLP-1-2011-IE-COMENIUS-CNW.

Dockett, Sue and Bob Perry. 2005. "Starting School in Australia is 'a bit safer, a lot easier and more relaxing.' Issues for parents from culturally and linguistically diverse backgrounds". *Early Years* 25 no. 3: 271–281.

Dolan, Pat, John Canavan and John Pinkerton (eds). 2006. *Family Support as Reflective Practice*. London: Jessica Kingsley.

Donaldson, Margaret. 1978. *Children's Minds*. London: Fontana.

Elango, Sneha, Jorge Luis Garcia, James J. Heckman and Andres Hojman. 2015. Early Childhood Education. Chicago: Center for the Economics of Human Development at the University of Chicago. https://cehd.uchicago.edu/ECE-US

Elsley, Susan. 2017. *Review of Societal Attitudes of Children for the Scottish Child Abuse Inquiry*. Edinburgh: Scottish Parliament.

Entwistle, Doris R. 1995. "The role of schools in sustaining early childhood program benefits". *Future of Children* 5 no. 3: 133–144.

Esser, Florian, Mieke S. Baader, Tanja Betz and Beatrice Hungerland (eds). 2016. *Reconceptualising Agency and Childhood: New Perspectives in Childhood Studies*. London: Routledge.

Evans, Judith L. 1996. "Quality in programming: Everyone's concern". *Co-ordinators Notebook* No. 18. Washington, DC: World Bank. Available at: https://pdfs.semanticscholar.org/2e39/91492db14b0214515894fdce6bfcc67144d9.pdf

Hanson, Karl and Olga Nieuwenhuys (eds). 2012. *Reconceptualizing Children's Rights in International Development: Living Rights, Social Justice, Translations*. Cambridge: Cambridge University Press.

Heckman, James J. 2017. "The Heckman Equation". The Heckman Equation. https://heckmanequation.org/the-heckman-equation/.

Hill, Malcolm. 2012. "Interpersonal and interagency working: The rough with the smooth". In *Children's Services: Working Together*, edited by Malcolm Hill, Sir George Head, Andrew Lockyer, Barbara Reid and Raymond Taylor, 62–74. Harlow, UK: Pearson Education.

Isaacs, Barbara. 2010. *Bringing the Montessori Approach to Your Early Years Practice*, 2nd ed. Abingdon: Routledge.

Jeffrey, Bob and Peter Woods. 2003. *The Creative School: A Framework for Success, Quality and Effectiveness*. London: Routledge Falmer.

MacNaughton, Glenda. 2003. *Shaping Early Childhood: Learners, Curriculum and Contexts*. Maidenhead: Open University Press.

MacNaughton, Glenda. 2004. "The politics of logic in early childhood research: A case of the brain, hard facts, trees and rhizomes". *The Australian Educational Researcher* 31 no. 3: 87–104.

McNair, Lynn J. 2016. "Rules, rules, rules and we're not allowed to skip". PhD Thesis, University of Edinburgh, Edinburgh.

Montessori, Maria. 1912. *The Montessori Method: Scientific Pedagogy as Applied to Child Education in "The Children's Houses"*, with Additions and Revisions by the Author, Translated from the Italian by A. E. George. London: William Heinemann.

Moore, A. 2013. "Love and fear in the classroom: How 'validating affect' might help us understand young students and improve their experiences of school life and learning". In *The Uses of Psychoanalysis in Working with Children's Emotional Lives*, edited by Michael O'Loughlin, 285–304. Maryland: Rowan and Littlefield.

Moore, Shannon, Wende Tulk and Richard Mitchell. 2005. "Qallunaat crossing: The southern-northern divide and promising practices for Canada's inuit young people". *The First Peoples Child & Family Review* 2 no. 1: 117–129.

Moosa-Mitha, Mehmoona. 2005. "A difference-centred alternative to theorization of children's citizenship rights". *Citizenship Studies* 9 no. 4: 369–388.

Moss, Peter. 2015. "There are alternatives: Contestation and hope in early childhood education". *Global Studies of Childhood* 5 no. 3: 226–238.

Nandy, Ashis. 1988. "Introduction: Science as a reason of state". In *Science, Hegemony and Violence: A Requiem for Modernity*, edited by Ashis Nandy, 1–23. Tokyo: The United Nations University.

O'Donnell, Margaret. 2003. "Transfer from special schools to mainstream: The voice of the pupil". In *Encouraging voices: Respecting the insights of young people who have been marginalised*, edited by Michael Shevlin and Richard Rose, 228–253. Dublin: National Disability Authority.

Raina, Vinod. 2011. "Between behaviourism and constructivism". *Cultural Studies* 25 no. 1: 9–24.

Ravenscroft, John, John M. Davis and Lynn J. McNair. 2018 (accepted/in press). "The continuing need for child led approaches within inclusive systems: A focus on transition across 8 European countries". In *Inclusive Practices, Equity and Access for Individuals with Disabilities: Insights from Educators across the World*, edited by Santoshi Halder and Vassillios Argyropoulos, 179–200. London: Palgrave.

Ravenscroft, John, Kerri Wazny and John M. Davis. 2017. "Factors associated with successful transition among children with disabilities in eight European countries". *PLoS One* 12 no. 6: e0179904. doi: https://doi.org/10.1371/journal.pone.0179904

Reynaert, Didier, Ellen Desmet, Sara Lembrechts, and Wouter Vandenhole. 2015. "Introduction: A critical approach to children's rights". In *Routledge International Handbook of Children's Rights Studies*, edited by Wouter Vandenhole, Ellen Desmet, Didier Reynaert, and Sara Lembrechts, 1–23. Abingdon: Routledge.

Sanagavarapu, Prathyusha and Bob Perry. 2005. "Concerns and expectations of Bangladeshi parents as their children start school". *Australian Journal of Early Childhood* 30 no. 3: 45–52.

Siraj, Iram, and Denise Kingston. 2015. *An Independent Review of the Scottish Early Learning and Childcare (ELC) Workforce and Out of School Care (OSC) Workforce*. London: University College London Institute of Education.

United Nations. 1989. *The UN Convention on the Rights of the Child*. Geneva: United Nations.

United Nations Educational, Scientific and Cultural Organization. 1990. *World Declaration on Education for All*. Paris: UNESCO.

Urban, Mathias and Beth Blue Swadener. 2016. "Democratic Accountability and Contextualised Systemic Evaluation: A Comment on the OECD Initiative to Launch an International Early Learning Study (IELS)". *Reconceptualising Early Childhood Education* 5 no. 1. http://receinternational.org/pdf/RECE_OECD_response_for_ICCPS.pdf.

Vinovskis, Maris A. 1996. "Changing perceptions and treatment of young children in the United States". In *Images of Childhood*, edited by C. Philip Hwang, Michael E. Lamb, and Irving E. Sigel, 99–112. Mahwah: Lawrence Erlbaum Associates.

Viruru, Radhika. 2001. *Early Childhood Education: Postcolonial Perspectives from India*. New Delhi: Sage.

Viruru, Radhika. 2005. "The impact of postcolonial theory on early childhood education". *Journal of Education* 35 no. 1: 7–29.

Walkerdine, Valerie. 1998. "Developmental psychology and the child-centred pedagogy: The insertion of Piaget into early education". In *Changing the Subject: Psychology, Social Regulation and Subjectivity*, edited by Julian Henriques, Wendy Hollway, Cathy Urwin, Couze Venn and Valerie Walkerdine, 153–202. London: Routledge.

White, E. Jayne. 2016. *Introducing Dialogic Pedagogy: Provocations for Early Years*. Oxon: Routledge.

33

IMMIGRANT CHILDREN'S LIFEWORLDS IN THE U.S. BORDERLANDS

Angeles Maldonado, Beth Blue Swadener and Casey Khaleesi

Introduction

I think we all come from Mexico, but we were born here ... so we are Mexican slash American.

—Juanito, age 8

Our work is situated in a children's rights-based framework, and we draw specifically from the United Nations Committee's General Comment No. 12, *The Child's Right to Be Heard* (2009), which emphasized children's right to participate in decisions affecting them and to have their views taken seriously: 'The views expressed by children may add relevant perspectives and experiences and should be considered in decision-making, policy-making and preparation of laws and/or measures as well as their evaluation' (p. 5).

We build on research that foregrounds younger people's views (e.g. Clark & Moss, 2001; Lundy & Swadener, 2012; MacNaughton, Hughes, & Smith, 2008; Perez, Medellin, & Rideaux, 2016; Soto & Swadener, 2005; Swadener, Peters, & Gaches, 2012). These projects highlight the ways young children can tell adults about their lives and experiences and the concerns that they have for people close to them and for their immediate environment.

This chapter draws from our conversations with 23 immigrant children, some of whom are in undocumented or mixed-status families. We look at ways that participation rights of migrant children can be strengthened and address several questions that have both substantive and methodological implications. What does it mean to be an immigrant child in Arizona? How are identities and imagined futures impacted? To explore these and other questions, our research applies Border Crit theory (Maldonado, 2013) and conducted activity-based conversational interviews with children living in Arizona. We inquired about their views and experiences in home, school, and community settings. We reflect and conclude with the implications for those doing research in the borderlands, within the reality of recent family separations in the name of enforcing federal immigration law without regard for children's human rights.

Context and Border Crit theory

We begin with the land. Arizona rests on land that has been possessed, exploited, and colonized. Much like brown bodies, its soil has been demarcated and cut, scarred to establish the current border route separating Mexico and the United States (a consequence of the 1848 Treaty of Guadalupe Hidalgo). As Karleen Pendleton Jiménez (2006) describes, "the land has been covered in blood for hundreds of years, often spilled as a result of racist ideologies. This is where our classrooms rest" and where we birth our children (p. 255). As Juanito asserts, "we all come from Mexico." The notion of belonging to two geographical spaces, two very culturally different worlds, and two or more languages is an all too familiar reality for many children living in the borderlands. Some of the many recent attacks against migrant families living in the southwest borderlands include inhumane immigration enforcement policies that impact children, unaccompanied minors, and other asylum seekers fleeing poverty and violence.

On April 8, 2018, U.S. Attorney General Jeff Sessions announced a new "zero-tolerance policy" calling for the prosecution of all individuals who entered the United States "illegally." The strict criminalization of migration has resulted in heinous acts by Immigration and Customs Enforcement (ICE), including the practice of separating children from their parents upon apprehension at the U.S./Mexico border. Immigrant families detained continue to be crowded into cells known as *hieleras* (ice chests) due to intentionally set extremely cold temperatures. Children, some as young as 3 months old, were transported to detention facilities for children. We are now learning that many of these facilities were unlicensed, and a myriad of reports have surfaced about child neglect and physical and sexual abuse within these sites, with one case of sexual abuse coming to trial at the time of this writing. This systemic and institutionalized public turmoil inflicted upon people living in the borderlands and nationwide is impacting children in serious ways and raises many issues regarding the lack of protection for children's fundamental human rights.

Border Crit is an emergent theoretical framework that emphasizes the importance of contextualizing the experiences of people of color living in the borderlands. It is inspired by Critical Race theory (CRT), was founded in response to critical legal studies (CLS), and maintains that race and racism is endemic to everyday life (Delgado & Stefancic, 2000). Tribal Critical Race theory (Tribal Crit), in contrast, maintains that colonization is endemic to everyday life (Brayboy, 2001) and Latino/a Critical Race theory (Lat Crit) emphasizes issues that affect Latina/o people in everyday life (Delgado Bernal, 2002; Espinoza, 1990; Hernandez-Truyol, 1997; Montoya, 1994, Villalpando, 2003). Finally, Border Crit (Maldonado, 2013) maintains and recognizes race, colonization, and borders as endemic and focuses on issues that impact and concern border communities.

The border is a highly politicized geographical space in which the violation of human rights is justified and rationalized under the fabricated knowledge that the border is a place of danger. It delineates through walls and policies who gets to belong by strategically attacking the identities of those it seeks to exclude. We believe it is imperative to understand both the political climate of the borderlands as well as its geographical history, as it sheds light on the ways in which this context impacts people who live there and illuminates those who benefit. Arizona, for example, straddles two countries and sits on indigenous land. Arizona was part of the state of Sonora, Mexico, until 1848, when the United States took possession through the Treaty of Guadalupe Hidalgo. It is ironic, therefore, that many regard Mexican migrants as outsiders. Border Crit theory seeks to expose and name the racial ideologies behind the symbolic parade of laws and immigration enforcement practices that dominate the borderlands.

The children we interviewed shared narratives that illustrate some of the concerns, struggles, and resiliency of migrant and transborder childhoods. We see narratives and stories as real and legitimate, though often undervalued, sources of knowledge and seek to complicate the often-simplified rationalization of injustice. Border Crit denounces the neutrality of law and government and seeks to unveil its contradictions through counterstories. Applying Border Crit theory, therefore, requires a reimagining of a world without borders.

Border Crit theory is grounded by direct action. It calls for researcher accountability to the communities they seek to represent, by raising ethical questions about the goals of their research. It urges us to reflect upon who is benefiting from the stories we tell, and the projects we undertake in research, to ensure that at the heart of our writing are the voices and perspectives of people of color, and that our research is tied to social justice movements and advocacy in solidarity with local impacted communities on both sides of the border.

Our conversations with children

Given the national political climate, we were deeply concerned with the ways in which children were being impacted by anti-immigrant laws and policies. We felt that documenting their experiences was increasingly necessary. At the same time, our primary concern was safeguarding children from additional trauma and triggers that could re-traumatize children or make them relive pain through our conversations (e.g., Block, Warr, Gibbs, & Elisha, 2012). We intentionally did not lead with questions about legal status, threats to well-being, or other sensitive topics. Instead, we assumed and hoped that some of these topics would emerge organically. We recognize the inherent ethical challenges of talking with children about traumas they may have experienced. While we hope our research can serve as a tool for advocacy, we recognize the need to balance that with respect for the real lives of the children with whom we interact. We are aware that children's lives are rich and complex and their daily experiences are not only focused on their migrant status. We ultimately decided to talk with children about their lived experiences in family, school, and community contexts. As children told us about family and school, topics of language, safety, and family across the border came up in many of our conversations, with children raising these issues themselves.

We conducted 23 activity-based conversational interviews (Tay-Lim & Lim, 2013) with children aged 5–9 years old in an elementary school, their homes, and a community center. We tried to keep the interviews to approximately 30 minutes, though in some instances we allowed for flexibility in our time with children who wanted to keep sharing; we did not want to appear to be cutting them off or insensitive when they wanted to continue speaking. We offered art supplies and paper and asked children to do a drawing of their home, school, or community. Some were basic questions such as "Tell me about your family" or "What do you do to help at home?" We also asked children to tell us about a usual day at school or to tell us about their teachers or classes. As we continued the interviews, we found ourselves rewording and adjusting some of our questions by adding examples as prompts. For instance, the topic of language came up immediately as we asked children at the start of the interview if they preferred that we did the interview in English or Spanish. At times, there were children who would say Spanish but then switch to responding in English, or vice versa. This led us to ask about language more directly. We asked what they enjoyed about being bilingual, or what language they spoke at home.

Language then became a focal question for us, much as Norma Gonzalez (2005), in *I Am My Language*, argues that to speak of language is to speak of ourselves: "Language is at the heart literally and metaphorically, of who we are, how we present ourselves, and how others see us" (p. xix). In her work, she explored what identities children construct when they use language in particular ways. Children in the borderlands often tread linguistic terrains in which meanings are discovered and redefined.

When asked if there was anything they wished to change at school, many children said nothing. When we reworded the question in a way that offered them agency, they began to become more responsive. For example, we reworded our earlier question to "If you were principal, what would you do differently?" children began to offer a plethora of ideas, such as changing some of the discipline structures or the physical appearance and resources of the school, including adding a pool or better soccer field.

What we learned from children

> I came to theory because I was hurting—the pain within me was so intense that I could not go on living. I came to theory desperate, wanting to comprehend—to grasp what was happening around and within me. Most importantly I wanted to make the hurt go away. I saw in theory a location for healing. I came to theory young when I was still a child.
>
> *(hooks, 1994b, p. 59)*

The idea of children as theorists is not new, yet adults seldom regard them as creators or holders of knowledge. As we engaged with children, it was evident that they had their own clear ideas and a willingness to articulate how the world ought to be. We began our research seeking to explore and foreground children's "views and voices" but what we found was not just opinions and perspectives, but theories about their worlds and how to resolve identified problems or concerns. In this study, we wanted children to talk freely about their lives. We did, however, structure the interviews about three broad aspects of their lives: home, school, and community. We organize the findings around those three contexts; of course, what children shared often addressed more than one of these settings.

Home

For immigrant and Mexican American communities, *nuestras familias*, our families, are incredibly important. It has long been documented that many families migrate precisely to be reunited with family that left, often as a sacrifice, to flee violence or to secure better economic conditions or opportunities for one's children and family. It is not rare for families to exist apart. Children in the borderlands straddle borders and have relied on home as equivalent to where the family lives. Given the geographic physical instability created by one's migration status, the family becomes the constant upon which immigrant children rely.

Many of our conversations began with children choosing to make drawings of their family members or of their houses and describe the ways in which they live within these settings. Children shared the ways in which they helped their parents with chores or with their siblings. They also spoke about their neighborhoods, their desires for a pool (given the hot Arizona weather), and lamented their lack of access to parks and/or a fear of going outside. Overall one prevalent theme was about safety and the lack of safety in their living conditions, fearing the safety of their parents, or altruistic concerns for their families and their futures.

Many children discussed where they were "from," and in these conversations it became apparent that children felt anchored to their multiple languages, with yearnings and a sense of belonging to both the United States and to Mexico (even in situations when children were not born there). This notion of belonging to two worlds is reflected in the quote with which we began this chapter:

> I think we all come from Mexico, but we were born here ... so we are Mexican slash American.
>
> —*Juanito, age 8*

Juanito describes this intuitive understanding that though he was not physically born in Mexico, he still was somehow theoretically born there, and so in stating "we all come from Mexico" he is redefining identity to translate not only to where one is born, but to where one shares connections. Following this thought, Juanito went on to share with us that his grandparents were born in Mexico and his parents lived there:

Interviewer: But your grandparents live in Mexico.
Juanito: Yeah, and my mom and dad lived in Mexico.

In doing this, his definition is also including the idea that one's identity is also connected to where one's family is born. Additionally, we observed the ways in which children yearned for or missed family living in Mexico:

Interviewer: Do you get to go down and see your grandparents very often?
Juanito: Nnno. Um, mostly we're going to see one of 'em cuz I only have grandpas. I don't have any grandmas. I've never seen any of 'em, and one of 'em, um, died when ... and one of 'em died I think before I was born.

This was reflected not only in the quote above, but in many other interactions with children. We recalled Anzaldúa's (1999) yearning for family in Mexico and named this response of the children as a "transborder family imaginary." Many of the children understand that they have family that transgress Mexico and the United States, and that their identities are intertwined between both cultures and languages.

The display of code-switching and yearning for family in Mexico was a recurring theme in our conversations; many recounted a desire and hope to be with family or seeing family in Mexico or family they had been separated from because of their immigration status. One child also spoke about being afraid of her mother dying because she was very sick, and at the time the child's father found himself in immigration custody:

Interviewer: Is there anything that worries you?
Child: Uh-huh.
Interviewer: What?
Child: I worry in the night because I'm afraid that my mom's gonna die.
Child: Y a veces, um, um, y a veces, um, um, y a veces lloro. (And sometimes, um, um, and sometimes I cry.)
Interviewer: A veces lloras? Oh. Porque lloras? (You cry sometimes? Oh. Why do you cry?)
Child: Porque extraño mi papa. (Because I miss my dad.)

Other children also expressed fears about death, as some knew of family who had been killed or had died. One child described that a cousin was shot and had died. As evidenced in our conversations with children in Arizona, many spoke about home within the context of their parents and siblings. Home shifted and was defined with the transborder identities of their families.

Community

We also asked children about their community or neighborhood. The word community was perhaps one of the most challenging to explain and/or difficult for children to understand. We realized quickly the need to explain the concept through examples. Living undocumented in the borderlands often means living in neighborhoods that are over-policed, it means racial profiling and discrimination, it means criminalization, it means transient employment, low-wage jobs, long work hours, work insecurity, underpayment, sending your children to or attending underfunded schools, and it many times means lack of access to healthcare and/or working in jobs that expose undocumented migrants to injury and health hazards due to exposure to chemicals and poor or dangerous working conditions (Panikkar, Brugge, Gute, & Hyatt, 2015). Additionally, many migrant families, particularly recently arrived families, are struggling financially or living in impoverished neighborhoods with high crime rates.

Many migrant communities work in the shadows, or under the table, making earning a decent income challenging. Migrant communities also are less likely to have health insurance or seek public assistance (Toomey et al., 2014). Migrant families may fear calling the police, where the police and other agencies are known to actively collaborate with ICE, and may also restrict their interactions with community and governmental agencies.

While children did not speak directly about poverty or lacking resources, they did discuss a myriad of concerns over safety of themselves or their families, concerns over parents working late, or not having access to parks. One child explained that he had no neighbors and he was very afraid of snakes. We learned through the interview that the child was living in a very rural area in West Phoenix. Another boy described not being allowed to play outside because his mom was afraid of the traffic around their house, another about not going out at night for fear of being shot.

Children with a parent in immigration-related detention had partial information about this situation. As one 7-year-old girl expressed:

> Sometimes she [my mother] goes like to a meeting … it's an emergency place where kids can't go …. She went to go to like in a meeting about my dad … To get him out, how to get him out from there … he's in Eloy, Arizona … I feel sad … porque extrano a mi papa (because I miss my dad).

There are many challenges that migrant and impoverished communities experience, particularly those that left their countries of origin fleeing poverty or violence, who may arrive with very few resources and therefore seek support of local organizations and churches.

At the same time, children did discuss that their families frequented either community organizations or church spaces for family support. Some of the children we interviewed in an educational after-school program they frequented in the West Side of Phoenix, and others we recruited at a migrant rights organization in central Phoenix. We do know that these community spaces offered support to families in various ways.

While the fear of immigration agents was not directly conveyed by children we interviewed, we did encounter children who talked about not liking Trump, one about Sheriff Arpaio, and/or reflections about missing a parent who was in immigration custody, as described in the quote above: "Porque extrano a mi papa" (because I miss my dad). Despite the role that police play in carrying out anti-immigrant policies, some children spoke about becoming police officers when they "grow up." Some of their reasonings varied, but were intimately linked to altruistic desires to provide safety. For example:

Interviewer: Do you know what you want to be when you grow up?
Child: Mmmm, when I grow up I want to be a police.
Interviewer: You want to be a police? OK. Do you know anybody else who's a police?
Child: Um, a police came my school and showed me a dog police.
Interviewer: Oh …
Child: Like, he, he like, if you're lost and stuff, he will look, and find you.
Interviewer: Oh. And so, why do you want to be a police? You want to look for kids?
Child: Yeah, if they're lost.

We include this reflection to illustrate the contradiction, conflict, and active negotiation over the meaning of safety. When we speak about the transborder identity, we refer to a constant juggling of meaning and the recreation of new meanings. Having a transborder identity can often require people to entertain two seemingly contradictory ideas. The external world of the migrant child is often colored with the imposition of meanings that may not relate to one's direct experience or that may impact one's family or home life in a distinct way. Children are therefore required to juggle the meaning of a term and decide what meaning to apply. Therefore, code-switching is not limited to language, but is also consistently required when children belong to two social contexts and therefore meaning constructs. As depicted in the quote above, the child's concern over missing children, which likely reflects his knowledge (from his parents?) that "children are unsafe," inspired him to yearn for adopting a professional identity that he was taught (at school) to address this safety concern. This is interesting because of our knowledge about the role of police in enacting anti-immigrant enforcement policies.

School

English and Spanish. But she don't want to talk in English to us. Wait. Not English, Spanish, because we are, we need to know how to speak English.

—*6-year-old boy*

Immigrant children are not sheltered from hostility by classroom walls where diversity and culture are purported to be celebrated. They encounter bias and white supremacy within the curriculum, policies, and on the playground. According to the Southern Poverty Law Center's (2016) Teaching Tolerance project, fear and anxiety levels among children of color had escalated significantly since Trump's presidential campaign and his heightened anti-immigration rhetoric and unjust policies. Teachers reported an increase in racial tensions, intimidation, and bullying toward Mexican and Muslim students associated with ways in which Trump targeted them during his campaign and emboldened white students to act on their prejudices.

Teachers may collude with or even contribute to this school climate issue, as demonstrated by the conversation we had with one student who shared that her teacher (who is Hispanic) told her that she was "del rancho." To be "del rancho" means to be from a ranch, which implies that people who are "del rancho" are from the outskirts of society and considered "less" civilized.

Furthermore, policies such as the Structured English Immersion (SEI) model directly affects immigrant children in Arizona. SEI requires all instruction, text, and work produced by students be in English only, and until recently required blocks of segregated SEI, depending on English test scores. This model has received backlash from teachers, families, and researchers as to its validity regarding its effectiveness (Krashen, Rolstad, & Jeff, 2012). It has also been criticized for its infringement on children's civil rights (Rios-Aguilar, Gonzalez-Canche, & Luis, 2010) via linguistic imperialism (Jimenez-Silva, Bernstein, & Baca, 2016). Robert Phillipson (1992) describes linguistic imperialism this way:

> The working definition of English linguistic imperialism attempts to capture the way one language dominates another, with anglocentricity and professionalism as the central ELT (English Language Teaching) mechanisms operating within a structure in which unequal power and resource allocation is effected and legitimated.
>
> *(p. 54)*

As evidenced in the young boy's comment below, children transverse dichotomies from school and home, teachers and friends, south of the border (Mexico) and Arizona:

> Cuz, you know why? Cuz my brother's talking English but they don't. My mom gets mad at them cuz they, they want em a get talk in Spanish.
>
> *—6-year-old boy*

The SEI model, as compared to bilingual and multicultural models, strips away what could be considered one of the most prevalent cultural identifiers immigrant children have.

Children also spoke about their school day and what they did and didn't like about it. The majority stated that they loved their school and their teacher(s), and many were enthusiastic to tell us in extensive detail about their daily schedule. We got the sense that they liked knowing the structure and routine of their school day and speculated that this was due to the stability it provided when other aspects of life may have felt uncertain. Several children did, however, discuss discipline practices, including "positive discipline." For example, we asked what children might change about their school if they were the principal, and one boy responded:

> That when I am principal, I would … that they all let their kids be on green. That the teachers let the kids to, to always be on green.
>
> *—6-year-old boy*

The concept behind this boy's quote relates to the so-called "positive discipline" approach or behavior management plan used by many schools in the United States that has each student's name assigned to stoplight colors. Green means the student is following directions, yellow means they have been warned regarding a behavior, and red means they have reached a point where they will receive a consequence (Khaleesi, 2018). Being on red can result in a punitive action such as, but not limited to, loss of recess, time-out, phone call to parents, or being sent to the principal (Khaleesi, 2018). This may lead to the students' first contact with the juvenile detention system, which often leads to adult incarceration, and has been referred to as the "school-to-prison pipeline" (Nelson & Lind, 2015).

Implications for research in the borderlands

Angeles Maldonado reflects:

> And I suppose our migration story never leaves us … it becomes part of our iden-
> tity, and resurfaces in our everyday understandings of self, amidst a world that feels
> distant. We become either foreign to this land or foreign to the people who
> birthed us. We belong to two worlds and we exist reading between the lines,
> making sense of the in between. Recently, I observed tears fall off of a migrant
> child's cheek … and in that moment, I also cried … I saw myself … still healing,
> still making sense of the loss and nostalgia of walking away from the land that
> loved me but couldn't care for me and into a land that denounces all that
> I represent.

We recognize the traumatic impact that anti-immigrant policies have and are having and
will have on children for many years to come. These experiences, even those that are not
directly affected, harm migrant children's lifeworlds in many ways. Border Crit theory urges
us to interrogate simplified discourses and rhetoric about the identities of people living in
border communities. When we situate our research in Border Crit, we can ask more critical
questions, ensuring that our research sheds light on issues that are of importance to migrant
communities. When guided by anti-racist theories, our methods thereby become mindfully
constructed around aligning our work to the greater struggle for social justice, thus maintaining ethics and accountability visible in the how and why of our research.

We reject the falsely perceived neutrality of research. As Border Crit scholars, we cannot
just ask how immigrant children are doing in school. We must go beyond that and consider
context-driven and relevant questions, such as: How are children impacted when they live
in fear of losing their parents or know of their peers or neighbors who suddenly do not live
next door or are missing from their classrooms? How can migrant communities feel
grounded in a country that allows children to be detained, to have their rights violated, to
be separated from their parents at the border, and be exposed to physical and sexual abuse?
How do communities address new policies that are being crafted to bring the border into
the interior through enforcement policies that impact workplaces and neighborhoods? This
reframing and reconsideration of what could remain an isolated question on the education
status of migrant children forces us to see children more holistically, and to grapple with the
reality that families in the borderlands are living in uncertainty. Knowledge of workplace
raids and stories of parents being deported on their route to take children to school or to
the hospital circulate in the media. This reality impacts the lived experiences of migrant
families and has implications for how we do research.

In applying Border Crit, we recognize that the context and conditions in which children
are living can affect them in many implicit and explicit ways. It reminds us to give due
weight to the views and experiences of children of color living in the borderlands and to
complicate the discourse around migration. Border Crit urges us to view migrant children's
perspectives as legitimate sources of knowledge, creating a critical space for counternarratives. In the case of young children, it enabled us to note the creativity, agency, and resiliency of children inhabiting the challenging terrain of the borderlands. We see a need to
recognize that research carries serious ethical responsibilities to the communities and people
it touches. The suffering and struggle of migrant families should not be available as mere
data or findings in a paper. If we are asking what it is like to live as a Mexican/American,
we cannot unhear those stories, stories that are nested within larger discourses, political

struggles, and grassroots demands. Border Crit urges us to not be passive listeners and be willing to see "the researched" as more than participants. Applying Border Crit enabled us to see ourselves, the researchers, as accomplices for social justice, thereby helping us to effectively use this research as a weapon to expose social issues and produce unique insights into the human rights issues that children are living and negotiating every day.

This type of research carries a commitment to expose the daily violence and racism against migrant families. As Border Crit scholars, our work must be situated, rooted, and anchored within the greater struggle for human rights. We must lean into the discomfort and ambiguity that comes with navigating sensitive terrains where "truth," "right," and "wrong" are complex and messy. At times, this may include doing more listening, creating more confusion, raising more questions, and complicating more than resolving. It also means being flexible, and adjusting and reconsidering assumptions, with the goal of doing justice to the topic, to the people, to the children, to the families that are ultimately impacted, even if subtle in the ways in which we socially construct knowledge.

For these very reasons, as we proceed with this work, we have identified the need to dig deeper and not shy away from topics that are a vivid reality for migrant communities. We recognize the need to consult first and foremost with children, but also with their families. Children do not exist in isolation and are intimately affected by what happens to their parents. Impacted organizations and stakeholders are also key sources of grounded knowledge. Border Crit theory recognizes the need to have the research meet communities in the places and conversations where they are. As we applied the theory, we consistently evaluated and asked: What matters and is most important to migrant families? We believe our migrant rights communities on the ground hold a wealth of knowledge about migration as they interact and advocate, and struggle to fight against the systemic and persistent attacks against families of color.

Doing research with communities and stakeholders in liminal spaces must be collaborative. Stakeholders are not mere access points to exploit and utilize. Immigrant rights organizations and advocates see what these policies look like on the ground, who they hurt, and our work has to fill a purpose beyond our own academic pursuits. Migrant rights organizations continue to serve on the frontlines in defense of migrant communities. Within these spaces, children's lives are increasingly politicized and many continue to take a more visible presence in the struggle. Thus, when we observe migrant children also on the frontlines of this critical human rights struggle, we must listen and immerse ourselves within this reality. Our own concerns over children reliving trauma become complicated by the reality that trauma is not a one-time event, but rather a lived experience of communities in the borderlands.

A better set of questions then becomes: Who benefits from an untold story? What "facts" and master narratives remain unchallenged? The implications for those navigating research in the borderlands include coming to terms with this feeling of ambiguity, recognizing the permanence of racism (Bell, 1992), and embracing our duty to create—as Anzaldúa (1999) described, "*nuevas teorias*," new theories; we need a new language, a new set of words, a new unsterilized story about how we work toward justice and liberation. Border Crit theory is one tool among many with the goal of speaking truth to power and complicating discourses that are utilized to oppress migrant communities.

Conclusion

The U.S-Mexican border *es una herida abierta* where the Third World grates against the first and bleeds. And before a scab forms it hemorrhages again, the lifeblood of two worlds merging to form a third country—a border culture.

Borders are set up to define the places that are safe and unsafe, to distinguish us from them. A border is a dividing line, a narrow strip along a steep edge. A borderland is a vague and undetermined place created by the emotional residue of an unnatural boundary. It is in a constant state of transition. The prohibited and forbidden are its inhabitants.

(Anzaldúa, 1999, p. 3)

The immigrant identity is systematically criminalized, policed, forbidden, prohibited, and misconstrued. This *herida abierta*, open wound, that immigrant families living in the borderlands also carry is very much intentional and by design. In Arizona, and nationwide, the lives of migrant families continue to be attacked via inhumane border policies and immigration laws fueled by economic and political greed. Immigrant childhoods are impacted in serious ways. This research sought to honor the participation rights of children in research. As immigrant and children's rights advocates, but also as mothers, we believe research with immigrant children must illustrate that this "distinguishing" of "us from them" is orchestrated trauma and direct violence that must be denounced. The voices of and perspectives of children on family, community, and school illustrate just how resilient and powerful children are, amidst an uncertain and unjust terrain.

Our interviews underscored the significance of consulting and talking with children on issues that affect their daily lives. Themes of our conversations included child-generated theories on identity, migration, notions of home and related responsibilities, belonging, race, citizenship, status, bilingualism, family, community, neighborhood, education, schooling, friendship, and altruistic desires, including for the future. Applying Border Crit theory results in context-based race-conscious community-grounded research, providing insights into the incredible resourcefulness of children "code-shifting" to manage and negotiate the constant contradictions and dangers of their lives. We hope this writing illustrates the potential of counternarratives in making research relevant to collective pursuits of social justice and the significance in constructing knowledge that interrogates the location of power in the borderlands. While a small step, we cross in solidarity with migrant families, aligning our work with current efforts to resist and abolish nativist policies and laws that disregard the well-being, quality of life, and safety of children.

References

Anzaldúa, Gloria. 1999. *Borderlands =: La frontera*. San Francisco: Aunt Lute Books.

Bell, Derrick A. 1992. *Faces at the bottom of the well: The permanence of racism*. New York: Basic Books.

Block, Karen, Warr Deborah, Gibbs, Lisa, & Elisha, Riggs. 2012. Addressing ethical and methodological challenges in research with refugee-background young people: Reflections from the field. *Journal of Refugee Studies*, 26(1), 69–87.

Brayboy, B. 2005. Toward a tribal critical race theory in education. *Urban Review*, 37(5), 425–446. doi:10.1007/s11256-005-0018-y

Clark, Allison & Moss, Peter. 2001. *Listening to young children. The Mosaic approach*. London: National Children's Bureau.

Delgado, Richard & Stefancic, Jean. 2000. Introduction. In Richard Delgado & Jean Stefancic (eds.), *Critical race theory: The cutting edge* (2nd ed., pp. xv–xix). Philadelphia: Temple University Press.

Delgado Bernal, Dolores. 2002. Critical race theory, Latcrit theory, and critical raced gendered epistemologies: Recognizing students of color as holders and creators of knowledge. *Qualitative Inquiry*, 8(1), 105–126.

Espinoza, Leslie, & Harris, Angela P. 1997. Embracing the tar-baby: LatCrit theory and the sticky mess of race. *La Raza Law Journal*, 10(1), 499–559.

Gonazalez, Norma. 2005. *I Am My Language: Discourse of women and children in the borderlands*. Tucson: The University of Arizona Press.

Hernandez-Truyol, Berta Esperanza. 1997. Borders (en)gendered – Normativities, Latinas, and a LatCrit paradigm, 72 N.Y.U. *Law Review*, 882-927.

hooks, bell. 1994b. *Teaching to transgress: Education as the practice of freedom* (pp. 316–321). New York: Routledge.

Jimenez-Silva, Margarita, Bernstein, Katie A., & Baca, Evelyn C. 2016. An analysis of how restrictive language policies are interpreted by Arizona's Department of Education and three individual school districts' websites. *Education Policy Analysis Archives*, 24(105), 1–33.

Khaleesi, Casey. 2018. "It Makes me sad because I think … I can never be good enough": What students are saying about high-stakes testing. (Master's thesis). Retrieved from Arizona State University, ProQuest Dissertations and Theses database.

Krashen, Stephen, Rolstad, Kellie, & Jeff, MacSwan 2012. Review of "research summary and bibliography for structured English immersion".

Lundy, Laura, & Swadener, Beth Blue. 2012. Engaging with young children as co-researchers: A child rights-based approach. In Olivia Saracho (ed.) *Handbook of research methods in early childhood education* (Volume II, pp. 657–676). Washington, DC: Information Age Publishing.

MacNaughton, Gillian, Hughes, Patrick, & Smith, Kylie (Eds.). 2008. *Young children as active citisens: Principles, policies and pedagogies*. Newcastle, UK: Cambridge Scholars Publishing.

Maldonado, A. (2013). Raids, race, and lessons of fear and resistance: Narratives and discourse in the immigration movement in Arizona. (Doctoral dissertation). Retrieved from Arizona State University, ProQuest Dissertations and Theses database. (UMI 3590934).

Montoya, Margaret E. 1994. Law and literature: Mascaras, Trenzas, y Grenas: Un/masking the self while un/braiding Latina stories and legal discourse. *Harvard Journal of Law & Gender*, 17, 185.

Nelson, Libby & Lind, Dara. 2015. The school-to-prison pipeline, explained; Police officers in the classrooms are just the tip of the iceberg. Retrieved from www.vox.com/2015/2/24/8101289/school-discipline-race

Panikkar, Bindu, Dough, Brugge, David, M. Gute, & Raymond, R. Hyatt. 2015. "They see us as machines": The experience of recent immigrant women in the low wage informal labor sector. *PLoS One*, 10(11), e0142686. doi:10.1371/journal.pone.0142686

Pendleton Jiménez, Karleen. 2006. "Start with the land": Groundwork for Chicana pedagogy. In D. D. Bernal, C. A. Elenes, F. E. Godinez & S. Villenas (eds.), *Chicana/Latina feminist pedagogies and epistemologies for everyday life: Educación en la familia, comunidad y escuela* (pp. 219–30). Albany: SUNY Press.

Perez, Michelle S., Medellin, Kelly, & Rideaux, Kia S. 2016. Repositioning childhood lived experiences within adult contexts: A black feminist analysis of childhood/s regulation in early childhood care and education. *Global Studies of Childhood*, 6(1), 67–79.

Peters, Lacey. 2012. "When the bell rings we go inside and learn" children's and parents' understandings of the kindergarten transition. 175–76. Retrieved from Arizona State University, ProQuest Dissertations and Theses database.

Phillipson, Robert. 1992. Linguistic imperialism and linguicism. In *Linguistic imperialism* (pp. 50–57). Oxford: OUP.

Rios-Aguilar, Cecilia, Gonzalez-Canche, Manuel, & Luis, Moll 2010. Implementing Structured English Immersion (SEI) in Arizona: Benefits, costs, challenges, and opportunities. The Civil Rights Project/Proyecto Derechos Civiles. Retrieved from www.civilrightsproject.ucla.edu/research/k-12-education/language-minority-students/implementing-structured-english-immersion-sei-in-arizona-benefits-costs-challenges-and-opportunities?searchterm=implementing+sei

Soto, Lourdes D., & Swadener, Beth B. (Eds.). 2005. *Power and voice in research with children*. New York, NY: Peter Lang.

Southern Poverty Law Center SPLC. 2016. The Trump effect: The impact of the presidential campaign on our nation's schools. Retrieved from www.splcenter.org/20160413/trump-effect-impact-presidential-campaign-our-nations-schools

Swadener, Beth Blue, Peters, L., & Gaches, S. 2012. Taking children's rights and participation seriously: Cross-national perspectives and possibilities. In Veronica Pacini-Ketchabaw & Larry Prochner (eds) *Resituating Canadian early childhood education*. New York: Peter Lang, 189–210.

Tay-Lim, Joanna, & Lim, Sirene. 2013. Privileging younger children's voices in research: Use drawings and a co-construction process. *International Journal of Qualitative Methods*, 12, 65–83.

Toomey, Russel B., Umaña-Taylor, Adriana J., Williams, David R., Harvey-Mendoza, Elizabeth, Jahromi, Laudan B., & Updegraff, Kimberly A. 2014. Impact of Arizona's SB 1070 immigration law on utilization of health care and public assistance among Mexican-origin adolescent mothers and their mother figures. *American Journal of Public Health*, 104(Suppl 1), S28–S34. doi:10.2105/ AJPH.2013.301655

United Nations. 2009. *United Nations Convention on the Rights of the Child, general comment No 12: The child's right to be heard.* Geneva: United Nations.

Villalpando, Octavio. 2003. Self-segregation or self-preservation? A critical race theory and Latina/o critical theory analysis of a study of Chicana/o college students. *International Journal of Qualitative Studies in Education*, 5, 619-646.

34

EXPLORING GLOBAL CITIZENSHIP WITH CANADIAN AND TANZANIAN CHILDREN THROUGH VOICE AND MULTIMODAL MEANING-MAKING

Jodi Streelasky

Introduction

Developing cross-cultural understandings with children in our contemporary global society is becoming increasingly important, and many countries, including Canada (Schweisfurth, 2006), have begun adding content to curriculum documents that address this topic. This transformative initiative aims to enhance students' knowledge of global cultures and their understanding of global citizenship. Oxfam (2015) defined global citizens as people who are aware of the wider world and have a sense of their own role as world citizens, and who value and respect diversity. In the Canadian province of British Columbia, the Ministry of Education Social Studies (2016) curriculum addresses global citizenship approaches to learning that focus on social justice, voice, cross-cultural understanding, and valuing diverse worldviews (Dill, 2013).

However, a current challenge is how to engage children in meaningful and relevant learning experiences that draw on a global citizenship approach and that are sustainable, engaging, and embrace the characteristics of empathy, understanding, and valuing diversity. Understanding the ways children thrive in an interconnected global landscape, and develop deeper understandings of other communities' languages, cultures, histories, schools, and familial networks is also significant to developing a global citizenship orientation. This research project is guided by the following two questions: (1) What do young children's multimodal representations of their valued school experiences in diverse, international settings reveal about their lives and what matters to them? (2) When these multimodal representations are shared with a different peer group across the world, what impact do these representations have on young children's understandings of their peers' lived experiences?

Geographical and cultural contexts

The Canadian elementary school where the research took place is located in North Vancouver, which is part of the larger metropolitan area of Vancouver in the province of British Columbia. Similar to most urban public Canadian schools, the student enrollment is culturally and linguistically diverse, and the school offers both English language instruction and French immersion classes for students. The school is located in a forested, mountainous area, and the neighborhood has a high socio-economic demographic. The school has two spacious playgrounds, a large soccer pitch, and a sprawling forested area with an outdoor classroom. The Canadian children involved in the study were enrolled in the same English instruction classroom at the beginning of the study and were at the school for the duration of the three-year project. However, in the second and third years of the study, four of the children were enrolled in French immersion classrooms at the school.

In the Tanzanian context, the research participants attended two public schools (pre-primary and primary) over the course of the project, both of which are located on the gated grounds of a large university in Dar es Salaam. The children reside in the low socio-economic neighborhoods surrounding the campus. The children were enrolled at the pre-primary school for the first two years of the study and the primary school during the third year of the study. Dar es Salaam is a major port city in East Africa and has a sub-Saharan climate with distinct rainy and dry seasons. The pre-primary and primary schools are painted in bright colors, and have large open-air corridors. The school has a small playground and soccer pitch, and flowering bushes and trees are part of the outdoor grounds. The African children involved in the project are all Tanzanian, and the schools provide English-medium instruction. At the beginning of the study, the children primarily communicated in Kiswahili. As the study progressed, the children began to communicate with me in English.

Purpose

In this project, 14 Canadian children and 14 Tanzanian children participated in the study that took place over their first three years of schooling. The children in both contexts were asked to share their valued school-based experiences through multiple modalities. As the study evolved, the children also began to share their valued experiences outside of school, which provided a more holistic view on their local cultural worlds (Fine and Sandstrom, 1988). At the beginning of the project, the children in both contexts were 4 and 5 years old. The purpose of this partnership was to: (i) introduce children to diverse global school cultures to develop an understanding of their international peers' school lives; (ii) provide children with a voice on what experiences matter to them at school; and (iii) inform the development of future international partnerships with young children in relation to global citizenship education and early childhood curriculum. In this project, Articles 12 and 13 from the UN Convention on the Rights of the Child (UNESCO, 1989) framed these overarching goals. Article 12 focuses on children's right to express their views, and recognises children as people who need to be listened to in matters that affect them. Article 13 articulates that children have the right to express their views and to impart information and ideas through any media of their choosing.

Theoretical framework

The theoretical and conceptual frameworks guiding this international research project include: (i) sociocultural theory (Vygotsky, 1978); (ii) funds of knowledge (Moll and Greenberg, 1990);

(iii) multimodality (Kress, 2003); and (iv) critical literacy (Luke, 2012). A sociocultural understanding of children draws on a sociological approach to childhood (James, Jenks, and Prout, 1998). This theory enables researchers to explore the social forces that shape children's meaning-making and to appreciate the diversity of human systems. Additionally, this theory allows researchers to examine the complex interactions of policy, school curriculum, and community and family systems in children's lives, and to understand children in ways that are not fundamentally reductionist in nature (Pence and Hix-Small, 2007). A funds of knowledge conceptual approach has been used to describe the intellectual resources of diverse cultural groups (Moll and Greenberg, 1990). This perspective acknowledges children's competences, values, and ways of knowing, all of which positions them as powerful informants on their own lives (Hardman, 1973). This understanding is particularly significant, as sub-Saharan African children have often been viewed by Western society as deficient, as opposed to being seen as knowledgeable co-constructors of their learning (Pence and Nsamenang, 2008).

This project was also informed by a multimodal perspective that focuses on how humans use different modes of communication to make meaning in the world (Stein, 2008). Kress (1997) argued that it is imperative that we understand the principles of meaning-making in all of the ways children do and that we honor their diverse ways of knowing. Finally, a critical literacy perspective framed this project, which recognises how the meanings embedded in texts reveal people's perspectives and motivations, and enables humans to examine how a text compares to their own realities (Luke, 2012).

In the following section, I briefly outline two areas of research that are significant to the project. The first area of literature provides an overview of global citizenship approaches to education with young children. The second area of literature focuses on the positioning of young children in research, and addresses the importance of including children's views in research projects in meaningful and developmentally appropriate ways.

Global citizenship education

A recent review of empirical studies on global citizenship education (Goren and Yemini, 2017) revealed that this approach is often described as a direct response by education systems to globalisation (Goren and Yemini, 2016; Resnik, 2009) or to social changes brought on by broader global processes such as immigration. Davies, Evans, and Reid (2005) described global citizenship education as "learning about the world," and being concerned with teaching children the importance of empathy, identity, and advocacy for people's voices—both locally and globally.

According to UNESCO (2015), global citizenship education can be addressed with young children by helping them understand that they belong to a broader global community and common humanity, and by emphasising the interconnectedness between the local and the global. This approach recognises that global citizenship education is a multifaceted approach, employing concepts and methodologies already applied in other areas, including human rights education, education for sustainable development, and education that focuses on the development of international understandings (UNESCO, 2014a). Global citizenship education also applies a lifelong learning perspective, beginning from early childhood and continuing through all levels of education and into adulthood, requiring both formal and informal approaches, and conventional and unconventional pathways to participation (UNESCO, 2014b).

As understandings of global citizenship education have evolved, there has been increasing focus on related teaching and learning practices, recognising that existing practices need to emphasise participatory and child-centered approaches that focus on inclusive teaching and learning practices (Kerr, 2002). Zhao (2010) posited that although educators are aware of the importance of imparting knowledge to students on the global nature of societal issues, and the relevance of appreciating the interconnectedness of people, there is a lack of support and resources on this topic, and little research has been conducted in this area.

Children's perspectives

In the field of early childhood education, there is a developing body of literature that addresses the importance of children's voices in education and research (Clark, 2005; Dockett, Einarsdottir and Perry, 2009; McTavish, Streelasky, and Coles, 2012). The current focus on valuing children's perspectives aligns with a paradigm shift in the way children are viewed, and has led to more inclusive and participatory practices connected to several political, social, and research agendas (Peters and Kelly, 2011). This understanding links to children's participatory rights under the UN Convention on the Rights of the Child (UNESCO, 1989), which provides an internationally accepted standard that applies to basic human rights affecting children (Smith, 2016). Freeman (1995) added that although the Convention is not the final word on children's rights, since it is a result of international compromise, it is more comprehensive than any prior international documents and represents a global consensus on the status of children. Melton (2005) added that the Convention is a nearly universally adopted expression of respect for children as people with voices that need to be heard, and is unparalleled in breadth as it addresses many domains of children's lives.

Methodology and analysis

In this project, I used a comparative case study approach (Stake, 2006) and participatory methods to identify the children's valued context-specific experiences (Kroes, 2009). My rationale for using a case study approach is based on Stake's (1978) perspective that cases can take us to places where we otherwise would not have the opportunity to go and see the world through the researcher's and participants' eyes. In my data collection and analysis, I also drew on the foundational components of critical ethnography (Denzin, 2001; Noblit, Flores, and Murillo, 2004) and visual ethnography (Rose, 2001).

In relation to my position as the researcher, my first visit to Dar es Salaam occurred in 2009 when I was a PhD student. At that time, I shared my doctoral research at the Pan African Reading for All Conference, which was held at a large university in Dar es Salaam. During that visit, I developed connections with early childhood faculty at the university and with other East African early childhood scholars. In 2015, as an assistant professor, I contacted early childhood faculty at that same Tanzanian university to inquire if they knew of early childhood educators who may be interested in participating in an international research project. They directed me to the headmistress of the pre-primary school on campus. Through email, I informed her of the group of children I was working with in Canada and inquired about her interest in doing a comparative analysis of the children's valued school experiences across global contexts. She responded positively to my request, and shared the details of the study with the Tanzanian children's families. The Tanzanian parents provided verbal consent (in Kiswahili) for their children's participation in the study.

In the Canadian context, I was already investigating a group of kindergarten children's valued school experiences, and the Canadian families had provided signed consent for their children to participate in the study. After connecting with the Tanzanian school, I asked the kindergarten teacher and children if they would be interested in learning about a group of children's valued school experiences in Tanzania. To provide the children with some context on Tanzania, I showed the children where Tanzania was on their classroom globe. The children verbally expressed their excitement to learn about a group of children across the world, and their families were informed of this change to the original project.

Throughout the three-year project, qualitative data collection methods were employed. For example, I used participant observations in both contexts. Yin (1994) contended that participant observations are frequently used in anthropological studies of different cultural groups in everyday settings, and several researchers (e.g., Dyson, 2003; Kendrick, 2003) have utilised participant observations when conducting studies with children. Semi-structured interviews also took place with the research participants during each year of the study. Although the Tanzanian children were learning English at school, they predominantly communicated in Kiswahili. Therefore, I required translation assistance from the headmistress. I also collected the children's multimodal texts, which provided a window into their valued experiences (Morphy and Banks, 1997).

During the three-year project, I visited the Canadian school approximately seven to eight times each year, where I participated in the daily routine of the children's school day, played with them outside at recess, informally met their families, and conducted semi-structured interviews with each child. Over the course of three years, I visited the Tanzanian school each spring for two weeks, where I took part in the children's daily routine, visited with their families as they dropped off their children at school, played with the children outside, and conducted individual semi-structured interviews with the assistance of a translator.

In the study, I analyzed the data inductively throughout the research process (Thomas, 2006). This occurred through multiple reads of the data to develop emerging themes (Corbin and Strauss, 2008) using a process of inductive coding. I also drew on critical ethnographic and visual ethnographic approaches to analyze the children's multimodal representations. Historically, the analysis of visual images has been based on a history of images produced in Western contexts (Kendrick, 2016). Since this study also included Tanzanian research participants, I drew on the aforementioned approaches (critical and visual ethnography), as these analytical perspectives take into account the agency of the image and the distinct social practices and activities of the maker (Rose, 2001).

Research project

In the first year of the study, developing a familiarity with the children and teachers in both contexts was a significant priority for me as I strived to achieve trustworthiness with both groups of participants. Therefore, when I visited the Canadian school, I participated in a range of everyday classroom and outdoor-based learning experiences. I was also able to observe and engage in discussions with the kindergarten teacher about her valued practices and pedagogical beliefs and the learning goals of the broader school community. Although my time was more condensed in the Tanzanian school site, I engaged in the same type of data collection techniques in that context. For example, I played with the children outside, observed and assisted in the classroom, and had discussions with the teacher about her practices and pedagogical beliefs, as well as the learning objectives of the Tanzanian curriculum.

At the end of my observation periods in the two schools, I spent two days at each site where I individually met with the children and asked them to share what learning experiences they valued at school. During these individual sessions, the children used a range of modes or assemblage of modes to share their perspectives. At each session, white paper, crayons, markers, paints, pencils, pens, and pencil crayons were available for the children to use. The students were also provided with the option to take a photograph with an iPhone of something they valued at school. In both settings, the children engaged in drawing and painting practices at school, so these were familiar meaning-making practices to them. Using technology in the classroom for educational purposes was occasionally implemented in the Canadian context, and technology use was not evident in the Tanzanian setting; however, the Canadian and Tanzanian children who chose to take photographs all skillfully manipulated the iPhone. The use of mobile phones as a tool of communication was evident in both cultures as I observed families using their mobile phones as they dropped off and picked up their children from school. I also observed the children competently use their parents' phones.

The data from the first year of the study revealed both groups of children's use of oral language, print and symbols, drawing, painting, photography, and gesture to represent their valued school experiences. In the Canadian context, 12 of the 14 research participants shared the value they placed on engaging in imaginative and collaborative outdoor play with their peers. The other two children chose to create texts that focused on indoor play with their classmates. Themes related to play, friendship, autonomy, and flexible learning environments were prevalent throughout all the multimodal texts created by the Canadian children. Figure 34.1 is a Canadian child's depiction of his most valued school based experience.

In the Canadian site, the children frequently mentioned their interest in the outdoors and their physical surroundings, and the importance of collaborative play. The kindergarten

Figure 34.1 Lorenzo's painting of himself and his peers on the playground

Explanation: "I made a picture of me, my brother, and Kai (classmate). We're on the swings on the little playground. It's good because it's sunny outside and you can see the trees and mountains. I like playing outside because you can do what you want with your friends – like building forts to keep away bad guys."

teacher's pedagogical beliefs and practices were grounded in the importance of play, particularly outdoor play that was unstructured and exploratory. This approach to learning aligns with the most recent reiteration of the British Columbia Ministry of Education Language Arts kindergarten curriculum (2016) that addresses the importance of play-based experiences and utilising natural outdoor learning environments. As I engaged with the children outside, it was evident that the topography of the playground and forest enabled them to be imaginative and collaborative meaning-makers. For example, they developed original games, made forts and bridges with tree branches and rocks, and made food for small animals with leaves, pine cones, flowers, and moss.

In the Tanzanian context, 9 of the 14 children stated that playing outside with their peers was what they valued most at school. Three children mentioned that eating a snack together was what they valued during their school day. One child shared that she liked practicing her English letters in her journal and had written the English vowels at the top of her drawing, and another child chose not to speak about her school experiences. Instead, that child shared how her aunt had recently moved in with her family, as her mother was very ill. She decided to draw a picture of her aunt cooking and cleaning in their home, and selling *mandazi* (fried dough) in a stall in the neighbourhood market. Figure 34.2 is a Tanzanian child's portrayal of snack time at school.

Based on my observations, the Tanzanian children's outdoor time during school hours was teacher-directed. However, the children also engaged in informal outdoor learning experiences (for approximately 15–20 minutes before or after school), where I observed the children play pick-up football, help water the flowers in the school's garden, and climb on the playground equipment. The children's snack time was also not considered by the teacher to be a formal part of the school day.

In the Tanzanian dataset, the children's explanations of their valued school experiences largely focused on outdoor collaborative play, interacting with their local environment and vegetation, playing football together, and engaging in communal eating where they were able to informally chat with one another. These findings represent a disconnect between the learning objectives outlined in the Tanzanian curriculum. In 2016, the Tanzanian Ministry of Education, Science, Technology and Vocational Training updated the nation's curriculum to emphasise "the 3Rs – focused on the development of basic skills and competences in reading, writing, and arithmetic" (p. 1). Additional areas of focus in the curriculum include developing skills in Kiswahili, English, science, and information and communication technology. Although the culture of schooling in Tanzania is based on a traditional model of learning, as mandated and practiced by the teachers, the children's valued experiences were strongly associated with learning experiences that enabled them to engage in self-directed learning and collaborative play in a natural, flexible learning environment.

At the conclusion of the first year of the study, the Canadian children and I discussed how we could share their multimodal texts and local school environments with their global peers. We decided to make two books using a book-making app that featured the children's school environments and valued school experiences in both contexts. The books included images of the children, their texts, their schools, and the children's outdoor play spaces. The book that featured the Tanzanian children was a dual-language book in English and Kiswahili. These books were shared with the children in both research sites.

As the Canadian children read the books, many of them asked specific questions about their Tanzanian peers' school worlds (e.g., Do they have a library? Can they bring their own snack from home?). Additionally, some of the Canadian children shared their surprise at the physical beauty of the Tanzanian schools and the artistic abilities of the children, as

Figure 34.2 Sarah's drawing of the cups and water cooler in the corridor outside of her classroom

Explanation: "I like having water, tea, and bread with my friends. It's nice because we can talk and laugh, and we get a break from schoolwork."

this seemed to contradict their perceptions of African children's surroundings and capabilities. As a group, we discussed the different UNICEF and World Vision commercials they had seen on television that portray African children as helpless and in dire need of support. This resulted in a conversation focused on the concept of generalisations and stereotypes, which seemed to resonate with the children. Overall, the research process in the first year of the study seemed to broaden the children's worldviews, their understanding of diversity and commonalities, and the Canadian children's perspectives on school cultures in other parts of the world.

In the second year of the study, I engaged in the same type of data collection methods in both contexts. Once again, I asked the children to share their valued school-based experiences to see if any changes were evident. In the Canadian dataset, the same 12 participants created multimodal texts that focused on their play in the forest, on the soccer pitch, and on

Figure 34.3 Siena's painting of herself and her brother playing soccer at recess

Explanation: "I like playing soccer outside with my brother. He's older, his name is Max. I like going in the forest too and playing with Denna [classmate]. It's fun outside because there's lots of things to do and I really like seeing my brother."

the playground. The other two children once again shared their interest in indoor-based learning experiences. Unlike the children's first year of school, when they were enrolled in the same class, the children were placed in four different Grade 1 classrooms in the second year of the study.

Based on my observations, and through conversations with the children's teachers, the children's Grade 1 year was not as play-based, and although outdoor learning occurred, it was not a primary focus of the learning program. The children's continued interest in out-door play, developing social relationships, and having autonomy and choice once again revealed the significance these participants placed on their sense of freedom at school when engaged in outdoor play with peers. Louv (2005) contended that when children engage with the outdoors and natural playscapes, "they find freedom, fantasy, and privacy – they are in a place distant from the adult world, a separate peace" (p. 7).

In the Tanzanian setting, significant differences in the children's valued school experiences were evident in the second year of the research. For example, 12 of the 14 children shared that playing outdoors with their peers was what they valued most at school. The same analysis techniques were used when examining the Tanzanian children's texts, and the dominant themes that emerged from the data continued to link to autonomy, collaboration and social relationships, and the importance of outdoor play. The other two children created drawings and shared stories centered on valuing traditional practices, such as copying letters from the blackboard. Similar to the Canadian children, the messages embedded in the Tanzanian children's texts linked to voice and power, and were connected to experiences that allowed them to engage in self-directed learning, further develop their social relationships, and engage in collaborative outdoor play.

In the second year of the study, the Canadian children and I discussed how we could share their multimodal texts in a different way. I specifically talked to the children about the possibility of displaying their work at a national art gallery. When I received approval to host an opening reception at the Gordon Smith Gallery of Canadian Art in North Vancouver, and have the children's work displayed in a subsequent two-week showing, I decided to pair the Canadian and Tanzanian children so they would have specific partners as the research continued. I created the partnerships based on my familiarity with the children and their similar valued interests. A videographer was also hired by the school district to document and create a short film of the opening event, which I shared with the Tanzanian children and their teachers on my next visit to East Africa.

Figure 34.4 Peter's drawing of the school playground

Explanation: "I like playing outside on the playground and going on the swings. I also like running around outside with my friends."

Following the public viewing of their work, the Canadian children began to ask detailed personal questions about their partner (e.g., Does Edith have brothers or sisters? What kind of house does Najma live in? Do the children in Tanzania have backyards at their homes?). It was evident that the children were interested in learning more about their partners' lives to develop a more holistic understanding of each other's worlds. These inquiries led to the research taking a new trajectory that focused on the children's lives outside of school.

In the third year of the study, I continued to visit the Canadian children's school on a regular basis, and before I returned to Tanzania for my third visit, the Canadian children created multimodal texts as gifts for their Tanzanian partners. Each text represented what mattered most to the Canadian children outside of school. During the individual sessions with the Canadian children, the data revealed a commonality across their drawings and paintings that focused primarily on their families. In addition, the children also created self-portraits and images of their homes and backyards (see Figures 34.5–34.7).

I shared the Canadian children's multimodal texts and their explanations of the texts with the Tanzanian children when I visited their primary school. One of the Tanzanian children, Fiaz, who was confident with his English abilities, told me to tell the Canadian children, "We love you, and we like your pictures." This process also provoked the Tanzanian students to ask personal questions about the Canadian children (e.g., Do they like playing with their brothers and sisters and cousins? Do they wear uniforms to school?). During my visits

Figure 34.5 William's drawing of his home and backyard

Explanation: "I want Blessing [Tanzanian partner] to see my house and backyard. So I made a picture of my house and the road in front. In the backyard, I have a basketball net and we have spikeball too, and a trampoline. I also made the ladder that goes to my neighbour's yard."

Figure 34.6 Angelica's drawing of her and her baby brother

Explanation: "I made a picture of me and my baby brother Roman. He is 6 months old and just ate an avocado for the first time. That's what I ate for the first time as a baby. Can you tell Azfa [Tanzanian partner] that my brother is almost crawling? He is starting to make sounds and talk too!"

with the Tanzanian children over the course of two weeks, I also shared the video of the art exhibit with them, which they requested to watch several times.

Findings

This research project, guided by Articles 12 and 13 of the United Nations Convention on the Rights of the Child (UNESCO, 1989), and global citizenship education (Davies, Evans, and Reid, 2005), focused on developing an understanding of children's perspectives on their valued school-based learning experiences in two diverse international contexts. In this study, the children's use of multimodal methods to share their valued experiences in their local, sociocultural worlds revealed more commonalities than differences. As revealed in the data, the importance of relationships and collaborative outdoor play were overarching valued experiences across both contexts. A more critical analysis of their texts centred on themes linked to power, autonomy, and choice. Additional key findings from the project revealed the disconnect between the traditional practices (e.g., reading, arithmetic) that the Tanzanian children participated in during the majority of their school day and the learning experiences they chose as meaningful.

In the Canadian context, a significant finding was the evolution of the children's perceptions of their Tanzanian peers as they began to view their partners as skilled artists who had significant things to say in regard to their school experiences. This revelation appeared to disrupt their beliefs

Figure 34.7 Taya's self-portrait

Explanation: "I made a picture of myself. I wanted to make it life-size so Najma [Tanzanian partner] will know what I look like in real life. What do you think she will think of my hair? It's a different colour and it's long, so it's a bit different from hers. I hope she likes it. I hope she's still at the school too because sometimes kids move. If she isn't there, I don't want another partner, I only want Najma as a partner, even if she's at another school in Tanzania."

and perceptions of sub-Saharan African children's lives and abilities. Providing the 28 children with opportunities to share their views on their lived experiences, particularly at school, seemed to provide them with a sense of empowerment and enabled them to see themselves as citizens who matter and have a voice. This research also provided insight on how a longitudinal comparative case study, framed by the UN Convention on the Rights of the Child, and a global citizenship education perspective, has the potential to provide a model for educators and researchers on how young children can develop cross-cultural insights and relationships with international peers.

Conclusion

The contributions of this study are extensive in relation to adding to the knowledge base in the fields of early childhood education, children's rights, cross-cultural studies, ethnography, and global citizenship education. In addition, this research has also contributed to the field methodologically by highlighting young children's capabilities to contribute to research projects in which they are involved (Dahlberg, Moss, and Pence, 2007). This occurred by positioning the children as powerful experts on their lives, and as capable and creative meaning-makers.

In conclusion, this study provides significant insight on young children's perspectives on their complex lives and experiences in two diverse international settings. Additionally, this project provides a conceptual framework for the ways educators and researchers can implement global partnerships with children to develop cross-cultural understandings, and outlines how educators and researchers can draw on the UN Convention on the Rights of the Child (UNESCO, 1989) in ways that are meaningful and relevant to children to enhance their knowledge and sense of global citizenship.

Based on the project's findings, the following recommendations could be considered when engaging in rights-based, participatory research with children in international settings: (i) children develop norms, values, attitudes, and behaviours early in life; therefore, young children's participation in international collaborations has the potential to develop children's cross-cultural understandings and disrupt stereotypes and essentialist views; (ii) children have the capacity to share their views in multiple ways and should be afforded this right as they have the ability to transform and reorient worldviews; and (iii) societies depend on schools to introduce meaningful models of learning; thus, engaging in cross-cultural learning with children from the onset of their formal education is a social investment on a global scale that may impact future generations.

References

British Columbia Ministry of Education. 2016. *Elementary English language arts curriculum.* Retrieved from: https://curriculum.gov.bc.ca/curriculum/english-language-arts/core/introduction.

Clark, Alison. 2005. "Ways of seeing: Using the mosaic approach to listen to young children." In *Beyond listening: Children's perspectives on early childhood services*, edited by Alison Clark, Trine Kjørholt, and Peter Moss, 29–50. Bristol, UK: The Policy Press.

Corbin, Juliet, and Anselm Strauss. 2008. *Basics of qualitative research: Techniques and procedures for developing grounded theory.* Thousand Oaks, CA: Sage.

Dahlberg, Gunilla, Peter Moss, and Alan Pence. 2007. *Beyond quality in early childhood education and care: Languages of evaluation*, 2nd ed. London, UK: Falmer Press.

Davies, Ian, Mark Evans, and Alan Reid. 2005. "Globalizing citizenship education? A critique of global education and citizenship education." *British Journal of Educational Studies* 53:66–89. doi:10.1111/j.1467-8527.2005.00284.x

Denzin, Norman K. 2001. *Interpretive interactionism*, 2nd ed. Thousand Oaks, CA: Sage.

Dill, Jeffrey S. 2013. *The longings and limits of global citizenship education: The moral pedagogy of schooling in a cosmopolitan age.* New York, NY: Routledge.

Dockett, Sue, Johanna Einarsdottir, and Bob Perry. 2009. "Researching with children: Ethical tensions." *Journal of Early Childhood Research* 7:283–98. doi:10.1177/1476718X09336971

Dyson, Anne Haas. 2003. *Brothers and sisters learn to write: Popular literacies in childhood and school cultures.* New York: Teachers College Press.

Fine, Gary Alan, and Kent L. Sandstrom. 1988. *Knowing children: Participant observation with minors.* Qualitative Research Methods Series 15. London: Sage.

Freeman, Michael. 1995. "Children's rights in a land of rites." In *The handbook of children's rights*, edited by Bob Franklin, 70–88. London: Routledge.

Goren, Heela, and Miri Yemini. 2016. "Global citizenship education in context: Teacher perceptions at an international school and a local Israeli school." *Compare: A Journal of Comparative and International Education* 46:832–853. doi:10.1080/03057925.2015.1111752

Goren, Heela, and Miri Yemini. 2017. "Global citizenship education redefined – A systematic review of empirical studies on global citizenship education." *International Journal of Educational Research* 82:170–83. doi:10.1016/j.ijer.2017.02.004

Hardman, Charlotte. 1973. "Can there be an anthropology of childhood?" *Journal of the Anthropological Society of Oxford* 4:85–99.

James, Allison, Chris Jenks, and Alan Prout. 1998. *Theorizing childhood.* Cambridge, UK: Polity Press.

Kendrick, Maureen. 2003. *Converging worlds: Play, literacy, and culture in early childhood.* Bern: Peter Lang.

Kendrick, Maureen. 2016. *Literacy and multimodality across global sites.* New York: Routledge.

Kerr, David. 2002. "Citizenship education: An international comparison across sixteen countries." *International Journal of Social Education* 17:1–15.

Kress, Gunther. 1997. *Before writing: Rethinking the paths to literacy.* London: Routledge.

Kress, Gunther. 2003. *Literacy in the new media age*. London: Routledge.

Kroes, Geneviève. 2009. *Aboriginal youth in Canada: Emerging issues, research priorities, and policy*. Report of the roundtable on Aboriginal youth workshop report. Canadian Policy Research Initiative. Retrieved from: http://publications.gc.ca/collections/collection_2009/policyresearch/PH4-50-2009E.pdf

Louv, Richard. 2005. *Last child in the woods: Saving our children from nature-deficit disorder*. Chapel Hill, NC: Algonquin Books.

Luke, Allan. 2012. "Critical literacy: Foundational notes." *Theory Into Practice* 51:4–11. doi:10.1080/00405841.2012.636324

McTavish, Marianne, Jodi Streelasky, and Linda Coles. 2012. "Listening to children's voices: Children as participants in research." *International Journal of Early Childhood* 44:249–67. doi:10.1007/s13158-012-0068-8

Melton, Gary. 2005. "Treating children like people: A framework for research and advocacy." *Journal of Clinical Child and Adolescent Psychology* 34:646–57. doi:10.1207/s15374424jccp3404_7

Moll, Luis, and James Greenberg. 1990. "Creating zones of possibilities: Combining social contexts for instruction." In *Vygotsky and education: Instructional implications and applications of sociohistorical psychology*, edited by Luis Moll, 319–48. Cambridge, UK: Cambridge University Press.

Morphy, Howard, and Marcus Banks. 1997. *Rethinking visual anthropology*. New Haven, CT: Yale University Press.

Noblit, George W., Susana Y. Flores, and Enrique G. Murillo, eds. 2004. *Postcritical ethnography: An introduction*. Cresskil, NJ: Hampton.

Oxfam. 2015. *Global citizenship in the classroom: A guide for teachers*. Oxford, UK: Oxfam International.

Pence, Alan, and Hollie Hix-Small. 2007. "Global children in the shadow of the global child." *International Journal of Educational Policy, Research, and Practice* 8:83–100.

Pence, Alan, and Bame Nsamenang. 2008. *A case for early childhood development in sub-Saharan Africa Working Paper No. 51*. The Hague, The Netherlands: Bernard van Leer Foundation.

Peters, Sally, and Janette Kelly. 2011. "Exploring children's perspectives: Multiple ways of seeing and knowing the child." *Waikato Journal of Education Te Hautaka Mātauranga O Waikato* 16:19–30.

Resnik, Julia. 2009. "Multicultural education – Good for business but not for the state? The IB curriculum and global capitalism." *British Journal of Educational Studies* 57:217–44. doi:10.1111/j.1467-8527.2009.00440.x

Rose, Gillian. 2001. *Visual methodologies*. London, UK: Sage.

Schweisfurth, Michele. 2006. "Education for global citizenship: Teacher agency and curricular structure in Ontario schools." *Educational Review* 58:41–50. doi:10.1080/00131910500352648

Smith, Anne B. 2016. *Children's rights: Towards social justice*. New York, NY: Momentum.

Stake, Robert. 1978. "The case study method in social inquiry." *Educational Researcher* 7:5–8.

Stake, Robert. 2006. *Multiple case study analysis*. New York: Guildford Press.

Stein, Pippa. 2008. *Multimodal pedagogies in diverse classrooms*. London, UK: Routledge.

Thomas, David R. 2006. "A general inductive approach for analyzing qualitative evaluation data." *American Journal of Evaluation* 27:237–46. doi:10.1177/1098214005283748

UNESCO. 1989. *United Nations convention on the rights of the child*. Paris, France: United Nations Educational, Scientific, and Cultural Organization.

UNESCO. 2014a. *Global citizenship education: Preparing learners for the challenges of the 21st century*. Paris, France: United Nations Educational, Scientific, and Cultural Organization.

UNESCO. 2014b. *Teaching respect for all*. Paris, France: United Nations Educational, Scientific, and Cultural Organization.

UNESCO. 2015. *Global citizenship education: Topics and learning objectives*. Paris, France: United Nations Educational, Scientific, and Cultural Organization.

The United Republic of Tanzania Ministry of Education, Science, Technology, and Vocational Training. 2016. *Curriculum for basic education: Standard I and II*. Dar es Salaam, Tanzania: Tanzania Institute of Education.

Vygotsky, Lev. 1978. *Mind in society: The development of higher psychological processes*. Cambridge, MA: Harvard University Press.

Yin, Robert. 1994. *Case study research: Design and methods*, 2nd ed. Beverly Hills, CA: Sage.

Zhao, Yong. 2010. "Preparing globally competent teachers: A new imperative for teacher education." *Journal of Teacher Education* 61:422–31. doi:10.1177/0022487110375802

35

CHILDREN'S PERSPECTIVES ON BELONGING IN ICELANDIC PRESCHOOLS

Johanna Einarsdottir and Sara M. Ólafsdóttir

Introduction and context

The Nordic countries have established social welfare and educational policies in regard to childhood and early education, often named the Nordic model or the social democratic model. This model includes, among other features, access to full-day early childhood programs during the years before children begin school, regardless of their family's income or parental employment. Behind these policies lie democratic values such as solidarity, civil rights, equity, and equality (Broström, Einarsdottir, and Samuelsson, 2018).

In Iceland, preschools are regarded as the first level of education, with almost all children attending preschool from the age of 2 until they start primary school in the fall of the year they turn 6. Governance of the education system is administered by both national and local authorities. The Ministry of Education, Science and Culture is responsible for implementing legislation, formulating educational policy, and publishing the national curriculum guidelines (Ministry of Education, Science and Culture, 2011). At the local level, municipalities take responsibility for preschools, most of which they oversee and operate.

The early childhood education curriculum guidelines in the Nordic countries illustrate both philosophy and practice and reflect the values of the society (Einarsdottir, Purola, Johansson, Broström, and Emilson, 2015). Democracy as a fundamental value is spelled out in the early childhood policy documents in all the Nordic countries. Democracy is presented as having two dimensions: being and becoming. Children are considered democratic beings, with an emphasis not only on allowing children to experience democracy in their preschool settings, but also on educating children to become democratic citizens. The other dimension concerns the relationship between the individual and the collective, wherein cooperation and children's rights to participation are emphasized. Another important concept in the Nordic curricula is care, which has two dimensions: care as fulfillment of basic needs and care as an ethical relationship. Care and learning are integrated in the curricula, which recognizes the social, emotional, and cognitive aspects of learning and well-being. Play also has a central role in Nordic ECE philosophy and practice; indeed, in Iceland the term play-school (*leikskóli*) is used to refer to all group-care services for children before starting compulsory school (Ministry of Education, Science and Culture, 2011).

The first decades of the new millennium have been characterized by social change, with major impacts on the education systems in the Nordic countries and elsewhere. These changes include globalization, immigration, marketization, neoliberalism, digitization, and increasing demands for accountability and standardized assessment (Broström et al., 2018). In the Western world, forces emphasizing accountability, evidence-based teaching methods, and standardized assessment to determine whether or not children have met particular learning objectives have become more conspicuous in recent years. The Organisation for Economic Co-operation and Development (OECD) cross-national assessment of early learning outcomes among 4- and 5-year-old children reflects this development (Moss et al., 2016; Moss and Urban, 2018). There are indicators that these trends are affecting the play-based ECE practices in Iceland and the other Nordic countries by shifting from play and holistic child-centered practices toward more structured and formalized teaching in preschools (Broström et al., 2018; Einarsdottir, 2019).

In recent years, immigration has dramatically affected Iceland, a country that was largely homogenous just a few decades ago. In 1998, only 3.1 percent of preschool children had a mother tongue other than Icelandic. In 2016, the number was up to 12.6 percent (Statistics Iceland, 2018). In the city of Reykjavik, where the present study was conducted, 18.9 percent of preschool children are of non-dominant Icelandic backgrounds. In some preschools, including the one in which the current study was conducted, the presence of children with a background other than Icelandic is around 50 percent. In the wake of substantial social changes and increasing diversity in the population of Iceland during a short period of time, the purpose of this chapter is to shed light on how the play-based Icelandic preschool and the values presented in the national curriculum guidelines support children's belonging in preschool.

The current study

The aim of the current study is to advance knowledge about children's belonging in preschool by engaging with a group of 5- and 6-year-old preschool children of diverse racial, ethnic, and linguistic backgrounds. In times of increasing migration and globalization in the Nordic countries, children's daily environments are becoming increasingly diverse. Therefore, research on children's belonging has become more topical than ever. In democratic societies, we see it as a crucial value that every child has the right to experience belonging, to be valued equally and with respect (Juutinen, Puroila, and Johansson, 2018; NordForsk, 2018).

Theoretical background

This study brings together the multidisciplinary field of childhood studies and the politics of belonging in the context of Icelandic early childhood education.

Childhood studies

Childhood studies can be traced to the last decades of the previous century when new ideas were emerging in the field of early childhood education. Early scholarship in the field presented views of childhood as a social construction instead of a universal experience and recognized the importance of the social and cultural context in which the child lives (James and Prout, 1997; Jenks, 1982; Qvortrup, 1994). Childhood studies places an emphasis on the being child of the present over the becoming child of the future. Children's voices and agency are privileged, as are their strengths and competence to influence their surroundings. They are seen as contributing members of society and experts on their own lives, with opinions that should be heard and considered (Hanson, 2017; Qvortrup, Corsaro, and Honig, 2009).

The UN Convention on the Rights of the Child added to the conceptual transformation regarding how children and childhood are viewed (United Nations, 1989). The Convention raised awareness of the agency of children and their place in society, and as a result children's rights and citizenship became an international focus. General Comment No. 7 (United Nations, 2005) addresses in particular the rights of young children under the age of 8. This convention established an important foundation for children's rights to participate in research, although it does not specifically mention research (Alderson, 2012). Hence, both the children's rights movement and childhood studies share intersecting interests and visions in which children's status as human beings and their place in society are reconsidered (Alanen, 2011; Quennerstedt and Quennerstedt, 2014).

Politics of belonging

The concept of belonging has been analyzed from different perspectives in the literature. Yuval-Davis (2006) draws attention to the distinction between belonging on a personal level – the *sense of belonging* – and belonging on a broader level – the *politics of belonging*. Sense of belonging refers to an individual's emotional attachment to other individuals and communities. Politics of belonging highlights that belonging involves ethical and political values, as well as power relations through which boundaries between individuals and groups are constructed. Thus, politics of belonging refers to how belonging operates between people and their environments, taking a collective rather than an individual approach to belonging and accounting for both belonging and exclusion (Juutinen, 2018; Juutinen et al., 2018; Sumsion and Wong, 2011; Yuval-Davis, 2006). In a similar vein, Press and colleagues explain belonging within the early childhood setting as mainly about relationships: connections with people, places, and things inside and outside the ECE setting, including the community and, more broadly, society (Press, Woodrow, Logan, and Mitchell, 2018, p. 4).

The current study relates to the ideology of politics of belonging in two ways: in understanding belonging and exclusion as relational rather than individual phenomena, and in defining belonging as a process of inclusion and exclusion among children in their everyday preschool practice (NordForsk, 2018). This view recognizes the importance of the diverse and dynamic relationships among people, places, and things in the preschool community and broader society. Belonging is also seen as closely related to the concepts of participation and democracy (Juutinen, 2018; Juutinen et al., 2018).

Methodology

The development of childhood studies and the children's rights movement in the past decades has highlighted the importance of incorporating and respecting children's perspectives in research as well as in everyday life. In this study, we regard children's participation as a process that involves children in matters that affect them. The role of the researchers in this participatory process is to listen, respond, and incorporate the children's perspectives on these matters (Breathnach, Danby, and O'Gorman, 2018).

The study was conducted with the oldest children (5- and 6-year-olds) in one preschool in Reykjavik. The preschool has 54 children in three age-divided classrooms. The preschool was chosen because of the diversity among the children. For 60 percent of the children, either one or both parents had a mother tongue other than Icelandic. Nine children participated in the study. Daníel, Ása, Harald and Lisa had both parents Icelandic. Adam's parents were from Lithuania, Ami's parents were from Latvia, Sofia's parents were from Ghana, and Christian's parents had come from the Philippines. Thomas had one parent with Icelandic background and another parent from Portugal.

After gaining consent from gatekeepers – the preschool authorities, the preschool director, the parents, and the preschool educators – the children were informed about what it might involve to participate in the study, as well as their right to withdraw from the research (Dockett, Einarsdottir, and Perry, 2012; Dockett, Perry, and Kearney, 2013). The study was introduced to the children through an informational leaflet in which the study was explained through pictures, and a short text clarified what was involved in the study. The researcher went through the leaflet with individual children, and each participant agreed by writing their names. All the children with permission from their parents agreed to participate. Their anonymity is protected by pseudonyms.

We tried to reduce the power inequality between the children and the researcher by conducting the study in the preschool context, which was a familiar and non-threatening environment for the children. We got to know the children and built mutual trust by making frequent visits to the preschool before the data construction began. We tried to reach out to diverse children in order to represent a multiplicity of voices, since children's experiences and perspectives are likely to vary considerably (Einarsdottir and Egilsson, 2016; Tisdall, 2012). With that goal in mind, we recruited a preschool with a diverse demographic makeup.

Methods and analysis

Data-gathering included individual interviews that were built on photographs that the children had taken, as well as group interviews. After a month of participant observations in the preschool, the researcher invited the children individually to show her around the preschool by taking a walking tour with a tablet computer. The children took photos with the tablets, which then served as a stimulus for the conversations that followed. This method was chosen because taking photographs can be an interesting and inviting way for children to participate in research; it can offer insights that may not be evident from other data, promote different kinds of discussion, highlight taken-for-granted elements in the lives of participants, and position the photographer as the expert in discussions of the photos (Dockett, Einarsdottir, and Perry, 2017; Rose, 2016).

For the most part, the individual conversations with the children who were not native Icelandic speakers were both short and not very rich, as their vocabulary was limited. We therefore decided to conduct group interviews as well, meeting with two to four children together at a time. During the group interviews, the children were invited to draw pictures from the preschool while they talked together and with the researcher. As the children drew, the researcher focused on listening to the children and paying attention to their narratives and interpretations (Einarsdottir, Dockett, and Perry, 2009).

The interviews were audiotaped and transcribed verbatim. Data were coded and analyzed in five separate but interrelated steps or phases (see Braun and Clarke, 2006). Analysis was conducted separately by the two researchers. The data were coded openly and systematically to identify themes, but the theoretical framework of the study was also kept in mind. To manage the coding process, the qualitative data analysis software ATLAS.ti was used for coding and categorizing. The first phase consisted of closely reading and rereading the data and writing notes. The second phase involved identifying segments of the data, examining the frequency of words, and generating initial codes generated. In the third phase, these codes were sorted and combined into overarching themes. The fourth phase consisted of reviewing and refining the themes, looking at how they support the data and the overarching theoretical perspective, and figuring out the overall story they tell. The fifth phase consisted of the final writing. In the presentation of the findings, direct quotations and descriptions are provided to afford readers an opportunity to evaluate to what extent the analysis and the researchers' interpretations reflect the data and reality.

Findings: what does belonging in the preschool community mean for children?

When the interview data were analyzed and interpreted regarding children's views on the conditions for belonging, several interconnected themes became visible. The photos the children took on the tablets when they walked around the preschool also give a picture of what it means for the children to belong in the preschool community. There was not much difference between the views of the children with dominant Icelandic identities and those with non-dominant Icelandic identities when it came to conditions for belonging in the preschool setting. The data were reduced into four main themes: (a) friendship; (b) participation; (c) solidarity; and (d) sense of identity.

Friendship

Friendship with other children and positive interactions with peers was the overarching theme in the dataset. According to all the children, having friends and positive relations with peers was vital for experiencing belonging in preschool, a finding that other studies have also shown (Einarsdottir, 2011, 2014a; Sheridan and Samuelsson, 2001). This theme does not come as a surprise, as early childhood settings are spaces where young children often form their first friendships and negotiate the connections that make up relationships (Parry, 2018).

When the children walked with the tablets around the preschool, they took many pictures of other children, and when they talked about the photos it was obvious that being a part of the group and having friends was very important to them. All the children said they had friends in preschool. Adam, for instance, took many photos of other children and explained that they were all his friends. He was then asked if all the children in preschool were friends:

R: You took many pictures – are all the children in preschool friends?
Adam: No.
R: Are not all the children friends?
Adam: No.
R: What does it mean to be a friend?
Adam: I don't know – just something.
R: What do you do when you are friends?
Adam: Just being a friend.

Participation

Politics of belonging refers to how belonging operates between people and their environments, and includes both belonging and exclusion (Juutinen et al., 2018; Yuval-Davis, 2006). The findings illustrate that for all the children, being able to participate and being included in activities with other children were important conditions for belonging. It was most painful for them if they were not accepted by the group and did not have friends to play with. Many of the children stated explicitly how difficult it was if someone was excluded and not allowed to participate in group play.

Adam did not always feel good in preschool and said that sometimes he would prefer to stay at home rather than come to preschool. Although he took many pictures of other children and explained that they were his friends because he played with them, he explained that not all the children in the preschool were friends. He also said that while he was often allowed to participate in play, other times he was excluded and not allowed to participate in play, as the following example illustrates:

R: Are you always allowed to join?
Adam: Not always. Sometimes they say: I cannot take part. – You cannot participate – sometimes.

    …

R: How do you feel when you are not allowed to join the play?
Adam: Not well.

The children that participated in the study said that they helped each other out or found solutions to their problems by themselves. They did not mention the educators; they were not part of the discussion about what the children would do if they were excluded or hurt. This is in line with Juutinen's (2018) study, which indicated that "constructing belonging verbally often emerged among friends; the educators were not part of it" (p. 28). However, the findings run counter to a recent Icelandic study where the children said that they needed the educators' support when dealing with challenging situations such as exclusion. They often told the educators and got support if they were excluded from their peer group (Ólafsdóttir and Einarsdottir, 2017). One reason why the children in the present study depended more on themselves than the educators could be that they are the oldest children in the preschool, which means they have had time to create mutual trust in the peer group and are becoming more competent in social relations. The findings of the current study resonate with the Icelandic national curriculum guidelines for preschools (Ministry of Education, Science and Culture, 2011). These guidelines indicate that preschool children should be competent social actors who are able to deal with challenges in a diverse society, stating, "Preschool practices should encourage children to show respect and concern for other people, develop feelings of solidarity, consideration and friendship" (p. 33).

Gender, age, and common interests were important issues for children's belonging, but at first sight ethnicity did not seem to play an important role in this group, where approximately 50 percent of the children had Icelandic identities and 50 percent non-Icelandic identities. When asked who their friends were, the children named friends of the same age and gender and those who had the same interests. Harald said, for instance, that the best thing about preschool was that Daniel was going to soccer practice with him. The discussion below describes a telling moment from a conversation with Daniel. He was hesitant and needed to stop and think when he was asked if all the children in the preschool were alike or different. He then explained that he and his friend Adam looked different but they were friends all the same:

Daniel: I and Harald are a bit alike.
R: Why are you alike?
Daniel: I don't know.
R: Are any of the other children different?
Daniel: I am thinking.
Daniel: I and Adam are very different … we are a bit different although we are friends.
R: How are you different?
Daniel: But I and my brother Jon are very much alike.
R: Yes.
Daniel: Although he – although he has darker hair than I. He has brown but I have red hair.
R: Yes.
Daniel: And my big brother he has more red hair than I.

When examining the data further and looking closer, it became evident that when the children talked about their *best friend*, ethnic identity was identified as an important component as power relations were unveiled. Then the group was split into two: native Icelandic-speaking children and children whose home languages were other than Icelandic. That is, Icelandic children's best friends were those of dominant Icelandic identity, and the children with non-dominant identities had best friends who had non-dominant identities. A plausible reason for this could be the alignment and/or misalignment of language and cultural practices. Zachrisen (2018) found in her study that it was challenging for children of different cultural and linguistic backgrounds to play together. This was especially the case in symbolic and imaginative play. The children who have dominant Icelandic backgrounds share common cultural values, language practices, and knowledge of play activities which can lead to the exclusion of children with non-dominant Icelandic backgrounds, as Thordardottir (2018) found in her study.

Solidarity

There was a clear sign of solidarity among the children who participated in the study. They showed empathy toward each other and sympathized with children who were in some way or another left out. They seemed to be very much aware of how difficult it was for a child to be excluded from the group, and some of them mentioned what they did or would do if someone was hurt and left out. Harald explained that sometimes children were excluded from play, and if that happened the others tried to be nice to them and comfort them. He gave an example of when a group of children made fun of Daniel:

R: How do you think Daniel felt then?
Harald: Not well, he started to cry … He said everyone was bad in preschool except for me and Adam.
R: What can you do when someone feels so unhappy?
Harald: You console him.
R: How did you do that?
Harald: I console him by saying something and hug him – somehow.

During a group interview, three children discussed friendship and incidents when a child had hurt another child. They reminded each other of the incident and explained what they would do or could do to console a child that had been excluded or hurt:

Asa: Once there was boys – boys who were teasing … Remember Sofia?
R: How did you feel then?
Asa: Not well. Ari was the most bad.…
R: But what do you do if someone is teasing and hurting other children?
Asa: Then I will console.
R: Yes.
Asa: I always console when someone cries. I say ooh and start to console them.

Both Asa and Harald have dominant Icelandic backgrounds. That is, they are proficient communicators in Icelandic language. They were able to verbalize what it meant to be a friend and explain what they did if someone was excluded in Icelandic without prompting or support. Sofia, on the other hand, is an emergent bilingual who speaks English at home with her family and Icelandic in school. She did not have the vocabulary to explain what she would do to show empathy and support in Icelandic, and therefore explained by hugging the girls who sat next to her.

Identity

In their conversations and when taking pictures around the preschool, some of the children attempted to position themselves and indicate their distinctness within the community of preschool, which can be regarded as their way of showing their belonging in the preschool setting. During group interviews, discussions about similarities and differences – different languages, countries, ethnicities, characteristics, and identities – seemed to unravel. During one group interview, four children with different backgrounds were drawing pictures of themselves when they began to talk about different hair and skin colors. Lisa drew a picture of herself as fair-skinned with blond hair, commenting that she likes to color her hair yellow. She said, "I have yellow hair … I love to paint my hair yellow." Thomas drew attention to his dark skin and explained that his skin was dark because he is often in Portugal. Ami, a fair-skinned boy from Latvia, obviously envied Thomas of his dark skin and said, "I am sometimes more black when I am in Latvia – sometimes." Thomas's response was, "I am never another color. Always brown."

The children also tried to position themselves in the preschool by material and ownership. One way to show that they felt at home and belonged in the preschool was to point out their own possessions when they walked around the preschool taking pictures. Many of the children took photos of their personal possessions in the preschool (e.g., artwork that they had created that was hanging on the walls). Lisa took a picture of her artwork that was hanging from a shelf and said, "This is mine." They also took photos of places that were pleasurable for them, such as the nap area, outdoor area, and art room.

This supports the findings of Juutinen et al. (2018), who found that belonging in the preschool community was not only constructed through social relations, but also in the children's relationship with the material environment. Several of the children took photos of their personal compartments in the clothing room, where their spare clothes and other personal things were kept. Some also took photos of their friends' compartments. They usually did not give much explanation as to why they chose to take these photos. However, some said the compartments were there to store their warm clothes, and others explained that they helped keep their things from getting lost. This compartment can be viewed as a transition space between the home and the preschool. This is where the children come in the morning with their parents, take off their outdoor clothes, and leave things that are not to be used during the day in the preschool. The compartments belonged to the preschool environment, but the content was their own. This is consistent with Hultman and Taguchi (2010), who have argued that children have a strong relationship with artifacts and spaces in educational settings. The material environment not only provides stable physical conditions for children's play, but also serves a powerful function in uniting and separating children.

Discussion – conclusion

In the wake of increasing globalization and substantial changes in the population of Iceland during a short period of time, this study aimed to explore the lived experiences of a group of 5- and 6-year-old preschool children and how they experience the politics of belonging in their preschool setting. Nine children with culturally, racially, ethnically, and linguistically varied backgrounds participated in the study. The theoretical standpoint of the study is the multidisciplinary field of childhood studies and the politics of belonging. Childhood studies views childhood as a social construction, privileges children's voices and agency, and assumes children have competences and rights to influence their surroundings (Qvortrup et al., 2009). The politics of belonging refers to how belonging operates between people and their environments, and involves the processes of inclusion and exclusion among children in their everyday preschool practice (Yuval-Davis, 2006).

We tried to reach out to diverse children in order to represent a multiplicity of children's voices. However, gaining access into preschool children's experiences and perspectives can be challenging – particularly for those children with non-dominant Icelandic backgrounds and limited ability to express themselves in Icelandic, as well as children who may come from a culture where it is not acceptable to talk about your feelings and experiences. Authors conducting research with, for instance, infants (Elwick, Bradley, and Sumsion, 2014; Pálmadóttir and Einarsdottir, 2016) and disabled children (Tisdall, 2012) have highlighted the challenges in understanding and interpreting the meaning-making of children who have limited verbal skills. In this study, we were aware of these variations among the children, and therefore gave them the opportunity to express themselves not only verbally through both individual and group interviews, but also through drawing and photographing. They were also invited to choose the space where they wanted to talk to the researchers. However, there is always uncertainty involved in the presentation of children's perspectives, and we as researchers can never be certain of how things appear to the child. The researchers' theoretical perspective, previous experiences, and ideological stance influence how they will understand and interpret children's actions and expressions (Pálmadóttir and Einarsdottir, 2016).

From our adult perspectives, the findings indicate that participation in the community of children was the most important condition for belonging in the preschool. All of the children mentioned that having friends and being accepted by the group was most important. This was the case for both the children with dominant Icelandic identity and the children of non-dominant Icelandic background. All the children reported that they had friends in preschool, and they mentioned children with varied backgrounds when they talked about their friends. Despite these interethnic relations, the findings suggest that belonging in preschool also involves power relations through which boundaries between individuals and groups are constructed. This became obvious when the children talked about their best friends. On that question, two groups of children emerged, containing, on the one hand, children with dominant Icelandic background and, on the other, children with non-dominant Icelandic background. Thus, best friends of the children who had dominant Icelandic backgrounds were from the Icelandic group, and likewise for the children with non-dominant Icelandic backgrounds. Those who shared a common culture, heritage, and fluency in the native language stuck together, which is consistent with recent Nordic studies (Thordardottir, 2018; Zachrisen, 2018).

In the minds of the children, belonging was not only closely related to the concepts of democracy and participation, but also to the concept of care. Being able to participate and being included in activities with the other children was an important condition for belonging, and the children obviously felt deeply for those who were excluded and not allowed to participate in play with other children. They expressed solidarity and compassion and explained what they did to comfort and console a child if they were hurt or not included in play. This is consistent with other Nordic studies which show that children are encouraged to comfort each other, show compassion for others, and pay attention when someone needs help (as cited in Johansson, Emilson, and Puroila, 2018). This finding furthermore resonates with Icelandic and Nordic educational policies, where care has been found to be an important institutional function of preschool and where one dimension of care involves the ethical and emotional relationship between the child and other people within the community (Einarsdottir et al., 2015).

The children did not mention their educators when they discussed difficult situations or times when someone was excluded. This does not mean that the educators left the children alone to deal with these problems, but more likely it reflects the Nordic preschool tradition, characterized by the free child and free play, where the educators stay in the background when children are playing and only intervene if necessary. The children seemed to have assimilated the values of care and learned from their educators (Einarsdottir, 2014b; Einarsdottir and Wagner, 2006; Markström and Halldén, 2009).

Iceland, like other Nordic countries, is facing enormous social change, including immigration, marketization, digitization, and increasing demands for accountability and standardized assessment. The population of preschool children in Iceland is becoming more diverse. In times of increasing diversity, it is important that we reach out for our new citizens, to learn from them and value their contributions. The findings from this study indicate that we can do better. The children with non-dominant backgrounds and the children with dominant Icelandic identities did not seem to integrate, although there were no signs of unfriendliness. Hence, we need to focus on the opportunities provided by being a part of a diverse group of children in preschool.

Another challenge facing early childhood education in Iceland is the push-down of formalized pedagogical approaches. This sea change has swept over early childhood settings in the Western world, and there are already signs of it in the Nordic countries (Broström et al., 2018). The findings from this study with a diverse group of preschool children indicate that relationships with people, places, and things in the preschool community are of utmost importance to the children. The findings also offer evidence of how children learn compassion and empathy for other children in a play-based preschool, indicating that if they are given the opportunity, children of different backgrounds will learn to live together. In that way, early childhood settings can contribute substantially to building more socially just societies (Sumsion and Wong, 2011). The findings support the values presented in the Icelandic national curriculum guidelines for preschools (Sumsion and Wong, 2011), and hence the national policy of early childhood education, where care and learning are integrated and the social aspect of learning and well-being is recognized.

This study is a part of the research project "Politics of belonging: Promoting children's inclusion in educational settings across borders" (NordForsk, 2018).

References

Alanen, Leena. 2011. "Editorial: Critical childhood studies?" *Childhood* 18 (2):147–150.

Alderson, Pricilla. 2012. "Right-respecting research: A commentary on 'the right to be properly researched: Research with children in a messy, real world'." *Children's Geographies* 10 (2):233–239.

Braun, Virginia, and Victoria Clarke. 2006. "Using thematic analysis in psychology." *Qualitative Research in Psychology* 3:77–101.

Breathnach, Helen, Susan Danby, and Lyndal O'Gorman. 2018. "Becoming a member of the classroom: Supporting children's participation as informants in research." *European Early Childhood Education Research Journal* 26 (3):393–406.

Broström, Stig, Johanna Einarsdottir, and Ingrid Pramling Samuelsson. 2018. "The Nordic perspective on early childhood education and care." In *International handbook of early childhood education, Springer international handbooks of education*, edited by Marilyn Fleer and Bert van Oers, 867–887. Switzerland: Springer.

Dockett, Sue, Johanna Einarsdottir, and Bob Perry. 2012. "Young children's decisions about research participation: Opting out." *International Journal of Early Years Education* 12:1–13.

Dockett, Sue, Johanna Einarsdottir, and Bob Perry. 2017. "Photo elicitation: Reflecting on multiple sites of meaning." *International Journal of Early Years Education* 25 (3):225–240. doi: 10.1080/09669760.2017.1329713.

Dockett, Sue, Berry Perry, and Emma Kearney. 2013. "Promoting children's informed assent in research participation." *International Journal of Qualitative Studies in Education* 26 (7):280–828. doi: 10.1080/09518398.2012.66289.

Einarsdottir, Johanna. 2011. "Reconstructing playschool experiences." *European Early Childhood Education Research Journal* 19 (3):389–404.

Einarsdottir, Johanna. 2014a. "Children's perspectives on play." In *Handbook of play and learning in early childhood*, edited by Elizabeth Brooker, Suzy Edwards, and Mindy Blaise, 319–329. Newbury Park, CA Sage.

Einarsdottir, Johanna. 2014b. "Children's perspectives on the role of preschool teachers." *European Early Childhood Education Research Journal* 22 (5):679–698.

Einarsdottir, Johanna. 2016. "Research with children – In retrospect." In *Just do good research. Commentary on the work and influence of Bob Perry*, edited by Sue Dockett and Amy MacDonald, 39–46. Albury: Peridot.

Einarsdottir, Johanna, Sue Dockett, and Bob Perry. 2009. "Making meaning: Children's perspectives expressed through drawings." *Early Child Development and Care* 179 (2):217–232. doi: 10.1080/03004430802666999.

Einarsdottir, Johanna, Sue Dockett, and Bob Perry. 2019. *Listening to children's advice about starting school and school age care*. London: Routledge.

Jenks, Chris. 1982. *Sociology of childhood*. London: Batsford Academic and Educational Ltd.

Einarsdottir, Johanna, and Snæfríður Thora Egilsson. 2016. "Embracing diversity in childhood studies: Methodological and practical considerations." In *Diversity: Intercultural Learning and Teaching in the Early Years*, edited by Ann Farrell and Ingrid Pramling Samuelsson, 35–53. Oxford: Oxford University Press.

Einarsdottir, Johanna, Anna-Maija Purola, Eva Johansson, Stig Broström, and Anette Emilson. 2015. "Democracy, caring and competence: Values perspectives in ECEC curricula in the Nordic countries." *International Journal of Early Years Education* 23 (1):97–114. doi: doi: 10.1080/09669760.2014.970521.

Einarsdottir, Johanna, and Judith T. Wagner, eds. 2006. *Nordic childhoods and early education: Philosophy, research, policy, and practice in Denmark, Finland, Iceland, Norway, and Sweden*. Greenwich, CT: Information Age.

Elwick, Sheena, Ben Bradley, and Jennifer Sumsion. 2014. "Infants as others: Uncertainties, difficulties and (im)possibilities in researching infants' lives." *International Journal of Qualitative Studies in Education* 27 (2):196–213.

Hanson, Karl. 2017. "Embracing the past: 'Been'. 'Being' and 'becoming' children." *Childhood* 24 (3):281–285.

Hultman, Karin, and Hillevi Lenz Taguchi. 2010. "Challenging anthropocentric analysis of visual data: A relational materialist methodological approach to educational research." *International Journal of Qualitative Studies in Education* 23 (5):525–542.

James, Allison, and Alan Prout, eds. 1997. *Constructing and reconstructing childhood: Contemporary issues in sociological study of childhood.* London: Falmer.

Jenks, Chris. 1982. *Sociology of childhood.* London: Batsford Academic and Educational Ltd.

Johansson, Eva, Anette Emilson, and Anna-Maija Puroila. 2018. "Mapping the field: What are values and values education about?" In *Values education in early childhood settings: Concepts, approaches and practices,* edited by Eva Johansson, Anette Emilson, and Anna-Maija Puroila, 13–31. Cham: Springer.

Juutinen, Jaana. 2018. "Inside or outside? Small stories about the politics of belonging in preschools." Ph. D., Faculty of Education, University of Oulu.

Juutinen, Jaana, Anna-Maija Puroila, and Eva Johansson. 2018. "'There is no room for you!' The politics of belonging in children's play situations." In *Values education in early childhood settings: Concepts, approaches and practices,* edited by Eva Johansson, Anette Emilson, and Anna-Maija Puroila, 249–264. Cham: Springer.

Markström, Ann-Marie, and Gunilla, Halldén. 2009. "Children's strategies for agency in preschool." *Children & Society* 23 (112–122).

Ministry of Education Science and Culture. 2011. "The Icelandic national curriculum guide for preschools." Retrieved October 1, 2018 from: www.stjornarradid.is/verkefni/menntamal/namskrar/.

Moss, Peter, Gunilla Dahlberg, Susan Grieshaber, Susanna Mantovani, Helen May, Alan Pence, Sylvie Rayna, Beth B. Swadener, and Michel Vandenbroeck. 2016. "The organisation for economic co-operation and development's iternational early learning study: Opening for debate and coontestation." *Contemporary Issues in Early Childhood* 17 (3):343–351.

Moss, Peter, and Mathias Urban. 2018. "The organisation for economic co-operation and development's international early learning study: What is going on." *Contemporary Issues in Early Childhood* 1–6. doi: 10.1177/1463949118803269.

NordForsk. 2018. "Politics of belonging: Promoting children's inclusion in educational settings across borders." Project number: 85644.

Ólafsdóttir, Sara, and Johanna Einarsdottir. 2017. "Þeir vilja ekki leika bara tala saman": Sýn barna á hlutverk fullorðinna í leik." *Netla – veftímarit um uppeldi og menntun.* Retrieved from http://netla.hi.is/serrit/2017/innsyn_leikskolastarf/002.pdf.

Pálmadóttir, Hrönn, and Johanna Einarsdottir. 2016. "Video observations of children's perspectives on their lived experiences: Challenges in the relations between the researcher and children." *European Early Childhood Education Research Journal* 24 (5):721–733.

Parry, John. 2018. "Making connections: Young children exploring early friendships through play." In *Young children's play and creativity: Multiple voices,* edited by Gill Goodliff, Natalie Canning, John Parry, and Linda Miller, 113–126. New York: Routledge.

Press, Frances, Christine Woodrow, Helen Logan, and Linda Mitchell. 2018. "Can we belong in a neo-liberal world? Neo-liberalism in early childhood education and care policy in Australia and New Zealand." *Contemporary Issues in Early Childhood.* doi: 10.1177/1463949118781909.

Quennerstedt, Ann, and Mikael Quennerstedt. 2014. "Researching children's rights in education: Sociology of childhood encountering educational theory." *British Journal of Sociology of Education* 35 (1):115–132.

Qvortrup, Jens. 1994. *Explorations in sociology of childhood.* Copenhagen: Sociologisk Institut Köbenhavns Universitet.

Qvortrup, Jens, William A. Corsaro, and Michael-Sebastian Honig, eds. 2009. *The Palgrave handbook of childhood studies.* London: Palgrave Macmillan.

Rose, G. 2016. *Visual methodologies: An introduction to the researching with visual materials,* 4th ed. Los Angeles, CA: Sage.

Sheridan, Sonja, and Ingrid Pramling Samuelsson. 2001. "Children's conceptions of participation and influence in pre-school: A perspective on pedagogical quality." *Contemporary Issues in Early Childhood* 2 (2):169–194.

Statistics Iceland. 2018. Retrieved December 1st from: www.statice.is/.

Sumsion, Jennifer, and Sandie Wong. 2011. "Interrogating 'belonging' in belonging, being and becoming: The early years. Learning framework for Australia." *Contemporary Issues in Early Childhood* 12 (1):12–45. doi: 10.2304/ciec.2011.12.1.28.

Thordardottir, Thordis. 2018. "Communication and respectability in two Reykjavik preschools: The role of children's literature and popular culture in peer-group stratification." In *Diversity and social justice in early childhood education: Nordic perspectives.*, edited by Anette Hellman and Kirsten Lauritsen, 63–91. Newcastle: Cambridge Scholars Publishing.

Tisdall, E. Kay M. 2012. "The challenge and challenging of childhood studies? Learning from disability studies and research with disabled children." *Children & Society* 26 (3):173–267.

United Nations. 1989. "Convention on the rights of the child." Retrieved September 19th 2018 from www.ohchr.org/en/professionalinterest/pages/crc.aspx.

United Nations. 2005. *Convention on the rights of the child: General Comment No 7. Implementing child rights in early childhood.* Retrieved July 6th 2012 from www2.ohchr.org/english/bodies/crc/docs/Advance Versions/GeneralComment7Rev1.pdf.

Yuval-Davis, Nira. 2006. "Belonging and the politics of belonging." *Patterns of Prejudice* 4 (3):197–214. doi: 1080/00313220600769331.

Zachrisen, Berit. 2018. "Play in an ethnically diverse preschool: Conditions for belonging." In *Values in early childhood education: Citizenship for tomorrow*, edited by Eva Johansson and Johanna Einarsdottir, 132–146. Oxon: Routledge.

36

HOW TO CREATE AN OPEN LISTENING CLIMATE

Using the Lundy model of child participation with adults

Alison Moore

Introduction

The rights model of participation developed by Lundy (2007) is at the core of this chapter. Lundy's model, based on the United Nations Convention on the Rights of the Child (hereafter UNCRC), conceptualises Article 12. It presents an accessible interpretation of Article 12 and associated provision rights. Lundy's voice model provides a theoretical and practical understanding of Article 12 based on four interrelated elements – *space, voice, audience* and *influence* – to help adults working with children create an open listening climate.

This chapter draws on the findings from an empirical innovative study exploring practitioner and parent understanding of child voice in children's centres in the UK. The study examined how child voice can be authentically heard in ways that create an open listening climate to stimulating professional dialogue and advancing our understanding of rights-based pedagogy, in order to influence both policy and practice. Although the context in which the study was conducted was in relation to vulnerable children, the Lundy model of child participation (hereafter the Lundy model) lends itself to work with children across all fields. The Lundy model was developed to use within child participation and eliciting child voice. I have adopted and used it with practitioners and parents.

Research context and purpose

The study informing this chapter was carried out between 2012 and 2018 in a large city in the West Midlands of England. It included two children's centres. Children's centres (DfE, 2013, p. 5) in England provide services for families such as:

- early years provision (early education and childcare);
- health services relating to young children and families;
- training and employment services; and
- information and advice services for parents and prospective parents.

Children's centres were set up by the Blair/Gordon ministry (1997–2010) to consider new ways of developing and delivering policies around early intervention, child poverty and social exclusion, supporting the government's commitment to children and tackling disadvantage. Key elements to these policies were that they covered both the needs of children and parents.

The city in which the study was conducted has a very diverse population and includes some of the most economically challenged districts in the country, with a high percentage of children living in poverty (2015). Driving the study was a commitment to make a change to children's lived experiences and those of the parents trying to make a lasting impact on children's well-being. Five parents and 16 practitioners took part in the study. This chapter will focus on the data from the semi-structured parent interviews, which captured their views on the impact the involvement with the children's centre has had to their lives and that of their children.

The study began by reflecting on my previous professional experiences as a family support worker, community development worker and children's centre district manager. In my earliest roles, I had first-hand experience of the processes and procedures within a social services context and the complexities of the circumstances that families were living in. I struggled to recall a situation where the voice of the child was placed at the centre of the decision-making process, hence a driving factor of this study. Discovering Lundy's (2007) model of child participation gave me the tool I was searching for, to place the child at the centre when developing a listening climate. I truly came to grasp its significance as a key contributor to understanding and implementing the UNCRC, and specifically conceptualising Article 12.

Lundy's leading work on children and young people's participation in decision-making has, for instance, served to provide a comprehensive framework included in the Irish National Strategy (DCYA, 2015). In a personal conversation with Dr Sheila Long, lecturer in early childhood education and care, Institute of Technology Carlow, she suggested that Lundy's research is 'beginning to have impact at a national and international level' and believes there is 'potential for the Lundy model to effect change at the systemic level, yet to be explored by early childhood practitioners themselves'. The Lundy model, as such, served as the catalyst for the study design, methods and data collection.

The following five research questions guided the study:

1.   What does a listening climate look like in children's centres?
2.   Where do practitioners feel their practice is at the present time?
3.   What changes need to happen in order to create a more collaborative, open listening climate?
4.   What strategies may be adopted to improve the listening climate and pedagogical practice across teams in children's centres?
5.   What support do practitioners need to change practice where a listening climate is not present or not embedded in practice?

Guided by the literature and my extensive experience in the field, this study sought to explore parent and practitioner perceptions of the current listening climate in children's centres, in order to develop our pedagogical practice.

Theoretical underpinning and methodology

Framework

Bronfenbrenner's bioecological model of development (Bronfenbrenner and Morris, 2006) provides the theoretical and conceptual framing for the study, outlining the complex *layers* of a child's environment, the relationships, the interactions and their impact on the child's development, providing a holistic view of the complex lived experiences of children and families.

Praxeology

When considering the most appropriate methodological framework in which to conduct the study, I took inspiration from research conducted by Pascal and Bertram (2009, 2012, 2013) and Oliveira-Formosinho and Formosinho (2012), who advocate for the use of participatory methodology within early childhood research that they call *praxeology*. Their paradigm reflects a worldview that places emphasis on collaboration, democracy, empowerment, respect, inclusion and participant voice. Pascal and Bertram (2012) argue that a praxeological worldview is more 'profound and intensely participatory and thus more authentically democratic' (p. 480). They assert this because at the heart of praxeological research is a strong ethical code that includes the need for redistributed power in relation to participation and the voice of participants, particularly those potentially more marginalised in research. The *praxeological* paradigm, and how this then translates into practice, resonates with my own study and positioning as a researcher.

Lundy model

Lundy's (2007) voice model informed both the data collection and data analysis, emphasising a rights-based approach to the research. Lundy developed the voice model in response to findings from research conducted on behalf of the Northern Ireland Commissioner for Children and Young People (Kilkelly et al., 2005, cited in Lundy, 2007). The findings from the large-scale research project, conducted with school-age children, identified several areas where children felt their views were not being taken into account or taken seriously expressing concerns that they were not *having a say in decisions that were about them*, revealing direct violation of Article 12 (UNGA, 1989). Acknowledging that 'Article 12 cannot be viewed in isolation … the meaning of individual provisions of the UNCRC can only be understood when they are read and interpreted in conjunction with the other rights protected in the Convention' (Lundy 2007, p. 932). Lundy proposed:

> that the successful implementation of Article 12 requires consideration of the implications of four separate factors:

- *Space*: Children must be given the opportunity to express a view.
- *Voice*: Children must be facilitated to express their views.
- *Audience*: The view must be listened to.
- *Influence*: The view must be acted upon, as appropriate

The model and accompanying checklist for participation provided the tool to take into the field. The intent of the study was to examine how child voice is authentically heard in ways that create an open listening climate to facilitate change and improve pedagogy in children's centres. However, for this chapter, the focus will be on parent voice. Engaging with the most significant adult in the child's life (in the main, the parent) is important if we are to have a holistic worldview of the child within the home environment. Practitioners need *inviting into* the child's lived experiences.

Ethical perspectives

I took into consideration the British Educational Research Association (BERA, 2011, 2018) and the EECERA ethical code for early childhood researchers (Bertram et al., 2015). The set of ethical principles within the EECERA code of practice resonates with the current study and supports the spirit of participatory research with a strong value base. The code of practice promotes high standards within research 'involving children or vulnerable young people and adults' (Bertram et al., 2015, p. 7), promoting Articles 3 and 12 of the UNCRC.

Consideration was given throughout the study to my positionality within the research. I considered the ethical perspective of the insider–outsider researchers (Breen, 2007; Chavez, 2008; Merton, 1972). I also drew inspiration from Dwyer and Buckle (2009 cited in Kerstetter, 2012) and their notion of 'the space between', where the relationships between the participants and researcher is multidimensional and open to change, depending on any given situation. I found this to be true within this current study. As a result, part of my ethical consideration was where to conduct the interviews. The choice was given, and four out of the five parents chose to have the interviews conducted at their homes. The remaining one took place in the parents' room in the children's centre. This choice was offered being aware of the power differential between a researcher and its participants.

Data management and analysis

I draw on the research of Richie and Lewis (2003), who suggest the use of a systematic and flexible approach to analysis. Data collection and data analysis were carried out simultaneously. As the data were collected from each parent interview, a thematic approach to analysis was applied, using Braun and Clarke's (2013) six stages to thematic analysis. The data were considered based on themes categorised from Lundy's (2007) voice model, listed above. The coding framework facilitated the interpretation of the data using Geertz's (1973) notion of thick descriptions. This process of thematic analysis was not to gain representative results, as each parent and child's experience was different, but to explore and gain a deeper understanding and meaning; as Rubin and Rubin (1995) suggest, 'coding encourages hearing the meaning in the data' (p. 240).

Findings

The parent interviews provided varied and valuable insights. There were many similarities across the narratives that were shared. As parents told their stories, their individual experiences and those of their children came through, and shared themes emerged:

* relationships;
* children's needs;
* knowledge; and
* support networks.

The four factors

The four factors from Lundy's model formed the structure for the analysis of the data collected. The above-mentioned themes that emerged from the interviews are grouped under these four factors, with the individual parents referred to, noted in brackets, e.g. (P1) for parent 1.

Space

All parent stories placed an emphasis on the environments that the children's centres created, for parents and children. The *space* was clearly important to them and they were able to describe why this was. Specialist services, such as infant massage or bumps to babies and stay-and-play were considered a great opportunity, developing early relationships with the staff and other parents at the centres, as well as with their baby, as expressed by Parent 2:

> Services and staff were very approachable ... key to this was the consistency of staff ... [I] felt in control of [my] own situation but knew staff were there to help if needed.
>
> *(P2)*

The location of their children's centre to their home and the flexibility and variety of services were considered key to their success. Stay-and-play, crèche and nursery provision were considered essential, as they had had an impact on the children's development. These services provided the routines and structures that parents now understood to be essential for themselves and their children, including the ability to set boundaries for behaviour.

Generally, parents expressed their deep-felt appreciation for the children's centre, the space, and the level of support they received when they most needed it. For one parent, she expressed the importance of life beyond the centre, and how important developing networks in the community is for parents and children:

> It is important that the children's centre is there, as a support network, the fact that I know they are there and can help ... It is important to have a support network in the community ... especially if you are new to the area.
>
> *(P5)*

> This place has had an effect on me from the day I come, right up until now.
>
> *(P4)*

All parents interviewed referred to the critical periods in their lives and they reflected on how these experiences had impacted on their children's development and their wider family structures. The children's centre was clearly identified as the *space* they needed, at that time, for emotional as well as practical support.

Voice

The data reflected a strong link between space and voice; as suggested by Lundy (2007), 'these elements are interrelated. There is a significant degree of overlap between (a) Space and Voice [and] (b) Audience and Influence' (p. 933). All parents referred to critical incidents in their lives that they had experienced. These critical incidents, while often different in nature and consequence, had similar effects on their emotional well-being and that of the children. All parents' stories included aspects of:

- lack of self-confidence;
- poor self-esteem;
- postnatal depression; and
- depression.

Parents referred to periods of isolation as a result of lacking in confidence or knowing what to do. Several mothers had also experienced significant transitions in their lives, having often moved cities or addresses, which one parent referred to as 'sofa-surfing' (P4). These experiences had a major impact on attachment and bonding with their babies. In some cases, there had been social care interventions providing support, prior to the children's centre involvement.

The key issues that emerged in all the parent interviews was their determination to make changes in the children's and their own lives. They perceived that the children's centre would be able to help them achieve these aspirations for change:

> I want to make a home for my son.
>
> *(P1)*

> I thought I need to do this for myself and my child ... I am a changed person from where I was [before coming to the centre].
>
> *(P4)*

All the parents had experience of home visits, made by the family support team from the children's centres, prior to them attending services. They felt that this first encounter had been important in establishing relationships, a rapport and trust. They felt for the first time that their 'voice' had been heard. Their experiences reflected a supportive approach, with parents often relating back to examples where they had felt this had not been the case with other agencies or professionals they had previously encountered. Parents mentioned that these visits were valued as they gave the opportunity for visiting practitioners to observe and listen to the children, carry out development checks, and at times role-model home play. Parents expressed that this first positive experience meant that they felt they wanted to attend the services at the centre:

> Before I started at the children's centre, I guess, I was alone in my way of thinking ... he [family support worker] said, 'You know you can go in, and there are all these services that you can go to' ... he walked in with me ... and we went from there, slowly, slowly.
>
> *(P4)*

Parents all referred to one parenting programme or another that they had attended and felt had had an impact on them, expressing their new understanding that their child had a voice even at the early stages of development:

> I attended Triple P [Australian parenting programme] and PHP [promoting happier parenting] and I've never looked back.
>
> *(P3)*

> I wanted to attend programmes before she was born as I wanted to be active and socialise once I had her ... I attended Bumps to Babies, and then weaning sessions followed.
>
> *(P2)*

I came to other services and even attended Freedom [specialist domestic abuse pro-
gramme] ... I only wanted to come once, I came three or four times ... OK,
I didn't realise this was for me, but it was.

(P4)

The accounts that parents gave in their stories showed a range of services were on offer to
meet the varying needs of parents and children. A number described how they did not initially think the programme was for them, but the practitioners had obviously both seen and
heard their individual needs and guided them to the relevant support programme. As
a result of being heard, they all expressed a greater awareness and understanding of their
children's needs alongside their own.

Audience

The need for trusting relationships between parents and practitioners and with the children
was voiced by all the parents and was a recurring theme throughout the narratives. Parents
also discussed healthy friendships in relation to friendships that had been established with
their peers. The concept of a healthy friendship was considered important, and reference
was made to parents having experienced negative influences in their lives:

I lived with criticism from my mom ... resulting in self-doubt.

(P1)

I made the decision to move to Birmingham away from past and bad influences.

(P3)

I got into all sorts of different relationships and each one of them was no good for me.

(P4)

All the parents talked about the practitioners as being friendly and supportive and that the
centres were welcoming. Not being judged was a key factor to parents and children having
had positive experiences, as well as the notion of sustained and quality relationships with professionals and friendships made while attending the children's centre. This was a prominent
thread across the stories.

Stay-and-play, crèche support and home visits were viewed as crucial services, indicating
they felt this was where they and their children were listened to:

I started to attend stay-and-play and I've never looked back ... my son gained confidence, independence and socialised and integrated with other children.

(P3)

Ensuring that parents and children have an appropriate and effective *audience* is essential
when considering Article 12 and developing the concept of an *open listening climate*.

Influence

The reflections expressed by parents gave inference to the connections between the practitioners within the service(s) provided, as described above, and the impact on the children
and their lives. Parents mentioned the varied services and routes they were guided through
as a result of being listened to and their needs being understood. Parents could see the benefits of multi-agency interventions at the right time.

There was an acknowledgement that the children's centres were not able to provide all of the required support but ensured there was effective signposting or referral processes in place:

> The children's centre set up the opportunity for me to volunteer with Home Start … I got help with English, maths and then an access course for my degree.
>
> *(P3)*

> I've got my course, I didn't think I would be walking out as a parent and having some form of place to go to study … I thought I would walk out unemployed.
>
> *(P4)*

All of the parents expressed their gratitude for the support and guidance they received, which helped them to develop aspirations for themselves and their children, emphasising the role the practitioners had played in supporting them to make positive choices that, as a consequence, had a positive *influence* on their and their child's lives. Examples of a range of parenting programmes were given and the importance of continued learning and gaining qualifications:

> I feel I can contribute to core group meetings and I have confidence to challenge the social worker … I feel in control now.
>
> *(P1)*

Each mother cited the opportunity to volunteer as a key component for changing their lives which was a turning point for them:

> I wanted to give back to my community … the opportunity to become a Sparkler Parent Mentor volunteer came up … we are the voice for other women and for the children's centre.
>
> *(P5)*

All the parents acknowledged that the children's centre had a big part to play in their lives, and as a result they had all made different choices and taken a different life course than they would have done without the support they received. What parents did show was that they had developed independence and self-reliance. They had gained the confidence to make their own decisions that had a positive influence on the lives and future aspirations of their children.

Discussion

This chapter, drawing on research from a wider study, has given a glimpse into the experiences of five parents and their children who have accessed support services at a children's centre.

Applying Lundy's voice model in a context of researching with parents and children in children's centres has provided a structure and platform from which practitioners can start to develop a greater understanding of the UNCRC and how to apply it in everyday practice. Lundy's suggestion that to fully understand Article 12, a number of other relevant articles within the Convention have to be considered – Article 2 (non-discrimination), Article 3 (best interests), Article 5 (adult/parental guidance and child's evolving capacities), Article 13 (freedom of expression) and Article 19 (protection from violence, abuse and neglect) – resonates with the wider study, emerging findings and my own experiences in the field.

This model has shown itself to be not only an accessible framework with parents and children in order to empower change, but a key contributor to understanding and implementing the UNCRC within practice in children's centres, and specifically conceptualising Article 12.

The findings helped give a narrative of the parent and child journey in the children's centres. Connell (2013) recounts that 'the only true knowledge of an experience comes from those living in the world of the experience' (p. 34).

These narratives provide us with a greater understanding of the individual component parts of their experiences, highlighted as key themes that help us to develop a holistic worldview of the child and family.

Key themes

This section briefly discusses the themes from the narratives. These included relationships, children's needs, knowledge and support networks.

Relationships

The use of a rights-based method has provided an opportunity for practitioners to consider how they engage with parents and children. The findings suggest developing trusting and collaborative relationships with parents and children is key. If we are to truly uphold and embed the rights of the child in the hope of facilitating change and improving our pedagogical environments, there must be a focus on relationships.

All the parents, either inexplicitly or explicitly, referred to having lost trust in agencies they had previously encountered, resulting in a feeling of mistrust or lack of trust in any subsequent support services they were involved with.

The practitioner's first encounter with the parent and child is pivotal for the relationship and ongoing developing partnership to be successful. The parents described the positive influence the centres have had on their lives and those of their children. Casey (2012) makes the connection between the need to listen to and understand the parents and their experiences as children, to then find out and understand the experiences of their children. The Lundy model formed the framework by which the practitioners could start to build the bigger picture to support child and parent using the four interrelated elements of the model: space, voice, audience and influence.

Parents referred to the importance of their children developing friendships, reflecting their understanding of their child's emotional well-being alongside their own needs. Developing a firm relationship with the parents helped them understand that they were in a better position to help their children. The importance of having a sense of *belonging* initially to the centre, then with the wider community, was strongly conveyed.

Children's needs

The findings showed that all the parents had gained an understanding of the needs of their child with the support of practitioners at the children's centre. For many mothers, the home visits provided by family support at the centres were acknowledged as a key link to establishing trusting relationships, described above, as well as the chance to discuss the children's needs.

Ferguson (2017) examined the phenomenon of children becoming 'invisible' within the day-to-day practice in the context of social work practice and child protection. Ferguson sought to deepen the understanding of encounters between practitioners, children and their families that seemingly renders some children 'invisible', and therefore potentially exposed to greater risk. This is equally relevant to an early years context, and Ferguson emphasised that making a child 'visible' within practice required the use of a range of approaches. This he considers important to ensure genuine engagement with the child that goes beyond just having sight of the child.

All the parents developed an awareness of the potential detrimental effects that their own stress factors and experiences could have had and could continue to have on their child's development. This increased awareness of their child's needs enabled the practitioners to engage in dialogues with the parents, described by Easen et al. (1992) as 'developmental partnerships' (p. 285). He considers that practitioners bring the 'general child development theory' and the parents bring the 'personal theory' (p. 285). This identifies what both the practitioners and parents bring to the partnership for the mutual benefit of meeting the needs of the child.

This is in line with what Bronfenbrenner refers to as 'bi-directional influences' (Bronfenbrenner and Morris, 2006) when defining the relationships a child encounters or systems within their environment.

Knowledge

In an unpublished lecture given at the Pen Green Centre of Excellence Corby UK, Pascal (1996) stated that:

> When we draw children, parents and families into our early childhood centres [I] think we should be sure that what we are about is making these people strong, providing them with the means to appreciate their destinies, giving them a measure of control and influence about what goes on, encouraging them to stop accepting their lot and start creating the world they would like to be part of.
>
> *(cited in Whalley et al. 2013, p. 11)*

This statement remains as strong today as it did then. The parent narratives described, in different ways, that they wanted a better life for their child and a better start than they felt they had. There was a collective acknowledgement that working with the children's centres would support their own learning, and in turn that this would have an impact on their child's development and education. This early 'developmental partnership' and positive dialogue with the parents gave practitioners a firm foundation on which to build upon. The fact that the parents felt valued was evident. All the parents, at some point in their relationship with the centres, accessed parenting or adult learning programmes and they acknowledged they valued the groups that were on offer.

As previously mentioned, using the Lundy model as a tool for opening dialogue with parents had helped practitioners gain a greater holistic view of the family and the child, a view supported by Katz et al. (2007, p. 9), who recognise that addressing the needs of the parent is required if the needs of the child are to be met.

Support networks

The sense of belonging to a group or centre was a strong need reflected across the four key themes and voiced by all the parents. The experiences the parent and child have can be described as a journey. The approach to engagement needs to be flexible depending on the circumstances that the parents are in, and that can change very quickly. Parents and children need to be able to access and benefit from a range of opportunities that best support their needs at any given time.

There was a strong sense of wanting to *give back* support for other parents facing similar or the same situations. This was made possible by parents accessing volunteering opportunities that for some led on to further education and employment. There was an overwhelming feeling of pride expressed by the parents in what they had achieved with the help of the centre, but also acknowledgement that they had been able to change the life course of their child as a result.

For one parent, the opportunity to take her volunteering experience further led onto a specialist parent befriending and mentoring programme. This was one possible route open for parents but may not be the right route for all parents. What is important is that children's centres work alongside parents and children to provide these positive experiences.

Conclusion

This chapter has, with data from the wider research study, supported practitioners within children's centres to develop a greater understanding of the children and families they support. Further, the chapter has illustrated a new way of interpreting and applying Lundy's model that has opened a door to an alternative way of engaging in dialogue with parents and children. Applying a rights-based approach to the work with parents and children has illustrated the importance of working respectfully and valuing everyone's contribution.

I wish to end by acknowledging that the participation and protection rights included in Lundy's model and my research are part of the overall UNCRC, the UNCRC being one of the nine core international human rights treaties. Alison Moore and Aline Cole – Albäck (presentation, Children's Rights in Early Childhood, CREC Learning Circle April 2017). My research is, as such, a piece of a jigsaw of a much bigger international human rights framework.

The study and findings discussed in this chapter, although set in an English context and in children's centres, will resonate with and have relevance to practitioners working with children, parents and researchers in many countries. With my research, I started out exploring the use of the Lundy model as a tool for practitioners to engage with the concepts of participation and an open listening climate across two children's centres in the UK. The impact of my research has led to the consortium leading all of the children's centres in the city, where the research took place, expressing interest in cascading the findings to a citywide audience with a view to adopting the methodology and the way I applied the Lundy model in my research.

References

BERA (British Educational Research Association). 2011. *Ethical Guidelines for Educational Research.* London: BERA.

BERA (British Educational Research Association). 2018 *Ethical Guidelines for Educational Research.* Accessed June 6th 2002 http://www.bera.ac.uk/researchers-resources/publications/ethical-guidelines-for-education-research-2018

Bertram, Tony, Júlia Formosinho, Collette Gray, Chris Pascal, & Margy Whalley. 2015. *EECERA Ethical Code for Early Childhood Researchers.* Accessed May 20th 2015 http://www.eecera.org/about/ethical-code

Birmingham Child Poverty Commission 2015. *A Fairer Start for All Children and Young People* An Independent Report Accessed September 20th 2018 http://www.childrenssociety.org.uk

Braun, Virginia and Victoria Clarke. 2013. *Successful Qualitative Research: A Practical Guide for Beginners.* London: Sage Publications.

Breen, Lauren. J, 2007. *The Researcher 'In the Middle': Negotiating the Insider/Outsider Dichotomy.* Australian Community Psychologist, 19 (1): 163–174.

Bronfenbrenner, Urie & Pamela A. Morris. 2006. The Bioecological Model of Human Development. In *Handbook of Child Psychology. Theoretical Models of Human Development.* Vol. 1. doi10.1002/9780470147658.chpsy0114

Casey, Louise. 2012. (DCLG) Department for Communities and Local Government. *Listening to Troubled Families.* Accessed 10th July 2017 http://www.communities.gov.uk/communities/troubledfamilies

Chavez, Christina. 2008. Conceptualizing from the Inside: Advantages, Complications and Demands on Insider Positionality. *The Qualitative Report,* 13: 474–494.

Connell, Patricia. 2013. *A Phenomenological Study of the Lived Experiences of Adult Caregiving Daughters and Their Elderly Mothers.* Published Doctoral Thesis: Accessed May 5th 2016. ufdcimages.uflib.ufl.edu /UF/E0/00/12/63/00001/connell_p.pdf

DCYA (Department of Children and Youth Affairs) Ireland. 2015. 2020 *National Strategy on Children and Young People's Participation in Decision-Making Ireland.* Accessed 10th April 2016 http://dcya.gov.ie/documents/playandrec/20150617NatStratParticipationReport.pdf

DfE (Department of Education). 2013. *Sure Start Children's Centres: Guidance for Local Authorities.* Statutory guidance on early childhood services and Sure Start Children's Centres. Accessed July 10th 2017 www.gov.uk/government/publications/sure-start-childrens-centres

Dwyer, Sonia C. and Jennifer L. Buckle. 2009. The Space between: On Being and Insider-Outsider in Qualitative Research. *International Journal of Qualitative Methods,* (March 2009): 54–63 Accessed July 22nd 2018 http://doi.org.10.1177/160940690900800105

Easen, Patrick, Pippa Kendall, & Janet Shaw. 1992. *Parents and Educators: Dialogue and Development Through Partnership* December 1992, 6 (4): 282–296. https://onlinelibrary.wiley.com/doi/pdf/10.1111/j.1099-0860.1992.tb00395

Ferguson, Harry., 2017. How Children Become Invisible in Child Protection Work: Findings from Research into Day-to-Day Social Work Practice. *British Journal of Social Work,* 47: 1007–1023.

Geertz, Clifford. 1973. Thick Description: Toward an Interpretive Theory of Culture. In Clifford Geertz (editor). *The Interpretation of Cultures: Selected Essays,* 311–323. New York: Basic Books.

Katz, Ilan, Judy Corlyon, Vincent La Placa, & Sarah Hunter. 2007. *The Relationship between Parenting and Poverty.* London: Joseph Rowntree Foundation.

Kerstetter, Katie., 2012. Insider, Outsider, Ore Somewhere in between: The Impact of Researchers' Identities on the Community-Based Research Process. *Journal of Rural Social Sciences,* 27 (2): 99–117.

Kilkelly,U., R. Kilpatrick, & ,L. Lundy et al. 2005. *Children's Rights in Northern Ireland (Belfast) Northern Ireland Commissioner for Children and Young People.*

Lundy, Laura., 2007. 'Voice' is not enough: Conceptualising Article 12 of the United Nations Convention on the Rights of the Child. *British Educational Research Journal,* 3 (6): 927–942.

Merton, Robert K., 1972. Insiders and Outsiders: A Chapter in the Sociology of Knowledge. American Indian Studies. *The American Indian Quarterly,* 33 (4): 440–461.

Oliverira-Formosinho, Julia, & Joao Formosinho. 2012. *Pedagogy-In-Participation: Children Association Educational Perspective.* Porto: Porto Editora.

Pascal, Christine, & Tony Bertram. 2009. Listening to Young Citizens: The Struggle to Make Real a Participatory Paradigm in Research with Young Children. *European Early Childhood Education Research Journal,* 17 (2): 249–262.

Pascal, Christine, & Tony Bertram. 2012. Praxis, Ethics and Power: Developing Praxeology as a Participatory Paradigm for Early Childhood Research. *European Early Childhood Education Research Journal,* 20 (4): 477–492.

Pascal, Christine, & Tony Bertram. 2013a. Small Voices, Powerful Messages: Capturing Young Children's Perspectives in Practice-Led Research. In Martyn Hammersley, Rosie Flewett, Martin Robb and Alison Clark (editors). *Issues in Research with Children and Young People.* Milton Keynes: Sage Publications/Open University Press.

Pascal, Christine, & Tony Bertram. 2013b. *The Impact of Early Education as a Strategy in Countering Socio-Economic Disadvantage. Research paper for Ofsted's 'Access and achievement in education 2013 review'.* Accessed October 11th 2013. www.crec.co.uk/doc/Access.pdf

Richie, Jane, & Jane Lewis. 2003. *Qualitative Research Practice: A Guide for Social Science Students and Researchers*. London: Sage.

Rubin, Herbert J., & Irene Rubin. 1995. *Qualitative Interviewing: The Art of Hearing Data*. London: Sage Publications.

UNGA (United Nations General Assembly). 1989. *"Convention on the Rights of the Child."* UN Treaty Series 1577, 3. www.refworld.org/docid/3ae6b38f0.html

Whalley, Margaret, Cath Arnold, & Robert Orr (editors). 2013. *Working with Families in Children's Centres and Early Years Settings*. London: Hodder Education.

37

WHAT DO CHILDREN EXPECT OUT OF RESEARCH PARTICIPATION?

Sue Dockett and Bob Perry

Introduction

Respect for children's rights and competences has been a distinctive feature of much early childhood research in recent decades (Clark and Moss, 2001; Einarsdóttir, 2014; Flewitt, 2005). This research draws from the theoretical bases of sociology of childhood and children's rights. Sociology of childhood discourse is characterised by regard for children as 'persons in their own right' (Prout, 2000, p. 308); subjects rather than objects of research (Hunleth, 2011); social actors who influence and are influenced by their social contexts (Christensen and Prout, 2005); constructors of meaning through their many and varied interactions (Ansell, Robson, Hajdu and van Blerk, 2012); experts on their own lives (Clark and Moss, 2001); and, with appropriate support, competent to share this expertise (James and Prout, 1997).

Children's rights discourse recognises children as rights-holders with not only the ability to influence their own lives, but also the entitlement to do so. The United Nations Convention on the Rights of the Child (CRC) (United Nations, 1989) provides the framework of much of the current research with young children that utilises a rights-based paradigm. In particular, two articles of the Convention − Articles 12 and 13 − are most often cited in relation to the engagement of children in research. These articles provide to 'the child who is capable of forming his or her own views the right to express those views freely in all matters affecting the child' and that these views be given 'due weight' (Article 12), and 'the right to freedom of expression; this right shall include the freedom to seek, receive and impart information and ideas of all kinds' in ways of the child's choosing (Article 13). Indeed, Article 12, paraphrased as 'the right of all children to be heard and taken seriously', has been identified as one of four general principles of the CRC (UN Committee on the Rights of the Child, 2009).

However, the indivisibility of rights outlined in the CRC also requires researchers to consider the relevance of other articles as they frame research with children. In particular, attention is drawn to Article 3.1, which states that 'the best interests of the child shall be the primary consideration', and Article 3.6, which 'obliges those who work with children to ensure that professional standards are established and implemented' (Beazley, Bessell, Ennew and Waterson, 2011, p. 163). Further, the CRC includes provision for children's access to information (Article 17), appropriate direction and guidance to support the exercise of their rights (Article 5) and protection from exploitation (Article 36).

In addition to the CRC itself, the UN Committee on the Rights of the Child has published a range of General Comments that analyse and elaborate the provisions of the CRC. Among these, General Comment 7 affirms the rights of the youngest children, recognising that 'early childhood is a critical period for the realization of these rights' (UN Committee on the Rights of the Child, 2006, p. 1), and General Comment 12 (UN Committee on the Rights of the Child, 2009) affirms not only the right for children's views to be heard and taken seriously, but also for appropriate support and guidance to be provided as children form their views (Lundy, McEvoy and Byrne, 2011).

Taken together, the CRC and General Comments position children as rights-holders, entitled to participate in high-quality research that is relevant to and for them, undertaken with regard for the best interests of the children involved, with opportunities to express their views in ways that are appropriate for them, and that do not exploit either the children or the data they contribute. Further, children have the right to access information and to support and guidance to inform their decision-making as they exercise their rights.

Background

Over a period of more than two decades, we have engaged with children in a range of contexts, seeking their perspectives of their early childhood settings, schools and communities, and their transitions among these. The perspectives shared by children have contributed to developing understandings of transition to school and school-aged care (Dockett and Perry, 2014a, 2016b; Perry and Dockett, 2011), learning environments (Dockett and Perry, 2012, 2016a) and child-friendly communities (Dockett, Main and Kelly, 2011; Dockett, Perry and Kearney, 2012). In several instances, children's perspectives have contributed to changes in policy as well as practice (Dockett and Perry, 2014a, 2015; Victorian Department of Education and Training, 2017).

These projects have employed the methodological framework of participatory rights-based research (Dockett and Perry, 2014b). This framework embodies both the CRC and recognition of the subjectivity and agency of children. Five key characteristics of participatory rights-based research have been identified (Beazley et al., 2011, p. 161):

1. Research is genuinely respectful of children, regarding them as partners in the research. This respect extends to the nature of participation, which must be meaningful for children.
2. Research is grounded in ethical practice and children's participation is bound by the same ethical principles as research with adults, notably voluntary participation and avoidance of exploitation.
3. Research is systematic and valid. Data are generated systematically in ways that can be justified and replicated.
4. Analysis is rigorous, using techniques that are appropriate.
5. Research prioritises local knowledge and expertise, focusing on children's own experiences and opinions within a specific context.

In addition, we contend that participatory rights-based research is also characterised by:

6. Reporting and dissemination that respects children's rights and aims to make a positive difference to their lives (Dockett and Perry, 2014b).

461

Children's expectations

Drawing on one recent project and the extant literature, we explore children's expectations of their participation in research, including their expectations about participation choices, what was to be shared and with whom, and how this was to occur – as well as the strategies they used to convey these expectations. Our intention in sharing these is to question assumptions about research with children and to reflect on what can be learned about children's expectations of research participation.

The core element of Article 12 of the CRC refers to children's rights to express their views in matters that affect them. This also includes the right of children to decline to express their views. Participatory rights-based research acknowledges the role of child choice – children are invited, but not compelled, to express their views. Research methods that offer children a genuine choice acknowledge the context-dependent nature of such choices (Kjørholt, 2004) and build in multiple opportunities for children to assess their input and to decide whether, as well as how, their involvement may continue.

To ground our discussion, we report interactions with four children participating in a study of their experiences of starting school. We use these as illustrative rather than representative. In our discussion, we use the inclusive term *children*, but in both the example and the following discussion we aim to recognise and celebrate the diversity of children's experiences, understandings and engagement with research. Following this, we also explore the different yet complementary positions around child perspectives and children's perspectives (Sommer, Pramling Samuelsson and Hundeide, 2013) in promoting research with children.

Thinking about starting school

The context for the following interactions was a project exploring perceptions of starting school. The project methodology involved multiple visits to the school site by the same researchers over a period of six months, with emphasis on ongoing informal observations and conversations with adults and children about their experiences and expectations around starting school. At the beginning of the project, information was distributed to teachers and parents, and they were encouraged to talk with the children about whether or not they (the children) were interested in participating in conversations with the researchers.

After these discussions, and after several visits to the school, researchers discussed the project with the class group. This discussion invited children to think about, and ask questions about, research as we described what was involved and the purpose of this particular project. The term 'survey' was discussed, with children concluding that a survey was 'about asking questions' and 'writing some answers'. Several children noted that they had seen their parents writing some answers on paper and suggested that they may have been completing surveys. Children posed a number of questions about the survey booklets they were shown and offered a range of comments about their starting school experiences. Questions included: 'Can we keep it?' and 'Can I draw my friends?'. Comments included: 'I don't like drawing', 'Writing hurts my hand' and 'This is big school'.

Vignette

Four 5-year-old children (two girls and two boys) who indicated interest in participating and whose parents had provided consent for involvement in the project formed one group. The children had all been at school for approximately six months. They met with Sue in one classroom while the remaining class group occupied the next room. Concertina doors between the rooms remained open. The class teacher intermittently walked through the room to access materials from her desk.

The small group conversation started with a reminder about the project and reference to the previous class discussion. Children were given a copy of the survey booklet, which included an information/consent form. Following from previous research investigating documentation to support children's informed consent (Dockett et al., 2012), this form included text and visual information about the project and what participation might involve, as well as multiple opportunities for children to indicate their willingness to participate or withdraw their involvement.

The form was discussed with the children prior to their decisions about participating in the project. The form provided a space for children to write their name or, if they chose, use some other image/letter combination so that they would know it was their booklet. They were invited to circle a 'thumbs up' sign if they wished to participate, a 'thumbs down' sign to indicate that they did not wish to participate, or another neutral sign which indicated that they were not sure about participation. During the discussion, the children identified the signs and indicated that they knew which sign was associated with which option. They also noted that they could come back to those signs at any time if they wished to change their mind about participation, or they could make the signs with their hands and the researcher would understand their choice. Several minutes were spent practising the hand signals and confirming their meaning. The two girls – Martha and Rose – indicated that they wished to participate by writing their names and circling a 'thumbs up' sign on their consent form. The two boys – Abel and Matt – also wrote their names on their booklets. Abel then started to circle the 'thumbs up' sign but looked hesitantly at the researcher. He moved his pen to the 'thumbs down' sign and looked up again.

Sue:	Would you like to talk about starting school, or would you like to do something else?
Abel:	[nods]
Sue:	Write in the booklet?
Abel:	[shakes his head]
Sue:	Something else?
Abel:	[nods] [looks around as teacher passes by, starts to move his pencil back to the 'thumbs up' sign]
Sue:	If you would like to do something else, it is OK. You can put a circle around any sign you like, and it is OK.
Abel:	[circles the 'thumbs down' sign]
Sue:	At the bottom of the page, it says 'Could we ask you again later?' What do you think? If you think no, you can put a cross. If you think yes, you can put a tick.
Abel:	[draws a cross]
Matt:	[has been observing the interaction between Abel and Sue] Can I put a cross too? Can I do something else?
Sue:	Yes, you can choose. [Matt pumps fist in air as he stands up to leave]
Teacher:	[to Sue] Are you sure that is OK? [both boys look to the teacher and Sue]

When Sue nods to affirm their right to decline participation, the boys leave the room and join other class activities. Martha and Rose were eager to continue their involvement and talk about starting school. They indicated their willingness to be involved by moving quickly into the survey. Three forms of the survey were offered: a written booklet listing a series of questions and lines of 'thumbs up', neutral and 'thumbs down' signs; a series of laminated cards with the same signs that could be 'posted' in response to the questions; and a large laminated card with three large signs and a whiteboard marker to circle the relevant response. The girls chose the written booklet, and Rose noted, 'We know what to do, 'cause you told us'.

As each of the seven survey statements were read, the girls circled a sign to indicate their responses. In response to a question about accessing help at school, Martha looked at the researcher, sighed and said, 'We'll have to think about that one'. This became a common response for Martha; for several questions, she circled a sign to indicate a 'yes', 'sometimes' or 'no' response, but in response to follow-up questions used the same sentence, 'We'll have to think about that one'. When asked if she would like to come back to that question, Martha shook her head and repeated her comment.

In contrast, Rose quickly circled the 'yes' sign and moved on to a question about friends, commenting, 'I already told my mum about my friends'.

Martha: What about Mrs S [teacher]?
Rose: She knows we are friends too.

The girls continued to respond to the survey questions, sharing their experiences. Rose commented, 'It was scary when I was outside [waiting to come into the school] because there were lots of people looking at me'. Martha said she was happy to circle the signs because 'I don't like writing'.

The second element of the survey invited children to draw something they liked about school. Both Rose and Martha were enthusiastic about this and spent some time choosing the coloured textas they would use to start their drawings. They became quite involved in drawing and appeared to be concentrating on the task, conversing with each other about what they would draw. Rose commented, 'This is more funner than the other things, 'cause we get to do what we think and we can draw what we like'.

At one point, Rose paused during the drawing and looked around. The researcher commented, 'That's an interesting drawing. Will you tell me what it is you like about school?' Rose's reply was inaudible. After a few minutes, the researcher asked again. Rose replied, 'I already told you that'; adopting a teacher-like voice, she added, 'Maybe you weren't listening properly'.

The girls spent several more minutes drawing. They took time to discuss with each other which colours they wanted to use, what they might draw and how this would happen. With the drawing complete, Rose held it up to show the researcher, who asked, 'Would you like to keep the drawing or are you happy for me to keep it?' Martha also held up her drawing and replied, 'You can have a look at it, but I'm gonna take it home'. 'Me too', said Rose. 'Is it OK if I take a photo of the drawing?' asked the researcher. 'Sure', the girls replied. They positioned the drawings on the table for a photo. Once it was taken, Martha leaned over and said, 'Can we see?'

Rose: Let me look. [looks at digital image] Mm. That's OK.
Martha: Where does it go now?
Sue: If you think it is OK, it might go in the report. In the report, we will tell others about what you have said, but we won't tell your names or your school.
Rose: What does that mean?

Sue:	We will write a report that says what children and parents and teachers have said about starting school. We will send it to the people who want to help kids when they start school and they will help tell others about what is important.
Martha:	What about the pictures?
Sue:	If you say it is OK, we could put the drawings in the report.
Rose:	With our names?
Sue:	No, not your real names. But if you tell me what you would like to say about the drawing, we can put that in as well.
Martha:	OK. [points to her drawing] I don't want to say anything. Just nothing.
Rose:	I just love it.
Sue:	What is it that you love?
Rose:	I really love it a lot. My picture. [points to the drawing]. You can write that.

Several other versions of the same survey had been developed to provide a choice for children in how they engaged with the task. Recalling the earlier conversation about these other versions, Rose asked, 'Can we do those ones as well?' Rose and Martha then proceeded to play a matching game using cards to respond to the survey questions. When asked which version they preferred, Rose replied, 'The one with the writing, the one like grown-ups do, with writing and stuff'. The game quickly moved to one that was unrelated to the topic of starting school as the girls generated a range of seemingly unrelated questions to be answered by placing a card on the desk. They soon dissolved into laughter, which ceased as the teacher re-entered the room and announced that it was almost home time.

Participation choices

Children's understanding of the voluntary nature of participation can be undermined by several factors, including their perceived obligations to parents and/or teachers and their sense of how adults will react if they withdraw (Bray, 2007; Bruzzese and Fisher, 2003; Ondrusek, Abramovitch, Pencharz and Koren, 1998). When research is conducted in schools or early childhood settings, children may believe that they have little choice about participation, partly because their participation in classroom activities is expected (David, Edwards and Alldred, 2001). In the example above, both Abel and Matt expressed surprise that they could choose to opt out of the activity.

The initial expectation that participation was not voluntary may have been exacerbated by the nature of the activity – a written booklet with spaces for children to share their experiences. This is not an unfamiliar task and is akin to much of the 'work' required of children in schools. While this may make it familiar, it also embeds the task within discourses of school education (David et al., 2001). In such situations, children are likely to expect that such 'work' is to be completed, and to be completed in a particular way.

When children do choose to participate, they expect to be listened to and for researchers to remember what has been said. Rose made this very clear when she adopted a teacher-like voice to indicate that the researcher should have been aware of what had been said previously. This too may reflect the context and language of school.

Knowing that parents or guardians have signed consent forms authorising their participation may generate the expectation that children have no choice to exercise (Ashcroft, Goodenough, Williamson and Kent, 2003). This can be despite researchers providing opportunities for children to record their own consent (Wiles, Heath, Crow and Charles, 2005). While seeking children's informed consent to participate in research is a central tenet of participatory rights-based research, so too is offering multiple opportunities for children to review their participation. In this example, even though the boys had initially agreed to participate and had written their names to indicate this, when provided with a second opportunity they declined. Abel signalled this with his non-verbal actions, notably his hesitant look to the researcher when he was about to circle the 'thumbs down' sign. His potential reversion to the 'thumbs up' sign with the approach of the teacher suggests that he did not expect to be able to decline participation. Matt's fist pump when he was told he could decline participation also suggests a victory of some sort.

What is to be shared, and with whom and by whom?

Research with children is relational, influenced by perceptions of children (Todd, 2012) as well as the nature of relationships within any given context (Horgan, 2017). While a wide range of methods has been described as suitable for use when researching with young children, Gallagher (2008) reminds us that it is the relations between the researcher and the researched, rather than the methods themselves, which generate participatory research.

This is particularly evident in educational settings, where relationships are predominantly based on power differentials. Here, adults (parents and teachers) have assumed that they have the right to know what children have said or done within the research (Christensen and Prout, 2002; Dockett, Einarsdóttir and Perry, 2009; Hill, 2005). Children too are not always convinced by promises of confidentiality, with some expecting that information given to researchers will be shared with their parents (Ashcroft et al., 2003; Hurley and Underwood, 2002).

Implicit in Rose's comment that 'I already told my Mum about my friends' and that Mrs S 'knows we are friends too' is the expectation that what was documented on the survey might be shared with both her mother and her teacher. This was despite what the researcher at least had assumed were clear statements that the information shared was to be confidential and that any information discussed with parents or teachers would not be attributed to individual children. Once again, the educational context may be influential here, as 'work' undertaken at school is expected to be shared with the teacher. However, this was not necessarily the case with the drawings, with Martha and Rose both indicating that they wished to take them home rather than to provide them to the researcher.

Both Rose and Martha were prepared to share photographs of their drawings with the researcher and, when it was explained, with a broader audience. However, before agreeing to this, they were interested in knowing what use would be made of the photograph of their drawing and to where this would go. Rose questioned whether their names would be on the photograph but did not seek a detailed explanation of the use of pseudonyms. In other studies (Conroy and Harcourt, 2009), children have questioned the use of pseudonyms and presented a case for the use of their own names to recognise their contributions (Dockett et al., 2012). Possibly adopting a gatekeeper role, Martha was happy to share her drawing but did not want to add any commentary.

On several occasions during the discussion, Martha commented, 'We'll have to think about that one'. Each time she said this, she moved to the next question, effectively closing the previous discussion. It seemed that Martha was using this strategy to be her own gatekeeper – choosing what points or issues she wished to pursue and declining to comment on others. Perhaps she was using a phrase she had heard others use. Regardless of the source of the response, Martha expected that this strategy would be accepted and that no further prompting would be asked (Farrell, 2005).

How sharing information was to occur

Both Martha and Rose were keen to keep their drawings. They agreed to have them photographed and, after some discussion, to have them included in the research report. It is not clear that they understood the notion of a research report, and they did not seek further information about the report or its function.

Martha chose not to add any commentary to her drawing, while Rose's comment deflected attention from the topic of discussion – starting school – to her pleasure at her drawing. This was understood by the researcher as both girls exerting their own power through regulating the intensity and nature of their participation (Danby and Farrell, 2005; Morrow, 2008). Their verbal and non-verbal interactions suggested that they had reached the limits of their interest in that particular task and were ready to move to something else. However, they did seek to continue the interactions by referring to the card versions of the task and using these to play a game. It is quite possible that they knew the end of the day was near and were using the game to avoid participating in further class activities before packing up and going home.

Strategies used to convey expectations

While much of the interaction reported relates to the two girls, all four children used a range of strategies to convey their expectations. The children's body language and levels of engagement provided indications of their willingness to participate (Flewitt, 2005). Abel's hesitant glance at the researcher and Matt's fist pump provide clear examples of their expectations. Martha and Rose utilised a range of verbal strategies to convey their expectations. Martha used the comment 'We'll have to think about that one' seemingly to signal her personal gatekeeping role. She did not change this statement when asked follow-up questions, indicating that she expected this to put an end to the conversation. She employed a similar strategy when she declined to offer any commentary on her drawing. Rose's commentary on her drawing suggested a strategy of diversion, indicating that she had chosen to engage no further with the topic of starting school.

When discussing the potential incorporation of their drawings into the report, both girls were interested to know more about what this involved. Rose was explicit in her question 'What does that mean?' when told that the photos of their drawings could be included. She expected a response to this question from the researcher that would enable her to make an informed decision.

Discussion

The four children who participated in these interactions used several strategies to convey a range of expectations about their participation choices, the information they chose to share and how this was to be achieved. We recognise that these children bring different experiences and expectations to the interactions and do not propose that they are representative of children as a group. However, their actions prompt us to ask a range of reflective questions about children's expectations of their participation in research and to offer these as possible implications for future studies. While there may be many answers to each question, such reflection helps us to consider the role of child perspectives and children's perspectives in research and to consider how we promote the principles of participatory rights-based research (Beazley et al., 2011). On this basis, we ask:

- Do children expect to have a genuine choice about participation when parents have already provided consent? For example, how can we balance sharing the information that parents and teachers have provided permission to talk with children with offering the children a genuine choice?
- What impact does the context have on the research? Does research in schools set up expectations that children have limited choices about participation, or that information will be shared with adults? What actions might influence this and what strategies do we have to respond appropriately?
- How do the activities in which children are asked to participate impact on their choices? For example, do school-type tasks promote school-type expectations about completion and participation?
- What opportunities are provided for children to access information about the research and their participation that make sense to them? How do we engage with children about their expectations of the research?
- How do researchers actively listen to children's perspectives? What strategies are used to support verbal and non-verbal interactions and to convey to children that adults are listening? How can listening progress to constructing shared understandings and shared meanings?
- How do we recognise and respect the range of strategies children use to manage their participation in research? For example, do we acknowledge children as potential gate-keepers as they choose what information is shared, with whom and how?
- What opportunities are provided to consider, and how do we respond to, children's expectations about the artefacts they create in research activities?

There will be many instances where children express their views or share their experiences in very clear terms. There will also be other times when seeking to understand these expressions requires interpretation or inference on the part of the adults.

While promoting the inclusion of children's voices, distinctions have been made between child perspectives in research and children's perspectives. Sommer et al. (2013) describe taking a child perspective as seeking to understand a child's point of view, noting that 'the adult's intention is directed towards an understanding of children's perceptions, experiences, utterances and actions in the world ... a child perspective is not the child's experience' (p. 463). This definition recognises children as unique individuals and ascribes the role of adults as seeking to build some shared meaning through interactions. On the other hand, children's perspectives 'represent children's own experiences, perceptions and understandings of their life world' (p. 463). The difference between these two perspectives lies in who formulates the perspective. A child perspective is based on inferences and interpretations made by adults, drawn from shared interactions and meaning-making among those adults and the children involved. It recognises the role of interaction in the construction of knowledge and meaning. Children's perspectives rely on children's reporting of their own experiences through their interactions (verbal and non-verbal). Such input is central to recognising children's rights and to supporting their expression of these rights. While these positions may seem to be in opposition, they are often complementary and together contribute to children's perspectives being acknowledged and their rights supported. It is important for children to have opportunities to express their thoughts and feelings and to describe their own experiences. It is equally important for adults to listen to children, seek to understand their expressions, and help construct meaning and understanding around these.

In offering the questions noted previously and reflecting on the interactions reported in this chapter, we recognise that adults and children may well have different expectations about research and research participation. As prompts to reflect on this, we have reported both children's perspectives (their words and actions) and researcher interpretation based on shared interactions.

Conclusion

The CRC (United Nations, 1989) and subsequent General Comments acknowledge children as rights-holders and promote actions that support the 'best interests of the child'. Central to these notions is supporting children's rights to be heard in matters that are relevant for them. Much is known about what researchers expect from researching with young children. Each time a project involving children's participation is conceptualised and described to a funding body or ethics committee, researchers outline their expectations for engaging with children in research. These expectations often include accessing perspectives not available to adults or seeking data about children's lived experiences. However, little is known about children's expectations of research participation.

Reflection on the interactions included in this chapter suggests that young children hold a range of expectations about research participation relating to their choices, the nature of their participation and control over that participation. Research conducted in educational settings can contribute to expectations of limited choice – particularly when tasks resemble work activities undertaken in that setting. The surprise expressed by the two boys suggests that, in their context, such choice is not routinely available. The children involved in this project expressed expectations about the nature of their participation. While overall control resided with the adult researcher, the children exercised both power and control as they responded in different ways.

The principles of participatory rights-based research offer a framework to explore the expectations of all involved in research with young children. Research that is genuinely respectful of children acknowledges their rights to make informed choices about participation and the nature of that participation, regardless of the context in which the research occurs. The same ethical practice that guides research with adults is applicable to research with children. The cornerstone of such practice is voluntary participation and the avoidance of exploitation. One implication of this is that researchers need to be very aware of the potential influence of educational contexts on children's participation. While it may be convenient to engage with children in these contexts, there is the possibility that researchers may exploit children's expectations that they are required to engage in activities designed by adults in such situations.

These same principles advocate for systemic and valid generation of data, accompanied by rigorous data analysis. We suggest that rich and reliable data are generated when children's decisions are respected and when they feel that their perspectives are listened to and taken seriously. This is likely to occur when research prioritises children's own experiences and opinions, but does not exclude the generation of child perspectives as adults and children construct shared understandings. The final characteristic of participatory rights-based research involves disseminating and reporting research in ways that aim to make a positive difference to their lives. We suggest that exploration of children's expectations of research participation contributes to this through increasing awareness of the ways in which they position themselves and are positioned by researchers in such endeavours. In particular, it requires researchers to question the ways in which they recognise children as rights-holders; seek to engage children in high-quality research that is relevant to and for them; and offer opportunities to express their views in ways that are appropriate for them and do not exploit either the children or the data they contribute.

References

Ansell, Nicola, Elsbeth Robson, Flora Hajdu, and Lorraine van Blerk. 2012. "Learning from Young People about their Lives: Using Participatory Methods to Research the Impacts of AIDS in Southern Africa." *Children's Geographies* 10 (2): 169–186.

Ashcroft, Richard, Trudy Goodenough, Emma Williamson, and Julie Kent. 2003. "Children's Consent to Research Participation: Social Context and Personal Experience Invalidate Fixed Cutoff Rules." *American Journal of Bioethics* 3 (4): 16–18.

Beazley, Harriot, Sharon Bessell, Judith Ennew, and Roxana Waterson. 2011. "How Are Human Rights of Children Related to Research Methodology?" In *The Human Rights of Children: From Visions to Implementation*, edited by Antonella Invernizzi and Jane Williams, 159–178. London: Taylor and Francis.

Bray, Lucy. 2007. "Developing an Activity to Aid Informed Assent when Interviewing Children and Young People." *Journal of Research in Nursing* 12 (5): 447–456.

Bruzzese, Jean-Marie, and Celia B. Fisher. 2003. "Assessing and Enhancing the Research Consent Capacity of Children and Youth." *Applied Developmental Science* 7 (1): 13–26.

Christensen, Pia, and Alan Prout. 2002. "Working with Ethical Symmetry in Social Research with Children." *Childhood* 9 (4): 477–497.

Christensen, Pia, and Alan Prout. 2005. "Anthropological and Sociological Perspectives on the Study of Children." In *Researching Children's Experience*, edited by Sheila Greene and Diane Hogan, 42–60. London: Sage.

Clark, Alison, and Peter Moss. 2001. *Listening to Young Children: The Mosaic Approach*. London: National Children's Bureau and Joseph Rowntree Foundation.

Conroy, Heather, and Deborah Harcourt. 2009. "Informed Agreement to Participate: Beginning the Partnership with Children in Research." *Early Child Development and Care* 179 (2): 157–165.

Danby, Susan, and Ann Farrell. 2005. "Opening the Research Conversation." In *Ethical Research with Children*, edited by A. Farrell, 49–67. London: Open University Press.

David, Miriam, Rosalind Edwards, and Pam Alldred. 2001. "Children and School-Based Research: 'Informed Consent' or 'Educated Consent'?" *British Educational Research Journal* 27 (3): 347–365.

Dockett, Sue, Johanna Einarsdóttir, and Bob Perry. 2009. "Researching with Children: Ethical Tensions." *Journal of Early Childhood Research* 7 (3): 283–298.

Dockett, Sue, Sarah Main, and Lynda Kelly. 2011. "Consulting Young Children: Experiences from a Museum." *Visitor Studies* 14 (1): 13–33.

Dockett, Sue, and Bob Perry. 2012. "'In Kindy You Don't Get Taught': Continuity and Change as Children Start School." *Frontiers of Education in China* 7 (1): 5–32. doi:10.3868/s110-001-012-0002-8

Dockett, Sue, and Bob Perry. 2014a. *Continuity of Learning: A Resource to Support Effective Transition to School and School Age Care*. Canberra, ACT: Australian Government Department of Education.

Dockett, Sue, and Bob Perry. 2014b. "Participatory Rights-Based Research: Learning from Young Children's Perspectives in Research that Affects their Lives." In *Handbook of Research Methods in Early Childhood Education: Review of Research Methodologies, Volume II*, edited by Olivia Saracho, 675–710. Charlotte, NC: Information Age.

Dockett, Sue, and Bob Perry. 2015. "Transition to School: Times of Opportunity, Expectation, Aspiration and Entitlement." In *Rethinking Readiness in Early Childhood Education: Implications for Policy and Practice*, edited by Will Parnell and Jeanne Iorio, 123–140. New York: Palgrave Macmillan.

Dockett, Sue, and Bob Perry. 2016a. "Imagining Children's Strengths as They Start School." In *Disrupting Early Childhood Education Research: Imagining New Possibilities*, edited by Will Parnell and Jeanne Iorio, 139–153. New York: Routledge.

Dockett, Sue, and Bob Perry. 2016b. "Supporting Children's Transition to School Age Care." *Australian Educational Researcher* 43 (3): 309–326. doi:10.1007/s13384-016-0202y

Dockett, Sue, Bob Perry, and Emma Kearney. 2012. "Promoting Children's Informed Assent in Research Participation." *International Journal of Qualitative Studies in Education* 26 (7): 802–828. doi:10.1080/09518398.2012.666289

Einarsdóttir, Johanna. 2014. "Children's Perspectives on the Role of Preschool Teachers." *European Journal of Early Childhood Education* 23 (4): 679–697. doi:10.1080/1350293X.2014.969087

Farrell, Ann. 2005. *Ethical Research with Children*. Maidenhead: Open University Press.

Flewitt, Rosie. 2005. "Conducting Research with Young Children: Some Ethical Issues." *Early Childhood Development and Care* 175 (6): 553–565.

Gallagher, Michael. 2008. "Power Is Not an Evil: Rethinking Power in Participatory Methods." *Children's Geographies* 6 (2): 137–150.

Hill, Malcolm. 2005. "Ethical Considerations in Researching Children's Perspectives." In *Researching Children's Experience: Approaches and Methods*, edited by S. Greene and D. Hogan, 61–86. London: Sage.

Horgan, Deidre. 2017. "Child Participatory Research Methods: Attempts to Go 'Deeper'." *Childhood* 24 (2): 245–259. doi:10.1177/0907568216647787

Hunleth, Jean. 2011. "Beyond on or with: Questioning Power Dynamics and Knowledge Production in 'Child-Oriented' Research Methodology." *Childhood* 18 (1): 81–93.

Hurley, Jennifer C., and Marion K. Underwood. 2002. "Children's Understanding of Their Research Rights before and after Debriefing: Informed Assent, Confidentiality, and Stopping Participation." *Child Development* 73 (1): 132–143.

James, Allison, and Alan Prout. 1997. *Constructing and Reconstructing Childhood: Contemporary Issues in the Sociological Study of Childhood* (2nd ed). London: Falmer Press.

Kjørholt, Anne Trina. 2004. *Childhood as a Social and Symbolic Space: Discourses on Children as Social Participants in Society*. Trondheim: Department of Education, Norwegian Centre for Child Research.

Lundy, Laura, Lesley McEvoy, and Bronagh Byrne. 2011. "Working with Young Children as Co-Researchers: An Approach Informed by The United Nations Convention on the Rights of the Child." *Early Education and Development* 22 (5): 714–736. doi:10.1080/10409289.2011.596463

Morrow, Virginia. 2008. "Ethical Dilemmas in Research with Children and Young People about Their Social Environments." *Children's Geographies* 6 (1): 49–61.

Ondrusek, Nancy, Rona Abramovitch, Paul Pencharz, and Gideon Koren. 1998. "Empirical Examination of the Ability of Children to Consent to Clinical Research." *Journal of Medical Ethics* 24 (3): 158–165.

Perry, Bob, and Sue Dockett. 2011. "'How 'Bout We Have a Celebration?' Advice from Children on Starting School." *European Early Childhood Education Research Journal* 19 (3): 375–388.

Prout, Alan. 2000. "Children's Participation: Control and Self-Realisation in British Late Modernity." *Children and Society* 14 (4): 304–315.

Sommer, Dion, Ingrid Pramling Samuelsson, and Karsten Hundeide. 2013. "Early Childhood Care and Education: A Child Perspective Paradigm." *European Early Childhood Education Research Journal* 21 (4): 459–475.

Todd, Liz. 2012. "Critical Dialogue, Critical Methodology: Bridging the Research Gap to Young People's Participation in Evaluating Children's Services." *Children's Geographies* 10 (2): 187–200.

United Nations. 1989. *The United Nations Convention on the Rights of the Child*. New York: United Nations.

United Nations Committee on the Rights of the Child. 2006. *General Comment No. 7 Implementing Child Rights in Early Childhood*. www.refworld.org/docid/460bc5a62.html

United Nations Committee on the Rights of the Child. 2009. *The Right of the Child to Be Heard*. www.refworld.org/docid/4ae562c52.html

Victorian Department of Education and Training. 2017. *Transition: A Positive Start to School – Resource Kit*. Melbourne, VIC: State of Victoria (DET).

Wiles, Rose, Sue Heath, Graham Crow, and Vikki Charles. 2005. *Informed Consent in Social Research: A Literature Review*. ESRC National Centre for Research Methods. www.ncrm.ac.uk/research/outputs/publications/methodsreview/MethodsReviewPaperNCRM-001.pdf

38

'OTHERNESS' IN RESEARCH WITH INFANTS

Marginality or potentiality?

Ioanna Palaiologou

Introduction

The participatory ideology in research and practice with children is now considered as a democratising process by involving children directly in all aspects concerning their lives, offering a rich narrative of children's everyday experiences and altering our thinking about the ways in which academic research and early childhood practice are conducted (e.g. Christensen and James, 2017). Following this line of thinking, alongside other researchers (e.g. Clark, 2010), I have been adamant that my research with young children will always stay faithful to participatory principles by considering that much knowledge can be produced with and by the children through telling their stories (voices). However, this commitment to participatory research with infants (from birth to 3 years) somehow, as will be explained in this chapter, feels like a dystopia. Thus, over the last few years, I have been questioning the realms of participatory research when seeking ways that infants can become participants in research, where their agency is respected (Gallacher and Gallagher, 2008), their voices (verbal and non-verbal) are heard, and they become constructors of knowledge (Murray, 2016). Therefore, the remaining questions for me are how to stay faithful to the principles of participatory research and how infants' voices can be represented in research, because I am cautious of White's (2011) warnings:

> How much more challenging is such seeing when the subject of our gaze is an infant or toddler who speaks a distinct corporeal language that has long been forgotten by the adult, and who draws from a sociocultural domain that is only partially glimpsed by the early childhood teacher or researcher.
>
> *(p. 63)*

In reflecting on these issues, this chapter extends my previous thinking on research with young children (Palaiologou, 2012, 2014, 2017, 2019; Salamon and Palaiologou, 2019), and first will critically examine key features of children's rights that seem to promote the ideal of participatory research with infants in the current era. The central quest to participatory research with infants, I will argue, is how to equalise what I consider to be an inevitable asymmetrical relationship between researchers and researched. With growing interest in participatory ideology, researchers not only have been investigating how to recognise and respect the diverse voice(s) of the children by avoiding categorising them as developmentally immature, but also looking to see how children and researchers can use a whole range of methods as partners in the research. Participatory research in its current ideological form challenges the notion of *otherness* in research where children are represented by adults as dissimilar, and thus separate from the process and/or remain unfamiliar and different in research. However, by examining theoretical and methodological issues of participatory principles in research with infants and exploring the consequent challenges of investigating infants' spaces and lives, the central argument presented in this chapter is that infants will always be different in research (others).

Furthermore, it is proposed that recognising the concept of otherness (being different and having a different voice, as will be explained later) in research with infants is not necessarily marginalisation so long as their distinctiveness (infants' voice is different from adults' voice) is recognised and respected. In that sense, it will be argued that participatory research cannot be achieved with infants as the asymmetries between researchers and infants cannot be equalised. Finally, it will be concluded that accommodating the concept of otherness when undertaking research with infants offers potential benefits and provides the opportunity for ethical praxis and relationships through developing ethical proximity (i.e. adults being responsive and emotionally attuned to children's spaces and lives).

I address this issue by drawing on examples from two research projects with infants that employed qualitative methodology, mainly naturalistic observations. The first project (vignettes Jack and Ellie) aimed to investigate how adults can understand infants' (birth to 2 years) playful moments and the ways they respond to and encourage them. Using naturalistic observations, 15 infants were observed in their homes for a period of six months. The researcher visited the homes twice a week for about two hours over a period of six months. The second project (vignettes Peter and Edith) aimed to investigate object recognition of infants (from 5 months to 3 years). The key aims were to identify whether, how and when infants recognise objects when showing them photographs rather than showing them miniature toys (such as toy animals or household objects). The project used a set of miniature toys of animals and household toys that were the same in photographs. There were 25 infants involved and the researcher visited them in the day-care centre they were attending. In the first couple of visits, the researcher played with the infants with the miniature toys, but in subsequent visits the researcher showed the photo cards.

Both projects were conducted in an English urban city and the infants involved came from diverse sociodemographic backgrounds and were selected randomly. In both projects, the institutional ethical protocols were considered and all requirements were fulfilled.

The context of participatory research and implications in research with infants

In the 30 years since the publication of the UNCRC, much emphasis has been placed at government policy level, as well as within academic discourse, on the participatory principles of the UNCRC Declaration, and specifically from the combination of Articles 3.3, 12, 13 and 36. Subsequently, it seems that when developing agendas either at policy level or research that involves children, the quest to include children's participation (voice(s)) has been considered to be central. This has led to methodological (Punch, 2002) and ethical (Powell, Graham and Truscott, 2016) considerations that focus on the importance of constructing knowledge and learning from and with children in ways that reflect the agentic ideology of childhood 'in their own construction of knowledge' (Murray, 2016, p. 718). As a result, academic research has seen the flourishing of methods, mainly qualitative, which highlight children's involvement in research by the positioning researchers and children as active co-participants within the process and co-producers of knowledge (e.g. Groundwater-Smith, Dockett and Bottrell, 2015). Consequently, there has been the identification of key elements of participatory research with children that distinguishes it from non-participatory research. These are the control of research process and/or problem identification, information-gathering, the decisions about action following from the information, and how the researcher and the researched can become symmetrical partners in the research process (Christensen and Prout, 2002).

On the one hand, this body of research attempts to understand the world from a child's point of view, with such learnings being contextualised by bridging the lived worlds of adults and children, focusing on applaudable and innovative methods to be used *with* and *by* the children, and being child-led (e.g. Clark and Moss, 2001). On the other hand, there has been discourse about the role of adults and the desired symmetrical relations of adults and children in participatory research as a 'pretence that children are in charge' (Hammersley, 2015, p. 579). Although such contributions appreciate the potential pedagogical value of a symmetrical relationship, they suggest that children 'carrying out investigations is unacceptable and indeed unethical to pretend that this work would normally be equivalent to inquiries carried out by professional researchers' (Hammersley, 2015, p. 579.). Such views make the case that children's participation and voice in research might be assumed or is being presented by adults (James, 2007), and suggest, instead of seeking participation (which arguably might be a fallacy), a need to focus on ethics as 'resources to think a little more complicatedly about the practice of fieldwork' (Thrift, 2003, p. 11).

This line of argument is shared by those researching infants' lives (Elwick and Sumsion, 2013; Elwick, Bradley and Sumsion, 2014a, 2014b; Sumsion, 2014), with Elwick et al. (2014a) discussing the (im)possibilities of identifying the difficulties that arise from the complexities of capturing the 'infant's own perspective', especially for non-verbal children:

> Researchers are aiming to capture or move closer to what can be thought of as the 'infant's (children's) perspective'; arguably a difficult if not impossible entity to ascertain given that researchers necessarily have to draw on personal knowledge, adult concepts and theoretical understandings to construct plausible interpretations of the infant's 'expression of meaning'.
>
> *(p. 203)*

This body of research therefore suggests moving beyond seeking participatory methods in research with infants as '[infants'] 'voice' … is extremely limiting to focus on the word and neglect the body; thus narrative research that relies on the story being told through conversational speech inhibits our understanding of these young children and their experiences' (Fincham, 2016, pp. 89–90). Instead, these contributions urge us to seek alternative ways of (re)examining what voice(s) mean for infants, and suggest to focus on the search either for ethical practices (Elwick et al., 2014a, 2014b) or to 'include any sound, gesture, movement, or word that has potential to be recognised by [an] other' (White, 2011, p. 64).

Research *with* and *by* infants: recognise but not know how

Thus, participatory research has been problematised and questioned as to the extent it can be achieved and implemented *with* and *by* children, including how children can be involved in the research design, be engaged with data collection and analysis via appropriate child-led methods and ethics, and participate in dissemination of the findings (e.g. Gallacher and Gallagher, 2008; Murray, 2017; Punch, 2002;). In participatory research, the overriding aim is for children and researchers to hold equal parts and to be co-positioned (at the axiological level), with both becoming active co-participants (at the methodological level) within the research process and co-producers of knowledge (at the epistemological level). The relevance of engaging with reflexive embodiment and reflexivity are thus emphasised as important elements for participatory methodology to become operational (Powell et al., 2016).

Here, however, it is argued that the relevance of co-producing knowledge with infants (research *with* and *by* infants) has axiological, methodological and epistemological fragmentation as the cognate skills needed by infants to partake in the research process (i.e. the methodology) and to achieve the co-production of knowledge (i.e. the epistemology) are considered to be still developing (Elwick et al., 2014a, 2014b; Salamon and Palaiologou, 2019). It is important to state, however, that in this discussion I am positioning infants as 'individuals with their own point of view and their own hopes to do interesting and enjoyable things for themselves' (Trevarthen, 2014, p. xiii) and consider they have intentions and conscious interest in knowledge and understanding the world around them. Moreover, I appreciate and acknowledge that infants have a cleverness in their communication and development of relationships, and with their use of corporeal language they make conscious attempts to be affectionate, sensitive, emotionally attuned to others, and playful about the physical world and the people around them. Nevertheless, '[t]he essence of participation is exercising voice and choice and developing the human, organisational and management capacity to solve problems as they arise in order to sustain improvement' (Saxena, 2011, p. 31) requires knowledge, understanding and a set of skills that infants are still developing. In any discussion on participation, we cannot ignore that infants start life as dependant on intimate care and protection to become mobile, confident, eager to explore the world and become emotionally attuned to others. Equally, the importance of emotionally attuned sensitive support for the infants' development is critical towards their conscious understanding of their agency. For infants' agency to flourish, social relationships are of key importance, but it requires care and protection that is responsive to infants' efforts and their development. Consequently, participatory research with infants should acknowledge the developmental nature of their agency and not take it as a given.

This leads me to conclude that the notion that participatory research can be conducted *with* and *by* infants is fallacious, as researcher–infant encounters are not symmetrical counterparts at the core architectures of participatory research (axiologically, methodologically and epistemologically). Christensen and Prout (2002) instead propose that in participatory research with young children, a code of ethics where reflexivity and professional judgement are used would be a core requirement to create symmetry. They claim that this notion of symmetry has been based in 'dialogue between researchers and the children who take part in research … a dialogue that recognises both intra-and intergenerational commonality, but also honours difference' (p. 495). This view was endorsed in a later study where infants were researched using photo documentation methods and ethical symmetry was sought, leading Salamon (2015) to conclude that infants as participants in research can be achieved only if the researcher 'acknowledges the inherent differences of infants as research participants' and is aware of 'the potential power imbalances between researcher and participant' (pp. 1027–8).

It seems, therefore, that those who subscribe to the achievement of ethical symmetry in participatory research emphasise respect for children, the differentiation of the child from the adult, and communication between researcher and children (Dockett and Perry, 2007). This communication or dialogue requires, however, a level of linguistic representation of mental schemata, symbols and mental models that are used to communicate and explore abstracts and knowledge. Even visual language used with young children in research (as in the photo documentation methods) is not always 'transparent and universally understood; it is culturally specific' (Kress and van Leeuwen, 2006, p. 4), and although there are claims that visual representations enhance dialogue with children, caution has to be exhibited as some knowledge cannot be constructed and represented either visually or verbally:

> Even when we can express what seem to be the same meanings in either image-form or writing or speech, they will be realised differently. For instance, what is expressed in language through the choice between different word classes and clause structure, may, in visual communication, be expressed through the choice between different uses of colour or different compositional structures. And this will affect meaning. Expressing something verbally or visually makes a difference.
>
> *(Kress and van Leeuwen, 2006, p. 2)*

When referring to research *with* and *by* infants, the notion of enacting this dialogue (verbal or visual) is problematic, therefore, because dialogue rests upon essentialist notions of difference ('I need the other to communicate') and communication of meanings and translation of these meanings into signs, symbols, images, other visual or verbal schemata. Infants, it is argued, are not yet in a cognate position to engage in such a level of verbal or visual encounters with the researchers and translate meaning into signs or symbols (verbal and/or visual) (Guasti, 2017). In that sense, ethical symmetry with infants becomes, at best, difficult to achieve. Instead of trying to bridge symmetrically the imbalanced encounters between researches and infants within the ideology of participatory research, I suggest instead that the challenge is to recognise the difference (otherness) of infants' voices.

Thus, there remain two crucial points about participation: the concept of other in research with infants is not about being merely who stands next to us, but the being with whom we have to research (research about), and since they are different from us we could not understand them fully, and are thus unable to interpret their actions or emotions in the true sense of participatory research (co-construction), as demonstrated in the two vignettes below.

Vignette: Jack
Jack is 6 months old and he is observed at home when the mother is present. The researcher starts interacting with Jack by playing 'peekaboo'. Jack starts engaging with the researcher and laughs with the game. Suddenly, he starts crying, the researcher stops, and the mother picks him up to comfort him. The mother cannot understand why he is crying and says to the researcher that she thought Jack was enjoying playing peekaboo, so she is not sure why he is crying. She does not think it is the game, but something else.

Both the researcher and the mother in this example cannot explain why suddenly Jack started to cry when it appeared to both he was being engaged in an activity that he enjoyed. In any explanations of this observation, one only can assume potential scenarios as Jack cannot explain to them as probably an older (verbal) child would have done.
Vignette: Ellie
Ellie is 7 months old and she has been playing with a picture book that the researcher has given her. She throws the book to the floor and the mother picks it up for her, but she repeats this pattern at least four times. Then the mother (with the instructions of the

researcher) takes the book away and gives her toy key rings that make noise. Ellie takes the toy key rings and starts the same pattern of behaviour, throwing the toy on the floor, which the mother then picks up. It seems she is not interested in the object, but the actual action, and thus the researcher asks the mother to take away the toy and replace it with a teddy bear toy. Ellie throws away the teddy bear and shows discomfort. She places firmly her hands on her face and starts rubbing her chin. The mother picks up the teddy bear and gives it back to her, but once again Ellie throws away the teddy bear (not on the floor as with previous toys, but in a non-targeted direction). She points at the picture book that is next to the researcher and mutters angry noises.

In this incident, we can only assume that Ellie did not want the teddy bear as maybe it was not making the same noise as when the toy key rings or the picture book was hitting the floor or that she did not like the teddy bear. Yet Ellie's mother had nominated these objects to the researcher as her favourite ones.

In both examples, the adults had to be responsive and emotionally attuned to the infants, and could only assume what happened and conclude that both infants withdrew from the research based on past observations and knowledge of Jack's and Ellie's patterns of behaviours. As shown in these two vignettes, when researching infants, it is always the adults that conclude why a situation emerged, thus making it very difficult, if not impossible, to construct knowledge with infants. This does not necessarily mean that participatory research with infants is fatally jeopardised, but it should mean that we need to rethink what can be achieved with infants by acknowledging their developmental and agentic nature as interwoven construction and move away from conflicting examinations of one or the other. As such, instead of trying to engage infants as co-constructors in research, what should be questioned is how we can research infants' lives we do not fully understand and how we have the right to research them. I argue that these questions have not been comprehensively addressed, which leads me to assert that otherness must be recognised and not seen as the marginalisation of infants from research.

If we avoid or ignore recognising the notion of otherness, we may not be aware that we run the risk of projecting adultomorphic perspectives to infants' spaces and lives. Thus, it is proposed that researchers should seek for the potentialities of interpretations of infants' lived experiences within the researcher–infant encounter, acknowledge the asymmetrical relationships of researchers and infants, and recognise the concept of otherness in ethical praxis when researching infants' spaces and lives as a key element in becoming emotionally attuned and responsive towards them and their diverse voices.

Ethical praxis and otherness

Most examples of participatory research have involved children above the age of 3, but there is limited research engaging discourses for infants. As children's rights apply to all children from birth, the issue of how we enact participatory research with infants has not yet been explained fully. In attempts to understand participatory ideology with infants, researchers have tried to (re)conceptualise how participation can be enacted based on both their developmental immaturity and their agentic nature (Elwick et al., 2014a, 2014b). All such work concluded that researching infants' lives is not about knowing with and by infants (epistemological practices), but should be about ethical practices, 'being conscious of the impossibilities of knowing with certainty what meaning they [researchers] may be making of those experiences' (Elwick et al., 2014a, p. 211) and recognising their difference (otherness).

In the light of this, there has been discourse on the nature of otherness in research as infants will always remain different (other) from the adults (Lahman, 2008). Moreover, researchers have started conceptualising the idea of 'other' in research with infants and the role of respect for the other being envisioned in ethics (Elwick et al., 2014a, 2014b; Salamon and Palaiologou, 2019), with all such contributions seeking to examine ways researchers can avoid colonising infants' space and lives. In the quest of ways for how we avoid claims that we can fully understand and interpret infants' spaces and lives, it has been argued that:

> instead of examining methods as parts of participation, research should prioritise the structure of the complex union between methodology and ethical practices. This union should reflect an ethical commitment to creating conditions for engagement by the community for their own purposes.
>
> *(Palaiologou, 2014, p. 691)*

This union between methodology and ethical practices is exemplified in the notion of ethical praxis that seeks to examine research in a holistic way, with an in-depth understanding of the historicity, culture and social environments of the researched. Core to ethical praxis is the idea that researched context has a unique identity and social environments cannot be standardised (Palaiologou, 2014). Thus, I argued that ethical praxis when researching infants should allow for emotional responsiveness (permeability) and emotional relatability to infants (Palaiologou, 2019; Salamon and Palaiologou, in press). I propose that researchers should acknowledge that participatory rights tend to be adultomorphic with their aims, achievements and context, even if they have been done for the protection of children. Instead, I am suggesting that the principle of children's rights should be mirroring how adults can empower infants not to be invisible in our society, with the adult task being to recognise infants as others and not to impose onto/into the infants' own spaces and lives.

As researchers will not be able to know what the actual otherness of the infants is, rather we tend to imagine *we know how* on the basis not only of relevant own experiences, but also from a desire to achieve the enactment of participatory rights as encompassed in the UNCRC Declaration. I am instead arguing that rather than the researcher being concerned with participatory ideology that suggests we can construct knowledge with and by infants that somehow places the infants as knowns and adults as articulating their knowing, we should instead recognise the potentialities of otherness at the core of subjecthood in research:

> [R]ecognising the unique and context specific differences of participants [infants], and acknowledging the subjectivity of the researchers … [g]iven the unique nature of working with infants, in research and pedagogical capacities, critical reflection, interrogating one's own practices, and understandings about ethical praxis is essential.
>
> *(Salamon and Palaiologou, In press, p. xx)*

In this discussion, I have attempted to extend these discussions by arguing that recognition of the otherness of infants when researching their lived experiences cannot be done without recognising that they are and always will be the other (infants) who do not think and feel the same as adults. In that sense, recognition of the infant as 'other' is not marginality or a collapse of participatory rights, but rather one that embraces the acknowledgement and existence of the infants as other (differentiation). There is a real difference, yet this should not be limited to the implementation of the current ideology of participatory research with or by infants as this is a dystopia. Instead, I consider research needs to be conceptualised in terms of context relatedness of infants' spaces and lives. Consequently, I propose that by accepting the otherness of infants as ethical praxis, researchers can seek for ethical research about infants.

Research *about* infants: recognise the notion of 'otherness'

The concept of 'other' has been examined by several disciplines, such as sociology (Bauman, 1993), philosophy (Levinas, 1985, 1991) and psychology (Lacan, 1936/2000; Benjamin, 1998). Sociologists mainly examine the concept as how we construct social identities, while philosophers focus on the place the other and the 'I' are having in human relationships and their interactions. Psychology, and mainly the psychoanalytical school, examine the 'other' in relation to self when relating to others, and the recognition of the other, as Benjamin (1998) describes: 'in the intersubjective conception of recognition, two active subjects may exchange, may alternate in expressing and receiving, co-creating a mutuality that allows for and presumes separateness' (p. 29).

The concept has also been debated in research ethics (Whiteman, 2018), in research with children (Christensen and Prout, 2002; Lahman, 2008), and with infants and toddlers (Elwick et al., 2014a; Salamon and Palaiologou, In press). In all approaches, the concept has been examined mainly from sociological or philosophical lenses and associated with equality and justice. Despite the different approaches from each school of thought, however, the espoused common parameters of otherness are differentiations, recognition and respect of similarity/differentiation, the (im)balance-(a)symmetry between self and other, and how relationships are established and maintained. In the discussion I undertake here, there is no intention to enter the discourse of the varied approaches of 'otherness', but instead to investigate the key parameters of being different (to others) in relation to research about infants and to explore the implications. As I will discuss more fully, however, these elements can become potentialities in research with infants by embracing the parameters of otherness as a value-added component in the ethics of research with infants. Ramos de Miranda et al. (2017) propose that:

> research with children implies an overcoming of the I–other dichotomy in the direction of a plural I–others relationship. It is a plural otherness beyond the duality of the I–other as the plurality of others is a plurality of 'Is', a diversity of perspectives. This child's voice is not that which can be lent to him or her as an abstraction. His/her body is made of flesh and not of the conceptual structures that mold it. The thinking is his/her own; it cannot be derived from a cogito that judges universally. The child's voice is different from the voice of the adult, and the child speaks in a manner that is strange to the researcher.
>
> *(p. 497)*

Such a view could not be more relevant for conducting research *about* infants. As shown earlier, we can assume that we understand and interpret infants' voice(s) (verbal and non-verbal) into words in research. This sets infants apart (otherness) not only from adults, but also from other older children who are verbally articulate, have started to construct their self-identity, and are making attempts to find out how they fit in society by voicing themselves literally or metaphorically with their actions, as will be shown in the vignettes below. Thus, I suggest we need to recognise and embrace this otherness, and the inevitability of asymmetrical relationships should be noted at the methodological and epistemological level.

At the methodological level, where older children can be part of the research design (i.e. choose methods such as a visual aid, to handle a camera or make a drawing), infants have limited skills and dispositions to do so (especially those in their first year of life). It is always the adults that choose the research tools and that are in control of the process. The control that remains within infants is for them to partake in the research. This itself creates an asymmetry as the researcher occupies the infants' space with adult-oriented methods that are often assumed as infant-friendly rather than child-led. At the outset, infants give the impression that they hardly care what the adult is with respect to them, but from the inset the primacy of the adult is the face of the executioner in terms of feeding, cleaning and taking the infant to places. When researching infants as ethical considerations, we need to recognise the physical asymmetries such as the size of the body of the adult, the movement of the infant, and the space the infant occupies when research is taking place compared to the space the adult occupies.

Vignettes: Peter and Edith – asymmetry in physicalityPeter
Peter (5 months old) is on the floor with the researcher. The mother is present. The researcher shows him different toy animals, naming them. After three minutes, Peter appears to be distressed and dis-coordinated. The researcher stops and the mother comes to comfort him by picking him up and walks with him around the room.
Edith
Edith is 2 years and 6 months. She is in the room with the researcher. The researcher is using the same animals as with Peter and gives Edith an animal, asking her to name them. When Edith cannot name them, the researcher names the toy animal for her. After 5 minutes, Edith picks up an animal toy and throws it away by saying, 'No, no'. She gets up from the floor and walks away, going in the corner of the room where the wooden blocks are, and starts playing with them.

In Peter's vignette, it is the adult who is in control of Peter's space and needs to be responsive and attuned to his emotions by reading his mood. In the second vignette, Edith became a participant in the research, but she is in control of the physical space and able to move away. In both examples, Peter and Edith are in control of their involvement in research, and thus in control whether they want to take part and for how long, and not the researcher. This creates an imbalance between them and the researcher. However, whereas Edith can move away independently, Peter needs the adult to be responsive and emotionally attuned and 'move' him away by stopping the research. In Peter's vignette, the adult is in control of his moves, which creates an imbalance as Peter depends on the adult's responsiveness for his movements.

At an epistemological level, while it has shown that it is possible to construct knowledge with older verbal children, with infants (especially non-verbal) this construction is impossible as it will always be the explanation of the adult (as in the examples with Peter and Ellie). At this point, infants cannot interpret their own lives with words due to the cognate asymmetry between them and the adults who will interpret on their behalf. This interpretation will always be adult-oriented, and thus subjective, as they are supposed to know and yet are not the ones who actually know. As such, I argue that researchers should reflect on asymmetrical relationships as ethical matters rather than striving to balance them. I draw on what Levinas (1985) argues about relationships of responsibility to the other:

> I speak of responsibility as the essential, primary and fundamental structure of subjectivity. For I describe subjectivity in ethical terms. Ethics, here, does not supplement a preceding existential base; the very node of the subjective is knotted in

ethics understood as responsibility. I understand responsibility as responsibility for the Other, thus as responsibility for what is not my deed, or for what does not even matter to me; or which precisely does matter to me, is met by me as face.

(p. 95)

In reflecting upon the notion of ethical praxis, relationships to be formed need the construction of self and self-identity (I need the other to relate myself), and it must be remembered that researchers are in a stage where they have constructed self-identity, and as such can place themselves in relation to others. Infants, as Benjamin (1998) and Winnicott (1971), among others, suggest, are still developing means (physical, cognitive, emotional) to separate from dualistic relationships (dependency on carer) and place themselves in the society (agency). However, core to participatory research (and one of its major strengths) is the acceptability and recognition of the concept of self of the participants and the creativity that this brings, which makes such research pluralistic. Such an ambition is challenging at best with research about infants unless we acknowledge that as adults, we do not fully understand them and make ethical decisions that any knowledge acquired about infants is based on adult-oriented explanations.

Conclusions

In this discussion, I have argued that participatory research with infants is troublesome, if not impossible, to be achieved. Equally, however, the recognition of otherness in research with infants does not constitute marginalisation so long as their distinctiveness is recognised, valued, and attention is paid to including the parameters of otherness in the ethical praxis that underpins the research. Recognising otherness and its asymmetrical relationships (such as the physical, cognate and self-identity of infants) offers the capacity to develop and sustain relationships where researchers and infants exist in an ethical proximity (i.e. adults to be responsive and emotionally attuned) with each other instead of trying to equalise these asymmetries. Further to the ideology arising from the UNCRC Declaration of children's rights, we need to open the debate that participation should not be limited to what adults can provide or reciprocate to balance adult–infant relationships. Instead, it is proposed that we should accept the otherness of infants and recognise that their developmental and agentic nature are interconnected and impact on each other. Rather than being concerned how to comprise participatory ideology in research with infants, we should accept that 'relationships with the other is not symmetrical ... in the relation to the face, it is asymmetry that is affirmed ... [the other] is above all the one I am responsible for' (Levinas, 1991 pp. 104–5), and seek to conceptualise as participatory these asymmetrical relationships when seeking ways of sustaining ethical relationships in research with infants. Such relationships might be neither reciprocal nor symmetrical in nature, but should become an ethical imperative when seeking to exemplify participatory ideology when researching infants.

References

Bauman, Zygmunt. 1993. *Postmodern Ethics*. Cambridge, MA: Basil Blackwell.

Benjamin, Jessica. 1998. *Shadow of the Other: Intersubjectivity and Gender in Psychoanalysis*. NY: Routledge.

Christensen, Pia and Alison James (Eds). 2017. *Research with Children: Perspectives and Practices* (3rd ed.). Abingdon, Oxon: Routledge.

Christensen, Pia, and Alan Prout. 2002. "Working with ethical symmetry in social research with children." *Childhood*, 9 (4): 477–497.

Clark, Alison. 2010. *Transforming Children's Spaces: Children's and Adults' Participation in Designing Learning Environments*. London: Routledge.

Clark, Alison and Peter Moss. 2001. *Listening to Young Children: The Mosaic Approach*. London: Joseph Rowntree Foundation.

Dockett, Sue, and Bob Perry. 2007. "Trusting children's accounts in research." *Journal of Early Childhood Research*, 5 (1): 47–63.

Elwick, Sheena, Ben Bradley and Jeniffer Sumsion. 2014a. "Infants as other: Uncertainties, difficulties and (im)possibilities in researching infants' lives." *International Journal of Qualitative Studies in Education*, 27 (2): 196–213.

Elwick, Sheena, Ben Bradley and Jeniffer Sumsion. 2014b. "Creating space for infants to influence ECEC practice: The encounter, écart, reversibility and ethical reflection." *Educational Philosophy and Theory*, 46 (8): 873–885.

Elwick, Sheena and Jennifer Sumsion. 2013. "Moving beyond utilitarian perspectives of infant participation in participatory research: Film-mediated research encounters." *International Journal of Early Years Education*, 21 (4): 336–347.

Fincham, Emmanuel. 2016. Words and bodies: Reimagining narrative data in a toddler classroom, in Will Parnell, and Jeanne Marrie Iorio (Eds) *Disrupting Early Childhood Education Research: Imagining New Possibilities*, London: Routledge, pp. 86–101.

Gallacher, Lesley-Ann and Michael Gallagher. 2008. "Methodological immaturity in childhood research?: Thinking through 'participatory methods'." *Childhood*, 15 (4): 499–516.

Groundwater-Smith, Susan, Sue Dockett and Dorothy Bottrell. 2015. *Participatory Research with Children and Young People*. London: SAGE.

Guasti, Maria Teressa. 2017. *Language Acquisition: The Growth of Grammar* (2nd ed). London: The MIT Press.

Hammersley, Martyn. 2015. "Research ethics and the concept of children's rights." *Children and Society*, 29: 569–582.

James, Alison. 2007. "Giving voice to children's voices: Practices and problems, pitfalls and potentials." *American Anthropology*, 109 (2): 261–272.

Kress, Gunther and Theo van Leeuwen. 2006. *Reading Images: The Grammar of Visual Design* (2nd ed). London: Routledge.

Lacan, Jacques. 1936/2000. The mirror stage, in Paul du Gay, Jessica Evans and Peter Redman (Eds) *Identity: A Reader*, Buckinghamshire: Open University Press, pp. 44-50.

Levinas, Emmanuel. 1985. *Ethics and Infinity*. Pittsburgh: Duquesne University Press.

Levinas, Emmanuel. 1991. *Entre Nous: On Thinking of the Other*. London: Athlone.

Lahman, Maria K. E. 2008. "Always othered: Ethical research with children." *Journal of early Childhood Research*, 6 (3): 281–300.

Murray, Jane. 2016. "Young children as researchers: Children aged four to eight years engage in important research behaviour when they base decisions on evidence." *European Early Childhood Education Research Journal*, 24 (5): 705–720.

Murray, Jane. 2017. "Welcome in! How the academy can warrant recognition of young children as researchers." *European Early Childhood Education Research Journal*, 25 (2): 224–242.

Palaiologou, Ioanna. 2012. Ethical praxis when choosing research tools for use with children under five, in I. Palaiologou (Ed) *Ethical Practice in Early Childhood*, London: SAGE, pp. 32–46.

Palaiologou, Ioanna. 2014. ""Do we hear what children want to say?" Ethical Praxis when choosing research tools with children under five." *Early Child Development and Care*, 184 (5): 689–705. doi: 10.1080/03004430.2013.809341

Palaiologou, Ioanna. 2017. "The use of vignettes in participatory research with young children." *International Journal of Early Years Education*, (Special Edition: Hearing Young Children's Voices through Innovative Research Approaches). 15 (3): 308–332. doi: 10.1080/09669760.2017.1352493

Palaiologou, Ioanna. In press 2019. Going beyond participatory ideology when doing research with young children: The case of ethical permeability, in Z. Brown and H. Perkins (Eds) *Beyond the Conventional: Using Innovative Methods in Early Childhood Research*, London: Routledge, pp. 31-46.

Powell, Mary, Ann Anne Graham and Julia Truscott. 2016. "Ethical research involving children: Facilitating reflexive engagement." *Qualitative Research*, 16 (2): 197–208.

Punch, Samantha. 2002. "Research with children. The same or different from research with adults?"." *Childhood*, 9 (3): 321–341.

Ramos de Miranda, Francine, Israel Fabiano Pereira de Souza, Paulo Roberto Haidamus de Oliveira Bastos, Maria Angélica Marcheti, Maria Lúcia Ivo, Alexandra Maria Almeida Carvalho, Isabelle Campos de Azevedo, Marcos Antonio Ferreira Júnior. 2017. "Research with children: Reading of Emmanuel Levinas and the others." *Revista Bioética*, 25 (3): 493–501.

Salamon, Andi. 2015. "Ethical symmetry in participatory research with infants." *Early Child Development and Care*, 185 (6): 1016–1030.

Salamon, Andi and Ioanna Palaiologou. In press. Infants' and toddlers' rights in early childhood settings: Research perspectives informing pedagogical practice, in Frances Press and Sandra Cheeseman (Eds) *(Re)conceptualising Children's Rights in Infant-Toddler Early Childhood Care and Education: Transnational Conversations*, Australia: Springer.

Saxena, N.C. 2011. What is meant by people's participation? in Andrea Cornwall (Ed) *The Participation Reader*, London: Zed Books, pp. 31–33.

Sumsion, Jennifer. 2014. "Opening up possibilities through team research: An investigation of infants' lives in early childhood education." *Qualitative Research*, 14 (2): 149–165.

Thrift, Nigel. 2003. Practising ethics, in Michael Pyke, Gillian Rose and Sarah Whatmore (Eds) *The International Handbook of Student Voice*, London: SAGE, pp. 105–120.

Trevarthen, Colwyn. 2014. Forward, in Lynne Murray (Ed) *The Psychology of Babies: How Relationships Support Development from Birth to Two*, London: Robinson, pp. vii–viii.

United Nations. 1989. *The Convention on the Rights of the Child Defence International and the United Nations Children's Fund*. Geneva: United Nations.

White, Jayne. 2011. "Seeing" the toddler: Voices or voiceless? in Jayne White (Ed) *Educational Research with Our Youngest*, New York: Springer, pp. 63–82.

Whiteman, Natasha. 2018. What if they're bastards? Ethics and the imagining of the other in the study of online fan cultures, in Ron Iphofen, and Martin Tolich (Eds) *The SAGE Handbook of Qualitative Research Ethics*, London: SAGE, pp. 510–525.

Winnicott, Donald. 1971. *Playing and Reality*. London: Tavistock.

39

CHILDREN AS RESEARCH CONSULTANTS

The ethics and rights of no research about them without consulting *with* them

Sonya Gaches and Megan Gallagher

Introduction

What happens when adults seek to better understand children's worlds? Historically, adult researchers have largely turned to other adult outsider perspectives based upon interviews and observations from family members, teachers and researchers (Smith, 2013). Lahman (2008) notes that children have traditionally been seen as 'unfamiliar and different in research' (p. 282). Their perspectives are often portrayed as memories of adults, as younger, less-capable adults, and those over whom adults have control (Clark, 2005; Corsaro, 2005; James and Prout, 1997; Qvortrup, 1994). Based upon the United Nations Convention on the Rights of the Child (UNCRC) Article 12, researchers are increasingly recognising that the voices of children need to be given due weight in this research, resulting in a move away from research *on* children to research *with* children (Harcourt, Perry and Waller, 2011; Morrow and Richards, 1996; Smith, 2013).

Yet even with increased attention on prioritising young children's views and for young children's perspectives to be given due weight, adults are still entering into the research process based upon and privileging their adult perspectives, from designing the research questions to developing the research methodologies. The research project discussed in this chapter sought to disrupt this further privileging of adult perspectives by seeking the consultative advice from a group of children regarding further research we, adult researchers, were thinking of pursuing regarding younger children's learning, community engagements and hopes for their futures. Specifically, this project's research questions asked: (1) What guidance can child research consultants provide regarding (a) questions adult researchers want to pursue with children and (b) the types of methodologies that might be effective with younger children? (2) How can the words and ideas of children inform the larger research community's approach to investigating the worlds of children and childhood?

This chapter will focus on the ongoing ethical dilemmas and processes that were present as this research consultation proceeded. We will first present some of the ethical issues of research *with* children that led to this consultation. Then we will describe our perspectives on the ethical processes we experienced with the children throughout the consultation. We will conclude the chapter by reflecting upon how we are fulfilling the purpose of the consultation and potential future impacts for our own and the greater education and research communities' work with children.

One important ethical dilemma to acknowledge at the outset is that those writing this chapter are the adults in this consultation *with* children. While the children's words and actions will be ever-present, we describe here our adult perceptions of this process as we were guided by the children and our own prior experiences (James, 2007).

Ethical issues of research *with* children

Child consultancy is not a new concept. Over the past few decades, there have been numerous scholars and community activists who have worked with children as consultants in various contexts, including development of policy (Lundy, Orr and Marshall, 2015; Una Children's Rights Learning Group, 2010), utilisation of children's spaces (Blanchet-Cohen and Elliot, 2011), children's healthcare (Coyne, 2008; Schalkers, Dedding and Bunders, 2014) and throughout the research processes (Clark, 2011; Lundy, McEvoy and Byrne, 2011).

While these consultations are important steps towards more fully embracing children's rights approaches, a great deal of prior and current research on and about children is driven by adult perspectives that view childhood as a particular time in life preparing children to *become* capable and competent (Cannella, 2002; James, 2007; Smith, 2011, 2013). Children in this conceptualisation are seen as vulnerable and in need of protection, which is reinforced by articles in the UNCRC addressing 'provision (to necessary, not luxury, goods, services and resources)' and 'protections (from neglect, abuse, exploitation and discrimination)' (Alderson, 2008, p. 17). It can be argued that due to biology and the powerful positions of many adults, young children do require some specialised care and considerations, as do older children and youth at particular times and in certain circumstances. For these reasons, children and those defined as legal minors are considered 'vulnerable populations' when seeking ethics approvals for research (Ketefian, 2015; see also Health Research Council of New Zealand, 2015; National Health and Medical Research Council, 2015; U.S. Department of Health & Human Services (DHHS), n.d.).

One approach taken by other vulnerable populations (e.g. indigenous communities, refugees, etc.) in addressing their unique ethical needs is community engagement in the consultative process (Dickert and Sugarman, 2005). Community engagement such as this creates spaces for the enactment of children's participation rights as framed by the UNCRC, where children have the right to have their voice given due weight in matters that affect them and to express these views in manners of their choice and as appropriate for their age and abilities (UNCRC Articles 12 and 13; General Comment No. 7).

Throughout this chapter, we make a distinction between community consultation, community consent and individual consent (Dickert and Sugarman, 2005). Individual consent is the process by which individuals agree to participate in research based upon information they receive from the researchers (MacNaughton and Hughes, 2008). Community consent seeks the approval or permission for research projects to be conducted within that community, whereas through community consultation the community or vulnerable group advises the researchers regarding the appropriateness of the research, potential specialised cultural or linguistic considerations, methodologies, and other matters the specialised communities deem important. While this distinction will be discussed more fully throughout this chapter, it is important to note that the line between consent and consultation can become quite blurred and lead to ethical dilemmas when consultants have particularly strong reactions to the proposed research. If researchers are authentically and genuinely seeking the consultative input from the community/vulnerable group, they must be prepared to dramatically adjust their plans and/or be prepared to negotiate with the consultative group to find common ground. Otherwise, the consultation becomes tokenistic and merely a symbolic, disingenuous gesture that could do more harm than good, with children becoming disappointed or disillusioned when no change comes from their consultation (Dickert and Sugarman, 2005; Hill, 2006; Lundy, 2007, 2018; Shier, 2001).

To address some of these challenges, Dickert and Sugarman (2005) suggest four ethical goals of community consultations:

Enhanced protection: Consultants identify risks or hazards that researchers had not previously considered and/or consultants can advise potential safeguards and protections.
Enhanced benefits: Consultants identify potential benefits of the research for the research participants or the community/vulnerable group at large. This includes the community's input on research questions and methodologies that would be of benefit to that particular group.
Legitimacy: Consultants provide their views and concerns as unique members of this community/vulnerable population before the research protocol is fully developed.
Shared responsibility: Consultants take an active role in conducting the research and/or consultants assume some of the moral responsibilities for the research itself.

These four goals also highlight further potential ethical issues, such as who counts as a member of this community, how well any subset of a group can represent the perspectives of the larger community, how to address multiple viewpoints from within the community, and when researchers can override or dismiss concerns the consultants express. With the children as the community consultants, this project was primarily focused on addressing the first three of these goals: enhanced protection, enhanced benefits and legitimacy. As adult researchers, we did not enter into this consultative process with the expectations that our child consultants would conduct any of the ongoing research or assume moral responsibility for that research.

While the culture of childhood has often been deemed as a subset culture to that of the dominant culture (Hirschfeld, 2002) and children are classified as among these specialised, vulnerable populations, no similar community consultations are required, nor generally sought, for further research in their cultural community. Why could this be so? We would argue that adult researchers fall back to those historical and traditional conceptualisations of children and childhood that originally placed children in this vulnerable population category at the outset. As those who have been deemed *becomings* (Cannella, 2002; James, 2007; Smith, 2011, 2013), children have not been seen as capable and competent to provide this consultative knowledge.

We ask instead: What if we were to alternatively see children as capable and competent? Anne Smith (2013) noted that 'if children are treated as competent and active participants *now*, rather than as vulnerable and incompetent, then they are likely to *be* competent and active' (p. 66, emphasis in original). This perspective has powerfully influenced a renewed focus in the recently revised national early childhood curriculum for Aotearoa New Zealand through its aspirational statement that sees all *tamariki* (children) as 'competent and confident learners and communicators, healthy in mind, body and spirit, secure in their sense of belonging and in the knowledge that they make a valued contribution to society' (Ministry of Education, 2017, p. 5). Thus, this research consultation takes a childhood studies theoretical perspective (Corsaro, 2005; James, 2007; Smith, 2013) that children *are* competent and capable, and therefore they are important insiders with whom we, adult researchers, are ethically obligated to consult for enhanced protections, enhanced benefits and legitimacy for further research within their community.

We also felt an obligation to proceed as ethically and thoughtfully as possible throughout this consultative process itself. In the sections that follow, we will describe our processes and perceptions of how this ethical consultation with children unfolded. These sections are then followed by our collaborative evaluation of this consultative process and future implications and possibilities for further consultations with children.

The consultative process

The consultative process itself and the children's recommendations are multilayered and multifaceted. The primary purpose was to receive guidance from the children regarding the enhanced protections, enhanced benefits and legitimacy for a later research project. In this particular chapter, we are highlighting the rationale behind the consultations, the process and the ethics of the consultation itself. Therefore, it is once again important to note that while we are privileging the actions and words of these child consultants, we are presenting our adult perspectives on and experiences with the consultative process. It is hoped that through sharing these experiences, we can provide guidance and support to the research and teaching communities in recognition of a moral and ethical imperative of no research about them without consulting *with* them.

Sonya's researcher story and perspectives

The first step in this consultation was determining my consultants. One ethical question is how well any subset of community members can represent the greater community (Dickert and Sugarman, 2005). Acknowledging that no one subset of children can completely represent the vast perspectives and experiences for *all* children, I set about finding a group of children in the same region of the country with a similar demographic representation to that of most communities in that region, and found a classroom of 7–9-year-old children on the South Island of Aotearoa New Zealand. We acknowledge that the population of children is an older cohort than that of the population with whom the further research would be conducted (3–5-year-olds). However, a similar research consultation conducted previously (Swadener, Peters and Gaches, 2013) indicated that 7–9-year-olds, as insiders to childhood cultures, were able to provide keen insights and recommendations for research with their younger peers. Furthermore, this prior consultation had found that particular school-based routines of collaboration, discussion and scaffolded recording of ideas had facilitated a focus on the content of the consultation rather than on learning a new process and eliciting information from that process.

In the current education climate with busy classrooms and teachers, the next ethical dilemma was whether children should be giving up valuable educational time for adult-centric research curiosity (Smith, 2011). The only people who could really determine this were the children themselves. A university colleague recommended Megan, and we found that we were kindred spirits who shared similar views on children's empowerment and rights-based learning experiences. In fact, while I had taught for many years in a primary classroom halfway around the world, Megan and I shared many similar classroom processes and routines that prioritised children's voice and participation in their own learning.

Consenting process

Ethical research consents in Aotearoa New Zealand include a university research ethics consent as well as a mandated Māori research consultation. This Māori research consultation acknowledges the partnership of the local indigenous population and in many regards runs parallel to and informed the intentions of this research consultation. In fact, it was the definition of consultation found on the university's Māori consultation website that originally provided guidance for this project. This definition, attributed to Justice McGechan, states:

> Consultation does not mean negotiation or agreement. It means: setting out a proposal not fully decided upon; adequately informing a party about relevant information upon which the proposal is based; listening to what the others have to say with an open mind (in that there is room to be persuaded against the proposal); undertaking that task in a genuine and not cosmetic manner. Reaching a decision that may or may not alter the original proposal.
> *(www.otago.ac.nz/research/maoriconsultation/otago003272.html)*

Thus, as previously presented, the intention of this research consultation was to listen deeply to children's feedback regarding my proposed further research with an open mind, ready to make modifications to or even no longer pursue that further project.

Subsequent to the university requirements and after receiving written consent from the school principal, I began the process of relationship-building with the children of Megan's classroom (Smith, 2013) by spending a full day in Megan's classroom. The day started wonderfully with the semi-formal introductions influenced by traditional Māori greetings. The children recited their class poem and sang a *waiata* (song) and I responded with my own *pepeha* (formal introduction of who I am and from whom and where I've come) and *waiata*. This had a dual purpose in my mind. It followed the cultural traditions and practices for the region but it also exposed me to the children as a vulnerable learner and definite non-expert (Gollop, 2000) as I am recently arrived in Aotearoa New Zealand and am still a beginning student of *te reo me ngā tikanga Māori* (Māori language and customs). As children assisted me in remembering keywords in my *pepeha* I had legitimately stumbled to remember, they were able to view me as someone who was willing to listen to and be guided by them. The rest of that day was spent getting to know the children, the routines of the class, and becoming more than a visitor, but neither a teacher nor friend.

When I returned a couple of weeks later, I wasn't sure how or if the children would remember me. My name being yelled across the ball court in happy greeting upon my arrival put these concerns to rest. Many of the children were eager to catch up with me and hear about what I had been doing during my absence, while a few others still looked at me a bit shyly and uncertainly. Now that Megan had obtained formal, written, individual parental consents, this visit entailed an introduction to the consultation and the beginnings of the children's individual consent process. Smith (2013) includes the question of 'can the investigators explain the research clearly enough so that anyone they ask to take part can give informed consent or refusal' (p. 73) as one of the two ethical questions basic to research concerning children. Describing this consultative process to adults had, at times, proved challenging, so Megan and I had carefully worked out how to approach the individual consent process with the children as we wanted to ensure as best as possible that they did actually sufficiently understand the project and their freedom to choose whether or not to participate, rather than merely individually consenting because of the power that school participation generally required.

Thankfully, Megan had already done some work around 'scientists', who they are and what they do, as part of her regular planned curriculum. This classroom topic created an opening to discuss the kind of research I do to better understand what happens in the lives of children and teachers. As part of a regularly occurring class meeting time, I introduced the consultation project to the children. Plenty of time was provided to answer any and all questions the children may have had, and then each child received a small brochure (one sheet of folded paper) that contained regularly occurring individual consent language, albeit in more child-friendly language. The brochure also had a place for children to record their own thoughts, questions and concerns for later individual (or group, if they preferred) follow-up. Children were encouraged to share the brochure with their families/*whānau* and anyone they felt could provide them guidance. This brochure also contained a place for their signature of individual consent (Harcourt et al., 2011). Children received a second brochure to keep.

All along the way, we reassured children that they could step in and out of the consultative process. While we had to receive a written individual consent from them for any participation to begin, they could choose to withdraw at any time and they could also choose to rejoin (Harcourt et al., 2011). This in-and-out power of individual consent disrupted the usual established power dynamic of committing to an adult agenda without really understanding what this could entail. While all children ultimately decided to individually consent and join the consultation, a few took a bit longer to decide, and only 3 of the 22 children ever stepped out of the consultative processes throughout the project.

Confidentiality

Confidentiality was another important area of consideration in our ethical approach. To ensure the confidentiality of the children and the group itself, Megan worked with the children during regular class time using established group decision-making processes to create their consultancy group name. Thus, they became the Smart Consultancy Group. Following a class discussion on what code names (pseudonyms) were, why and how they'd be used, each child created their own code name. The children's unique personalities and interests appeared as the code names varied from popular culture references (e.g. Agent Chaspin, Flash) to family events (e.g. Chook after the family recently acquired chickens) to names important to the children (e.g. father's name, the principal's name). Pinning specially prepared name badges to their chests proved to be a signal that it was now time to refer to each other only using their code names so that all audio recordings[1] of the sessions would be confidential (with only an occasional peer or teacher slip-up). Children's posture and demeanour changed once their badge was attached as they would often straighten and acquire a more serious, intense facial expression. They were settling into serious work and they took it seriously.

Worthiness of potential future research

Once these ethical processes of consent and confidentiality were addressed, we began the consultation work itself. The second of Smith's (2013) two ethical questions that are basic to research concerning children asked whether or not the research itself was worth doing. This was the first task for the Smart Research Group, which also addressed Dickert and Sugarman's (2005) enhanced benefits ethical goal of community consultation: Was my intended focus for further research with younger children worthy of investigation? Would this research be of benefit for this specialised (and 'vulnerable') community? Furthermore, if the overall focus of the further research was sound, were we asking meaningful questions about children's lives or were there other more important questions to be pursued? The children's answers to these questions were indeed high-stakes as they would potentially be determining the fate of my own research agenda. At this point, the lines between consult-ation and community consent became blurred (Dickert and Sugarman, 2005). If the Smart Research Group provided feedback that the further research was not worthy, that consult-ation could have become community dissent. In order for this consultation to be genuine, authentic and ethically sound, I felt I had to be willing to walk away from this further pro-ject or work with these consultants to determine if there was another, worthier focus.

So that each child's voice could be heard and more vocal children's opinions didn't over-ride those who were quieter (Smith, 2013), we utilised a classroom collaboration routine already a part of this setting. Megan and the children called this a bus stop process. Children worked in already established small groups and rotated among chart papers each entitled with that chart's focus:

- Should we be finding things out from 3- and 4-year-olds?
- Should we be finding out how and where younger children learn?
- Should we be finding out how younger children are involved in their communities?
- Should we be finding out younger children's hopes for their future?
- What else should we be asking?

At each chart paper stop, the children wrote their responses to the questions on sticky notes they then attached to the chart. Children weren't required to respond, and at times children chose to passively no longer consent to be involved by withdrawing from the activity in favour of chatting with friends or participating in other classroom experiences, such as draw-ing or reading. However, each question still had more sticky notes than there were children in the class, indicating that while some children may not have contributed, others contrib-uted multiple times. Another ethical dilemma is whether or not these multiple contributions swayed the overall feedback. This dilemma was addressed by providing multiple opportun-ities and modalities for children's input here and as follows. In this instance, a child's mul-tiple postings were interpreted as a particularly strong sentiment. As will be seen later, strong sentiments can be presented in other manners that were then also given due weight and consideration.

Overall, the children were very much in favour of the further research project. There were 24 responses (see Table 39.1). Only five responses indicated a negative response. Four of these five responses took a relatively deficit perspective of younger children, stating that 'they wont consentrat' (they won't concentrate), 'the don't understand' (they don't under-stand) and 'they mit have no idera' (they might have no ideas), and 'there silly' (they're silly). However, when reviewing the data together later, the whole group indicated that these weren't of great enough concern to stop the further research, as the younger children would not be in any danger or exposed to risks, thus addressing enhanced protection goals (Dickert and Sugarman, 2005). Rather, the consultants were concerned that the researcher would get much out of the research experience. The consultants' positive responses included that the younger children might have really good/important ideas and that the younger children are smart. Therefore, the researcher would likely learn a lot from these children. One child felt that we should not only ask younger children, but children of their own age, because 'You should know what they're going to do when their (*sic*) grown-ups so that if it's not real you can turn it into something real'. Furthermore, children provided predominantly positive comments for all of our sub-questions.

At the end of the initial bus stop charting activity, I typed all the responses into a large table. A few days later (Lundy, 2018), I returned to the classroom and we projected the chart on the class interactive whiteboard and discussed each response. Seeking feedback promptly was an important ethical step to ensure that our adult translations and understandings of the children's written words were as the child had intended. The children also had the opportunity to add any further comments. This further typing (additions, revisions, translations) happened in real time using the projected document so that children could clearly see how their input was being prioritised.

As a former classroom teacher, I was impressed with how attentive and engaged the children were during this rather lengthy process. While one or two students tuned out at times, the rest of the children were highly engaged, with a great deal of discussion and sharing from nearly everyone. This was clearly a project that they felt was worthy of their attention and participation.

Appropriate methodology

A few weeks later, I returned and was welcomed once again by many greetings and hugs. I truly felt part of this community. Now that the children had indicated that the further research project was one worth pursuing and that we were asking meaningful questions for their community, I was seeking their consultative advice on how I should go about finding out this information from the younger children. While I had some basic ideas drawn from previous research conducted with younger children (Dockett and Perry, 2005; Docket, Einarsdóttir and Perry, 2011; Einarsdóttir, 2005; Gollop, 2000; Thomas and O'Kane, 1998, 1999), it was ethically important to be guided by the Smart Research Group in determining which methods might be most appropriate for younger children in this part of the world at this time.

Therefore, I came to this consultative session accompanied by six pots and four different kinds of counters (Thomas and O'Kane, 1998, 1999) (see Figure 39.1). After a brief introduction to this next part of the consultancy, the children appeared very eager to provide their ideas. It was a beautiful day, and Megan, the children and I decided that it would be very nice to conduct the pots and beans activity outside, sitting at a lunch table in the shade of their huge tree. Megan and I had previously discussed having the children participate in the pots and beans decision-making in partnerships that were a regular part of their class routine. The children acknowledged in the whole-group introduction that they felt this would be a good idea as well. During this introductory whole-group discussion and the logistical planning, the children were once again very involved and there was a real sense of collaboration.

Table 39.1 Children's bus stop responses to 'Are we, adult researchers, asking meaningful relevant questions?'

Question posed to children	Affirmative Responses	Negative Responses
Should we be finding things out from 3- and 4-year-olds?	Finding out things from 3- and 4-year-olds • Yes • Will • Because thay might have a good idea • Yes because it will be fun for them • It will help them lern • You have to be happy • Yes because they have impotent erise (ideas) • Yes they might have relly good ideas • Yes because it will help them learn in a lot of ways • Yes because they dotn no tings • Because they sat me • Yes • Yes because they grow when they get older and then they might be adults • Yes because they grow when they get older and then they might be adults • Yes because they have to be shiat • Yes because they are smart • They might fidget • Yes, so we can learn more • You should ask 8 & 9 year olds. You should know what they're going to do when their grown-ups so that if it's not real you can turn it into something real	• No • No because they wont consentrat • No because they don't understand • No they mit have no idera • I don't think it's a good idea because there silly
Should we be finding out	• Yes, because it will be diferen • Other pepale learna so children lerna	(no negative responses provided)

how and where younger children learn?	• Kids learn from books
	• Yus because if you tell them what they already know, they wont laerng
	• Yes because you ned to grow
	• Yes
	• Yess because it's good for them to learn
	• Yes because if they go thow the chalindjs (go through the changes) when thay littltle thay no when when thay are older
	• Yes so thay can lean more
	• There mum and dad teacs things
	• Let them lean from peoplore that reacorck (research) people
	• Yes becase adolts can no
	• Let them resreck (research)
	• Let them lean from older peopol
	• So they know what researck mean
	• Yes because the teachers would know
	• Yes toecous they tack the hichashes
	• Yes because YES!
	• Yes so you can no win your older
	• Yes because the teachers would like to know
	• Yes ecause it will help them learn
	• I think is a good idy because you no wot there thing and then you can get then on the rit hcrak
	• Yes because we can ask them how they learn
	• Yes because yes of course
	• Yes because then you can help them
	• Becase its in portent
	• Yess because you'll now how much theyv learnt
	• Yes becase its fun
	• Yes because you can help
	• Yes so you know how much they know
	• Triy and triy agen

(Continued)

Table 39.1 (Cont.)

	• Yes because when they go to school they will get a head start	• No
	• Yes! Because we can aks them how they learn	• No because when they're busy they'll say go away.
	• How do they learn maths if they learn maths	
Should we be finding out how younger children are involved in their communities?	• So they can help people	• I don't know … what if they say I don't know
	• They think of good ideas	
	• Yes resin	
	• Yes, because it can help (community) people learn better	
	• Communities	
	• Yes because you will get a lot of ansise (answers)	
	• They learn more	
	• Yes because she can aske people more grat queshins	
	• It helps them lerm	
	• Yes, I tech it is good so they lone (learn)	
	• Yes decase you can lerm other places and good and bad	
	• Yes because it will help Sonya work	
	• Yes because if we do we will learn more	
	• Yes because if they are baybies they will learn to do things	
	• Yes because if they are baybies they will learn to do things	
	• Yes because it will help her do her work	
	• Things [are] in are comynerdy (community)	
	• Yes because you can find out what they do	
	• Yes it sounds like a good idea	
	• Yes, so people can help them do what they do	
	• Yes, so they can get help from people	
	• Yes because it might help them know what to do when they get older	
	• Yes because when they are older they might live by themselves and they might need to know what to do.	
	• Yes, because when they live on their own they might not know how to get money and food. They might need to know how to get settled into a house and how much everything costs and how to work at their	

jobs and how to drive their car and how to get credit. And learn how to get onto an airplane and helicopter.

- If they live by themselves they'll need how to tell time.
- Yes because sometimes my mom and dad don't how much money they need to buy food
- Yes because it will help them learn to count money.

Should we be finding out younger children's hopes for their future?	- Yes because you will help htem	- N|O
	- Yes because thay will learn	- No becose it mit be to mash (because it might be too much)
	- YES! Because it might be important to them. And it might be fun	
	- Yes because it will help them learn	- No
	- Yes	
	- Yes	
	- Grat kids that will listen	
	- Yes cos it's helpful	
	- Yes because Sonya and us will get to do more research	
	- Yes	
	- Yes because if it is a little something that does not cost much we can get it for them	
	- Yes because they would have things to do when there grownup (Victoria)	
	- Yes	
	- Yes becos it well hollp the loodell ceds loon (help the little kids learn)	
	- Yes because you a good	
	- Yes because they mite say there a research	
	- It's good for them	
	- Yes because they now how thay are	
	- Yes because they will need money to live	
	- Yes because we want to know where they want to live	
	- Yes because we might want to know what they want to be	
	- Can they grow up	
	- What they want and not what the parents are giving them	

Table 39.1 (Cont.)

	• Yes, you have to know them first to be able to work with them	
	• Yes, it would be good for them to have things for them to do when they're grown up	
	• Yes because with the future it's important to know all the details of what the world is going to be like	
What else should we be asking?	• Fob they eit (what they eat)	• No because no
	• Everthing	• No bece they mit have a important meeting (because they might have an important meeting)
	• Doing maths	
	• Learning	
	• What tv (What they watch on TV)	
	• Yes because yes	
	• What they play with	
	• What they want not what there parents wanted them to have	
	• Having fun	
	• Get it growing so it will win	
	• Ask them when's there birthday	
	• Growing their brains	
	• What do they play with	
	• What thay want iinstd of the perins giving them	
	• Yes, because they will have a hepy ever after	
	• Yes, hoe do they goy (grow?) up	
	• Have a cod name a good cod name	
	• Be stooped (tell them don't be stupid)	
	• You could make them badt's (badges)	
	• Ask them what sort of food they like	
	• You shod see 8 and 9 year oldds	
	• Ha they food and a nice tidey hose	
	• Reading – Can they read? What do they like to read?	
	• What do they like and what do they not like?	

All responses are presented as written on the chart paper sticky-notes. Comments in parentheses are translations of written words provided by the child who wrote the response.

Figure 39.1 'Pots and beans' used with the Smart Research Group

I proceeded to take my materials outside accompanied by the first partnership. They helped me set everything up, admiring the different types of counters I had brought, and then settled into their decision-making and feedback. Each child received six counters that they could place however they pleased into the six pots, which were labelled:

- Talk with children.
- Talk with children while they play/draw.
- Children draw their ideas.
- Children photograph their ideas.
- Show children pictures.
- Your own idea.

Children were asked to tell me either while or after they placed their counters in the pots why these were the pots they chose. This was particularly important for the category of 'Your own idea' since we didn't want children limited by our adult-centric prior research thoughts.

The children's feedback and further ideas can be found in Table 39.2. Children were quite excited to participate in this consultation, judging by the manner in which they exuberantly came running out to the table and were quite chatty about their selections and rationale. The one lone exception was the child who came out rather slowly and grudgingly at his partner's insistence. However, when I reminded him that participating was his choice, he perked up and returned to the classroom. His partner shrugged and continued on with the activity.

Overall, the three most popular responses were to talk with children, to talk with children while they drew pictures or played with toys, and have children photograph their ideas. One child, who Megan reports and I observed is generally very quiet, was particularly adamant about the need for children to photograph their ideas and then talk to the researcher about their pictures. As with the multiple sticky note ethical dilemma, we felt this was significant feedback from an individual child that was then included in creating the research protocol for the later research. A similar stance was taken for the original idea of taking children to a nature spot to talk with them (and draw) due to this child's particular passionate appeal. She wanted to ensure that participating younger children would feel safe

Table 39.2 Children's responses in the pots and beans activity

Student	Talk with children	Talk with children while they play/draw	Children draw their ideas	Children photograph their ideas	Show children pictures	Own idea
Jelly		6				
Boof	1	1		1	1	2 - talk to other children so they can learn
Victoria	1	1	1	1	1	she doesn't know but she'll tell teacher later
Robert	5				1	
Ed		3	3			
Cuckoo	1	1	1	1	1	you take them out to nature in a personal spot and talk to them and draw
Sharpy	N*	N	N	N	N	
Flash	1	2	1	1	1	
Ruby	3			2	1	
DJ		6				
Princess			2	2	1	They could write about it.
Daisy			3	3		
Hunter	4				2	
Agent Chaspin		6				
Rosco			1	5		
John		6				
Rosealla		2	1	2	1	
Mini-man	2	2	2			
Chook	ab°	ab	ab	ab	ab	
Einstein		2	2	1	1	you could have them write about it
Spike	3		1	1	1	
Paul	1	1	1	1	1	explain how....use equipments to show your ideas (use legos)
Totals	22	39	19	21	13	8

* Chose to not participate in this session
° Absent from school that day

and secure being in a natural, familiar environment when working with the researcher. In the whole-group feedback that occurred later, the rest of the children in the Smart Research Group responded very positively to the inclusion of these two individual points.

After this pots and beans session, I revised a general research protocol that had been created as part of a cross-national related research project, Children's Views and Voices (see Maldonado et al., Chapter 33 in this volume), based upon the overall consultation with the Smart Research Group. During my final consultation session, I shared the proposed research protocol once again using the classroom interactive whiteboard. The children and I went through each point in the protocol, verifying that what I was including is what they intended. The children were once again very engaged in the discussion and their focus was primarily on when this protocol was going to be used and by whom. A couple of the children were even volunteering their younger siblings for the further research. One child was even quite adamant that I contact her sister's childcare centre, told me the centre's name and provided me with directions on how to find it. My takeaway from that moment was that these children felt confident enough in the appropriateness, safety and validity of the research that they were willing and eager for their own siblings to be involved. That is a strong endorsement of the consultative process, its enhanced protections, its enhanced benefits and the legitimacy of its outcome.

Megan's classroom teacher story and perspective

From my perspective as a teacher, the ethical process was thorough, and it has prompted me to reflect on my teaching practice, school policy and wider educational systems with an ethical lens. We started from the premise that the students in my classroom were capable, knowledgeable citizens who could contribute valuable insight for the proposed research (Smith, 2013). I believe the success of the dialogue with participants rested on two things: (1) the time spent building relationships both outside and inside the project work itself; and (2) the clarification of the project aims, different roles and concepts participants needed to understand, especially that of consent.

Most of the students involved in this project started school in a play-based learning environment and the sense of student agency underpinning their learning in the junior school continued through to their current classroom. They had an expectation that their voices would be heard on different topics and that they would be involved in democratic processes within their classroom.

Before the initial research, Sonya spent time in the classroom, and she was greeted with our class welcoming ceremony, which reflects traditional Māori welcoming practices. After introductions were made, Sonya participated alongside students in classroom activities, getting a feel for how we worked as a learning community and building relationships. The children quickly warmed to Sonya as a part of our classroom to the point that at the time of writing, four months after the completion of the project, they still ask after her and wonder when she will visit again. Sonya became a trusted adult who they were helping by sharing their ideas and knowledge as part of the Smart Research Group. This relationship was one where the balance of power was more evenly distributed between the adults and children: children decided if they would participate and what they would share, adults decided when sessions would take place and established methods that were more likely to engender useful data using their knowledge of the students and other research (Thomas and O'Kane, 1998, 1999).

The students, being capable and knowledgeable citizens, were involved in a session where the project aims were outlined and consent was discussed fully. We continued to talk about consent in the classroom and what it meant in the intervening days before data-gathering began. It was vital that this concept was understood, and from my perspective it is not a concept that is commonly discussed with young people. Some students were keen to be involved almost immediately, while others took a few days to decide. Either way, they were encouraged to talk with their teacher and parents/*whānau* if they wanted clarification. Their individual consent was sought at the beginning of each session and they were entitled to leave at any time. Being able to exercise the right to participate or not is a right I feel students experience less often in most school settings. It is something that I have reflected on since undertaking this project.

As a teacher having participated in this project, there are implications for schools that may need to be considered, such as how deep our democratic processes go, what students can opt in and opt out of, and who holds the power and why. When teachers or schools undertake practitioner research, do we engage students as participants with rights to consent, do we take our findings back to them for verification, do we ask their permission to share their work with other teachers? Student agency and student voice are currently hot topics in the education sector, but I now question how ethically sound our processes are around these constructs and how often students are viewed as capable and knowledgeable people in their own right.

Since completing the project, the learning from participating has been expressed at various times in the classroom. One notable impact was when the class were participating in a trial of a standardised maths test. Earlier in the year, they had completed a similar maths test where many of the students had expressed negativity and for some anxiety. When presented with this trial, I explained that we were doing this to help the researchers decide if this test would help teachers know what Year 4 students were able to do in maths. One of the students made the connection, 'Oh, like we did when we were in the Smart Research Group'. This generated a lot of positive commentary, and subsequently the participation was positive – there were no complaints or expressed anxiety.

Conclusion

This research consultation was based upon the positioning of children as capable and competent and as members of a specialised community. Ethical research standards recommend, and at times require, consultation with specialised communities for research to be conducted with those communities. We are taking the stance that not only must children's perspectives be given due consideration in matters that affect them (UNCRC Article 12) (United Nations, 1989), but there is also a similar moral and ethical imperative to seek their guidance and consultation in research with and about them.

Our experiences with this particular research consultation demonstrate that children are indeed capable and competent when invited to actively participate in the real research process as collaborative, contributing consultants. We entered into the consultation, which focused on three of Dickert and Sugarman's (2005) ethical goals, which we feel were met. The Smart Research Group identified there were no risks or hazards in pursuing the proposed further research and provided recommendations for how younger children would feel safe and secure during the further research process. They identified the enhanced benefits of the further research by indicating that seeking answers to the proposed questions would help better meet the needs of younger children. The Smart Research Group were able to be a legitimate part of the research process, from establishing veracity of the proposed further research project itself through to the creation and their approval of the research protocol that will be submitted for ethical approvals and cross-national collaborations in further similar research with children.

Finally, where Dickert and Sugarman's (2005) fourth ethical goal, shared responsibility, was not an intended focus of this consultation, we found that the Smart Research Group did assume some of the moral responsibilities for the research itself. They were aware and eager that what they were sharing would have an influence on children now and in the future. They knew that their guidance and consultation for this further research could have a real-world impact on children's lives potentially globally now and in the future, and that their words and ideas would be recorded, published and listened to by adults in many contexts, including internationally. This became especially apparent when they transferred their experiences in this consultation to their actions in a maths research task they were required to undertake in the classroom. Their understanding that being an active participant in the research process made a difference to the outcome of the research meant that they wanted to engage with this required task. Having been through the process of being listened to by a researcher provided them with a sense of comfort in what had previously been a difficult and unsettling experience. The children of the Smart Research Group now saw themselves as capable, competent, active participants who are making a valued contribution to society.

Future impacts and ethical actions

When children know their voices are being heard and given due weight, they expect to be treated as active participants in the world around them. Moving forward, this consultancy process will be driving the further democratic processes in the classroom and further research with younger children. In school settings, this consultative process challenges administrators and teachers to recognise students as capable and competent members of the learning community whose powerful voices must be heard and acted upon. Guidance from this consultation has already been utilised in grant applications and related ethics applications. Any publications related to the consultation with the Smart Research Group will be forwarded to the children's teacher and school. Sonya also intends to return to the group with other updates from international collaborations and research conference presentations. This was serious work that requires ongoing recognition and researcher accountability. Personally and professionally, as a researcher, this process will always be used alongside other consultative processes, such as the already-required Māori consultation. Furthermore, it is hoped through the sharing of this consultative process that the ethical standard in all research involving children includes similar child-based research consultations, as is already the standard in research involving other 'vulnerable' populations. This reinforces the position of no research about them without consulting *with* them.

Note

1 All sessions with the children were audio-recorded and later transcribed. This was an important ethical step as we wanted to be able to best represent children's actual statements and not be over-reliant on the written responses from children or our field notes.

References

Alderson, Priscilla. 2008. *Young Children's Rights: Exploring Beliefs, Principles and Practice*. 2nd ed. London: Jessica Kingsley Publishers.
Blanchet-Cohen, Natasha and Enid Elliot. 2011. "Young children and educators engagement and learning outdoors: A Basis for rights-based programming." *Early Education and Development*, 22(5), 757–777.

Cannella, Gaile. 2002. *Deconstructing Early Childhood Education: Social Justice and Revolution*. New York: Peter Lang.

Clark, Alison. 2005. "Listening to and involving young children: A review of research and practice." *Early Child Development and Care*, 175(6): 489–505.

Clark, Cindy Dell. 2011. *In a Younger Voice: Doing Child-Centered Qualitative Research*. New York, NY: Oxford University Press.

Corsaro, William. 2005. *The Sociology of Childhood*. 2nd ed. London: Sage.

Coyne, Imelda. 2008. "Children's participation in consultations and decision-making at health service level: A Review of the literature." *International Journal of Nursing Studies*, 45(11), 1682–1689.

Dickert, Neal and Jeremy Sugarman. 2005. "Ethical goals of community consultation in research." *American Journal of Public Health*, 95(7): 1123–1127.

Docket, Sue, Jóhanna Einarsdóttir and Bob Perry. 2011. "Balancing methodologies and methods in researching with young children." In *Researching Young Childrens Perspectives: Debating the ethics and Dilemmas of Educational Research with Children*, Edited by Edited by Deborah Harcourt, Bob Perry and Tim Waller, 68–82. London: Routledge.

Dockett, Sue and Bob Perry. 2005. "Children's drawings: Experiences and expectations of school." *International Journal of Innovation and Equity in Early Childhood*, 3(2): 77–89.

Einarsdóttir, Jóhanna. 2005. "Playschool in pictures: Children's photographs as a research method." *Early Child Development and Care*, 175(6): 523–541.

Gaches, Sonya and Megan Gallagher. 2018. "Children as research consultants: Creating an interview protocol with children for younger children." Paper presented at Reconceptualizing Early Childhood Education (RECE) Conference, Copenhagen Denmark, October 14- 18.

Gollop, Megan M. 2000. "Interviewing children: a research perspective." In *Children's Voices: Research, Policy and Practice*, edited by Anne B. Smith, Nicola J. Taylor and Megan M. Gallop, 18–36. Auckland: Pearson.

Harcourt, Deborah, Bob Perry and Tim Waller. 2011. *Researching Young Children's Perspectives: Debating the Ethics and Dilemmas of Educational Research with Children*. London: Routledge.

Health Research Council of New Zealand. 2015. Special considerations." www.hrc.govt.nz/ethics-and-regulatory/applying-ethical-approval/specific-considerations

Hill, Malcom. 2006. ""Children's voices on ways of having a voice: Children's and young people's perspectives on methods used in research consultation." *Childhood*, 13(1): 69–89.

Hirschfeld, Lawrence A. 2002. "Why don't anthropologists like children." *American Anthropologist*, 104(2): 611–627.

James, Alison. 2007. "Giving voice to children's voices: practices and problems, pitfalls and potentials." *American Anthropologist*, 109(2): 261–272.

James, Alison and Alan Prout. 1997. *Constructing and Reconstructing Childhood*. London: RoutledgeFalmer.

Ketefian, Shaké. 2015. "Ethical considerations in research: Focus on vulnerable groups." *Invest. Educ. Enferm*, 33(1): 164–172.

Lahman, Maria. 2008. "Always othered: Ethical research with children." *Journal of Early Childhood Research*, 6(3): 281–300.

Lundy, Laura. 2007. "'Voice'is not enough: conceptualising Article 12 of the United Nations Convention on the Rights of the Child." *British educational research journal*, 33(6): 927–942.

Lundy, Laura. 2018. "In defence of tokenism? Implementing children's right to participate in collective decision-making." *Childhood*, 2018: 0907568218777292.

Lundy, Laura, Lesley McEvoy, and Bronagh Byrne. 2011. "Working with young children as co-researchers: An approach informed by the United Nations Convention on the Rights of the Child." *Early education & development*, 22(5): 714–736.

Lundy, Laura, Karen Orr and Chelsea Marshall. 2015. Towards better investment on the rights of the child: The view of children, .Centre for Children's Rights, Queen's University Belfast, Belfast.

MacNaughton, Glenda and Patrick Hughes. 2008. *Doing Research in Early Childhood Studies: A Step by Step Guide*. Berkshire, England: Open University Press.

Ministry of Education. 2017. *Te Whāriki: He Whāriki Mātauranga mō ngā mokopuna o Aotearoa: Early Childhood Curriculum*. Wellington: Author.

Morrow, Virginia and Martin Richards. 1996. "The ethics of social research with children: An overview." *Children and Society*, 10: 90–105.

National Health and Medical Research Council. 2015. *National statement on Ethical Conduct in Human Research*. Australia: National Health and Medical Research Council. www.nhmrc.gov.au/guidelines-publications/e72

Office of the United Nations High Commissioner for Human Rights. 2005. *United Nations Converntion on the Righs of the Chid, General Comment No. 7*. Geneva, Switzerland:Author.

Qvortrup, Jens. 1994. "Childhood matters: An introduction." In *Childhood Matters: Social Theory, Practice and Poltics*, edited by Jens Qvortrup, Marjatta Bardy, Giovanni Sgritta and Helmut Wintersberger, 1–24. Aldershot, England: Avebury.

Schalkers, Inge, Christine WM Dedding, and Joske FG Bunders. 2014."'[I would like] a place to be alone, other than the toilet'–Children's perspectives on paediatric hospital care in the Netherlands." *Health expectations*, 18(6): 2066–2078.

Shier, Harry. 2001. "Pathways to participation: Opening, opportunities, and oblications." *Children and Society*, 15: 107–117.

Smith, Anne. 2011. "Respecting Children's Rights and Agency: Theoretical Insights into Ethical Research Procedures." In *Researching Young Children's Perspectives: Debating the Ethics and Dilemmas of Educational Research with Children*, edited by Deborah Harcourt, Bob Perry and Tim Waller, 11–25. London: Routledge.

Smith, Anne. 2013. *Understanding Children and Childhood*. 5th ed. Wellington: Bridget Williams Books.

Swadener, Beth, Lacey Peters and Sonya Gaches. 2013. "Taking Children's Rights and Participation Seriously: Cross-national Perspectives and Possibilities." In *Re-situating Canadian Early Childhood Education*, edited by Veronica Pacini-Ketchabaw and Larry Prochner, 187–210. New York: Peter Lang.

Thomas, Nigel and Claire O'Kane. 1998. "The ethics of participatory research with children." *Children & Society*, 12: 336–348.

Thomas, Nigel and Claire O'Kane. 1999. "Children's participation in reviews and planning meetings when they are 'looked after' in middle childhood." *Child and Family Social Work*, 4: 221–230.

U.S. Department of Health & Human Services (DHHS). (n.d.) Vulnerable populations. www.hhs.gov/ohrp/regulations-and-policy/guidance/vulnerable-populations/index.html.

Una Children's Rights Learning Group. 2010. *Children's Rights in Una and Beyond: Transnational Perspectives* (Una Working Paper 7). Belfast, Northern Ireland: Una. Retrieved from www.unaglobal.org/en/page/reports.

United Nations. 1989. *United Nations Convention on the Rights of the Child*. New York: UNICEF.

40

USING THE UNCRC AS A FRAME OF REFERENCE FOR ETHICAL RESEARCH WITH YOUNG CHILDREN

Aline Cole-Albäck

Introduction

There are hundreds of different images of the child. Each one of you has inside yourself an image of the child that directs you as you begin to relate to a child. This theory within you pushes you to behave in certain ways; it orients you as you talk to the child, listen to the child, observe the child.

(Malaguzzi, 1994, p. 52)

The quote above is taken from a seminar presented by Professor Malaguzzi to an audience of education professionals; however, it would have been equally fitting to an audience of childhood researchers. Regardless of the image(s) of the child that directs us, what children are entitled to is research conducted in an ethical way, whether research is about or for, with or by children.

The premise of this chapter is that if we recognise that children have rights, then the United Nations Convention on the Rights of the Child (UNCRC) (UN, 1989) ought to inform research with children (Bell, 2008). However, much of the academic debate to date has focused on jurisprudence and the legal implementation of the UNCRC, with limited discussions on how children's rights are relevant outside of the legal and political sphere (Reynaert et al., 2009, 2012) and how the UNCRC can be used as a frame of reference to inform research ethics guidelines and ethical practice in the field (Bell, 2008). This chapter will address this gap drawing on a PhD research study.

It will be argued here that an ethics framework informed by children's rights offers a more comprehensive view of what constitutes ethical research with children. The reason for suggesting this is because childhood research informed by rights has as its starting point an image of the child as a subject (not object) of equal worth to adults, not only worthy of respect, but *entitled* to respect at every stage of the research process. A rights-based ethics framework also necessitates specific research design considerations, according to Lundy and McEvoy (2012). They suggest that for research with children to qualify as rights-based, there are criteria that need to be met: the research aims should be informed by the

UNCRC, the research process should comply with the UNCRC, the outcomes should build the capacity of children and duty-bearers, and the process should further the realisation of children's rights.

The first section of the chapter briefly outlines the context of the study and the countries involved, before introducing the structured rights-based ethical approach to the research process used in the study. The ensuing phenomenologically inspired analysis and discussion will illustrate through positive or affirmative examples how the UNCRC can guide researchers when reflecting on how to engage ethically in research with very young children.

Research context and methodology

The data informing this chapter are from a research study into children's rights in early childhood education, gathered in England and Finland (2016–2017). Two settings in each country took part, involving 13 staff and 16 2-year-old children. The reason for choosing England was because this is where I live and work, and where I hope to make a direct difference, and the reason for choosing Finland was because of its high status in the league tables (OECD, 2015) and different history of engagement with children's rights due to its political and sociocultural heritage. Choosing two countries with distinctive histories of engagement with rights was expected to provide a richer database than a single-country study would. Interestingly, data revealed differences in experiences but common concerns regarding ethical issues. The reason for choosing the age group was because of the growing number of 2-year-olds in formal or out-of-home care across Europe (DfE, 2018; UNICEF, 2008). As this is a relatively recent phenomenon, there is still limited research with this age group, particularly taking a rights-based research approach (Rayna and Laevers, 2011).

English context

Under New Labour (1997–2010), there was a growing commitment to children's rights, as evident in several government publications (DCSF, 2009, 2010). New Labour laid the foundation for a more explicit rights-based approach to childhood provision through legislation such as the Children Act 2004 and the *Every Child Matters* reform programme (DfES, 2003). However, since the formation of the Cameron ministry in 2010 and the archiving of the *Every Child Matters* agenda, and the subsequent May ministry in 2016, children's rights are again less visible in government initiatives and policies (CRAE, 2015, 2016).

Despite the current situation on the (in)visibility of the UNCRC and children's rights, it must be recognised that there are many Acts protecting children and guaranteeing them basic health and education rights in England. However, without incorporation of the UNCRC, children's rights risk being largely invisible in the national discourse, as pointed out by the Equality and Human Rights Commission (EHRC, 2016). Despite the political reluctance to openly engage with children's rights (CRAE, 2017), the ethics guidelines for educational research in Britain recognise their importance: 'The Association requires researchers to comply with Articles 3 and 12 of the United Nations Convention on the Rights of the Child' (BERA, 2011, p. 6).

Finnish context

The context in Finland is somewhat different in that Finland is one of 13 EU states that has a national policy framework in place on children's rights (EUFRA, 2014). The plan called *A Finland Fit for Children* is used in conjunction with other policies and initiatives (Ministry of Social Affairs and Health, 2005). It was developed based on the feedback Finland got in 2000 from the Committee on the Rights of the Child (UN CRC, 2000). However, in the national research guidelines, only Article 12 is referred to (TENK, 2009, p. 6). Interestingly, in the new National Core Curriculum for ECEC (Finnish National Agency for Education, 2016), the document explicitly refers to the UNCRC and uses rights language in a very accessible way. The subchapter on underpinning values refers to 12 of the articles of the UNCRC.

Phenomenological inspiration

This study was inspired by what Giorgi (2000) calls 'scientific phenomenology' (p. 12) in that it sought 'experience-sensitive understanding' of a particular issue or social phenomenon (Van Manen, 1997, p. xi), admittedly with a specific rights focus, as opposed to 'philosophical phenomenology' that is primarily interested in the nature or essence of the phenomenon per se and its universal meaning.

The bulk of the data was collected through participant observations, rather than from interviews, as typically is the case in phenomenology (Danaher and Briod, 2005; Patton, 2015). The Canadian phenomenologist Max Van Manen recognises observations as a means of especially gaining access to young children's experiences, where interviewing may not be an appropriate method due to the age of the children. Van Manen (1997) calls them 'experiential anecdotes' (p. 68). To systematically structure the observations, as illustrated in the first *experiential anecdote* below, Van Manen's (1997, 2014) five 'lifeworld existentials' were used: lived other (relationality), lived body (corporeality), lived space (spatiality), lived time (temporality) and lived things (materiality).

To frame the discussion, Kraus's (2013, 2015) reformulation of the phenomenological term 'lifeworld' (*Lebenswelt*) was used, as well as his interpretation of the concept 'life conditions' (*Lebenslage*). These terms were further expanded on by introducing the concept of 'life interactions' (*Lebensinteraktion*).

Honouring its phenomenological origin, the term 'lifeworld' (*Lebenswelt*) is used to mean more than just 'a simple orientation towards a person's life situation' (Kraus, 2015, p. 2). In agreement with Kraus, 'lifeworld means a person's subjective construction of reality, which he or she forms under the condition of his or her life circumstances' (p. 4), which can be communicated to others through verbal or non-verbal communication. Kraus's term 'life conditions' (*Lebenslage*) was, however, adapted as 'life conditions' was considered too broad, as it encompasses everything outside of the person's lifeworld, all of a person's material as well as immaterial circumstances. Kraus's notion of life conditions was therefore adapted. Life conditions are here taken to represent a person's material or external circumstances solely. In the case of this study, a child's external circumstances, in which subjective experiences take place, are, for instance, their living conditions at home, socio-economic status, neighbourhood, type of nursery the child attends, curriculum or approach to play and learning taken in the nursery, resources available, routines, and so forth.

The immaterial or social and relational aspects of a person's circumstances are brought to the fore by giving these aspects of a person's circumstances its own category, 'life interactions' (*Lebensinteraktion*) in order to draw more attention to the importance of inter-personal interactions to experiences, as children can only grow and develop to their fullest potential in relationship with others, feral children or the stories of Romanian orphans cases in point. Life interactions are, in other words, the connections children develop in relation to adults and children they encounter or share their daily lives with. These interactions can be anywhere along a continuum, from fleeting and unimportant to deep and meaningful attachments to primary and secondary caregivers. Interactions with researchers, for instance, may be fleeting but need to be meaningful to be ethical.

The notion of a person's subjective reality is, as such, aligned with the term 'lifeworld', the term 'life condition' is aligned with material circumstances in a person's life, and the term 'life interaction' is aligned with relational aspects of a person's experiences.

Embedding rights in an ethical research process

There is a generally agreed discourse on ethical responsibilities towards child partici-pants today, even if university and national and international guidelines may differ. The UNCRC has undeniably played a role in this shift towards more respectful, par-ticipative ways of researching children. However, Bell's (2008) analysis of several con-temporary research ethics guidelines for research involving children revealed that there was a general lack of direct reference in these guidelines to rights principles such as those articulated in the UNCRC. This is an important omission if we, as mentioned above, consider that a rights-inspired lens brings to the fore important ethical issues. The *EECERA Ethical Code for Early Childhood Researchers* (Bertram et al., 2015) does refer to rights principles by stating, 'researchers should operate within the spirit of Art-icle 3 [best interest] and Article 12 [voice and participation] of the UNCRC' (p. 7). But what does 'operate within the spirit' mean? The next part of this chapter endeav-ours to elucidate that. For the sake of legibility, ethical considerations during the research process described below have been spilt into four stages; however, in reality, the process is overlapping and less stage-like:

1 introduction stage;
2 access stage;
3 process stage; and
4 completion stage.

To illustrate how rights correlate to ethical aspects grappled with during the research pro-cess, the relevant UNCRC articles have been noted in brackets. The ensuing discussion will clearly demonstrate the link between children's rights and ethical research practices.

Introduction stage

The introduction stage is about finding out about the research and building trust. In both England and Finland, after gaining access from adult gatekeepers at county and setting level, information letters were sent out to families to invite them to take part in the study and to obtain written consent to engage with their child. The research in the settings started with two *play days*, days to get to know the children and staff, and familiarise myself with everyday life in the setting. The play days were also the starting point for most of the children to get information about the research that was going to take place (Article 17). Because of the young age of the children, the information given was that I wanted to find out what made them happy or sad, what they liked or did not like when in the setting (Article 17). I also explained I was going to take notes and sometimes film their day, if that was OK with them. This is a fundamental point for me as a childhood researcher, to inform the children that they genuinely have the power to say no, to ask me to stop or go away, without having to give a reason, the same right I would accord any adult participant, as the image I hold of 2-year-olds is that of someone of equal worth to adults, deserving the same courtesy.

The play days were an equally important starting point for the children to get to know me, for the children to form their first impressions of me as a person and professional (Article 3.3).

Part of the introduction stage is also for the children to get familiar with research tools: pens, pads, laptops, cameras, and so forth. Learning about and allowing access to research equipment was an important aspect of the methodology. All children used the GoPro camera with utmost care, respecting it was an expensive piece of equipment, and proud to have the opportunity to use it responsibly (Article 29.1d). The impact it had on the children was quite remarkable. I had not anticipated it to be as empowering as it turned out to be (Article 5).

Experiential anecdote, 25 November 2016

A group of children come back to the 2-year-old room (lived time – they have been playing in another part of the building). When Chris sees me in the book area, reading with a child, he walks up to me and says he wants to film (lived things – researcher equipment). He stands very close to me and looks expectantly up at me (lived body – proximity). I push my pen and notepad to the side to make some space for Chris and reach for my camera case. Chris watches as I take my camera out of its case. I hand it to him, and we secure the strap around his wrist. He switches the camera on. Chris chooses to film Jimi (early years worker) who is playing with some children (lived space – what is happening). This is an adult Chris enjoys spending a lot of time with. When Chris is done filming, he switches the camera off, turns to me, standing tall, looking intently at me, and says with a great big smile, 'I'm a big boy!' as he hands the camera back to me (lived other – relationality).

There were empowering experiences across the four settings of how the resources I brought with me not only helped develop trust and a sense of connection, but also helped draw children in and have a sense of ownership in the research process itself.

Access stage

This aspect of research is about equitable opportunity. The initial approach had been to allow children to come to me, and those who chose to engage with me were understood to be the children choosing to opt in. This is in line with what Corsaro (2018) calls the 'react-ive method' (p. 54), as the researcher sits down and waits for children to react to them, waits for the children to take the initiative to engage. However, I quickly began to question this approach as it became apparent that it disadvantaged the quieter or more reserved child (Article 2). The more reserved children sometimes needed a non-verbal invitation from me (a smile or nod, offering of a pen and pad, or GoPro) for them to join in the first time. In both England and Finland, some children never asked directly to film independently, but when I picked up on their non-verbal cues (long looks at the camera or at me, hovering nearby or hesitantly approaching) (Article 13), and I gave them the opportunity to join in, they were keen to accept. More confident children asked directly, as Tony did one morning in setting 3. He asked if he could film (Article 12), asked for confirmation he was about to press the correct button (Articles 17 and 13), and as he started filming exclaimed with a great big smile, 'I'm filming, I am!' I had expected that the camera would fuel children's curiosity and draw them in to the research process, but did not anticipate that my (different) pen and notepad would do so in equal measure. The children either wrote directly on my researcher notepad or made their own notes on their identical pad. They chose to either keep their notes or hand them to me, to add to mine. To an outsider, they may seem like mere scribbles, but as my image of the child is that of a competent participant, I saw their notes as valuable contributions, in line with their age and maturity.

Process stage

An important aspect to consider at this stage is assent and dissent. A distinction is made here between consent from adult gatekeepers and a child's assent. The concept of assent is, however, a contested concept. It has been discussed in detail by other scholars (e.g. see Alderson, 2012; Dockett et al., 2013), and will therefore not be discussed in greater detail here, simply defined. Assent is understood as 'a sense of agreement obtained from those who are not able to enter into a legal contract' (Ford et al., 2007, p. 20). It is seen as a negotiated process, not a one-off event, whereby verbal and non-verbal communication is continually taken into consideration (Articles 12 and 13). Due to the young age of the children, this was deemed the most appropriate way of ascertaining if children were happy to participate (assent) or not (dissent). It must be recognised, however, that children in care settings are used to complying with adult requests and may not be accustomed to saying 'no' to adults, which is why dissonance between children's verbal and non-verbal communication is important to note. I made a point of frequently reminding the children that they had the right to say 'no' to being observed or filmed, and to say 'stop' if they changed their mind. An older 2-year-old in setting 3 exercised his right to say 'stop' on a number of occasions until he realised he truly had that right, regardless of whether he said it in a whisper or in a loud voice (Article 12). In setting 4, a child told me on one occasion to go away – 'Mene pois!' – as I approached her, indicating her desire for privacy in her play (Article 16). This was particularly pleasing as she was the quietest and most reserved of the 2-year-olds in that group, and I felt that if she felt confident enough to tell me to go away, I had managed to gain the children's trust. There is, as such, a relational aspect to assent and dissent, and this interpersonal connection need not take long to develop, as I experienced in the first week of the research process in setting 2.

Chris, the oldest 2-year-old in the group (2 years, 9 months) and I had an instant positive rapport that I believe was the reason I was allowed privileges others may not have been

---

Experiential anecdote, 23 November 2016

Only a couple of children are getting ready to go outside today, as it is bitter cold. I get dressed and walk out in the garden, about to switch on my GoPro camera, as I approach Chris, who is the first child outside. He is looking around the sandpit, moving with confidence, seemingly searching for something, with his back turned against me. As I approach him, I call out, 'Can I film you, Chris?' Without looking up, he replies with an emphatic, 'No!' but when he turns around and sees me, he says, 'Oh! Yes!'

---

accorded (Article 3.3). I also believe he understood the research process, that observing and taking notes or filming was part of the data collection process, the reason why I was there, as he in his play stated, glancing over at me, that some toy food he was preparing was for me, for later, when I had finished filming.

I initially always explicitly asked the children permission to film or take notes, but as the research progressed and my presence and role in the setting became part of the children's lifeworld, a wave of the pen and pad or gesture with the GoPro was quickly acknowledged by the children as quite ordinary. Children's assent was never taken for granted, but their verbal assent (Article 12) was often replaced with their non-verbal assent (Article 13) in what seemed like a very natural ongoing negotiated process. My image of the 2-year-old child is as such that they are competent communicators, and it is for adults to both listen to words and take notice of their non-verbal communication to understand them. When filming continued over an extended time, I always, verbally or with a gesture, kept reminding children that I was filming (Article 17). It was also a deliberate choice to hold the camera rather than place it on a tripod and let it run. In the pilot setting in England, one child did not want to be filmed, and whenever she came into a room and saw the blinking camera in my hand, she always chose to come and stand next to me, out of the field of vision. Had the camera been on a tripod, left to run at a distance, she may not have been aware of it, and so not have been able to make that informed choice (Article 5).

An important aspect throughout the research process is to do no harm, for the children to feel safe (Article 19). Safe in the sense that the views they expressed, verbally or non-verbally, were never criticised and were met with a compassionate response, if sensitive issues were divulged, such as when Jessica, in setting 2, talked about being sad when she had been reprimanded by her key person (field notes, 25 November 2016). As a rule, not filming a child in distress was also adopted as a duty of care. It was presumed that the child wanted privacy (Article 16) and comforting (Article 3.2), away from the camera gaze when upset, at times also seeking comfort from me, the researcher.

Completion stage

Member-checking, feedback and dissemination are aspects of this stage. The children were made aware throughout the fieldwork that the end result would be many documents for adults to read and a film they and adults would be able to watch. Children that had been filmed were all given the opportunity to view the footage they were in, respond to it, and say whether they felt it was OK to show it to Mummy and Daddy and other adults in the setting (Articles 17 and 42). All children responded positively to the viewings and gave their assent to letting others view the footage too. They did so either verbally, with an affirmative sound or a nod (Articles 12 and 13). Interestingly, some children asked to be able to view footage before the final edit (Article 12), and Adam (2 years, 1 month) surprised me by also expressing a 'dissemination request'. Adam said he wanted his Nanny and Granddad to see the footage too, which I was happy to comply with.

Another very interesting life interaction and meaningful connection to a child during the member-checking process occurred many months after the fieldwork in setting 1.

Only a few of the children showed a great level of interest in the notes I had written up. Most, now 3-year-old children, when given the opportunity to view them, just said 'no' or simply turned on their heels and walked off to play (Articles 12 and 13). The children were free to guide me in how involved they wanted to be. Much time had sometimes elapsed when I came back to settings for member-checking and final conversations, and as the

---

Experiential anecdote, 19 June 2017

When sitting on the floor, going over observations with the manager, one of the focus children kept coming up to us to see what we were doing. This was a child who had been a little reserved at first when I had arrived in the setting six months previously. I explained that we were reading through notes I had been taking when I had been there before. He asked, 'Where is mine?' I looked for his notes, found them and held them up. He reached for them and looked around for something. He then looked at the pen in my hand. I asked him if he wanted my pen to make some notes too, and handed him my pen. He took it with a smile and started making marks on the back page. With great concentration, he made some what at first appeared random marks, but reading upside down I suddenly realised he had written the first two letters of his name. He went on to write all the letters of his name, and with a great big smile handed the pen and papers back to me. It felt quite poetic that he had 'signed off' his observations.

---

children had been so young at the time of the initial interactions, many children said they did not remember me. I could, however, not help but register that even if children said they did not remember me, some looked at me with a quizzical look, as if they maybe had some fragment of memory or feeling of connection. Often these children immediately wanted me to play with them, or started telling me of recent events, as if I (actually) was a familiar person in their lives.

These are but a few examples of the correlation between the articles of the UNCRC and corresponding research stages, listed with some examples from practice in Table 40.1.

Table 40.1 Ethical rights–based research process with young children

Research stage	Process	UNCRC article
1. IntroductionFamiliarisation	Opportunity planned for child to get to know the researcher before study to form an initial opinion to decide if they feel they want to engage with the researcher.	Right to suitability of researcher (Article 3.3)
Building trust	Give child the time it takes to build trust, which can be immediate or require time.Justify your chosen role as researcher, on a continuum from 'non-participant' to 'atypical adult' observer.	Right to suitability of researcher (Article 3.3)
Learning about research process	As some children attend part-time, make sure to inform all children about the research process in person.	Right to information (Article 17)
Learning about the tools	Explore research tools together: camera, special pen, pad, activities, games or any other resources to be used.Explore rules of use,	Right to learning and development (Article 29)

(Continued)

Table 40.1 (Cont.)

Research stage	Process	UNCRC article
	expectations (e.g. camera strap around wrist, holding it steady, keeping it clean).	
2. AccessOpportunity to participate in the research process	Equity of access. Make sure children who do not verbally ask are offered opportunity to be included, to learn and take turns using tools, as some children may lack confidence to come forward.Include key person if child needs familiar adult present to feel at ease with researcher in the beginning.Consider what to do if a child wants to take part but parents say no.Special considerations given to children with additional needs and children with other home languages.Plan research experiences at age-appropriate level.	Right to inclusion, non-discrimination (Article 2) Right to participation (Article 12) Right to special care (Article 23) Right to learning and development (Article 29)
3. ProcessOngoing explicit assent and dissent	Explicitly give children permission to say no to being observed and filmed, or being asked questions: 'You can say no or stop'.	Right to verbal expression (Article 12)
Ongoing implicit assent and dissent	Once familiar and comfortable with the process, implicit non-verbal agreement may be given by a child with a nod, smile or glance of recognition.Silence, facial expression or body language may indicate dissent.	Right to non-verbal expression (Article 13)
Ongoing implicit assent and dissent	Look for dissonance between spoken words and non-verbal expressions that may contradict verbal assent (compliance).	Right to non-verbal expression (Article 13)
Data collection:Filming and being filmedBeing filmed and observedConversations	Duty of care not to film/observe children in distress – the right to well-being – do no harm.The presence at all times of a well-known adult for comfort and well-being during the research process.Allow expression of views and non-verbal communication without fear of being told off or criticised.Step back at times so the child is not	Right to well-being (Article 3.2) Right to be safe (Article 19) Right to privacy (Article 16) Right to information (Article 17) Right to verbal expression (Article 12)

(Continued)

Table 40.1 (Cont.)

Research stage	Process	UNCRC article
	under the researcher gaze all the time, even if they do not say 'no' or 'stop'.Draw children's attention to the flashing red light if they walk in on filming in process, as well as during filming, as children may forget they are being filmed.Spontaneous or planned conversations one-to-one with confident children, or with a key person, or other children present for children to feel more at ease.	
Benefit	Empowering by sharing the process, having a say, contributing to note-taking, filming and conversations.	Right to guidance (Article 5)
Harm	Is the research process exploitative or respectful, and will it ultimately benefit children?	Right not to be exploited (Article 36)
4. CompletionMember-checking	Showing notes, footage and end product to participating children for verbal and non-verbal feedback, taking note of tone of voice and facial expressions of approval or disapproval, as well as dissonance between spoken words and non-verbal expressions.	Right to verbal (Article 12) and non-verbal expression (Article 13)
Final feedback	Feedback at final completion – infants and toddlers may well have forgotten who you are, or have moved on, when you come back, but still consider feeding back.	Right to information (Article 17)
Disseminationconfidentiality	Inform of intended use of video footage, showing of film to parents and staff (or any other audience). Inform of intent to write about their experiences for others to read – publications.Protect the future adult by considering where visual data may end up if shared; university open-source learning systems (Moodle), online parent platforms (Tapestry), social media (Facebook, Instagram, YouTube).	Right to information (Article 17) Dissemination (Article 42) Right to privacy (Article 16)

This is by no means an exhaustive list, but serves as an illustration of how the UNCRC can inform both research ethics guidelines and ethical researcher practices.

Discussion

When we as researchers enter children's worlds in a setting, we are invited into a space of shared routines and a web of relationships and values. It is a physical and social space that is in constant flux, and as researchers we only get a glimpse of how children experience this space at a specific moment in time (Raittila, 2012). Just as we enter a space with its own unique history, we bring with us our own histories that have shaped who we are, why we wish to explore a specific issue or phenomenon in this context, and the image of the child we hold. Even if we try to suspend our judgement, we need to recognise that we are not neutral, as qualitative researchers are 'the instrument of both data collection and data interpretation' (Patton, 2015, p. 57). To help in the interpretation of and reflections on the ethical responsibilities researchers face in research with young children, a phenomenological perspective can be illuminative.

Phenomenological inspiration

As my research study was with early verbal children, who have not got the ability to fully articulate their *lifeworld* or subjective perspective, it required a more relational *life interaction* and interpretivist approach to develop my understanding of my issue of concern: young children's rights. Making a distinction between *lifeworld*, *life conditions* and *life interactions* helped me analyse ethical implications participatory research may have on children.

During one of the focus groups with parents, as we were watching a video clip where a child exercised their right to say 'stop' to being filmed, one mother exclaimed:Is that where Danny's got 'Stop Mummy!' from?! He says, 'No, stop! Stop!' all the time.

My philosophy, together with a change in material circumstances, life condition, the bringing in of a camera, and our life interactions in the setting, had in a matter of days become part of Danny's subjective reality, his lifeworld. Danny had subsequently brought his subjective reality from the setting to the home environment, where in this case it was respected, as the parents saw being assertive as something positive; however, I cannot help wondering what the outcome could have been had it been in a socioculturally different home environment? Taking a *lifeworld*, *life conditions*, *life interactions* perspective opened my eyes to the fact that my interactions in settings could have unanticipated consequences. This perspective puts children's best interests more visibly at the core of the research process.

Relational perspective

If we recognise that when we enter settings as researchers we become part of children's life conditions and life interactions, which has a bearing on children's subjective reality, their lifeworld, we cannot escape the ethical responsibility it carries to reflect on the impact we may have on the children taking part in our research.

Warming (2011) suggests 'a "least adult role" approach, enhances the possibilities of successfully achieving empathetic and empowering representation of young children's perspectives' (p. 39). In the least adult role, the researcher endeavours to participate in a childlike way by:

- playing with the children;
- submitting to the authority of their adult carers;

- abdicating from adult authority and privileges; and
- letting children define and shape the researcher's role.

Warming insists that it is only through the least adult role that researchers can gain access to areas of children's lifeworld that would otherwise be inaccessible. However, I was in both England and Finland in similar positions of complicity with children, as Warming (2011) describes, gaining deeply personal insights, without the need for abdicating 'adult authority and privileges' (p. 43).

It should also be questioned if children really buy into what may be understood as an adult-constructed illusion, as the adult researcher can at any point in time reclaim their abdicated authority and privileges. It is, as such, a notion with an element of pretence or even deception. Rogers and Evans (2008) admit that the children in their study had, to their surprise, not bought into their role as *lesser adults*. They suggest it is because the notion of a lesser adult does not fit with children's experiences of the world, lifeworld, because children position adults 'according to the discourse within which they are operating' (p. 49).

There are therefore ethical questions to be answered: How ethical is it to try to be a lesser adult? Just as children have the right to staff that are suitable, according to Article 3.3, it could be argued that children have, by extension, the right to researchers who are suitable in personality, understanding and sensitivity towards their lifeworlds, life conditions and life interactions. Maybe a more honest researcher role is Corsaro's (2018) notion of 'atypical adult' or non-authoritarian adult (p. 55). This recognises irrefutable power relationships and inescapable generational issues (Mayall, 2000).

Rights-based ethical research approach

Rights-based research is, as such, about respecting children's evolving capacity and a question of ethical relationships, as adults in line with Article 5 help children exercise the rights as expressed in the UNCRC. With young children in the early years, it is foremost about listening according to Article 12 and noticing, according to Article 13, about the harmony between verbal and non-verbal communication as we try to understand children's lifeworld. It is about providing information children can understand, according to Article 17, to be able to make informed decisions, and about including all children interested in taking part, despite challenges so as not to discriminate, according to Articles 2 and 23, and in the research process protecting children from any possible harm (Article 19) or from simply being used for the purpose of a research project (Article 36).

Furthermore, if we really seek to embed rights in our research practices and adopt a 'children's rights-based approach' to our research, we need to consider Lundy and McEvoy's (2012, p. 78) five elements or principles mentioned in the introduction. This is a tall order, but a very useful framework to distinguish between 'rights-based' research and rights-inspired or 'rights-informed' approaches to research with children (p. 79). Both have their value, but the distinction needs to be made for clarity. In my original study, I can only claim it to be rights-informed, as we are now, as the next step, beginning to explore how to build the capacity of staff (duty-bearers). By adopting an ethical approach to research as described in this chapter, using the UNCRC as a frame of reference at the various stages of the research process, childhood researchers can move in the direction towards a more conscious rights-informed and children's rights-based research.

Conclusion

In 2008, Bell stated that ethics guidelines were only beginning to reference children's rights; however, when they were, they lacked definition and were seldom correlated with ethical research practices. I believe this is still much the case. This chapter has, with data from a research study, shown the correlation between ethical research practices and articles of the UNCRC, and thus how children's rights can be brought to the fore in research guidelines and research practices with children. The examples are by no means exhaustive, but a starting point for reflecting on how the UNCRC can be used as a frame of reference, thus firmly setting the researcher's eyes on what is in the best interest of the child. Bringing attention to the correlation between children's rights and ethical research practices will hopefully encourage childhood researchers to adopt a more rights-inspired approach to childhood research, and thus 'protect and promote children's rights throughout the research process' (Bell, 2008, pp. 11–12) and support the realisation of the UNCRC.

What this chapter has also tried to convey is the importance of respecting children's life conditions and lifeworld: 'To be ethical, adults must enter a child's world with respect, humility and caution' (Broström, 2006, p. 250). By unpicking the terms 'lifeworld' (*Lebenswelt*) and 'life conditions' (*Lebenslage*) and adding the concept of 'life interactions' (*Lebensinteraktion*), greater attention is given to the impact researcher interactions in the field have on children's lifeworld, and the ensuing ethical responsibility researchers carry towards their young participants. Treating children as competent social actors with rights creates new ethical challenges, especially in institutions where children traditionally are expected to comply with adult requests (Freeman and Mathison, 2009). 'Our understandings of research with children and, indeed, of ethics in research with children, are embedded within our understandings of children and childhood' (Farrell, 2005, p. 5). We are coming back to the opening quote. We, as researchers, or any adult working with children, therefore need to first of all turn the spotlight inward, to recognise what image of the child we have, to understand where we are coming from, before we can truly see the individual child in our attempt to understand their subjective reality, or lifeworld, and life conditions. In my view, the 2-year-old children in the research study were all competent decision-makers within their environment, skilful communicators, and adept participants. Inspired by phenomenology and Kraus' distinction between 'life conditions' (*Lebenslage*) and 'lifeworld' (*Lebenswelt*), together with the concept of 'life interactions' (*Lebensinteraktion*), gave me a more nuanced understanding of ethical rights-based research with young children.

I wish to give the final word to one of the great child rights scholars of our time, Emeritus Professor Michael Freeman from University College London:

> Those who espouse children's rights have a vision of a better world for children and through this a better world for all. This requires us to gain a better understanding of the lives of children, of what is important to them and how they perceive and construct their social worlds.
>
> *(Freeman, 2012, p. 37)*

Acknowledgements

With thanks to all the children and adults who took part in the study referred to in this chapter and deepest gratitude for the unwavering support from my PhD supervisors, Professor Chris Pascal and Professor Tony Bertram at the Centre for Research in Early Childhood (CREC) in Birmingham, England.

References

Alderson, Pricilla. 2012. "Children's Consent and 'Assent' to Healthcare Research." In *Law and Childhood Studies: Current Legal Issues Volume 14*, edited by Michael Freeman, 174–190. Oxford: Oxford University Press.

Bell, Nancy. 2008. "Ethics in Child Research: Rights, Reason and Responsibilities." *Children's Geographies* 6 (1): 7–20. doi: 10.1080/14733280701791827.

BERA (British Educational Research Association). 2011. *Ethical Guidelines for Educational Research*. London: BERA.

Bertram, Tony, Julia Formosinho, Collette Gray, Chris Pascal, and Margy Whalley. 2015. *EECERA Ethical Code for Early Childhood Researchers*. http://eecera-ext.tandf.co.uk/documents/pdf/organisation/EECERA-Ethical-Code.pdf

Broström, Stig. 2006. "Children's Perspectives on their Childhood Experiences." In *Nordic Childhoods and Early Education: Philosophy, Research, Policy and Practice in Denmark, Finland, Iceland, Norway, and Sweden*, edited by Johanna Einarsdottir and Judith T. Wagner, 223–256. Greenwich: Information Age.

Corsaro, William. A. 2018. *The Sociology of Childhood*. 5th ed. London: Sage.

CRAE (Children's Rights Alliance for England). 2015. *UK implementation of the UN Convention on the Right of the Child: Civil Society Alternative Report 2015 to the UN Committee – England: Report Summary*. London: CRAE.

CRAE (Children's Rights Alliance for England). 2016. *State of Children's Rights in England 2016: Briefing 1: Executive Summary*. London: CRAE.

CRAE (Children's Rights Alliance for England). 2017. *Barriers and Solutions to Using Children's Rights Approaches in Policy*. www.crae.org.uk/media/123572/Barriers-and-solutions-to-using-childrens-rights-in-policy-E.pdf

Danaher, Tom, and Marc Briod. 2005. "Phenomenological Approaches to Research with Children." In *Researching Children's Experiences: Approaches and Methods*, edited by Sheila Greene and Diane Hagan, 216–235. London: Sage.

DCSF (Department for Children, Schools and Families). 2009. *United Nations Convention on the Rights of the Child: Priorities for Action*. Nottingham: DCSF Publications.

DCSF (Department for Children, Schools and Families). 2010. *UNCRC: How Legislation Underpins Implementation in England: March 2010*. www.gov.uk/government/publications/united-nations-convention-on-the-rights-of-the-child-uncrc-how-legislation-underpins-implementation-in-england

DfE (Department for Education). 2018. *Early Education and Childcare: Statutory Guidance for Local Authorities*. www.gov.uk/government/publications/early-education-and-childcare-2

DfES (Department for Education and Skills). 2003. *Every Child Matters: CM 5860*. London: TSO.

Dockett, Sue, Bob Perry, and Emma Kearney. 2013. "Promoting Children's Informed Assent in Research Participation." *International Journal of Qualitative Studies in Education* 26 (7): 802–828. doi: 10.1080/09518398.2012.666289.

EHRC (Equality and Human Rights Commission). 2016. *Children's Rights in the UK: Updated Submission to the UN Committee on the Rights of the Child in Advance of the Public Examination of the UK's Implementation of the Convention on the Rights of the Child: April 2016*. www.equalityhumanrights.com/en/file/18726

EUFRA (European Union Agency for Fundamental Rights). 2014. *National Policy Framework (Action Plan or Strategy)*. http://fra.europa.eu/en/publication/2015/mapping-child-protection-systems-eu/national-policy

Farrell, Ann. 2005. "Ethics and Research with Children." In *Ethical Research with Children*, edited by Ann Farrell, 1–14. Maidenhead: Open University Press.

Finnish National Agency for Education (Utbildningsstyrelsen). 2016. *The National Core Curriculum for ECEC 2016 (Grunderna för Planen för Småbarnspedagogik)*. Helsingfors: Utbildningsstyrelsen.

Ford, Karen, Judy Sankey, and Jackie Crisp. 2007. "Development of Children's Assent Documents Using a Child-Centred Approach." *Journal of Child Health Care* 11 (1): 19–28. doi: 10.1177/1367493507073058.

Freeman, Melissa, and Sandra Mathison. 2009. *Researching Children's Experiences*. New York: Guilford Press.

Freeman, Michael. 2012. "Towards a Sociology of Children's Rights." In *Law and Childhood Studies: Current Legal Issues Volume 14*, edited by Michael Freeman, 29–39. Oxford: Oxford University Press.

Giorgi, Amedeo. 2000. "Concerning the Application of Phenomenology to Caring Research." *Scandinavian Journal of Caring Sciences* 14 (1): 11–15. doi: 10.1111/j.1471-6712.2000.tb00555.x.

Kraus, Björn. 2013. *Erkennen und Entscheiden: Grundlagen und Konsequenzen eines erkenntnistheoretischen Konstruktivismus für die Soziale Arbeit.* Weinheim: Beltz Juventa.

Kraus, Björn. 2015. "The Life We Live and the Life We Experience: Introducing the Epistemological Difference between "lifeworlds" (Lebesnwelt) and "life conditions" (Lebenslage)." www.socwork.net/sws/article/view/438

Lundy, Laura, and Lesley McEvoy. (Emerson). 2012. "Childhood, the United Nations Convention on the Rights of the Child, and Research: What Constitutes a 'Rights-Based' Approach?." .In *Law and Childhood Studies: Current Legal Issues Volume 14*, edited by Michael Freeman, 75–91. Oxford: Oxford University Press.

Malaguzzi, Loris. 1994. "Your Image of the Child: Where Teaching Begins." *Child Care Information Exchange* 96: 52–61. www.reggioalliance.org/downloads/malaguzzi:ccie:1994.pdf

Mayall, Berry. 2000. "The Sociology of Childhood in Relation to Children's Rights." *International Journal of Children's Rights* 8 (3): 243–259. doi: 10.1163/15718180020494640.

Ministry of Social Affairs and Health (Social- och Hälsovårdsministeriet). 2005. *A Finland Fit for Children: The National Finnish Plan of Action Called for by the Special Session on Children of the UN General Assembly.* http://julkaisut.valtioneuvosto.fi/handle/10024/74560

Organisation for Economic Co-operation and Development (OECD). 2015. *PISA 2015: Results in Focus.* www.oecd.org/pisa/pisa-2015-results-in-focus.pdf.

Patton, Michael Q. 2015. *Qualitative Research and Evaluation Methods.* 4th ed. London: Sage.

Raittila, Raija. 2012. "With Children in their Lived Place: Children's Action as Research Data." *International Journal of Early Years Education* 20 (3): 270–279. doi: 10.1080/09669760.2012.718124.

Rayna, Sylvie, and Ferre Laevers. 2011. "Understanding Children from 0 to 3 Years of Age and its Implications for Education: What's New on the Babies Side: Origins and Evolutions." *European Early Childhood Education Research Journal* 19 (2): 161–172. doi: 10.1080/1350293X.2011.574404.

Reynaert, Didier, Maria Bouverne-de Bie, and Stijn Vandelvelde. 2009. "A Review of Children's Rights Literature Since the Adoption of the United Nations Convention on the Rights of the Child." *Childhood* 16 (4): 518–534. doi: 10.1177/0907568209344270.

Reynaert, Didier, Maria Bouverne-de Bie, and Stijn Vandelvelde. 2012. "Between 'Believers' and 'Opponents': Critical Discussions on Children's Rights." *International Journal on Children's rights* 20 (1): 155–168. doi: 10.1163/157181812X626417.

Rogers, Sue, and Julie Evans. 2008. *Inside Role-Play in Early Childhood Education: Researching Young Children's Perspectives.* New York: Routledge.

TENK (Tutkimuseettinen Neuvottelukunta) (Finnish National Board on Research Integrity). 2009. "Ethical Principles of Research in the Humanities and Social and Behavioural Sciences and Proposals for Ethical Review." www.tenk.fi/en/ethical-review-in-finland

UN CRC (UN Committee on the Rights of the Child). 2000. *UN Committee on the Rights of the Child: Concluding Observations, Finland, 16 October 2000, CRC/C/15/Add.132.* www.refworld.org/publisher,CRC,FIN,3ae6afd514,0.html

UN (United Nations). 1989. "Convention on the Rights of the Child." *UN Treaty Series* 1577: 3. www.refworld.org/docid/3ae6b38f0.html

UNICEF (United Nations International Children's Emergency Fund). 2008. *The Child Care Transition: Innocenti Report Card 8.* Florence: UNICEF Innocenti Research Centre.

Van Manen, Max. 1997. *Researching Lived Experiences: Human Science for an Action Sensitive Pedagogy.* 2nd ed. London: Routledge.

Van Manen, Max. 2014. *Phenomenology of Practice: Meaning-Giving Methods in Phenomenological Research and Writing.* Walnut Creek: Left Coast Press.

Warming, Hanne. 2011. "Getting Under their Skins? Accessing Young Children's Perspectives through Ethnographic Fieldwork." *Childhood* 18 (1): 39–53. doi: 10.1177/0907568210364666.

41

COMBINING CHILDREN'S PARTICIPATION RIGHTS IN RESEARCH WITH PROFESSIONALISATION OF EDUCATORS AND TEACHERS

Critical analysis of a transition study design

Petra Büker

Introduction

In Germany, children's perspectives have been highlighted in a range of research contexts in recent years (Heinzel, 2012; Kordulla, 2017). In line with international developments in the field of early years education and primary education (Dockett, Einársdottir and Perry, 2019; Murray, 2017), children are no longer considered as research *objects*, but rather as *subjects*. Thus, they are regarded as 'experts in their own environments' (Kordulla, 2017, p. 101), who are able to, and should, comment on their experiences and desires regarding family, kindergarten, school, leisure activities and other relevant aspects of life. Not only researchers, but also professionals working in kindergartens and primary schools, often have a growing interest in children's perspectives. However, there remains a distinct lack of knowledge and practical experience concerning how the results of research projects involving children can be used as stimuli to impact professionalisation processes in kindergartens and primary schools (Büker, 2019; Büker, and Höke 2019). Two problems are apparent here. First, the results obtained from children's surveys are still too rarely used regarding the aim of systematically developing and improving teaching practice and the professionalisation of teaching staff (Gräsel, 2010). This is related to the fact that in teaching practice, there is little reflection regarding questions and methods concerning the *transfer* of research results (Donie and Kammermeyer, 2019; Gräsel, 2010). Second, the implementation of children's right to participate in all matters that may affect themselves, as described in the 1989 UN Convention on the Rights of the Child (UNCRC) (UN General Assembly, 1989; United Nations (UN), 1989) is realised insufficiently if the voices of children are heard but their opinions have no direct influence on any changes affecting pedagogical practice.

The following chapter addresses both mentioned problems and combines them under the aspect of participation-oriented and transfer-oriented research with children. Based on experiences made with the accompanying children study of the so called buddY pilot project, which aimed to strengthen children's competence to participate actively in transition processes from kindergarten to school (Büker, 2019; Büker and Bethke, 2014), the chapter analyses type and extent of opportunities for children's participation in research. This includes the analysis of children's possibilities to affect pedagogical innovation and professionalisation of educators and teachers. For the critical analysis of the methodological design of the pilot project, the 'hierarchical model of children's research participation rights' developed by Mayne, Howitt and Rennie (2018) is used. Specific reference is made to Articles 12, 13 and 29 of the 1989 UNCRC. It will be shown critically that even if the pilot project and the accompanying study had pursued the aim of children's participation, existing opportunities of participation and exertion of influence have not been used. The integration of children in research, on the one hand, and the professionalisation of educators and teachers, on the other, remained as two unconnected processes because of an insufficient concept of transfer. Regarding this, the chapter closes with a discussion of how further research settings should be designed so that they respect the UNCRC right of children's participation and grant them at a maximum degree, while at the same time the professionalisation of pedagogical staff is enhanced. This includes rethinking the role children play in research and optimisation of pedagogical practice and creating opportunities for their voices to be heard by adults – all happening in close collaboration with the children.

The chapter starts with an introduction to the main reasons, aims and design of the buddY pilot project (second section). To enable a better understanding of the setting, the special German context regarding transition from kindergarten to primary school is outlined. This is followed by an overview of the design of the accompanying qualitative-oriented buddY children study, including children aged 5–7 years. A special focus is placed here on the description of the transfer concept of the study (third section). In the fourth section, the right of the child to participation in research is highlighted with reference to Articles 12 and 13 of the 1989 UNCRC, as well as the role of adults with particular reference to Article 29. The theoretical background and the currently unsatisfactory situation regarding the implementation of children's rights to participation in research are also briefly discussed here. In 2018, Mayne, Howitt and Rennie developed a children's rights-based hierarchical model for the participation of children in research. This enables a systematic determination of the type and extent of participation of children in research projects. After a brief presentation of this model in the fourth section, the buddY study is classified into this hierarchical model in the fifth section. The closer analysis strives to answer the critically reflexive question concerning the extent to which the child's right to participation is fully implemented in the study design.

This chapter concludes with a discussion of the following question: *How can children be supported regarding their right to participation while at the same time enhancing the professionalisation of educators and teachers?* (sixth section). Out of this analysis, perspectives for future research designs are outlined that contribute to rights-based research with young children. Thus, the chapter deals not with the question of *what* we could learn about children's views on transition processes. Because of this, there is not a detailed report of findings from the buddY children study (details in Büker and Bethke, 2014; Büker and Höke, 2019). Much more, the chapter rather focuses on the question of *how* the rights of the child to participation in research can be applied so that children could become an integrative part of the process of optimising pedagogical practice in kindergartens and primary schools.

The buddY pilot project and the buddY children study

Transition from kindergarten to primary school in Germany: initial situation for the pilot project

In Germany, kindergartens and primary schools belong to different systems, each following their own traditional logic within these systems (Bührmann and Büker, 2015). Kindergartens educate children aged between a few months and 6 years. To this day, attendance is not obligatory. Aged 6, children enter primary school, which is compulsory for everyone. Until now, every institution has had its own mandate, its own policy and its own organisational structures. Kindergarten and primary school have different pedagogic traditions and specific views on children, learning, playing, performance and working with parents. Because of this, the transition equates to a *caesura* that receives considerable attention in Germany. Children experience a rite of passage from 'kindergarten child' to 'pupil' as one of the major changes in young children's lives (Wildgruber and Griebel, 2016).

These different systems are also applied at the level of the professions. While in several countries people who work in kindergarten and primary school are both called 'teachers' (e.g. nursery school teachers or preschool teachers), in Germany their professions have different names. Professionals who work in kindergarten are called *Erzieher* (educators) and those in primary school are called *Lehrer* (teachers).

Triggered by the poor performance of German school pupils in international comparative studies (known in Germany as the 'PISA shock'), major efforts have been made to improve the quality of education over the past 15 years – from early years education onwards. Given the fact that, particularly at transition points within the education system, the social and ethnic background of the family have a significant impact on the educational opportunities of children and young people (Maaz, Neumann and Baumert, 2014), many research and teaching practice initiatives were launched in Germany focusing on the transition from kindergarten to primary school. Conceived as pilot projects, they were aimed at achieving optimisation of childhood educational biographies, enhancing the professionalisation of educators and teachers as well as of the institutions themselves. Overall, in recent years, various new forms of cooperation have been developed and evaluated within the framework of scientific accompanying research from the point of view of educators and teachers, management staff, and parents (Höke et al., 2017; Wildgruber and Griebel, 2016). However, there have only been a few of these pilot projects that systematically included the children's perspectives in Germany (e.g. Kordulla, 2017; Müller, 2014). In view of the child's right to participation in all matters affecting the child, as documented in the 1989 UNCRC, the implementation of that right in transition research can be described as a major current deficit.

Aim and concept of the model project

The pilot project initiated and funded by the buddY e.V[1] aimed to strengthen children's competence in dealing with the transition process. Eight regional cooperation networks made up of kindergartens and primary schools in the Paderborn and Detmold areas (in the German federal state of North Rhine-Westphalia) were supported in the period from 2013 to 2015. This included training courses, process support, and coaching in developing innovative forms of children's participation in optimised transition processes, and in incorporating these into the professionalisation process of the institutions and professions. There was a focus on the establishment of a buddy system (children helping their peers in transition processes). The English term 'buddy', meaning 'good friend', 'mate' or 'pal', is used here to describe the peer learning principle that aims to foster the assumption of mutual responsibility. Alongside peer learning, the objective of the pilot project is to foster the development of democratic abilities as a key competence for social participation (Franzen, 2016). Against the background of this guiding principle, a diverse range of transition activities were developed and tested: exploration of the school building by kindergarten children, mixed-age learning workshops for kindergarten and primary school children in the fields of science, arts and literature, and buddy models. This means that older children take on the role of a buddy for a child starting school soon. The Centre for Primary Education and Early Childhood Education at the University of Paderborn conducted the accompanying scientific research study.

Design of the buddY children study

In line with the guiding principles 'democracy' and 'participation', children were consistently involved in managing innovative ways of transition, as well as in the evaluation of those. In the following, the empirical study will not be described regarding further details of methods and gained findings, but rather regarding the overall design of the accompanying study under the aspect of involvement of the children. This constitutes a basis for the analysis in the fourth section.

First, within the framework of a qualitative action research study (Prengel, Heinzel and Carle, 2004), a survey was conducted including $n = 26$ children aged between 5 and 7 years in four structured group discussions. This cohort was made up of a total of $n = 15$ kindergarten children in the final year of kindergarten and $n = 11$ schoolchildren in the first year of primary school. The survey took conscientiously into account the current ethical standards in children's research (Bertram et al., 2015). Especially, the informed consent, the voluntary participation in the survey and a child-oriented research design were considered here. The study focused on the opportunities for participation in the previously experienced activities in the view of the children. In addition, the children were asked to report retrospectively which strategies of participation they found and how they arranged participation in peer learning settings. Moreover, they were asked to formulate ideas for improvements of transition activities in the future. Based on a special theoretical participatory and transition framework (Büker and Bethke, 2014), a content-analytical evaluation of the children's statements was done (Mayring, 2011). The data demonstrate children's competence to give firm and detailed statements to the conditions of success of transition. Main findings show that it is essential for them to have the possibility to get deeply involved into planning and implementation of transition activities, to get the opportunity to contribute spontaneous ideas during activities, and to be able to choose their partner on their own. Furthermore, children want to be self-effective in challenging differentiated learning tasks and to get feelings of self-competence, but do not want to be controlled too closely by teachers (Büker and Höke, 2019). Fifteen determinants for success were formulated that seemed to be of particular relevance to the children. These were divided into content-related, methodical, social and organisational aspects of the transition activities.

In a first transfer step, the 15 determinants for a successful transition design formulated from the perspective of the adult researchers were subjected to communicative validation with the children.

To make the findings accessible to children, a special interactive questionnaire was developed that presents the success factors in child-friendly formulated items. These were visualised by pictograms. Moreover, smiley scales were used that symbolised the hierarchy of the importance of the various items. For example, the success factor 'Ensuring task quality: the learning tasks to be solved within a transition activity should provide internal differentiation as appropriate. Regarding the heterogeneity of the different participants' backgrounds' was reformulated in the child-friendly item: 'When kindergarten children and primary school children do something together then every child should find the tasks quite hard but possible to solve' (Büker and Bethke, 2014, p. 39). A few months later, $n = 4$ children who had taken part as kindergarten children in a group discussion were surveyed again in individual interviews using the tool described above, shortly after they had started primary school. This resulted in corrections being made in terms of shifts in emphasis and differentiations to the success factors, enabling clearly formulated 'quality criteria for a successful transfer from the child's perspective' to be developed.

Transfer and dissemination concept

The feedback of the children's perspectives to the educators and teachers was transformed into a 'Children's Declaration on Transition Design' (see Figure 41.1). A particular challenge encountered in this transfer phase was to ensure that the voices of the children were effective as stimuli for professionalisation. A public feedback event was thus held at which the social actors from the cooperation networks involved, as well as multipliers from kindergartens and schools, were presented the Children's Declaration in the form of a paper scroll with the title 'This is important to us!' The aim was that the pedagogical staff should deal intensively within their cooperation networks with the children's views by reading the Children's Declaration, comparing its content with the adults' perspectives, and thus reflect on their tasks and roles. Ideally, it was intended that this should prompt a fundamental discussion about learning and education in transition, which should have a clarifying effect and should evoke implications for further collaboration in the field of transition. The work on the children's opinions incorporated in the Children's Declaration should thus have a professionalisation effect (for a more detailed description of the professionalisation opportunities provided by the examination of children's perspectives within the framework of multi-professional teamwork, see Bührmann and Büker, 2015; Bührmann, Büker and Höke, 2017).

It was also intended that the children's opinions should be made available to a larger user group for use in training and further education. In the spirit of sustainability of the project, there was thus an extended dissemination phase. Taking the limitation of the small, non-representative sample into account, the children's statements from the buddY study were combined with the results from the children's survey of another pilot project (Kordulla, 2017; Büker and Höke, 2019). Both gave information to the design of a self-assessment tool for use in cooperation in the transition from kindergarten to primary school. This online tool was developed in 2017 and referred to as the *Paderborner Qualitätsstern* (Paderborn quality rating), and was used as the basis for an advanced training programme (Höke, Büker and Bührmann, 2017).

Before continuing with the analysis of type and extent of opportunities for children's participation in research based on reflections on the experiences gained in the implementation of the transfer concept in the buddY pilot project, it is useful to take a closer look on the right of the child to participation in research first.

Declaration for transition process
This is important for us!

What children tell us about professional support for wellbeing and learning in transition process from kindergarten to school

Level of organization

- We want to be active in solving tasks. Therefore the groups should not be that large.
- We want to meet in the kindergarten as well as in primary school.
- We want to act (play and solve tasks) without adults. If something is vague, we will ask for support.

Level of methods

- We want to reflect the experiences and feelings after doing the activities.
- We have suggestions for improvements in cooperation, which should be considered in process of planning.
- We want to know what will happen next. The procedure of the activity should be known by every child.

Level of content

- We want to plan the activities ourselves. Spontaneous ideas should be involved in the activities.
- We want the tasks to be compatible with our needs and our personality.

Level of togetherness

- We want to feel comfortable in the group. It would be great if there would be children from kindergarten and primary school of mixed age in the group.
- We want to organize our togetherness ourselves. We establish rules and manage them within the group.
- We want to choose our partner for the activity on our own. Therefore it is necessary to come in contact with unknown children also.
- We can carry responsibility in our group. We need space and time for choosing the leader of the group.

These are perspectives of children who were surveyed about the transition process from kindergarten to primary school (buddy model project) within the evaluation study of the University of Paderborn.

Prof. Dr. Petra Büker
University of Paderborn
Institute of Education Science
Education in Primary School and Early Childhood
pbueker@mail.uni-paderborn.de

Figure 41.1 Declaration for transition process

The 1989 UN right of the child to participation

The right of the child to participate in research

In recent years, greater significance has been attached both at the international and the German national level to the integration of children and their perspectives in research projects (Dockett et al., 2019; Heinzel, Kränzl-Nagl and Mierendorff, 2012). Thus, often within the paradigm of action and evaluation research, the perspectives of children regarding needs, interests, ideas and appraisals of teaching measures, materials, etc. were collected with the aim of increasing the adaptivity of these. A second aim is to precipitate a professionalisation through the relating of child and adult perspectives (Büker, 2019; Kordulla, 2017). In the field of basic research, there is growing anthropological interest in finding out what children think. However, also in survey studies (e.g. World Vision and UNICEF studies), which have become more popular in recent years, children are interviewed with the aim of finding out how children are doing in our society. At the international level, there is a paradigm shift from conducting research *about* children to conducting research *with* children (Heinzel, 2012).

In my view, at least three key lines of argument could be identified for conducting research with children: (1) Theoretical argumentation based on recognition of rights, with reference to Article 12 of the 1989 UNCRC, the right of children to free expression of their own opinions on all matters affecting them, is taken into account. This is a position of *respect* for the child (Prengel, 2016). Furthermore, childhood theory-based argumentations have a significant influence. (2) Around new childhood social studies, the aim is that the voice of *the child as a competent social actor*, as an expert in his or her world, should be heard (James, Jenks and Prout, 1998). Ultimately, the involvement of *all social actors* builds a main quality criterion in the context of a *qualitative research paradigm* itself. (3) This is also reflected in the relevant ethical standards for research with children (Bertram et al., 2015).

A closer look at the 1989 UNCRC shows how comprehensively the right of the child to participation is formulated in Articles 12 and 13.

Yet it is not only a matter of enabling expression of opinion. In relation to Article 12 of the 1989 UNCRC, the OECD states point out in their 'Common Understanding of Early Learning and Development' (2015) that it is of utmost importance that the view of the child would be taken into account in the realisation of a child-friendly and family-oriented early childhood education and care system.

This highlights the problem that the right to participation is not an issue that is adequately addressed solely by the integration of children's perspectives in society, in education facilities and research. For the research context, this means that merely by 'capturing' children's perspectives, as is commonly the case in so-called child-centred studies devised by adults (Sommer, Samuelsson and Hundeide, 2010), the right to participation is not sufficiently honoured (see below).

This becomes more apparent if we also consider the statements given by UNICEF in its fact sheet *The Right to Participation* (2014), which draws attention to the risk of so-called pseudo-participation: genuine participation only exists if children *understand* the context and the possible effects of the expression of their opinions and if their recommendations and concerns can have an *active influence* on the developments of future measures.

Adults in general and educational institutions play a decisive role *as enablers* here. This is referred to in Article 29(a) and (b) in the 1989 UNCRC. Parents, teachers and researchers play a critical role by either supporting the development of children's agency and autonomy in participation through caring, trusting relationships or by reinforcing 'a sense of dependency' (Ghirotto and Mazzoni, 2013, p. 301) and heteronomy.

On insufficient implementation of the child's right to participation in research

For the field of participative research with children, this means that within the framework of the UNCRC, children as co-researchers are entitled to be involved in processes that affect them. This includes consistently involving them in all phases of the research process: from finding the research question, to planning and realisation through to transfer of the results into policymaking as well as in modified teaching practice (Lundy, McEvoy and Byrne, 2011).

Up to now, there are few international studies that involve children of kindergarten and primary school age in this comprehensive understanding as co-researchers (Mayne and Howitt, 2014). It is not possible to give a full survey of children's rights-based research here. Exemplary mentioned studies with young children carried out in Austria (Arztmann et al., 2017), Sweden (Bergström, Jonsson and Shanahan, 2010), the UK (Kellett, 2011; Kellett et al., 2004; Murray, 2017), Ireland (Lundy et al., 2011) and Australia (Dockett and Perry, 2011; Fleet and Britt, 2011; Harcourt and Conroy, 2011) highlight the important opportunities in the field of participative research with children (Harcourt, Perry and Waller, 2011).

At an international level, there is increasing emphasis on the fact that early childhood researchers should give children the opportunity to be involved in research relating to topics that affect children in accordance with their right to participate (Groundwater-Smith, Dockett and Bottrell, 2015). Even if a systematic analysis is not available yet for the German research context, it can still be assumed that there is a lack of full implementation of participatory rights in research (Eßer and Sitter, 2018). Currently, in the German research context, initial theoretical studies show that the difficulties on a structural level are to be located in the field of *generational asymmetry* and the related *imbalance of power*. Adult researchers generally tend to plan and take responsibility for the research process in combination with maintaining control and prerogative of interpretation. This is accompanied by differences in level of knowledge. Methodical research knowledge in particular is not part of children's common, everyday knowledge (Eßer and Sitter, 2018). Furthermore, the fear on the part of the adult researchers of putting too much strain on the children holds them back from involving them to any great degree. Spriggs and Gillam (2017) point out that by participating in the research process, children could possibly be party to information that they would not have received otherwise, and which could possibly overwhelm them. Involving children in research therefore requires constant interplay between children's right to participation and other rights protected in the Convention, especially their right to protection (Lundy, 2007; Mayne et al., 2018). Recognition of such relationalism must play an important role in the redrafting of research ethics standards for participatory research with children. Overall, it can be concluded that there is an urgent need for an improvement in quality for the implementation of rights to participation within the exploratory field of research with children.

A hierarchical model of children's research participation rights based on information, understanding, voice and influence (Mayne, Howitt and Rennie)

An important step towards achieving such an improvement in quality is thinking about the active participation of children in the research process systematically and from the very start.

In this context, systematic models of implications of Article 12 of the UNCRC are helpful. Lundy's model, presented in her 2007 paper '"Voice" is not enough', is one of the most adopted academic papers on children's rights. Her model of child participation is based on four key concepts: space and voice (referring to the right to express a view) as well as audience and influence (referring to the right to have views given due weight). Mayne et al. (2018) developed a model that allows researchers to define and reflect in a systematic way on the degree of compliance with the UNCRC in research projects with children of preschool and primary school age. In this model, there is a linking of the levels of social participation (with reference to Hart, 1992) in which children's research participation rights are itemised into four core elements, shown in the form of a matrix (see Figure 41.2). For the analysis in this chapter, the model of Mayne et al. (2018) is used because, as a hierarchical model, it allows researchers to define the degree of successful implementation of Article 12.

Vertically, the matrix of Mayne, Howitt and Rennie shows what has become known as the 'ladder of participation', with its eight levels of participation of young people in society according to Hart (1992). Hart regarded participation as a skill that can be acquired through involvement in meaningful projects. On the lower rungs of the ladder, separated by a horizontal black line, are the levels classified as manipulation, decoration and tokenism. These are described by Hart as non-participatory and thus false forms of participation. In the worst case, children experience participation as an illusion in such token settings (Hart, 1992, p. 10). On the lowest rungs of the ladder, children have little or no agency; they are denied the right to self-determination. It is only from the fourth rung upwards that we can speak of (increasingly complex) levels of true participation in the sense of the 1989 UNCRC. These occur in cases where children are assigned a clearly defined role by adults in participation settings that they understand based on information provided (level 4), where children are specifically asked about their views in certain projects and their opinions are taken seriously (level 5), and where they are not only heard, but are also involved in the planning and implementation of projects, as well as in decision-making processes (level 6). Both of the highest participation levels are characterised by the fact that the project is initiated by the children themselves, whereby the balance of power in the generational relationship between children and adults are reversed and they implement their own ideas (level 7) and invite adults to share in the decisions at their own discretion (level 8). This idealised level is evocative of the project method according to Dewey's theory (Büker et al. 2018, p. 112). Hart's levels of participation are used in the model developed by Mayne, Howitt and Rennie as a way of describing levels defining the relationship between opportunities for self-determination and being directed by others, as well as between freedom and control for the participants in a research project. This also allows statements to be made systematically about the quality of the implementation of children's research participation rights. The latter refers to the 1989 UNCRC as well as to statements on the Rights of the Child 2006 published by the United Nations Committee on the Implementation of Children's Rights in Early Childhood. These were differentiated in four key participation rights by the authors, which appear on the horizontal axis of the model: the right to information, understanding, voice (having a say) and influence.

According to Mayne, Howitt and Rennie, these aspects of children's rights are thus to be seen in a hierarchical context since information forms the basis for the understandable communication of research intentions, aims and methods. In sight of the authors, it is only such understanding that enables children to express their own opinions in a detailed way on the issue in question and to influence decision-making in a significant way, based on the data made available by the children. Understanding and agency are thus the two key dimensions that define the honouring of children's rights (Büker et al., 2018, p. 112).

Hart's Ladder of Participation

Hierarchy of children's research participation rights

	Rung on Hart's ladder	Hart's participation categories	Level Descriptors	Participation rights			
				Information provided to the child: **Information**	Appropriate to the child's capacities: **Understanding**	Express views and relate experiences: **Voice**	Carries weight in decision-making processes: **Influence**
Rights-based Participation	8	Child-initiated and directed, shared decisions with adults	**Child-initiated and directed with significant influence, decisions shared with adults.** Child's voice having greatest influence with adults overseeing	Information created by children	Understanding greater than adults	Voice equal to that of adults'	Significant influence
	7	Child-initiated and directed	**Child-initiated and directed but facilitated by adults.** Significant scope for child voice and influence	Information greater than adults'	Understanding equal to that of adults'	Significant voice	Selected influence
	6	Adult-initiated, shared decisions with children	**Adult-initiated and scaffolded, decisions shared with children.** Selected scope for child voice with scaffolded influence	Information equal to that of adults'	Significant understanding	Selected voice	Scaffolded influence
	5	Consulted and informed	**Consulted, informed with understanding, heard.** Volunteers with a measure of voice and influence	Significant information	Selected understanding	Scaffolded voice	Restricted opportunities for influence
	4	Assigned but informed	**Assigned, informed with understanding.** Volunteers but restricted to a practical yet symbolic role	Selected information	Scaffolded understanding	Restricted opportunities for voice	Negligible influence
Non-participation	3	Tokenism	**Assigned, somewhat informed.** May offer opinions but no action is taken	Scaffolded information	Restricted opportunities for understanding	Negligible voice	No influence
	2	Decoration	**Assigned, largely unaware, not consulted**	Restricted opportunities for information	Negligible understanding	No voice	No influence
	1	Manipulation	**Assigned, unaware, possibly misled** to facilitate involvement	Negligible information	No understanding	No voice	No influence

Figure 41.2 Hierarchy of children's research participation rights, showing its relationship to Hart's ladder of participation (Mayne et al., 2018, p. 6)

In research projects, both dimensions are largely in the hands of adults. The fields in the matrix describe different types of distribution and availability of information (from negligible to complete information, as well as information provided by the children as co-researchers) (first column), information appropriate to the child in terms of his or her individual level of understanding (second column), the way in which opinions can be expressed and experiences can be related (third column), and the way children can influence decisions (fourth column). The darker the fields are shaded, the higher the degree of the dimension of understanding and agency are, thus the more consistent they are with the implementation of the rights of the child to participation.

Classification of the buddY children study in the hierarchical model

Attempts to classify the accompanying study of the buddY pilot project described in section 2 into the hierarchical model developed by Mayne, Howitt and Rennie provide critical reflection on the type and extent of opportunities for children's participation. Here, it should be noted that the project was not launched on the initiative of the children, but by the foundation providing the funding. The focus of the foundation was thus also on the evaluation of the buddY participation concept funded by it. The research questions 'How do children rate the innovative measures and methods in the transition design?', 'How do they rate their opportunities for participation?' and 'What wishes, needs and ideas do they express with regard to an ideal design of the transition phase?' (Büker and Bethke, 2014) were formulated by a team of adults, consisting of the foundation's coordinator, researchers, educators and teachers. At the beginning of the study, the children received significant information about the study. It was explained to them why they were being consulted and why their opinions are important. The implementation of children's rights to information and understanding can thus be located on level 5 (see markings in Figure 41.3).

The children participating in the buddY study received supported opportunities for expressing their opinions through the provision of special scaffolding measures. A pre-test was thus conducted to evaluate in advance if the interview questions for the group discussion were suitable regarding the cognitive and language development requirements of the children. The children also had opportunities to express their opinions verbally, in picture form or using body language. A special method was developed for the individual interviews in the second survey phase, as described previously, which involved the use of pictograms and smiley scales. This was done to ensure that a true communicative validation of the results from the first survey phase could be affected and to enable participation on the basis of extensive and profound understanding at level 5 of the model. In the area of opportunities for having influence, the design of the buddY study may be located at level 4 and/or at most at level 5. Although the design explicitly foresaw a transfer and dissemination concept, unfortunately it was omitted to invite the children themselves to the public feedback and to give them an opportunity to speak at this event for themselves. The Children's Declaration described above was handed over by the foundation's coordinator to the kindergartens and schools. Researchers and funders were conceptualised as advocators of the children and acted as mediums for the children's voices. What can be seen here is that there were tensions between the ideals of participatory pedagogy, participatory research, the researcher's agenda and the funder's agenda. It should be noted that a self-critical analysis shows that the way the results obtained from the children's survey were dealt was primarily with the view to the professionalisation of the educators and teachers, as well as the optimisation of teaching practices. Originally, the children were asked to participate as experts, but

Hart's Ladder of Participation

Hierarchy of children's research participation rights

	Rung on Hart's ladder	Hart's participation categories	Level Descriptors	Participation rights			
				Information provided to the child: Information	Appropriate to the child's capacities: Understanding	Express views and relate experiences: Voice	Carries weight in decision-making processes: Influence
Rights-based Participation	8	Child-initiated and directed, shared decisions with adults	**Child-initiated and directed with significant influence, decisions shared with adults.** Child's voice having greatest influence with adults overseeing	Information created by children	Understanding greater than adults'	Voice equal to that of adults'	Significant influence
Rights-based Participation	7	Child-initiated and directed	**Child-initiated and directed but facilitated by adults.** Significant scope for child voice and influence	Information greater than adults'	Understanding equal to that of adults'	Significant voice	Selected influence
Rights-based Participation	6	Adult-initiated, shared decisions with children	**Adult-initiated and scaffolded, decisions shared with children.** Selected scope for child voice with scaffolded influence	Information equal to that of adults'	Significant understanding	Selected voice	Scaffolded influence
Rights-based Participation	5	Consulted and informed	**Consulted, informed with understanding, heard.** Volunteers with a measure of voice and influence	Significant information	Selected understanding	Scaffolded voice	Restricted opportunities for influence
Rights-based Participation	4	Assigned but informed	**Assigned, informed with understanding.** Volunteers but restricted to a practical yet symbolic role	Selected information	Scaffolded understanding	Restricted opportunities for voice	Negligible influence
Non-participation	3	Tokenism	**Assigned, somewhat informed.** May offer opinions but no action is taken	Scaffolded information	Restricted opportunities for understanding	Negligible voice	No influence
Non-participation	2	Decoration	**Assigned, largely unaware, not consulted**	Restricted opportunities for information	Negligible understanding	No voice	No influence
Non-participation	1	Manipulation	**Assigned, unaware, possibly misled** to facilitate involvement	Negligible information	No understanding	No voice	No influence

Figure 41.3 Levels of participation within the buddY study

their voices became means of providing information for the training of adults. The children involved in the study could not experience the effectiveness and influence on the change processes for themselves. The integration of children in research, on the one hand, and the professionalisation of educators and teachers, on the other, remained as two unconnected processes because of a short-circuited transfer and dissemination concept.

Discussion: how could further research settings be designed combining children's participation and professionalisation of educators and teachers?

In this chapter, a pilot project with an accompanying children's study was described that pursued the ambitious aim to let children participate in their individual and collective transition process. Big efforts were made to find innovative pedagogical and didactical ways to allow democratic learning during the transition from kindergarten to school.

Furthermore, big efforts were made to find a methodological design that is appropriate to bring children's opinions to light. This article shows that theoretical models that operationalise the UNCRC provisions, such as the hierarchical model from Mayne, Howitt and Rennie, could be very helpful for a critical reflection of type and extend for children's opportunities to participation. There is no doubt that such models have limitations. For instance, within the used hierarchical model, it is not always possible to differentiate the given levels in an exact way. However, despite those limitations, such models offer a systematic framework that provides orientation and systematic planning and reflection of children's rights-based research. In the case of the buddY project, the analysis shows that children were given information, understanding and voice, but the aim to involve children participation in the design of transition processes was only partially achieved. The higher levels in the model were not reached because children did not get the opportunity to present their opinions personally, and thus they weren't involved in the transfer and dissemination process.

Markable and sustainable consequences were drawn from the pilot project. Especially, the self-assessment tool described above offers strong promise for professionalisation of educators and teachers. The voices of the children were consequently integrated into the design of this tool so that many children can profit from them by joining optimised transition activities in the future. But nevertheless, the UNCRC right to have a *direct* impact on further measures and decisions and to feel what significant influence would mean to them was refused to the children that joined in the buddY study. The focus of the dissemination was on the adults. The buddY project is an example of the argument given above that children's participation rarely meets its own ideals. The result of the analysis gives reason to reflect how the UNCRC rights of information, understanding, voice and influence could be granted in pedagogy and research, while at the same time be combined with professionalisation processes in pedagogical institutions.

Conclusion

In my opinion, the solution includes three aspects: attitudes, structures and didactics. First, the adult researcher should be prepared to postpone the intergenerational order in favour of the child's agency. This, in turn, implies a critical reflection on the image of the child held by the researcher. If research is carried out with the intention of supporting children in their participation competence while at the same time professionalising adults, then all the involved social actors (children, parents, educators, teachers and policymakers) must regard and respect each other *as partners* (Harcourt and Conroy, 2011). Special attention needs to be paid to the transfer and dissemination phase of research: ensuring that children's voices are heard is not something that can be achieved simply by depending on the goodwill of those involved, but rather requires *structures*. For example, children can be delegates in every educators meeting. Structures must be developed that implement the presentation of findings by children themselves as a normal element of the participatory research design. In the process of developing new teacher training measures based on findings of children's studies, children themselves should be engaged as critical experts in a communicative validation. To make all these participatory elements accessible for children, the research process has to be designed as an interaction process with the child and as a systematic learning process for the children – taking into account the age and stage of development of the child. This requires *didactic-pedagogical competencies* that are indeed new for the research context (Büker et al., 2018, p. 113). The right of the child to participation is not only fulfilled by the act of participation, but also includes the right of the child to a conscious, framed learning and experience process in the field of learning to participate – beginning from planning to hear children's voices up to transferring them into professionalisation processes.

For the design of future research settings this means that there are a range of diverse new tasks which need to be accompanied by strengthening children's rights-based research quality standards. Mayne et al. (2018) demand, 'While it is not clear why researchers have been slow to shift their style of research to more participatory methods, it is time to expect more from those who plan new research projects that involve young children' (p. 1). Coming from an adult-dominated research tradition, the ideas given in this article may seem as hard work here. Nonetheless, it is the right of children that this work will be done.

Note

1 buddY e.V. is a foundation set up by the Vodafone Foundation Germany, which aims to establish a 'new learning culture'. In 2016, buddY e.V. was renamed Education Y.

References

Arztmann, Doris, Doris Harrasser, Karin Schneider, and Veronika Wöhrer. 2017. "Rahmenbedingungen und Vorgangsweisen." In *Partizipative Aktionsforschung mit Kindern und Jugendlichen. Von Schulsprachen, Liebesorten und anderen Forschungsdingen*, edited by Veronika Wöhrer et al., 49–84. Wiesbaden: Springer VS.

Bergström, Kerstin, Lena Jonsson, and Helena Shanahan. 2010. "Children as co-researchers voicing their preferences in foods and eating: methodological reflections." *International Journal of Consumer Studies* 34: 183–189.

Bertram, Tony, Julia Formosinho, Colette Gray, Chris Pascal, and Margy Whalley. 2015. *EECERA Ethical Code for Early Childhood Researchers*. Accessed 11 February 2019. http://eecera-ext.tandf. co.uk/documents/pdf/organisation/EECERA-Ethical-Code.pdf

Bührmann, Thorsten, Petra Büker, and Julia Höke. 2017. "'Wir sind jetzt alle Lernbegleiter' – Nivellierungstendenzen in der multiprofessionellen Teamarbeit im Übergang Kita-Grundschule." In *Profession und Disziplin - Grundschulpädagogik im Diskurs*, edited by Susanne Miller et al., 212–217. Wiesbaden: Springer VS.

Bührmann, Thorsten, and Petra Büker. 2015. "Organisationsentwicklung und multiprofessionelle Teamarbeit im Kinderbildungshaus. Eine systemische Perspektive." *Diskurs Kindheits- und Jugendforschung* 10(2): 149–165.

Büker, Petra. 2019. "Partizipation von Kindergarten- und Grundschulkindern an Übergangsgestaltung, Übergangsforschung und am Transfer in optimierte Praxis: Erfahrungen aus einer Kinderbefragungsstudie im Rahmen des Modellprojekts ‚buddY'." In *Grundschulpädagogik zwischen Wissenschaft und*

Transfer, edited by Christian Donie et al. Wiesbaden: Springer VS (Jahrbuch Grundschulforschung 21).340-343.

Büker, Petra, and Cathleen Bethke. 2014. *Evaluationsstudie im Rahmen des buddY-Modellprojektes: Übergang von der Kita in die Grundschule. Eine qualitative Kinderbefragung. Abschlussbericht.* Accessed 11 February 2019. http://kw.uni-paderborn.de/fileadmin/fakultaet/Institute/erziehungswissenschaft/ Grundschulpaedagogik-und-fruehe-Bildung/Projekte/Abschlussbericht_Endfassung_02.02.2015.pdf.

Büker, Petra, and Julia Höke. 2019. "Children's voices as a bridge between educators in kindergarten and teachers in primary school: Potential of children's perspectives to support professional development." In *Children's Perspectives on Transition to School: From Research to Practice*, edited by Sue Dockett, Jóhanna Einársdottir, and Bob Perry, 116–132. London, New York: Routledge.

Büker, Petra, Birgit Hüpping, Fiona Mayne, and Christine Howitt. 2018. "Kinder partizipativ in Forschung einbeziehen – ein kinderrechtsbasiertes Stufenmodell." *Discourse. Journal of Childhood and Adolescence Research* 13(1): 109–114.

Dockett, Sue, Jóhanna Einársdottir, and Bob Perry, eds. 2019. *Children's Perspectives on Transition to School: From Research to Practice.* London, New York: Routledge.

Dockett, Sue, and Bob Perry. 2011. "Researching with young children: Seeking assent." *Child Indicators Research* 4(2): 231–247.

Donie, Christian, and Gisela Kammermeyer, eds. 2019 in press. *Grundschulpädagogik zwischen Wissenschaft und Transfer.* Wiesbaden: Springer VS. (Jahrbuch Grundschulforschung, 26).

Eßer, Florian, and Miriam Sitter. 2018. "Ethische Symmetrie in der partizipativen Forschung mit Kindern." *Forum Qualitative Sozialforschung/Forum: Qualitative Social Research* 19(3), Art. 21.

Fleet, Alma, and Clare Britt. 2011. "Seeing spaces, inhabiting places: Hearing school beginners." In *Researching Young Children's Perspectives: Debating the Ethics and Dilemmas of Educational Research with Children*, edited by Deborah Harcourt, Bob Perry, and Tim Waller, 143–162. London: Routledge.

Franzen, Nina. 2016. "Eltern und Erzieher. Partner beim Schulstart." *Grundschule* 15(7): 10–12.

Ghirotto, Luca, and Valentina Mazzoni. 2013. "Being part, being involved: The adult's role and child participation in an early childhood learning context." *International Journal of Early Years Education* 21(4): 300-308.

Gräsel, Cornelia. 2010. "Stichwort: Transfer und Transferforschung im Bildungsbereich." *Zeitschrift für Erziehungswissenschaft* 13(1): 7–20.

Groundwater-Smith, Susan, Sue Dockett, and Dorothy Bottrell. 2015. *Participatory Research with Children and Young People.* London: SAGE Publications Ltd.

Harcourt, Deborah, and Heather Conroy. 2011. "Informed consent: Processes and procedures in seeking research partnerships with young children." In *Researching Young Children's Perspectives: Debating the Ethics and Dilemmas of Educational Research with Children*, edited by Deborah Harcourt, Bob Perry and Tim Waller, 38–51. London: Routledge.

Harcourt, Deborah, Bob Perry, and Tim Waller, eds. 2011. *Researching Young Children's Perspectives: Debating the Ethics and Dilemmas of Educational Research with Children.* London: Routledge.

Hart, Roger. 1992. *Children's Participation: From Tokenism to Citizenship.* Florence: UNICEF International Child Development Centre. Accessed 11 February 2019. www.unicef-irc.org/publications/pdf/chil drens_participation.pdf.

Heinzel, Friederike, ed. 2012. *Methoden der Kindheitsforschung.* Weinheim: Beltz Juventa.

Heinzel, Friederike, Renate Kränzl-Nagl, and Johanna Mierendorff. 2012. "Sozialwissenschaftliche Kindheitsforschung – Annäherung an einen komplexen Forschungsbereich." *Zeitschrift für Religionspädagogik* 11(1): 9–37.

Höke, Julia, Thorsten Bührmann, Petra Büker, Rebecca Hummel, Kapriel Meser, Susanne Miller, and Robert Stölner. 2017. "Bildungshäuser als ,Dritter Raum' im Übergang zwischen Kita und Grundschule – Kritische Blicke auf ein Jahrzehnt Intensivkooperation." *Zeitschrift für Grundschulforschung* 10(1): 91–106.

Höke, Julia, Petra Büker, and Thorsten Bührmann. 2017. *Paderborner Qualitätsstern© zur Einschätzung der Kooperation im Übergang Kita – Grundschule.* Paderborn: Universität Paderborn. Accessed 11 February 201918. https://blogs.uni-paderborn.de/paderborner-qualitaetsstern/

James, Allison, Chris Jenks, and Alan Prout. 1998. *Theorizing Childhood.* Cambridge: Polity Press.

Kellett, Mary. 2011. "Empowering children and young people as researchers: Overcoming barriers and building capacity." *Child Indicators Research* 4(2): 205–219.

Kellett, Mary, Ruth Forrest (aged ten), Naomi Dent (aged ten), and Simon Ward (aged ten). 2004. "'Just teach us the skills please, we'll do the rest': Empowering ten-year-olds as active researchers." *Children & Society* 18(5): 329–343.

Kordulla, Agnes. 2017. *Lernen mit- und voneinander. Peer-Learning im Übergang von der Kita in die Grundschule unter besonderer Berücksichtigung der Kinderperspektiven.* Bad Heilbrunn: Klinkhardt.

Lundy, Laura. 2007. "Voice' is not enough: conceptualising Article 12 of the United Nations Convention on the Right of the Child." *British Educational Research Journal* 33(6): 927–942.

Lundy, Laura, Lesley McEvoy, and Bronagh Byrne. 2011. "Working with young children as co-researchers: An approach informed by the United Nations Convention on the Rights of the Child." *Early Education & Development* 22(5): 714–736.

Maaz, Kai, Marko Neumann, and Jürgen Baumert, eds. 2014. *Herkunft und Bildungserfolg von der frühen Kindheit bis ins Erwachsenenalter.* Wiesbaden: Springer VS.

Mayne, Fiona, and Christine Howitt. 2014. "Reporting of ethics in early childhood journals: A meta-analysis of 10 journals from 2009 to 2012." *Australasian Journal of Early Childhood* 39(2): 71-79.

Mayne, Fiona, Christine Howitt, and Léonie Rennie. 2018. "A hierarchical model of children's research participation rights based on information, understanding, voice, and influence." *European Early Childhood Education Research Journal* 36(2): 1–13.

Mayring, Philip. 2011. *Qualitative Inhaltsanalyse. Grundlagen und Techniken.* 11th ed. Weinheim: Beltz.

Müller, Ulrike Beate. 2014. *Kinder im verzahnten Übergang vom Elementar- zum Primarbereich.* Opladen (u. a.): Verlag Barbara Budrich.

Murray, Jane. 2017. "Welcome in! How the academy can warrant recognition of young children as researchers." *European Early Childhood Education Journal* 25(2): 224–242.

OECD, Network on Early Childhood and Care. 2015. *Early Learning and Development: Common Understanding.* Accessed 11 February 2019. www.oecd.org/edu/school/ECEC-Network-Common-Under standings-on-Early-Learning-and-Development.pdf.

Prengel, Annedore. 2016. *Bildungsteilhabe und Partizipation in Kindertageseinrichtungen.* Vol. 47 of *WIFF Expertisen.* München: DJI.

Prengel, Annedore, Friederike Heinzel, and Ursula Carle. 2004. "Methoden der Handlungs-, Praxis- und Evaluationsforschung." In *Handbuch der Schulforschung*, edited by Werner Helsper, and Jeanette Böhme, 181–197. Wiesbaden: Springer VS.

Sommer, Dion, Ingrid Pramling Samuelsson, and Karsten Hundeide. 2010. *Child Perspectives and Children's Perspective in Theory and Practice.* Volume 2. Dordrecht, Heidelberg, London and New York: Springer.

Spriggs, Merle, and Lynn Gillam. 2017. "Ethical complexities in child co-research." *Research Ethics*: 1–16. doi: 10.1177/1747016117750207

UN General Assembly. 1989. "Convention on the rights of the child." *United Nations*, November 20. Accessed 11 February 2019. www.refworld.org/docid/3ae6b38f0.html.

UNICEF. 2014. *Fact Sheet: The Right to Participation.* Accessed 11 February 2019. www.unicef.org/crc/ files/Right-to-Participation.pdf.

United Nations Committee on the Rights of the Child. 2006. *A Guide to General Comment 7: 'Implementing Child Rights in Early Childhood'.* Geneva, Switzerland: United Nations Children's Fund and Bernard van Leer Foundation. Accessed 11 February 2019. www.unicef.org/earlychildhood/files/Guide_ to_GC7.pdf.

Wildgruber, Andreas, and Wilfried Griebel. 2016. *Erfolgreicher Übergang vom Elementar- in den Primarbereich. Empirische und curriculare Analysen.* München: DJI.

42

YOUNG CHILDREN'S RIGHT TO PLAY DURING THEIR TRANSITION FROM EARLY CHILDHOOD EDUCATION TO PRIMARY SCHOOL IN CHILE

Daniela S. Jadue-Roa and Matías Knust

Introduction

In this chapter, we draw on research findings to discuss and analyse adherence by the State of Chile to specific aspects of the United Nations Convention on the Rights of the Child (UNCRC) (United Nations, UN Committee on the Rights of the Child, 1989) relating to young children's rights to be heard, to education, play and foregrounding of their best interests. The chapter opens with an overview of early childhood education (ECE) policies in Chile and their relationship to the UNCRC, followed by a literature review concerning childhood, play and transitions. We draw on findings from an empirical study about young children in Chile making the transition from ECE into primary school education (PSE), and we identify four important associations for positive transition made by children in the study: (1) space and free play; (2) free play and peer relationships; (3) space and play resources; and (4) space, relationships and sense of belonging. Based on these findings, we advocate for Chilean children's voices to be heard concerning their outdoor playful experiences in ECE and PSE settings. We argue that when young children express their need to play outdoors in ECE and PSE, their educational provision should accommodate such play, and therefore teachers should have access to professional development to understand that need and how to accommodate it. This argument is fundamental to compliance with young children's UNCRC rights, to be heard, to participate, to play, to education and to their best interests.

The UNCRC and Chilean ECE policies

The UNCRC articles have been interpreted differently across countries, and consequently, since 2001, the UN Committee has elaborated and disseminated General Comments (GCs)

Table 42.1 Summary of General Comment Nos. 1, 7, 14 and 17 (adapted from Viviers, 2014)

General Comment	Description
No. 1 (2001) Article 29 (1): The Aims of Education (UN, 2001)	Emphasises that education should be a child-friendly, child-centred and inclusive experience, integrating the cognitive, emotional, social and physical aspects of children's learning and development trajectories.
No. 7 (2005) Implementing Child Rights in Early Childhood (UN, 2005)	Defines early childhood as the period below the age of 8 years and emphasises the responsibility of State Parties to respect children's rights from this early stage onwards. It draws on the characteristics of children's learning and development to exemplify how children's rights to well-being, education and social integration must be addressed.
No. 14 (2013) The Right of the Child to have His or Her Best Interest taken as a Primary Consideration (Article 3, para. 1) (UN, 2013a)	Specifies that the child's and children's best interest should be acknowledged as a 'substantive right', 'principle' and 'rule of procedure' in legal procedures, education and social welfare institutions, among others.
No. 17 (2013) The Right of the Child to Rest, Leisure, Play, Recreational Activities, Cultural Life and the Arts (Article 31) (UN, 2013b)	Strengthens the argument in favour of spaces for children to recreate, play and rest according to their own interests and needs in all spaces that they inhabit, including educational provision, community parks and social services, among others. Special attention is drawn to the educational transition experience between ECEC and PSE, calling the State Parties' attention to provide with adequate provisions for this early childhood (as defined in the Convention) period, regardless of their curriculum structure.

to different articles of the Convention to support their implementation (Viviers, 2014). The UNCRC and the GCs guide this chapter, particularly GC Nos. 1, 7, 14 and 17 (Table 42.1). These GCs interrelate and draw the attention of State Parties to how they may secure the particular rights of young children indicated above.

Childhood policies have an early origin in Chile (Rojas Flores, 2010). However, it was not until 1970 when the National Board of Early Childhood Centres (JUNJI, Spanish acronym) was founded by law No. 17301 (MINEDUC, 1970). Then, during General Pinochet's military dictatorship (1973–1990), the National Foundation of Assistance to the Community (FUNACO, Spanish acronym) was founded in 1975 to coordinate and support the social work of volunteers for the social welfare of children from disadvantaged families. Chile's ratification of the UNCRC in 1990 was an important milestone for children and childhood policies, and characterised Chile's return to democracy in the same year. FUNACO was then replaced by the ECE foundation Fundación INTEGRA, implicitly integrating education and care (Hermosilla, 1998). In 2009, Chile created a multisector strategy called *'Chile*

Crece Contigo' [Chile Grows with you], recognised nationally and internationally, which established integrated health, social, educational and legal services to protect children from conception to the age of 8 years old, and their families.

More recently, in relation to education, Chile has introduced: (a) a national policy for childhood from birth to 18 years old (Consejo Nacional de la Infancia, 2016); (b) the ECE Sub-Secretary (2015) and the Childhood Sub-Secretary (2018); (c) the Early Childhood Intendency (2016); (d) compulsory kindergarten (2013); (e) increasing ECE coverage (2014–2018); (f) official recognition of ECE centres law (2015); (g) inclusion of ECE educators in the national practitioners' law (2016); and (h) a government organisation for childhood advocacy (2018). These policies have highlighted Chilean ECE in public discourse but have accentuated tensions between ECE and PSE.

Currently, Chile has three important institutions that provide ECE up to the age of 6: JUNJI and Fundación INTEGRA, which address the needs of children from birth to 4 years old, and the Ministry of Education (MINEDUC), which supervises the transition levels – pre-kindergarten and kindergarten – in PSE provision. PSE in Chile starts at 6 years and young children usually move within their school setting to a different classroom and playground. Transitions between ECE and PSE are therefore embedded in the political context (Moss, 2013). PSE was enshrined in law in 1860 in Chile, and the first public kindergarten, influenced by Froebel, was created in 1906 (Cerda Díaz, 2007). The Chilean ECE system is informed by several philosophical approaches, including Froebel, Montessori and High Scope (Peralta, 2005). In the 1970s, a group of Chilean ECE educators created the *'Curriculum Integral' [Integral Curriculum]*, which prevails today, encompassing aspects of those different approaches grounded in the country's sociocultural context (Cerda Díaz, 2007). Conversely, the PSE curriculum follows Chile's national curriculum exclusively.

Since the 1990s, national curricula for both ECE and PSE have constantly been subjected to revision and reform (Mella, 2003; Peralta, 1999), and consequently changes made to those guiding documents have resulted in overlapping learning goals and discontinuities (Jadue-Roa & Whitebread, 2012). Although continuity and progression between ECE and PSE have recently been considered problematic in Chile, discourse has tended to focus more on the curricula than their impact on young children's learning (MINEDUC, 2004, 2017).

In the context of this chapter, concerned with ECE and PSE in Chile, it is important to consider the impact of UNCRC and GC Nos. 1, 7, 14 and 17 (Table 42.1) on ECE and PSE policies and pedagogical practices regarding play, educational transitions and young children's learning trajectories.

Play and transitions in childhood

Early childhood is the period from birth to 8 years (Viviers, 2014). In this chapter, we adhere to the children's rights approach that aligns with the new sociology of childhood theoretical perspective (Qvortrup, 2002). We understand young children as individuals and a collective, acknowledging that each child has subjectivities and whose meanings are negotiated and constructed within social groups (Bruner, 1996). We regard childhood as a social construction and recognise children as agents who co-construct their own lives and produce and reproduce culture (Löfdahl, 2014; Mayall, 2002). We value play as an essential part of children's lives and their own constructions of their cultures, as indicated in GC No. 17 (United Nations, UN Committee on the Rights of the Child, 2013b). This perspective chimes with work undertaken by Corsaro and Molinari (2005) which showed that peer interactions during play are essential to understand young children's constructions of meanings and sense of belonging. Wood (2014) adds that during free play, young children learn how to interact, enact roles, negotiate ideas and subjectivities, understand emotions, and create their own agendas and cultures.

Play, participation and agency

Accordingly, young children should be enabled to participate and their voices heard in all matters concerning them. In education for children up to 8 years, play should be at the core (Clark, 2010; Einarsdóttir, 2014) because it is children's fundamental activity, vital for childhood experiences, learning and growth (Fleer, 2017). Humans learn best when they are genuinely interested in what and how they are learning, and intrinsic motivation is the motor of play (Broström, 2007). Children's agency is central to their free play, its impact on playful learning and positive experiences of transition to school (Saltmarsh, 2014). However, the borderline between free play and structured play in schools is fragile (Sylva et al., 2010). Accommodation of children's own choices of play activities and also the teacher's pedagogical intentions, without resorting to instructional play, remains an unresolved issue (Grau et al., 2018). Instructional play is valued, yet it dismisses children's own interests and cultures (Fleer, 2017; Wood, 2014). The challenge for pedagogy is free play that has children's own motivations and interests at its core, while also enabling children to meet curriculum goals.

Playful pedagogies

Careful observation of children's play over time and conversing with them about their play may be useful tools for informing playful learning as part of pedagogical practice (Hedges, 2011). Fleer (2017) and Wood (2014) suggest that an essential duty of researchers and educators is to observe and document children's play over time to understand their perspectives on play, their interests, and their ideas about culture. Einarsdóttir (2014) and Fleer (2017) argue that children elaborate their perspectives on play based on agentic choices guided by their own interests. In this way, it may be possible to begin to address the tension between children's own play imperatives and curricular goals determined by adults. Fleer (2017) argues that children's perspectives are essential for the joint construction of a play-based curriculum. Playful pedagogies may be an effective mechanism for securing children's learning in a positive climate and assuring later academic success (Whitebread & Bingham, 2011): Weisberg, Hirsh-Pasek, and Micknick Golinkoff (2013) suggest that including guided play in the design of the pedagogical environment enables children to reach curriculum goals.

Transition from ECE to PSE

Internationally, a rich seam of literature highlights discontinuities between young children's experiences of ECE and PSE (Moss, 2013; Whitebread & Bingham, 2011). However, when attempts to reduce disjuncture between the two phases centre on leveraging ECE to secure young children's 'school readiness', there is evidence that young children's cognitive and emotional needs are disregarded (Whitebread & Bingham, 2011). Nevertheless, the UN (2015) currently regards ECE as preparation for PSE.

Teachers and play

Research exploring teacher professional development about play is scarce. Nevertheless, there are studies exploring teachers' perspectives on play, and a common concern among educators across many cultures is the tendency for ECE curricula to become too academic (Ryan & Northey-Berg, 2014). This point resonates with Chilean children's concerns about the transition from ECE to PSE and how this may affect their play (Jadue-Roa et al., 2016; Rupin, Muñoz, & Jadue-Roa, 2018). Findings suggest that ECE educators and PSE teachers should work together to construct a playful pedagogy in ECE and early in PSE, including free outdoor play. Such a model implies some reconstruction of the identities of ECE educators' and PSE teachers' identities to develop a shared identity of a professional supporting children's initial education (Jadue-Roa et al., 2016).

Outdoor spaces for play

Children's free play, especially outdoors in natural environments, is fundamental for the development of consciousness (Maturana, 2003). School playgrounds can be spaces with strong potential to promote children's well-being through free play and connection with nature (Bagot, Allen, & Toukhsati, 2015; Collado & Staats, 2016). Researching 'the "space between" the environment and (the child as) a human agent' during young children's play may enable adults to understand their agentic actions in different contexts where affordances are historically, socially and culturally mediated (Waters, 2017, p. 40). Offering young children play opportunities indoors and outdoors respects their right to play, and their exposure to natural landscapes impacts positively on motor development (Fjørtoft, 2001). Even in South Korean ECE, where there is relatively little available outdoor space, young children engage in outdoor play, albeit for fixed periods of time (Kwi-Ok, 2017).

Kindergartens in countries including Norway, Sweden, Denmark and Germany commonly make provision for young children to play outdoors in nature (Lysklett, 2013). Equally, in Australia and New Zealand, playgrounds in kindergartens and schools have been transformed into natural play areas where children educate themselves in explorative, fun, risky and flexible spaces (Wynne & Gorman, 2015). Significant learning and development benefits are reported from young children's outdoor play, including enhanced confidence, motivation, concentration, encouragement of language development, communication skills, reasoning, observation skills, creativity, social skills and friendship (Bateman & Waters, 2018; Chawla, 2015). Including children's voices in the design of outdoor space is an emergent field of interest for researchers and practitioners; for example, the 'Spaces to Play' project (Clark & Moss, 2005), which demonstrated that children were knowledgeable about their outdoor spaces and their input was essential to design a quality space for them to play freely and learn.

Young children's rights to play in Chilean ECE and PSE

In Chile, as a result of increasing education policy concerns about children's readiness for school and later academic success, play has only recently become a focus for discussion in the context of education (Grau et al., 2018). It is a contested area, at the heart of which lies divergent perspectives of child, children and childhood that guide ECE and PSE. This point is reflected in the national curricula at both levels in Chile: play is a key principle in the ECE curriculum but only features in arts and physical education elements of the PSE curriculum (MINEDUC, 2013, 2018). Little is understood by Chilean teachers working at either level about the UNCRC and its implications for pedagogical practices (Pardo and Jadue-Roa, forthcoming). Therefore, understanding children's rights to education, play and being heard during transition from ECE to PSE is not yet an issue for Chilean public discourse or teacher training, as recommended in GC No. 7 (UN, 2005). Addressing this lacuna is essential to the provision of a continuous and progressive transition experience for young children between ECE and PSE (Jadue-Roa, 2019). The study set out below makes a contribution to achieving this: it illuminates young children's views of their outdoor play experiences during their transition from ECE to PSE in Chile. Their views reveal the paucity of play opportunities they found when starting first grade, indicating that their rights to free play and being heard were ignored, and their best interests were not served by existing transition practices.

The study

The qualitative cross-sectional study focused on transition as a feature of the Chilean educational system in 2015 (Jadue-Roa et al., 2016). It was conducted in six schools (two municipal, two partially subsidised and two private) in two different regional urban areas of Chile. A purposive sample of 41 young children participated in semi-structured group interviews, each including three or four children: 24 in kindergarten aged 5–6 and 17 in PSE first grade aged 6–7. Drawing elicitation was used to explore the children's perspectives about their transition experiences. Narratives were co-constructed with the children during interviews, and analysis involved contrasting and comparing the children's narratives and a thorough process of code validation, resulting in a coding framework based on children's accounts (Jadue-Roa, Whitebread, & Guzmán, 2018). Because a rights approach underpinned this study, stringent ethical procedures were essential and included asking children for ongoing assent throughout the fieldwork (Harcourt, Perry, & Waller, 2011; Jadue-Roa, 2017; Lundy & McEvoy, 2012).

Main findings

This study revealed children's perspectives on their transition experience, including – but not limited to – several elements: relationships (with peers and adults), spaces (indoors and outdoors), identity, resources and interrelations that children established between free play in outdoor spaces, and other elements. Four important associations concerning the outdoor play environment emerged: (1) space and free play; (2) free play and peer relationships; (3) space and play resources; and (4) space, relationships and sense of belonging.

    1. Space and free play:

R: So what do you think you will do in first grade?
Ch1: Work, work, work and more work ... We will not be able to play.
R: Oh! This means that you won't be able to play in first grade?
Ch1: No ... no.
Ch2: Exactly, they don't allow it.
R: And during breaks? (Ch2 nods)
R: During breaks, yes?
Ch1: They don't allow to do anything! Not even during breaks!

Vignette 1: kindergarten children (school 5)

In vignette 1, children's expectations about play are quite pessimistic. They accepted, but were disappointed by, their situation, which demonstrates disregard of their right to play, even during break time. However, vignette 2 shows that this view cannot be generalised: children also saw break times as time to play freely:

R: Wow! It seems like everyone likes the classroom areas. And do you like breaks too?
Ch1: Yes.
R: And how many breaks do you have?
Ch1: Three.
R: Three breaks! How lucky!
Ch1: Actually, during the three breaks I mostly play football, with a ball made of plastic bags like this.
R: And do you play with your classmates?
Ch1: Yes.
R: And what is more fun? Kinder or first grade?
Ch2: First grade.
R: Why?
Ch2: Because we have more breaks.
Ch3: Because we have a lot of space to run.

Vignette 2: kindergarten children (school 6)

Both examples indicate that through their expectations, children construct the idea that fun and play are different from learning. Young children often develop emotional and contextual clues to differentiate 'play' from 'work' as they transition from ECE to PSE (Fleer, 2017), and their views of play and learning become separated in time and space by breaks *or* class activity and outdoors *or* indoors. This finding suggests that PSE teachers in Chile could strengthen their knowledge expertise about outdoor play and learning in practical ways, as Viviers (2014, p. 202) suggests, in allusion to GC No. 17: 'listen to children while playing; create environments that facilitate children's play; allow children to play freely and play with children' (United Nations, UN Committee on the Rights of the Child, 2013b).

2. Free play and peer relationships:

Ch1: You play with them in the playground.
R: What things do you play in the playground, for example?
Ch1: Football, because today we will do a cyberclub, because we can't play football anymore.
R: Why?
Ch1: Because aunty [educator] [said] ... We can't play.
R: You can't play anymore ... Maybe because there are too many children in the playground?
Ch1: And ... no, that's not the reason, it's because ... we all have to play.

Vignette 3: kindergarten children (school 4)

Here, where children own their decision concerning play, they also own their decisions on relationships and value those opportunities to learn about each other. They understand that

Figure 42.1 Vignette 3: kindergarten and first grade

these opportunities are for everyone, so they know that it is important to negotiate their choices respectfully. There were different moments during the interview when children talked about their peer relationships; nevertheless, when those moments were related to their free play time, they referred to their friendships and elements for building them (vignettes 4 and 5).

R: OK, Ch1, tell me … you said that you were there with your friend … what's her name?

Ch1: Felicity …

R: Felicity. What are you doing there?

Ch1: We were there in the football field.

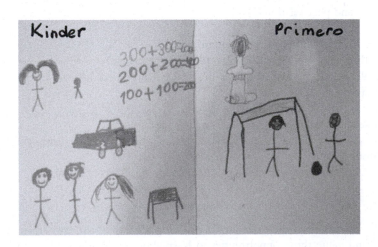

Figure 42.2 Vignettes 4 and 5: kindergarten and second grade

R: In the field ... this is kindergarten, right?

Ch1: Yes.

R: And what were you doing?

Ch1: We were walking ... and then we had a race.

R: And is she your friend in first grade?

Ch1: Yes, still.

R: Are you in the same classroom group?

Ch1: Yes.

R: And do you still play the same things?

Ch1: Hide and seek, 'pinta', races ...

Vignette 4: first grade children (school 4)

R: What things do you like to do in kinder?

Ch1: Play with my classmates, play during breaks, and doing a lot of things and activities ...

R: [...] and what things do you play during breaks?

Ch1: 'Pinta', sometimes to the monster ...

R: All by yourself?

Ch1: No, sometimes with all my classmates.

R: Playing all together?

Ch1: Sometimes not ... now we are figh (she stops talking before she finishes) ... Sometimes we fight and we are not together ...

R: What games do you play during break time?

Ch2: To the balls, balls fight.

R: Balls fight ... oh, not football?

Ch3: Nooo.

R: And how do you play balls fight? Can you explain it to me?

Ch2: You have to hold it with your hand and throw it like this.

R: To whom? Your classmates?

Ch2: Yes, and you have to hide, you have to bend over.

Ch3: To avoid the ball.

R: But that hurts, right?

Ch4: No, we don't throw them strongly, but ...

Ch2: They are air balls ... air balls ...

R: Ahh, those thin coloured ones.

Ch1: We throw them hard anyways ...

Vignette 5: kindergarten children (school 2)

Children indicate here that free time is essential for them to learn how to relate to others. They reveal important characteristics of friendship such as: helping, protecting, commitment and sharing, and helping children to understand limits within relationships and reflect about the impact of their actions on others. As Corsaro and Molinari (2005) advocate, older children may relate to and protect younger children, serving as models and partners in children's transition to PSE. This finding resonates with GC No. 17: 'play and recreation create the opportunities for the formation of friendships and can play a key role in strengthening civil society, contributing towards the social, moral and emotional development of the child, shaping culture and building communities' (United Nations, UN Committee on the Rights of the Child, 2013b).

Figure 42.3 Vignette 6: we can play better

3. Space and play resources:

R: Which playground do you like more? The one in kindergarten or in first grade?
Ch1: I like better the one in kinder, because we had balls.
Ch2: I prefer the one in first grade.
R: Why?
Ch2: Because we can play better because we have more space.

Vignette 6: first grade children (school 1)

R: So, what games do you play now since you don't have a ball to play football?
Ch1: Sometimes they bring balls.
R: From home?

Figure 42.4 Vignette 7: sometimes they bring balls

Ch1: Sometimes I play with bottles.

R: Bottles? Plastic bottles?

Ch1: (nods)

Ch2: When we finish drinking the juice ...

Ch1: Or a milk.

Ch2: Yes! And I give it to them so they can play.

R: That's great!

Vignette 7: first grade children (school 1)

Space and resources that may or may not be available for children's games are another important element for their play and interactions. Here, discontinuities of their transition were identified by children after moving to first grade. Children found that possibilities for playing different games were restricted to the physical resources available within the settings. Most outdoor areas in the Chilean study settings had concrete flooring, few play structures and almost no vegetation. Some years ago, Chilean policymakers proposed reductions of outdoor play space in ECE centres and PSE (in kindergarten to 3 m^2 per child and in PSE to 2.5 m^2 per child) (MINVU, 1992). However, the functioning guide for ECE centres in Chile (JUNJI, 2013) establishes that playgrounds must have natural elements (grass, trees and plants) and equipment, although it explicitly excludes ropes, swings and climbing structures in kindergartens.

Ch1: And this is the playground.

R: OK, tell us, why do you like this playground so much?

Ch1: Because it has play facilities [structures].

R: Ahhh, like the slide.

Ch2: But we don't have swings! (pointing at Ch1's drawing)

R: Did you imagine that you had swings?

Ch1: Because we have play facilities [structures] and those are like swings, slides ...

Vignette 8: kindergarten children (school 6)

Vignette 8 indicates that participating children were not able to discuss their experiences of playing games such as skipping, playing with rings, or ball games, which may have been because participating PSE schools have few – if any – of these resources.

4. Sense of belonging and identity:

Ch3: There was a tree and a car ... and the car was a metal one, and that is the entrance [car door space].

R: Why did you like that car?

Ch3: Because it had a steering wheel that moved. I liked the colour, the wheels, the traffic light, everything.

R: OK, and what else did you have there? I see a ...

Ch3: There was a tunnel.

R: And what did you do there?

Ch3: We hid just in case ... because there was a game that we made up that had a monster, and the one that is the monster has to go after the others. So we go into the tunnel and the monster can't see us.

Figure 42.5 Vignette 9: tree and car

Vignette 9: first grade children (school 6)

Interwoven with the first three important associations that the study children revealed regarding play as they moved from ECE to PSE provision was a fourth. In vignette 9, the young children's narratives suggest that their sense of belonging and identity development during this transition was integral to their play opportunities, especially self-chosen social and pretend play. Equally, in vignette 10, young children claimed they needed various resources outdoors to support their imaginative and social play.

Ch1: My drawing is because I like to go out for break time and here with her we went to play at the tree we have there […]

R: Who is your classmate?

Ch1: Lizzy (…) we were playing that the tree was a little house and we had to bring the son home because the wolf was coming.

R: A son? And the wolf was coming? Really? (the child nods after every question) And here, what is this?

Ch1: A slide of the son, but because he was not there the son could not be there because he was trapped with the wolf.

R: I see, you had to save the son from the wolf! And who is the son? Is someone imaginary or there is another kid?

Ch1: John …

Figure 42.6 Vignette 10: the tree was a house

Vignette 10: kindergarten children (school 2)

Learning from children's views on play

The four associations that young children highlighted in this study enable adults to learn about the importance children place on play as part of their transition from ECE to PSE. First, participating children valued space and free play: fundamental elements for children's learning and development (Jadue-Roa & Whitebread, 2012; Whitebread et al., 2012). For children in Chile starting PSE, the physical environment changes, and children in this study indicated that they were anxious about how such changes might increase control by an external (adult) agent – usually their teacher – and may limit time, space and opportunities they had to choose play activities.

Second, the children regarded free play and peer relationships as an important association. They saw possibilities of interacting and learning to socialise in free play as an important aspect of transition from ECE to PSE, a finding that resonates with Corsaro and Molinari's (2005) study about young children's transitions in Italy. The third important association that the children in this study highlighted was their need for space and play resources, including swings and slides. Studies elsewhere have identified that such resources in outdoor spaces enable children to learn to self-regulate and increase their autonomy (Lysklett, 2013; Wynne & Gorman, 2015). Consequently, it may be argued that establishing well-resourced outdoor spaces as part of the PSE national curriculum in Chile should be a policy priority.

The fourth and final important association that children in the study identified was space, relationships and sense of belonging. The interconnections arising from children's peer inter-actions in outdoor free play are characterised by ownership and 'dynamic and multi-faceted processes' of belonging, as children create and recreate situations, and negotiate, fantasise and socialise within with their sociocultural contexts (Löfdahl, 2014; Woodhead & Brooker, 2008, p. 3). To secure young children's rights of identity, belonging and well-being, we need to acknowledge that their sense of belonging is constantly constructed and co-constructed, evolving according to space, time and opportunities to hand.

These four important associations were expressions of the young Chilean participants' need to continue to play outdoors as they moved from ECE to PSE, yet they indicated they lost such opportunities in PSE.

Reflections on outdoor space provision for young children's play

In the final section of the chapter, we revisit our argument that young children's outdoor play should be accommodated in educational provision and addressed in initial teacher preparation to secure their UNCRC rights to education, to be heard, to participate, to play, and to foreground their best interests. We structure our argument according to four core issues that were evidenced in the study. First, time and space for free outdoor play, especially in natural spaces, is fundamental for children to develop and learn holistically in playful, imaginative ways (Maturana, 2003; Warden, 2017). However, increasing focus on ECE as leverage for school readiness is leading to teachers attributing less pedagogical value to young children's risky play (Ryan & Northey-Berg, 2014). For children to develop healthily, they need competent practitioners who are able to secure their emotional well-being by providing opportunities for self-initiated play in a rich nature-based landscape (Bateman & Waters, 2018).

Second, taking into account young children's views when designing their educational spaces is essential because children have knowledge that adults do not (Birkeland, 1998; Clark, 2010). This consultation is a democratic right and an essential pedagogical strategy for aligning young children's rights to play and education (Fleer, 2017; Viviers, 2014). It will enable them to explore and learn deeply about the world on their own terms.

Third, a coherent, progressive curriculum based on children's rights, participation and interests needs to be co-constructed between practitioners, children and other specialists in order to secure young children's optimal learning (Casey, 2017; Clark, 2010; Fleer, 2017). To achieve this goal, play must feature prominently in ECE and PSE teacher preparation (Ryan & Northey-Berg, 2014). This possibility is beginning to be explored in Chile (Grau et al., 2019).

Fourth – and finally – for ECE and PSE teachers to support young children to be protagonists of their own play and learning requires teacher education that is grounded in the UNCRC and relevant GCs. Doing so would upskill teachers to appreciate and facilitate young children's constructions of their own cultures and definitions of childhood (Löfdahl, 2014), and as the study outlined in this chapter indicates, such constructions are likely to include outdoor free play in natural environments as children move from ECE to PSE.

References

Bagot, Kathleen, Felicity Catherine Louise Allen, & Samia Toukhsati. 2015. "Perceived Restorativeness of Children's School Playground Environments: Nature, Playground Features and Play Period Experiences." *Journal of Environmental Psychology* 41: 1–9. www.sciencedirect.com/science/article/abs/pii/S0272494414001029?via%3Dihub.

Bateman, Amanda, & Jane Waters. 2018. "Risk-Taking in the New Zealand Bush: Issues of Resilience and Wellbeing." *Asia-Pacific Journal of Research in Early Childhood Education* 12(2): 7–29.

Birkeland, Loise. 1998. *Pedagogiske Erobringer: Om Praksisfortellinger Og Vurdering i Barnehagen*. Oslo: Pedagogisk Forum.

Broström, Stig. 2007. "Transitions in Children's Thinking." In *Informing Transition in the Early Years*, edited by Dunlop Aline-Wendy & Fabian Hilary, 61–73. Berkshire: Open University Press.

Bruner, Jerome. 1996. *The Culture of Education*. Cambridge, MA and London: Harvard University Press.

Casey, Theresa. 2017. "Outdoor Play and Learning in the Landscape of Children's Rights." In *The Sage Handbook of Outdoor Play and Learning*, edited by Waller Tim, Ärlemalm-Hagsér Eva, Ellen Beat, Hansen Sandseter, Lee-Hammons Libby, Lekies Kristi, & Shirley Wyver, 362–376. London, Thousand Oaks, New Delhi: SAGE.

Cerda Díaz, Leonor. 2007. *Un Siglo de Educación Parvularia En Chile: Un Vistazo a Su Historia y Desarrollo. [A Century of Early Childhood Education in Chile: An Insight to its History and Development]*. Curicó: Mataquito.

Chawla, Louise. 2015. "Benefits of Nature Contact for Children." *Journal of Planning Literature* 30 (4): 433–452.

Clark, Alison. 2010. *Transforming Children's Spaces: Children's and Adults' Participation in Designing Learning Environments*. London and New York: Routledge.

Clark, Alison, & Peter Moss. 2005. *Spaces to Play: More Listening to Young Children Using the Mosaic Approach*. London: National Children's Bureau.

Collado, Silvia, & Henk Staats. 2016. "Contact with Nature and Children's Restorative Experiences: An Eye to the Future." *Frontiers in Psychology* 7: 1885. doi:10.3389/fpsyg.2016.01885.

Corsaro, William A., & Luisa Molinari. 2005. *I Compagni: Understanding Children's Transition from Preschool to Elementary School*. Sociology of Education Series, edited by Aaron M. Pallas New York: Teachers College Press.

Dockett, Sue, & Bob Perry. 2005. "A Buddy Doesn't Let Kids Get Hurt in the Playground Starting School with Buddies." *International Journal of Transitions in Childhood* 1: 22–34.

Einarsdóttir, Johanna. 2014. "Children's Perspectives on Play." In *The SAGE Handbook of Play and Learning in Early Childhood*, edited by Brooker Liz, Mindy Blaise, & Edwards Susan, 319–329. Los Angeles, London, New Delhi, Singapore, Washington, DC: SAGE.

Fjørtoft, Ingunn. 2001. "The Natural Environment as a Playground for Children: The Impact of Outdoor Play Activities in Pre-Primary School Children." *Early Education Journal* 29 (1): 111–117.

Fleer, Marilyn. 2017. *Play in the Early Years*. 2nd ed. Cambridge: Cambridge University Press.

Grau, Valeska, David Preiss, Katherine Strasser, Daniela Jadue-Roa, Magdalena Müller, & Lorca Amaya. 2019. "Juego Guiado y Educación Parvularia: Propuestas Para Una Mejor Calidad de La Educación Inicial." "[Guided Play and Early Childhood Education: Suggestions for Better Early Childhood Education Quality."] In *Propuestas Para Chile. Concurso Políticas Públicas 2018*, 251–282. Santiago, Chile: Pontificia Universidad Católica de Chile. https://politicaspublicas.uc.cl/wp-content//uploads/2019/03/Libro-completo-en-PDF_final.pdf.

Grau, Valeska, David Preiss, Katherine Strasser, Daniela S. Jadue-Roa, Veronica López, & David Whitebread. 2018. *"Informe Final: Rol Del Juego En La Educación Parvularia: Creencias y Prácticas de Educadoras Del Nivel de Transición Menor".* ["Final Report: The Role of Play in Early Childhood Education: Beliefs and Perspectives of Pre-Kindergarten Educators."] Santiago, Chile: MINEDUC (Chilean Ministry of Education). https://centroestudios.mineduc.cl/wp-content/uploads/sites/100/2018/10/Informe-final-FONIDE-FX21615-Grau_apDU.pdf

Harcourt, Deborah, Bob Perry, & Tim Waller. 2011. "Researching Young Children's Perspectives: Debating the Ethics and Dilemmas of Educational Research with Children." Oxon and New York: Routledge.

Hedges, Helen. 2011. "Rethinking SpongeBob and Ninja Turtles: Popular Culture as Funds of Knowledge for Curriculum Co-Construction." *Australasian Journal of Ealry Childhood* 36 (1): 25–29.

Hermosilla, Blanca. 1998. *La Educación Parvularia En La Reforma: Una Contribución a La Equidad. [Early Childhood Education Reform: A Contribution to Equity]*. Santiago, Chile: MINEDUC. http://ww2.educarchile.cl/UserFiles/P0001/File/edu_parvularia.pdf.

Jadue-Roa, Daniela, Gabriela Bargellini Báez, Elisabeth Díaz Costa, Marlene Rivas Muena, & Benjamin Gareca Guzmán. 2016. "Informe Final: Transición y Articulación Entre La Educación Parvularia y La Educación General Básica En Chile: Características y Evaluación." [Final Report: Transition and Articulation between ECE and PSE in Chile: Characteristics and Evaluation]. Santiago, Chile. https://centroestudios.mineduc.cl/wp-content/uploads/sites/100/2017/07/INFORME-FINAL-F911436.pdf.

Jadue-Roa, Daniela S. 2017. "Ethical Issues in Listening to Young Children in Visual Participatory Research." *International Journal of Inclusive Education* 21 (3). doi:10.1080/13603116.2016.1260829.

Jadue-Roa, Daniela S. 2019. "Children's Agency in Transition Experiences: Understanding Possibilities and Challenges." In *Listening to Children's Advice about Starting School and School Age Care*, edited by Sue Dockett, Johanna Einarsdottir, & Bob Perry, 36–41. Abingdon: Routledge.

Jadue-Roa, Daniela S., & David Whitebread. 2012. Young Children's Experiences through Transition between Kindergarten and First Grade in Chile and Its Relation with Their Developing Learning Agency. *Educational and Child Psychology* 29(1), 32.

Jadue-Roa, Daniela S., David Whitebread, & Benjamin Gareca Guzmán. 2018. "Methodological Issues in Representing Children's Perspectives in Transition Research." *European Early Childhood Education Research Journal* 1 (20). www.tandfonline.com/doi/abs/10.1080/1350293X.2018.1522764.

JUNJI. 2013. "Guía de Funcionamiento Para Establecimientos de Educación Parvularia: Reglamento Interno Junta Nacional de Jardines Infantiles." [Practice Guide of ECE Centres: Internal Regulations of JUNJI]. Santiago, Chile: Junta Nacional de Jardines Infantiles, Ministerio de Educación. www.bien estararmada.cl/prontus_bienestar/site/artic/20131211/asocfile/20131211120520/m_fsz_01_guia_de_ funcionamiento_para_establecimiento_de_educaci__n_parvularia.pdf.

Kwi-Ok, Nah. 2017. "The Rise of Outdoor Play and Education Issues in Preschools in South Korea." In *The Sage Handbook of Outdoor Play and Learning*, edited by Waller Tim, Eva Ärlemalm-Hagsér, Ellen Beate, Hansen Sandseter, Lee-Hammond Libby, Kristi Lekies, & Shirley Wyver. London, Thousand Oaks and New Delhi: SAGE.

Löfdahl, Annica. 2014. "Play in Peer Cultures." In *The SAGE Handbook of Play and Learning in Early Childhood*, edited by Liz Brooker, Mindy Blaise, & Susan Edwards, 342–353. Los Angeles, Washington, DC, London, New Delhi and Singapore: SAGE.

Lundy, Lauren, & Lesley McEvoy. 2012. "Children's Rights and Research Processes: Assisting Children to (in) Formed Views." *Childhood* 19 (1): 129–144.

Lysklett, Olav. 2013. *Ute Hele Uka: Natur- Og Friluftsbarnehagen*. Norway: Universitetsforlaget.

Maturana, Humberto. 2003. *Amor y Juego: Fundamentos Olvidados de Lo Humano, Desde El Patriarcado Hasta La Democracia*. Santiago, Chile: LOM Ediciones.

Mayall, Berry. 2002. *Towards a Sociology of Childhood: Thinking from Children's Lives*. Buckingham: Open University Press.

Mella, Orlando. 2003. "12 Años de La Reforma Educacional En Chile. Algunas Consideraciones En Torno a Sus Efectos Para Reducir La Inequidad." ["12 years from the Educational Reform in Chile. Some Considerations about its Impact to Reduce Inequity."] *REICE - Revista Electrónica Iberoamericana Sobre Calidad, Eficacia y Cambio En Educación* 1 (1). www.ice.deusto.es/rinace/reice/vol1n1/Mella.pdf.

MINEDUC. 1970. *Ley 17301. [Law 17301]*. www.leychile.cl/Navegar?idNorma=28904.

MINEDUC. 2004. "Resolución Sobre Articulación Entre Educación Parvularia y Educación General Básica." [Resolution about Articulation between ECE and PSE."] Edited by Ministerio de Educación Departamento Jurídico Gobierno de Chile. Santiago de Chile.

MINEDUC. 2013. *Bases Curriculares. Primero a Sexto Básico. [Curriculum. From First to Sixth Grade]*. Santiago, Chile. www.curriculumnacional.cl/614/articles-22394_bases.pdf.

MINEDUC. 2017. *Decreto 373: Establece Principios y Definiciones Técnicas Para La Elaboración de Una Estrategia de Transición Educativa Para Los Niveles de Educación Parvularia y Primer Año de Educación Básica. [Decree 373. Establishes Principles and Technical Definitions for the Elaboration of an Educational TRansition Strategy for ECE and PSE.]* Santiago, Chile.

MINEDUC. 2018. *Bases Curriculares. Educación Parvularia. [Early Childhood Education Curriculum]*. Santiago, Chile: Gobierno de Chile. https://parvularia.mineduc.cl/wp-content/uploads/sites/34/2018/ 03/Bases_Curriculares_Ed_Parvularia_2018.pdf.

MINVU. 1992. *Decreto 47. Fija Nuevo Texto de La Ordenanza General de La Ley General de Urbanismo y Construcciones. [Decree 47. Determines New Text about General Commands of the General Law or Urbanism and Construction]*. www.leychile.cl/Navegar?idNorma=8201.

Moss, Peter. 2013. *Early Childhood and Compulsory Education*. London and New York: Routledge.

Pardo, Marcela, & Daniela S. Jadue-Roa. forthcoming. "Emerging Inclusion of the Child Rights Approach in ECEC Undergraduate Programs in Chile: Any Possibilities for the Enactment of Children's Rights for Infants and Toddlers in ECEC Programs?" In *Conceptualising and Reconceptualising Children's Rights in Infant-Toddler Early Childhood Education and Care: Transnational Conversations*, edited by Press Frances & Cheeseman Sandra. New York: Springer.

Peralta, E. Maria Victoria. 1999. "La Reforma Curricular de La Educación Parvularia: Una Gran Oportunidad de Construir Para Los Párvulos Chilenos La Pedagogía Del Siglo XXI." ["The ECE Educational Reform: A great Opportunity for Constructing the XXIst Century Pedagogy for Young Children."] *Revista Perspectiva* 13: 5–10.

Peralta, E. Maria Victoria. 2005. *El Currículo En El Jardín Infantil (Un Análisis Crítico). [Curriculum in Ealry Childhood Centres. A Critical Analysis]*. 3rd ed. Santiago, Chile: Editorial Andrés Bello.

Qvortrup, Jens. 2002. "Sociology of Childhood: Conceptual Liberation of Children." In *Childhood and Children's Culture*, edited by Mouritsen Flemming & Qvortrup Jens, 43–78. Odense: University Press of Southern Denmark.

Rojas Flores, Jorge. 2010. *Historia de La Infancia En El Chile Republicano 1810-2010 [History of Childhood in the Republic of Chile: 1810-2010]*. Santiago de Chile: Junta Nacional de Jardines Infantiles, JUNJI.

Rupin, Palo, Carla Muñoz, & Daniela S. Jadue-Roa 2018. "El Juego Dentro y Fuera Del Aula: Miradas Cruzadas Sobre Prácticas Lúdicas Infantiles En Momentos de Transición Educativa." [Play inside and outside the classroom: Multiple Perspectives of Childhood Playful Practices through Educational Transitions."] Santiago, Chile: MINEDUC (Chilean Ministry of Education). https://centroestudios.mineduc.cl/wp-content/uploads/sites/100/2018/10/Informe-final-FONIDE-FX11651-Rupin_apDU.pdf

Ryan, Sharon, & Kaitlin Northey-Berg. 2014. "Professional Preparation for a Pedagogy of Play." In *The SAGE Handbook of Play and Learning in Early Childhood*, edited by Liz Brooker, Mindy Blaise, & Susan Edwards, 204–215. Los Angeles, London, New Delhi, Singapore and Washington, DC: SAGE.

Saltmarsh, Sue. 2014. "Childhood Studies and Play." In *The SAGE Handbook of Play and Learning in Early Childhood*, edited by Liz Brooker, Mindy Blaise, & Susan Edwards, 91–102. Los Angeles, London, New Delhi, Singapore and Washington, DC: SAGE.

Sylva, Kathy, Edward Melhuish, Pam Sammons, Iram Siraj-Blatchford, & Brenda Taggart, eds. 2010. *Early Childhood Matters: Evidence from the Effective Pre-School and Primary Education Project*. Abingdon: Routledge.

United Nations. 2015. Sustainable Development Goal 4. https://sustainabledevelopment.un.org/sdg4.

United Nations, UN Committee on the Rights of the Child. 1989. "Convention on the Rights of the Child." www.ohchr.org/Documents/ProfessionalInterest/crc.pdf.

United Nations, UN Committee on the Rights of the Child. 2001. *General Comment No. 1 (2001) Article 29 (1): The aims of education*. CRC/GC/2001/1. Geneva: United Nations.

United Nations, UN Committee on the Rights of the Child. 2005. *Implementing Child Rights in Early Childhood General Comment no. 7 (2005) UN/CRC/GC/2005/1*. Geneva: United Nations.

United Nations, UN Committee on the Rights of the Child. 2013a. *General Comment no. 14 on the right of the child to have his or her best interests taken as a primary consideration. CRC/C/GC/13*. Geneva: United Nations.

United Nations, UN Committee on the Rights of the Child. 2013b. *General Comment no. 17 on the right of the child to rest, leisure, play, recreational activities, cultural life and the arts (art. 31) to have his or her best interests taken as a primary consideration. CRC/C/GC/17*. Geneva: United Nations.

Viviers, André. 2014. *General Comments of the Committee on the Rights of the Child. A Compendium for Child Rights Advocates, Scholars and Policy Makers*. UNICEF South Africa. www.unicef.org/southafrica/SAF_resources_crcgeneralcomments.pdf.

Warden, Claire. 2017. "Nature Pedagogy – An Exploration of the Storied Narratives Which Illustrate Its Application Across Spaces Inside, Outside and Beyond." In *The Sage Handbook of Outdoor Play and Learning*, edited by Waller Tim, Eva Ärlemalm-Hagsér, Ellen Beate, Hansen Sandseter, Libby Lee-Hammond, Kristi Lekies, & Shirley Wyver, 279–291. London, London, Thousand Oaks and New Delhi: SAGE.

Waters, Jane. 2017. "Affordance Theory in Outdoor Play." In *The Sage Handbook of Outdoor Play and Learning*, edited by Waller Tim, Eva Ärlemalm-Hagsér, Ellen Beate, Hansen Sandseter, Libby Lee-Hammond, Kristi Lekies, & Shirley Wyver, 40–54. Los Angeles, London, New Delhi and Singapore: SAGE.

Weisberg, Deena Skolnick, Kathy Hirsh-Pasek, & Roberta Micknick Golinkoff. 2013. "Guided Play: Where Curricular Goals Meet a Playful Pedagogy." *Mind, Brain, and Education* 7 (2): 104–112. doi:10.1111/mbe.12015.

Whitebread, David, Marisol Basilio, Martina Kuvalja, & Mohini Verma. 2012. "The Importance of Play." *Toy Industries of Europe*, no. April.

Whitebread, David, & Sue Bingham. 2011. "School Readiness; a Critical Review of Perspectives and Evidence." Occasional Paper N°:2. http://tactyc.org.uk/occasional-paper/occasional-paper2.pdf.

Wood, Elizabeth. 2014. "The Play-Pedagogy Interface in Contemporary Debates." In *The SAGE Handbook of Play and Learning in Early Childhood*, edited by Liz Brooker, Mindy Blaise, & Edwards Susan, 145–156. Los Angeles, London, New Delhi, Singapore and Washington, DC: SAGE.

Woodhead, Martin, & Liz Brooker. 2008. "A Sense of Belonging." *Early Childhood Matters* 111: 3–6. https://issuu.com/bernardvanleerfoundation/docs/enhancing_a_sense_of_belonging_in_the_early_years/2.

Wynne, Samantha, & Ronald Gorman. 2015. *Nature Pedagogy*. Osborne Park: Association of Independent Schools of Western Australia.

EPILOGUE
Imagining child rights futures

Jane Murray, Beth Blue Swadener and Kylie Smith

Introduction

Child rights work is an ongoing endeavour across the world. It is undertaken by children, families, advocates, early childhood educators, NGOs, policymakers and researchers, and *The Routledge International Handbook of Young Children's Rights* celebrates and takes stock of that endeavour as it marks the 30th anniversary of the adoption of the United Nations Convention on the Rights of the Child (United Nations (UN), 1989) by illuminating the rights of infants and children younger than eight years. Children's rights are an important path that we can journey on together so that we can all experience better times: they remind us to consider the best ways we can value children. If we respect children's rights, they have the potential to benefit us all now and in the future. In the three decades spanning 1989–2019, almost every country government in the world has acknowledged that children's rights are important. However, that acknowledgement is not universal, and even where the importance of children's rights has been recognised by states' ratification of the Convention, that recognition has rarely translated to full enactment, as many of the chapters in this book have revealed.

Our handbook provides a snapshot of a moment in time that marks the 30th anniversary of the Convention, across diverse local and national spaces. Our imaginings for the book were threefold. First, we wanted to acknowledge and celebrate the work that is being undertaken to enact children's rights through policy, practice and research. Second, we sought to bring critique to the child rights space and raise questions about the lack of progress for the realisation of rights for many children across the world. *Which children have the opportunities and possibilities to realise their rights?* This is an ongoing question and challenge for the United Nations and for signatories to the convention. The distribution of wealth globally and locally means that many children continue to live in poverty, resulting in little or no opportunity to access provision, protection and participation rights. Third, we want to pose possibilities and provocations for how progressing child rights might be considered in the future. We are grateful to the children, parents, educators, authors, policymakers, NGOs, advocates and researchers whose experiences have come together in this book to make our imaginings real. Our handbook is just one book, so it cannot cover all the work that has been carried out and continues to be undertaken in the field of young children's rights. This handbook does, however, bring together important current ideas, innovations, practices, policies, research, outputs and trends that capture and reflect the zeitgeist in young children's rights, three decades after the adoption of the Convention (UN, 1989).

Limitations to young children's rights

The rights of children younger than 8 years have tended to be less respected than the rights of older children, young people and adults, and this has been the case for different reasons. Those reasons include – but are not limited to – violence, conflict and their effects, adult imperatives concerned with economics rather than people, assumptions that younger children are always more vulnerable than others, that their size matches their capacity to think and act, and that their preverbal communication is a proxy for incapacity. Perhaps most disappointing of all is that the Convention itself marginalises the rights of infants and younger children by empowering adults to make decisions on some children's behalf. The Convention articulates that adults – not the children themselves – should decide the extent of the child's capacity to exercise his or her own rights. The Convention also exhorts adults to decide on behalf of children whether they are 'capable of forming (their) own views freely in all matters affecting' them, and it empowers adults to decide what 'weight' to give the child's views, 'in accordance with the age and maturity of the child' (UN, 1989, Article 12). By assuming that age and maturity are commensurate with capacity, Articles 5 and 12 deny infants and young children full agency as rights-holders. Yet from birth, children *are* rights-holders, a point made explicitly, albeit retrospectively, by the United Nations in General Comment 7 (United Nations Committee on the Rights of the Child (UNCRC), 2005). To secure respect for younger children's rights as 'social actors from birth' (UNCRC, 2005, p. 2), the assertions in General Comment 7 may need to be incorporated more prominently in a revised Convention.

Evidence and policy

In the 30 years since the Convention was adopted, the important role of our early life experiences for our own lifetime outcomes and the generations that follow us has been established by powerful research evidence (e.g. see Shonkoff & Richter, 2013). To date, that evidence has led to unprecedented policy focus, which has tended to align with economic imperatives (e.g. the 2015 United Nations Target 4.2 that 'by 2030, all girls and boys have access to quality early childhood development, care and pre-primary education so that they are ready for primary education') (United Nations (UN), 2015). It is important for us to be mindful that young children's rights appropriately concern many other aspects of their lives that young children may also value at least as much as education, such as rights to family life, play and freedom of expression (e.g. Articles 9, 13, 31). More research evidence is needed concerning a wider range of aspects of early childhood development to persuade policymakers of the importance of respecting the full range of young children's rights in policy and ensuring that policy translates to practice.

Young children's rights: addressing challenges, imagining futures

The content that we have curated in the handbook indicates that while the UNCRC (UN, 1989) is the most ratified global policy document, being a signatory is not enough. It is also important to remember that at the time of writing, the US has still not ratified the UNCRC. Accountability for signatories and UN sanctions is one area that requires urgent attention. Further, consideration also needs to be attended to how individual and collective complaints are undertaken *by* and *for* children. As children and youth organise for climate justice and their future on the planet, against violence in schools and communities, and for more safe spaces to play – indeed, for the right to a space to call childhood – giving their views due weight in policy and practice is critical. Neither can we make assumptions that adults are always the best people to gauge young children's capacities.

What are the realities of children who are living in poverty, are homeless, or are disconnected from education that would enable them to access the UN and complaints processes? As global wealth gaps widen and child poverty continues to grow in the Global North as well as the Global South, provision rights of young children worldwide require more attention and may be used as an advocacy tool by local communities, NGOs and others concerned about child well-being. Neither can protection rights be taken for granted. Young children experience violence on an epidemic scale: of the tens of thousands of children murdered each year across the world, each year infants and young children aged 0–4 years are twice as likely as other children to be homicide victims (World Health Organization (WHO) and International Society for Prevention of Child Abuse and Neglect (ISPCAN), 2006). Young children have also experienced many of the harsh realities of increased armed conflict in recent years in countries including Syria and Yemen, leaving the survivors with lasting symptoms, including post-traumatic stress (Save the Children, 2019; Slone & Mann, 2016).

Children crossing borders and seeking asylum – on their own and with families – will continue to need support to ensure how their rights are attended to, particularly as there is a growing discourse of border 'security' and 'protection' across wealthy nations. Article 22, which focuses on children seeking refugee status, and other provisions of the CRC might be better leveraged in advocating for children in these circumstances. Demonisation of religions and racial vilification are layered within this discourse. These phenomena are emerging in contexts of narrowing and far-right ideologies and resettlement processes that require children to live in institutional settings, separated from their families, and suffering from lost recognition of their citizenship. For example, Australia is exploring not repatriating children in Syrian refugee camps if their parents were fighting or aligned with ISIS and/or have basic housing, nutrition, clothing and educational needs unmet.

In respect of young children's participation rights, children were not consulted in the writing of the UNCRC, but they are being listened to by a growing number of researchers, child ombudspersons, municipalities and advocacy groups, as some of the chapters in the participation section attest. Two of the editors of this handbook were involved in an international project (Lundy et al., 2014) that involved interviewing young children in five nations about their views of what should have been included regarding children's right to education. Children aged 5–9 years old were concerned about education that included animal rights and humane treatment, caring for and about others, preventing bullying, addressing poverty, and understanding refugee issues. Child Friendly Cities have provided creative ways to learn from the views of their youngest citizens for many years, and provide examples for other municipalities for ways that children as young as infants and toddlers might be consulted (Melaine, MacNaughton, & Smith, 2008; Smith, Alexander, & Mac-Naughton, 2008).

The rapid growth and diversification of technology will also be an important and in some ways unknown space for the UN going forward to ensure children have access to the digital space to be able to communicate and learn across transnational spaces, but also to protect children from child pornography and child trafficking.

As we consider the imagined, yet very real, futures of young children, it is important to address larger issues of climate change and climate justice in the current geological era of human-generated impact on the environment that has been named as the Anthropocene (Crutzen & Stoermer, 2000). Use of this construct signifies that humans are a 'global geological force' (Steffen, Crutzen, & McNeill, 2007, p. 614). A powerful example of children taking collective action for the future of their planet is the #FridaysForFuture movement, begun by Greta Thunberg, a Swedish teen whose organising led to a global movement to demand adult action on climate change. As she stated, 'because we children can't vote but have to go to school, this is a way that I can make my voice heard' (Mitra, 2019, p. 47, cited in Goebel, 2019, p. 26). At the time of writing this 2,000 registered #FridaysForFuture events have taken place in 125 countries, on all continents, involving at least 1.6 million people (FridaysForFuture, 2019). While this example focuses primarily on actions of youth, young children worldwide are engaging with an array of activities and advocacy for the sustainability of their communities and world – from saving animals from extinction, to protecting the oceans, to recycling and green practices closer to home.

Notions of the Anthropocene are also tied to the 'more than human' in early childhood research and practice (e.g., Taylor & Pacini-Ketchabaw, 2015). Such framings have direct relevance to how young children experience life and their rights, sharing common worlds that transcend beyond human exceptionalism (Taylor, 2017). Young children's lifeworlds are interconnected with their physical environment, including nature, animals and material objects. In other words, children's rights are not freestanding from their wider, more-than-human experiences, and this will likely create growing tensions in emphasis on human/individual rights versus more inclusive and embedded rights going forward.

Conclusion

In capturing the zeitgeist in young children's rights, our handbook highlights that there is much work still to do three decades after the adoption of the Convention (UN, 1989) if young children's rights are to be respected. While our handbook showcases a wide range of research in children's rights, early childhood and related fields, more research evidence is needed to persuade policymakers of the importance of respecting the full range of young children's rights in policy and ensuring that policy translates to practice. We advocate for a revised Convention that regards children as capable social actors from birth, and we hope that future books and resources about young children's rights will include more contributions from children and will find better ways to accommodate the many varied means young children use to express their thoughts and ideas about matters affecting them. Finally, we call for the Convention to be universally ratified across the world and for all states to find ways to assume their full responsibilities by ensuring that all children's rights are enacted, including those of our youngest citizens.

References

Crutzen, Paul J., & Eugene F. Stoermer. (2000). The "Anthropocene." *Global Change Newsletter*, 41, 17–18.

FridaysForFuture. (2019). "FridaysForFuture." www.fridaysforfuture.org/

Goebel, Janna. (2019). *What Matter(s) in Education beyond the Human?* Unpublished essay, Tempe, AZ: Arizona State University.

Lundy, Laura, Elizabeth Welty, Natasha Blanchet-Cohen, Natasha Dympna Devine, Beth Blue Swadener, & Kylie Smith. (2014). What if children had been involved in drafting the United Nations Convention on the Rights of the Child? In Alison Diduck, Noam Peleg, & Helen Reece (Eds.), *Law and Michael Freeman*. Leiden, Netherlands: Brill Publishers.

Melaine, Saballa, Glenda MacNaughton, & Kylie Smith. (2008). Working with children to create policy: The case of the Australian Capital Territory's children's plan. In G. MacNaughton, P. Hughes, & K. Smith (Eds.), *Young Children as Active Citizens: Principles, Policies and Pedagogies* (pp. 62–76). London: Cambridge Scholars Publishing.

Mitra, M. N. (2019). "Winter grown-ups have failed us". *Earth Island Journal*, 33, 46–48. Retrieved from http://login.ezproxy1.lib.asu.edu/login?url=https-//search-proquest-com.ezproxy1.lib.asu.edu/doc view/2158129340?accountid=4485.pdf

Save the Children (2019) "Stop war on children." www.savethechildren.org/content/dam/usa/reports/ ed-cp/stop-the-war-on-children-2019.pdf

Shonkoff, Jack P., & Linda Richter. (2013). "The powerful reach of early childhood development: A science-based foundation for sound investment." In Pia Rebello Britto, Patrice L. Engle, & Charles M. Super (Eds.), *Handbook of Early Childhood Development Research and Its Impact on Global Policy* (pp. 24–34). New York: Oxford Press Limited.

Slone, Michelle, & Shiri Mann. (2016). "Effects of war, terrorism and armed conflict on young children: A systematic review." *Child Psychiatry and Human Development*, 47, 950–965. doi:10.1007/s10578-016-0626-7

Smith, Kylie, Kate Alexander, & Glenda MacNaughton. (2008). *Respecting Children as Citizens in Local Government: Participation in Policies and Services Project*. Report. City of Port Phillip, Victoria (pp. 1–195).

Steffen, Will, Paul J. Crutzen, & John R. McNeill. (2007). "The anthropocene: Are humans now over-whelming the great forces of nature". *AMBIO: A Journal of the Human Environment*, 36(8), 614–622.

Taylor, Affrica. (2017). "Beyond stewardship: Common world pedagogies for the anthropocene". *Environmental Education Research*, 23(10), 1448–1461.

Taylor, Affrica, & Veronica Pacini-Ketchabaw. (2015). "Learning with children, ants, and worms in the anthropocene: Towards a common world pedagogy of multispecies vulnerability". *Pedagogy, Culture & Society*, 23(4), 507–529.

United Nations (UN). (1989). "Convention on the Rights of the Child." www.unicef.org.uk/Docu ments/Publication-pdfs/UNCRC_PRESS200910web.pdf

United Nations (UN). (2015). "Sustainable development goals." https://sustainabledevelopment.un.org/? menu=1300

United Nations Committee on the Rights of the Child (UNCRC). (2005). *Implementing Child Rights in Early Childhood General Comment No. 7 (2005) UN/CRC/GC/2005/1*. Geneva: United Nations.

World Health Organisation and International Society for Prevention of Child Abuse and Neglect. (2006). "Preventing child maltreatment: A guide to taking action and generating evidence." www. who.int/violence_injury_prevention/publications/violence/child_maltreatment/en/

INDEX

University of Winchester Libraries
Sparkford Rd., SO22 4NR Winchester
01962 827306
library@winchester.ac.uk